CW00551075

JOHN PAGUS ON ARISTOTLE'S *CATEGORIES*

ANCIENT AND MEDIEVAL PHILOSOPHY

DE WULF-MANSION CENTRE
Series I

XLV

Series editors

Russell L. Friedman
Jan Opsomer
Carlos Steel
Gerd Van Riel

Advisory Board

The "De Wulf-Mansion Centre" is a research centre for ancient, medieval, and Renaissance
philosophy at the Institute of Philosophy of the Catholic University of Leuven,
Kardinaal Mercierplein, 2, B 3000 Leuven (Belgium).
It hosts the international project "Aristoteles latinus" and publishes
the "Opera omnia" of Henry of Ghent and the "Opera Philosophica et Theologica" of
Francis of Marchia.

John Pagus on Aristotle's *Categories*

A Study and Edition of the *Rationes super Praedicamenta Aristotelis*

Heine Hansen

Ancient and Medieval Philosophy - Series 1 - volume XLV

ERRATA

Part One   Introductory Study

Page 22*, n. 33. The end of this footnote should read:

…1989), 65*. For all other aspects of the basic description of the manuscript, see Franceschini, "Giovanni Pago," 174, esp. n. 8 (see my n. 44 below). I have modified Franceschini's description only slightly.

Page 32*, n. 52. The beginning of this footnote should read:

Less complete lists of this material can be found in Franceschini, "Giovanni Pago," 476–80. The specific passages…

Page 57*, n. 10. This footnote should read:

John Pagus, *Rat. sup. Praed.* I (9.1–15). This and the following passage are also translated and discussed in Giorgio Pini's recent survey "Reading the *Categories* as an Introduction to Logic: Later Medieval Discussions about its Place in the Aristotelian *Corpus*," in *Medieval Commentaries on Aristotle's Categories*, ed. Lloyd A. Newton (Leiden: Brill, 2008), 153–54. I have allowed myself to adopt several of the phrases and formulations in Pini's translation.

Page 66*, n. 30. The beginning of this footnote should read:

Andrews, *Peter of Auvergne's Commentary*, 11–12; id., "Thomas of Erfurt," 804; Pini, "Transcendentals," 143–46 (see my n. 35 below). In general, see Sten Ebbesen and Jan Pinborg, "Bartholomew of Bruges and his Sophisma on the Nature of Logic," *CIMAGL* 39 (1981), viii–ix. For the date…

Page 74*, n. 65. The beginning of this footnote should read:

This general analysis and assessment of the role of the notion in these thinkers and its subsequent success is basically also that of Pini, "Transcendentals," 147–48. One commentator is…

(cont.)

Part Two   Edition

Due to an error in compiling the critical apparatus, information pertaining to Ezio Franceschini's 1933 edition of excerpts from Pagus' commentary has been all but omitted. The following conjectural readings had already been proposed by him:

27.13:	<duo>	231.14:	<nec>
27.18:	ibi	238.4:	<quaeritur>
50.25:	tertio	251.2:	<verum>
93.16:	secundo	264.2:	potestate
163.31:	contra	267.9:	in *Physicis*
172.1:	non dicitur	267.17:	<octavo>
228.6:	operationum	267.26:	<decimo>

Similarly, the following readings based on *F* were suggested by him as conjectures:

9.21:   accipiuntur
10.1:   totam
10.26: de denominativis

Finally, the following additions should be made to the apparatus:

51.4   causa] *Franceschini* : cum *P*
75.27   dictum] *Franceschini* : dictu *P*
159.15   unum] *Franceschini* : un *P*
244.21   quem] *Franceschini* : quam *P ut v.*
250.11   relativis] *Franceschini* : relatis *P ut v.*
267.31   hic] non *add. Franceschini*

Bibliography

Page 282. After the second complete entry, add the following:

Ebbesen, Sten, and Jan Pinborg. "Bartholomew of Bruges and his Sophisma on the Nature of Logic." *Cahiers de l'Institut du Moyen-Âge Grec et Latin* 39 (1981), iii–xxvi + 1–80.

Page 286. After the first entry, add the following.

—. "Reading the *Categories* as an Introduction to Logic: Later Medieval Discussions about its Place in the Aristotelian *Corpus*." In *Medieval Commentaries on Aristotle's Categories*, ed. Lloyd A. Newton, 145–81. Leiden: Brill, 2008.

 LEUVEN UNIVERSITY PRESS

JOHN PAGUS ON ARISTOTLE'S *CATEGORIES*

A Study and Edition of the Rationes super Praedicamenta Aristotelis

HEINE HANSEN

LEUVEN UNIVERSITY PRESS

ISBN 978 90 5867 913 0
D / 2012 / 1869 / 43
NUR: 732

GPRC
Guaranteed
Peer Reviewed
Content
www.gprc.be

For my mother and sister

CONTENTS

PREFACE

This book is intended as a contribution to the history of philosophy. Its chief aim is to help ameliorate the unfortunate lack of edited commentaries on Aristotle's logic from the first half of the thirteenth century by providing an edition of one of the earliest known logical commentaries written by a Parisian arts master: John Pagus' *Rationes super Praedicamenta Aristotelis*.

The book has two parts. Part one contains an introductory study, part two the edition. The first chapter of part one focuses on the various historical and philological aspects of the commentary. First, I briefly survey the sparse biographical data on Pagus and his known works. Second, I deal with his commentary on the *Categories* in more detail and discuss its manuscript sources, its formal features, the many authoritative sources it makes reference to, its relation to other known commentaries from the period, and its date of composition. The second chapter of part one analyses some of the main philosophical and interpretive themes in the commentary. Among the topics discussed are Pagus' positions on perennial questions such as what categories are, which categories there are, what type of items they collect, and whether or not they can overlap. Many of the issues treated in this chapter are by no means unique to Pagus, and in order to better appreciate and understand his approach considerable attention is also paid to the views of some of his ancient predecessors and, especially, to those of his near contemporaries Nicholas of Paris and Robert Kilwardby.

Part two contains the critical edition. The first chapter of this part gives the *ratio edendi* and *sigla*. The second chapter provides the first full edition of what remains of Pagus' text. It is based mainly on MS Padua, Biblioteca Universitaria 1589, ff. 24ra–67vb, which is the sole known source for most of the commentary. Editing a text on the basis of a single witness is always a difficult task, and I harbor no illusion of having solved, or even detected, all of the textual problems. I have worked hard to locate and solve as many as I could, but attentive readers might well find more and come up with further conjectural emendations of their own.

The book is a revised version of my doctoral dissertation, submitted to the Faculty of Arts, University of Sydney in 2009. The work on the dissertation was carried out under the banner of *The Reception of Aristotle's Categories in the Byzantine, Arabic and Latin Traditions*, an international research project funded by a grant from the Australian Research Council. I should like to acknowledge the debt of gratitude I owe to the four main investigators of this project. First of all, to Paul Thom, my academic supervisor, whose acute comments, suggestions, and advice benefited the work immensely, and without whose friendly encouragement and continuous support it would not have been possible. Secondly, to Sten Ebbesen, who first taught me many of the skills here applied and who initially alerted me to Pagus' commentary and supplied me with a microfilm copy. He subsequently took the time to read through the several parts of the book and made many valuable suggestions. Finally, to John Marenbon and Tony Street for their support and generous hospitality during my visits to Cambridge.

Many other colleagues, scholars, and friends around the world lent me their help and support in various ways during my work on this material. I am especially grateful to Carlos Steel, but also owe warm thanks to Robert Andrews, Dominique Angeloro, David Bloch, Charles Burnett, Alessandro Conti, William Courtenay, Silvia Donati, Jakob Fink, Karin Margareta Fredborg, Griet Galle, Jules Janssens, Berenice Kerr, James Kerr, Claude Lafleur, Constant Mews, Robert Milne, Ana María Mora-Márquez, Cassandra Parkinson, David Piché, and Cecilia Trifogli.

I would also like to thank the editorial board of Ancient and Medieval Philosophy - Series 1 for accepting the manuscript, the anonymous referees for their comments on it, and Beatrice Van Eeghem at Leuven University Press for her assistance in preparing it for publication.

Travel grants from the Augustinus Foundation, Knud Højgaard Foundation, Nordea Denmark Foundation, Politiken Foundation, Oticon Foundation, and Sigurd Jacobsen Memorial Fund eased the financial burden of moving to the other side of the planet to study philosophy. I would like to thank these foundations and the Australian Research Council for making it all possible.

Finally, a very special thanks to my mother and my sister for their continuous love and support, and to Louisa for the many lovely distractions (they are, indeed, my favorite).

Part One
Introductory Study

CHAPTER ONE
THE AUTHOR AND HIS WORK

INTRODUCTION: LOGIC IN THE THIRTEENTH CENTURY

The role assigned to logic in the philosophy of the Middle Ages was a fundamental and important one. As the anonymous author of an early thirteenth-century handbook of logic puts it, the discipline could be aptly described as

> the art of arts, the science of sciences, which alone produces knowledge and makes it clear whether someone has it.[1]

Underlying this claim is the conception of logic as the discipline which investigates and prescribes the basic methodological tools needed in any field of rational inquiry. Logic is, the author also says, a sort of pathway to all other branches of scientific knowledge.[2]

The basis of logic, as it was conceived at the time, was Aristotle's logical writings, and at its centre lay the theory of the syllogism:

> Dialectic deals with the syllogism as such, as in the *Prior Analytics*, but its subjective parts are dealt with in the *Posterior Analytics*, the *Topics*, and the *Sophistical Refutations*, and its integral parts in the *Categories* and the *Perihermeneias*. Thus, since the whole concern of dialectic revolves around the understanding of the syllogism (which can be seen from the fact that in all the books belonging to logic the topic treated is the syllogism and its subjective or integral parts), what is above all to be taught and learned is therefore the nature of the syllogism or, if you will, of argumentation.[3]

---

[1] Anon., *Dialectica Monacensis* (ed. de Rijk, 462): "Dialectica est ars artium, scientia scientiarum, quae sola facit scire et scientem apparere." Cf. Lambert of Lagny, *Logica* (ed. Alessio, 4). Notice that when I quote from printed editions of Latin texts I do not necessarily preserve the editor's spelling or punctuation. Similarly, I tacitly standardize the orthography of manuscript sources. When I have introduced conjectures, this is always signalled. All translations into English are, unless otherwise noted, my own.

[2] Anon., *Dialectica Monacensis* (ed. de Rijk, 461): "dialectica sit quasi via in omnes alias scientias." Cf. Nicholas of Paris, *Philosophia* §38 (ed. Lafleur, 462). For a good brief discussion of the medieval conception of logic, to which my introduction here is partly indebted, see Gyula Klima, *John Buridan* (Oxford: Oxford University Press, 2009), 8–12.

[3] Anon., *Dialectica Monacensis* (ed. de Rijk, 461): "Dialectica autem est quae tractat de syllogismo simpliciter, ut in *Libro priorum*, sed de partibus subiectivis in *Libro posteriorum* et in *Topicis* et *Elenchis*, de partibus vero integralibus in *Libro Praedicamentorum* et *Perihermeneias*. Quia ergo tota intentio dialecticae versatur circa cognitionem syllo-

Logic is centrally concerned with syllogistic argumentation or reasoning, the topic of Aristotle's *Prior Analytics*. The integral parts of such reasoning, what it is composed of, namely, terms and propositions, are discussed in the *Categories* and the *Perihermeneias* respectively. The subjective parts, that is to say, the various types, of such reasoning are considered in the final three books: demonstrative reasoning in the *Posterior Analytics*, dialectical reasoning in the *Topics*, and sophistical reasoning in the *Sophistical Refutations*.

The schoolmen were generally convinced that with these six texts Aristotle had given an adequate treatment of what logic is about, but the logical canon also included other authoritative works, most importantly Porphyry's *Isagoge*, the anonymous *Book of Six Principles*, and Manlius Boethius' monographs *On division* and *On topical differences*. These books were, however, seen as auxiliary rather than essential to the discipline. They were, as it was often said, of the well-being (*de bene esse*) rather than of the being (*de esse*) of logic.[4]

Together with these auxiliary texts, the *Categories* and the *Perihermeneias* made up what was known as the old art (*ars vetus*). Apart from the twelfth-century *Book of Six Principles*, these were texts that had been available, studied, and taught for centuries. By contrast, the *Prior* and *Posterior Analytics*, the *Topics*, and the *Sophistical Refutations* did not become widely available in Latin translation until sometime in the first half of the twelfth century and were thus referred to as the new art (*ars nova*). Together the old and new art, it was generally assumed, adequately covered the field of scientific logic, and one of the main ways of doing logic in the Middle Ages consisted in writing a commentary on all or some of these authoritative works.

There were, nonetheless, also some characteristically medieval innovations in the field. These were presented above all in the various treatises on the properties of terms, and eventually came to be characterized as the logic of the moderns (*logica modernorum*).[5] As the name suggests, the medieval logicians were in some sense tilling new ground in these texts, but this "modern logic" seems to have never really been properly integrated into the system.[6] Presumably, the schoolmen

---

gismi (quod patere potest ex hoc quod in omnibus libris logicae agitur de ipso syllogismo et de partibus eius subiectivis aut integralibus), idcirco potissimum docenda et discenda est natura syllogismi sive argumentationis." Cf. Boethius, *in Isag.*[1] 1 5 (ed. Brandt, 12–15); *in Cat.* 161b (ed. Migne).

[4] See, for example, Robert Kilwardby, *Notulae super Librum Praedicamentorum*, Proem (Cambridge, Peterhouse 206, f. 42va; Madrid, Bibl. Univ. 73, f. 11rb). Cf. P. Osmund Lewry, *Robert Kilwardby's Writings on the* Logica Vetus: *Studied with Regard to their Teaching and Method* (PhD diss., University of Oxford, 1978), 207, n. 3.

[5] L.M. de Rijk, *Logica Modernorum*, vol. 1 (Assen: Van Gorcum, 1962), 14–17.

[6] This is indicated by the facts that these innovations and texts never figure in the various divisions of logic that abound in thirteenth-century logical texts and that the material

viewed their innovations and the treatises in which they were presented as akin
to the non-Aristotelian texts of the old art — they were appendices to or auxiliary
extensions of Aristotle's logic.[7]

Along with grammar and rhetoric, logic constituted the part of philosophy
known as linguistic (*sermocinalis*) or rational (*rationalis*) philosophy.[8] The field of
inquiry of this branch of philosophy was traditionally taken to be speech (*sermo*)
in its various aspects,[9] and in accordance with this construal logic was understood
as the discipline concerned with speech in its capacity for being the bearer of truth
and falsehood; it is, it was said, the art of discerning the true from the false.[10] The
three disciplines — but logic especially — were the fundamental components of
the philosophical training (usually administered in the faculty of arts), which was
a mandatory prerequisite for admission into the higher faculties of law, medicine,
and theology.

Logic was, in sum, the cornerstone of the schooling with which everyone began
(and many ended) their university-level education, and it was to be learned above
all by studying the logical writings of Aristotle. Of the several places one could do
so, the most prominent was unquestionably the faculty of arts at the University of
Paris. Founded around the turn of the thirteenth century, this university remained
the leading centre of learning in the arts, as well as in theology, throughout the
Middle Ages (its only serious rival being the University of Oxford), and many of
the most important thinkers of the High Middle Ages in the Latin West were
trained there and taught there for some time.

As a consequence, the logical commentaries of the Parisian arts masters must
be regarded as texts of considerable importance for the understanding and assessment of theoretical developments in the thirteenth and fourteenth centuries

was never properly integrated in the logical handbooks. See Sten Ebbesen, "What Counted
as Logic in the Thirteenth Century?" in *Methods and Methodologies*, ed. Margaret Cameron and John Marenbon (Leiden: Brill, 2011), 99–101.

[7] Cf. de Rijk, *Logica Modernorum*, vol. 1, 15; Ebbesen, "What Counted," 99–101.

[8] The idea that logic can be aptly described as a linguistic science was to be called into
question later, but for the logicians that will concern us in this book, who were all active
before or around the middle of the thirteenth century, the conceptions of logic as a linguistic science and as a rational science would seem to have been both acceptable and compatible. See, for example, Anon., *Dialectica Monacensis* (ed. de Rijk, 461–62); Nicholas of
Paris, *Philosophia* §§26–29 (ed. Lafleur, 459–60); Robert Kilwardby, *Notulae super Librum
Perihermeneias*, Proem (Cambridge, Peterhouse 206, f. 65vb; Madrid, Bibl. Univ. 73, f. 44ra;
Venice, Biblioteca Marciana L.vi.66 [2528], f. 1r).

[9] Anon., *Dialectica Monacensis* (ed. de Rijk, 461). Cf. Nicholas of Paris, *Philosophia* §29
(ed. Lafleur, 460); Lambert of Lagny, *Logica* (ed. Alessio, 3).

[10] Anon., *Dialectica Monacensis* (ed. de Rijk, 462): "Dialectica est ars discernendi
verum a falso, et est a causa finali data ista descriptio; finis enim dialecticae est cognoscere
quid sit verum et quid falsum." Cf. Lambert of Lagny, *Logica* (ed. Alessio, 3).

and for the history of medieval logic and philosophy in general. There is, however, a conspicuous gap in our present knowledge of these works, namely, those composed during the first half of the thirteenth century. We know some of the figures that seem to have been important in this period, and we even know that several of their logical commentaries survive, but there are almost no modern editions of these texts.[11] And so, where the main theoretical developments and figures (Siger of Brabant, Boethius of Denmark, Peter of Auvergne, Radulphus Brito, etc.) of the final three or four decades of the century have been relatively well-researched, we still have no clear picture of what exactly took place in the first half.[12]

The *Rationes super Praedicamenta Aristotelis* by John Pagus is believed to be one of the earliest known literary products from the arts faculty at Paris, and is therefore an important source for the understanding of this early period. But, although he is one of the very first figures from the period whose work is known to us, and thus one of the earliest known logicians of the thirteenth century,[13] Pagus remains a relatively unknown figure. Before proceeding to discuss his commentary, therefore, it will be useful to sum up what is known about his life and works.

1. JOHN PAGUS: LIFE AND WORKS

1.1. Life

The only firm date attached to Pagus' name in our sources is found in a letter dating from 6 May 1231.[14] The letter, from Pope Gregory IX, recommends Geoffrey of Poitiers (d. 1231) and William of Auxerre (d. 1231) to King Louis IX. Geoffrey and William were returning to France after having spent time in Rome attending to university affairs during the academic strike of 1229–31. The Pope reassures the French King that during their stay at the Apostolic See the masters have done nothing running counter to the best interest of the Court. He then proceeds to commend a master John Pagus (*magistrum Iohannem Pagium*) as someone else who may have undeservingly incurred the King's suspicion due to certain detrac-

---

[11] As recently deplored by Henrik Lagerlund, "The Assimilation of Aristotelian and Arabic Logic up to the Later Thirteenth Century," in *Handbook of the History of Logic*, ed. Dov M. Gabbay and John Woods, vol. 2, *Mediaeval and Renaissance Logic* (Amsterdam: Elsevier, 2008), 302.

[12] Sten Ebbesen, "The Paris Arts Faculty: Siger of Brabant, Boethius of Dacia, Radulphus Brito," in *Medieval Philosophy*, ed. John Marenbon, vol. 3 of *Routledge History of Philosophy*, ed. G. H. R. Parkinson and S. G. Shanker (London: Routledge, 1998), 271.

[13] He has even been called the principal Parisian logician of the first half of the thirteenth century. See Alain de Libera, *L'art des généralités* (Paris: Aubier, 1999), 35.

[14] Heinrich Denifle and Emile Châtelain, *Chartularium Universitatis Parisiensis*, vol. 1 (Paris: Delalain, 1899), 145–46.

tors. The letter suggests that Pagus was somewhat closely involved in the contro-
versies surrounding the University of Paris at the time, though it does not clearly
indicate the exact nature of his involvement. It is possible that he was among the
university representatives who went to Rome upon the Pope's request, or that he
accompanied William of Auxerre on his journey there at the beginning of 1230.[15]
However it came about, the papal letter firmly establishes Pagus as a master of arts
in 1231. A few years later, ca. 1234–35, he must have taken up the study of theology,
since he appears to have lectured on the *Sentences* of Peter the Lombard as a bachelor of the *Sentences* (*Baccalarius sententiarius*) in 1243–45.[16]

Both as a logician and as a theologian, Pagus seems to have enjoyed some re-
nown. His repute in the former capacity is attested to by Henri d'Andeli's *The
Battle of the Seven Arts*, a satirical poem, which, judging from the circumstantial
evidence, dates from the second quarter of the thirteenth century (probably from
after 1236).[17] Here Pagus appears alongside John Pointlasne (fl. ca. 1250) and, possibly, Nicholas of Paris (d. before 1263) as the vanguard of the armed forces of
Dame Logic, which under the command of someone called Pierre of Courtenay,
are marching from Paris to take up battle against the humanist grammarians of
Orléans.[18] This picture of Pagus as a prominent logician in the first half of the thirteenth century is corroborated by the fact that his *Appellationes* constitutes the
principal source of Lambert of Lagny's *De appellatione* (ca. 1263–65).[19]

---

[15] Fernand Van Steenberghen, *Aristotle in the West: The Origins of Latin Aristotelianism* (Leuven: E. Nauwelaerts, 1955), 100–101.

[16] This is the date argued for by Victorin Doucet in Alexander of Hales, *Summa theologica*, vol. 4, *Prolegomena* (Quaracchi: Collegium S. Bonaventurae, 1948), cccliii. Marie-
Dominique Chenu, "Maîtres et Bacheliers de l'Université de Paris v. 1240: Description du
Manuscrit Paris, Bibl. Nat. lat. 15652," *Études d'Histoire Littéraire et Doctrinale du XIIIe
siècle* 1 (1932): 34 suggests a slightly earlier date: "Nous sommes ainsi reportés aux alentours de 1240, plutôt qu'aux alentours de 1245." Pagus' time as a bachelor of the *Sentences*
coincides with that of Odo Rigaldus (d. 1275), and the difference of opinion between Doucet
and Chenu is due to a disagreement about the correct date of Odo's time as a bachelor of
the *Sentences*; on this matter, see Doucet, *Prolegomena*, ccxxviii–ccxxix.

[17] See Henri d'Andeli, *The Battle of the Seven Arts*, ed. and trans. Louis John Paetow
(Berkeley: University of California Press, 1914), 33–34.

[18] Henri d'Andeli, *The Battle of the Seven Arts* vv. 49–54 (ed. Paetow, 41–42): "Ses genz
manda devers Tornai / Par dant Pierron de Cortenai / Uns logicïens molt tres sages. / La
fu mestre Jehans li pages / et Pointlasne, cil de Gamaches / Mestre Nichole aus hautes
naches." Nothing appears to be known of this Pierre of Courtenay; but cf. Paetow's note
to line 50. For the identification of Pointlasne, see Paetow's note to line 53. The identification of "Master Nicholas with the prominent buttocks" as Nicholas of Paris is very likely
but uncertain; see H.A.G. Braakhuis, "Obligations in Early Thirteenth Century Paris: The
Obligationes of Nicholas of Paris(?) (MS Paris, B. N. lat., 11412)," *Vivarium* 36 (1998): 154.

[19] See Alain de Libera, "Le traité *De appellatione* de Lambert de Lagny (Lambert de
Auxerre)," *AHDLMA* 48 (1982): 232–35.

His reputation as a theologian is attested to by an anonymous *Tractatus de fide secundum diversos magistros* found in a Münster manuscript (Münster, Universitätsbibliothek 257, ff. 54r–74r). Here, in the main text as well as in the margin, reference is made to a number of thinkers active in the first half of the thirteenth century, such as Phillip the Chancellor (d. 1236), Alexander of Hales (d. 1245), Hugh of St. Cher (d. 1263), Albert the Great (d. 1280), and Guerric of St. Quentin (d. before 1245). Along with these thinkers, Pagus is explicitly referred to a handful of times.[20]

He seems to have been a somewhat controversial figure. More specifically, his name is bound up with the ten theological theses that were condemned in Paris on 13 January 1241 and again, apparently, in strengthened form on 5 January 1244.[21] Indeed, as one of the manuscripts preserving the list of condemned theses, the fourteenth-century Vat. lat. 692, explicitly refers to them as "the errors of Pagus" (*errores Pagi*), there has been speculation that it was Pagus' lectures on the *Sentences* that occasioned the reinforced strictures.[22] Although the correctness of this *en bloc* ascription of the ten theses cannot, I think, be established with certainty at the present stage of research, other sources, dating from Pagus' own time, supply strong evidence that he entertained at least two of them.[23] If the attribution to

---

[20] See Franz Pelster, "Literargeschichtliches zur Pariser theologischen Schule aus den Jahren 1230 bis 1256," *Scholastik* 5 (1930): 46–78; Doucet, *Prolegomena*, cxli–cxlii. Pelster, "Literargeschichtliches," 78 dates the treatise to shortly before 1248.

[21] See Victorin Doucet, "La date des condamnations parisiennes dites de 1241: Faut-il corriger le Cartulaire de l'Université?" in *Mélanges Auguste Pelzer*, Recueil de Travaux d'Histoire et de Philologie 3ᵐᵉ Série, 26ᵐᵉ Fascicule (Leuven: Éditions de l'Institut Supérieur de Philosophie, 1947), 183–93.

[22] MS Vat. lat. 692, f. 179v. Another manuscript (Paris Nat. lat. 16360) connects the theses with a certain *frater Stephanus* — perhaps a reflection of the double condemnation; see Doucet, "La date," 184; 192–93.

[23] (1) Anon., *Tractatus de fide secundum diversos magistros* (Münster, Universitätsbibl. 257, ff. 72vb–73va): "Aliter secundum Pagum: (...) Spiritus Sanctus dupliciter potest considerari, vel prout est extremum vel prout est nexus Patris et Filii. Prout est nexus, sic se habet in ratione medii (...) Amor enim in ratione medii non procedit a Patre et Filio, sed procedit a Patre in Filium ut ab amante in amatum, et secundum hanc rationem Spiritus Sanctus (...) est spiritus Filii, sed non a Filio." (Cited from Doucet, *Prolegomena*, ccviii). This corresponds to the third of the condemned theses, namely, *Chartularium* I, 128 (ed. Denifle and Châtelain, 171): "Tertius, quod Spiritus Sanctus, prout est nexus vel amor, non procedit a Filio, sed tantum a Patre." (2) MS Paris, Bibl. Nat. lat. 15652, f. 54rb: "Et tangit opinionem Pagi, quod quidam fuerunt statim mali. Sed hoc error." (Cited from Johannes Gründel, "Die Sentenzenglosse des Johannes Pagus (circa 1243–1245) in MS Padua, Bibl. Ant. 139," *Münchener Theologische Zeitschrift* 9 (1958): 182, n. 42.) This corresponds to the fifth of the condemned theses, see *Chartularium* I, 128 (ed. Denifle and Châtelain, 171): "Quintus, quod malus angelus in principio suae creationis fuit malus et nunquam fuit nisi malus."

him of an anonymous gloss-commentary on the *Sentences* found in a manuscript in Padua is correct, it would also seem that he later retracted both of those views, perhaps in response to the strengthened condemnation of 1244.[24]

1.2. Works

A number of works relating to Pagus' career both as a logician and as a theologian have survived. His extant logical works consist of a treatise on supposition theory, the *Appellationes*,[25] part of a treatise on syncategorematic terms, the *Syncategoremata*,[26] and the commentary on Aristotle's *Categories* edited here, the *Rationes super Praedicamenta Aristotelis*.[27]

As to theological works, two introductory lectures (*introitus*) to a course on the *Sentences* of Peter the Lombard, as well as substantial parts of the lectures proper, are ascribed to Pagus in a collection of theological works contained in Paris, Bibl. Nat. lat. 15652 and Paris, Bibl. Nat. lat. 15702 — a collection that appears to be the work of a student preparing for his bachelor's degree in theology at the University of Paris between the years 1243 and 1247.[28] As the material ascribed to Pagus contains two explicit references to Pagus himself, it can, however, hardly be regarded as a direct *reportatio*, but is rather an adapted version of some such written account of his course.[29] Due to close literal resemblances, Johannes Gründel has suggested that an anonymous gloss-commentary on the *Sentences*, which he discovered in Padua, Bibl. Ant. 139, is a later authorial redaction of this

---

[24] See Gründel, "Sentenzenglosse," 171–85.

[25] Edited in Alain de Libera, "Les *Appellationes* de Jean Le Page," AHDLMA 51 (1984): 193–255; the treatise is preserved in two manuscripts, namely, Paris, Bibl. Nat. lat. 11412, ff. 83r–87r and Paris, Bibl. Nat. lat. 15170, ff. 63r–65r.

[26] Partially edited in H.A.G. Braakhuis, *De 13de eeuwse tractaten over syncategorematische termen*, vol. 1, *Inleidende studie* (Meppel: Krips Repro, 1979), 168–246; the treatise is preserved in a single manuscript, namely, Paris, Bibl. Nat. lat. 15170, ff. 46r–48r, 65r–70v.

[27] For a list of the logical works which have been attributed to Pagus and other relevant literature, see Olga Weijers, *Le travail intellectuel à la Faculté des arts de Paris: Textes et maîtres (ca. 1200–1500)*, vol. 5, *Répertoire des noms commençant par J (à partir de Johannes D.)*, Studia Artistarum 11 (Turnhout: Brepols, 2003), 136–37. For the commentaries on the *Isagoge*, the *Perihermeneias*, and the *Book of Six Principles* that have been attributed to him, see sections 2.1 and 2.5 below, as well as the appendix to part one.

[28] On this collection, see Doucet, *Prolegomena*, cccxlv–ccliv; Chenu, "Maîtres et Bacheliers," 11–39. The date given here is that argued for by Doucet; Chenu places its composition between 1240 and 1245.

[29] MS Paris, Bibl. Nat. lat 15652, f. 54rb: "Et tangit opinionem Pagi, quod quidam fuerunt statim mali. Sed hoc error." Ibid., f. 59va: "Ad aliud, quod illa innocentia et rectitudo sunt quasi habitudines naturales, secundum Pagum hoc est gratis data." (Cited from Gründel, "Sentenzenglosse," 182, n. 42; 183, n. 45).

material.[30] As these glosses contain an explicit retraction of an earlier position taken by its author on the question of the procession of the Holy Spirit — a position which is explicitly ascribed to Pagus in another source and identical to one of the ten condemned theses mentioned above — Gründel further suggests that the authorial redaction postdates the condemnation of 1244.[31]

2. THE COMMENTARY ON THE *CATEGORIES*

2.1. Manuscript Sources

There are two known manuscript sources for Pagus' commentary on the *Categories*. A small fragment containing extracts of the very beginning of the commentary is found in:

> F = MS Florence, Biblioteca Medicea Laurenziana, Gadd. Plut. 89 Sup. 76, ff. 2ra–3rb. 13th cent.

This manuscript contains mainly translations of the *ars vetus* and the *ars nova* and has been described by the editors of *Aristoteles Latinus*.[32] The anonymously transmitted fragment was identified by Sten Ebbesen in 1973, but the find was never published.

The main source for the commentary is:

> P = MS Padua, Biblioteca Universitaria 1589, ff. 24ra–67vb. Early 14th cent.

This manuscript contains a set of commentaries on the *ars vetus*. It measures ca. 245 x 180 mm and consists of 164 parchment leaves in all. The modern numeration in Arabic numerals counts 173 folios but is faulty as it skips from 29 to 39. The old numeration in Roman numerals is in five parts: I–XXI (ff. 3–23), I–XXVIII (ff. 24–68), I–XIII (ff. 69–81), I–XII (ff. 82–93), I–LXXX (ff. 94–172; folio 173 is blank). The text is neatly executed in what appears to be an Italian hand of the early fourteenth century[33] with paragraph letters, paragraph marks, and underlining of lemmata in red. There are two columns to a page for the first four parts (ff. 1–93) and one column for the remaining part (ff. 94–172). The contents are the following:

---

[30] Gründel, "Sentenzenglosse," 171–85.

[31] Gründel, "Sentenzenglosse," 185. For the condemned thesis, see n. 23 above.

[32] See L. Minio-Paluello, *Aristoteles Latinus: Codices. Pars posterior* (Cambridge: Cambridge University Press, 1955), 924–25.

[33] René A. Gauthier, *Preface* in Thomas Aquinas, *Expositio Libri peryermenias*: *Editio altera retractata* (Rome: Commissio Leonina, 1989), 65*.

(1) Fragment of a commentary on Porphyry's *Isagoge* (ff. 1ra–2va)

Inc. Cum sit necessarium, Grisairie, etc. Iste liber, cuius subiectum dicitur universale, dividitur in duas partes: in prooemium et tractatum. Secunda pars incipit ibi: *Videtur autem neque genus* etc.

Expl. ...confirmat quod dixerat locum esse principium generationis, dicens: *et enim*, pro quia, quia *patria* et locus *est principium generationis quemadmodum*, pro sicut, *pater.* Deinde cum dicit... (incomplete)

(2) A commentary on Porphyry's *Isagoge* (ff. 3ra–22va)

Title. Incipit Liber Porphyrii (2nd hand) + Johannis Bridam, scriptus Parisius per Enricum de Franbruc, scholarem in logica et utique in philosophia. Amen. (3rd hand)

Inc. Sicut dicit Philosophus, creata est anima intellectiva ad totius sapientiae Primi imaginem omnium species in se gerens...

Expl. Nam cum genus non *sit animal* etc. Exemplum est generis de quo praedicatur substantia vel aliquid huiusmodi. *Cumque differentia sit rationalis...* (incomplete)

Colophon. Explicit Liber Porphyrii (2nd hand)

+ Indices of notabilia and questions (ff. 22vb–23rb) (2nd hand)

(3) A commentary on Aristotle's *Categories* (ff. 24ra–67vb)

Title. Incipit Liber praedicamentorum Aristotelis (2nd hand)

Inc. Incipiunt Rationes super Praedicamenta Aristotelis secundum Iohannem Pagum. "Ars imitatur naturam in quantum potest,"...

Expl. ...modi septimi, secundum quem vir dicitur habere uxorem vel e converso. Deo gratias. Amen. Amen. Amen. Deo gratias.

Colophon. Expliciunt Rationes super Praedicamenta Aristotelis secundum Iohannem Pagum.

+ Indices of notabilia and questions (ff. 68r–68v) (2nd hand)

(4) A commentary on Aristotle's *Perihermeneias*

(a) Commentary on Book 1 (ff. 69ra–81rb)

Title. Incipit Liber perihermeneias primus (2nd hand)

Inc. Primum oportet constituere etc. In principio huius libri sicut et in aliis sex sunt inquirenda. Primo quae sit causa materialis, secundo quae sit formalis causa, tertio quae sit causa efficiens...

Expl. Hoc quemadmodum dictum est, quia, scilicet, in illis de praesenti est veritas determinata, in illis de futuro indeterminata.

Colophon. Explicit sententia super primum Perihermeneias (4th hand)

+ Indices of notabilia and questions (f. 81v) (2nd hand)

(b) Commentary on Book 2 (ff. 82ra–93rb)

Title. Incipit Liber perihermeneias secundus. Amen. (2nd hand)

Inc. Quoniam autem est de aliquo. In primo libro determinatum est de enuntiatione in se et absolute considerata non concreta ad aliquam materiam vel talem, in secundo libro determinat de enuntiatione concreta ad aliquam materiam vel talem, ut...

Expl. Ad tertium dicendum quod triplex {*lege:* duplex} est modus: processivus, ut quando aliquis movetur de loco ad locum, et talis motus non de necessitate inest animali, immo contingenter, et est motus naturalis.

Colophon^a. Explicit Scriptum super Librum Perihermeneias Aristotelis. Deo gratias. Amen.

Colophon^b. Explicit secundus liber Perihermeneias (2nd hand) + secundum Bridam, bonum et utique utilem (3rd hand)

+ Indices of notabilia and questions (f. 93va) (2nd hand)

(5) A commentary on the *Liber sex principiorum* (ff. 94r–172v)

Title. Incipit Liber sex principiorum (2nd hand) + a magistro Iohanne Bridam, Parisius utique scriptus (3rd hand)

Inc. Quoniam omnes doctrinae diversitatem recipiunt penes differentia syllogismorum {*lege:* differentiam subiectorum}, ideo necesse est rationalem philosophiam penes diversitatem sui subiecti diversitatem recipere. Quoniam igitur subiectum...

Expl. ...et notandum quod bene dicitur quod est moveri secundum naturam et non substantiam, quoniam non est generatio cuiuslibet, sed substantiae mobilis; non enim est generatio substantiarum incorporearum, quia non sunt mobiles secundum naturam. Amen.

+ Eight lines of extracts from Boethius' *Consolation of Philosophy* added by another hand in the white space after the commentary.

Colophon. Explicit scriptum super totam artem veterem (...) super Prae(...) secundum magistrum Iohannem Pagum. Deo gratias. Amen.

As we can see, only item (3), the commentary on the *Categories*, has a visible ascription in the original hand at the beginning of the commentary. The ascription in the colophon at the end of the commentary also appears to be in the original hand. The commentary is, in both cases, attributed to John Pagus.

The later third-hand additions to the second-hand titles in the upper margin or colophons of items (2), (4b), and (5) appear to ascribe these three commentaries to John Buridan, but such an ascription is, as everyone agrees, wholly impossible.[34]

The colophon to item (5) is of great importance. Unfortunately, it is almost completely faded and illegible. It was first noticed by the late Victorin Doucet. On the basis of Doucet's handwritten notes, an entry on Pagus was included in the *addenda et corrigenda* to Charles Lohr's catalogue of medieval Latin Aristotle commentaries. The central piece of information in this entry is the following:

> The manuscript Padova BU 1589 contains not only Pagus' commentary on the *Praedicamenta*, but a complete *Scriptum super totam artem (veterem)* per magistrum Johannem Pagum (f. 172v).[35]

Apparently, then, not only item (3), but also items (2), (4), and (5) are to be ascribed to Pagus. Subsequently, René A. Gauthier included a brief discussion of the Padua material in his impressive preface to the revised Leonine edition of Aquinas' commentary on the *Perihermeneias*. Referring to his correspondence with the director of the Biblioteca Universitaria in Padua, Gauthier offered the following reading of the colophon:

> Explicit scriptum super totam artem veterem secundum magistrum Iohannem Pagum. Deo gratias. amen.[36]

---

[34] See, for example, Gauthier, *Preface*, 65*.
[35] See Charles Lohr, "Medieval Latin Aristotle Commentaries: Addenda et Corrigenda," *Bulletin de Philosophie Médiévale* 14 (1972): 124.
[36] Gauthier, *Preface*, 65*.

It seems, however, that something important has been missed here. The colophon runs over two lines. On the suggested reading, the first line breaks shortly after the centre of the page (after *veterem*), which is also approximately where the second line ends. Recall, however, that everything in this section of the manuscript is written in a single column. So why did whoever wrote the colophon (it is unclear whether it is, in fact, in the original hand) leave almost half of the first line blank? It appears that he didn't, but that the end of the line has become almost completely invisible. Read under ultra-violet light, however, the following can be deciphered:

> Explicit scriptum super totam artem veterem (…) super prae(…) | secundum magistrum Iohannem Pagum. Deo gratias. Amen.

It seems that the "super prae" can only be a part of the title of item (3), Pagus' commentary on the *Categories*, namely, *Rationes super Praedicamenta Aristotelis*. This suggests that the colophon should be reconstructed as follows:

> Explicit scriptum super totam artem veterem. <Rationes> super prae<dicamenta Aristotelis> | secundum magistrum Iohannem Pagum. Deo gratias. Amen.

In any case, it seems clear that the colophon singles out the commentary on the *Categories*, and that this commentary is most likely the only item in the manuscript that it intends to ascribe to Pagus. In other words, the only information that the note really adds to what we know from the rest of the manuscript is the attribution to John Pagus of the title of *magister*.[37]

Another important thing to notice is that despite its apparent unity, on close study item (3), the commentary on the *Categories*, turns out to be made up of two different commentaries. One supplies full treatment of chapters 1–11 of Aristotle's text, as well as a partial treatment of chapter 12, before breaking off mid-sentence. The other supplies a partial treatment of chapter 12 plus full treatment of chapters 13–15. While the shift of commentary has left no outward sign in the manuscript, it emerges quite clearly from the occurrence of a stretch of garbled text followed by an easily detectable change in the formal features of commentary style at the bottom of f. 65va. It seems that at some stage someone found himself with an incomplete commentary and added the final part of a different commentary. He

---

[37] As it turns out, the staff at the Biblioteca Universitaria actually appears to have seen that the colophon isn't legible in its entirety. In a letter to the *Commissio Leonina*, dated 1 December 1987 and signed by the director of the library, Mr. Luigi Frisini, the following transcription of it is given: "Explicit scriptum super totam artem veterem […] secundum magistrum Iohannem Pagum. Deo gratias amen." The letter also mentions that the note is legible only under ultra-violet light. I thank Prof. Claude Lafleur for informing me of this letter.

located the exact place in Aristotle's text where the original commentary breaks off but seems to have made no attempt to tamper with the material so as to make a meaningful transition. The lack of any sort of indication in the manuscript of this shift of commentary suggests that it had already occurred in the source from which the scribe was copying.

Something similar is the case with item (2), the commentary on the *Isagoge*. Here, however, there seems to be material from three different commentaries. There is a shift of commentary in the middle of the discussion of the fourth of Porphyry's five predicables, the unique property (*proprium*). This shift reveals itself by the fact that there is a double exposition (*sententia*) of this chapter as well as a change in commentary style beginning with the second of these expositions (f. 20rb). It seems that there may be yet another shift of commentary beginning with the so-called *Communitates* (*Isag.* 13.7ff.). The reason for suspecting it is that according to the author of the second commentary it was customary not to bother with this concluding part of Porphyry's text, and yet, in the manuscript, the beginning of a treatment of it is actually found.[38] This treatment takes up merely two and a half columns starting on f. 22rb and only covers the very beginning of the *Communitates* (up to *Isag.* 14.13) before breaking off mid-sentence. Again, the differences in commentary style suggest that here we are dealing with material from a third commentary.

There are other manuscript sources for some of the items contained in the Padua manuscript, but they are scarce. Besides the small fragment of the commentary on the *Categories* already mentioned, they are as follows. Item (2), the commentary of Porphyry's *Isagoge*, is found in MS Vat. lat. 5988, ff. 63r–81v.[39] In contrast to the Padua manuscript, this manuscript seems to preserve the original commentary in its entirety.[40] The commentary is ascribed by a secondary hand to Peter of Ireland, whose commentary on the *Perihermeneias* is also preserved in the manuscript.[41] Item (4), the commentary on the *Perihermeneias*, is also found

---

[38] MS Padua, Biblioteca Universitaria 1589, f. 20va: "ista pars non solet legi." Lewry, *Kilwardby's Writings*, 255–56, notes this discrepancy and briefly discusses the apparent tendency to omit the *Communitates*.

[39] For a description of this manuscript, see Karen Elisabeth Dalgaard, "Peter of Ireland's Commentary on Aristotle's *Perihermeneias*," CIMAGL 43 (1982): 3–44.

[40] Except for what appears to be roughly a folio's worth of missing text between f. 75v and f. 76r (the end of the sixth and the beginning of the seventh *lectio*).

[41] A full edition of Peter's commentary can be found in Petrus de Ybernia, *Expositio et Questiones in Librum Aristotelis Peryermenias seu de Interpretatione*, ed. Michael Dunne. Philosophes Médiévaux 34 (Leuven: Peeters, 1996). Gauthier, *Preface*, 67*–68*, dates this commentary to ca. 1260.

in a second manuscript, namely, Palermo, Bibl. Com. 2 Qq. D. 142, ff. 37ra–51va.[42] In this case, however, it is the Padua manuscript which preserves the commentary in its entirety.

Little of the material has been edited. A short excerpt of the prologue of item (2) has been edited by Claude Lafleur.[43] All questions found in item (3), along with a few solutions, were excerpted by Ezio Franceschini in a groundbreaking 1933 article.[44] A list of the questions found in item (4) and a short excerpt of the commentary were published by H.A.G. Braakhuis.[45]

Since Victorin Doucet's discovery of the note on f. 172v of the manuscript, it appears to have been generally assumed that the four commentaries it contains, that is to say, not only the commentary on the *Categories*, but also items (2), (4), and (5), should be attributed to Pagus.[46] Several problems with this global attribution have since been noted,[47] but it still seems to be widely accepted.[48] However, since on close scrutiny the note appears to single out the commentary on the *Categories* and may well intend to ascribe only that item to Pagus, and since the four com-

---

[42] Andrea Tabarroni, "Lo Pseudo Egidio (Guglielmo Arnaldi) e un'inedita continuazione del commento di Tommaso al *Peryermenias*," *Medioevo* 14 (1988): 404–5, n. 46. For a description of the manuscript, see G.M. Cao et al., *Catalogo di manoscritti filosofici nelle biblioteche italiane*, vol. 7, *Novara, Palermo, Pavia*. Corpus Philosophorum Medii Aevi, Subsidia 8 (Florence: Leo S. Olschki, 1993), 48–50.

[43] Claude Lafleur, "Une figure métissée du platonisme médiéval: Jean le Page et le Prologue de son Commentaire (vers 1231–1240) sur l'*Isagoge* de Porphyre," in *Une philosophie dans l'histoire: Hommages à Raymond Klibansky*, ed. Bjarne Melkevik and Jean-Marc Narbonne (Québec: Les Presses de l'Université Laval, 2000), 105–60.

[44] Ezio Franceschini, "Giovanno Pago: Le sue *Rationes super Praedicamenta Aristotelis* e la loro posizione nel movimento Aristotelico del secolo XIII," *Sophia* 2 (1934): 172–82; 329–50; 476–86.

[45] H.A.G. Braakhuis, "The Chapter on the *Liber Peryarmenias* of the Ripoll '*Student's Guide*': A Comparison with Contemporary Commentaries," in *L'enseignement de la philosophie au XIIIᵉ siècle: Autour du "Guide de l'étudiant" du ms. Ripoll 109*, ed. Claude Lafleur and Joanne Carrier (Turnhout: Brepols, 1997), 320–23.

[46] A notable exception is Lewry, *Kilwardby's Writings*, 207, n. 9; 270, n. 3.

[47] Lewry, *Kilwardby's Writings*, 256; 270, n. 3; Tabarroni, "Lo Pseudo Egidio," 404–5, n. 46; C. H. Kneepkens, "*Significatio generalis* and *significatio specialis*: Notes on Nicholas of Paris' Contribution to Early Thirteenth-Century Linguistic Thought," in *Medieval Analyses in Language and Cognition*, ed. Sten Ebbesen and Russell L. Friedman (Copenhagen: The Royal Danish Academy of Sciences and Letters, 1999), 38–40; David Piché, *Le problème des universaux à la Faculté des arts de Paris entre 1230 et 1260* (Paris: Librairie Philosophique J. Vrin 2005), 134–35.

[48] Gauthier, *Preface*, 65*; Claude Lafleur, "La *Philosophia* d' Hervé le Breton (alias Henri le Breton) et le recueil d'introductions à la philosophie du ms. Oxford, Corpus Christi College 283 (Première partie)," *AHDLMA* 61 (1994): 196–97, n. 97; Braakhuis, "Chapter," 305–6; Weijers, *Travail intellectuel*, vol. 5, 136–37.

mentaries are furthermore so stylistically diverse that they clearly do not constitute a unitary course on the old art (see the appendix to part one), there appears to be no reason to think that items (2), (4), and (5) were written by Pagus, and the attribution may, I submit, safely be rejected.

2.2. Formal Features

The *Rationes super Praedicamenta* is a literal commentary. More specifically, it is a literal commentary of the so-called *lectio* variety. This format appears to have become the standard vehicle of exegesis at some point during the second quarter of the thirteenth century and takes its name from the fact that it breaks up the text under interpretation into a number of lectures (*lectiones*).[49]

In principle, this type of commentary provides a comprehensive exposition of the authoritative text where every passage is dealt with, line by line, in a uniform way. This is achieved by progressively subjecting each passage to a series of standard exegetical operations — the exact number and choice of which may vary from commentator to commentator. As a result, each *lectio* naturally divides into a number of more or less clearly defined components. In addition, it is customary for commentaries of this type to contain a prologue in which more general preliminary matters are determined. The prologue may simply be an integral part of the first *lectio* or form a more autonomous whole.

Pagus' *Categories* commentary adheres to the standard format rather strictly. Judging from its well-articulated composition and the many references to authoritative texts it incorporates, it is certainly no mere *reportatio* of a lecture series, but the product of considerable editorial work. As it is found in the manuscript, it consists of 48 *lectiones*. The last 3 ½ of these are demonstrably from a different commentary, but the complete original is likely to have contained much the same number. It is a work of roughly 70,000 words.

The prologue forms an integral part of the first *lectio*, and the remaining *lectiones* are, as a rule, rigidly structured units made up of the following four elements in the specified order: (1) a division (*divisio*), (2) an exposition (*sententia*), (3) a literal exposition (*expositio litteralis*), and (4) a series of questions (*quaestiones*).[50] The quantity of text dealt with in a given *lectio* may vary from a couple of lines to several pages, so that while every passage of the authoritative text receives a uniform treatment, more emphasis may be put on select passages.

---

[49] For a general introduction to the different formats used by medieval commentators, see, e.g., Olga Weijers, *Le maniement du savoir: Pratiques intellectuelles à l'époque des premières universités (XIIIe-XIVe siècles)* (Turnhout: Brepols, 1996).

[50] In the first two *lectiones*, elements (2) and (3) merge; in the third *lectio*, the same is initially the case, but then element (3) is added as a separate element after element (4); beginning with the fourth *lectio*, the structure as here described is in place.

Each *lectio* opens with a lemma, followed by a succinct introductory statement serving to locate that piece of text in its immediate context. This leads directly on to the division, which is an extremely detailed structural analysis of Aristotle's text, beginning with the text as a whole and terminating in the identification of atomic parts of, roughly, sentence length. The analysis is begun in the first *lectio* and carried out progressively throughout the commentary.

The second component is the exposition (*sententia*). This part of the *lectio* is basically a successive paraphrase of each of the atomic parts identified in the division. As the contents of each of these parts have already been described in outline in the division, and since the parts are generally rather short, there is some repetition here. Yet, what the procedure serves to do is to expound in more detail the contents of each part. This frequently involves explicating the argumentative structure of the part, supplying premises and conclusions if needed, and noting which of these Aristotle actually posits. Again, the procedure is carried out in rather formulaic terms.

The third component is the literal exposition (*expositio litteralis*). This is basically a running gloss on Aristotle's text and serves to explain in detail how the interpretation of the contents put forward in the division and exposition may be derived from the text. This is done by explicating the links between parts, periods, and sentences, spelling out the referents of pronouns, offering synonyms for difficult words, rearranging the word-order, etc.

The fourth and final component is the section devoted to questions (*quaestiones*). Of the four elements that constitute a *lectio*, this part displays the least fixed structure. Thematically, questions range from those closely tied to the exegesis of the text, such as questions why Aristotle proceeds the way he does, why he uses the expressions he does, or how to avoid some undesirable consequence of what he says, etc., to those of more theoretical import with only a faint grounding in the actual text, e.g., what is the nature of truth? Structurally, this section is sometimes divided into two main parts according to a thematic grouping of the questions, such as, for example, those pertaining to purely exegetical matters and those of a more general nature. At other times, the structuring principle is based on the structural features of the text itself. Such ordering is frequently announced at the outset. In some cases, it is detectable but not explicitly announced, and in yet others it is neither announced nor detectable. Sometimes questions and answers alternate, at other times a series of questions is followed by a series of corresponding answers. An answer may on occasion prompt a further question or objection to be worked through before proceeding to the next question.

The complexity of the questions range from very simple ones, taking up no more than a line or two, to elaborate constructions involving one or more arguments for a given standpoint, one or more arguments to the contrary, a magisterial solution, and, finally, refutations of the arguments to the contrary of that solution. Questions of medium complexity, involving some but not all of the elements mentioned, are frequent. Some questions may take up more than a page in the printed edition, but they remain rather simple structurally and never reach the complexity achieved in the question commentaries that became common in the second half of the thirteenth century. A very pronounced feature of this section is the frequent use of and reference to authoritative texts in the formulation of the question. The texts are often invoked as contradicting the *Categories* or used to supply one or more of the premises in arguments whose conclusions contradict what Aristotle says there, but they may also be cited in support of a solution to a given question.

Pagus' commentary does not follow the practice of devoting a separate part of the *lectio* to an in-depth explication of how the passage under exposition fits into the overall structure of the authoritative text or of the passage's own internal structure (*ordo, ordinatio*). If such matters are brought up (which they frequently are), they are dealt with in the question section. Another component absent from the commentary is the listing of key points (*notabilia*) to be taken from the passage dealt with in a given *lectio*.[51]

As is clear, this type of commentary aims at being comprehensive. Its overriding concern is to elucidate Aristotle's text chapter by chapter, line by line, paying close attention to details of argumentative structure and literal content, as well as to questions arising out of these more narrow exegetical concerns. As such, it imparts to the reader a very thorough and detailed knowledge of what is usually a rather difficult text. These concerns are largely determined by the specific educational context in which this type of commentary evolved, and a present-day reader is likely to find a literal commentary rough going. To the modern mind, it simply looks boring, and the exposition may — at times perhaps justifiably — appear to pay excessive attention to irrelevant or self-explanatory detail at the cost of neglecting matters of more theoretical concern. It is certainly true that a literal commentary lacks some of the salient features of a systematic treatise, but this does not mean that there isn't a systematic approach to the topic it deals with un-

---

[51] The commentary from which the ending has been supplied is of a somewhat simpler sort. It partitions the authoritative text into parts in a way equivalent to a *lectio* commentary, but does not employ the word *lectio*. For each main part, it provides the initial words, followed by an introductory statement serving to locate the part in its immediate context. There is no division. Instead, there is a general exposition of the text, in which each subpart is first identified by its initial words and then examined. Once the entire piece of text has been expounded in this manner, there follows a series of numbered questions followed by a corresponding series of numbered answers. This section displays a very uniform structure, and individual questions do not reach the levels of complexity evidenced by some of the questions in the initial commentary. An edition of this fragment can be found in the appendix to part two.

derlying the exposition, nor does it imply that its author does not have interesting things to say about issues of perennial philosophical interest. It is, however, often the case that such views will have to be teased out of the text, sometimes to appear only in outline.

2.3. Authoritative Sources

Throughout his commentary, Pagus pursues a program of exegesis that aims not only at a comprehensive exposition of Aristotle's text, but also at an interpretation under which the *Categories* is consistent internally as well as externally, that is, with points of doctrine drawn from a larger body of works recognized as authoritative in Pagus' immediate historical context. Indeed, it is, as was noted previously, a prevalent feature of the commentary that a vast number of other texts are brought to bear on the interpretation of the *Categories*. The authoritative sources explicitly invoked fall into two main groupings: texts written by Aristotle and texts not written by Aristotle.[52]

The texts written by Aristotle come from all corners of the corpus: logic, natural philosophy, metaphysics, ethics, etc. All of the texts belonging to the *ars nova* are represented as are a number of the *libri naturales* — references to the *Topics* and the *Physics* being especially numerous.

Work	References	Work	References
Perihermeneias	7	*Meteora*	6
Prior Analytics	1	*De anima*	11
Posterior Analytics	17	*De morte et vita*	2
Topics	31	*De animalibus*	1
Sophistici elenchi	8	*Metaphysics*	7
Physics	35	*Nicomachean Ethics*	12
De generatione et corruptione	1	Unspecified	18

Table 1. Explicit references to the writings of Aristotle[53]

Not all of the references have been placed. Some are almost verbatim quotations, while others are merely *ad sensum* or very general in nature. Many of them appear to have been commonplace. This can be gleaned from the fact that they are frequently phrased in a way that does not actually correspond to Aristotle's text but rather to the formulations found in the *Auctoritates Aristotelis*, a compilation

---

[52] The specific passages Pagus refers to are collected in the index locorum.

[53] The unspecified references (*dicit Aristoteles, dicit Philosophus, dicitur alibi*, etc.) distribute as follows: *Topics* 3; *Physics* 6; *De generatione et corruptione* 1; *Metaphysics* 2; *Nicomachean Ethics* 1; plus five that have not been placed. Three of the eight references to the *Sophistici elenchi* seem to actually be to the *Topics*.

of authoritative quotations from the writings of Aristotle, Averroes, Boethius, and others. The *Auctoritates* was compiled after 1267 but undoubtedly had precursors. It seems that Pagus was acquainted with and used one of these.

To the extent that it can actually be determined which translations lie behind the references to Aristotle's works, they seem to be the following.[54] For the *Posterior Analytics*, the translation used is that of James of Venice.[55] For the *Topics*, it is that of Boethius.[56] For the *Physics*, it would again seem to be James of Venice's translation.[57] For the first three books of the *Meteora*, the translation used

---

[54] For a convenient list of the Latin translations of Aristotle's works, see Appendix B1 in *The Cambridge History of Medieval Philosophy*, ed. Robert Pasnau (Cambridge: Cambridge University Press, 2010), vol. 2, 793–97. The list is a slightly revised version of the table in Bernard G. Dod, "Aristoteles Latinus," in *The Cambridge History of Later Medieval Philosophy*, ed. Norman Kretzmann, Anthony Kenny, and Jan Pinborg (Cambridge: Cambridge University Press, 1982), 74–78.

[55] See John Pagus, *Rationes super Praedicamenta* XXX, q. 5 (ed. Hansen, 178.5–9): "Et dicendum quod duplex est ignorantia, scribitur in primo *Posteriorum*. (...) Alia est (...), et hanc appellat Aristoteles deceptionem factam per syllogismum." The reference is to *Posterior Analytics* I 16.79b23–25; in James' translation (ed. Minio-Paluello and Dod, Aristoteles Latinus 4.1, 34): "Ignorantia autem non secundum negationem sed secundum dispositionem dicta est quidem *per syllogismum facta deceptio*"; in John's translation (ed. Minio-Paluello, AL 4.2, 133): "Ignorantia autem quae non secundum negationem sed secundum dispositionem dicta est quidem per syllogismum dicta fallacia"; in Gerard of Cremona's translation (ed. Minio-Paluello, AL 4.3, 217): "Ignorantia autem quae est non secundum modum negationis sed sicut dispositio et forma deceptio est per viam syllogismi"; in William of Moerbeke's translation (ed. Dod, AL 4.4, 302): "Ignorantia autem non secundum negationem sed secundum dispositionem dicta est quidem quae per syllogismum fit deceptio."

[56] See, for example, John Pagus, *Rat. sup. Praed.* IX, q. 1 (55.28–29): "Sed omne univocum comparabile, scribitur in primo *Topicorum*." The reference is to *Topics* I 15.107b17; in Boethius' translation (ed. Minio-Paluello, AL 5.1, 26): "Nam *univocum omne comparabile*"; in the anonymous twelfth-century translation (ed. Minio-Paluello, AL 5.3, 205): "Univocum enim omne *comparatum*." See also John Pagus, *Rat. sup. Praed.* XIII, q. 3 (83.15–16): "Scribitur in *Topicis* quod ignis flamma magis est ignis quam ignis carbo, et lux quam flamma." The reference is to *Topics* V 5.134b28–35a5, and the rendering of the three kinds of fire as *carbo*, *flamma*, and *lux* is that of Boethius (ed. Minio-Paluello, AL 5.1, 102); the anonymous translation (ed. Minio-Paluello, AL 5.3, 245) has *pruna*, *flamma*, and *splendor*.

[57] See, for example, John Pagus, *Rat. sup. Praed.* XXXIII, q. 5 (140.4): "Infinitum est cuius quantitatem sumentibus semper est aliquid sumere extra." The reference is to *Physics* III 6.207a7–8; in James' translation (ed. Bossier and Brams, AL 7.1.2, 128): "*Infinitum* quidem igitur hoc *est cuius* secundum *quantitatem* accipientibus *semper aliquid est* accipere *extra*"; in Michael Scot's translation (ed. Venet., 115rb): "Infinitum igitur est illud ex quo cum aliquid accipitur possibile est semper accipere aliquid extra illud in quantitate." In fact, Pagus' wording most closely resembles what, according to Bossier and Brams' apparatus, is found in MS Oxford, Corpus Christi 111 (*Oc*): "*Infinitum* igitur *est cuius quantitatem* accipientibus *semper est aliquid sumere extra*." For another example, see John Pagus,

is that of Gerard of Cremona;[58] for the fourth book, that of Henry Aristippus.[59] With respect to the *De anima*, ten out of the eleven places referred to are actually included in some form in the *Auctoritates Aristotelis*. Whether it be directly or

Rat. sup. Praed. XXII, q. 5 (135.12–13): "unumquodque non prohibitum fertur ad locum proprium." The reference is to *Physics* IV 1.208b11–12; in James' translation (ed. Bossier and Brams, AL 7.1.2, 136): *"fertur* enim *unumquodque* in sui *locum non prohibitum"*; in Michael Scot's translation (ed. Venet., 122va): "quodlibet enim eorum transfertur ad suum locum quem habet nisi impediatur ab aliquo."

[58] See John Pagus, *Rat. sup. Praed.* XLI, q. 6 (239.12–14): "et hoc est quod scribitur in primo *Meteorum* quod elementa corrumpuntur et generantur ad invicem, et unum est in potentia et alterum." The reference is to *Meteora* I 3.339a37–b1; in Gerard's translation (ed. Schoonheim, 8): "Dico ergo quod ignis et aer et aqua et terra *generantur et corrumpuntur* et alterantur ab *invicem*, et omne elementum ex eis est in elemento alio *potentia"*; in William of Moerbeke's translation (ed. Vuillemin-Diem, AL 10.2.2, 10): "Dicimus itaque ignem et aerem et aquam et terram fieri ex invicem, et unumquodque horum in unoquoque existere potentia."

[59] See John Pagus, *Rat. sup. Praed.* XLI, q. 7 (239.23–25): "Scribitur in quarto *Meteorum*: Cum quattuor sint qualitates, duae passivae, aridum et umidum, et duae activae, calidum et frigidum, calidum est maxime activum." The reference is to *Meteora* IV 1.378b10–13; in Henry's translation (ed. Rubino, AL 10.1, 7): "Quoniam quidem quattuor causae determinatae sunt elementorum, harum quidem iuxta coniugationes et elementa quattuor contingit esse, quarum sane *duae activae, calidum et frigidum, duae* profecto *passivae, aridum et umidum"*; in Gerard's translation (ed. Schoonheim, 144): "Capita primitiva elementorum quattuor sunt quattuor, sicut elementa composita, ex quibus sunt duo elementa agentia et duo elementa patientia. Verum duo elementa agentia sunt caliditas et frigiditas, et duo quidem elementa patientia sunt umiditas et siccitas"; in Moerbeke's translation (ed. Vuillemin-Diem, AL 10.2.2, 105): "Quoniam autem quattuor causae determinatae sunt elementorum, harum autem secundum coniugationes et elementa quattuor accidit esse, quarum duo quidem factiva, calidum et frigidum, duo autem passiva, siccum et umidum." Note that on one occasion, the language is reminiscent of what we find in the commentary of Alfred of Sareshel; see John Pagus, *Rat. sup. Praed.* XXXII (187.14–17): "et est durum, ut scribitur in quarto *Meteorum*, quod de difficili cedit impressioni, molle vero quod cedit de facili non circumfluendo (et dicit 'non circumfluendo' propter aquam et huiusmodi alia umida)." The reference is to *Meteora* IV 7.382a11–14; in Henry's translation (ed. Rubino, AL 10.1, 16): "Est nempe durum non cedens in se ipsum, secundum epipedum, molle vero cedens in non circumstando; namque aqua non molle; haut enim cedit compressioni epipedum in profunditatem, ceterum contracircumstat"; in Moerbeke's translation (ed. Vuillemin-Diem, AL 10.2.2, 114): "Est autem durum quidem quod non cedit in se ipsum secundum superficiem, molle autem quod cedit non econtracircumstando; aqua enim non mollis; non enim cedit compressione superficies in profundum, sed econtracircumstat"; Alfred comments (ed. Otte, 66): "Umidum facile *cedit impressioni*, et hoc molle dicimus; aridum resistit, et hoc durum appellatur." Pagus has *circumfluendo* rather than *circumstando* here. This is not recorded as a variant reading in Rubino's apparatus, but note that Albert the Great's commentary on the passage (ed. Hossfeld, 249a) glosses both occurrences of the verb *circumstare* by forms of *circumfluere* ("*circumstando* sive circumfluendo"; "*circumstat* et circumfluit"), so it might well have been a common gloss.

indirectly, the translation behind the quotations is usually that of James of Venice.⁶⁰ On one occasion, however, it would appear to be that of Michael Scot.⁶¹ The explicit references to the *Metaphysics* are not very numerous and are never literal enough to determine exactly which translation was used. Several of them take the form of commonplaces.⁶² They are not confined to the parts covered by James of

---

⁶⁰ See, for example, John Pagus, *Rat. sup. Praed.* x, q. 1 (61.4–5): "Accidentia maximam partem conferunt ad cognoscendum subiectum." The reference is to *De anima* I 1.402b21–22; in James' translation (ed. Decorte and Brams, Aristoteles Latinus Database 12.1): "*accidentia conferunt* magnam *partem ad cognoscendum* quod quid est"; in Michael Scot's translation (ed. Crawford, 14): "accidentia adiuvant maxime in sciendo quid est aliquid"; Moerbeke (ed. Gauthier, 3) has made no revision to James' text here; the word-order and the use of *subiectum* in Pagus seem to point to a florilegium like Anon., *Auct. Arist.* (ed. Hamesse, 174): "*Accidentia* magnam *partem conferunt ad cognoscendum* quod quid est, id est *subiectum* sive definitio subiecti." See also John Pagus, *Rat. sup. Praed.* XIII, q. 1 (82.29–30): "excellentia sensibilium corrumpit sensum." The reference is to *De Anima* II 12.424a28–32; in James' translation (ed. Decorte and Brams, ALD 12.1): "Manifestum autem est ex his et propter quid *sensibilium excellentia*e *corrump*unt ea quibus sentimus; si namque sit fortior eo quo sentimus motus, solvitur ratio (hoc autem *sensu*s est), sicut et symphonia et tonus percussis fortiter cordis"; in Michael Scot's translation (ed. Cornford, 318): "Et manifesta est ex hoc causa propter quam sensibilia intensa corrumpunt instrumenta sensuum, quae sit etiam quoniam, quando motu sentientis fuerit fortior eo, dissolvetur sua intentio (et hoc erit sensus), sicut dissolvitur consonantia cordarum et neumata, cum tanguntur fortiter"; in Moerbeke's revision (ed. Gauthier, 168): "Manifestum autem ex his et propter quid sensibilium excellentiae corrumpunt sensitiva; si namque sit fortior sensitivo motus, solvitur ratio, hoc autem erat sensus, sicut et symphonia et tonus percussis fortiter cordis"; in Anon., *Auct. Arist.* (ed. Hamesse, 182): "excellens sensibile *corrumpit sensum.*"

⁶¹ See John Pagus, *Rat. sup. Praed.* XI, q. 3 (67.11–12): "substantia dicitur tribus modis: materia, forma et compositum." The reference is to *De anima* II 1.414a14–15; in Michael Scot's translation (ed. Crawford, 165): "*substantia dicitur tribus modis,* sicut diximus, *materia* scilicet et *forma et compositum* ex eis"; in James' translation (ed. Decorte and Brams, ALD 12.1): "tripliciter enim dicta substantia, sicut diximus, quorum hoc quidem species, illud autem materia, aliud autem ex utrisque"; in Moerbeke's revision (ed. Gauthier, 82): "tripliciter enim dicta substantia, sicut diximus, quarum hoc quidem species, illud vero materia, aliud autem ex utrisque"; in Anon., *Auct. Arist.* (ed. Hamesse, 177): "Triplex est substantia rerum, scilicet materia, forma et compositum."

⁶² For example, John Pagus, *Rat. sup. Praed.* VI, q. 4 (42.8): "secundum quod dicit Aristoteles quod ens et verum convertuntur." The adage is based on *Metaphysics* II 1.993b30–31; in James of Venice's translation (ed. Vuillemin-Diem, AL 25.1, 37): "quare unumquodque sicut se habet ad esse, sic et ad veritatem"; in the *composita* (ed. Vuillemin-Diem, AL 25.1a, 120): "quare unumquodque sicut ad esse sic ad veritatem se habet"; in the *media* (ed. Vuillemin-Diem, AL 25.2, 37): "quare unumquodque sicut habet esse, ita et veritatem"; in Michael Scot's translation (ed. Venet., 29vb): "quapropter necesse est ut dispositio cuiuslibet rei in esse sit dispositio sua in rei veritate"; in Moerbeke's revision of the *media* (ed. Vuillemin-Diem, AL 25.3.2, 44): "quare unumquodque sicut se habet ut sit, ita et ad veritatem";

Venice's translation (and the anonymous revision known as the *composita*) in its present state (books I to IV 4). Since Pagus refers to Averroes' commentary, he was presumably acquainted with Michael Scot's accompanying translation from the Arabic, but he also refers to a passage from book I that is missing from this translation.[63] The references to the *Ethics* are all *ad sensum* — sometimes to the extent that they are difficult to place.[64] All would, however, seem to be to the first three books. Most of them are to book II (which Pagus twice refers to as "the first book of the *Old ethics*"),[65] and there is one reference to book III. It has been thought otherwise,[66] but the *Ethica nova* (book I) is, in fact, also referred to.[67] Although the

Anon., *Auct. Arist.* (ed. Hamesse, 118): "Unumquodque sicut se habet ad entitatem, sic se habet ad veritatem."

[63] See John Pagus, *Rat. sup. Praed.* XXXVI, q. 2 (210.5–6): "Sapiens ergo ordinare debet et non ordinari, ut scribitur in *Metaphysica*." The reference, which, it should be noted, was a commonplace, is to *Metaphysics* I 2.982a17–19; in James of Venice's translation (ed. Vuillemin-Diem, AL 25.1, 8): "non enim oportet ordinari sapientem sed ordinare"; in the *composita* (ed. Vuillemin-Diem, AL 25.1a, 92), the *media* (ed. Vuillemin-Diem, AL 25.2, 9), and Moerbeke's revision of the *media* (ed. Vuillemin-Diem, AL 25.3.2, 15): "non enim ordinari sed sapientem ordinare oportet"; in Anon., *Auct. Arist.* (ed. Hamesse, 116): "Sapientis non est ordinari, sed ordinare oportet, id est sapientis est regere et non regi."

[64] For example, John Pagus, *Rat. sup. Praed.* XL, q. 3 (232.9–11): "Et quando dominatur sensualitas <et> succumbit ratio, homo male operatur, ut scribitur in *Ethicis*, sed e converso, bene"; cf. ibid., XXV, q. 2 (149.10–11): "et scribitur quod quando praedominatur ratio <et> succumbit ancilla sensualitas, tunc bene operatur homo, si e converso, male." The language is not that of Aristotle's *Nicomachean Ethics*, but similar to what one finds in twelfth-century texts such as the *Liber poenitentialis* of Alan of Lille (ed. Migne, PL 210, 284a): "Sed hae fenestrae frequenter obturantur, dum in creaturis creator non legitur, dum homo a divina illustratione deseritur, dum ratio sensualitati ancillatur, dum sacra scriptura contemnitur"; and the anonymous *Liber de stabilitate animae* (ed. Migne, PL 213, 917b): "Duas naturas deus in anima posuit, unam superiorem, id est rationem; aliam inferiorem, id est sensualitatem"; and ibid. (ed. Migne, 919c): "Habet enim ratio ancillam naturaliter lascivam et petulcam, incontinentem et impudicam, sensualitatem videlicet, cuius quidem officium esset, si legem sibi a deo constitutam vellet custodire, dominae suae rationi in omnibus et per omnia oboedire. Ipsa enim tunc tantum recte incedit, cum a magisterio et imperio rationis non recedit."

[65] See John Pagus, *Rat. sup. Praed.* X, q. 3 (62.4–5): "Scribitur in primo *Veteris ethicae* quod omnis actio circa singularia, et passio similiter"; and ibid., XXXI, q. 6 (184.9–11): "Et hoc est quod scribitur in primo *Ethicae veteris* quod quales sunt operationes, tales sunt habitus ex operationibus derelicti in anima."

[66] Franceschini, "Giovanno Pago," 484.

[67] See John Pagus, *Rat. sup. Praed.* XL, q. 2 (231.18–20): "Aliud est bonum morale, scilicet bonum acquisitum, de quo scribitur in *Ethicis* quod non qui facit bona bonus est, sed qui bonum facit et hoc ipso gaudet bonus est." The reference must be to *EN* I 9.1099a17–18; in Burgundio of Pisa's translation (ed. Gauthier, AL 26.2a, 81): "Cum praedictis enim nullus est bonus, qui non delectatur bonis operationibus"; in Grosseteste's translation (ed. Gauthier, AL 26.3a, 153) and Moerbeke's revision (ed. Gauthier, AL 26.3b, 386): "Cum dictis

references are all far from being literal quotations, the underlying translation can on one occasion be seen to be that of Burgundio of Pisa.[68] On another occasion, one encounters a word (*multifarie*) that is actually found in Grosseteste's rather than Burgundio's translation of the relevant passage,[69] but there does not, on the whole, seem to be sufficient evidence to warrant the conclusion that Pagus actually knew the *translatio Lincolniensis*.[70]

---

enim nullus est bonus, qui non gaudet bonis operationibus." Although it is not the passage primarily referred to, Franceschini, "Giovanni Pago, 484, n. 60, nevertheless has a point when he mentions EN II 2.1104b5–6; in Burgundio's translation (ed. Gauthier, AL 26.1, 8): "Qui quidem enim removetur a corporalibus voluptatibus et hoc ipso gaudet, castus"; in Grosseteste's translation (ed. Gauthier, AL 26.3a, 166) and Moerbeke's revision (ed. Gauthier, AL 26.3b, 399): "Qui quidem enim recedit a corporalibus voluptatibus et hoc ipso gaudet, temperatus." Clearly, the phrase *et hoc ipso gaudet* is taken from this passage, which is the only place in the *Ethics* where it occurs.

[68] John Pagus, *Rat. sup. Praed.* XLII, q. 2 (243.15–16): "scribitur in *Ethicis*, quod tria requiruntur ut simus boni: scire, velle et impermutabiliter operari." Cf. ibid., XL, q. 2 (231.20–21): "scribitur ibidem quod tria requiruntur ad hoc ut simus boni: scire, velle, impermutabiliter operari." The reference is to EN II 3.1105a28–33, and the use of *velle* and *-mutabiliter* points to Burgundio's translation (ed. Gauthier, AL 26.1, 10): "Sufficit igitur ea qualiter habentia, fieri; ea autem quae secundum virtutes fiunt, non si illa qualiter habent, iuste et caste operantur, sed si qui operatur qualiter habens operatur; prius quidem si *sciens*; deinde si *volens* propter haec; tertium autem si firme et *immutabiliter* habens, *operatur*"; in Grosseteste's translation (ed. Gauthier, AL 26.3a, 168) and Moerbeke's revision (ed. Gauthier, AL 26.3b, 400): "Quae autem secundum virtutes fiunt, neque si haec qualiter habeant, iuste vel temperate operata sunt, sed et si operans qualiter habens operetur; primum quidem si sciens, deinde si eligens, et eligens propter haec, tertium autem et si firme et immobiliter habeat et operetur."

[69] See John Pagus, *Rat. sup. Praed.* XLIV, q. 4 (255.19–20): "Bonum dicitur uno modo, scribitur in *Ethicis*, malum vero multifarie." The reference is to EN II 5.1106b34–35; in Burgundio's translation (ed. Gauthier, AL 26.1, 14): "Boni quidem enim simpliciter, mali autem omnifariam"; in Grosseteste's translation (ed. Gauthier, AL 26.3a, 171) and Moerbeke's revision (ed. Gauthier, AL 26.3b, 403): "Boni quidem enim simpliciter, *multifarie* autem mali." The date of Grosseteste's translation of the *Nicomachean Ethics* is uncertain, but it is usually placed around 1246–47; see D.A. Callus, "The Date of Grosseteste's Translations and Commentaries on Pseudo-Dionysius and the Nicomachean Ethics," *Recherches de Théologie ancienne et médiévale* 14 (1947): 186–210.

[70] The reference just mentioned was a commonplace. It occurs, for example, twice in the *Summa* of Alexander of Hales (in the parts presumably written before Grosseteste's translation), once as "bonum enim est uno modo, malum autem omnifariam," and once as "bonum est uno modo, malum autem *multifariam*" (see Doucet, *Prolegomena*, cxiv). It is also implicitly invoked in Kilwardby's commentary on the *Categories* (which presumably also antedates Grosseteste's translation); see Robert Kilwardby, *Not. sup. Praed.* XVII, q. 31 (Cambridge, Peterhouse 206, f. 63ra; Madrid, Bibl. Univ. 73, f. 38rb): "est enim bonum uno modo, malum autem *multifariam*." Since Pagus' reference is actually closer to what we find in Alexander of Hales and Kilwardby than to any of the translations (he has *bonum, uno*

The source material drawn upon that does not stem from the *Corpus Aristotelicum* displays a surprising variety. Besides numerous references to the other set texts of the arts course, Porphyry's *Isagoge*, the anonymous *Book of Six Principles*, and Priscian's *Institutiones grammaticae*, as well as to Boethius' commentaries and logical monographs, we find, as table 2 shows, references to, among others, a number of medical works, some theological treatises, and Averroes' commentaries on the *De anima*, the *Physics*, and the *Metaphysics*.

Author/Work	References	Author/Work	References
Anon., *Liber de causis*	2	Dionysius, *De caelesti hierarchia*	1
Anon., *Liber sex principiorum*	15	Euclid, *Elementa*	1
Anselm, *De veritate*	2	Haly, *Super Librum tegni Galeni*	2
Augustine, *in Iohannis evangelium*	1	Hippocrates, *Aphorismi* [Galen]	1
Ps.-Augustine, *Categoriae decem*	3	Horace, *Epistolae*	1
Ps.-Augustine, *De spiritu et anima*	1	Isaac Israeli, *Liber febrium* [Galen]	1
Averroes		Ps.-Isaac Israeli	1
in De an.	3	Isidore of Seville	
in Metaph.	1	*Etymologiae*	1
in Phys.	5	*Sententiae* [Boethius]	1
Avicebron, *Fons vitae*	2	John Damascene, *De plantis*	1
Avicenna, *Liber canonis*	1	Johannitius, *Isagoge*	2
Boethius		† Morebus † (not found)	1
Ars geometriae	1	Nicholas of Amiens, *Ars fidei*	
Consolatio philosophiae	3	*catholicae*	4
De divisione	4	Nicolaus Logicus (not found)	1
De hypotheticis syllogismis	1	Peter Helias, *Summa super Priscianum*	1
De topicis differentiis	4	Philaretus, *Liber pulsuum*	2
in Cat.	14	Plato, *Timaeus*	5
*in Int.*¹	1	Porphyry, *Isagoge*	17
*in Int.*²	1	Priscian, *Institutiones grammaticae*	15
*in Isag.*²	4	Richard of St. Victor, *De trinitate*	
Institutio arithmetica		[John Chrysostomus]	2
(Nicomachus)	1	Vergil, *Georgica* [Boethius]	1
Not found	7		

Table 2. Explicit references to other authors[71]

Again, not all of the references have been placed. As can been seen from the table, Boethius is here the predominant source, followed by Porphyry, Priscian, and the author of the *Book of Six Principles*.

---

modo, malum rather than *boni, simpliciter, mali*), and since the use of *multifariam* appears to have been common, Pagus' use of *multifarie* could well, it seems, be independent of Grosseteste's translation.

   [71] Square brackets around a name, e.g., [Galen], indicate that Pagus misattributes the quotation to this author. Cruces, e.g., † Morebus †, indicate that I take the transmitted text to be corrupt.

The nine references to Averroes (referred to as *Commentator*) are noteworthy. They turn out, however, to be repetitive. The three references to his commentary on *De anima* are to one and the same passage, and the five references to the *Physics* commentary are to two passages, one cited twice, the other three times. The quotation of the passage from the *De anima* commentary is far from verbatim and approaches the form of an adage, and the same goes for at least one of the quotations from the *Physics* commentary.

The references to specifically theological works such as Nicholas of Amiens' *Ars fidei catholicae* and Richard of St. Victor's *De trinitate* are also worth noting, especially since such references are not found in any of the known roughly contemporary commentaries on the *Categories*. Here, they mostly occur in questions that deal with issues connected to ones discussed in theological contexts,[72] and to some extent appear to come in bundles. The two references to Richard of St. Victor are to one and the same passage, and both occur alongside a reference to Plato's *Timaeus* 28a. On the second occasion, there is also an explicit reference to a theorem from Nicholas of Amiens, and this theorem turns out to be implicitly invoked on the first occasion as well.[73] Several of these references are somewhat imprecise. The quotation from Richard of St. Victor is on both occasions attributed to John Chrysostomus, and the piece of doctrine ascribed to Dionysius is not actually found anywhere in the *Dionysiaca*, although ideas similar to it were apparently invoked in connection with *De caelesti hierarchia* I 3.[74]

The references to medical authors (Haly, Iohannitius, Philaretus, Avicenna) are also a curious feature without parallel in the other *Categories* commentaries from the period. There are two references to Galen,[75] both of which appear to be

[72] See John Pagus, *Rat. sup. Praed.* XI, q. 2 (66.14–28); XV, q. 4 (94.8–25); XXX, q. 4 (177). The first question is whether substance is really a *per se* being, seeing as only God (*Primum*) can be a *per se* being strictly speaking; the second is whether the truth of a thing (*veritas rei*) and the truth of an utterance (*veritas orationis*) are one and the same; the third is whether correlatives such as father and son can be defined in terms of each other without circularity.

[73] See John Pagus, *Rat. sup. Praed.* XI, q. 2 (66.16); XV, q. 4 (94.13–14). It is perhaps worth noting that Alexander of Hales opens the first tract of his *Summa theologica* with a longish quotation of the relevant passage from Richard of St. Victor, and that a little later in the same question he implicitly invokes the theorem from Nicholas of Amiens (nothing is its own cause); see Alexander of Hales, *Summa theologica* I 1.1.1 (ed. Collegium S. Bonaventurae, vol. 1, 40–41).

[74] John Pagus, *Rat. sup. Praed.* XI, q. 1 (65.29). Cf. Thomas Aquinas, *Scriptum super tertium librum Sententiarum* d. 35, q. 2, a. 2, sol. 1 (ed. Moos, vol. 3, part 2, 1198): "Sicut autem mens humana in essentiam rei non ingreditur nisi per accidentia, ita etiam in spiritualia non ingreditur nisi per corporalia et sensibilium similitudines, ut dicit Dionysius."

[75] John Pagus, *Rat. sup. Praed.* XXXII, q. 1 (188.14) and XXXIV, q. 2 (198.12). The manuscript has g. (f. 56va) and G (f. 58ra).

misattributions. One ascribes to him a version of the adage that blood is a friend of nature,[76] and the other turns out to be to the *Aphorisms* of Hippocrates rather than to Galen's commentary on it.

Finally, the reference to Nicholas the Logician is intriguing. It does not seem to be to the *Quaestiones Nicolai Peripatetici* to which both Robert Kilwardby and Albert the Great refer.[77] As Franceschini suggested, it may perhaps then be a reference to Nicholas of Paris.[78] It cannot, however, be found in the one known *Categories* commentary associated with Nicholas' name,[79] and it has not been possible to track it down.

2.4. Contemporary Commentaries

Besides the many references to authoritative sources, Pagus on several occasions makes explicit mention of other expositions of Aristotle's text. Although always to anonymous characters denominated as "some people" or "others," these references bear witness to the fact that he is not operating in an interpretive vacuum. This, however, is hardly surprising. Literal commentaries are, much like modern textbooks, not usually works of great originality but rather the working, re-working, and fine-tuning of a mass of material accumulated in the course of a long tradition. Indeed, it appears to have been not at all unusual for a commentator to tacitly employ the commentary of one or more of his predecessors as source material, or even as a template, for his own commentary.

---

[76] John Pagus, *Rat. sup. Praed.* XXXIV, q. 2 (198.11–12): "et reducit sanguinem, qui est amicalis naturae, dicit Galenus." The standard version of the adage seems to have *amicus naturae*. See, for example, William of Conches, *Glose super Boetium* (ed. Nauta, 42), where it occurs in a reference to Boethius' commentary on *Categories* 8.9b12–14 (ed. Migne, 247c). It is the exact same passage of Aristotle's text that Pagus is discussing. The expression is not actually found in Boethius, but the reference suggests that the saying had become connected with the exposition of this part of the *Categories* early on in the commentary tradition. A gloss in a fourteenth-century manuscript of the *Alexandreis* of Walter of Châtillon ascribes the adage to "the physicians" (*physici*); see Walter of Châtillon, *Alexandreis* (ed. M. L. Colker, 500–501). I have not been able to find the phrase in Galen, but it does occur in Constantine's translation of Isaac's *Liber febrium* II 8 (ed. Lyon, f. 214vb): "Sanguis autem est amicus naturae."

[77] Edited in Stanisław Wielgus, "Quaestiones Nicolai Peripatetici," *Mediaevalia Philosophica Polonorum* 17 (1973), 57–155. Cf. Robert Kilwardby, *Not. sup. Praed.* (Cambridge, Peterhouse 206, f. 59va; Madrid, Bibl. Univ. 73, f. 33va); Albert the Great, *De praedicamentis* V 12 (ed. Donati and Steel, 125). I would like to thank Carlos Steel for kindly supplying me with a provisional version of his and Silvia Donati's forthcoming edition of Albert the Great's paraphrase.

[78] Franceschini, "Giovanno Pago," 479, n. 41.

[79] Found in MS Munich, Bayerische Staatsbiliothek Clm. 14460, ff. 42r–62r. More on this commentary below.

In the present case, tracing these explicit as well as tacit trails of tradition has proved a somewhat difficult and arduous task. This is mainly due to three things. First, there is a dearth of known commentaries on the *Categories* from the first half of the thirteenth century. Secondly, of the small number of known commentaries only a few have been previously edited. Finally, the dating and relative chronology of the material is rather difficult to fix with precision. Table 3 offers an overview of this material and the dates usually assigned to it.

Author / Work	Date
Anonymus D'Orvillensis, *Commentary on Aristotle's* Categories	ca. 1200
John Pagus, *Rationes super Praedicamenta*	ca. 1231–35
*Nicholas of Paris (attr.), *Rationes super Praedicamenta*	ca. 1230–40
(*)Robert Kilwardby, *Notulae super Librum Praedicamentorum*	ca. 1237–45
Anonymus Domus Petri 206, *in Praedicamenta*	ca. 1240–50
*Anonymus Domus Petri 205, *in Praedicamenta*	ca. 1250
William of Montoriel, *Summa Libri praedicamentorum*	ca. 1250
Albert the Great, *De praedicamentis*	ca. 1253

* = the work is unedited; (*) = the work has been partly edited; all other works have been edited.

Table 3. Commentaries on the Categories *from ca. 1200–1250*[80]

Of the commentaries listed, Pagus' commentary shows the closest proximity to the three commentaries that follow it on the list: that attributed to Nicholas of Paris, that of Robert Kilwardby, and that of the Anonymus Domus Petri 206. The four commentaries all occupy a similar theoretical space, and many points of doctrine can be found that are common to varying sets of them. It is, however, difficult to determine whether this is, in fact, because of any direct influence or whether it is merely due to a shared tradition.

---

[80] For the Anonymous of D'Orville, see Sten Ebbesen, "Anonymus D'Orvillensis' Commentary on Aristotle's *Categories*," CIMAGL 70 (1990): 229–423. For Pagus, see Gauthier, *Preface*, 66*, but cf. below. For Nicholas, see Olga Weijers, *Le travail intellectuel à la Faculté des arts de Paris: Textes et maîtres (ca. 1200–1500)*, vol. 6, *Répertoire des noms commençant par L–M–N–O*, Studia Artistarum 13 (Turnhout: Brepols, 2005), 191. For Kilwardby, see Lewry, *Kilwardby's Writings*, 6. For the Anonymous of Peterhouse 206, see Heine Hansen, "Anonymus Domus Petri 206's Commentary on Aristotle's *Categories*," CIMAGL 78 (2008): 111–203. On the Anonymous of Peterhouse 205, see Lewry, *Kilwardby's Writings*, 89–111. For William of Montoriel, see Robert Andrews and Timothy B. Noone, "Willelmus de Montoriel: *Summa libri Praedicamentorum*," CIMAGL 64 (1994): 63–100. For Albert the Great, see Carlos Steel, "Albert's Use of Kilwardby's *Notulae* in his Paraphrase of the *Categories*," in *Via Alberti: Texte, Quellen, Interpretationen*, ed. Ludger Honnefelder, Hannes Möhle, and Susana Bullido del Barrio (Münster: Aschendorff, 2009), 502–3.

The commentary attributed to Nicholas of Paris is a *lectio* commentary contained in MS Munich, Bayerische Staatsbibliothek Clm. 14460, ff. 42–62.[81] The commentary is a work of approximately 48,000 words and contains 11 *lectiones* with a prologue integrated into the first *lectio*. The *lectiones* fall into three separate sections of which the first is made up of alternating division (*divisio*) and exposition (*sententia*) of stretches of text. Then follows a section devoted to the explication of the rationale behind the internal structure of the passage under discussion as well as its place in the text as a whole (*ordinatio*). Lastly there is a section made up of alternating series of questions and corresponding solutions. As in Pagus' commentary, questions range from very simple ones to more elaborate dialectical structures involving objections and counter-objections to a given thesis. References to authoritative works are less frequent than in Pagus and the range of works referred to narrower. They include the *ars vetus* and the *ars nova* as well as the *De anima*, the *Physics*, and the *Metaphysics*. In contrast to Pagus' commentary, there appear to be no explicit references to the writings of Averroes. The commentary seems to be more or less complete except for some missing questions and solutions at the end of Lectio IV (bottom of f. 49vb), where the manuscript has approximately 20 lines left blank. An origin in a classroom context betrays itself when in the fourth *lectio* a reference to the previous one takes the form: "it was said yesterday" (*heri dictum est*), and the commentary is, if not in fact a mere *reportatio*, certainly the product of less editorial effort than Pagus' commentary.[82]

Nicholas' commentary is the one that bears the closest resemblances to that of Pagus. Most notably, in these two commentaries there are numerous sequences of questions which are basically the same (although the internal ordering of each sequence may vary slightly).[83] These shared sequences or clusters occur throughout the commentaries, but they grow longer and more frequent with the beginning of the chapter on quantity (*Categories* 6). The same question may take on a more

---

[81] On this manuscript, see Martin Grabmann, "Die Logischen Schriften des Nikolaus von Paris und ihre Stellung in der Aristotelischen Bewegung des XIII. Jahrhunderts," in Martin Grabmann, *Mittelalterliches Geistesleben*, vol. 1 (Munich: Max Hueber, 1926), 222–48. The biographical information supplied by Grabmann is outdated and faulty, see instead Gauthier, *Preface*, 66*–67* and Weijers, *Travail intellectuel*, vol. 6, 191. For lists of the works attributable to Nicholas, see Charles H. Lohr, "Medieval Latin Aristotle Commentaries: Authors Narcissus–Richardus," *Traditio* 28 (1972): 298–99 and Weijers, *Travail intellectuel*, vol. 6, 193–97.

[82] I am currently preparing an edition of this commentary. As I will argue in the introduction to it, Grabmann's attribution of it to Nicholas of Paris is correct. I would like to thank Robert Andrews and Griet Galle for helping me complete the transcription of this material.

[83] Compare, for example, John Pagus, *Rat. sup. Praed.* XVI, qq. 1–7; XXII, qq. 2–6; XXIX, qq. 3–7; and XXXV, qq. 7–10 to Nicholas of Paris, *Rationes super Praedicamenta* IV qq. 1–7 (Munich, Bayer. Staatsbibl. 14460, f. 48rb–vb); V, qq. 10–15 (f. 51ra–va); VII, qq. 8–11 (f. 54rb–va); and IX, qq. 1–5 (f. 57va–vb), respectively.

elaborate form in one commentary or the other,[84] and the two commentators may also offer either partly or completely different solutions to a problem.[85] Nonetheless, in many cases we are clearly dealing with the same philosophical contents presented in different ways. Consider, for example, the following passages:

Nicholas of Paris, *Rat. sup. Praed.* v, q. 13 (Munich, Bayer. Staatsbibl. 14460, f. 51rb–va)	John Pagus, *Rat. sup. Praed.* XXII, q. 4 (134.14–24)
Item. Dicit: "Videtur esse circa locum contrarietas; sursum enim ad id quod est deorsum contrarium est." Contra. **Sursum et deorsum sunt differentiae positionis, non** ergo erunt differentiae **loci** vel ubi, quia "**Diversorum generum** et non subalternatim positorum **etc.**"	Consequenter quaeritur: Videtur quod male posuit exemplum de sursum et deorsum. Quia **sursum et deorsum sunt differentiae positionis, non** igitur **loci**, cum "**Diversorum generum etc.**" Maior patet, quia situs est ordinatio vel positio partium, ut dicit auctor *Sex principiorum*, sed haec ordinatio est secundum sursum et deorsum, ut homo habet caput sursum et pedes deorsum.
Ad aliud dico quod sursum et deorsum sunt differentiae loci. Et obicis quod sunt differentiae positionis; non ergo loci. Dico **quod sursum et deorsum uno modo dicunt** ordinationem partis ad partem respectu **eiusdem totius**, secundum quod dicitur quod pedes hominis sunt sub brachiis, et brachia sub capite. Alio modo sursum et deorsum possunt dicere ordinem **partium** respectu **diversorum totorum**, sicut corporis locati ad aliud, secundum quod dicitur corpus meum esse sub caelo. **Et sic sunt differentiae loci.**	Et dicendum **quod sursum et deorsum** dupliciter considerantur. **Uno modo** prout **dicunt** ordinem partium **eiusdem totius** in suo toto, et sic sunt differentiae positionis, ut obicitur. Aliter considerantur prout dicunt ordinationem vel respectum **partium diversorum totorum, et sic sunt differentiae loci**, et sic loquitur hic, quod per exempla patet; dicit enim quod terra est deorsum et caelum sursum, et illa sunt diversa tota.

As is clear, here we are dealing with the same material arranged and phrased in slightly different ways. The question is introduced differently, but the objection to Aristotle's example is the same, and almost verbatim. Pagus, as is his habit, provides a supporting argument for one of the premises, drawn here, as is usually the case, from an authoritative text, and he further exemplifies by means of the

---

[84] For an example where Pagus is more elaborate, see John Pagus, *Rat. sup. Praed.* XVII, q. 3 and Nicholas of Paris, *Rat. sup. Praed.* IV, q. 14 (Munich, Bayer. Staatsbibl. 14460, f. 49rb–va). For an example where Nicholas is more elaborate, see John Pagus, *Rat. sup. Praed.* XXXII, q. 1 and Nicolas of Paris, *Rat. sup. Praed.* VIII, q. 5 (Munich, Bayer. Staatsbibl. 14460, ff. 55vb–56ra).

[85] Compare, for example, John Pagus, *Rat. sup. Praed.* XXII, q. 2 and XXXV, q. 5 to Nicholas of Paris, *Rat. sup. Praed.* v, q. 10 (Munich, Bayer. Staatsbibl. 14460, f. 51ra–rb) and VIII, q. 25 (f. 57ra), respectively.

human body. The solutions to the objection are also the same. Nicholas determines the question, reiterates the objection, and then solves it by distinguishing two meanings of "up" and "down." Pagus moves directly to the solution. Nicholas exemplifies both of the two meanings he distinguishes. Pagus only gives an example of the second meaning, but he has already exemplified the first meaning in his argument in support of the major premise of the objection. Notice how these exemplifications of the first meaning are again quite similar in the two texts.

The passage is in many ways representative of the nature of the parallels between the two commentaries. They are not always as close as is the case here, and they are never so close that one commentator can be seen to have merely copied the other verbatim. They consist rather in shared philosophical or exegetical problems and positions presented in very similar ways. They are quite numerous and frequently come in clusters, and they are clearly not completely incidental. No hard evidence has, however, been found that they are due to the direct influence of one commentator on the other rather than to a shared (proximate or remote) source. Nor is it immediately clear which direction the influence took, if indeed there was one. It is clear, however, that if there was one, it was only partial. For the fact is that the clusters of shared questions are usually flanked by sequences of questions where the two commentaries have little to nothing in common, and the two commentators may well, as already mentioned, resolve the same problem differently. It is difficult to say which of the two commentaries antedates the other, but the wide range of authoritative texts invoked by Pagus (including the works of Averroes) may perhaps suggest that his commentary is the later one.

The *Notulae super Librum praedicamentorum* attributed to Robert Kilwardby is a work of approximately 64,000 words.[86] Of the commentaries considered here, it is the one that comes closest to Pagus' commentary in terms of size. It is a *lectio* commentary containing a separate prologue and 21 *lectiones*. The internal structure of the *lectiones* is less articulated and rigid than in Pagus' commentary, as Kilwardby prefers to mix the exegetical manoeuvres other writers separate as *divisio, sententia*, and *ordinatio*. In addition, Kilwardby scrupulously accounts for the adequacy (*sufficientia*) of Aristotle's way of proceeding, but he rarely bothers to supply a literal gloss on a piece of text. The question section is a series of alternating questions and answers, sometimes with an inserted list of points to note.

---

[86] Kilwardby's commentary is preserved in two manuscripts: MS Cambridge, Peterhouse 206, ff. 42ra–65va and MS Madrid, Biblioteca Universitaria 73, ff. 10vb–43vb. For these, see Lewry, *Kilwardby's Writings*, 14–22. On the commentary itself, see ibid., 260–80. On the date of Kilwardby's course, see ibid., 6. For an edition of the first *lectio* of the *Categories* commentary, see ibid., 367–78. The long-awaited critical edition of this commentary is still under preparation under the direction of Prof. Alessandro Conti who generously shared Lewry's preliminary edition of the text. When quoting the commentary, I usually quote from Lewry's transcription but supply a reference to the two manuscripts. Where omissions or misreadings have been noted, I have tacitly corrected them.

As in Pagus, the questions may take up no more than a few lines or they may grow to include a series of objections and counter-objections to a given proposition. The feature of explicitly referring to authoritative texts, which is so pronounced in Pagus' commentary, is less predominant in Kilwardby, although the range of quotations that he does invoke appears to be roughly equivalent (save for the references to medical literature and theological authors such as Nicholas of Amiens). He has explicit references to Averroes' commentary on the *Metaphysics*, and has a large number of references to Aristotle's *Metaphysics* (41) and *Physics* (23), but only a few to the *Topics* (5).[87] The commentary survives in its entirety and was presumably composed during Kilwardby's regency in arts at the University of Paris approximately between the years 1237 and 1245.

Kilwardby also raises many of the same questions that Pagus does. Their answers are often very different.[88] Nonetheless, on many occasions they give very similar answers, and there are sometimes rather close parallels. For example:

John Pagus, *Rat. sup. Praed.* I, q. 1 (11.20–12.26)

Robert Kilwardby, *Not. sup. Praed.* Proem, q. 1 (Cambridge, Peterhouse 206, f. 42ra–b; Madrid, Bibl. Univ. 73, ff. 10vb–11ra)

Primum est **an de primis generibus** possit esse **scientia**.
Quod non videtur.
(...)
Item. "Scire est causam rei cognoscere," scribitur in primo *Posteriorum*. Solum ergo **illorum est scientia quorum acceptio per causam est possibilis**. **Sed primorum** decem **generum non est possibilis acceptio per causam, cum sint** prima. **Ergo** de ipsis **non** est **scientia**.
(...)
Ad aliud. Prima genera decem habent principia ex quibus componuntur, scilicet materiam et formam (et probat Aristoteles in *Metaphysica* quod habent principia supra se), **et ideo possibilis est eorum** acceptio **per** causas.

Dubitatur hic primo **an** sit **scientia de generibus primis**.

Et apparet quod non sic: **Quorum** non **est acceptio possibilis per causam, illorum** non **est scientia** (haec patet ex definitione "scire"). **Sed primorum generum non est acceptio possibilis per causam, cum sint** principia ita quod non principiata. **Ergo** illorum **non** erit **scientia**.
(...)
Ad primum quidem dicimus quod generum primorum est scientia et est illorum acceptio possibilis per causam. Est enim unumquodque eorum ex materia et forma aggregatum, sicut patebit in sequentibus, **et ideo possibilis est eorum** cognitio **per** sua principia.

It is not really clear, however, if the parallels involve views which are truly characteristic of one or other of the two commentators and so can be taken as hard evidence that one of them drew directly on the other.

---

[87] For the authoritative works referred to in Kilwardby's commentary, see Lewry, *Kilwardby's Writings*, 262–63.

[88] Compare, for example, Robert Kilwardby, *Not. sup. Praed.* VII, q. 12 (Cambridge, Peterhouse 206, f. 48vb; Madrid, Bibl. Univ. 73, f. 19ra–b); IX, q. 1 (f. 52rb–va; f. 24ra); XI, q. 9 (f. 55rb; f. 28ra); and XII, q. 2 (f. 56ra; f. 29ra) to John Pagus, *Rat. sup. Praed.* XIV, q. 2; XXI, q. 2; XXVI, q. 4; and XXIX, q. 5, respectively.

Views referred to by Kilwardby as common or held by some people are on occasion identical or very similar to positions embraced by Pagus. Consider, for example, the following excerpt, where the topic under discussion is the fourth type
of quality that Aristotle lists in *Categories* 8. Kilwardby says:

> Next, it may be asked what the difference between form and figure, straight-
> ness and curvature is.
>
> With regard to form and figure it is said that they differ because form be-
> longs to animate things, figure to inanimate things.
>
> Furthermore, form is consequent on the interior disposition of the parts,
> figure on the exterior disposition.[89]

The two differences Kilwardby here recounts are close to those found in the two
alternative answers given to the same question by Pagus.[90] Kilwardby, however,
dismisses these answers as being at odds with Porphyry's *Isagoge* and proceeds to
work out an independent solution.[91] But again, it is not clear that the two rejected
views are truly characteristic of Pagus. The first way of distinguishing between
form and figure appears to have been a staple of the commentary tradition, and is
found, for example, in the Anonymus D'Orvillensis and in the *Dialectica Monacensis*.[92] Similarly, a version of the second way of distinguishing between form and
figure is also embraced by Nicholas of Paris.[93] What can be said is that this critical
attitude to points of doctrine similar to ones that are common to Pagus and the
earlier tradition (or to Pagus and Nicholas) also surfaces elsewhere in Kilwardby's
commentary, and while it is never clear that Pagus is being targeted specifically,

[89] Robert Kilwardby, *Not. sup. Praed.* XIII, q. 24 (Cambridge, Peterhouse 206, f. 58rb;
Madrid, Bibl. Univ. 73, f. 31vb): "Consequenter quaeratur quae sit differentia inter formam
et figuram, rectitudinem et curvitatem. De forma et figura dicitur quod differunt, quia
forma est rei animatae, figura rei inanimatae. Amplius, forma est consequens interiorem
dispositionem partium, figura vero exteriorem."
[90] John Pagus, *Rat. sup. Praed.* XXXV, q. 1 (203.28–4.2).
[91] Robert Kilwardby, *Not. sup. Praed.* XIII, q. 24 (Cambridge, Peterhouse 206, f. 58rb;
Madrid, Bibl. Univ. 73, f. 32ra). The reference to Porphyry is to *Isagoge* 11.13–17. The explanation of the difference between form and figure advanced by Kilwardby is later adopted
by Roger Bacon, *Summulae dialectices* I 2.223 (ed. de Libera, 216).
[92] Anon. D'Orvillensis, *in Cat.* (ed. Ebbesen, 362): "Sed inter haec est differentia quod
forma est dispositio partium rei animatae, figura est dispositio partium rei inanimatae."
Anon., *Dialectica Monacensis* (ed. de Rijk, 522): "Item. Quarta species qualitatis est forma
et circa aliquid constans figura. Dicitur autem forma circa res animatas id idem quod est
figura circa inanimata."
[93] Cf. Nicholas of Paris, *Rat. sup. Praed.* VIII, q. 22 (Munich, Bayer. Staatsbibl. 14460, f.
56vb–57ra). Nicholas explicitly rejects the first solution.

it may perhaps be taken to suggest that Kilwardby's commentary is the later commentary, as is also usually assumed.[94]

Finally, Anonymus Domus Petri 206 is my name for the author of a course on the *ars vetus* found in MS Cambridge, Peterhouse 206 — a manuscript which also contains some of Kilwardby's logical commentaries. The commentary on the *Categories* that is part of this course is a *lectio* commentary containing 17 *lectiones* and no prologue. It appears to be complete except that most of the question section is missing in Lectio XV. In its present state, it is a work of approximately 22,500 words. It is thus significantly shorter than the other three commentaries that concern us here. The *lectiones* are rigidly structured and fall into three parts: division (*divisio*), exposition (*sententia*), and a section of alternating questions and solutions (*quaestiones/solutiones*). Questions and solutions are mostly rather basic and rarely take up more than a few lines, and the commentary has, on the whole, a rather elementary air about it. References to authoritative works are rare and, except for a very general reference to the *Metaphysics*, are confined to the *ars vetus* and the *ars nova* — a trait that is perhaps due to the very succinct format and elementary character of the commentary.[95]

Most of the questions found in the Anonymus Domus Petri 206 can also be found in some or all of the other three commentaries discussed here, and the answers are often very similar but usually considerably shorter. On a couple of occasions, the commentary holds a view identical or similar to one that Nicholas refers to as held commonly or by "some people" (*quidam*).[96] It has a somewhat similar relation to Robert Kilwardby's commentary, and it shares points of doctrine

---

[94] Compare, e.g., Robert Kilwardby, *Not. sup. Praed.* IV, q. 4 (Cambridge, Peterhouse 206, f. 44va; Madrid, Bibl. Univ. 73, f. 13va–vb) to John Pagus, *Rat. sup. Praed.* V, q. 10; Nicholas of Paris, *Rat. sup. Praed.* I, q. 23 (Munich, Bayer. Staatsbibl. 14460, f. 43va–vb); and Anon. D'Orvillensis, *in Cat.* (ed. Ebbesen, 271).

[95] An edition of this commentary can be found in Hansen, "Anonymus Domus Petri," 119–203. For the course to which this commentary belongs, see Lewry, *Kilwardby's Writings*, 65–73.

[96] Compare, for example, Anon. Domus Petri 206, *in Cat.* VI, q. 3 (ed. Hansen, 149–50): "Praeterea quaeritur quare potius definit quantitatem in singulari quam in plurali. Et videtur quod potius deberet definire in plurali quam in singulari: Ibi {ibi *scripsi* : ubi *ed.*} est constructio proleptica. Et in constructione proleptica divisum debet poni in plurali et dividentia in singulari. Ergo etc. (...) Ad tertium dicendum est quod Auctor definit quantitatem prout est genus, et quia quantitas est genus in singulari et non in plurali, et ideo etc." with Nicholas of Paris, *Rat. sup. Praed.* IV, q. 6 (Munich, Bayer. Staatsbibl. 14460, f. 48vb): "Aliter dicunt quidam quod hic est prolepsis. Ad hoc quod obicis respondent quod ponitur pro genetivo plurali genetivus singularis propter hoc ut denotetur divisio generis in species." Compare also Anon. Domus Petri 206, *in Cat.* IX, q. 5 (ed. Hansen, 167) with Nicholas of Paris, *Rat. sup. Praed.* VII, q. 2 (Munich, Bayer. Staatsbibl. 14460, ff. 53vb–54ra).

with Pagus'.[97] Its precise temporal relation to these commentaries is not, however, very clear. It might be slightly earlier, it might be contemporary or it might be the product of a slightly later, but conservative, elementary course on the *Categories*. There is nothing to suggest that it was directly influenced by Pagus' commentary, or that it had any direct influence on Pagus'.

In summary, Pagus' commentary is longer and contains a much higher number of *lectiones* than those of his near contemporaries. It also contains many more references to authoritative sources, and the range of texts referred to is wider. It has many questions and theoretical commitments in common with the commentary attributed to Nicholas of Paris especially, but also with that of Robert Kilwardby, who, however, can be seen to be critical of the line taken by Pagus on several points and who seems to draw more heavily on Aristotle's *Metaphysics*. It was tentatively suggested that Nicholas' commentary may antedate that of Pagus and that Kilwardby's commentary may postdate it. It may be that Pagus knew Nicholas' commentary and that Kilwardby knew Pagus' (and perhaps Nicholas'), but here a few of the caveats made at the outset must be reiterated. As was stated there, information about the interpretation of the *Categories* in the first decades of the thirteenth century is scarce. This makes it difficult to determine where points of convergence between the commentaries surveyed here should be put down to tradition, to a common source, or to direct influence. This complication is further accentuated by the fact that the relative chronology of these commentaries will have to be teased out of the texts themselves, as the biographical information we possess about their respective authors does not allow us to fix it with sufficient precision. Fortunately, other Aristotelian commentaries by some of the masters in question are known to exist. There is, however, as already pointed out, a serious lack of modern editions available, and studies are scarce. The material may be there to establish a more precise and solid chronology, but we are still in the initial stages of this task.

Finally, it should be mentioned that there is other material relevant to the reception of the *Categories* in the first half of the thirteenth century, some of which has been edited (see table 4).

---

[97] See Hansen, "Anonymus Domus Petri," 115–16.

Author / Work	Date
Anon., *Dialectica Monacensis*	ca. 1200–25
Peter of Spain, *Tractatus*	ca. 1220–45
Anon., *Ripoll Compendium*	ca. 1240
Anon., *De communibus artium liberalium*	ca. 1250
Roger Bacon, *Summulae dialectices*	ca. 1250
Anon., *Communia Visitatio*	ca. 1250
Lambert of Lagny, *Logica*	1250–67

Table 4. Edited summulae and examination compendia up to ca. 1260[98]

Again, doctrinal agreements between Pagus' commentary and each of these texts have been noted, but evidence of any direct influence on or from his commentary has not been found.

2.5. Date of Composition

In his 1933 edition of excerpts from Pagus' *Categories* commentary, Ezio Franceschini placed its date of composition between 1230 and 1240. As the *terminus post quem* he took the assumed date of the Latin translations of Averroes' commentaries on the *De anima*, the *Physics*, and the *Metaphysics* — to all of which Pagus refers. The *terminus ante quem* was derived from the following facts: (1) Pagus cites the fourth book of Aristotle's *Meteora* in the twelfth-century translation made by Henricus Aristippus and not that of William of Moerbeke, which was perhaps completed ca. 1260; (2) Pagus seems to have been unfamiliar with Robert Grosseteste's translation of the somewhat popular pseudo-Aristotelian treatise *De lineis indivisibilibus*, which Franceschini took to date from between 1240 and 1250; (3) with respect to the *Nicomachean Ethics*, Pagus seems to know neither Averroes' middle commentary, the translation of which Franceschini took to date from 1240, nor the compendium known as the *Summa Alexandrinorum*,

---

[98] Few of the dates assigned in this table are securely fixed. On the now assumed date of the *Dialectica Monacensis*, see L.M. de Rijk, "The Aristotelian Background of Medieval *transcendentia*: A Semantic Approach," in *Die Logik des Transzendentalen*, ed. Martin Pickavé, Miscellanea Mediaevalia 30 (Berlin: Walter de Gruyter, 2003), 9; for a summary of the problems concerning the date of Peter of Spain, see Angel D'Ors, "Petrus Hispanus O.P., Auctor Summularum (II): Further documents and problems," *Vivarium* 39 (2001): 244–45, n. 66; the date of the *Ripoll Compendium* is also quite uncertain, see Lafleur and Carrier, *L'enseignement de la philosophie*. For the *De communibus artium liberalium*, see Claude Lafleur and Joanne Carrier, "Un instrument de révision destiné aux candidats à la licence de la Faculté des arts de Paris, le *De communibus artium liberalium* (vers 1250?)," *Documenti e studi sulla tradizione filosofica medievale* 5 (1994): 140–44; on Roger Bacon and Lambert of Lagny, see Gauthier, *Preface*, 53*; on the so-called *Communia Visitatio*, see Sten Ebbesen, "*Communia Visitatio* and *Communia Feminae*," CIMAGL 73 (2002): 167–77.

translated in 1243 or 1244, nor Grosseteste's complete translation of Aristotle's text, which Franceschini took to date between 1240 and 1250, and which is now usually dated to ca. 1246–47.[99]

In his erudite preface to the Leonine edition of the *Perihermeneias* commentary of Thomas Aquinas, Gauthier suggested that Franceschini's dating could be made a little more precise. Taking Franceschini's dating of the *Categories* commentary as his point of departure, Gauthier adjusted the *terminus post quem* slightly. Since the work is presumably the product of Parisian teaching activity, it is unlikely, due to the academic strike between April 1229 and April 1231, to have originated in that period, and since there seems to be *"une bonne connaissance"* of the works of Averroes, a date prior to the strike is not very probable. Thus, the commentary may be taken to postdate April 1231. As to the *terminus ante quem*, Gauthier suggests that it be pushed back to around 1235, which is the approximate date when Pagus must have begun his study of theology. Thus, the commentary probably originated in the period ca. 1231–35.[100]

Gauthier's suggested dating is neat, but it suffers from a serious flaw. Since he took the entire contents of the Padua manuscript to be the work of Pagus, the proposed dating was supposed to apply to all the commentaries. The problem is that the commentary on the *Perihermeneias* contains an explicit reference to Robert Kilwardby.[101] Since Kilwardby's grammatical and logical commentaries are generally thought to date from ca. 1237–45, a view Gauthier appears, roughly, to share when he places Kilwardby's *Perihermeneias* commentary around ca. 1240, an obvious inconsistency results.[102]

The problem seems to be exacerbated in the case of the commentary on the *Isagoge*. According to Lewry, this "commentary from its form can hardly be earlier than 1240, or from its mode of citing book 12 of the *Metaphysica* later than 1271."[103] Pressing the issue of its formal features, David Piché has recently proposed a date around 1260 for this commentary.[104] Indeed, such a date does seem to make it less surprising that the author of the commentary apparently knew William of Luna's

---

[99] Franceschini, "Giovanno Pago," 482–84; Callus, "Date of Grosseteste's Translations"; Dod, "Aristoteles Latinus," 61.

[100] Gauthier, *Preface*, 66*.

[101] Padua, Bibl. Univ. 1589, f. 77va. This was noted long ago; see Lewry, *Kilwardby's Writings*, 270. The commentary also contains a reference to Peter of Spain (f. 84vb, l. 6 from the top). The reference would seem to be to *Tractatus* XI, 15–16 (ed. de Rijk, 205–7); see Tabarroni, "Lo Pseudo Egidio," 404–5, n. 46.

[102] For the date of Kilwardby's course, see Lewry, *Kilwardby's Writings*, 6; 354; Gauthier, *Preface*, 66*.

[103] Lewry, *Kilwardby's Writings*, 256.

[104] Piché, *Problème des universaux*, 134–35.

translation of Averroes' middle commentary on the *Posterior Analytics*,[105] and it also seems more consonant with the fact that he is fully familiar with the doctrine of second intentions.[106] The theory of second intentions became of paramount importance in the second half of the thirteenth century but is completely absent from the *Categories* commentaries of Pagus and his near contemporaries.

The formal features that ground Piché's proposed date for the commentary on the *Isagoge* are not mirrored in Pagus' *Categories* commentary. In fact, as was pointed out above, there appears to be no good reason to think that the commentaries in the Padua manuscript actually constitute a single course, or, for that matter, that, apart from the commentary on the *Categories*, they were written by Pagus. This, of course, gets rid of the problems that beset Gauthier's suggested dating, which means that this dating may be kept with regard to the commentary on the *Categories*.

Nevertheless, one might consider refraining from drawing the sharp distinction between Pagus' career as a student of theology and as a lecturer on Aristotelian logic that Gauthier's dating relies on. Among later arts masters, at least, it seems to have been not uncommon to continue to lecture in the faculty of arts while studying theology.[107] It is, as already mentioned, a unique feature of Pagus' *Categories* commentary in comparison to those of his contemporaries that on a handful of occasions he refers to specifically theological authors such as Nicholas of Amiens and Richard of St. Victor, and the same goes for his numerous mentions

---

[105] See Gauthier, *Preface*, 75*–81* for the problems pertaining to the dating of William's translations. According to Gauthier, the earliest witnesses to this translation (apart from the present commentary on the *Isagoge*) appear to date from the middle of the 1270s. For the most recent discussion of the problems, see Roland Hissette, *Preface* in Averroes, *Commentum medium super libro Praedicamentorum Aristotelis* (Leuven: Peeters, 2010), 3*–27*.

[106] See, for example, Padua, Bibl. Univ. 1589, f. 5vb: "Ad primum dicendum quod universalia multis modis sumuntur. Possunt enim accipi prout dicunt essentias quasdam separabiles, nunquam tamen separatas, et sic dicuntur partes entis et metaphysico pertinent. Alio modo universalia possunt accipi prout nominant intentionem fundatam in rebus secundum modum {secundum modum *scripsi* : secundo modo *ms*} praedicandi vel ordinandi, et sic logico pertinent; sic enim dicimus quod logica est de secundis intentionibus applicatis primis." For the role these notions came to play in the interpretation of the *Categories*, see Giorgio Pini, *Categories and Logic in Duns Scotus: An Interpretation of Aristotle's* Categories *in the Late Thirteenth Century* (Leiden: Brill, 2002).

[107] It is known, for example, to have been the case with Radulphus Brito later in the century; see William J. Courtenay, "Radulphus Brito: Master of Arts and Theology," CIMAGL 76 (2005), 134. See also id., *Teaching Careers at the University of Paris in the Thirteenth and Fourteenth Centuries*, Texts and Studies in the History of Mediaeval Education 18 (Notre Dame: University of Notre Dame, 1988).

of God (*Deus, Primum, Prima Causa*).[108] These features could suggest that he had already begun his studies in theology when he gave the recorded course on the *Categories*, but the evidence is perhaps not decisive.

It is probably best, therefore, to keep Gauthier's suggested *terminus post quem*, but Pagus' becoming a bachelor of theology may, I think, be proposed as the better *terminus ante quem*. If his progress in the faculty of theology followed what came to be the normal sequence of studies,[109] and if, as seems likely, he lectured on the *Sentences* of Peter the Lombard as a bachelor of the *Sentences* in 1243–45,[110] he presumably became a biblical cursor around 1241. As this career step seems to have made a continued regency in arts difficult, if not impossible,[111] this yields a plausible time frame between 1231 and 1241 — a slight modification of France-schini's original dating.

---

[108] See John Pagus, *Rat. sup. Praed.* VI (40.1–2); VI, q. 3 (41.11–17); XIV, q. 1 (87.23–24); XIV, q. 3 (88.25–28; 89.7–11); XIV, q. 4 (89.1–6; 12–15) [Deus]; XI, q. 2 (66.15–21); XV, q. 4. (94.15–17); XXVIII, q. 4 (165.16–18; 23–25); XXVIII, q. 6 (166.18–19; 22–24) [Primum]; XI, q. 2 (66.22–26); XIV, q. 3 (88.23–24); XXVIII, q. 1 (164.5–7); XXVIII, q. 6 (166.19–21); XXXIII, q. 4 (193.21–23); XLIV, q. 7 (257.13–21) [Prima Causa]. Cf. XLIII, q. 2 (250.3–4).

[109] For a brief overview of how the university career structure came to look, see John Marenbon, *Medieval Philosophy: An Historical and Philosophical Introduction* (London: Routledge, 2007), 206–9.

[110] Doucet, *Prolegomena*, cccliii.

[111] Courtenay, *Teaching Careers*, 22.

CHAPTER TWO
PAGUS' INTERPRETATION OF THE *CATEGORIES*

INTRODUCTION: ARISTOTLE'S *CATEGORIES*

It should be stated from the outset that the objective of the present chapter is not to give a complete account or summary of all the topics discussed by Pagus in his commentary. Indeed, given the variety and richness of the themes touched upon by both Aristotle in the *Categories* and Pagus in his commentary, such an account would quickly grow too large for an introductory study. Instead, the more modest aim will be to introduce and explore some of the main philosophical themes and interpretive ideas in Pagus' approach to the theory of categories that lies at the center of Aristotle's short but rich text.

Although it has proved a long-lived and deeply influential work, Aristotle's *Categories* is in many ways an enigmatic and, at first encounter, bewildering text. Therefore, in order to better appreciate the discussion that follows, it is worthwhile recalling some of the peculiarities of the text and some of the difficulties that beset its interpretation, and to place the themes to be discussed in this wider context.

The *Categories* opens very abruptly and in contrast to many of Aristotle's other writings contains no explicit statement of the field of philosophical inquiry it is supposed to belong to. Nor, more specifically, is there any indication of what its intended subject matter might be. Thus, while it seems clear that the central concern is some sort of categorization, it is never made unequivocally clear exactly what kind of items Aristotle is proposing to categorize. What is more, there is not even an explication of how one is to understand the presumably central notion of a category. From an interpretive viewpoint, all of these issues are matters of some importance. Certainly, how one thinks they should be settled will have considerable bearing on how one understands what Aristotle actually says in his text. Unsurprisingly, perhaps, they are also among the most controversial issues surrounding the interpretation of the text and have been much disputed by scholars throughout the centuries.[1] Accordingly, sections 1–3 of the present chapter will try to get a clear understanding of Pagus' take on these fundamental interpretive issues: How does the *Categories* fit into the *Corpus Aristotelicum*? What is the text about? And how is the notion of a category to be explicated?

---

[1] For a modern introduction to some of the main problems of interpretation surrounding the *Categories*, see Jonathan Barnes, "Les catégories et les *Catégories*," in *Les Catégories et leur histoire*, ed. Otto Bruun and Lorenzo Corti (Paris: Librairie Philosophique J. Vrin, 2005), 11–80. See also Christopher Shields, *Aristotle* (London: Routledge, 2007), 146–95.

A further complication arising from the abrupt opening of the *Categories* is that its structure and plan remain somewhat obscure. It is relatively clear that the text has three main parts. As John Ackrill puts it in the introductory note accompanying his 1963 translation:

> The *Categories* divides into three parts. Chapters 1–3 make certain preliminary points and explanations. Chapters 4–9 treat of the doctrine of categories and discuss some categories at length. Chapters 10–15 deal with a variety of topics, such as opposites, priority, and change.[2]

This division is an old one, and it also constitutes the first step in the detailed structural analyses propounded by medieval commentators, to whom the first of the three parts was known as the *Antepraedicamenta*, the second as the *Praedicamenta*, and the third as the *Postpraedicamenta*. Like most of his contemporaries, John Pagus ascribes to this traditional view. The problem, however, lies in accounting for how the three parts fit together.

The first part, the *Antepraedicamenta*, contains, as Pagus' contemporary Nicholas of Paris puts it, some definitions, some divisions, and some rules.[3] Since Aristotle simply posits these, without introduction or specification of import, the task of accounting for their theoretical relevance is left to the reader or commentator. Modern scholars frequently regard with some scepticism the prospect of completeing this task in a convincing manner,[4] but for Pagus, as for many medieval commentators, these "preliminary points and explanations" provide, in some sense, the principles of the theory of categories and thus constitute an important and fundamental part of the treatise. Consequently, sections 4–6 of the present chapter look in detail at Pagus' understanding of the key notions of this part of Aristotle's text and their role in the theory of categories. Section 4 looks at his interpretation of the definitions of equivocals, univocals, and denominatives that Aristotle gives in chapter 1; section 5 looks at his construal of the division of beings that Aristotle presents in chapter 2; and section 6 looks at his understanding of the two rules that Aristotle lays down in chapter 3.

In the middle part of the treatise, the *Praedicamenta*, Aristotle first introduces and exemplifies his list of categories in chapter 4. He proceeds, in chapters 5–8,

---

[2] Aristotle, *Categories and De interpretatione*, trans. J.L. Ackrill (Oxford: Clarendon Press, 1963), 69.

[3] Nicholas of Paris, *Rat. sup. Praed.* 1 (Munich, Bayer. Staatsbibl. 14460, f. 42ra): "Prima pars dividitur in tres partes ita quod in prima parte ponit quasdam definitiones, in secunda ponit quasdam divisiones, in tertia ponit quasdam regulas. Prima incipit hic: *Aequivoca dicuntur* (1.1a1), secunda: *Eorum quae dicuntur* (2.1a16), tertia: *Quando autem alterum de altero* (3.1b10)."

[4] See, for example, Barnes, "Catégories," 16.

to delimit and discuss in more detail the four initial categories on his list: substance, quantity, relation, and quality. This is followed by a few scattered remarks pertaining to the remaining six categories in chapter 9. The final three sections of the present chapter will be devoted to Pagus' interpretation of this part of the text. Section 7 looks at some of the main philosophical issues surrounding the list of categories, which Aristotle so famously presents without any justification or indication of how it was arrived at. Section 8 discusses some of the main themes relating to the understanding of the first and most fundamental category on the list, the category of substance. Finally, section 9 presents the main lines of Pagus' interpretation of the major non-substantial categories: quantity, relation, and quality.

The third and final part of Aristotle's text, the *Postpraedicamenta*, has, as Ackrill observes, "only a loose connection to what precedes."[5] Although many medieval commentators try to find some sort of meaningful link, they generally do not see Aristotle's discussion in this part of the *Categories* of the notions of opposition, priority, simultaneity, change, and having, as central to the theory of categories that precedes it, and they would certainly agree with a recent introduction to Aristotle that "the main thrust of Aristotle's theory emerges in the first two sections, *Categories* 1–9."[6] In addition, since Pagus' commentary in its current state only covers some of this part of Aristotle's text, his interpretation of it will be left out of consideration here.

In sum, the discussion which follows falls into three main segments. Sections 1–3 deal with Pagus' take on some important preliminary issues. Sections 4–6 discuss his construal of the foundation laid down in the *Antepraedicamenta* (*Categories* 1–3). Sections 7–9 deal with themes central to his understanding of Aristotle's list of categories and the four major categories presented and discussed in the *Praedicamenta* (*Categories* 4–9). Many of the issues discussed are by no means unique to him, and in order to better appreciate and understand his approach, considerable attention will also be paid to the views of some of his ancient predecessors and, especially, to those of his near contemporaries Nicholas of Paris and Robert Kilwardby.

1. THE *CATEGORIES* AND LOGIC

Scholasticism had flourished in the Greek-speaking world from ca. 150 to 550 AD, and the medieval Latin schoolmen were in many respects its direct descendants. This was mainly due to the work of Anicius Manlius Severinus Boethius (ca. 480–

---

[5] Aristotle, *Categories*, trans. Ackrill, 69–70.
[6] Shields, *Aristotle*, 151.

524), a Roman aristocrat who took it upon himself to create a Latin scholastic library that could match contemporary Greek standards. Although this large-scale
project never saw completion, Boethius had, by the time he was put to death, man-
aged to translate a number of Aristotelian logical texts and compose several commentaries and monographs (including a translation of and a commentary on the
Categories), thus bequeathing to western Europe a partial philosophical library
that was to exercise an enormous influence.

According to the ancient scholastics, the *Categories* was to be considered a
work of logic and grouped with the rest of Aristotle's logical writings. They conceived of this body of writings, the *Organon*, as it came to be known, as a system-
atically ordered whole moving from the study of simple expressions (terms) in the
Categories, to that of compound expressions (propositions) in the *Perihermeneias*,
to that of compounds of propositions (syllogisms) in the *Prior Analytics*, and from
there to that of the different applications of the syllogism dealt with in the *Posterior Analytics*, *Topics*, and *Sophistical Refutations*.[7] By the time of Boethius, this
general conception of Aristotelian logic was already one of long standing, and he
duly rehearses it in his first commentary on Porphyry's *Isagoge*.[8]

The Latin scholastics thus inherited the view of the *Categories* as a logical text
from their Greek predecessors, and it constitutes a fundamental premise in their
interpretation of Aristotle's text as well as their theorizing about categories in
general. Indeed, as translations of Aristotle's physical and metaphysical writings
slowly became available to thinkers in the Latin West, the logical nature of the
Categories appears to have become increasingly accentuated in order to distinguish the theorizing it contains from discussions of categories in other fields of
philosophical inquiry such as metaphysics.[9]

In keeping with this traditional construal of Aristotle's text, John Pagus begins
his commentary with a division of logic. He does not offer a straightforward version of the account sketched above (terms form to make propositions, propositions form to make syllogisms), but proposes an account in terms of the different
kinds of unity displayed by the items studied in the different texts of the *Organon*.
Taking as his point of departure an adage from Aristotle's *Physics*, he proceeds

---

[7] See, for example, Simplicius, *in Cat.* 15.13–25.

[8] Boethius, *in Isag.*[1] 1 5 (ed. Brandt, 12–15); cf. *in Cat.* 161b (ed. Migne). The conception
of the *Organon* as a systematic whole appears to be already assumed by Porphyry, *in Cat.*
56–58.

[9] For a survey of the distinction between the logical and metaphysical study of categories in the thirteenth century, see Pini, *Categories and Logic*, 19–44. Since the survey
is based on edited or partly edited commentaries, it mostly covers the second half of the
century.

to draw a parallel between certain structural features displayed by reality and human language respectively:

> "Art imitates nature to the extent that it can," it says in the second book of the *Physics*. There is, therefore, a threefold unity in speech corresponding to the threefold unity found in things. For in things there is a unity through in-division, and this is found in angels. A second unity results from the union of matter with form, and this is found in composite things such as those made out of the elements. A third unity is achieved through order and causality, and in this way the parts of the universe have unity, for they are ordered and one causes the other.
>
> To this threefold union there corresponds a threefold unity in speech. To the first unity, namely, that found in simple things, the term corresponds, for the term has unity through indivision since the logician divides no further than the term. Likewise, there is a second unity in speech, which corresponds to the second unity found in things, and this unity is found in the proposition, for the proposition is composed of a name and a verb as of matter and form; and this unity corresponds to that found in composites of matter and form such as things made out of the elements. There is also a third unity in speech, which is achieved through order and causality, and this unity is found in the syllogism, for the premises stand in relations of causality and order to the conclusion; and this unity corresponds to the unity of the universe.[10]

There are three types of unity found in the world and mirrored on the plane of human speech: (1) unity through indivision, (2) unity resulting from the union of matter with form, and (3) unity through order and causality. In accordance with this observed structural parallelism, logic divides into its several branches in so far as there is one or more books devoted to items of speech displaying each of these three kinds of unity:

> From what has been said, therefore, the division of the branch of rational phi-losophy known as logic is clear. For as far as the first kind of unity is con-cerned, we have the *Categories*, where the incomplex is treated of, which has unity through indivisibility. As far as the second kind is concerned, we have the *Perihermeneias*, in which the proposition is treated of, which has unity through the composition of form with matter. In regard to the third kind of unity, we have the other books in which the syllogism is treated of, in which there is unity through order and causality.[11]

---

[10] John Pagus, *Rat. sup. Praed.* I (9.1–15).
[11] John Pagus, *Rat. sup. Praed.* I (9.16–22).

Logic is concerned with language and can therefore be divided according to the types of unity that linguistic items display. These types of unity are the same as the basic types found in extramental reality, and so the division is to some extent grounded in extralinguistic fact.

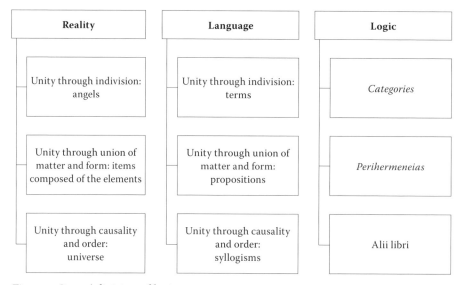

Figure 1. Pagus' division of logic

This model appears to have enjoyed some success in the decades around the middle of the thirteenth century. A slightly different version of its first two columns occurs in the *Logica* of Lambert of Lagny, who employs the parallelism in his exposition of Aristotle's definition of the syllogism in order to explain how the syllogism can be said to be *a* discourse (in the singular).[12] It may be, Lambert points out, that taken separately, each of the two premises and the conclusion of a syllogism is in itself one discourse through the unity of composition,

> but the whole that is conjoined from the premises and the conclusion is one discourse with the unity of ordering, and the syllogism is denominated from that unity of ordering rather than from any other, in that neither premises nor conclusion are considered in or by themselves, but the premises of the syllogism are considered in so far as they are ordered to implying the conclusion.

---

[12] Lambert of Lagny, *Logica* v (ed. Alessio, 109–10).

And so it is clear that the syllogism is one discourse, and it is clear also by what unity it is one.[13]

Apart from Lambert's handbook, the model is found as a straightforward division of logic in at least three other logical commentaries, all of which are, unfortunately, of uncertain origin. The commentaries, which are presumably roughly contemporary with Pagus' commentary on the *Categories*, are: (1) a commentary on the *Six Principles* found with works of Nicholas of Paris in a Munich manuscript, (2) a commentary on the same work found in the Padua manuscript that contains Pagus' commentary on the *Categories*, and (3) a commentary on the *Prior Analytics* found in a Cambridge manuscript containing, among other things, commentaries by Robert Kilwardby.[14]

Like Lambert, the three commentaries offer different examples for the first two kinds of unity found in reality. For the first kind of unity they offer the point, as does Lambert, but they add either the soul (*anima*) or the intellect (*intelligentia*) as a second example. For the second kind they, like Lambert, simply offer man. More interestingly, perhaps, the three commentaries all concur in adding an additional column to the model. The Padua *Six Principles* commentary briefly mentions the "acts of understanding that are signified by language" (*intellectus qui significantur per sermonem*) and that are divided in accordance with (*proportionaliter*) the things of which they are understandings.[15] The Peterhouse *Prior Analytics* com-

---

[13] Lambert of Lagny, *Logica* v (ed. Alessio, 110): "Quaedam conclusio et quaelibet praemissarum est oratio per se unitate compositionis, sed totum coniunctum ex conclusione et praemissis est oratio una unitate ordinationis, et ab ista unitate ordinationis denominatur syllogismus magis quam alia, eo quod non considerantur praemissae in se vel per se, nec conclusio similiter, sed considerantur praemissae in syllogismo secundum quod ordinantur ad inferendam conclusionem; et sic patet quod syllogismus est oratio una et patet etiam qua unitate sit una."

[14] The manuscripts are (1) Munich, Bayer. Staatsbibl. 14460, ff. 174–188; (2) Padua, Bibl. Univ. 1589, ff. 94r–172v; and (3) Cambridge, Peterhouse 206, ff. 81ra–97vb. For (1), see Grabmann, "Nikolaus von Paris," 222–48; for (2), see chapter one, section 2.1 above; for (3), see Lewry, *Kilwardby's Writings*, 16–22; 65–73.

[15] Anon., *in LSP* (Padua, Bibl. Univ. 1589, f. 94r): "Potest etiam aliter haberi illa diversitas, quoniam sermo sive intellectus qui {qui *scripsi* : quem *ms, ut v.*} significantur per sermonem, cum a rebus causantur, proportionaliter ipsis rebus dividuntur. Quoniam igitur triplex est unitas rerum, et triplex unitas sermonum sive intellectuum. Est enim quaedam unitas rerum per indivisibilitatem, sicut punctus est unus, intelligentia est una. Est iterum alia rerum unitas per compositionem, sicut homo est unum et aliae res compositae ex materia et forma. Est iterum alia unitas ordine quemadmodum universum est unum; universi enim una pars secundum naturam aliam antecedit et aliquo modo continet. Hoc igitur modo est triplex unitas sermonis. Est enim quidam sermo unus per indivisibilitatem, sicut sermo incomplexus. Alius sermo est unus per compositionem, sicut enuntiatio. Tertius

mentary explicitly refers to the *Perihermeneias* and on the basis of a three-tiered
semantic model in which expressions are signs of concepts (identified with the in-
telligible species) that, in turn, are signs of things, argues that the threefold unity
found on the ontological level has counterparts on both the conceptual and linguistic level.[16] The Munich *Six Principles* commentary also adds an extra column
but speaks rather of faculties of the soul (*potentiae animae*). To each of the three
kinds of unity displayed by human language there corresponds, the author main-
tains, a faculty of the soul. The first faculty is that by which the soul apprehends
the items that are signified by simple expressions; this, according to the author,
is the faculty of imagination (*fantasia vel imaginatio*). The second faculty is the
"intellect that combines or divides" (*intellectus componens vel dividens*), which
faculty is signified, the author says, by propositions. The third faculty is that which
"brings together or orders" (*conferens sive ordinans*); this is the faculty of reason
(*ratio*), or the intellect which reasons or brings together (*intellectus ratiocinans
sive conferens*), and this faculty is signified by the syllogism.[17] Generally speaking,
we seem to be dealing here with additions to the original, simpler model. These
conceptual or intellectual columns do not appear wholly integrated into the model
and seem to a smaller or larger degree to involve a conflation between structural
parallels between language and the world, on one hand, and semantic links between them, on the other.

    Apart from this initial division of logic, Pagus also alludes to a different way of
dividing Aristotle's logic. The outcome is, unsurprisingly, the same, but the basis
of division is different. It is the kind of division later made famous by Thomas
Aquinas, according to whom the human intellect

---

sermo est unus per ordinem et causalitatem, sicut syllogismus — quod patet per suam
definitionem: "Syllogismus est oratio in qua quibusdam positis per ea quae posita sunt etc."
In syllogismo enim principia priora sunt conclusione et causa eiusdem."

  [16] Anon., *in APr.* (Cambridge, Peterhouse 206, f. 81ra): "Voces sunt signa intellectuum,
id est specierum intelligibilium in anima rerum, et intellectus sunt signa rerum, ut dicit
Aristoteles in *Libro perihermeneias*. Sed signum et signatum debent habere proportionem
et convenientiam, quia sicut est in signo ita debet esse in signato. <Ergo> sicut est in re, ita
debet esse in intellectu, hoc est specie intellectuali illius rei, et sicut est in intellectu, ita
debet esse in voce quae est signum illius. Sed in rebus est triplex unitas..." (The rest of the
paragraph is, unfortunately, rather corrupt).

  [17] Anon., *in LSP* (Munich, Bayer. Staatsbibl. 14460, f. 174ra): "Et huic triplici unitati
sermonis respondet triplex potentia animae: una qua apprehendit significata incomplexi,
ut fantasia vel imaginatio; alia vero est componens, quae significatur {significatur : -antur
ms. a.c.} per enuntiationem, et haec est intellectus componens vel dividens; tertia vero est
conferens sive ordinans, quae significatur {significatur : -antur *ms. a.c.*} per syllogismum,
et haec est ratio sive intellectus ratiocinans sive conferens."

first apprehends something about a thing, namely, its quiddity, which is the first and proper object of the intellect. Then it understands the properties, accidents, and relationships that accompany the essence of the thing, and here it has to compound and divide one apprehended object from another. Then it must proceed from one composition and division to another, and this is to reason.[18]

In his *Posterior Analytics* commentary, Aquinas uses this doctrine as a basis for a division of logic. There is a need, he says, for an art that directs reason in its acts, and this art is logic. Accordingly, there is a branch of logic devoted to each of the three operations of the intellect. The *Categories* bear on the first operation (here referred to as the "cognition of indivisibles or noncomplexes, by means of which the intellect grasps what a thing is"), that is, the nonpropositional apprehension of the universal nature or essence of individual things. The *Perihermeneias* is concerned with the second operation, namely, the combination or division of the simple apprehensions to form affirmative or negative complexes or propositional judgements. And the remaining books of the *Organon* are devoted to the third operation, namely, the further composition of affirmative or negative complexes into (syllogistic) arguments.[19]

Pagus seems to accept that the operations of the intellect supply a valid basis for a division of logic, but he expressly denies the link between the *Categories* and simple apprehension. He does so in response to the objection that the intellect needs no art to direct it in the apprehension of its first and proper objects, since such apprehension occurs naturally. Since the ten highest genera — substance, quantity, quality, etc. — are universals, and, as such, proper objects of the intellective faculty, no art is needed to guide the intellect in the apprehension of them. Pagus concedes that this is so, but, he posits, there are in fact three intellectual operations subsequent to simple apprehension:

---

[18] Thomas Aquinas, *Summa theologiae* LXXXV 5, 5 (ed. Leonina, 341): "intellectus humanus non statim in prima apprehensione capit perfectam rei cognitionem, sed primo apprehendit aliquid de ipsa, puta quidditatem ipsius rei, quae est primum et proprium obiectum intellectus, et deinde intelligit proprietates et accidentia et habitudines circumstantes rei essentiam, et secundum hoc necesse habet unum apprehensum alii componere vel dividere et ex una compositione vel divisione ad aliam procedere, quod est ratiocinari." (trans. Eleonore Stump, *Aquinas* (London: Routledge, 2003), 270; modified). This doctrine of three successive operations of the intellect would appear to have its roots in the third book of Aristotle's *De anima*. However, Aristotle only mentions the first two operations explicitly." Cf. Aristotle, *De anima* III 6.430a26–b6; Anon., *Auctoritates Aristotelis* 6, 152–53 (ed. Hamesse, 187). See also René-Antoine Gauthier's comments in the *apparatus fontium* to Thomas Aquinas, *Expositio Libri posteriorum* I 1.46 (ed. Leonina, 4–5).

[19] Thomas Aquinas, *Expositio Libri posteriorum* I 1.32–50 (ed. Leonina, 4–5).

Reason orders that which has been apprehended, combines or divides that which has been ordered, and from that which has been combined or divided it puts together other combinations or divisions.[20]

In these three operations subsequent to apprehension the intellect may err, and so logic provides the necessary guidance. He explicitly aligns the doctrine of the categories with the first of the three operations:

This doctrine does not direct the intellect in the apprehension of the ten primary genera, but directs it with regard to the first operation, which is that of ordering. For it teaches how to order a thing belonging to a genus in its genus.[21]

Presumably, the doctrine of the *Perihermeneias* serves to guide the intellect in the second operation, whereas the *Prior Analytics*, *Posterior Analytics*, *Topics*, and *Sophistical Refutations* are intended to direct it in the third operation. If this surmise is correct, then, for Pagus, the operations of the intellect and the books of the *Organon* are to be aligned as shown in figure 2.

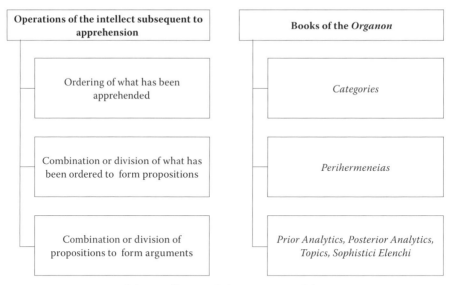

Figure 2. Operations of the intellect and the structure of the Organon

In fact, this model is found in other roughly contemporary sources. It appears in the *Ripoll Compendium* and seems to occur in Albert the Great, who at the very

---

[20] John Pagus, *Rat. sup. Praed.* I, q. 1 (12.19–20).
[21] John Pagus, *Rat. sup. Praed.* I, q. 1 (12.20–23).

beginning of his commentary on the *Categories* mentions precisely these three intellectual operations and explicitly aligns the first of them, the act of ordering, to the *Categories*.[22] Given the later success of divisions of logic based on intellectual operations, the allusion to some such model in Pagus' commentary deserves to be noticed. It should also be pointed out, however, that it is only mentioned very briefly.

For Pagus, in summary, logic falls under rational philosophy and is in some sense concerned with language.[23] Consequently, it may be divided according to the types of unity that language displays. The *Categories* deals with what, from the point of view of the logician, are the minimal units of discourse, namely, simple expressions such as "man" and "whiteness," which, ultimately, are studied as possible constituents (integral parts) of syllogisms. From another perspective, logic may also been seen as directing the human intellect in its various operations. And if so, Pagus takes it, the doctrine of the *Categories* should be seen as directing the intellect in its act of ordering the universal natures it has apprehended in the preceding act of simple apprehension. These two conceptions of the *Categories* are probably compatible, but no attempt is made to bring them together. They would also appear to have some bearing on the question of the subject matter of Aristotle's text, to which we now turn, and, as we shall soon see, the answer Pagus gives to this question does in fact involve references both to language and to the notion of ordering.

2. THE SUBJECT MATTER OF THE *CATEGORIES*

The problem of determining what type of item Aristotle intends to deal with in his *Categories* is one, which, famously, has exercised readers and commentators throughout the centuries. Are the objects of categorization linguistic, conceptual, or ontological? From antiquity to the present day, all of these options, as well as hybrids thereof, have found their champions among interpreters of Aristotle's text.

The cause of such interpretative diversity lies, to a certain degree, in the object of interpretation itself. In contrast to many other Aristotelian writings, the *Cat-*

---

[22] Anon., *Ripoll Compendium* §512 (ed. Lafleur, 141–42). Cf. Albert the Great, *De praedicamentis* I 1 (ed. Donati and Steel, 1): "Dictum est etiam hoc quod ratio, quae est virtus unum cum alio complectens, non potest devenire ad instrumentum quo cognitionem incogniti eliciat ex cognito nisi tribus actibus, qui sunt ordinare unum ad alterum, componere unum cum altero et colligere composita secundum decursum qui fit ex uno in alterum; sic enim et non aliter accipiet cognitionem incogniti per id quod est cognitum. (...) Et ideo hic ordinanda ad subici et praedicari sunt determinanda secundum omnem sui diversitatem, quae consistit in decem generibus praedicabilium sive praedicamentorum."

[23] Cf. John Pagus, *Rat. sup. Praed.* I, q. 3.

egories does not, as already mentioned, contain an explicit statement of the field of philosophical inquiry to which it is supposed to belong, or, more specifically, of what its intended subject matter is. To complicate matters, throughout his discussion Aristotle notoriously shifts between talk of linguistic items, on the one hand, and the ontological items denoted by them, on the other — so unconcernedly, in fact, that he has sometimes been charged with a gross confusion of the formal and material modes of speech.

The topic was much disputed in antiquity, but from at least the time of Porphyry (ca. 232–305) consensus seems to have formed in favour of an inclusive interpretation, on which the *Categories* is about simple significative expressions in their capacity of signifying extramental things via concepts.[24] Porphyry presumably advanced this view in his now lost major commentary on the *Categories*, but in his partly extant minor commentary he offers a simplified version, which leaves aside the conceptual element and includes only the linguistic and ontological terms.[25]

Porphyry anchors his interpretation in an account of the origin of names according to which simple expressions were imposed first to designate objects of sense and thought, and subsequently to classify expressions themselves on the basis of their grammatical features. Expressions of the first imposition are words such as "stone" or "animal," while those of the second imposition are words such as "noun" and "verb." The *Categories* is concerned with simple expressions of the former type, not in respect of their grammatical features, but in so far as they are significative of things, and not in so far as these things are numerically or specifically different, but in respect of their generic differences.[26] As Porphyry explains:

> Since beings are comprehended by ten generic differences, the words that indicate them have also come to be ten in genus, and are themselves also so classified.[27]

The multitude of sensible reality is, in other words, comprised under ten highest genera, and this fact is mirrored on the linguistic level in so far as there are ten simple expressions signifying these ten genera. The theory advanced in the *Categories* is a theory about linguistic items, but the fundamental distinction between the ten simple expressions with which it operates is one that carves sensible reality

[24] See, e.g., Porphyry, *in Cat.* 57.19–59.33; Dexippus, *in Cat.* 6.28–10.31; Ammonius, *in Cat.* 9.17–13.2; Simplicius, *in Cat.* 9.4–13.17.

[25] Simplicius, *in Cat.* 13.11–17; Porphyry, *in Cat.* 58.3–7. For possible pedagogical motivations behind this simplified account, see Sten Ebbesen, *Commentators and Commentaries on Aristotle's Sophistici Elenchi: A Study of Post-Aristotelian Ancient and Medieval Writings on Fallacies*, vol. 1 (Leiden: Brill, 1981), 141.

[26] Porphyry, *in Cat.* 57.19–58.12; Boethius, *in Cat.* 159a–60a

[27] Porphyry, *in Cat.* 58.12–14 (trans. Strange, 34; slightly modified).

at the joints, since these ten expressions correspond precisely to the ten highest kinds of beings in the sensible world.

This two-component Porphyrian account is one that, via Boethius, was to be highly influential on the medieval interpretation of Aristotle's text. Boethius explicitly adopts it in his initial determination of the subject matter of the *Categories*, and although in the rest of his commentary he does not, as has been pointed out by Monika Asztalos, always follow Porphyry in leaving out the mediating concepts, it is the position for which he was to be oft cited as an authority by the medieval scholastics.[28]

Pagus does not explicitly quote Boethius in his initial determination of the subject matter of the *Categories*, but most of his near contemporaries do, and the Porphyrian interpretation as relayed by Boethius still looms large in the background. Discussions of the subject matter of Aristotle's text had, however, become dominated by a new set of concerns brought about by the recent influx of translations of previously unavailable Aristotelian writings.

Prime among these concerns is what appears to be a global interest in construing each of the authoritative texts of the scholastic philosophical corpus as offering a scientific treatment of its subject matter in accordance with certain basic conditions of Aristotle's theory of scientific knowledge as presented in the *Posterior Analytics*.[29]

One way this interest manifested itself was in the practice of beginning one's inquiry into a given text by raising a series of questions concerned with what may be seen as the foundational issues of such an enterprise. It is not entirely clear when this tendency first began to surface, but as far as the *Categories* is concerned,

---

[28] Monika Asztalos, "Boethius on the *Categories*," in *Boèce ou la chaîne des savoirs*, ed. Alain Galonnier (Leuven: Peeters, 2003), 195–205. See, e.g., Anonymus D'Orvillensis, *in Cat.* Proem (ed. Ebbesen, 251): "patet per verba Boethii, qui in commento super hunc librum ait: '(…) intendit enim de decem primis vocibus decem prima rerum genera significantibus prout res significant'"; Robert Kilwardby, *Not. sup. Praed.* Proem (Cambridge, Peterhouse 206, f. 42ra; Madrid, Bibl. Univ. 73, f. 10vb): "Est igitur, ut dicit Boethius, scientia *Praedicamentorum* de decem vocibus decem prima rerum genera significantibus"; Nicholas of Paris, *Rat. sup. Praed.* 1 (Munich, Bayer. Staatsbibl. 14460, f. 42va): "ut per Boethium patet, qui dicit quod Aristoteles agit hic de decem vocibus decem prima rerum genera significantibus"; Albert the Great, *De praedicamentis* I 1 (ed. Donati and Steel, 1–2): "propter quod dicit Boethius quod haec scientia, *Libri* scilicet *praedicamentorum*, est de decem primis vocibus prima genera rerum significantibus." Cf. Boethius, *in Cat.* 161a (ed. Migne): "Ut igitur concludenda sit intentio, dicendum est in hoc libro de primis vocibus prima rerum genera significantibus in eo quod significantes sunt dispositum esse tractatum."

[29] The *Posterior Analytics* was translated by James of Venice in the second quarter of the twelfth century, but was quite slow to be fully incorporated into the philosophical corpus. See Dod, "Aristoteles Latinus," 54–55; 75.

the Anonymus D'Orvillensis, writing around the turn of the thirteenth century, shows no interest in the problematic, whereas once we reach the fourth decade of the century, we find, in the commentaries of Nicholas of Paris, John Pagus, and Robert Kilwardby, sets of questions devoted precisely to this thematic.[30]

Two topics discussed by all three (and most other commentators to follow) have direct bearing on the issue of the subject matter of Aristotle's text:

(1) How does a scientific theory of categories meet the requirement of unity, given that the unity of a science derives from the unity of its subject matter and that there are ten categories?

(2) How does a scientific theory of categories fall within the ambit of logic, and given that there are other branches of knowledge, e.g., metaphysics, that also deal with categories, how does the logical theory meet the requirement of having a unique subject matter?[31]

The first question is, as Pagus indicates, anchored in *Posterior Analytics* II 3.90b20–21, where, on the medieval reading of the text, Aristotle posits a one-to-one correspondence between a science and its object (in medieval terminology: its subject). Pagus answers the question as follows:

> This science is one because it is not of the ten genera as of its subject, but rather of the sayable, which is one subject.[32]

This formulation of the subject matter recurs throughout the commentary, sometimes in slightly augmented forms. For example:

> This science is not of the ten categories, but of the incomplex sayable.[33]

And:

[30] For the date of the Anonymus D'Orvillensis, see Sten Ebbesen, "Anonymus D'Orvillensis' Commentary on Aristotle's *Categories*," CIMAGL 70 (1990): 229–45. Indeed, it is possible that the author did not even know the *Posterior Analytics*; see id., "Two Nominalist Texts," CIMAGL 61 (1991): 430.

[31] John Pagus, *Rat. sup. Praed.* I, qq. 2–3; Nicholas of Paris, *Rat. sup. Praed.* I, Proem; q. 1 (Munich, Bayer. Staatsbibl. 14460, f. 42ra–va); Robert Kilwardby, *Not. sup. Praed.* Proem, qq. 2–3 (Cambridge, Peterhouse 206, f. 42rb–va; Madrid, Bibl. Univ. 73, f. 11ra–rb). It was indicated above but deserves to be stressed that these questions are not confined to commentaries on the *Categories*. They are, *mutatis mutandis*, raised in connection with just about any text of the curriculum. For an example, see Robert Kilwardby, *Notulae super Librum Porphyrii* Proem, q. 3; q. 6 (Cambridge, Peterhouse 206, f. 33rb–va; Madrid, Bibl. Univ. 73, f. 1rb–va).

[32] John Pagus, *Rat. sup. Praed.* I, q. 2 (13.11–12).

[33] John Pagus, *Rat. sup. Praed.* I, q. 1 (13.1–2).

the incomplex sayable capable of being ordered in a genus, which is the subject matter of this science.[34]

As was long since noted, variations on this last formulation were to become standard in the thirteenth-century interpretation of the *Categories*.[35] The full formulation Pagus offers — the incomplex sayable capable of being ordered in a genus (*dicibile incomplexum ordinabile in genere*) — is all but identical to that used by Nicholas of Paris, who answers (1) in much the same way:

> And because a science derives its unity from the unity of its subject matter, Aristotle does not treat of them in so far as they are ten in number but in so far as they are united in something common, namely, the incomplex sayable capable of being ordered. Thus, the material cause — or the subject matter — of the book is the incomplex sayable capable of being ordered.[36]

A very similar answer is found in Robert Kilwardby, according to whom the subject matter is not the ten highest genera as they are distinct from one another but rather as they concur and are united in the incomplex sayable capable of being ordered.[37]

The notion of the sayable plays a recurrent role in all three commentaries, not only as what gives unity to the scientific treatment of categories, but also in mat-

---

[34] John Pagus, *Rat. sup. Praed.* VI, q. 1 (40.20–23).

[35] Lewry, *Kilwardby's Writings*, 91. See also Alessandro D. Conti, "Thomas Sutton's Commentary on the *Categories* according to MS Oxford, Merton College 289," in *The Rise of British Logic*, ed. P. Osmund Lewry (Toronto: Pontifical Institute of Mediaeval Studies, 1985), 175–76; Robert Andrews, *Peter of Auvergne's Commentary on Aristotle's* Categories (PhD diss., Cornell University, 1988), 9–18; id., "Thomas of Erfurt on the *Categories* in Philosophy," in *Was ist Philosophie im Mittelalter?*, ed. Jan A. Aertsen and Andreas Speer. Miscellanea Mediaevalia 26 (Berlin: Walter de Gruyter, 1998), 806–7; Pini, *Categories and Logic*, 158–60; id., "The Transcendentals of Logic: Thirteenth-Century Discussions on the Subject Matter of Aristotle's *Categories*," in Pickavé, *Logik des Transzendentalen*, 145–52; Sten Ebbesen, "Les *Catégories* au moyen âge et au début de la modernité," in Bruun and Corti, *Les "Catégories" et leur histoire*, 257–67. The fullest accounts are found in Andrews, *Peter of Auvergne's Commentary*, and Pini, "Transcendentals."

[36] Nicholas of Paris, *Rat. sup. Praed.* I, Proem (Munich, Bayer. Staatsbibl. 14460, f. 42ra): "Et quia una est scientia ab unitate subiecti, non determinat de his in quantum decem sunt, sed in quantum uniuntur in hoc communi quod est dicibile incomplexum ordinabile. Est ergo causa materialis sive subiectum huius libri dicibile incomplexum ordinabile."

[37] Robert Kilwardby, *Not. sup. Praed.*, Proem q. 2 (Cambridge, Peterhouse 206, f. 42rb; Madrid, Bibl. Univ. 73, f. 11ra–rb): "Non sunt ergo genera prima secundum se distincta subiectum, sed magis ut sint {sint *scripsi* : sit *mss*} ad unum, dicibile incomplexum {incomplexum *scripsi* : ipsum *mss*} ordinabile, in quo quidem conveniunt et uniuntur ipsa genera prima."

ters of more detailed exposition. In none of them, however, does the notion appear
to be explicitly defined. What exactly is a sayable?

We may approach the issue by considering Pagus' answer to the second of the
two questions mentioned above: How does a scientific theory of categories pertain
to logic? The problem, as Pagus formulates it, is the following. Given that logic is
a branch of knowledge concerned with language, how does the study of the ten
primary genera pertain to it when these are in fact things (*res*), that is, items belonging to the ontological rather than the linguistic order?[38] The solution, he offers, is simply that:

> This science is not of the ten categories in so far as they are things, but in so
> far as they are sayables. But because the sayable, considered as such, falls under
> language, the rational philosopher is able to treat of them.[39]

The point is further explicated in order to solve a problem often raised in the late
ancient disputes on the subject matter of the *Categories* and reiterated by Boethius:
Why is it that some of the attributes Aristotle ascribes to the items he deals with
are demonstrably attributes of ontological rather than of linguistic items?[40] According to Pagus:

> Aristotle is here concerned with the ten highest genera in so far as they are sig-
> nified through language; and in this way they are sayables. Thus, the ten genera
> can be considered in two ways: either in so far as they are things only or in so
> far as they are things taken as falling under expressions, or signified through
> expressions. For this reason, some attributes (such as being able to receive con-
> traries) are proved of them in so far as they are things only, whereas others are
> proved of them in so far as they are things taken as falling under expressions.[41]

Whatever the merits and consistency of this solution, it strongly suggests that a
sayable is what can be expressed in or signified through language, and that, in the
present context, this is to be construed as something belonging to the ontological
order.[42]

The distinction between items belonging to the ontological order considered
as such and these same items considered in relation to language is employed by
Kilwardby in order to explain how the highest genera are studied in metaphysics
and logic respectively:

---

[38] John Pagus, *Rat. sup. Praed.* I, q. 3 (13.20–23).
[39] John Pagus, *Rat. sup. Praed.* I, q. 3 (13.27–29).
[40] Boethius, *in Cat.* 162d.
[41] John Pagus, *Rat. sup. Praed.* I, q. 3 (14.1–6).
[42] Cf. John Pagus, *Rat. sup. Praed.* XI (63.4–6).

The first philosopher's concern is with the ten primary genera irrespective of their relation to speech, whereas the logician's concern is with them in respect of this relation. For the first philosopher considers them in so far as they are parts and species of being, whereas the logician considers them in so far as they function as predicates and subjects.[43]

Nicholas of Paris makes a similar point. He begins his commentary on the *Categories* by drawing a series of distinctions between how the common sciences (*scientiae communes*), metaphysics and logic, are both concerned with being in its entirety and in its parts, and one of the differences he lists is that:

Metaphysics is concerned with being in its entirety and the parts of being simply qua being. Logic, in contrast, is concerned with being in its entirety and the parts of being in so far as they are signified through language.[44]

According to Nicholas, the distinction may be generalized. Like metaphysics, logic as a whole is concerned with being (an idea whose background would seem to be Aristotle's remark in *Metaphysics* IV 2.1004b18–26 that the philosopher and the dialectician concern themselves with the same subject matter). But whereas metaphysics considers the ontological plane in itself, logic considers it in its relation to the linguistic plane. The notion of the sayable captures this idea of an ontological item considered not in itself but in relation to language.

It has been claimed that the interpretation of the *Categories* as concerned with the sayable turns the Porphyrian/Boethian approach on its head.[45] In fact, the thinkers currently under discussion seem to take it as little more than a difference of perspective and appear to see no opposition here.[46] Consider, for example, the way Nicholas continues his explication of how the logician considers being:

---

[43] Robert Kilwardby, *Not. sup. Praed.* Proem, q. 1 (Cambridge, Peterhouse 206, f. 42rb; Madrid, Bibl. Univ. 73, f. 11ra): "Intentio primi philosophi stat super hoc praeter relationem ad sermonem, intentio vero logici per relationem, quia primus philosophus considerat haec prout sunt partes et species entis, logicus vero prout in praedicatione et subiectione consistunt."

[44] Nicholas of Paris, *Rat. sup. Praed.* 1 (Munich, Bayer. Staatsbibl. 14460, f. 42ra): "Metaphysica est de toto ente et partibus entis simpliciter in quantum ens, logica vero est de toto ente et partibus entis in quantum significantur per sermonem."

[45] Conti, "Sutton's Commentary," 175.

[46] Pini, "Transcendentals," 147.

Thus, logic considers the parts of being in a determinate number, namely, ten, whence Boethius in his commentary on this book says that Aristotle here treats of the ten expressions signifying the primary genera of things.[47]

Likewise Kilwardby, who within a few lines moves from positing that the subject matter of the *Categories* is simple significative discourse to the claim, quoted above, that it is not the ten highest genera as they are distinct from one another, but rather the incomplex sayable capable of being ordered, in which they concur and are united.[48] As for Pagus, we saw in the previous section how in his introductory division of logic he takes the *Categories* to be about the minimal units of speech, namely, uncombined expressions such as "man."

In light of this, one way to interpret the notion of the sayable is to construe it as a sort of pair made up of an ontological component, on one hand, and a corresponding linguistic component, on the other. Emphasis may shift from one component to the other, but nothing much depends on it. As is clear from key junctures in his commentary, Kilwardby applies a different terminology depending on which component is taken as primary so that if one wishes to emphasize the linguistic component one may speak of "simple significative discourse" (*simplex sermo significativus*) and if one intends to stress the ontological component one may say "incomplex sayable" (*dicibile sine complexione*). In Nicholas and Pagus, no such distinction in terminology appears to be strictly enforced, and so one can find them clearly emphasizing the linguistic component of the pair and saying, for example, that the sayable signifies.[49]

The sayable, Pagus explicitly says, is a thing of reason (*res rationis*). The claim is merely made in passing, and no explanation is offered. The idea recurs in the

[47] Nicholas of Paris, *Rat. sup. Praed.* I (Munich, Bayer. Staatsbibl. 14460, f. 42ra): "Considerat ergo partes entis in quodam numero determinato, scilicet denario, unde dicit Boethius super Commentum huius libri quod Aristoteles determinat hic de decem vocibus decem prima rerum genera significantibus."

[48] Robert Kilwardby, *Not. sup. Praed.* Proem, q. 2 (Cambridge, Peterhouse 206, f. 42rb; Madrid, Bibl. Univ. 73, f. 11r): "Ad quod notandum quod unitas istius scientiae est ab unitate generis subiecti; genus autem subiectum est simplex sermo significativus, quae quidem significatio non absolvitur ab ordine, quae quidem ordinatio non est separata a rebus. Non sunt ergo genera prima secundum se distincta subiectum, sed magis ut sint {sint *scripsi* : sit *mss*} ad unum, dicibile incomplexum {incomplexum *scripsi* : ipsum *mss*} ordinabile, in quo etiam conveniunt et uniuntur ipsa genera prima."

[49] Cf., e.g., John Pagus, *Rat. sup. Praed.* VI, q. 1 (40.20–23); Nicholas of Paris, *Rat. sup. Praed.* II, q. 7 (Munich, Bayer. Staatsbibl. 14460, f. 45rb): "Dicibile incomplexum significans formam non ordinabile nec potest subici nec praedicari in linea praedicamentali nec cadit in lineam praedicabilem nisi sit principium et simplex quemadmodum punctus cadit in praedicamento quantitatis non quia quantitas sed quia principium quantitatis."

commentaries of Nicholas of Paris and Robert Kilwardby, but the closest one gets to an explication of the rationale behind it would appear to be the reason Nicholas offers for why Aristotle's *Categories* pertains to rational philosophy, that is, logic:

> The *Categories* fall under rational philosophy, for in it Aristotle deals with the ten expressions signifying the ten highest genera of things, and the imposition of words is from reason and neither from nature nor from custom. Thus, I say that it falls under rational philosophy.[50]

This is in line with Nicholas' fundamental division of philosophy:

> There is a threefold principle immediately causative of things, namely, nature, custom, and reason, and in accordance with this there is a threefold diversity of things. For some things are natural, some customary, and some rational. Accordingly, philosophy divides into natural philosophy, moral philosophy, and rational philosophy.[51]

This suggests that the sayable is a *res rationis* because the coupling of its two components is rationally generated. It is not something that is, so to speak, found in the nature of things, but something that comes to be when man uses his reason to impose names on things and thereby links an item in the ontology with a linguistic expression.

On the semantics that were apparently standard at the time, a significative expression is linked to the entity it ultimately signifies via a mediating concept.[52] In Boethius' commentary, as was mentioned above, this mediating element between thing and expression is mentioned only occasionally. The same holds true of Pagus' commentary, as well as those of Nicholas and Kilwardby. It is nonetheless possible that in the final analysis the sayable is to be construed as also including a conceptual component. Kilwardby, at least, explicitly takes it as comprising

---

[50] Nicholas of Paris, *Rat. sup. Praed.* I (Munich, Bayer. Staatsbibl. 14460, f. 42ra): "Supponitur autem rationali philosophiae, quia determinat hic de decem vocibus prima rerum genera significantibus, et impositio vocis a ratione est neque {neque *scripsi* : et *ms*} a natura neque more; ideo dico quod iste liber supponitur rationali philosophiae."

[51] Nicholas of Paris, *Philosophia* §6 (ed. Lafleur, 455): "Est autem triplex principium immediate causans res, scilicet natura, mos et ratio, et secundum hoc est triplex rerum diversitas; sunt enim quaedam res naturales, quaedam morales, quaedam rationales. Et secundum hoc dividitur philosophia in naturalem, moralem et rationalem."

[52] Cf. John Pagus, *Rat. sup. Praed.* xv, q. 1 (93.9–15); Nicholas of Paris, *Rat. sup. Praed.* I, q. 2 (Munich, Bayer. Staatsbibl. 14460, f. 42va): "Voces sunt notae passionum in anima, quae dicuntur intellectus; ergo voces sunt notae intellectuum. Intellectus autem sunt notae vel signa rerum. Ergo voces sunt signa rerum, quia quidquid est signum signi in quantum signum est signum significati."

not only a linguistic and an ontological component but also a conceptual one.[53] Pagus and Nicholas never explicitly mention the issue, so their precise view on the matter is not quite clear. Nicholas does, however, point out that even if expressions signify things by virtue of signifying concepts that in turn signify things, there is a very important difference between the pair (word, thing) and the pair (word, concept), namely, that there are concepts of fictitious entities such as the chimera to which there is no corresponding thing in extramental reality. This difference is important, he insists, because "the incomplex sayable capable of being ordered in a category must signify something that is a thing and a part of being."[54]

The remaining components of the formula, "incomplex sayable capable of being ordered," function as restrictions. The notion of the incomplex (*incomplexum*) has its origin in *Categories* 2, where Aristotle introduces the following division:

> Of things that are said, some involve combination while others are said without combination. Examples of those involving combination are "man runs," "man wins"; and of those without combination "man," "ox," "runs," "wins."[55]

On Pagus' interpretation, things that are said (*eorum quae dicuntur*) are, of course, sayables, and so here Aristotle is taken to be dividing the sayable, the second dividend being what is under consideration in the *Categories*. The division is, Pagus says, a division of being, not qua being, but qua sayable, and he explicitly contrasts it with the same division as it is found in the *Perihermeneias* by saying that in the latter context it is a division of concepts.[56]

[53] Robert Kilwardby, *Not. sup. Praed.* I, q. 3 (Cambridge, Peterhouse 206, f. 43rb; Madrid, Bibl. Univ. 73, f. 12ra): "hic est intentio, ut diximus, de his quae antecedunt ad dicibile quantum ad id quod vocis est." Ibid., II, q. 1 (f. 43vb; f. 12vb): "hic sit sermo de antecedentibus ad dicibile quantum ad id quod intellectus est." Ibid., III, q. 2 (f. 44ra; f. 13ra): "determinat hic de illis quae antecedunt ad dicibile quantum ad id quod rei est." Kilwardby is using the expressions *dicibile* and *praedicabile* interchangeably. Thus, the reference (*ut diximus*) in the first passage is to earlier in *Lectio* I (f. 42va–b; f. 11va): "Et prima harum in tres secundum quod tria sunt in constitutione praedicabilis secundum quod praedicabile est; est enim in praedicabili aliquid de voce, aliquid de intellectu, aliquid de re. Determinat igitur in prima parte principia praedicabilis sive antecedentia ad praedicabile quantum ad id quod vocis est, in secunda, ut ibi: *Eorum quae dicuntur* etc. (2.1a16), quantum ad id quod intellectus est, in tertia, ut ibi: *Eorum quae sunt* etc. (2.1a20), quantum ad id quod rei est. Et patet sufficientia ex iam dictis, cum non sint plura in constitutione praedicabilis secundum quod tale."

[54] Nicholas of Paris, *Rat. sup. Praed.* I, q. 2 (Munich, Bayer. Staatsbibl. 14460, f. 42vb): "Vel potest dici quod aliquid componitur intellectui cui nihil respondet in re extra, ut chimera, et tamen per nomen significatur intelligibile vel imaginabile, licet non sit res eius. Sed oportet quod dicibile incomplexum ordinabile in praedicamento significet aliquid quod sit res et pars entis."

[55] Aristotle, *Categories* 2.1a16–19 (trans. Ackrill, 3).

[56] John Pagus, *Rat. sup. Praed.* III, qq. 7–8.

The addition of "capable of being ordered in a genus" (*ordinabile in genere*) restricts the notion further. Underlying it is the conception of categories as generic hierarchies, or Porphyrian trees, to which I shall return later.[57] It serves to exclude various items that may be construed as sayables but cannot be subsumed under a genus, items such as One, Being, and God.[58]

In keeping with all this, Aristotle's list of ten categories is construed as a division of the incomplex sayable capable of being ordered. This, in turn, prompts the question of what type of division this is, which brings us back to the question of the unity of the subject matter of the *Categories*. The answer that Pagus gives is that it is simply a division of a universal whole into its (subjective) parts.[59] This seems to suggest that there is something univocal to the ten categories, namely, the incomplex sayable capable of being ordered, and thus that the unity of the logical science of the categories is a univocal unity.[60] Kilwardby gives the same answer,[61] but neither of them discusses the issue at any length. Nicholas initially relays the same answer to the question, but he interestingly ends up by specifying the whole that is divided as universal *or* analogical. That he does, in fact, favour the second option is unequivocally stated elsewhere in his commentary:

> The incomplex sayable is univocal to all ten, whence we can say that "substance is an incomplex sayable," "quantity is an incomplex sayable," and so on. Capable of being ordered, however, is not univocal to them, but analogical. For substance is predicated *in quid* according to both thing and mode, in the other categories, however, the *quid* is according to mode only and not according to thing. Hence, in the category of substance the *quid* is absolute, in the other categories it is relative, and the other categories take on the mode of substance. And for this reason I claim that the incomplex sayable capable of being ordered

---

[57] This was correctly seen by Pini, "Transcendentals," 147. Pini errs, however, when he goes on to claim that the "formula *ordinabile in genere* posits the identity between what is signified by a simple expression and what is hierarchically ordered in a genus."

[58] John Pagus, *Rat. sup. Praed.* I (10.21–23); VI (39.25–40.2); VI, q. 3 (41.15–17).

[59] John Pagus, *Rat. sup. Praed.* VI, q. 1 (40.20–23).

[60] For the different kinds of unity, see Aristotle, *Metaphysics* V 6.1016b31–35. Cf. also Robert Andrews, *Peter of Auvergne's Commentary*, 15–18. Pini, "Transcendentals," 150, incorrectly places the emergence of the question of what kind of unity belongs to the subject matter of the *Categories* in the 1270s–80s.

[61] Robert Kilwardby, *Not. sup. Praed.* V, q. 5 (Cambridge, Peterhouse 206, ff. 44vb–45ra; Madrid, Bibl. Univ. 73, f. 14rb): "Sed adhuc remanet dubitatio, cuius fuerit haec divisio: *Singulum incomplexorum* etc. (4.1b25) Et dicimus quod est divisio totius universalis in suas partes subiectivas vel generis in species, et non remanent divisum ens vel unum, substantia etc. ea quae dividunt, sed remanet sermo simplex sive dicibile sine complexione divisum, et ea quae dividunt sermo significans substantiam etc. vel dicibile quod est substantia etc."

is analogically common to all ten and is said primarily of substance, secondarily of all the other categories, because they take on the mode of substance.[62]

According to Nicholas, then, the logical science of categories is one by analogy.
The incomplex sayable *capable of being ordered* is analogically common to the ten
categories, and the multiplicity of analogy does not, he claims, impede scientific
unity.[63] Since Pagus turns out to share Nicholas' idea that the order within the accidental categories is dependent on the order within the category of substance, his
exact position on the issue is not entirely clear.[64]

Either way, for Pagus and his contemporaries the notion of the sayable is clearly
instrumental in giving unity to the logical treatment of the highest genera, and,
as we have seen, it also lends uniqueness to it *vis-a-vis* metaphysics. Furthermore,
since it has one foot on the linguistic plane, so to speak, and one planted in extramental reality, it is able not only to justify the inclusion of a theory of categories within the linguistic discipline of logic but also to help explain why Aristotle
spends so much time actually talking about things (*res*). It is, in sum, a rather
potent interpretive notion, which may also be why it would prove so successful
throughout the thirteenth century.[65]

----

[62] Nicholas of Paris, *Rat. sup. Praed.* I, q. 1 (Munich, Bayer. Staatsbibl., f. 42va–vb): "Re-
spondendum per interemptionem, dicendo quod dicibile incomplexum [non] est univocum
ad omnia decem, unde possumus dicere 'substantia est dicibile incomplexum,' 'quantitas
est dicibile incomplexum,' et sic de aliis. Sed ordinabile non est univocum, sed analogum.
Substantia enim praedicatur in quid secundum rem et secundum modum, in aliis autem
praedicamentis est quid secundum modum et non secundum rem. Unde in substantia est
quid absolutum, in aliis autem praedicamentis est quid respectivum et cetera induunt
modum substantiae. Et propter hoc dico quod dicibile incomplexum ordinabile est commune analogum ad omnia decem quod per prius dicitur de substantia, per posterius autem
de omnibus aliis praedicamentis eo quod induunt modum substantiae." For the idea that
the order within the accidental categories is dependent on that of substance, see ibid., IV,
q. 2 (f. 48va): "Ad aliud dicendum quod dividebat substantiam per modum substandi et per
partes ordinabiles quia cetera praedicamenta recipiunt modum ordinandi a substantia;
non autem divisit sic quantitatem et qualitatem quia non habent modum ordinandi a se,
sed ab alio."
[63] Nicholas of Paris, *Rat. sup. Praed.* I, q. 1 (Munich, Bayer. Staatsbibl. 14460, f. 42va):
"Unde omnia decem uniuntur in hoc tanquam in communi uni analogo, et non univoco et
aequivoco; nihil enim est univocum ad decem praedicamenta. Et multiplicitas analogiae
non impedit unitatem scientiae. Ideo dicimus hanc scientiam esse unam." Cf. Aristotle,
Metaphysics IV 2.1003b11–15.
[64] See John Pagus, *Rat. sup. Praed.* XVI, q. 4.
[65] One commentator is known to have explicitly rejected this interpretation of the
Categories prior to Scotus, namely, the anonymous author of a commentary found in MS
Cambridge, Peterhouse 205, ff. 10va–20va, and MS Oxford, Bodleian, Can. Misc. 403, ff.
15ra–30rb. According to the Anonymus Domus Petri 205, as I call him, the subject matter

3. THE NOTION OF A CATEGORY

What, then, is a category? This is, if not *the* central question of category theory, certainly one of the more important ones. The matter is not entirely straightforward, as is evident from the fact that even in recent times accounts have ranged from simply stating that the answer is immediately obvious to declaring the task of defining the notion an impossible one.[66] Again, Aristotle is of little help. Indeed, it is a curious feature of the *Categories* that the word category (*praedicamentum*) occurs only a couple of times, and that the notion is nowhere explicated.[67]

Around the turn of the thirteenth century, it appears to have been not uncommon to address the issue by giving a list of the many senses of the word *praedicamentum*.[68] Like most of his near contemporaries, however, Pagus does not do this. Nor does he explicitly raise the question of what a category is or expound the notion of a category at any length. He does, however, tell us very succinctly what he takes a category to be:

A category is an ordering of predicables according to predication and subjection.[69]

This definition, which appears to have been a traditional one,[70] immediately prompts two further questions. First, what is a predicable? Secondly, what is meant by ordering according to predication and subjection?

Pagus does not explicitly answer the first question, but Nicholas of Paris, who offers a cognate definition, does:

---

of the *Categories* is simply being (*ens*); see Lewry, *Kilwardby's Writings*, 91; Ebbesen, "Les *Catégories*," 262–63. The commentary has been tentatively attributed to John Sackville, see Lewry, *Kilwardby's Writings*, 117–21, buf cf. Piché, *Problème des universaux*, 46–48. For Scotus, see Pini, *Categories and Logic*, 160–63.

[66] See Jan Westerhoff, *Ontological Categories: Their Nature and Significance* (Oxford: Clarendon Press, 2005), 22–23.

[67] Apart from the title, which cannot be credited to Aristotle, the word *katēgoria* occurs only three times (3a37; 10b19; 10b21). In the Latin translations, the first occurrence (3a37) is rendered by *praedicatio*, the latter two by forms of *praedicamentum*. On the difficulties of determining exactly what Aristotle takes categories to be, see Michael Frede, "Categories in Aristotle," in *Essays in Ancient Philosophy* (Oxford: Clarendon Press, 1987), 29–48.

[68] See, e.g., Anon. D'Orvillensis, *in Cat.* (ed. Ebbesen, 253–54); Anon., *Tractatus Anagnini* (ed. de Rijk, 224–25). The feature recurs in Roger Bacon's *Summulae dialectices* I 2.66–84 (ed. de Libera, 195–98).

[69] John Pagus, *Rat. sup. Praed.* VI, q. 3 (41.19–20) Cf. ibid., XLI, q. 1 (237.15).

[70] See, for example, Anon., *Logica "Cum sit nostra"* (ed. de Rijk, 432); Anon., *Logica "Ut dicit"* (ed. de Rijk, 388); Roger Bacon, *Summulae dialectices* I 2.82 (ed. de Libera, 196).

A category is a collection of predicables, and a predicable is the same as an incomplex sayable capable of being ordered.[71]

Given the way Pagus determines the subject matter of Aristotle's text, this seems a likely interpretation of what he means. Predicables in this sense will include individuals, since, as we shall see, he takes these to be capable of being ordered in a genus and contained in a category.

As to the second question, the background is to be found in Porphyry's *Isagoge*. Since this text was read and taught as an introduction to the *Categories*, this material could be presupposed in an exposition of Aristotle's text. In the chapter on species, Porphyry says the following:

> In each category there are some most general items, and again other most special items; and there are other items between the most general and the most special. Most general is that above which there will be no other superordinate genus; most special, that after which there will be no other subordinate species; and between the most general and the most special are other items which are at the same time both genera and species (but taken in relation now to one thing and now to another).[72]

He goes on to exemplify by means of the category of substance:

> What I mean should become clear in the case of a single category. Substance is itself a genus. Under it is body, and under body is animate body, under which is animal; under animal is rational animal, under which is man; and under man are Socrates and Plato and particular men. Of these items, substance is the most general and is only a genus, while man is the most special and is only a species. Body is a species of substance and a genus of animate body. Animate body is a species of body and a genus of animal. Again, animal is a species of animate body and a genus of rational animal. Rational animal is a species of animal and a genus of man. Man is a species of rational animal, but not a genus of particular men, only a species.[73]

This is the seed from which the famous Porphyrian tree grew. It does not yet, as Jonathan Barnes rightly points out, bear much resemblance to a tree and may perhaps be better characterized as a chain, as Ammonius does.[74]

---

[71] Nicholas of Paris, *Rat. sup. Praed.* 1 (Munich, Bayer. Staatsbibl. 14460, f. 42ra): "Praedicamentum enim est collectio praedicabilium, praedicabile autem idem est quod dicibile incomplexum ordinabile."

[72] Porphyry, *Isagoge* 4.15–20 (trans. Barnes, 5–6; slightly modified).

[73] Porphyry, *Isagoge* 4.21–5.7 (trans. Barnes, 6; slightly modified).

[74] Porphyry, *Introduction*, trans. Jonathan Barnes (Oxford: Clarendon Press, 2003), 109–10; Ammonius, *in Isag.* 70.13.

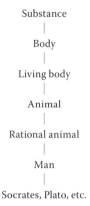

Figure 3. The Porphyrian chain

The tree does not appear until we specify the divisive differentiae for each level of the line. Traditionally, this looks as follows.

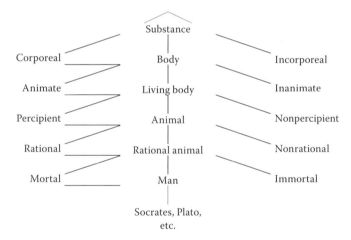

Figure 4. The Porphyrian tree

This is the sort of structure underlying the notion of ordering (*ordinatio*): the generic hierarchy extending downwards from a most general genus to the individuals. Obviously, the tree only models one path through the hierarchy of substance, namely, that relative to the species man, and each hierarchy will consist of the totality of such paths extending from a highest genus to its most special species.

Strictly speaking, however, categorial membership is not equivalent to generic inclusion. Pagus explicitly distinguishes the two:

The differentia, the point, and the unit are not in a category, but they are in a genus. The reason is that a category is an ordering of predicables according to predication and subjection, and in this way only species and individuals are in a category. But there are four ways in which something can be in a genus. One way is as what participates in the notion of that genus, and in this way species and individuals are in a genus — and to participate is to admit of the definition of the participated, as Aristotle says in the fourth book of the *Topics*. The second way something can be in a genus is as completive of the items in that genus, and in this way the differentia is in a genus. The third way something can be in a genus is as a way to the things in that genus, and in this way motion is in a genus; for with regard to the species generation motion is a way to substance, with regard to alteration it is a way to quality, and with regard to augmentation it is a way to quantity. Finally, something can be in a genus as a principle of the items in that genus, and in this way form and matter are in the genus of substance. The point, the unit and the like are not in a category, but they are in a genus.[75]

The distinction appears to be partly based on the type of items collected. Pagus seems to drawing on the distinction between (a) a thing taken as falling under language (*res sub sermone*) and (b) a thing as such, that is, between (a) a predicable or sayable (*dicibile*), which is a thing of reason (*res rationis*), and (b) a thing *simpliciter*, which is a thing of nature (*res naturalis*, *res naturae*).[76] The relation to language is, as Nicholas of Paris explains in his commentary on the *Isagoge*, a necessary condition for predication:

> I concede that universals are both things and names. (...) But in so far as they are things and the name is disregarded, they fall under the explorations of the metaphysician. Under the present science, by contrast, they fall only in so far as they are things falling under signs. For if they were not names, they could not be predicated, which is an act of speech and name.[77]

In other words, the predication "S is P" involves linguistic signs "S" and "P" but expresses a relationship between ontological items S and P. We may say that "P"

---

[75] John Pagus, *Rat. sup. Praed.* VI, q. 3 (41.18–30).

[76] Cf. John Pagus, *Rat. sup. Praed.* XI (63.4–6); XLI, q. 2 (237.20–22).

[77] Nicholas of Paris, *Rat. sup. Porph.* II, q. 10 (Munich, Bayer. Staatsbibl. 14460, f. 5va–vb): "Ad aliud concedo quod universalia sunt res et nomina (...) Sed in quantum res, circumscripto etiam nomine, cadunt in speculatione metaphysici. In hac autem scientia non cadunt nisi in quantum sunt res sub signo. Si enim non essent nomina, non possent praedicari, qui est actus sermonis et nominis."

predicates and P is predicated or that "P" serves to predicate P. A genus may collect ontological items in themselves, but a category collects them only in so far as they fall under their linguistic signs, that is, in so far as they are sayables. Like the items it collects, a category is a thing of reason (*res rationis*).[78]

Whereas a genus can collect different items in different ways, an item can be in a category only by falling in the categorial line (*linea praedicamentalis*), that is, the predicative chain mirroring the stem of a Porphyrian tree. In speaking of "ordering according to subjection and predication," then, Pagus has in mind not only a very specific kind of order, but also a very specific type of predication. Indeed, since he restricts categorial inclusion to species and individuals, the kind of predication involved will be the subtype of essential predication known as *in quid* predication.

In saying that only species and individuals are in a category, Pagus is not using the word "category" in accordance with the definition set out above. He is not referring to an entire coordination of predicables, but only to the topmost item of such a coordination. According to Radulphus Brito, who wrote at the turn of the fourteenth century, this ambiguity was common:

> A category can be taken either (a) as the most general genus in some coordination or (b) as the entire coordination proceeding from the most general genus all the way to the individuals, just like we sometimes say that the most general genus in some coordination is a category, while at other times we call the whole coordination a category.[79]

In the second sense, (b), a category will, of course, also include a highest genus.

There are some notable features of the category system flowing from all of this. First, a category collects things of reason (sayables), and can, strictly speaking, be distinguished from the generic hierarchy that underlies it. In a sense, of course, the two partly collect the same things, since a category collects the species and individuals collected by the generic hierarchy, but only in so far as they are taken in relation to language. Presumably, this is also why, in practice, the distinction is

---

[78] John Pagus, *Rat. sup. Praed.* XLI, q. 1 (237.15).
[79] Radulphus Brito, *Quaest. sup. Praed.* q. 4 (ed. Venet., 39va): "Dicendum quod praedicamentum potest accipi pro genere generalissimo in aliqua coordinatione vel pro tota coordinatione quae est a generalissimo usque ad individua, sicut aliquando dicimus quod genus generalissimum est praedicamentum in aliqua coordinatione, aliquando autem totam coordinationem vocamus praedicamentum." Cf. Anon. D'Orvillensis, *in Cat.* (ed. Ebbesen, 254): "Dicitur iterum praedicamentum collectio generalissimorum et eorum contentorum; unde dicit Porphyrius: 'In unoquoque praedicamento sunt generalissima et specialissima et eorum media.' Dicitur etiam praedicamentum genus generalissimum."

often ignored. Pagus can frequently be found to use "genus" and "category" interchangeably, and in this he is much like his contemporaries.

Secondly, there is a sense in which the categories are not exhaustive. There are a nonnegligible number of items that are not subject to categorial inclusion; the material and formal principles of substances, for example. Pagus also appears to exclude the differentiae that make up the branches of the underlying generic trees. This is a stronger version of an idea found in the commentaries of his contemporaries according to which the differentiae, although not properly included in a category, are nonetheless subject to lateral (*a latere*) inclusion.[80]

Thirdly, since a category is either a maximally general item or an entire hierarchy made up of such an item and everything falling under it, there can be no relation of containment between categories. No category contains another one.

4. EQUIVOCALS, UNIVOCALS, DENOMINATIVES

Having discussed Pagus' take on these fundamental preliminary issues, let us now turn to his interpretation of the *Antepraedicamenta* (*Categories* 1–3). As already mentioned, Pagus upholds the traditional view that the *Categories* divides into three parts, but he rephrases it slightly to suit his overall interpretation of the subject matter of Aristotle's text:

> The *Categories* divides into three parts. In the first of these, Aristotle treats of the principles of the sayable, that is, of the *antepraedicamenta*. In the second part, he treats of the items into which the sayable divides, that is, of the *praedicamenta*. In the third part, he treats of items consequent on the sayable, that is, of the *postpraedicamenta*.[81]

The *Antepraedicamenta* provide, in some sense, the foundation on which the system of categories is built. They establish, as Pagus says, the principles of the sayable, and are thus important for the system Aristotle presents.

The *Antepraedicamenta* begin with a series of three definitions of the technical notions of equivocals, univocals, and denominatives.[82] There are two topics

---

[80] See, for example, Robert Kilwardby, *Not. sup. Praed.* VII, q. 2 (Cambridge, Peterhouse 206, f. 48ra; Madrid, Bibl. Univ. 73, f. 18ra): "Et propter hoc, quia differentiae cadunt sic a latere et non sunt adeo vere in praedicamento sicut et genera et ut species, solum per se et primo determinat de generibus et speciebus in genere substantiae, et non de differentiis nisi prout conveniunt cum secundis substantiis." Cf. Lambert of Lagny, *Logica* II (ed. Alessio, 50).

[81] John Pagus, *Rat. sup. Praed.* I (10.8–11).

[82] I refer to these notions in terminology derived from their Latin designations. Equivocals (Lat. *aequivoca*), univocals (Lat. *univoca*), and denominatives (Lat. *denominativa*)

of perennial dispute regarding these definitions. First, exactly what type of items are they definitions of? Secondly, what is the wider role of these notions in the theory of categories?

One currently widespread interpretation is that Aristotle intends to define things, and so the definitions amount, roughly, to the following. Things are equivocal when they have only a name in common and the account of being (Gk. *logos tēs ousias*, Lat. *ratio substantiae*) corresponding to the name is different for each. Similarly, things are univocal when they have a name in common and the account of being corresponding to the name is the same for each. Finally, things are denominative, when they get their name from something else, but with a difference of ending (Gk. *tēi ptōsei*, Lat. *solo casu*).[83] The interpretation has much in its favour, but it is also clear that from Aristotle's definitions one can relatively easily derive definitions of equivocal, univocal, and denominative names.

At the time Pagus wrote his commentary, it was customary to speak of both things and names as equivocal and to distinguish between them by saying that the name relative to which two or more things are equivocal is an equivocating equivocal (*aequivocum aequivocans*), while the relevant things are equivocated equivocals (*aequivoca aequivocata*). Similarly with regard to univocal names and univocal things.[84] Pagus explicitly uses the terminology in his discussion of equivocals:

> Something is said to be equivocal in two ways, that is, as either equivocating (*aequivocans*) or equivocated (*aequivocatum*). Aristotle is here defining the equivocated in relation to the equivocating.[85]

This is in line with the favoured modern interpretation. The main difference in Pagus' exposition is that he introduces a distinction between a name according to matter (*secundum materiam*) and a name according to species (*secundum speciem*) in order to explain how two or more equivocal things can be said to have a name in common. Underlying the problem, as well as the distinction, is Aristotle's definition in *Perihermeneias* 2.16a19–20 of the name as "a spoken sound that is significant" (*vox significativa*), which Pagus takes to mean that a name is a composite

are also known, respectively, as synonyms (Gk. *synōnyma*), homonyms (Gk. *homōnyma*), and paronyms (Gk. *parōnyma*). Similarly, the related notions of equivocity, univocity, and denomination are known, respectively, as homonymy, synonymy, and paronymy.

[83] Aristotle, *Categories* 1.1a1–15 (trans. Ackrill, 3). Cf. Ackrill's comments, ibid. 71–73.

[84] See, for example, Robert Kilwardby, *Not. sup. Praed.* I, q. 1 (Cambridge, Peterhouse 206, f. 42vb; Madrid, Bibl. Univ. 73, f. 11va): "Non enim definit nomina aequivoca aut univoca, aequivocantia aut univocantia, sed magis res aequivocatas aut univocatas sub nominibus." See also Anon. D'Orvillensis, *in Cat.* (ed. Ebbesen, 255–57).

[85] John Pagus, *Rat. sup. Praed.* I, q. 8 (15.7–8).

of a phonetic component, the spoken sound (*vox*), and a semantic component, a concept or understanding (*intellectus*). This seems to imply that when I use "dog" of both Fido and Sirius, say, I am not using the same name, since there is a different semantic component involved in each case. It appears, in other words, as if no name can be equivocal. This is met by saying that we can speak of the spoken sound as a name according to matter, and of the spoken sound conjoined to a concept as a name according to species. When Aristotle says that equivocal things have a name in common, he is using "name" in the former sense.[86]

This analysis of names recurs in the exposition of the definition of univocals. However, this definition is expounded as a definition of names rather than things. Nothing much seems to hang on this inelegancy. The resultant definition can presumably be translated so as to parallel the definition of equivocals. What is common to univocal things, one could say, is a name according to both matter and species.[87]

As with the definition of univocals, Pagus takes the definiton of denominatives to be a definition of linguistic items. This appears to have been the standard approach at the time, although there seems to have been considerable disagreement about the details of interpretation. Central to the discussion was the question of how to interpret the phrase *solo casu* occurring in Aristotle's definition. Writing around the middle of the century, Roger Bacon lists three possible interpretations: (1) change in ending (*in fine*), (2) derivation (*formatio*), and (3) the "fall" (*cadentia*) of a form towards matter and subject.[88]

On (1), nouns in oblique cases will come out as denominatives of the same noun in the principal, that is, nominative, case. This reading is explicitly rejected by Pagus.[89]

On (2), the outcome will depend on the criteria by which one determines primacy. Thus, on the criteria employed by the grammarian "whiteness" will come out as a denominative of "white," whereas on those used by the logician the opposite will be the case, "white" will be the denominative of "whiteness." There are two versions of this idea. On (2a), the difference between the grammarian's and the logician's approach is epistemological in the sense that the grammarian takes as prior what is so in the order of experience, whereas the logician takes as prior

---

[86] John Pagus, *Rat. sup. Praed.* I, q. 9. Robert Kilwardby advances a different analysis, on which see Lewry, *Kilwardby's Writings*, 267–72.

[87] See John Pagus, *Rat. sup. Praed.* II (17.7–9).

[88] Roger Bacon, *Summulae dialectices* I 2.30–35 (ed. de Libera, 190–91). See also Jennifer Ashworth, "*Catégories*, 1 dans le '*Guide de l'étudiant*,'" in Lafleur and Carrier, *L'enseignement de la philosophie*, 294–95.

[89] John Pagus, *Rat. sup. Praed.* III, q. 5. Cf. Albert the Great, *De praedicamentis* I 4 (ed. Donati and Steel, 11).

what is so in the order of understanding. Nicholas of Paris opts for this explanation, as does Lambert of Lagny.[90] On (2b), the difference lies in the fact that the
grammarian employs purely linguistic criteria, while the logician bases primacy
on purely ontological grounds. This idea occurs in Robert Kilwardby's commentary. Roger Bacon lists both (2a) and (2b), and traces of both versions can be found
in Pagus' commentary.[91]

On (3), denomination becomes unquestionably grounded in ontology. This interpretation is embraced by Pagus and Kilwardby. The author of the *Ripoll Compendium* also advances a version of it.[92] The "fall" in question, Pagus says, is one
that occurs on the ontological (*a parte rei*) rather than the grammatical level (*a
parte vocis*).[93] He glosses Aristotle's definition as follows:

> *Denominatives are called* such as, *differing from some* principal name *merely
> by a fall*, that is, by a falling of a form towards a subject, *have their appellation*,
> that is, signification, *according to* that *name*.[94]

Kilwardby explains what is meant in saying that a denominative name differs from
the cognate principal name "merely by the falling of a form towards a subject" in
the following way:

---

[90] Nicholas of Paris, *Rat. sup. Praed.* I. q. 13 (Munich, Bayer. Staatsbibl. 14460, f. 43rb):
"Ad aliud dicendum quod grammaticus est artifex sensibilis tantum, et concreta no-
tiora sunt secundum sensum ipsis abstractis; ideo dicit quod a 'iustus' derivatur 'iustitia.'
Logicus autem est intellectualis et maioris abstractionis quam grammaticus; et ideo ab-
stracta magis ei sunt nota, et propter hoc dicit quod a 'iustitia' 'iustus' et non e converso."
Cf. Lambert of Lagny, *Logica* III (ed. Alessio, 64–66).

[91] Robert Kilwardby, *Not. sup. Praed.* I, q. 9 (Cambridge, Peterhouse 206, f. 43va; Madrid, Bibl. Univ. 73, f. 12va): "Post haec quaeritur quare logicus aliter appellat denominativa
quam grammaticus et opposito modo. Et dicendum quod grammaticus attendit deriva-
tionem et formationem, unde quae prima sunt in derivando simpliciter ponit esse prima;
quoniam ergo a 'iusto' formatur 'iustitia,' scilicet a genitivo 'iusti' addito '-tia' fit 'iustitia,'
propter hoc 'iustitia' est denominativum a 'iusto.' Sed logicus non considerat huiusmodi
proprietates sed prioritatem vel posterioritatem in essendo vel in causando, et in hac via
est prius 'iustitia' 'iusto.'" Cf. Roger Bacon, *Summulae dialectices* I 2.31–34 (ed. de Libera,
190–91); John Pagus, *Rat. sup. Praed.* III, q. 3.

[92] Anon., *Ripoll Compendium* §539 (ed. Lafleur, 151): "Item quaeritur quid est dictum,
'Denominativa different solu casu.' Ad quod dicimus quod idem est 'solu casu,' id est incli-
natione vel contractione vel concretione ad subiectum. 'Albus' enim denominativum est
secundum logicum et dicit in concretione ad subiectum illud quod dicit 'albedo' in abstractione." For Pagus and Kilwardby, see following notes.

[93] John Pagus, *Rat. sup. Praed.* III, q. 5. Cf. Peter of Spain, *Tractatus* III 1 (ed. de Rijk, 27).

[94] John Pagus, *Rat. sup. Praed.* III (21.10–12). Cf. ibid., III (24.13–16).

It is to be said that denominatives signify an accident as related to a subject, and so with "a fall," whereas the principal name signifies the same thing without relation to a subject, and so without "a fall." And in this way the denominatives "differ" from the principal name "merely by a fall," that is, "merely by a falling towards matter."[95]

Pagus, in turn, supplies a brief analysis of the underlying semantics. Basically, a word (*dictio*) has two semantic components: what is signified (*significatum*) and a way of signifying (*modus significandi*). The former component is primary (*praecedit*) and is determined by the word stem (*principium*), whereas the latter component is determined by the word ending (*finis*). A denominative name shares the primary semantic component with its cognate principal name but differs with regard to the secondary component. The two expressions signify the same thing but in different ways.[96] With regard to the pair "whiteness" (*albedo*) and "white" (*album*) we may say that what is signified is the form whiteness. The principal name, "whiteness," signifies this form in itself, the denominative, "white," signifies it as joined to a subject.[97]

From what has been said, it is evident that Pagus does not attempt a uniform exposition of Aristotle's three definitions, in the sense of reading all of them as being of things rather than expressions or vice versa. The interpretation is held together, nonetheless, in so far as it takes all three definitions to centrally involve both things and expressions, that is, as defining either expressions as they apply to things or things as they fall under expressions, and this dual perspective, we have

---

[95] Robert Kilwardby, *Not. sup. Praed.* I, q. 7 (Cambridge, Peterhouse 206, f. 43rb–va; Madrid, Bibl. Univ. 73, f. 12rb): "Sequitur quaestio de denominativis, et quaeritur primo qualiter differunt solo casu. Et dicendum quod denominativa significant accidens ut habet relationem ad subiectum, et ita cum casu, principale vero significat idem praeter relationem ad subiectum, et ita sine casu; et sic differunt *solo casu*, id est sola cadentia ad materiam, a principali." Kilwardby is not, *pace* Ashworth, "*Catégories*, 1," 294–95, speaking of "la matière des *voces*."

[96] John Pagus, *Rat. sup. Praed.* III, q. 4. Cf. Nicholas of Paris, *Rat. sup. Praed.* I, q. 14 (Munich, Bayer. Staatsbibl. 14460, f. 43rb–va): "Ad aliud dicendum quod denominativa semper conveniunt in significato cum suis abstractis, differunt autem in modo significandi, et quia a parte principii semper dinoscitur significatum, et non per finem, ideo conveniunt in principio et differunt in fine ut denotetur diversus modus significandi."

[97] The meaning of words such as "white" and "whiteness" was a recurrent problem in medieval philosophy. For historical background and an in-depth discussion of late thirteenth-century debates concerning the matter, see Sten Ebbesen, "Concrete Accidental Terms: Late Thirteenth-Century Debates about Problems Relating to such Terms as '*album*,'" in *Meaning and Inference in Medieval Philosophy: Studies in Memory of Jan Pinborg*, ed. Norman Kretzmann (Dordrecht: Kluwer, 1988), 107–74. Solutions invoking *modi significandi* can be traced back to at least the early twelfth century.

already seen, is one that the thinkers of this period took to be relatively unprob-lematic.

As to the role of the notions of equivocity, univocity, and denomination within the framework of categorial theory, Pagus accounts for it by mapping them onto the notion of the sayable (*dicibile*). This yields what he calls the *partes dicibilis*, that is, the types or modes of being sayable. A sayable, he says, is either in a genus (*in genere*) or not in a genus (*extra genus*). If it is of the latter sort, it will be things such as being and one, and it will be equivocal. If a sayable is of the former sort, it will either be sayable of something in the same genus, and so univocal, or it will be sayable of something in a different genus, and so denominative.[98]

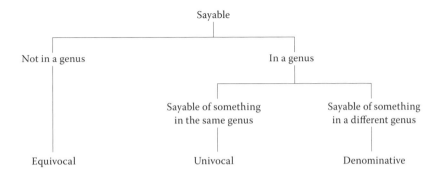

Figure 5. Types of sayable

He uses a related idea to account for the order in which Aristotle defines these no-tions. The categories (that is, the highest item in each categorial line) are subject, he says, to three comparisons. First, they can be compared to their superiors, in which case the result in something equivocal. Secondly, they can be compared to their inferiors, in which case the result is something univocal. Finally, they can be compared to their co-laterals, in which case the result is something denomi-native.[99]

This way of accounting for the order of presentation and the role of the notions has partial late ancient antecedents.[100] Pagus' proximate source may have been Nicholas of Paris:

The ten genera can be compared to being, which transcends all genera. They can also be compared to the things belonging to their genus, as substance to

---

[98] John Pagus, *Rat. sup. Praed.* I (10.21–25).
[99] John Pagus, *Rat. sup. Praed.* II, q. 5 (20.1–5).
[100] Porphyry, *in Cat.* 61.10–12; Simplicius, *in Cat.* 33.23–27; Boethius, *in Cat.* 166c. See Andrews, *Peter of Auvergne's Commentary*, 44–46.

the things belonging to its genus, quantity to the things belonging to its genus, and so on. They can furthermore be compared to things belonging to a different genus, as substance can be compared to quantity and quality. By the first comparison the equivocal is caused, and this is excluded from all categories. By the second comparison the univocal arises, and this is upheld in each of the categories (for there is univocal predication in all categories). From the final comparison the denominative arises, and according to this substance is said to be of a certain quality or quantity.[101]

The account appears to have become quite popular, and versions of it recur in many later thirteenth-century discussions of the *Categories*.[102] Robert Kilwardby employs the same idea but phrases it in a slightly different manner:

> First, the ten highest genera are equivocal relative to the names "being" and "one." Secondly, subaltern genera and species are univocal relative to the names of the highest genera. Finally, the last nine genera, falling towards substance, are denominative of substance.[103]

In sum, the role that the concepts of equivocity, univocity, and denomination play in the theory of categories is the following. Equivocity is an extra-categorial relation involved when a transcendental is predicated of the several categories. We may say that the highest genera are equivocal relative to the name "being," that being is equivocally predicated of them, or that it is an equivocal sayable relative to the several categories. Univocity, in turn, is an intra-categorial relation involved

---

[101] Nicholas of Paris, *Rat. sup. Praed.* I, q. 8 (Munich, Bayer. Staatsbibl. 14460, f. 43ra–rb): "Vel aliter dicendum, et melius, sicut dictum est, quod determinat de decem vocibus decem prima rerum genera significantibus, et ista decem genera possunt comparari ad ens, quod transcendit omne genus. Item possunt comparari ad res sui generis, ut substantia ad res sui generis, quantitas ad res sui generis, et sic de aliis. Possunt etiam comparari ad res alterius generis, ut substantia ad quantitatem et qualitatem. A prima comparatione causatur aequivocum, quod abicitur ab omni praedicamento; a secunda comparatione oritur univocum, quod salvatur in quolibet praedicamento (in omni enim praedicamento est praedicatio univoca); ab ultima comparatione {ultima comparatione *scripsi* : altera denominatione *ms., ut v.*} oritur denominativum, secundum quod substantia dicitur qualis vel quanta."

[102] Andrews, *Peter of Auvergne's Commentary*, 45. See, e.g., Lambert of Lagny, *Logica* III (ed. Alessio, 64–65); Peter of Auvergne, *Quaest. sup. Praed.* q. 7 (ed. Andrews, 7). Cf. also Anon., *Ripoll Compendium* §535 (ed. Lafleur, 150).

[103] Robert Kilwardby, *Not. sup. Praed.* I, q. 1 (Cambridge, Peterhouse 206, f. 42vb; Madrid, Bibl. Univ. 73, f. 11va): "Et patet etiam ex iam dictis ratio ordinis, cum primo sint sub his nominibus, 'ens' et 'unum', genera prima univoca, consequenter genera subalterna et species sub nominibus primorum generum univoca, ultimo alia genera ad substantiam cadentia substantiam sint denominativa."

when a categorial item is predicated of its categorial inferiors. We may say, for example, that items in the genus of substance are univocal relative to the name "substance," that substance is univocally predicated of them, or that it is a univocal sayable relative to its categorial inferiors. Finally, denomination is an intercategorial relation involved when an item in an accidental category is predicated of an item in the category of substance. Whiteness, say, is an item in the category of quality. It can be predicated of its several categorial inferiors (the different types of whiteness), and here univocity is involved. It can also be predicated of the items that bear it or in which it inheres (which in the final analysis will be substances). To do this, however, one does not use the abstract noun "whiteness" but rather the denominative "white." We may say that whiteness is denominatively predicated of its bearers or that it is a denominative sayable relative to them.[104]

Regardless of how it is phrased, the interpretation requires that the notion of account (*ratio*) that Aristotle invokes in the definitions of equivocals and univocals be understood in a wider sense than the strict sense of definition by means of genus and differentia, since neither being, nor substance, quantity, etc., have a superordinate genus by means of which such a definition could be given. Like other late ancient commentators, Boethius explicitly draws attention to this as regards the univocity of the highest genera and advances an interpretation on which an account may be either a definition in the strict sense or a mere description.[105] Kilwardby follows suit and expressly embraces an inclusive interpretation of "account" (*ratio*) as it occurs in the definitions of equivocals and univocals:

> Note that "account" is here used in the sense in which it is refers indiscriminately to a true definition or a description or in so far as it is used of any phrase more explanatory than the name, or any account whatsoever.[106]

Nicholas of Paris makes a similar point by glossing the first occurrence of "account" (*ratio*) with "delineation" (*notificatio*), but Pagus simply glosses its occurrences by "definition" (*definitio*), and in his discussions of equivocity and univocity he seems to have recourse solely to definitions in the strict sense of the word.[107]

---

[104] Cf. John Pagus, *Rat. sup. Praed.* XLIV, q. 6 (256.26–30).

[105] Boethius, *in Cat.* 166a–b. Cf. Ammonius, *in Cat.* 20.14–22; Simplicius, *in Cat.* 29.16–24.

[106] Robert Kilwardby, *Not. sup. Praed.* I, q. 3 (Cambridge, Peterhouse 206, f. 43rb; Madrid, Bibl. Univ. 73, f. 12ra): "Item, nota quod sumitur hic 'ratio' communiter ad rationem quae est vera definitio sive descriptio sive prout dicitur ratio sermo maioris declarationis quam nomen sive pro qualicumque ratione." Cf. Albert the Great, *De praedicamentis* I 2 (ed. Donati and Steel, 7); I 3 (ibid., 8).

[107] Nicholas of Paris, *Rat. sup. Praed.* I (Munich, Bayer. Staatsbibl. 14460, f. 42rb): "Dicit ergo quod *aequivoca dicuntur quorum solum nomen commune est*, et *secundum* illud

His exposition may still be consistent, however, since he seems on occasion to use the word "definition" to refer to what strictly speaking should be spoken of in terms of description.[108]

5. THE ONTOLOGICAL SQUARE

In the second chapter of the *Categories*, Aristotle introduces a fourfold division of "things that are" (*eorum quae sunt*). The division is generated by letting two basic relationships, being said of a subject and being in a subject, and their negations crosscut. On the traditional interpretation, being said of a subject picks out universals while its negation picks out particulars, being in a subject picks out accidents while its negation picks out substances. This suggests the following definitions: (1) A is a universal if and only if, for some B, A is said of B; (2) A is a particular if and only if, for no B, A is said of B; (3) A is an accident if and only if, for some B, A is in B; and (4) A is a substance if and only if, for no B, A is in B. The division then yields the result shown in table 5.

Said of a subject	In a subject	Item	
+	-	(I)	Universal substance
-	+	(II)	Particular accident
+	+	(III)	Universal accident
-	-	(IV)	Particular substance

Table 5. Division of things that are

On the basis of Aristotle's text, the following exemplification of types (I)–(IV) seems natural. Type (IV) items are items such as particular men and horses, while type (I) items are the species and genera, such as man and horse, to which type (IV) items belong. Type (III) items are attributes such as whiteness and grammatical knowledge, which are the genera and species of type (II) items, which are their particular instances, e.g., a particular whiteness, a particular grammatical knowledge.[109]

---

nomen ratio substantiae, id est notificatio, est *diversa, ut animal homo et quod pingitur.*" Cf. ibid. VIII, q. 1 (f. 55va): "Ad primum dicendum quod ista definitio non est definitio propria, eo quod non est per priora, sed est quaedam descriptio et notificatio qualitatis per posterius. Unde non est definitio potissima, eo quod non est per priora."

[108] Cf., for example, what he says of the opening lines of *Categories* 8, which contain Aristotle's "definition" of quality. See John Pagus, *Rat. sup. Praed.* XXXI (179.1–5); XXXI, q. 4 (183.11–16).

[109] This traditional interpretation of type (II) items has been disputed in recent years. For a discussion of the main arguments and defence of the traditional interpretation, see

Pagus belongs to this tradition of interpretation. He explicitly recognizes the division as a division of being in so far as it contains all forms plus their ultimate subject.[110] The ultimate subjects are, of course, type (IV) items, which, like Aristotle, Pagus takes to be the foundation of items of the remaining three types and as such a necessary condition for their existence.

> All the other things are either in or said of primary substances. Thus, primary substances are the foundation and subject of all the other things. But if the subject is destroyed, so is that which is contained in it. Thus, if primary substances do not exist it is impossible for any of the other things to exist.[111]

This is what may be called the key thesis of the *Categories* ontology. It is argued that the position is problematic:

> Aristotle here says that if primary substances are destroyed so are the others that are contained in them.
>
> To the contrary, it is self-evident that the destruction of the destructible does not cause the destruction of the indestructible. Thus, since primary substances are destructible and universals indestructible, the destruction of primary substances will not be the cause of the destruction of universals. Thus, even if the former are destroyed, the latter can remain.
>
> Likewise, the destruction of what is omnispatial and omnitemporal is not consequent on the destruction of what has definite spatial and temporal location. Thus, since singulars have definite spatial and temporal location whereas universals are omnispatial and omnitemporal, as it says in the *Posterior Analytics*, the destruction of universals is not consequent on the destruction of singulars.
>
> But to the contrary, it says in the second book of *On the soul* that the reproductive faculty is given to animals in order that through it the divine and desirable being that is the being of the species be continued so that what was in itself incapable of preservation be preserved in the individuals. Thus, primary substances are the cause of the continuation of the universals. But everything that by its existence is the cause of something else's continuation in being is by its extinction the cause of that things extinction. Thus, the extinction of the singulars is the cause of the extinction of universals, and so, if primary substances do not exist it is impossible for any of the other things to exist.[112]

Michael V. Wedin, *Aristotle's Theory of Substance: The* Categories *and* Metaphysics *Zeta* (Oxford: Oxford University Press, 2000), 38–66.

[110] John Pagus, *Rat. sup. Praed.* IV, q. 1 (28.3–6).

[111] John Pagus, *Rat. sup. Praed.* VIII (49.16–20).

[112] John Pagus, *Rat. sup. Praed.* VIII, q. 4 (51.1–16).

Pagus solves the puzzle by distinguishing two kinds or modes of being that a universal has.

> It is to be said that the universal has a double being, namely, natural and rational. Natural being is the actual being that it has in the singulars, and in this way the universals are destroyed if the primary substances are destroyed. Rational being is a defective or aptitudinal being, and in this way if the primary substances are destroyed the universals aren't destroyed but are rather indestructible according to following quote from Porphyry: "The destruction of what is superior is not consequent on the destruction of what is inferior." And so the solution to the objections is clear.[113]

Actual being for a universal requires instantiation; an actually existing universal is an instantiated universal. Rational being, by contrast, does not require extramental instantiation; a universal having this kind of being exists, it would seem, as a universal concept, and may do so irrespective of whether there is any remaining actual instantiation or not.[114] The universal *dodo*, say, has rational being but no actual being. On the level of actual being, then, the primacy of primary substances with regard to their substantial universals holds. If a universal substance actually exists, there will be some particular substance of which it is said.[115]

With regard to accidents, the primacy of primary substances follows directly from the facts that accidents require bearers and that the primary bearers of accidents are primary substances:

> Doing and all other accidents can be in something in two ways: either primarily or secondarily. It is therefore to be said that doing and all other accidents can be in something in two ways, as I just said. They are in primary substances in the first way (...), but as a consequence and secondarily they are in secondary substances.[116]

Pagus attributes this idea to Porphyry, whose *Isagoge* contains a few scattered remarks that may be taken to this effect.[117] Boethius advances it at more length in his commentary on the *Categories*:

> Every accident comes first to individuals, subsequently to secondary substances. For because Aristarchus has knowledge of grammar and Aristarchus

---

[113] John Pagus, *Rat. sup. Praed.* VIII, q. 4 (51.17–22).
[114] Cf. John Pagus, *Rat. sup. Praed.* VIII, q. 4 (51.23–33).
[115] Cf. John Pagus, *Rat. sup. Praed.* XXIX, q. 3 (170.20–31).
[116] John Pagus, *Rat. sup. Praed.* X, q. 3 (62.7–11).
[117] See Porphyry, *Isagoge* 13.18–21; 17.8–10.

is a man, man has knowledge of grammar. In this way every accident comes first to an individual, but secondarily the relevant accident will be thought to also come to the species and genera of substance.[118]

An accident, in other words, is in a secondary substance if and only if it is in a primary substance of which that secondary substance is a species or genus. Thus, if an accident exists, there will be a particular substance in which it is.

Accidents, Pagus holds, also depend for their individualization on the individualization of substance, which presumably means that a particular accident is made particular by the primary substance it is in.[119] Strictly speaking, then, it would appear that what is in a primary substance is a particular accident. This, in turn, suggests that a universal accident is in a subject if and only if it is said of an item (a particular accident) which is in a subject.

While he recognizes Aristotle's division as a division of things that are, Pagus, in keeping with his overall interpretation of the *Categories*, understands its role relative to the notion of the sayable (*dicibile*). As we saw previously, *Categories* 1 introduced three types of sayable (*partes dicibilis*): the equivocal, the univocal, and the denominative. *Categories* 2 is now understood to determine the nature of these types in their mutual relationships (*natura partium inter se*). One type, the equivocal, is the dividend. The dividers in Aristotle's fourfold division, Pagus then finds, indicate three dispositions (*habitudo*), comparisons (*comparatio*), orders (*ordo*), or orderings (*ordinatio*) across the two remaining types, the univocal and the denominative. The combination of being said of and not being in is said to not only pick out universal substances but also to indicate their disposition or ordering towards particular substances. Similarly, the combination of not being said of and being in is said to pick out particular accidents and indicate the disposition or ordering of accidents towards substances. Finally, the combination of being said of and being in is said to pick out universal accidents and indicate their disposition or ordering towards particular accidents.[120] The interpretation can be visualized as follows:

---

[118] Boethius, *in Cat.* 182c–d (ed. Migne): "Principaliter vero individuae substantiae dictae sunt quod omne accidens prius in individua, post vero in secundas substantias venit; nam quoniam Aristarchus grammaticus est, homo vero est Aristarchus, est homo grammaticus. Ita prius omne accidens in individuum venit, secundo vero loco etiam in species generaque substantiarum accidens illud venire putabitur." Cf. Boethius, *in Cat.* 189c–d.

[119] John Pagus, *Rat. sup. Praed.* XVI, q. 4 (99.15–17).

[120] John Pagus, *Rat. sup. Praed.* IV, qq. 3–4. Cf. ibid., IV (25.3–12).

Figure 6. Pagus' interpretation of Aristotle's division

The said-of relation now yields two distinct dispositions, D1 and D3, relative to the distinction between substance and accident. The motivation for this seems to lie in the parasitic nature of accidents. For an accident to be is for a substance to bear it — *accidentis esse est inesse*, as the adage has it. And not only are accidents dependent on substances for their being, they are also dependent on them for their individuation. D3, Pagus seems to take it, is dependent on or derivative of D1.[121]

One way of interpreting this construal of the fourfold division is to say that Aristotle's division provides the underlying ontological framework for the predicative relations with which categorial theory is concerned. What is predicable is a form or universal nature in so far as it falls under discourse (is an incomplex sayable). Such forms or natures and their subjects, the four fundamental types of entity Aristotle's division picks out, stand in certain basic ontological relationships, which determine three basic predicative relations: univocal substantial predication, univocal non-substantial predication, and denominative accidental predication.

6. THE ANTEPREDICAMENTAL RULES

Categories 3, the third and final part of the *Antepraedicamenta*, is, according to Pagus, about the actual ordering of one sayable in relation to another. More specifically, he takes Aristotle to posit two rules governing such ordering. The first rule concerns the ordering of sayables belonging to the same genus, the second rule pertains to the ordering of sayables belonging to different genera.[122]

The first rule (R1), as Pagus expounds it, is as follows:

(R1) Whenever one thing is predicated of another as of a subject, whatever is predicated of the predicate is predicated of the subject.[123]

---

[121] John Pagus, *Rat. sup. Praed.* XVI, q. 4.
[122] John Pagus, *Rat. sup. Praed.* V (33.6–8).
[123] John Pagus, *Rat. sup. Praed.* V (33.16–17).

When it is objected that the qualification "as of a subject" is superfluous since every predicate is predicated of a subject, "subject" is explicated as meaning "subjacent in the same categorial line."[124]

This explication occurs again when, as was customary, it is brought up for discussion whether or not the proposed rule licenses fallacious inferences such as "Animal is predicated of man; genus is predicated of animal; therefore, genus is predicated of man."[125] Not surprisingly, Pagus holds that it doesn't. However, in order to render the rule immune to such counterexamples, its compass needs to be restricted. He suggests two ways of doing this. The first consists in drawing a distinction between substantial and accidental predication and restricting the rule to the former type. The second way is to simply insist upon the previously proposed explication of the qualification "as of a subject" as meaning "subjacent in the same categorial line."[126] Since in both cases the restriction is taken to range over both the dependent and the main clause, the counterexample no longer applies. It should be noted, however, that the two ways of restricting the rule are not equivalent. The reason for this is that, while predications in the categorial line may perhaps be taken as the primary instances of substantial predication, substantial predication is not confined to such predications — the differentia is predicated essentially but does not fall in the categorial line. So while it follows that if A is predicated of B in the categorial line, then A is predicated essentially of B, the converse does not hold. Thus, on the first interpretation, the rule states that substantial predication is transitive, whereas on the second interpretation it states simply that predication in the categorial line is transitive. While in his exposition and glossing of the rule Pagus explicates the rule in this latter way, he effectively takes it in the former way when applying it at other points in his commentary.[127]

The second rule (R2), as Pagus reads it, is as follows:

(R2) The species and differentiae of genera, which are different and not subordinate, are themselves different.[128]

---

[124] John Pagus, *Rat. sup. Praed.* v, q. 2.

[125] John Pagus, *Rat. sup. Praed.* v, q. 5. Cf. Dexippus, *in Cat.* 26.13–16; Ammonius, *in Cat.* 31.3–6; Simplicius, *in Cat.* 52.9–11; Boethius, *in Cat.* 176c–d.

[126] John Pagus, *Rat. sup. Praed.* v, q. 5. Cf. Robert Kilwardby, *Not. sup. Praed.* IV, q. 2 (Cambridge, Peterhouse 206, f. 44va; Madrid, Bibl. Univ. 73, f. 13va).

[127] See, for example, John Pagus, *Rat. sup. Praed.* v (33.26–34.3).

[128] Pagus used the composite Latin translation, and he here reads *diverse species et differentiae sunt* with *CsCh* rather than the standard *diversae secundum speciem et differentiae sunt*, which, admittedly, corresponds better to Aristotle's Greek. See John Pagus, *Rat. sup. Praed.* v (34.12–14).

What the rule postulates, in other words, is that, for some distinct and nonsubordinate genera, A and B, it is never the case that, for some C, both C is a species of A and C is a species of B, nor is it ever the case that, for some D, both D is a differentia of A and D is a differentia of B.

With regard to the differentia, Pagus points out that the rule is vulnerable to the following counterexample:

> Animal and plant are different and not subordinate genera, and they have the same differentia, namely, animate.[129]

The solution, he suggests, lies in the proper interpretation of "subordinate":

> It is to be said that genera are called subordinate in two ways. Either because the one falls under the other or because there is a third genus under which they both fall. Thus, even though animal does not fall under plant or vice versa, they nonetheless both fall under substance, and so they are subordinate.[130]

It should be noticed that Pagus says that animal and plant both fall under substance. This suggests that the relevant third genus may be the highest genus under which the two genera in question fall. On this interpretation, what the rule amounts to is simply that the same differentia cannot be found in two different highest genera.

This may seem like rather strong medicine for the problem at hand. To see this, consider the traditional visualization of the Porphyrian tree as depicted in figure 4 above. Take the genus, which for lack of a readily available name is designated by its definition "animate body." Let's call it A. If we continue down the tree, we see that A is divided by the differential pair (percipient, nonpercipient). We also see that the addition of the differentia percipient constitutes the subordinate genus animal. We do not see that the addition of nonpercipient produces the subordinate genus plant, but this is presumably the case.[131] Now, the constitutive differentia of a given genus will be a differentia of any subordinate genera or species that genus may have, as Aristotle explicitly points out immediately after positing the above rule:

> However, there is nothing to prevent genera subordinate one to the other from having the same differentiae; for the higher are predicated of the genera below

129 John Pagus, *Rat. sup. Praed.* v, q. 6 (36.10–11).
130 John Pagus, *Rat. sup. Praed.* v, q. 6 (36.12–14).
131 See Porphyry, *Isagoge* 10.15–17; Roger Bacon, *Summulae dialectices* I 2.115–19 (ed. de Libera, 203).

them, so that all differentiae of the predicated genus will be differentiae of the subject also.[132]

As the schoolmen seem to have agreed, Aristotle is here speaking of constitutive, not divisive, differentiae.[133] It is obvious, then, that animal and plant share the differentia animate precisely because they are both subordinate to the genus A of which animate is a constitutive differentia. All that is needed to render the proposed rule immune to the counterexample is that it be modified to allow for such cases.

This, however, is not what Pagus is doing when he solves the problem by saying that two genera are subordinate if there is some third genus under which they both fall, and then suggests that this genus is substance. The thing to notice is that this solution allows two genera to have the same differentia even in cases where they do not share this differentia in virtue of either (a) one of them being subordinate to the other or (b) there being some third genus of which the shared differentia is constitutive and to which they are both subordinate.

There is, in fact, evidence that the interpretation of "subordinate" that Pagus is retailing here was, if not designed, then certainly applied to allow for precisely such cases. The main object of concern appears to have been the differentia rational. According to the standard conception of the structure of the generic hierarchy crowned by substance, substance is divided immediately by the differential pair (corporeal, incorporeal). Rational, the medievals were convinced, held of items falling on both sides of this initial divide. On the one hand it holds of the corporeal substance rational animal, on the other hand it applies to incorporeal substances such as intelligences (angels, for example) and souls.[134] In this case, unlike the case of animate holding of both animal and plant, there is no common superordinate genus from which the relevant differentia is inherited.

---

[132] Aristotle, *Categories* 3.1b20–24 (trans. Ackrill, 5).

[133] See, e.g., Nicholas of Paris, *Rat. sup. Praed.* 1 (Munich, Bayer. Staatsbibl., 14460, f. 42rb); Robert Kilwardby, *Not. sup. Praed.* IV, q. 5 (Cambridge, Peterhouse 206, f. 44va–b; Madrid, Bibl. Univ. 73, f. 13vb). The issue of how to read the passage was much discussed in antiquity; see Porphyry, *in Cat.* 84.10–86.4; Dexippus, *in Cat.* 27.2–28.5; Simplicius, *in Cat.* 58.23–59.32; Boethius, *in Cat.* 178d–80a. The discussion has, in fact, spilled over into the modern commentaries; see Aristotle, *Categories*, trans. Ackrill, 77; Aristotle, *Kategorien*, trans. Klaus Oehler (Berlin: Akademie Verlag, 2006), 237–40.

[134] I here ignore the related issue of whether the differentia rational is in fact constitutive of the species man and not of rational animal as Porphyry claims. For this issue, see, e.g., Robert Kilwardby, *Not. sup. Porph.* (Madrid, Univ. Bibl. 73, f. 7vb); Roger Bacon, *Summulae dialectices* I 2.121–23 (ed. de Libera, 203–4); John Duns Scotus, *Quaest. in Porph.* q. 29 (ed. Andrews et al., 179–87).

Robert Kilwardby, who refers to rational as a "difficult counterexample" to (R2), relates that some people had tried to solve it precisely by interpreting "subordinate" in the way Pagus proposes.[135] In fact, the Anonymus D'Orvillensis, writing ca. 1200, lists five solutions to the puzzle, the last two of which he deems authoritative. One of them is ascribed to Aristotle:

> In the *Topics*, Aristotle solves the question by supplementing the rule in the following manner: "[The species and differentiae of] genera, which are different and not subordinate and not contained under the same highest genus, are themselves different."[136]

Those are not Aristotle's exact words, but the solution is, indeed, modelled on the *Topics*. In book 6, chapter 6, Aristotle gives the prospective participant in a dialectical dispute the following piece of advice:

> Consider also if the differentia mentioned belongs to a different genus, neither contained in nor containing the genus in question. For it seems that the same differentia cannot hold of two genera neither of which contains the other.[137]

A few lines later, however, he adds the following modification:

> Or perhaps it is not impossible for the same differentia to hold of two genera neither of which contains the other, and we ought to add, "if they do not both fall under the same genus." Thus, terrestrial animal and winged animal are genera neither of which contains the other, and biped is a differentia of both. So we ought to add, "if they do not both fall under the same genus"; for both of these are subordinate to animal.[138]

---

[135] Robert Kilwardby, *Not. sup. Praed.* IV, q. 4 (Cambridge, Peterhouse 206, f. 44va; Madrid, Bibl. Univ. 73, f. 13va): "Sed adhuc remanet instantia difficilis de hac differentia, rationale, quae est differentia in corporea substantia et incorporea, quae sunt diversa genera et non subalternatim posita. Hac ergo ratione coacti, ponunt quidam substantiam corpoream et incorpoream esse subalternatim posita, non quia unum ponatur sub altero, sed quia ambo ponuntur sub reliquo tertio, et sic dicunt Aristotelem intendere hic de subalternatione."

[136] Anon. D'Orvillensis, *in Cat.* (ed. Ebbesen, 271): "Super hanc quaestionem duplex est solutio, una Boethii et alia Aristotelis. Hanc enim solvit Aristoteles in *Libro topicorum* per suppletionem quandam, hoc modo: 'Diversorum generum et non subalternatim positorum et non contentorum sub eodem generalissimo diversae sunt etc.'"

[137] Aristotle, *Topics* VI 6.144b12–14 (trans. Pickard-Cambridge, 243; slightly modified).

[138] Aristotle, *Topics* VI 6.144b20–26 (trans. Pickard-Cambridge, 243; slightly modified).

The idea, then, that a given differentia may in some cases occur several times in one generic hierarchy finds some support in Aristotle. Kilwardby, nonetheless, finds the suggested interpretation of the rule in *Categories* 3 unconvincing. Rather, he suggests, the problem should be solved simply by stating that rational is not in fact a differentia but rather a *per se* accident of the intelligences. This is necessary, he claims, in view of the idea that the ultimate differentia of a given species is supposed to convert with that species.[139]

Pagus does not enter into these issues, which ultimately touch upon a key point of Aristotelian metaphysics, but his solution to the less troublesome counterexample seems to imply a theoretical possibility that Kilwardby, with explicit reference to the *Metaphysics*, deems problematic. One should notice, however, that the polarity here reflects a genuine tension in the *Corpus Aristotelicum* between a classificatory and definitional ideal according to which the ultimate differentia entails all preceding differentiae and genera, and a more wavering approach evidenced by the passage from the *Topics*.

We have seen how (R2) was interpreted in order to circumvent certain counterexamples that may be brought against it with regard to differentiae. With regard to species, the rule would again appear to be problematic. It implies, at the very least, that a given species or genus can fall under no more than one of the ten highest genera to which entities reduce. The ten highest genera, in other words, must be mutually exclusive. Since the categories mirror these highest genera, the rule implies categorial exclusivity. Such proscription of overlapping categories is generally

---

[139]   Robert Kilwardby, *Not. sup. Praed.* IV, q. 4 (Cambridge, Peterhouse 206, f. 44va; Madrid, Bibl. Univ. 73, f. 13va–b): "Quod credimus esse falsum. Unde dicimus, sicut praescripsimus in Porphyrio, quod rationale in incorporeis est per se accidens et non differentia, sed solum in corporeis. Istud tamen latuit Porphyrio, ut credimus. Unde si quis respiciat Aristotelem et Averroem in septimo, ponit istud necessario esse verum, cum sit aliqua differentia in aeque cum specie quam constituit, apta tamen nata dici de pluribus. Huic etiam concordat quod dicit Aristoteles, quod ultima differentia adveniens generi erit substantia solius rei." Cf. Aristotle, *Metaph.* VII 12.1038a19–20; Averroes, *in Metaph.* VII 43 (ed. Venet., 195a-96b). Kilwardby's move seems to require that "rational" be taken as equivocal and not used of men and intelligences in the same sense. This was the view held by Albert the Great and John Duns Scotus, see Albert the Great, *De Praedicamentis* I 6 (ed. Donati and Steel, 16): "In veritate tamen rationale non convenit incorporeo secundum unam et eandem rationem, sed hoc determinare est *Libri causarum*." John Duns Scotus, *Quaest. sup. Praed.* q. 29 (ed. Andrews et al., 183): "Ad rationem dico quod 'rationale' est aequivocum intelligentiis et nobis. Ipsae enim intelligunt per species innatas, non autem per acquisitas; ideo non indigent sensibus ad scientiam, nos indigemus, per Aristotelem primo *Posteriorum*, quia omnis nostra cognitio ortum habet a sensu. Ipsae intelligunt complexas sine discursu, nos autem cum discursu, ut dicitur tertio *De anima*: 'Omne nostrum intelligere est cum continuo et tempore.'" On Albert's solution and his relation to Kilwardby in this context, see Steel, "Albert's Use," 485–92.

thought to be an attractive structural constraint on a category system,[140] and it is an issue that Pagus and his contemporaries were sensitive to. As they were also aware, however, Aristotle's text poses certain problems in this regard.

The problems divide, roughly, into two groups. The first group consists of cases where Aristotle assigns to a given category an item that other authoritative sources place (either explicitly or implicitly) in a different category; body (*corpus*), for example, is listed in the *Categories* as a quantity, whereas the idea that it falls under substance lies at the very heart of the traditional conception of this category as explicated by Porphyry in his *Isagoge*.[141]

The second group is made up of cases where Aristotle, in different parts of the *Categories*, seems to take the same item as falling now under one, now under another category; an example of this is knowledge (*scientia*), which in his treatment of the category of quality Aristotle lists as belonging to this category, while in his discussion of the category of relatives he appears to count it among the items that fall under this latter category. Indeed, at the very end of his discussion of the category of quality, he even appears to regard such categorial overlaps as theoretically unproblematic:

> Moreover, if the same thing happens to be a quality and a relative there is nothing absurd in its being counted in both genera.[142]

Much like their modern colleagues, medieval interpreters were not impressed with this idea. Since two highest genera are no less disjoint than any other two co-ordinate genera, it is (so goes the objection in Nicholas of Paris' commentary) just as absurd for something to be both a relative and a quality as for it to be both a man and a donkey.[143]

As a solution, Pagus suggests that when Aristotle states that the same item may belong to different highest genera, this should be taken to mean only that they

---

[140] See, for example, Westerhoff, *Ontological Categories*, 57–59.

[141] For body as a quantity, see Aristotle, *Categories* 6.4b23–25; for body as a substance, see Porphyry, *Isagoge* 4.27–28; consider also Aristotle, *Categories* 2.1a27–29 and *Topics* v 2.130b3–4.

[142] Aristotle, *Categories* 8.11a37–38 (trans. Ackrill, 31; slightly modified). For knowledge as a relative, see *Categories* 7.7b23ff. For knowledge as a quality, see *Categories* 8.8b29. Since the Latin translation renders *epistēmē* sometimes with *scientia* and sometimes with *disciplina*, the medievals actually faced two similar problems in this regard.

[143] Nicholas of Paris, *Rat. sup. Praed.* IX, q. 14 (Munich, Bayer. Staatsbibl. 14460, f. 58rb): "Item, dubitatur de ultimo verbo huius capituli. Dicit si idem contingat esse relativum et quale non est inconveniens in utrisque generibus hoc annumerare. Contra. Sicut impossibile est idem esse hominem et asinum, ita impossibile est idem esse relativum et quale, eo quod relatio et qualitas e diverso divisa sunt."

may do so in different respects (*secundum diversos respectus*).[144] And when faced with cases of categorial overlap, Pagus, as a general rule, moves to solve the contradiction with (R2) by pointing out that the item with regard to which the overlap occurs can be considered (*potest considerari, consideratur*) or taken (*sumitur, accipitur*) in multiple or different ways (*tripliciter, quadrupliciter, diversimode*).[145] Thus, in the case of body:

> Body is taken in different ways. In one way, body is triple dimension, and so taken it is a quantity. In another way, body means the thing underlying this triple dimension, and so taken it is a substance.[146]

Clearly, here we are dealing not with one entity considered in different ways, but with two distinct entities, substantial body and quantitative body, of which the first underlies the second. The expression "body" is, in other words, equivocal. This solution was very common, and however it gets worked out in detail safeguards exclusivity.[147]

With regard to knowledge, Pagus offers a similar solution:

> Knowledge is compared to the one who knows, in whom it is as in the subject it denominates, and in this way it is a quality. It is furthermore compared to the object of knowledge of which it is, and in this way it is a relation.[148]

The way this is phrased makes it less plausible to suppose that two distinct entities, equivocally referred to as knowledge, are being singled out. Does this imply that the same entity (in this case, knowledge), if considered in different ways, can be found to have different essential determinations? Presumably not. In the present case such a conclusion seems to be avoided because of the fact that knowledge is relative merely according to expression (*secundum dici*) and not according to being (*secundum esse*). That is, knowledge is one of the items that satisfy Aristotle's initial description of relatives, framed in terms of linguistic criteria, but fail to satisfy his second, final delineation, which is given according to ontological crite-

---

[144] John Pagus, *Rat. sup. Praed.* XXXVII, q. 4 (217.11).

[145] John Pagus, *Rat. sup. Praed.* V, q. 10; XVII, q. 6; XXIV, q. 9; XXXVII, q. 4. Cf. ibid., XXXIII, q. 3.

[146] John Pagus, *Rat. sup. Praed.* V, q. 10 (37.20–22).

[147] Cf. Robert Kilwardby, *Rat. sup. Praed.* IV, q. 4 (Cambridge, Peterhouse 206, f. 44va; Madrid, Bibl. Univ. 73, f. 13va); Albert the Great, *De Praedicamentis* I 6 (ed. Donati and Steel, 15); Anon., *Ripoll Compendium* §562 (ed. Lafleur, 156); Roger Bacon, *Summulae dialectices* I 2.139 (ed. de Libera, 206); John Duns Scotus, *Quaest. sup. Praed.* q. 10 (ed. Andrews et al., 336–37).

[148] John Pagus, *Rat. sup. Praed.* V, q. 10 (37.17–19).

ria.[149] Such items are sometimes said to belong to the category of relatives as well as some other category, but they are, strictly speaking, not relatives essentially (*per se*), but merely accidentally (*per accidens*).[150]

As it turns out, all cases of overlap between the categories of quality and relatives occurring in Aristotle's text can be resolved in this way.[151] But while he dicusses almost all of these overlaps, and in each case distinguishes the different ways the item in question may be considered or taken, Pagus fails to make the point explicit. Indeed, the charge that they fail to make clear which of the different ways of considering the item in question actually corresponds to its essential (*per se*) categorial status may be levelled against most of his answers to questions of overlap.

We saw above how the term "subordinate" occurring in (R2) was interpreted in order to allow two distinct genera, A and B, of which neither is subordinate to the other, to share a differentia, D, by saying that A and B could also be said to be subordinate if, for some C, A is subordinate to C and B is subordinate to C. Strictly speaking, it seems that this should apply to the rule as a whole and thus allow cases where D is a species rather than a differentia. In other words, it seems that the rule will allow the same species to be found more than once within the same category.

---

[149] Aristotle, *Categories* 7.6a36–38; 8a31–33. Aristotle modifies his initial description because it is found to overgenerate in that it lets some substances come out as relatives. On the medieval distinction between relatives *secundum esse* and relatives *secundum dici*, see Robert W. Schmidt, *The Domain of Logic According to Saint Thomas Aquinas* (The Hague: Martinus Nijhoff, 1966), 156–60, and section 9 below.

[150] John Pagus, *Rat. sup. Praed.* XXVII, q. 2.

[151] Besides knowledge (*scientia*), the cases are state (*habitus*), disposition (*dispositio*) and learning (*disciplina*). Cf. Nicholas of Paris, *Rat. sup. Praed.* VI, q. 9 (Munich, Bayer. Staatsbibl. 14460, f. 52vb): "Ad aliud quod obicis de exemplis dico quod positio et habitus {habitus *scripsi* : situs *ms*} et disciplina non sunt ad aliquid secundum suum esse; esse enim eorum non est ad aliud quodammodo se habere. Sed sunt ad aliquid secundum id quod sunt sive secundum dici. Et licet sint ad aliquid secundum id quod sunt, tamen secundum esse eorum sunt in praedicamento qualitatis." Ibid., IX, q. 13 (Munich, Bayer. Staatsbibl. 14460, f. 58rb): "Ad primum dicendum quod cum dicit auctor quod genera sunt ad aliquid, species non, loquitur de ad aliquid secundum dici et secundum id quod sunt et non de vere relativis. Et non est inconveniens genus secundum id quod est esse ad aliquid, non tamen speciem; disciplina enim secundum suum esse, prout est quiescens in anima, qualificans suum subiectum, qualitas est, prout autem egreditur a doctore in discipulum, sic est ad aliquid secundum dici {dici *scripsi* : hoc dico *ms*}." Ibid., IX, q. 14 (Munich, Bayer. Staatsbibl. 14460, f. 58rb): "Ad aliud dicendum quod idem diversimode sumptum potest esse in diversis generibus, sicut habitus et dispositio secundum id quod sunt sunt ad aliquid, tamen secundum suum verum esse sunt qualitates {qualitates *scripsi* : ad aliquid *ms*}."

This scenario is also one that Aristotle mentions in the *Topics*. In book 4, chapter 6, he first outlines a dialectic strategy based on the principle that "whenever one species falls under two genera, the one is embraced by the other." But then he makes the following addition:

> Yet a principle of this kind gives rise to a difficulty in some cases. For some people hold that prudence is both virtue and knowledge, and that neither of its genera is embraced by the other — although certainly not everybody admits that prudence is knowledge. If, however, any one were to admit the truth of this assertion, yet it would still be thought to be necessary that the genera of the same object must at any rate be subordinate either the one to the other or both to the same thing, as actually is the case with virtue and knowledge. For both fall under the same genus; for each of them is a state and a disposition.[152]

Pagus, in fact, brings up prudence as a counterexample to (R2):

> Prudence falls under virtue, knowledge, and quality, and those are different and not subordinate genera.[153]

The formulation seems a bit careless. Virtue and knowledge are both qualities, that is, they are both subordinate to the highest genus quality. However that may be, the counterexample is met, not by saying that prudence can fall under both virtue and knowledge by virtue of their both falling under quality or, as Aristotle suggests, the species of quality that is state and disposition, but by distinguishing the different ways in which prudence may be taken:

> Prudence can be considered in three ways: either according to its formal being, and then it is the choice of good and the avoidance of evil and is contained under virtue; if it is taken according to its material being, which is the discernment of good from evil, it is contained under knowledge; in so far, however, as it is compared to its subject and qualifies and denominates it, it is a quality.[154]

The use of the notion of formal being seems to suggest that, properly speaking, prudence falls under virtue.[155] And the idea appears to be that prudence is the choice of good over evil, which requires, or is based on, the knowledge of how to correctly discern the two. By solving the problem in this manner, in other words, it does not seem that Pagus intends for his exposition of "subordinate" to allow

---

[152] Aristotle, *Topics* IV 2.121b28–37 (trans. Pickard-Cambridge, 204).
[153] John Pagus, *Rat. sup. Praed.* V, q. 10 (37.8–9).
[154] John Pagus, *Rat. sup. Praed.* V, q. 10 (37.12–16).
[155] Cf. John Pagus, *Rat. sup. Praed.* XXXVIII, q. 7.

for one and the same item to be a species of two different genera of which neither contains the other.

7. THE CONTENT OF THE CATEGORY SYSTEM

Having laid down the principles of the sayble in chapters 1–3, Aristotle in chapter 4 goes on to list what we may call the content of the category system, that is, the categories that he actually recognizes. As we have already seen, Pagus takes these to be the items into which the incomplex sayable capable of being ordered divides. Aristotle's list contains ten items:

Substance	Quantity	Relative	Quality	Where
When	Position	Having	Doing	Being affected

Table 6. Aristotle's categories

Aristotle, famously, makes no attempt to justify his list, nor does he give any clear indication of how he arrived at it.[156] As is well known, a number of medieval commentators tried to remedy this situation by giving derivations of the scheme, the most famous example being Thomas Aquinas.[157]

In medieval terminology such derivations are called *sufficientiae*. A characteristic feature of scholastic commentary practice, a *sufficientia* is the exegetical move of accounting for the adequacy of a list, distinction, division, procedure, etc., encountered in an authoritative text, by producing a division that somehow yields the list, distinction, etc., in question. The procedure, it deserves to be stressed,

---

[156] See, for example, Immanuel Kant, *Critique of Pure Reason* A81/B107 (trans. Guyer and Wood, 213): "Aristotle's search for these fundamental concepts was an effort worthy of an acute man. But since he had no principle, he rounded them up as he stumbled upon them, and first got up a list of ten of them, which he called categories (predicaments)."

[157] See Thomas Aquinas, *in Metaph.* v 9, 890; *in Phys.* III 5, 321. The topic of the *sufficientiae praedicamentorum* has received some attention in recent years. The fullest account to date is that found in Andrews, *Peter of Auvergne's Commentary*, 72–103 (Andrews' account is in need of revision as far as the first half of the thirteenth century is concerned). See also William E. McMahon, "Radulphus Brito on the Sufficiency of the Categories," *CIMAGL* 39 (1981): 81–96; id., "The Medieval Sufficientiae: Attempts at a Definitive Division of the Categories," *PSMLM* 2 (2002): 12–25; id., "Some Non-Standard Views of the Categories," in *La tradition médiévale des catégories*, ed. Joël Biard and Irène Rosier-Catach (Leuven: Peeters, 2003), 53–67; id., "Reflections on Some Thirteenth- and Fourteenth-Century Views of the Categories," in *Categories: Historical and Systematic Essays*, ed. Michael Gorman and Jonathan J. Sanford (Washington, DC: The Catholic University of America Press, 2004), 45–57; John F. Wippel, "Thomas Aquinas's Derivation of the Aristotelian Categories (Predicaments)," *Journal of the History of Philosophy* 25 (1987), 13–34.

is in no way confined to the case of Aristotle's ten categories. It was customary, for example, when commenting on Porphyry's *Isagoge*, to give a *sufficientia universalium* yielding the five universals: genus, species, differentia, proprium, and accident.[158]

While he is not above employing the *sufficientia* as an exegetical device, Pagus is not among the many commentators who apply it in order to account for the adequacy of the ten-category system.[159] The reason for this, if there is one, is unclear. It is almost certainly not historical. The practice of showing the adequacy of the categorial scheme by means of *sufficientiae* was current at the time, and exemplars can be found in the contemporary commentaries of Nicholas of Paris and Robert Kilwardby, as well as in the *Ripoll Compendium*.[160] The idea was, contrary to what has sometimes been suggested, already commonplace in the Latin commentary tradition prior to the second half of the thirteenth century.[161] The reason may, then, be philosophical, but if so, it was apparently not important enough to be mentioned. It is doubtful, therefore, that Pagus prefigures those later thinkers who would deny the possibility of using this method to show the sufficiency of Aristotle's scheme.

The *sufficientiae praedicamentorum* of the period are based on purely ontological criteria and distinctions. While he doesn't supply a *sufficientia*, Pagus does, nevertheless, invoke many of the ontological differentiations central to such at-

---

[158] This was already a common feature of commentaries on the *Isagoge* in the period that concerns us here; see Piché, *Probléme des universaux*, 149–56.

[159] He gives, for example, a *sufficientia* of the species of quantity; see John Pagus, *Rat. sup. Praed.* XIX, q. 8.

[160] Nicholas of Paris, *Rat. sup. Praed.* II, q. 3 (Munich, Bayer. Staatsbibl. 14460, f. 44vb); Robert Kilwardby, *Not. sup. Praed.* V, q. 1 (Cambridge, Peterhouse 206, f. 44vb; Madrid, Bibl. Univ. 73, ff. 13vb–14ra); Anon., *Ripoll Compendium* §546 (ed. Lafleur, 152). The *sufficientia* in the latter is, unfortunately, incomplete in its present state.

[161] *Pace* Andrews, *Peter of Auvergne's Commentary*, 74–75, and Jorge Gracia and Lloyd Newton, "Medieval Theories of the Categories," in *The Stanford Encyclopedia of Philosophy (Summer 2006 Edition)*, ed. Edward N. Zalta (URL = http://plato.stanford.edu/archives/sum2006/entries/medieval-categories/). McMahon, "Medieval Sufficientiae," 12 sums up "what we presently know about the *sufficientia* movement" in the following way: "For about 50 years, roughly 1260 to 1310, there was a strong interest in showing that there are ten and only ten categories. It appears to have begun with people like Albert [the Great] and Thomas [Aquinas], is continued under those who are generally sympathetic to their philosophical outlook, and fades away with the ascendancy of the terminist/nominalist movement." Speculating further on the origins of this trend in the Latin West, McMahon (ibid., 13) goes on to suggest that "there may be sources for Albert's divisions in early thirteenth century treatments of the categories, many of which are not yet edited." This is correct at least to the extent that *sufficientiae*, even if not identical to Albert's, are indeed found in the earlier commentary literature.

tempts of accounting for the adequacy of Aristotle's list. To see this, let us consider
the one offered by Nicholas of Paris.

> The division has this many members and no more, because everything that is
> is either a substance or an accident. Thus, the first member is substance. If, on
> the other hand, it is an accident, there are two possibilities. For it will be an
> accident that belongs either intrinsically or extrinsically — and by accidents
> that belong extrinsically I mean such as require another subject in addition to
> the subject they are in, as, for example, doing is in an agent and in addition to
> this requires another subject. If it belongs intrinsically, it is in substance either
> principally on the part of the matter, and in this way it is a quantity, or on the
> part of the form, and in this way it is a quality, or on the part of the compound,
> and in this way it is a relation. If, on the other hand, it belongs extrinsically,
> then it is not in substance primarily and immediately, but by the mediation of
> some intrinsic accident, either, that is, by the mediation of quantity, quality, or
> relation. If it is in substance by the mediation of quantity, then there are two:
> when and where. For when is in substance by the mediation of time, where by
> the mediation of place. If by the mediation of quality, there will once again be
> two, namely, doing and being affected. For doing is in substance by the media-
> tion of natural capacity, being affected by the mediation of natural incapacity.
> If by the mediation of relation, then there will once again be two, namely, posi-
> tion and having. For position is caused by the relation of part to part according
> to the idea that posture is a sort of position of parts and order of generation,
> while having is caused by the relation of apparel to body, according to which
> relation we call someone shod or armoured.[162]

---

[162] Nicholas of Paris, *Rat. sup. Praed.* II, q. 3 (Munich, Bayer. Staatsbibl. 14460, f. 44vb):
"Ad aliud dicendum quod tot sunt membra divisionis et non plura, quia omne quod est aut
est substantia aut accidens, et sic primum membrum substantia. Si vero sit accidens, hoc
est dupliciter; aut enim est accidens intrinsecus adveniens aut extrinsecus — et dicuntur
accidentia extrinsecus advenientia quae praeter subiectum in quo sunt aliud exigunt
subiectum, ut actio est in agente et praeter hoc exigit aliud subiectum. Si est intrinsecus
adveniens, aut inest substantiae principaliter a parte materiae, et sic est quantitas, aut a
parte formae, et sic est [quanti] qualitas, aut a parte coniuncti, et sic est relatio. Si vero
est extrinsecus adveniens, tunc primo et immediate non inest substantiae, sed mediante
aliquo intrinseco; aut ergo mediante quantitate {quantitate *scripsi* : qualitate *ms*} vel qualitate vel relatione. Si mediante quantitate insit substantiae, tunc sunt duo, quando et ubi;
inest enim quando substantiae mediante tempore, ubi vero mediante loco. Si mediante
qualitate, erunt iterum duo, scilicet actio et passio; actio enim inest mediante naturali
potentia, passio mediante naturali impotentia. Si mediante relatione, tunc iterum erunt
duo, scilicet situs et habere; causatur enim situm esse per relationem partis ad partem,
secundum quod dicitur <quod> positio est quidam partium situs et generationis ordinatio,

Nicholas goes on to suggest another way of arriving at the final six categories, but judging from the fact that, in contrast to those underlying the latter model, the distinctions grounding the first account recur throughout his commentary, he favours the first one.[163] Nicholas' *sufficientia* is shown in figure 7.

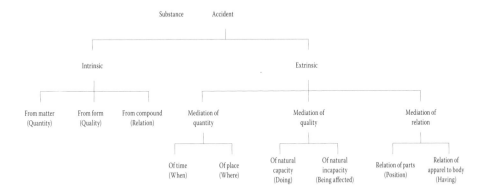

Figure 7. Nicholas of Paris' sufficientia of the categories

The top tier in Nicholas' model is the familiar Aristotelian distinction between substance and accident. The distinction on the second level between intrinsic and extrinsic accidents is not found in Aristotle, but has antecedents in Boethius' *On the Trinity*.[164] More important in the present context is its application in the anonymous *Book of Six Principles*:

> Now, of the items mentioned each constitutes the designation of an uncombined expression. As such, it will either be something that subsists or something contingent to it. Now, each of the things contingent to what exists either belongs to it extrinsically or is considered strictly internal to the substance (as,

---

habitus vero causatur per relationem ornamenti ad corpus, secundum quam relationem dicimus aliquem calciatum esse vel armatum esse."

[163] Nicholas of Paris, *Rat. sup. Praed.* II, q. 3 (Munich, Bayer. Staatsbibl. 14460, f. 44vb): "Et secundum hoc sumitur numerus accidentium extrinsecorum sic quod omne accidens extrinsecus aut est a parte formae, et sic est actio, vel a parte materiae, et hoc dupliciter, aut a parte materiae simpliciter, et tunc est passio, aut a parte materiae divisae, et tunc est positio, aut a parte coniuncti, et sic est habitus; et quia actio et passio sunt motus naturales et omnis motus naturalis habet fieri in loco et in tempore, ideo exigitur ubi, quod derelinquitur a loco, et quando, quod derelinquitur a tempore. Et sic patet numerus membrorum divisionis." For recurrences of the first model, see ibid., II, q. 4 (ff. 44vb–45ra); IX, qq. 15–17 (f. 58va).

[164] See Boethius, *De trinitate* IV (ed. Moreschini, 177).

for example, line, surface, and body). Now, each of those that require something external will of necessity be either an action, a being affected, a disposition, a being somewhere, a being sometime, or a having. Of those that subsist and those that require only that in which they exist an adequate treatment has already been given in the book entitled *On the categories*, of the rest I shall now treat.[165]

Leaving aside terminological differences, we find here the two top levels of Nicholas' model as well as the same distribution of categories. In fact, the passage also seems to be the source behind Nicholas' definition of the extrinsic accident as that which requires another subject in addition to the subject it is in.

Pagus explicitly refers to the final six categories as extrinsic. He also seems to accept the classification of the first three accidental categories as intrinsic.[166] Like Nicholas, in other words, he appears to adopt the distribution of categories found in the *Book of Six Principles*.

With regard to the subdivision of intrinsic accidents, let us first notice that the thinkers of this period generally seem to have assumed that a composite substance is in some sense the cause of its accidents.[167] Again, this is an assumption Pagus seems to share.[168] The same goes for the idea we have seen in Nicholas, and which can also be found in Kilwardby's commentary, that in the case of intrinsic accidents this holds in a systematic fashion so that such an accident flows from the hylomorphic constitution of substance either primarily on the part of its material component, in which case it is a quantity, or on the part of its formal component, in which case it is a quality, or on the part of the compound as a whole, in which case it is a relation.[169]

---

[165] Anon., *LSP* I 14–15 (ed. Minio-Paluello, 38): "Singulum vero eorum quae dicta sunt incomplexionis eius quae in voce est notatio est. Hoc vero erit vel subsistens vel contingens. Eorum vero quae existenti contingunt singulum aut extrinsecus advenit aut intra substantiam simpliciter consideratur (ut linea, superficies, corpus). Ea vero quae quod extrinsecus est exigunt, aut actus aut pati aut dispositio aut esse alicubi aut in mora aut habere necessario erunt. Sed de his quae subsistunt et quae solum in quo existunt exigunt, in eo qui *De categoriis* inscribitur libro sufficienter disputatum est, de reliquis vero continuo."

[166] John Pagus, *Rat. sup. Praed.* I, q. 6 (14.17–21).

[167] Nicholas of Paris, *Rat. sup. Praed.* II, q. 4 (Munich, Bayer. Staatsbibl. 14460, f. 44vb): "Ordo autem patet, quia ordinat haec secundum viam generationis, et ideo praeponit substantiam ante omnia alia; est enim primum principium a quo cetera causantur." Robert Kilwardby, *Not. sup. Praed.* V, q. 1 (Cambridge, Peterhouse 206, f. 44vb; Madrid, Bibl. Univ. 73, f. 14ra): "Substantia autem quia est per se ens et principium aliorum, est dispositio ceterorum ad causalitatem." Cf. Thomas Aquinas, *De esse et essentia* V.

[168] John Pagus, *Rat. sup. Praed.* XVI (97.1–2). Cf. ibid., IV, q. 7.

[169] John Pagus, *Rat. sup. Praed.* XXIV, q. 4 (144.7–9). Cf. Robert Kilwardby, *Not. sup. Praed.* V, q. 1 (Cambridge, Peterhouse 206, f. 44vb; Madrid, Bibl. Univ. 73, f. 14ra).

As regards the six extrinsic accidents, the question of their relation to the first four categories was usually raised when commenting on chapter 9 of Aristotle's text. Pagus gives the following account:

> The latter six depend on the initial four with regard to their being, since they come to be from their species, and, thus, the initial four being known, the rest are known as well. And that the latter six come to be from the species of the initial four is clear. For when and where come to be from species of quantity; when comes to be from time and where from place. Being affected and doing come to be from species of quality; doing comes to be from natural capacity and being affected from natural incapacity. Having and position come to be from relation, for having is the adjacency of relatives, as of items that cover the body in relation to the body, and position is the ordering of parts in relation to something, namely, the whole.[170]

The account is basically the same as the one encountered in Nicholas' *sufficientia*. Pagus does not employ Nicholas' language of mediation, but he does, on other occasions, like Nicholas, use the language of causation to describe the relation between the intrinsic accidents, on the one hand, and the relevant pairs of extrinsic accidents, on the other. This relation is sometimes specified further as efficient causation and opposed to formal causation in order to spell out that while accidental genera may be said to flow from or depend on either substance or species of other accidental genera, they are, nonetheless, distinct items which cannot be reduced to that from which they flow.[171]

It is clear, then, that all distinctions and relations underlying Nicholas of Paris' *sufficientia* of the categories are also invoked in Pagus' commentary. So while he does not supply a *sufficientia*, we can see that his basic conception of the underlying ontological structure of the category system is very similar to that of Nicholas. This conception can, consequently, be visualized as in figure 8.

---

[170] John Pagus, *Rat. sup. Praed.* XXXVIII, q. 2 (221.4–11).

[171] John Pagus, *Rat. sup. Praed.* XXXVIII, q. 7 (222.12–16); Robert Kilwardby, *Not. sup. Praed.* XVI, q. 4 (Cambridge, Peterhouse 206, f. 60rb; Madrid, Bibl. Univ. 73, f. 34va): "Reliqua duo solvuntur per hoc quod diversitas in causa efficiente non est causa diversitatis in genere, nec identitas causa identitatis. Unde quamvis naturalis potentia vel impotentia sint sub eodem genere, similiter qualitas activa et passiva, non tamen actio et passio, sed remanent genera diversa, quia identitatem causae efficientis non sequitur identitas in generibus sed identitatem causae formalis; sed non est eadem causa formalis actionis et passionis." Cf. Nicholas of Paris, *Rat. sup. Praed.* VI, q. 4 (Munich, Bayer. Staatsbibl. 14460, f. 52va): "Vel aliter possumus dicere quod ille sermo, 'Si causa etc.,' intelligitur de causa formali, tu autem obicis de causa efficiente; nam substantia est causa efficiens relationis, et qualitas."

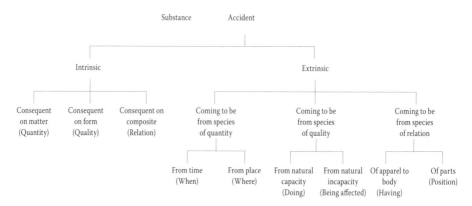

Figure 8. Pagus' basic conception of the category system

Both this scheme and the attempts to account for the adequacy of the category system raise some interesting questions relating to possible reductions of the system. Again, while he doesn't attempt a *sufficientia* of the categories, Pagus does touch on issues relating to possible reductions. Since categories are highest genera (or highest genera in so far as they fall under language), it is clear that the correctness of Aristotle's list depends on there being no more general genus to which one or more of the items on the list reduce.

Nicholas, as we saw, opened his *sufficientia* with the claim that "everything that is is either a substance or an accident." One possible reduction would then be to reduce all ten categories to one supercategory, namely, being (*ens*). The option is one that is explicitly ruled out by Porphyry:

> Being is not a single genus common to everything, nor are all things co-generic in virtue of some single highest genus, as Aristotle says. Let it be supposed, as in the *Categories*, that the first genera are ten — ten first origins, as it were. Thus, even if you call everything being, you will do so, he says, equivocally and not univocally. For if being were a single genus common to everything, all things would be said to be univocally. But since the first items are ten, they have only the name in common and not also the account which corresponds to the name.[172]

If there is an argument here, it may be something like the following: Every genus is predicated univocally of its species. Being is not predicated univocally of the categories. Therefore, being is not a genus of which the categories are species. The

---

[172] Porphyry, *Isagoge* 6.5–12 (trans. Barnes, 7; slightly modified).

premises would seem to be Aristotelian.[173] The same goes for the conclusion.[174] Pagus does not problematize the issue, but he clearly agrees with Porphyry. Not only does he invoke, in the course of his commentary, both of the aforementioned premises, he also explicitly refers to the above Porphyrian passage as support for the claim that there is nothing, that is to say, no superordinate genus, above the ten categories.[175]

Another reduction suggests itself if we look again at the opening claim of Nicholas' *sufficientia*: "everything that is is either a substance or an accident." Why not reduce the ten categories to two: substance and accident? Pagus touches on this question:

> It is asked why he divides in this way: Of the incomplex some signify substance, some quantity, etc., and not in the following way: Some signify substance, some accident, and then subdivided accident into quantity, quality, etc.
>
> And it seems that the latter procedure would have been more correct seeing as every division is dichotomous according to Boethius.
>
> The answer is that he divides the incomplex equally into these ten in order to indicate that they are genera to an equal degree and not according to prior and posterior. Thus, he better expresses his intended meaning in this way than if he had proceeded differently.
>
> The answer to the objection is that every division is dichotomous or capable of being reduced to one that is. In this way, the present division can be reduced in the following manner: Of the incomplex some signify substance, some accident. The first division is posited, however, because it better expresses the intended meaning.[176]

The ten dividends are genera to an equal degree, that is, they all occupy the same level of generality on different Porphyrian chains, namely, the topmost one. The answer will only run on the assumption that accident is not a genus. This, however, was taken for granted, as comes out more explicitly in Kilwardby's commentary, where the same question follows immediately upon the *sufficientia* of the categories. According to him, Aristotle proceeds the way he does

> in order to signify that each of the others, in so far as it is a first genus, is simultaneous with substance. Because of this, therefore, the division descends into substance and each of the others. For if a division into substance and accident

[173] Cf. Aristotle, *Topics* II 2.109b5–7; *Metaphysics* IV 2.1003a33–b10.
[174] See, e.g., Aristotle, *Metaphysics* III 3.998b22–27.
[175] John Pagus, *Rat. sup. Praed.* XXXI, q. 5 (183.18); I (10.21–23); II, q. 5 (20.1–2).
[176] John Pagus, *Rat. sup. Praed.* VI, q. 2 (40.24–41.9).

had first been made, and then into the others, it would seem as if the latter communicated in some genus.[177]

In sum, a twofold division of beings into substance and accident may be made, and a further ninefold division of accidents given, but there is a sense in which the procedure is misleading. It makes it look as if accident is a proper genus, which it is not.[178] The category system thus remains a ten-category, not a two-category, system.

8. SUBSTANCE

Fundamental among the ten categories in the system is the category of substance. The genus of substance collects, as Pagus explains, *per se* beings. A *per se* being in the relevant sense is a being that is not in something else. He distinguishes two variants:

> It is to be said that *per se* being refers in one way to that which is neither from something else nor in something else, and in this way the First Cause is a *per se* being; in a second way it refers to that which is not in something else even though it is from something else, such as substance.[179]

To be from something else is to have a cause. As the compass of the categorial scheme is restricted to entities bearing this property, God, the First Cause, finds no place in it:

> It is to be said that God is not in a category. To the objection [that each incomplex item signifies either a substance or a quantity, etc.] it is to be said that this division of incomplex items is given of that which is caused, not of the cause. Whence, since God is the cause of everything, he is not contained under said division.[180]

---

[177] Robert Kilwardby, *Not. sup. Praed.* v, q. 2 (Cambridge, Peterhouse 206, f. 45ra; Madrid, Bibl. Univ. 73, f. 14ra): "Cuius ratio est ut significet unumquodque aliorum a substantia in quantum est genus primum esse substantiae coaequaevum. Propter hoc ergo descendebat divisio immediate in substantiam cum quolibet aliorum. Si enim primo fieret divisio in substantiam et accidens, consequenter in alia, apparet quod alia communicaret genus aliquod."

[178] If one wants an argument for this, it can presumably be modelled on the argument that being is not a genus. See, e.g., Albert the Great, *De praedicamentis* IV 2 (ed. Donati and Steel, 82).

[179] John Pagus, *Rat. sup. Praed.* XI, q. 2 (66.24–26).

[180] John Pagus, *Rat. sup. Praed.* XIV, q. 4 (89.12–15).

The items collected by the first of the ten categories, then, are *per se* beings of the second variety only.

Drawing on the physical and metaphysical writings of Aristotle, the commentators of this period recognize at least three kinds of substance: matter, form, and composite.[181] They generally follow Boethius in saying that the items collected in the generic hierarchy of substance are composites.[182] The material and formal principles of these composites, in turn, enter into the hierarchical taxonomy only indirectly, that is, as principles of the composites that the generic hierarchy collects. In spite of this general idea, however, it seems also to be unanimously accepted that there are certain items that are not such compounds — such as souls and angels — that nonetheless fall in the hierarchy directly.[183]

According to the standard interpretation, Aristotle structures his discussion of the four main categories in chapters 5 to 8 in such a way that he first determines and delimits the nature of the items belonging to the category under consideration and then proceeds to specify a series of properties holding of them, culminating in the specification of a distinctive and convertible property. The discussion of substance begins with the following distinction:

> A substance — that which is called a substance most strictly, primarily, and most of all — is that which is neither said of a subject nor in a subject, e.g., the individual man or the individual horse. The species in which the things primarily called substances are, are called secondary substances, as are also the genera of these species. For example, the individual man belongs in a species, man, and animal is a genus of the species; so these — both man and animal — are called secondary substances.[184]

What we have here is not, Pagus says, a division of substance as such but rather an explication of what primary and secondary substances are. This, he argues, must be so on principled grounds:

---

[181] See, for example, Aristotle, *Metaphysics* VIII 1.1042a25–32; *On the Soul* II 1.412a6–9; II 2.414a14–16; Anon., *Auct. Arist.* 1.200 (ed. Hamesse, 131); 6.37 (ibid., 177).

[182] See, e.g., Nicholas of Paris, *Rat. sup. Praed.* II, q. 7 (Munich, Bayer. Staatsbibl. 14460, f. 25ra); Robert Kilwardby, *Not. sup. Praed.* VI, q. 1 (Cambridge, Peterhouse 206, f. 46ra; Madrid, Bibl. Univ. 73, f. 15rb–va); Anon. Domus Petri 206, *in Cat.* III, q. 8 (ed. Hansen, 135). See also Boethius, *in Cat.* 184a.

[183] See, for example, Nicholas of Paris, *Rat. sup. Praed.* II, q. 19 (Munich, Bayer. Staatsbibl. 14460, f. 45vb): "Item, inter substantiam et animam rationalem unum est medium tantum, scilicet incorporeum; ergo haec species, homo, pluribus substat quam haec, anima rationalis; ergo magis est substantia." Cf. John Pagus, *Rat. sup. Praed.* IV, q. 7 (30.23–31.3).

[184] Aristotle, *Categories* 5.2a11–19 (trans. Ackrill, 5–6).

It says elsewhere in the *Categories* that the dividers of something are in the dividend simultaneously and are equally participant of the dividend. Primary and secondary substances are not, however, equally participant of substance, but rather according to the prior and the posterior (this is obvious from the text, for primary substances are called substances primarily). Therefore, substances cannot be divided in this way.[185]

A similar line of reasoning is found in the commentary of Nicholas of Paris:

I claim that Aristotle does not make the division, but rather presupposes it, for the reason that the dividend is attributed properly to one of the members and improperly to the other; for substance is properly said of primary substance and improperly said of secondary substance. And so these members are not posited in the way of division but in the way of enumeration.[186]

The underlying worry here seems to be that intra-categorial univocity is threatened if substance is said according to the prior and posterior of its members, and so it is important to be clear about how substances are spoken of when it is said that some are primary, some secondary.

Nicholas deals with the problem within the framework of the Boethian theory of division.

There is a doubt with regard to the division, "Of substances some are primary, some secondary," namely, what kind of division it is. Either it is a *per se* division or a *per accidens* division. It is not a *per se* division, because it is not a division of a whole into its parts; nor of an expression into different significations, for substance does not signify multiple things; nor of a genus into its species, because a genus is said equally of its species, but substance is not said equally of primary and secondary substance, for primary substance is substance to a higher degree than secondary substance. Neither is it a *per accidens* division, because it is not of a subject into its accidents, for substance is not an accident, and therefore its dividers will not be accidents but substances; nor of an accident into its subjects, for substance is not an accident; nor of an accident into

---

185 John Pagus, *Rat. sup. Praed.* VII, q. 1 (44.16–20).

186 Nicholas of Paris, *Rat. sup. Praed.* II, q. 10 (Munich, Bayer. Staatsbibl. 14460, f. 45rb–va): "Ad aliud dico quod non proponit divisionem, sed supponit, eo quod divisum attribuitur proprie alteri membrorum, alteri improprie; substantia enim proprie dicitur de prima substantia, improprie dicitur de secunda substantia. Et ideo non ponuntur haec membra per modum divisionis, sed per modum enumerationis."

its accidents. Therefore, since this kind of division is neither *per se* nor *per accidens*, it seems that it is not a division at all.[187]

The answer he offers runs as follows:

> I say that the division, "Of substances some are primary, some are secondary," is not a *per se* but a *per accidens* division; for it is a division of a subject into its accidents; for it is accidental to substance to sub-stand primarily and sub-stand secondarily.
>
> To your objection, that the dividers of substance are substances and not accidents, it is to be said that this does not hold; for Aristotle is not dividing according to the thing but according to the act of sub-standing.[188]

The division of substances into primary and secondary is an accidental division in so far as it is a division of a subject according to an accidental feature, in this case the feature of sub-standing or underlying. In denying that substance can be divided in this way, Pagus seems to mean precisely that there is no such *per se* division of substance, or, more specifically, that it is not a division of a genus into its species. As he points out elsewhere:

> It is to be said that one can talk about substance in two ways, either according to being, and in this way it is not susceptible of degrees, as we learn later on, or in comparison to its act of sub-standing, and in this way it is well susceptible of degrees, as the substance which sub-stands more items is substance to a higher degree and that which sub-stands fewer items to a lesser degree.[189]

---

[187] Nicholas of Paris, *Rat. sup. Praed.* II, q. 8 (Munich, Bayer. Staatsbibl. 14460, f. 45ra): "Item, dubitatur de illa divisione, 'Substantiarum alia prima, alia secunda', cuiusmodi divisio sit. Aut sit divisio per se aut sit divisio per accidens. Non est divisio per se, quia non est divisio totius in partes nec vocis in significationes, eo quod substantia non multa significat, nec generis in species, quia genus aequaliter dicitur de speciebus, substantia autem non dicitur aequaliter de prima et secunda eo quod prima substantia magis est substantia quam secunda. Nec etiam est divisio per accidens, quia <non> est subiecti in accidentia, quia substantia non est accidens, ergo dividentia ipsam non erunt accidentia, sed substantiae, nec accidentis in subiecta eo quod substantia non est accidens, nec etiam accidentis in accidentia. Ergo, cum huiusmodi divisio neque sit per se neque sit per accidens, videtur quod nulla sit divisio." Cf. Boethius, *De divisione* 877b–78d (ed. Magee, 6–11).

[188] Nicholas of Paris, *Rat. sup. Praed.* II, q. 8 (Munich, Bayer. Staatsbibl. 14460, f. 45rb): "Ad aliud dico quod haec divisio, 'Substantiarum alia prima, alia secunda,' non est divisio per se, sed per accidens; est enim divisio subiecti in accidentia; accidit enim substantiae primo substare et secundo substare. Ad hoc quod obicis quod dividentia substantiam sunt substantiae et non accidentia dicendum quod non valet hoc; non enim dividit secundum rem, sed secundum actum substandi."

[189] John Pagus, *Rat. sup. Praed.* IX, q. 1 (56.1–4).

Since the predication of substance in the categorial line is presumably according to being, the fact that some substances are said to be primary in terms of the non-essential feature of underlying does not threaten the univocity of substance as it is predicated in the categorial line.[190]

The distinction between primary and secondary substance, is not (we have seen) a division of a genus into its species. Nor is it, Pagus seems to hold, extensionally equivalent to that between individual and universal substance. More specifically, he appears to claim that while it is the case that, for all A, if A is an individual substance, then A is a primary substance, it is not the case that, for all A, if A is a universal substance, then A is a secondary substance.

> Every individual belonging to substance is a substance as far as its mode of being is concerned and is said of nothing, as is the case with primary substance. In order to point out, therefore, that one cannot find an individual belonging to substance that is not a primary substance, Aristotle uses the verb "to be" in his definition of primary substance. There are, however, some universals that are substances as far as their mode of being is concerned, and yet they are not secondary substances. In order to point out, therefore, that not every universal is a secondary substance, he uses the verb "is said" in his definition of secondary substance. Here it should be noted that there are two requirements that something must meet in order for it to be a secondary substance, namely, that it is a substance as far as both its mode of being and its mode of being said is concerned.[191]

In speaking of universals that are substances as far as their mode of being, but not their mode of being said, is concerned, Pagus seems to be thinking of the differentiae of substances, which he takes to be universal, but not secondary, substances.

Thus, the piece of doctrine appears to be closely connected with what is sometimes referred to as the problem of the categorial status of the differentia.[192] The problem as it occurs in the commentary tradition on the *Categories* is in many

---

[190] Cf. Anon., *Ripoll Compendium* §542 (ed. Lafleur, 151): "Item, quaeritur quare non definitur substantia in genere. Ad hoc dicimus quod substantia magis convenit primae substantiae ratione qua substantia, quia magis debetur ei substare quam secundis substantiis. (…) Sed intelligendum: 'ratione qua substantia' dicit actum substandi, quia in veritate, cum substantia sit praedicamentum unum, genus est ad quodlibet contentum sub se, sed haec univocatio est secundum esse vel secundum essentiam ipsius substantiae."

[191] John Pagus, *Rat. sup. Praed.* VII, q. 3 (45.4–12).

[192] On this topic in Aristotle and his ancient commentators, see Donald Morrison, "Le statut catégoriel des differences dans l'*Organon*," *Revue philosophique de France et de l'Etrangér* 183 (1993): 147–78; Frans A.J. de Haas, *John Philoponus' New Definition of Prime Matter* (Leiden: Brill, 1997), 165–250; Porphyry, *Introduction*, trans. Barnes, 350–56.

cases better described as the problem of the generic or ontological status of the differentiae of substances, and it is, roughly, the following. On the standard interpretation of *Categories* 2, the property of being said of picks out universals, while its negation picks out individuals. Similarly, the property of being in picks out accidents, while its negation picks out substances. This seems to imply that, for all A, if A has the property of being said of but not that of being in, then A is a universal substance. In *Categories* 5, however, Aristotle, having argued that it is a characteristic common to all substances that they are not in a subject, goes on to make the following remark:

> This is not, however, peculiar to substance; the differentia also is not in a subject. For terrestrial and biped are said of man as a subject but are not in a subject; neither biped nor terrestrial is in man.[193]

By virtue of a conversational implicature, Aristotle's words are naturally taken to imply that the differentiae of substances are not themselves substances. However, seen against the backdrop of the canonical interpretation of *Categories* 2, he also seems to be denying that they are accidents, since he explicitly says that they are not in a subject.

Pagus, like many medieval commentators, approaches the problem by questioning Aristotle's presumable denial that the differentia is a substance. He supplies two quite similar reasons for why this cannot be correct, the second of which is the following:

> Everything that is is either a substance or an accident. The differentia is not an accident. Therefore, it is a substance. The minor premise is obvious, because it says in the first book of the *Physics* that no accident gives being to a substance. The differentia, as Porphyry says, gives being to a substance. Therefore, the differentia is not an accident.[194]

Assuming that (1) the division of beings into substances and accidents is exclusive and exhaustive, and that (2) this division can be superimposed on the tenfold generic scheme so that all items falling in one of the last nine genera are accidents, it seems that one must either accept as a metaphysical possibility that (3) accidents can be essential constituents of substances, or posit that (4) the differentia is a substance, in a way which can account for the distinction between substance and differentia that Aristotle appears to be drawing in the passage quoted above.

---

[193] Aristotle, *Categories* 5.3a21–24 (trans. Ackrill, 8; slightly modified).
[194] John Pagus, *Rat. sup. Praed.* XI, q. 3 (67.7–10).

Like many thirteenth-century commentators, Pagus is committed to assumptions (1) and (2), and to the rejection of (3). This leaves him with (4). He suggests two ways of solving the consequent exegetical tangle. The first one trades on the notion of a composite substance as opposed to its material and formal principles:

> It is to be said that substance is said in three ways: matter, form, and compound, as Aristotle says in the *De anima*. When he says, however, that the differentia is not a substance, this is true if substance is taken to mean the composite. It is, nonetheless, a substance which is a form, as it is objected. And so substance is equivocal.[195]

Alternatively, Pagus proposes, one might solve the problem by reference to the modes of being and being said that a (secondary) substance has:

> Substance has two modes, namely, a mode of being (for it is a *per se* being) and a mode of being said (because it is predicated *in quid*). Thus, it is to be said that the differentia of a substance, since it is a being *per se*, is a substance as far as its mode of being is concerned. It is not, however, a substance as far as its mode of being said is concerned, for it is predicated *in quale*, as Porphyry says.[196]

The substantial differentia has the mode of being of a substance, that is, it is a *per se* being in the second sense distinguished at the beginning of this section (it is not in something else even though it is from something else). It lacks, however, the mode of being said that a substance has, since it is not predicated *in quid* but *in quale*. It is, in other words, a universal substance but not a secondary substance since it fails to meet one of the two requirements for secondary substancehood.

Nicholas of Paris proposes to solve the problem by distinguishing between substance according to thing and substance according to its feature of sub-standing:

> I say that we can speak about substance in two ways, either according to thing or according to the act of sub-standing or ordering. Thus, the differentia is a substance in terms of what it is and not in terms of the act of sub-standing, because it does not sub-stand but stand laterally. I therefore concede the arguments to the conclusion that the differentia is a substance, and I say that the conjunction "substances and differentiae" is sound, because it does not conjoin the same thing to itself but rather substances that sub-stand in themselves to substances that stand laterally.

---

[195] John Pagus, *Rat. sup. Praed.* XI, q. 3 (67.11–14).
[196] John Pagus, *Rat. sup. Praed.* XI, q. 3 (67.15–19). Cf. Porphyry, *Isagoge* 3.5–12; 3.17–19; 11.7–12; 15.2–4; 18.16–17.

To your objection that every substance is either a primary or a secondary substance etc., it is to be said that in this context substance means that which sub-stands in itself and stands in the straight line; the differentia, however, stands laterally, and so it does not fall under this division.[197]

Here the distinction is not between mode of being and mode of being said, but between thing and act of sub-standing. The differentia is a substance according to thing, but it is not so in terms of the act of sub-standing. When speaking of being a substance according to thing, Nicholas seems to mean roughly the same as Pagus does when he speaks of a substance in terms of its mode of being. When speaking of the act of sub-standing, Nicholas is, of course, speaking in terms of the traditional modelling of the Porphyrian tree, where only primary and secondary substances sub-stand in the straight vertical line, whereas the differentiae are situated to the side of this line, that is, they stand laterally (*a latere*).

Robert Kilwardby seems to draw on both ideas. According to him, the differentia is not a substance according to the intention of substance (*intentionem substantiae*), which is to sub-stand. According to truth and the being of substance, he goes on to say, the differentia is nonetheless a substance, even though it is a quality according to mode.[198] This latter idea he attributes to Augustine, who is paraphrased as holding that the differentia is a *quid* in virtue (*virtute*) but a *quale* in speech (*dictione*). The reference is to the *Categoriae decem*, a fourth-century paraphrase of Aristotle's text erroneously attributed to Augustine, in which the succinct distinction between the ontological status and linguistic behaviour of the differentia is, in fact, adumbrated:

---

[197] Nicholas of Paris, *Rat. sup. Praed.* III, q. 5 (Munich, Bayer. Staatsbibl. 14460, f. 47ra): "Ad primum dico quod possumus loqui de substantia dupliciter, aut secundum rem aut secundum actum substandi vel ordinandi; differentia ergo secundum id quod est substantia est et non secundum actum substandi, eo quod non substat, sed a latere stat. Unde concedo rationes ad hoc quod differentia sit substantia, et dico quod ista copula bona est, quia non copulat idem sibi ipsi, sed copulat substantias per se <sub>stantes substantiis a latere stantibus. Ad hoc quod obicis, quod omnis substantia est prima vel secunda etc., dicendum quod dicitur ibi substantia quod per se substat et in recta linea stat, differentia autem a latere stat, et ideo non cadit in illa divisione."

[198] Robert Kilwardby, *Not. sup. Praed.* VII, q. 2 (Cambridge, Peterhouse 206, f. 47vb; Madrid, Bibl. Univ. 73, ff. 17vb–18ra): "Et dicendum quod, quia differentia hic nulli subicitur, quod non est substantia secundum intentionem substantiae, scilicet hanc quae est substare, et hoc est quod dicit Aristoteles quod differentia nulli subicitur. Et sic nomen differentiae significet formam solam, per relationem tamen ad materiam. Secundum veritatem tamen et esse substantiae est substantia, est tamen qualitas vel quale secundum modum. Et hoc est quod supra diximus in Porphyrio, quod dicit Augustinus differentiam esse virtute quid, dictione vero quale."

Now that the secondary substances, that is to say, genus and species, have been treated, only the differentia remains. Now, to someone considering the matter carefully it seems to be an accident of sorts, since when animal is said to be biped or mortal or rational, what is shown is not what it is, but rather what sort of so-and-so it is; and so, it appears to have the force of a quality. Yet, since the first differentia springs from the genus, and in this way the species follows, it should not be counted among the accidents. And it is for this reason that Aristotle said that it is mixed in terms of signification, though he deemed that in virtue it belongs among the substances.[199]

Now, the success of the distinction that Pagus seeks to draw depends crucially on whether this is, in fact, the correct determination of the predicative status of the differentia. This, however, was a well-known problem, routinely discussed in commentaries on the *Isagoge*.[200] The issue, briefly put, is this: On the one hand, the idea that the differentia is predicated *in quale* is, as we have seen, central to the Porphyrian conception of it; and the idea does, indeed, come from Aristotle. On the other hand, there are passages in the *Topics* where Aristotle appears to flatly contradict this by claiming that the differentia is rather predicated *in quid*.[201] In the present context, the problem is, of course, that if Aristotle is right in saying that the differentia is predicated *in quid*, then Pagus' proposed distinction between secondary substances and differentiae in the category of substance would seem to collapse:

It says in the seventh book of the *Topics* that if the definition is predicated *in quid*, so are its parts, namely, the genus and the differentia. Thus, the differentia has the mode of being said that substance itself has, which goes against the proposed solution.[202]

---

[199] Ps.-Augustine, *Categoriae decem* 68–69 (ed. Minio-Paluello, 148): "Monstratis ergo secundis usiis, id est genere et specie, differentia sola restabat, quae consideranti diligentius quasi accidens videtur esse; siquidem bipes vel mortale vel rationale cum animal dicitur, non quid sit sed quale sit potius demonstratur, ideoque videtur vim tenere qualitatis. Verum quando a genere prima oritur differentia, et sic sequitur species, in accidentibus non debet numerari. Atque ideo Aristoteles eam significatione quidem mixtam dixit esse, virtute autem inter usias habendam decrevit."

[200] See, for example, Nicholas of Paris, *Rat. sup. Porph.* v, q. 24 (Munich, Bayer. Staatsbibl. 14460, f. 14va; 15va); John Duns Scotus, *Quaest. in Porph.* q. 28 (ed. Andrews et al., 175–79).

[201] For an overview of the problem in Aristotle as well as references to the relevant texts, see de Haas, *Philoponus' New Definition*, 182–86.

[202] John Pagus, *Rat. sup. Praed.* XI, q. 4 (67.20–22).

The reference is to *Topics* VII 3.153a15–22, where Aristotle says precisely that. Pagus proposes the following way around the problem:

> It is to be said that being predicated *in quid* is ambiguous between being so properly and being so commonly. In the first way, the differentia is not predicated *in quid*; and this is how it is meant in the solution, whereas in the objection it is taken in the second way. And I call "properly *in quid*" that which is predicated essentially and has individuals immediately corresponding to it; and because the differentia does not have an individual immediately corresponding to it, it is not predicated *in quid*. To be commonly predicated *in quid* is to be predicated *in quale substantiale*, wherefore the differentia is predicated *in quid* because it is predicated *in quale substantiale*.[203]

Unfortunately, the exact import of the key notion here, that of having an immediately corresponding individual, is not clear. It does not seem to occur in any of the contemporary commentaries, nor does Pagus determine its precise content. The property, we are told, is one that belongs only to secondary substances.[204] It does not, as is clear from the above, pertain to the differentia, nor, it is said in another context, to an item such as white (*album*).[205] The issue may ultimately have to do with the primacy of the individuation and numeration of substance and the intuition that primary substances, concrete objects such as Socrates and Plato, are the only saturated entities, or *quids*, of the ontology, but how exactly it is to be cashed out is uncertain.

Having presented and explicated the division of substance into primary and secondary substance, Aristotle goes on to list six properties of the items belonging to this category: (1) not being in a subject; (2) being predicated univocally; (3) signifying a "this something"; (4) not having a contrary; (5) not being susceptible to degrees; and (6) being able to receive contraries while being numerically one and the same.

According to Pagus, the first three of these properties are attributed to substance in so far as it is a thing falling under discourse (*res sub sermone*), that is, a sayable (*dicibile*), or a thing of reason (*res rationis*), whereas the final three are ascribed to it in so far as it is a thing (*res*) or a natural thing (*res naturalis*).[206] The same distinction occurs in the commentaries of Nicholas of Paris and Robert Kilwardby, and it is obviously related to the ancient worry that some of the properties

---

[203] John Pagus, *Rat. sup. Praed.* XI, q. 4 (67.23–68.2).
[204] John Pagus, *Rat. sup. Praed.* XII, q. 5 (76.10–16).
[205] John Pagus, *Rat. sup. Praed.* XII, q. 6 (76.17–22).
[206] John Pagus, *Rat. sup. Praed.* XI (63.1–8).

Aristotle lists appear to hold of linguistic items, whereas others seem to hold of things (*res*).[207]

The distinctive and convertible property of substance is (6). This property, in other words, is supposed to hold of all and only substances. However, there is a worry here. How can it hold of secondary substances, when these are universals and universals are not numerically one? According to Pagus:

> It is to be said that a secondary substance is not numerically one in itself but through primary substance, for it depends on primary substance for its act of existing according to the author of the *Six Principles*, who says that all commonness proceeds from singularity. Therefore, since it has its being through primary substance, it is numerically one through primary substance, and in this way it is capable of receiving contraries and not in itself. You should distinguish, therefore, two possible ways of speaking of secondary substance: either in itself or in so far as it is in a primary substance. In the former way it is neither numerically one nor does it receive contraries, as the objection states, but only in the latter way, as we have seen.[208]

Kilwardby suggests that in themselves secondary substances have the property only potentially, but in so far as they exist in primary substances and are counted in them they have it actually.[209] Nicholas of Paris tries to sidestep the problem by means of some rather creative exegesis:

> To your objection that no secondary substance is numerically one, it is to be said that "one" indicates the union of secondary substances with primary sub-

---

[207] Nicholas of Paris, *Rat. sup. Praed.* III (Munich, Bayer. Staatsbibl. 14460, f. 46ra): "Et dividitur haec pars in duas partes. In quarum prima ponit proprietates substantiae prout est res rationis, in secunda parte ponit proprietates substantiae prout est res naturae; et hoc est quia ratio fundatur supra naturam. Prima incipit hic: *Commune est omni substantiae* (5.3a7), secunda hic: *Inest autem substantiis* etc. (5.3b25)." Robert Kilwardby, *Not. sup. Praed.* VII (Cambridge, Peterhouse 206, f. 46vb; Madrid, Bibl. Univ. 73, f. 16rb–va): "*Commune est autem omni substantiae* etc. (5.3a7) In parte ista dat proprietates et passiones ipsa ordinabilia in genere substantiae consequentes. Et dividitur in duas. In prima dat proprietates sive passiones quae insunt substantiae prout est aliquid secundum rationem, in secunda, ut ibi: *Inest autem substantiis* etc. (5.3b25), prout est aliquid secundum naturam. Et patet sufficientia et ordo per hoc quod prima pars dat consequentia substantiam in quantum est praedicabile, secunda autem in quantum est res." For the ancient worry, see Porphyry, *in Cat.* 58.21–29; Boethius, *in Cat.* 162d.

[208] John Pagus, *Rat. sup. Praed.* XIV, q. 1 (87.31–88.6).

[209] Robert Kilwardby, *Not. sup. Praed.* VII, q. 13 (Cambridge, Peterhouse 206, f. 48vb; Madrid, Bibl. Univ. 73, f. 19rb): "Sed istud totum solvitur per hoc quod potentia per se attribuitur secundis substantiis, actus autem ipsis in quantum sunt et numerantur in primis, et sic per se primis."

stances. Hence, the meaning is that it is a distinctive property of substance to be, when it is numerically the same or united with a thing that is one and numerically the same, capable of receiving contraries. By "one," then, Aristotle touches on secondary substances in so far as they are united with primary substances, by "numerically the same" he touches on primary substances. Hence, although Socrates is Socrates as well as (a) man, there is not therefore two items, but one, because man is united with Socrates.[210]

Differences aside, Pagus and his contemporaries seem to agree that secondary substances have the distinctive property only mediately, that is, in so far as they have actual existence in the primary substances whose essential natures they constitute.

9. ACCIDENTS

Substances are, as we have seen, *per se* beings, beings that are not in something else. Accidents, by contrast, are beings that *are* in something else; they are dependent entities requiring a bearer.

According to a traditional account, developed in the *Book of Six Principles*, accidents come in two varieties: intrinsic and extrinsic. The first are described as being "such as require only that in which they exist," and it is the three accidental categories of this type that Aristotle discusses in detail: quantity, relation, and quality.[211] Pagus, as already mentioned, subscribes to this account, and like Aristotle he does not have much to say about extrinsic accidents.

---

[210] Nicholas of Paris, *Rat. sup. Praed.* III, q. 12 (Munich, Bayer. Staatsbibl. 14460, f. 47vb): "Ad hoc quod obicis quod nulla substantia secunda est unum numero, dicendum quod li 'unum' notat unionem secundarum substantiarum ad primas, unde sensus est: proprie proprium est substantiae, cum sit idem numero et unitum cum re una et eadem numero, susceptibile esse {esse *scripsi* : est *ms*} contrariorum. Unde per li 'unum' tangit secundas substantias secundum quod unitae sunt cum primis, per li 'idem numero' tangit primas substantias, unde licet Socrates sit Socrates et homo, non propter hoc erunt duo, sed unum, quia homo unitum est cum Socrate."

[211] Anon., *LSP* I 14–15 (ed. Minio-Paluello, 38). The idea that the categories of quantity, relation, and quality are intrinsic seems to have been widely accepted at the time when Pagus was writing; see, e.g., Robert Kilwardby, *Not. sup. Praed.* V, q. 1 (Cambridge, Peterhouse 206, f. 44vb; Madrid, Bibl. Univ. 73, f. 14ra); Nicholas of Paris, *Rat. sup. Praed.* II, q. 3 (Munich, Bayer. Staatsbibl. 14460, f. 44vb); Anon., *Ripoll Compendium* §546 (ed. Lafleur, 152). The idea is somewhat surprising, (1) because Boethius, whose *On the Trinity* IV seems to be the source for the intrinsic/extrinsic distinction, actually counts relations among the extrinsically affixed accidents, and (2) because it is far from clear how relations can possibly be construed as accidents that "require only that in which they exist." For more on this

Aristotle begins his discussion of the nonsubstantial categories in chapter 6. He starts with the category of quantity and first posits two divisions of the domain. The first divides quantities into discrete quantities and continuous quantities, the second divides quantities into quantities whose parts lack relative position and quantities whose parts have relative position.

Pagus seems to take the first of the two divisions as central, and taking Aristotle's lead he explicates the two notions it involves as follows:

> The continuous is that whose parts join together at some common boundary, the discrete is that which does not have a common boundary at which its parts join together.[212]

While he is aware that it may be questioned, he also thinks that Aristotle's partition is essentially correct: discrete quantities are number and speech; continuous quantities are lines, surfaces, and bodies, as well as time and place.[213]

Aristotle offers no argument in support of his list, but Pagus thinks that its adequacy can, in fact, be accounted for:

> Every quantity is either continuous or discrete, as Aristotle says. If it's discrete, it will either have some sort of permanence with respect to its parts or it won't. In the first way we get number, in the second way we get speech. If it's continuous, it will either be a measure of substance under its essential being or of substance under its accidental being. If under its essential being, since substance can be measured according to the three dimensions body has, as Priscian says in his *Orthography*, namely, length, breadth, and depth, it may be measured only in respect of length, and in this way we get line, or in respect of breadth as well as length, and in this way we get surface, or in respect of length, breadth, and depth, and in this way we get body; for a line is length without breadth and depth, a surface is length and breadth without depth, whereas body has all three dimensions. If it measures substance under its accidental being, this will either be in so far as it is in movement or in so far as it is at rest. In the first way we get time, in the second way we get place.[214]

---

problem, see Heine Hansen, "Strange Finds," in *Logic and Language in the Middle Ages*, ed. Jakob L. Fink, Heine Hansen, and Ana María Mora Márquez (Leiden: Brill, forthcoming).

[212] John Pagus, *Rat sup. Praed.* XVI, q. 5 (100.1–5). Cf. Aristotle, *Categories* 6.4b22–5a14.

[213] The classification of time as a continuous rather than a discrete quantity might, for example, be disputed. On this, see John Pagus, *Rat. sup. Praed.* XIX, qq. 6–7. For a contemporary approach to this question that is similar to Pagus', see Paul Studtmann, "Aristotle's Category of Quantity: A Unified Interpretation," *Apeiron* 37 (2004): 73–74.

[214] John Pagus, *Rat sup. Praed.* XIX, q. 8 (120.6–18). Recall that body is equivocal between substantial body and quantitative body; see section 6 above.

Aristotle does, indeed, take his list to be exhaustive, for he claims that the seven items it contains are the only ones which are quantities in and of themselves (*per se*); all other items, if quantities at all, are only derivatively so (*per accidens*). Pagus tries to elucidate this distinction as follows:

> Something is said to be a quantity only derivatively if it does not measure in and of itself but through something else. This is made clear by the example of an ell. For if a piece of cloth is measured by an ell, the ell is a measure in and of itself, but if the piece of cloth which has been measured is then used to measure another piece, it is not a measure in and of itself, but through the ell.[215]

As is clear, both from the *sufficientia* of the species of quantity and from the exposition of the distinction between *per se* and *per accidens* quantities, the feature of being a measure is central to Pagus' construal of the category of quantity.[216] This is not an aspect of quantity that Aristotle has much to say about in the *Categories*, but Pagus is far from alone in emphasizing it.[217] The exact status of this feature became the topic of some controversy later in the century, but Pagus does not address the issue.[218]

As in the case of the category of substance, Aristotle rounds off the discussion of the category of quantity by specifying a series of properties that hold of the items belonging to the category. He lists three: (1) not having a contrary, (2) not being susceptible to degrees, and (3) being that according to which other things are said to be equal or unequal.

---

[215] John Pagus, *Rat. sup. Praed.* XX, q. 2 (122.27–23.1). Cf. Nicholas of Paris, *Rat. sup. Praed.* V, q. 2 (Munich, Bayer. Staatsbibl. 14460, f. 50vb).

[216] This feature presumably also applies to discrete quantities. For number, see John Pagus, *Rat. sup. Praed.* XVI, q. 5 (99.22–100.9); for speech, see Nicholas of Paris, *Rat. sup. Praed.* IV, q. 11 (Munich, Bayer. Staatsbibl. 14460, f. 49ra–rb). Cf. Robert Kilwardby, *Not. sup. Praed.* VIII, q. 8 (Cambridge, Peterhouse 206, ff. 49vb–50ra; Madrid, Bibl. Univ. 73, f. 20vb): "Omnis quantitas est mensura, et discreta quantitas est quantitas, ergo erit mensura, sed discretarum partium; aut igitur permanentium, et ita est numerus, aut non permanentium, et est oratio."

[217] Cf. Nicholas of Paris, *Rat. sup. Praed.* IV, q. 11 (Munich, Bayer. Staatsbibl. 14460, f. 49ra): "quantitas non mensuratur sed est mensura"; IV, q. 18 (f. 49va–vb): "Ad primum dicendum quod omnis quantitas est mensura"; V, q. 2 (f. 50vb): "Omnis enim quantitas est mensura." Robert Kilwardby, *Not. sup. Praed.* VIII, q. 8 (Cambridge, Peterhouse 206, f. 49vb; Madrid, Bibl. Univ. 73, f. 20vb): "Omnis quantitas est mensura"; VIII, q. 16 (f. 50va; f. 21vb): "Quantitas erat ut esset mensura substantiae; quod ergo non est mensura substantiae secundum se, nec est habens esse ultimum quantitatis." For Aquinas "measure of substance" constitutes what he calls the *ratio* of the category of quantity; see *Summa Theologiae* 1, q. 28, a. 2 (ed. Leonina, 321).

[218] See Andrews, *Peter of Auvergne*, 167–74.

Pagus follows Aristotle in taking the last of the three properties to be distinctive of quantity, although at first sight it may appear otherwise:

> It seems that this property does not belong to quantity alone.
>
> For something is said to be equal or unequal according to equality or inequality. But equality and inequality fall in the category of relation or perhaps of quality. Thus, this property belongs to relatives. Thus, it does not belong to quantity alone.
>
> And it is to be said that the preposition "according to" can express the disposition of the efficient cause, and it is used in this way when it is said that "it is a property of quantity etc." For quantity is the efficient cause of equality and inequality. Alternatively, it can express the circumstance of the formal cause, and it is used in this way when it is said that "something is said to be equal or unequal according to equality or inequality." For equality is the form of what is equal. And so, there is here, as we have seen, an equivocation in the use of "according to."[219]

Presumably, the idea is the following. Equality is a relation, and so falls under the category of relation. It is, however, a relation founded on quantity. That is to say, it is true that two items, A and B, are said to be equal because they stand in the relation of equality, but this is not, according to Pagus, what Aristotle has in mind. His point is rather that the relation of equality can only be founded on properties belonging to the category of quantity. Thus, if two items, A and B, are said to be equal, this is ultimately because they are "one" in quantity: there is a pair of instances of a given quantity property Q (a certain length, say) of which one is in A and the other in B, and these are the efficient cause of the relation in the sense that they are the properties on which the relation is founded. The interpretation seems to be in line with what Aristotle says in the chapter on relation in his philosophical lexicon in the fifth book of the *Metaphysics*:

> Those things are the same whose substance is one; those are similar whose quality is one; those are equal whose quantity is one.[220]

Sameness, we might say, is a relation founded on substance, similarity is a relation founded on quality, and equality is a relation founded on quantity. In this sense it is a distinctive property of quantity to be that according to which other things are said to be equal or unequal.

---

[219] John Pagus, *Rat. sup. Praed.* XXIII, q. 6 (140.18–27).
[220] Aristotle, *Metaphysics* V 15.1021a11–12 (trans. Ross, 1612; slightly modified).

Having discussed quantity, Aristotle in chapter 7 treats the category of relation. Most of Aristotle's discussion of this category deals with items that are towards something (*ad aliquid*) or relative (*relativa*) rather than with relations (*relationes*) as such. As a result, Pagus does not address the question of the nature of relations at any length. He does, however, appear to adopt a version of the view that a relation is a sort of property, which is in one of the two relata as its subject and so to speak "points to" the other as its term:

> Fatherhood has two respects, one towards the substance in which it is (...), the other to its term, that is, to the son (...); similarly with other correlative forms.[221]

On such a view, if David and Solomon are related as father and son, this is to be explained by an accident, paternity, which is in David but points to Solomon, and another accident, filiation, which is in Solomon but points to David. This kind of analysis of relational situations was very common in the Middle Ages.[222]

Aristotle begins the chapter by stating a criterion for being relative. Pagus glosses it as follows:

> *All such things are said to be towards something as are said to be just what* etc., that is, according to their being such, *of or than other things*, that is, in the genitive, *or in some other way*, that is, in some other case, *towards something else*.[223]

There is a sense in which this criterion relies on linguistic facts, on how things are expressed or called. This emerges more clearly from Aristotle's exemplification of it:

> For example, what is larger is called what it is *than* something else (it is called larger than something); and what is double is called what it is *of* something else (it is called double of something); similarly with all other such cases.[224]

---

[221] John Pagus, *Rat. sup. Praed.* XXX, q. 4 (177.13–15). Cf. ibid., XXIV, q. 3 (144.1–2).

[222] See Mark G. Henninger, *Relations: Medieval Theories 1250–1325* (Oxford: Clarendon Press, 1989), 4–6; Jeffrey E. Brower, "Medieval Theories of Relations," in *The Stanford Encyclopedia of Philosophy* (Winter 2010 Edition), edited by Edward N. Zalta. URL = <http://plato.stanford.edu/archives/win2010/entries/relations-medieval/>. Interestingly enough, Nicholas of Paris rejects it on the grounds that it turns relations into extrinsic accidents; see Hansen, "Strange Finds."

[223] John Pagus, *Rat. sup. Praed.* XXIV (142.1–3). The definition is found in Aristotle, *Categories* 7.6a36–37, ed. composita (ed. Minio-Paluello, 58): "Ad aliquid vero talia dicuntur quaecumque hoc ipsum quod sunt aliorum dicuntur, vel quomodolibet aliter ad aliud."

[224] Aristotle, *Categories* 7.6a37–b2 (trans. Ackrill, 17).

Double, in other words, is a relative. It is *called* what it is (according to its being such, as Pagus says), namely, double, *of* something, that is, with a complement in the genitive, and so satisfies the criterion. Aristotle lists a few more examples:

> The following, too, and their like are among relatives: state, disposition, perception, knowledge, position. For each of these is called what it is (and not something different) *of* something else. A state is called a state of something, knowledge knowledge of something, position position of something, and the rest similarly.[225]

Because of the linguistic nature of the criterion, the items satisfying it were known to Pagus and his contemporaries as relatives according to expression (*relativa secundum dici*).

The criterion turns out to overgenerate, since it lets certain secondary substances such as heads and hands come out as relative.[226] To avoid this consequence, Aristotle introduces a revised criterion towards the end of the chapter. Pagus glosses this second criterion as follows:

> Those things *are towards something for which being*, that is, their being such, *is the same as standing towards something in some way*, that is, in and of themselves.[227]

This criterion no longer refers to how things *are expressed* (*dici*) but to how they *are* (*esse*). Hence, to Pagus and his contemporaries items satisfying this second criterion were known as relatives according to being (*relativa secundum esse*).

Aristotle claims that whatever satisfies the second criterion also satisfies the first,[228] so all relatives according to being will also be relatives according to expression (but not, of course, vice versa). One consequence of this is that an ambiguity creeps in. Sometimes the label "relatives according to expression" is used to refer to all items satisfying the first criterion, regardless of whether they also satisfy the second. At other times the reference is exclusively to those items that satisfy the first criterion but fail to satisfy the second. In the following, when it is important

---

[225] Aristotle, *Categories* 7.6b2–6 (trans. Ackrill, 17; slightly modified).

[226] Aristotle, *Categories* 7.8a13–31.

[227] John Pagus, *Rat. sup. Praed.* xxix (169.5–6). The definition is found in Aristotle, *Categories* 7.8a28–33, ed. composita (ed. Minio-Paluello, 62): "Si igitur sufficienter eorum quae sunt ad aliquid definitio assignata est, aut nimis difficile aut impossibile est solvere quoniam nulla substantia eorum quae sunt ad aliquid dicitur; si autem non sufficienter, sed sunt ad aliquid quibus hoc ipsum esse est ad aliquid quodam modo se habere, fortasse aliquid contra ista dicetur."

[228] Aristotle, *Categories* 7.8a33–35.

to avoid this ambiguity, I shall therefore refer to the latter group of items as relatives *merely* according to expression.

There is an old tradition for associating the first of the two criteria with Plato.[229] Boethius, as so often, passed the idea on to the Latin West:

> This definition is thought to be by Plato, and it is corrected by Aristotle a little later on.[230]

Many medieval commentators followed suit: the first definition is due to other philosophers, sometimes specified as the Platonists or Plato himself; the second represents Aristotle's considered view. This considered view was usually taken to be essentially correct, so relatives according to being are often referred to as truly relative (*vere relativa*) or relatives according to truth (*secundum veritatem*). Pagus draws on all of these ideas in his exposition.[231]

The problem with the so-called Platonic definition, it was often claimed, is precisely that it fails to keep the categories mutually exclusive. For example, according to an anonymous twelfth-century commentator, who was a follower of Gilbert of Poitiers:

> Aristotle first offers a general description, following the account given by certain people who did not keep the genera distinct.[232]

According to Nicholas of Paris, the criterion basically undermines the whole enterprise of constructing a system of categories:

> The error of these people destroys the art; for it destroys the separation of the categories that the art establishes.[233]

---

[229] In the late first century BC, Boethus of Sidon had apparently claimed that Aristotle took it over from his teacher; see Simplicius, *in Cat.* 159.12–15. The claim seems somewhat questionable, which is perhaps why Porphyry relates it only in a weakened form, saying that it "is said to be a Platonic one"; see Porphyry, *in Cat.* 111.27–29.

[230] Boethius, *in Cat.* 217c (ed. Migne): "Huiusmodi auten definitio Platonis esse creditur, quae ab Aristotele paulo posterius emendatur."

[231] For the idea that the definition is due to other philosophers, see John Pagus, *Rat. sup. Praed.* XXIV (141.3–5); for mention of the Platonists or Plato in this context, see ibid., XXXVII (213.12–13; 217.7–8); for the reference to relatives according to being as true relatives, see, for example, ibid., XXVIII (162.32); XXX (173.1).

[232] Anonymus Porretanus, *in Cat.* (ed. Ebbesen, 86): "Agit enim hoc modo: prius ponit generalem descriptionem secundum assignationem quorundam genera non distinguentium, (...) deinde veriorem assignabit descriptionem."

[233] Nicholas of Paris, *Rat. sup. Praed.* VI (Munich, Bayer. Staatsbibl. 14460, f. 52ra): "Ordo capituli manifestus est in se, quia prius est ponere opinionem erroneam aliorum quam illam corrigere et propriam ponere, eo quod error illorum destruit artem; destruit

With the revised criterion for being relative, however, the desirable aim of mutually exclusive categories is supposedly achieved.

Ideas such as these might lead one to say that relatives merely according to expression fail *to be* relatives, and therefore do not belong to this category at all. Pagus, however, wants to maintain that in some sense they are and do. For him, apparently, being relative according to expression is never a purely linguistic matter — even for substances such as heads and hands. He tries to explain his position as follows:

> All other genera apart from relation are natures of some sort, but relation is a certain respect caused by a nature of some sort. But if the nature by which the relation is caused is such that some sort of respect is not really mixed in with it, then they are relatives according to expression. If, however, a respect is really mixed in with the nature, then they are relatives both according to expression and according to being, such as, for example, double and half. So relatives are not said to be according to expression because they are not so according to being at all, but because they are caused by some nature with which some sort of respect is not really mixed in, as are, for example, the parts of a substance.[234]

Pagus does not really explicate the view further. Perhaps, however, the main idea he is getting at is the one that Robert Kilwardby expresses when, speaking of relatives according to being, he says that

> the being of these is to stand in some way towards another; for they are not towards something through something added to their essence, but they are what they are towards something, not only according to mode or expression, but according to being and truth.[235]

Items such as state and disposition, by contrast, which Aristotle mentions in connection with his first criterion, but which also constitute one on the four main kinds of quality, are relatives according to expression only, because

---

enim separationem praedictamentorum quae habentur ex arte, et ideo si posuisset opinionem propriam, posset impediri veritas per illorum errorem."

[234] John Pagus, *Rat. sup. Praed.* XXVII, q. 4 (159.24–60.5).

[235] Robert Kilwardby, *Not. sup. Praed.* x (Cambridge, Peterhouse 206, f. 54ra; Madrid, Bibl. Univ. 73, f. 26rb): "Horum enim esse est ad aliud quodammodo se habere; haec enim non sunt ad aliquid per aliquid additum suae essentiae, sed id quod sunt, non solum secundum modum sive secundum dictionem, sed secundum esse et secundum veritatem, sunt ad aliquid."

they are qualities, and they are towards something through something added to their essence.[236]

Kilwardby goes on to explain:

> The best example of this last claim is a picture: considered in itself it is a quality (because it is colour), but compared to that of which it is an image it is a sort of likeness and thus a relation grounded in a quality; and this is how it is with knowledge and suchlike.[237]

Items that are relative merely according to expression are relative because something is added to their essence, whereas relatives according to being are essentially relative; their relativity springs from their very essence. The idea seems to be that knowledge, say, is an absolute item in the category of quality: it is a state of the knower. This state *has* a representational aspect (and it is in virtue of this aspect that it is said to be *of* something and satisfies Aristotle's first criterion for being relative), but it *is* not that aspect; the aspect is something added to, not included in, its essence. To be knowledge, therefore, is not, strictly speaking, "the same as standing towards something [an object of knowledge] in some way."

Admittedly, if this is what Pagus has in mind, he has not expressed himself too clearly, but an idea along these lines does seem to underlie his claim that

> there are some things whose being can be absolute, and if they are on occasion taken in comparison to something else, their being is not destroyed on account of this (...) But there are others whose being is always in comparison to something else, and if they lack this comparison, their being is destroyed; these are relatives.[238]

Being for some items essentially involves having a respect or "comparison" to something else, and if this respect or relation is taken away, so is their being (Pagus gives father and son as examples, and these are paradigmatic cases of relatives according to being; to be a father *is* "the same as standing towards something [a

---

[236] Robert Kilwardby, *Not. sup. Praed.* x (Cambridge, Peterhouse 206, f. 54ra; Madrid, Bibl. Univ. 73, f. 26va): "habitus et huiusmodi sunt ad aliquid, quia sunt qualitates, et per aliquid additum suae essentiae sunt ad aliquid."

[237] Robert Kilwardby, *Not. sup. Praed.* x (Cambridge, Peterhouse 206, f. 54ra; Madrid, Bibl. Univ. 73, f. 26va): "Optimum exemplum super hoc ultimo dictum est pictura, quae in se considerata qualitas est, quia color; comparando ad illud cuius est imago est similitudo quaedam, et sic relatio fundata in qualitate. Sic est de scientia et huiusmodi." Cf. John Pagus, *Rat. sup. Praed.* v, q. 10 (37.17–19).

[238] John Pagus, *Rat. sup. Praed.* XXII, q. 2 (133.25–34.1).

child] in some way"). Presumably, this is also why one can say, as Pagus does, that relatives according to being are relatives in and of themselves (*per se*), whereas relatives according to expression, that is, *merely* according to expression, are relatives only accidentally (*per accidens*).[239]

In sum, being relative merely according to expression is *not*, contrary to what one might think, a purely linguistic matter; it does have a basis in extralinguistic reality. The distinction between being relative according to being and being relative *merely* according to expression turns out, it would seem, to be rooted in a distinction between being essentially relative and being nonessentially — or accidentally — relative. Since an item that is accidentally relative *is*, in some attenuated sense, relative, relatives merely according to expression are, after all, also relatives according to being, albeit in this attenuated sense. That, at least, would seem to be the idea.[240]

Aristotle gives four properties that hold of relatives: (1) having a contrary, (2) being susceptible to degrees, (3) being said convertibly with its correlative, and (4) being simultaneous by nature with its correlative. On Pagus' interpretation, the latter two properties are distinctive of relatives: (3) of relatives according to expression, (4) of relatives according to being.[241] The same idea is found in Kilwardby.[242]

(3) consists in the idea that relative items come in pairs, so that for any relative item A there is a correlative item B such that A is said to be A in relation to B and B is said to be B in relation to A. The property, in fact, applies to all items satisfying the first of the two criteria for being relative, regardless of whether they are relatives according to being or not. A head is head of a headed and a headed is headed by a head, even though head is a substance and relative merely according to

---

[239]   John Pagus, *Rat. sup. Praed.* XXVII, q. 2 (158.25–26).

[240]   Ever since antiquity, interpreters have struggled to say clearly and convincingly what the difference between Aristotle's two criteria of being relative consists in, and which items do and which do not actually satisfy them; for two recent attempts, see David Sedley, "Aristotelian Relativities," in *Le style de la pensée*, ed. Monique Canto-Sperber and Pierre Pellegrin (Paris: Les Belles Lettres, 2002), 324–52, and Orna Harari, "The Unity of Aristotle's Category of Relatives," *Classical Quarterly* 61 (2011): 521–37.

[241]   John Pagus, *Rat. sup. Praed.* XXVI (151.1–4); XVIII (161.1–2).

[242]   Robert Kilwardby, *Not. sup. Praed.* XI , q. 6 (Cambridge, Peterhouse 206, f. 55rb; Madrid, Bibl. Univ. 73, ff. 27vb–28ra): "Ad aliud {aliud *P* : alia *M*} ergo dicendum quod dat duo propria, quorum primum est ex parte dicere, secundum ex parte esse {secundum...esse *scripsi* : *om. P* : secundum ex parte coniuncti vel esse *M*}. Unde etiam pertractanti patet sufficientia et ordo, cum non sint {sint *P* : sit *M*} ad aliquid dicta nisi secundum dictionem aut secundum esse {secundum esse *P* : secundum coniunctum vel esse *M*}, et communius {communius *P* : convenientius *M*} sunt ad aliquid quae secundum dictionem quam quae secundum esse."

expression. Similarly, a master is master of a slave and a slave is slave of a master, and these are relatives according to being.[243]

(4) claims that correlatives are simultaneous by nature. The interpretation of this property, or more specifically of Aristotle's use of "nature" in this context, was apparently controversial at the time.[244] Pagus takes a line, also taken by Kilwardby, which comes from the *Categoriae decem*.[245] He says:

> It is to be said, with Augustine, that relatives are simultaneous by nature, for nature is the same thing as birth, coming into being, or a sort of beginning which is the starting point of one relative as well as of the other. This is clear from a question that he raises in the same context. For he asks whether the master was always a master, and he replies that he wasn't but that he came to be a master when a slave came to be.[246]

As Kilwardby points out, the *Categoriae decem* actually speaks of "coming to be and passing away" (*ortu et occasu*).[247] So, on this interpretation (4) seems to consist in something along the following lines: if A and B are correlatives, then if an A comes into existence at some time *t*, a B comes into existence at *t*. Similarly, if an A goes out of existence at some time *t*, a B goes out of existence at *t*.

Having listed the property of simultaneity by nature, Aristotle immediately suggests that perhaps it doesn't hold of all relatives:

> For the knowable would seem to be prior to knowledge. For as a rule it is of actual things already existing that we acquire knowledge; in few cases, if any, could one find knowledge coming into existence at the same time as what is knowable. Moreover, destruction of the knowable carries knowledge to destruction, but knowledge does not carry the knowable to destruction. For if there is not a knowable there is not knowledge — there will no longer be anything for knowledge to be of — but if there is not knowledge there is nothing to prevent there being a knowable. Take, for example, the squaring of the circle,

---

[243] Aristotle, *Categories* 7.6b28–7b14.

[244] Cf. Anon. Domus Petri 206, *in Praed.* IX, q. 5 (ed. Hansen, 167); Nicholas of Paris, *Rat. sup. Praed.* VII, q. 2 (Munich, Bayer. Staatsbibl. 14460, f. 53vb).

[245] Ps.-Augustine, *Categoriae decem* 98 (ed. Minio-Paluello, 155).

[246] John Pagus, *Rat. sup. Praed.* XXVIII, q. 1 (164.8–12). Cf. ibid., XXVIII (162.26–29).

[247] Robert Kilwardby, *Not. sup. Praed.* XI, q. 12 (Cambridge, Peterhouse 206, f. 55va; Madrid, Bibl. Univ. 73, f. 28rb): "Unde 'simul natura' dicitur hic ut simul natura dicitur esse ab Augustino simul esse secundum ortum et occasum; haec enim posita se ponunt, destructa se destruunt." Cf. Ps.-Augustine, *Categoriae decem* 98 (ed. Minio-Paluello, 155): "Tunc ergo et vere et proprie ad aliquid dicitur cum sub uno ortu atque occasu et id quod iungitur et id cui iungitur invenitur."

supposing it to be knowable; knowledge of it does not yet exist but the knowable itself exists.[248]

As already mentioned, both Pagus and Kilwardby expressly state that the property in question holds only of relatives according to being. As we have also seen, Kilwardby explicitly says that knowledge is relative merely according to expression because considered in itself is a certain quality. This was a commonly held view, which Pagus seems to share.[249] On such an interpretation, it seems that it is as it should be that knowledge and its correlative, knowable, fail to be simultaneous by nature, since they are *not* relatives according to being. Indeed, this line of interpretation seems to have been quite common. For example, the anonymous author of the *Dialectica Monacensis* ends his discussion of the category of relatives by stating Aristotle's second criterion for being relative, followed by the remark that

> in accordance with this definition, the following property is assigned to relatives: relatives are simultaneous by nature. (...) But this property belongs to all those items that are relative according to truth and to those only.[250]

Since knowledge and knowable are relatives merely according to expression, that is, do not satisfy this second criterion, they do not seem to be genuine counterexamples. Thus, we find the Anonymus Domus Petri 206 saying that:

> Aristotle does not solve those counterexamples because they do not go against what has been proposed.[251]

The mid-thirteenth-century commentator William of Montoriel puts it as follows:

> You should know that the cases against which he posits counterexamples belong, according to the truth, to other categories and are not true relatives but only according to expression. For this reason they are not directly counterexamples to the property in question.[252]

---

[248] Aristotle, *Categories* 7.7b22–33 (trans. Ackrill, 21).

[249] Cf. John Pagus, *Rat. sup. Praed.* XXV (147.14–15); XXV, q. 1 (148.21–23).

[250] Anon., *Dialectica Monacensis* (ed. de Rijk, 520): "Iuxta hanc definitionem relativis hoc proprium assignatur: relativa sunt simul natura. (...) Sed id proprium convenit omnibus quae secundum veritatem sunt ad aliquid et solum illis, sicut patere potest per instantiam quam ponit Aristoteles contra hoc proprium."

[251] Anonymus Domus Petri 206, *in Cat.* IX, q. 7 (ed. Hansen, 167): "Ad aliud dico quod non solvit illas instantias quia non sunt contra propositum."

[252] Willelmus de Montoriel, *Summa libri Praedicamentorum* (ed. Andrews and Noone, 81): "Et sciatis quod ea in quibus ponuntur instantiae secundum veritatem sunt in aliis

Pagus seems to be following this traditional line in so far as he takes the property to be one that is characteristic of relatives according to being. But, as we shall see, he also wants to maintain that there is a sense in which knowledge and knowable are, in fact, simultaneous in the required sense.

He replies to the following objection:

> The prior and posterior, the cause and effect, are said in relation to something, but they aren't simultaneous by nature, as is obvious.[253]

by saying that

> the prior and posterior, and so on, can be considered in two ways. In one way, they can be considered according to what they are, and in this way one is prior to the other, as the objection goes, but in this way they are not said in relation to something. In another way, they are taken under the concepts of priority, causality, and so on, and in this way one is not prior to the other, and in this way they are relative and simultaneous.[254]

In the first of the two ways, the prior (that is to say, the thing that is prior, considered in itself, independently of its being prior) is neither relative to the posterior (that is to say, the thing that is posterior, considered in itself, independently of its being posterior) nor simultaneous with it. In the second way, however, where they are taken under the concept (*intentio*) of priority (which presumably means that they are considered in so far as they stand in the relevant relation and qua prior and posterior), they are correlative and simultaneous.

What seems to be the same idea is found in Kilwardby's commentary:

> To this we reply that the prior, under the concept by which it is prior, is simultaneous with the posterior under the concept by which it is posterior. That, however, to which priority belongs as an accident is prior to that to which posteriority belongs as an accident, and not simultaneous. Similarly also in other cases.[255]

---

praedicamentis et non sunt vere relativa sed secundum dici solum. Propterea non sunt directe instantiae contra praedictam proprietatem."

[253] John Pagus, *Rat. sup. Praed.* XXVIII, q. 2 (164.25–26).

[254] John Pagus, *Rat. sup. Praed.* XXVIII, q. 2 (165.3–6).

[255] Robert Kilwardby, *Not sup. Praed.* XI, q. 13 (Cambridge, Peterhouse 206, f. 55va; Madrid, Bibl. Univ. 73, f. 28rb): "Ad haec ergo dicimus quod prius, sub ratione illa qua est prius, est simul cum eo quod est posterius, sub ratione illa qua est posterius; id tamen cui accidit prioritas est prius eo cui accidit posterioritas et non simul. Similiter autem intellige et in aliis."

So basically, we seem to be dealing with a distinction between an item as such and an item in so far as it bears a relational property.

Pagus thinks that this distinction is relevant with respect to knowledge and the knowable:

> This solves a certain question that arises here, namely, why Aristotle posits these counterexamples without solving them. For if the knowable and knowledge are considered according to what they are, then the knowable is prior, and this is how the arguments that he gives proceed, and because in this way they infer something true, he leaves them unsolved. But if the knowable and knowledge are considered under these concepts, the knowable is not prior to knowledge but the two are simultaneous.[256]

If the terms are taken in one way, the arguments that Aristotle gives go through, if the terms are taken in another way, the arguments do not go through.

Such an interpretation raises the question of why Aristotle would actually posit such sophistical counterexamples. He does so, Pagus claims,

> in order to stress that this property does not belong to relatives according to what they are, and this is how the counterexample works, but belongs to relatives according to their being such.[257]

The property of being simultaneous in nature, the point seems to be, does not belong to the items related in themselves, but to them in so far as they are relatives, that is to say, by virtue of their co-relational properties. A father and his son are not simultaneous according to what they are (for example, the substances that we call David and Solomon), but they are simultaneous according to their being such (that is, father and son). The reason this becomes unclear in the case of knowledge and knowable, Pagus says, is because the expression "knowable" turns out to be ambiguous:

> It is to be said that "knowable" can name a thing alone, and in this way it isn't a relative nor does the destruction of knowledge carry the knowable to destruction, and this is how Aristotle uses it, because the substance that is knowable is not carried to destruction by the destruction of knowledge. If, however, it names a substance under the act of knowing, the destruction of knowledge does carry the knowable to destruction, but not the knowable according to its substance but under the form that is knowledge.[258]

---

[256] John Pagus, *Rat. sup. Praed.* XXVIII, q. 2 (165.7–11).
[257] John Pagus, *Rat. sup. Praed.* XXVIII, q. 3 (165.12–14).
[258] John Pagus, *Rat. sup. Praed.* XXVIII, q. 5 (166.10–14).

In so far as "knowable" means "actually known," the knowable is simultaneous with knowledge; it comes into existence when knowledge of it comes into existence and is carried to destruction when knowledge of it is carried to destruction. Kilwardby makes a similar point:

> "Knowable" is, therefore, said in two ways, namely, either potentially knowable and actually known, and in this way it is completely relative to knowledge; or potentially knowable and not actually known, and in this way it is not. Thus, if the knowable is posited as existing in so far as it is actually, it is necessary to posit knowledge as existing, but in the other way it is not necessary at all.[259]

The idea clearly involves some sort of modification of the standard interpretation, according to which the property of being simultaneous by nature holds of all and only relatives according to being. On this interpretation, it appears to have been commonly held that knowledge and knowable, being relative merely according to expression, do not constitute a real counterexample; the fact that they fail to be simultaneous by nature is as it should be. Pagus and Kilwardby follow the interpretation to the extent that they, too, take Aristotle to be introducing the property as one that is distinctive of relatives according to being, but, as we have just seen, they also want to maintain that there is a sense in which knowledge and knowable actually have the property. For such a position to be consistent, however, some additional move seems to be required. Either one will have to say that knowledge and knowable do, in fact, constitute a genuine counterexample: the property is not, after all, distinctive of relatives according to being, because there are relatives merely according to expression of which it holds. Or one will have to say that there is a sense in which both knowledge and knowable do, after all, satisfy Aristotle's second criterion for being relative, and that it is in this sense that they are simultaneous by nature. It is unclear, however, which, if any, of these moves Pagus (or Kilwardby) would want to make. What is clear is that Aristotle's difficulties in delimiting this category also create serious problems for the interpretation of the rest of his theory.

Having treated the category of relation, Aristotle in chapter 8 discusses quality. He begins by characterising the items belonging to this category as follows:

---

[259] Robert Kilwardby, *Not. sup. Praed.* xi, q. 15 (Cambridge, Peterhouse 206, f. 55vb; Madrid, Bibl. Univ. 73, f. 28va): "Scibile ergo dicitur dupliciter, scilicet potentia scibile et actu scitum, et sic se habet omnino ad scientiam; vel potentia scibile et non actu scitum, et sic non se habet. Et ita, si ponatur scibile in esse ut actu est, necesse est scientiam ponere in esse, alio modo nequaquam."

By a quality I mean that in virtue of which things are said to be qualified somehow.[260]

As Pagus explicitly points out, this is not a definition in the strict sense of the
word but a mere description. To explain the difference, he invokes a well-known
Aristotelian distinction:

> It says in the *Physics* that things are said to be prior to us and prior by nature.
> Hence, a definition properly speaking is given in terms of that which is prior as
> such, whereas a description is given in terms of that which is prior to us. And
> that's the way it is here, for quality taken in itself is prior to quality united to
> substance, but with respect to our cognition it is the exact opposite.[261]

It is unproblematic, in other words, to *describe* quality by means of things that are
qualified, and this is what Aristotle is doing.

Having posited his description of qualities, Aristotle goes on to make a claim
that has troubled his later interpreters considerably:

> But quality is one of the things spoken of in a number of ways.[262]

He then proceeds to list and discuss four kinds of quality. By saying that a thing, A,
is spoken of in many ways, Aristotle often means to say that the expression "A" is
not univocal. The problem is that if quality is a highest genus, it ought to be predicated univocally of the several kinds or species falling under it. As Pagus objects:

> Every genus is predicated univocally and not in many ways, as Porphyry says.
> Thus, since quality is a genus, it is not said in many ways.[263]

One solution is to interpret Aristotle's claim in the way proposed by John Ackrill:

> When Aristotle says that quality "is spoken of in a number of ways" he does
> not mean that the word "quality" is ambiguous but only that there are different
> kinds of quality.[264]

Pagus initially offers this same solution, but goes on to reject it:

---

[260] Aristotle, *Categories* 8.8b25 (trans. Ackrill, 24).
[261] John Pagus, *Rat. sup. Praed.* xxxi, q. 4 (183.12–16).
[262] Aristotle, *Categories* 8.8b26 (trans. Ackrill, 24).
[263] John Pagus, *Rat. sup. Praed.* xxxi, q. 5 (183.18–19).
[264] Aristotle, *Categories*, trans. Ackrill, 104.

But this solution doesn't seem adequate, because by parity of reason quantity will also be said in a number of ways since it too has many species. Thus, it is to be said that quality is said in a number of ways, not because it has numerous meanings, but because each of its species is called by a double name.[265]

This interpretation is also offered by Nicholas of Paris,[266] and it points to a curious fact about the four types of quality that Aristotle goes on to list, namely, that each of them is designated by a conjunction or disjunction of two terms: (1) state and disposition, (2) natural capacity or incapacity, (3) affective quality and affection, and (4) form and figure.

These designations, in turn, raise the more pressing question of how such pairs can actually constitute a single species. Pagus offers the following explanation:

It is to be said that contrariety belongs properly to quality, and so if it is found to belong to other things, this is due to the nature of quality, as, for example, fire is contrary to water because it is warm and water is cold. But that which has a contrary has being in an incomplete state before having it in a complete state, as, for example, when fire acts on water it is not capable of impressing its form at once because of the resistance of its contrary. (…) Thus, in order to designate this double being each species of quality is called by a double name. This is clear from the following example: the first species is state and disposition, and state designates complete being whereas disposition designates incomplete being.[267]

Nicholas of Paris, who takes the same approach, explains the point in a bit more detail:

Hence, qualities have contraries, and in those things which have a contrary being is prior to complete being. For qualities do not come to be quickly and instantly but successively and over time, and this is due to the resistance of the contrary, as is clear in the case of water. For water is naturally cold and fire is naturally hot, and coldness and heat are contraries. Hence, water is not made hot by fire straightaway, because fire is met with the resistance of the contrary, but heat is generated, and coldness reduced, successively. Therefore,

---

[265] John Pagus, *Rat. sup. Praed.* XXXI, q. 5 (183.24–27).

[266] Nicholas of Paris, *Rat. sup. Praed.* VIII, q. 4 (Munich, Bayer. Staatsbibl. 14460, f. 55vb): "Ad primum dico quod qualitas non dicitur multipliciter multiplicitate equivocationis vel analogiae nec etiam dicitur multipliciter propter hoc quod habeat multas species, quia concedo quod similiter debuisset dixisse quod relatio vel quantitas dicerentur multipliciter. Sed qualitas dicitur multipliciter quia species qualitatis circumloquuntur multiplici vocabulo."

[267] John Pagus, *Rat. sup. Praed.* XXXII, q. 1 (188.10–17).

because qualities do not come to be at once but over time, just as it is clear that water is not hot straightaway but is first tepid and then more and more warm until finally it is hot, and so because in qualities such as these being is prior to complete being, each species of quality is described by a double word in order to designate that in the case of quality incomplete being is prior to complete being.[268]

With regard to the four species of quality, then, one of the two names designates a sort of incomplete being, the other a sort of complete being.

In some cases, the incomplete is a sort of pathway (*via*) to the complete. Thus, with regard to the first species, Pagus says that

state and disposition are rooted in the same essence and with respect to the same subject. This is clear, for if you do works of charity once or twice, these acts effect in you a virtue according to disposition, and through frequent repetitions of these same acts what used to be a disposition will be turned into a state.[269]

A similar analysis holds, he claims, for the third species of quality: an affection may with time (*per moram temporis*) turn into an affective quality.[270] As Nicholas points out, these are also identical in essence:

States and dispositions are the same in essence; and similarly, affections and affective qualities are the same in essence.[271]

---

[268] Nicholas of Paris, *Rat. sup. Praed.* VIII, q. 5 (Munich, Bayer. Staatsbibl. 14460, f. 55vb): "Unde qualitas habet contrarium et in illis quibus est contrarium prius est esse quam completum esse. Non enim qualitas cito et in momento generatur, sed successive et in tempore, et hoc est propter resistentiam contrarii, ut patet in aqua. Aqua enim frigida naturaliter est et ignis naturaliter calidus (frigiditas et caliditas contraria sunt). Unde aqua non tam cito fit calida ab igne, eo quod ignis invenit resistentiam contrarii, sed successive generatur caliditas et remittitur frigiditas. Quia ergo qualitas non subito generatur sed in tempore, sicut patet quod aqua non tam cito est calida, sed prius est tepida et postea magis et magis donec ad ultimum sit calida, et ideo quia in huiusmodi qualitatibus prius est esse quam completum esse, circumloquitur quamlibet speciem duplici vocabulo ad denotandum quod in qualitate prius est esse incompletum quam esse completum."

[269] John Pagus, *Rat. sup. Praed.* XXXI, q. 6 (184.5–8).

[270] John Pagus, *Rat. sup. Praed.* XXXV, q. 2 (204.7–9). Cf. ibid., XXXIII, q. 5 (194.19–25).

[271] Nicholas of Paris, *Rat. sup. Praed.* VIII, q. 6 (Munich, Bayer. Staatsbibl. 14460, f. 56ra): "Sed habitus et dispositio conveniunt in essentia; similiter passio et passibilis qualitas conveniunt in essentia."

With the second and fourth species of quality, however, things are different. Nicholas continues:

> But in the case of the other two species, that is, natural capacity or incapacity and form and the figure surrounding something, they are not the same in essence, because figure is the closure of the sides or the lines, whereas that which lies in between and which is convex or curved is called form, and these are not the same in essence.[272]

This has consequences, since it would seem that one item's being the pathway (*via*) to the other in the present sense requires that the two items be the same in essence or rooted in the same essence. Thus, Pagus also says that

> a disposition is the pathway to a state, because through frequent repetitions of an act it is turned into a state, and something similar is the case with affections and affective qualities. With natural capacity or incapacity, however, it is not like this, nor with form or figure, because one is not a pathway to the other nor can one come to be from the other.[273]

So in these latter cases, we are not dealing with the same essence in some sort of incomplete and complete state of being.

Nonetheless, Pagus seems to think that there is some sense in which one item can be said to be incomplete and the other complete also in these cases.[274] With regard to natural capacity or incapacity, he says that

> they do not constitute a single species in so far as they are opposites, (…) but in so far as one is incomplete with respect to the other and the other is complete, and in every genus the incomplete can be reduced to the complete; and it is thus that they were able to constitute a single species in so far as one reduces to the other.[275]

For the fourth species, we have to look to Nicholas of Paris's commentary, where the following concern about this line of interpretation is raised:

---

[272] Nicholas of Paris, *Rat. sup. Praed.* VIII, q. 6 (Munich, Bayer. Staatsbibl. 14460, f. 56ra): "Aliae duae species non conveniunt in essentia, sicut naturalis potentia vel impotentia et forma et circa aliquid constans figura, quia figura est clausio laterum vel linearum, illud vero interiacens quod est convexum et curvum dicitur forma, et ista non sunt idem in essentia."

[273] John Pagus, *Rat. sup. Praed.* XXXII, q. 2 (188.23–27).

[274] For natural capacity or incapacity, see John Pagus, *Rat. sup. Praed.* XXXII, q. 4 (189.18–21); for form and figure, see ibid., XXXV, q. 3.

[275] John Pagus, *Rat. sup. Praed.* XXXII, q. 4 (189.18–21).

In the other species of quality, Aristotle posited the complete before the incomplete, for example, state before disposition, but here he does it the other way around and posits the incomplete before the complete (for, relative to figure, form is something incomplete).[276]

Nicholas seeks to alleviate the concern in the following way:

Figure is the limit of form, because the continuity of the space that lies in between could be extended infinitely but is limited and made finite by the closure of the lines, which is what we call figure. Hence, figure is a limit with respect to form. However, the limit should be posited after that which it limits, and it is with this in mind that Aristotle places figure after form. I still say, however, that figure is complete with respect to form, which is incomplete.[277]

So while the complete/incomplete distinction gives Nicholas and Pagus a useful tool for solving the problem of the "double species" in a uniform way at a general level, it cannot actually be applied to each of the four species in the same way, and so does not allow them to solve the problem in an entirely unified fashion. And ultimately, apart from this inelegance, one might wonder how, in the final analysis, items that are not the same in essence can actually constitute a single species.

However that may be, Pagus appears to take Aristotle's division of the genus of quality into these four immediate species as exhaustive. Thus, when Aristotle rounds off his discussion of them with the remark that "perhaps some other manner of quality might come to light," Pagus expounds this as follows:

It is to be said that because the properties of continuous quantities, such as, for example, straightness and curvature, belong to the fourth species of quality, some people have thought that the properties of discrete quantities, such as, for example, evenness and oddness, make up a new species of quality in a similar manner. But since their view is false, he said "perhaps."[278]

---

[276] Nicholas of Paris, *Rat. sup. Praed.* VIII, q. 23 (Munich, Bayer. Staatsbibl. 14460, f. 56vb): "Item, in aliis speciebus qualitatis posuit auctor completum <ante incompletum>, sicut habitum ante dispositionem, hic autem e converso ponit incompletum ante completum; est enim forma quid incompletum respectu figurae."

[277] Nicholas of Paris, *Rat. sup. Praed.* VIII, q. 23 (Munich, Bayer. Staatsbibl. 14460, f. 57ra): "Ad aliud dicendum quod figura est terminus formae, quia illa concavitas spatii interiacentis posset extrahi in infinitum sed terminatur et finitur per clausionem linearum, quae figura appellatur. Unde figura est terminus respectu formae. Sed terminus habet poni post terminatum, et hoc respiciens auctor posuit figuram post formam; tamen dico quod figura est completum respectu formae quae est incompletum."

[278] John Pagus, *Rat. sup. Praed.* XXXV, q. 6 (205.9–12).

The view that Pagus rejects here is apparently endorsed by Nicholas of Paris:

> It is to be said that straightness and curvature, which are properties of continuous quantity, are in the genus of quality. Similarly, evenness and oddness, which are properties of discrete quantity, ought to be in the genus of quality, and for this reason he says "perhaps some other manner of quality might come to light."[279]

By contrast, Pagus seems to think that evenness and oddness — if they are in fact qualities — might be considered as a sort of state or disposition of discrete quantity (that is, of numbers):

> If those items are qualities, they belong to the first species.[280]

It appears, then, that according to Pagus the genus of quality divides immediately into four, and only four, highest species.

As in the case of the other categories, Aristotle also gives a list of some properties belonging to qualities: (1) having a contrary, (2) being susceptible to degrees, and (3) being that according to which other things are said to be similar or dissimilar. The third of these properties is distinctive of quality and is to be understood along similar lines to the distinctive property of quantity. Thus, when the objection that this seems to turn similarity, which is actually a relation, into a quality is raised, Pagus replies:

> It is to be said that in so far as "according to" expresses the disposition of the efficient cause, it is a property of quality to be that according to which other things are said to be similar or dissimilar. For quality is the efficient cause of such things (which is clear from Boethius, since "similarity is the same quality in different things"). But when it is objected that "it is according to similarity etc.," this is true in so far as "according to" expresses the disposition of the formal cause and not of the efficient cause. For similarity is the form of what is similar, just as whiteness is the form of what is white. And so, the preposition "according to" is used equivocally.[281]

---

[279] Nicholas of Paris, *Rat. sup. Praed.* VIII, qq. 26–27 (Munich, Bayer. Staatsbibl. 14460, f. 57ra): "Ad aliud dicendum quod rectitudo et curvitas, quae sunt passiones continuae quantitatis, sunt in genere qualitatis. Similiter par et impar, quae sunt passiones <discretae> quantitatis, deberent esse in genere qualitatis. Et propter hoc dicit 'fortasse apparebunt alii modi qualitatis.'"

[280] John Pagus, *Rat. sup. Praed.* XXXV, q. 6 (205.12–13).

[281] John Pagus, *Rat. sup. Praed.* XXXVII, q. 2 (216.14–20).

Similarity, in other words, is a relation founded on quality and quality only, just like equality is a relation founded on quantity and quantity only. Thus, if two items, A and B, are said to be similar, this is ultimately because they are one in quality: there is a pair of instances of a given quality property Q of which one is in A and the other in B, and these are the efficient cause of the relation in the sense that they are the properties on which the relation is founded.

Aristotle's discussion of the categories of quantity, relation, and quality is followed, in chapter 9, by a few stray remarks about the categories of doing and being-affected, to the effect that items belonging to these two categories (1) have a contrary, and (2) are susceptible to degrees. Apart from that, the final six items on the list of categories receives no separate treatment.

According to contemporary scholarship, Aristotle's text must have suffered damage at this point, and subsequently someone — presumably an ancient editor — has inserted the following few lines to try to fill or justify the gap:[282]

> So much, then, is said about these; and about being-in-a-position too it has been remarked, in the discussion of relatives, that it is spoken of denominatively from the positions. About the rest, when and where and having, owing to their obviousness nothing further is said about them than what was said at the beginning, that having is signified by "having-shoes-on," "having-armour-on," where by, for example, "in the Lyceum" — and all the other things that were said about them. About the proposed genera, then, enough has been said.[283]

Unfamiliar with the methods of modern philology, Pagus takes these somewhat dubious remarks to be genuine Aristotle and tries to explain the lack of interest in the final six categories as follows:

> The latter six depend on the initial four with regard to their being, since they come to be from their species, and, thus, the initial four being known, the rest are known as well.[284]

As we saw in section 7, Pagus takes the extrinsic accidents to depend on or flow from the intrinsic ones. However, since he does not think that the final six categories are thereby reducible to the initial four, his interpretation hardly succeeds in completely getting rid of the problem.

---

[282] See, for example, Michael Frede, "The Title, Unity, and Authenticity of the Aristotelian *Categories*," in Frede, *Essays in Ancient Philosophy*, 13–14.

[283] Aristotle, *Categories* 9.11b8–10.11b16 (trans. Ackrill, 31).

[284] John Pagus, *Rat. sup. Praed.* XXXVIII, q. 2. Cf. ibid., I, q. 5.

It is difficult to fault Pagus for failing to make perfect sense of this particular aspect of the *Categories*, but it may, in closing, be pointed out that his way of dealing with the problem is characteristic of a tendency that permeates his entire commentary, namely, the sustained attempt to find some underlying theoretical assumption that can vindicate and make sense of the theses and claims put forth in the *Categories* — no matter how hopeless the possibility might look. In doing so, Pagus often goes well beyond the text, and while the resulting interpretation may on occasion look a bit strained or fail to be convincing, it is in many respects, as has hopefully become clear, certainly not devoid of philosophical interest.

APPENDIX
STYLISTIC COMPARISON OF THE COMMENTARIES IN MS PADUA, BIBLIOTECA UNIVERSITARIA 1589

For the dating of Pagus' commentary on the *Categories* it is a question of considerable importance whether or not the four commentaries found in the Padua manuscript actually constitute a single course on the *ars vetus*, and it is necessary to consider this matter at some length.

Before comparing the commentaries, however, a few things should be noted. First of all, it should be kept in mind that it is highly questionable whether the colophon on f. 172v can be taken to ascribe the full course to Pagus, as has hitherto been assumed. This is important, because this almost illegible note has been the motivation and main reason for thinking that these commentaries constitute a single course, attributable to Pagus.

Second, it should also be remembered that the first two commentaries of the course, namely, the commentary on the *Isagoge* and the commentary on the *Categories*, are incomplete in the Padua manuscript and have been supplied with endings from other commentaries to ensure complete coverage of the base text. The commentary on the *Isagoge* is, however, found in its entirety in another manuscript (MS Vat. lat. 5988, ff. 63r–81v). In other words, if the commentaries in the Padua manuscript do indeed constitute a single course, the course, as it is found here, has suffered some partial damage at some point during the process of transmission.

Third, on the few occasions where the commentaries are found in other manuscripts, they are not found together. The commentary on the *Isagoge* is found alongside Peter of Ireland's commentary on the *Perihermeneias* in MS Vat. lat. 5988, and the commentary on the *Perihermeneias* in found alongside logical commentaries by Gentilis of Cingulo and Durand of Auvergne in MS Palermo, Bibl. Com. 2 Qq. D. 142, ff. 37ra–51va.

In his important preface to the Leonine edition of the *Perihermeneias* commentary of Thomas Aquinas, René A. Gauthier suggested that the unity of the course contained in the Padua manuscript is confirmed by the unity of style of its various parts.[1] In fact, he claims, between the prologue of the commentary on the *Categories* and the prologue of the commentary on the *Perihermeneias* there are literary parallels that confirm that the two commentaries were written by one and the same author. It may, however, be argued that the evidence Gauthier adduces is simply too meagre to sustain the claim, and that there are, in fact, noticeable

---

[1] Gauthier, *Preface*, 65*–66*.

differences between the two passages he cites.[2] Nonetheless, it is worth looking at some of the prevalent stylistic features of the four commentaries in more detail in order to see whether or not they give any grounds for thinking that we are, in fact, dealing with a unitary course on the *ars vetus*. Since all four commentaries are *lectio* commentaries, the obvious way of doing this is by looking at how they apply this format.[3]

The first thing to notice is that the commentaries vary greatly as to the number of *lectiones* they contain, and so, the amount of text that they cover on average in each *lectio* also varies. In its extant form, the commentary on the *Categories* has 45 *lectiones* for the first 12 chapters of Aristotle's text. The commentary on the *Isagoge*, by contrast, has 12 *lectiones* for the whole of Porphyry's text, while the commentary on the *Perihermeneias* has 28 *lectiones* for the whole text, and the commentary on the *Book of Six Principles* has 38.[4] This means that on average the amount of base text covered per *lectio* is as follows for each of the four commentaries.

---

[2] Gauthier, *Preface*, 66*, compares parts of the introductory applications of the fourfold causal scheme in each of the two commentaries. Unfortunately, he does not spell out what exactly he takes the significant parallels to be. Now, since these applications of the fourfold causal scheme are a standard feature of this kind of commentary, the mere fact of their appearance proves little. Furthermore, due to their very nature such applications are often very similar across different authors. Note, however, that there are two noticeable differences between the applications in the two passages Gauthier cites. One, the commentator on the *Perihermeneias* counts three types of final cause (*propinquus, remotus, remotissimus*), whereas the commentator on the *Categories* counts only two (*intra et extra*). Two, the commentator on the *Perihermeneias* counts five types of *forma tractandi* (*definitivus, divisivus, probativus, improbativus, exemplorum positivus*), whereas the commentator on the *Categories* counts only three (*definitivus, divisivus, exemplorum positivus*). These differences are noteworthy, since there seems to be nothing in the texts commented on to account for them.

[3] All of them explicitly use the term *lectio* to refer to the main units of which they are made up; for the commentary on the *Isagoge*, see, for example, Padua, Bibl. Univ. 1589, f. 10va; for the commentary on the *Perihermeneias*, see, for example, ibid., f. 70rb; for the commentary on the *Book of Six Principles*, see, for example, f. 102r.

[4] The number for the commentary on the *Isagoge* is based on MS Vat. lat. 5988, which, in contrast to the Padua manuscript, contains the commentary in its entirety (except for what appears to be a missing or misplaced folio containing the end of Lectio VI and the beginning of Lectio VII).

Commentary	Words covered
Isagoge	ca. 440
Categories	ca. 190
Perihermeneias	ca. 210
Six Principles	ca. 120

Table 7. Average number of words covered per lectio

On average, the commentary on the *Isagoge* covers more than twice as much text per *lectio* as the commentaries on the *Categories* and the *Perihermeneias* and more than three and a half times as much as the commentary on the *Book of Six Principles*. Since there appears to be nothing in the authoritative texts themselves to really motivate these differences, it seems reasonable to consider them as differences in the application of the commentary format in question.

Also, when it comes to the basic makeup of the *lectiones* in each of the four commentaries, there are some noticeable differences, as can be seen in table 8.

	Isagoge	*Categories*	*Perihermeneias*	*Six Principles*
i.	*Divisio*	*Divisio*	*Divisio*	(*Divisio*)
ii.	*Sententia*	*Sententia*	*Sententia*	*Sententia*
iii.	*Notabilia*	*Expositio litteralis*	*Notabilia*	*Quaestiones*
iv.	*Quaestiones*	*Quaestiones*	*Quaestiones*	*Expositio litteralis*
v.	—	—	*Expositio litteralis*	—

Table 8. The basic standard structure of the lectiones

As we can see, the exegetical operations employed are not the same in all cases. The ones found in Pagus' *Categories* commentary have already been described in chapter one, section 2.2. They are: (i) a division of the text (*divisio*), (ii) a paraphrase of the text (*sententia*), (iii) a running gloss on the text (*expositio litteralis*), and (iv) some questions (*quaestiones*). If we compare this to the commentary on the *Isagoge*, we see that the author of this latter commentary does not supply a gloss on the text (*expositio litteralis*), but gives a list of numbered points of note (*notabilia*) instead. The commentary on the *Perihermeneias* also contains such lists of numbered points, but in contrast to the *Isagoge* commentary it also adds a gloss on the text at the end of the *lectio*.[5] Finally, while the commentary on the

---

[5] The sequence of operations given for this commentary in the table is the one most frequently found, but it is a notable feature of this commentary that the author is actually quite lax about the sequence of the final three components of the *lectio* and may on occasion omit one of them. Thus, in two cases the *notabilia* come after the questions and the gloss, and in five cases they are simply left out. In one case, there are no questions. There

Book of Six Principles basically has the same four components as the commentary on the *Categories*, it places the gloss at the end of the *lectio* (as did the commentary on the *Perihermeneias*) rather than before the questions. This commentary also has a clear tendency to divide the text less scrupulously than is the case in the other commentaries, and in more than a third of the *lectiones* it seems to simply leave out the division altogether, something that is not done in any of the other commentaries.

So, the exegetical operations applied in the four commentaries vary to some extent. What is more, even when the same operations are applied, the concomitant terminology is often different. Consider, for example, the section devoted to the division of the text (*divisio*). In several of the commentaries, the end of this section is explicitly signalled by what we may call a terminal formula. Thus, in 40 out of 45 cases this section of Pagus' commentary on the *Categories* ends with the phrase *haec est divisio lectionis*, to which is usually added the number of parts identified in the division, most frequently by the phrase *et sunt particulae* n or *et sunt* n *particulae*. The terminal forms used are found in table 9.

Terminal formula	Occurrences
Haec est divisio lectionis...	
+ *nothing.*	6
+ et sunt particulae *n.*	22
+ et sunt *n* particulae.	9
+ et sunt partes *n.*	1
+ et sunt *n* partes.	1
+ sub qua *n* particulae continentur.	1
Prima cum praecedentibus est praesentis lectionis, et sunt particulae *n.*	1
Ubi praesens lectio terminatur, et sunt particulae *n.*	1
None	3
Total	**45**

Table 9. Divisio. *The* Categories *commentary*

In the *Isagoge* commentary, things are different. Here there is usually no terminal formula, and in the few cases where the end of the division is explicitly signalled, one does not find any of the forms used in the *Categories* commentary.

----

is also a case in which the questions precede the *notabilia* and the gloss, and a case in which the gloss comes before the *notabilia* and the questions. In three *lectiones*, we find the standard structure but with some additional *notabilia* or *notabilia circa litteram* added after the gloss.

Terminal formula	Occurrences
Sunt igitur...	
+ in universo *n* particulae in praesenti littera.	1
+ *n* particulae in hac praesenti littera.	1
Unde in praesenti lectione sunt *n* partes.	1
None	9
Total	**12**

Table 10. Divisio. *The* Isagoge *commentary*

The *Perihermeneias* commentary differs from both of the previous commentaries. In this commentary, the end of the division is explicitly signalled in every one of its 28 *lectiones*. The formula most frequently employed, however, is *haec est sententia lectionis in generali*. To this the term *divisio* may be added in one way or another. When this is the case the formula most frequently reads *haec est divisio et sententia lectionis in generali*.

Terminal formula	Occurrences
Haec est sententia...	
+ in generali.	1
+ lectionis in generali.	17
+ et divisio lectionis in generali.	3
Haec est divisio...	
+ et sententia in generali.	1
+ et sententia lectionis in generali.	5
+ lectionis et sententia in generali.	1
Total	**28**

Table 11. Divisio. *The* Perihermeneias *commentary*

This habit of referring to the division as the *sententia in generali* is known from other commentaries, but among the commentaries contained in the Padua manuscript it is unique to the one on the *Perihermeneias*. Finally, in the commentary on the *Book of Six Principles*, the end of the division is (when a division is actually found) never explicitly signalled.

Similar differences are found with respect to the second of the exegetical operations shared by all four commentaries, the paraphrase (*sententia*). In the *Categories* commentary, the standard way of signalling the end of this section is by means of the formula *haec est sententia partis*, as can be seen in table 12.

Terminal formula	Occurrences
Haec est sententia…	
+ lectionis.	3
+ partis.	35
+ primae partis.	1
Et in hoc terminatur sententia lectionis.	1
Et terminatur sententia lectionis.	1
None	4
Total	**45**

Table 12. Sententia. *The* Categories *commentary*

In the commentary on the *Isagoge*, a wide variety of formulations are employed (see table 13), but one never finds the one that is standard in the commentary on the *Categories*.

Terminal formula	Occurrences
Et haec de *x* dicta sufficiant.	1
Et his habitis terminatur intentio huius partis.	1
Et hoc est processus litterae.	1
Et in his verbis completur intentio praesentis lectionis.	1
Et in hoc…	
+ terminatur…	
+ sententia lectionis.	3
+ capitulum de *x*.	1
+ imponit (auctor) finem dictis et terminatur…	
+ sententia lectionis.	1
+ lectio praesens.	1
+ intentio huius operis.	1
Et sic imponit finem dictis et terminatur tota sententia lectionis.	1
Total	**12**

Table 13. Sententia. *The* Isagoge *commentary*

The use of *intentio* in this context is unique to this commentary among the ones considered here, as is the phrase *imponit finem dictis et terminatur…* There is a small overlap with the commentary on the *Categories*, which contains one occurrence of the formula *et in hoc terminatur sententia lectionis* found here on three occasions, but this formula appears to have been so widespread among commentators that nothing of interest follows from this.

    In the commentary on the *Perihermeneias*, the end of this section is only signalled in half of the *lectiones*.

Terminal formula	Occurrences
Haec est sententia…	
+ lectionis.	2
+ lectionis in generali et (in) speciali.	12
None	14
Total	**28**

Table 14. Sententia. *The* Perihermeneias *commentary*

As can be seen from table 14, on two occasions the commentator uses the formula *haec est sententia lectionis*, which also occurs three times in the *Categories* commentary. Mostly, however, he adds the qualification *in generali et (in) speciali* in accordance with his distinction between *sententia in generali* (division) and *sententia in speciali* (paraphrase). Again, of the commentaries considered here this commentary is the only one to employ this terminology. As was the case with the division, the commentary on the *Book of Six Principles* does not explicitly signal the end of this section.

The next section of the *lectio* as it is structured in the commentary on the *Categories* is the literal exposition or gloss (*expositio litteralis*). As table 15 shows, it is usually simply introduced as such.

Introductory formula	Occurrences
Expositio haec est.	1
Expositio litteralis.	38
Expositio litteralis haec est.	1
Litteralis expositio.	2
Litteralis expositio haec est.	1
Total	**43**

Table 15. Expositio litteralis. *The* Categories *commentary*

As has already been mentioned, this component is absent from the commentary on the *Isagoge*. In the commentary on the *Perihermeneias* it is usually introduced by a different formula.

Introductory formula	Occurrences
Littera sic legatur.	25
Littera sic legatur et exponatur sic.	1
Littera facilis est et exponatur sic.	1
Total	**27**

Table 16. Expositio litteralis. *The* Perihermeneias *commentary*

The commentary on the *Book of Six Principles* consistently employs a similar but different formula:

Introductory formula	Occurrences
Littera sic exponitur.	38
Total	**38**

Table 17. Expositio litteralis. *The* Six Principles *commentary*

Here, the habits of the commentators emerge particularly clearly, and strikingly enough the forms employed never overlap.

The section devoted to questions is also introduced quite differently in each of the four commentaries. In the commentary on the *Categories*, the formulae employed are the following:

Introductory formula	Occurrences
Ad dictorum evidentiam...	
+ duo quaeruntur.	8
+ primo quaeritur...	4
Ad evidentiam dictorum duo quaeruntur.	2
Duo quaeruntur.	1
Hic duo quaeruntur.	1
Primo...	
+ dubitatur...	1
+ quaeritur...	27
Total	**44**

Table 18. Quaestiones. *The* Categories *commentary*

The most frequent way of introducing this section (*primo quaeritur*) is never found in any of the other commentaries. The closest we get is *sed primo quaeritur*, which, as we shall see, occurs twice in the commentary on the *Book of Six Principles*. Nor is the habit of introducing this section with the phrase *ad dictorum evidentiam* found in any of the other commentaries.

In the commentary on the *Isagoge*, there is, as with the other sections in this commentary, a wide variety of formulations (see table 19).

Introductory formula	Occurrences
n quaeruntur hic.	1
Circa hanc lectionem...	
+ incidunt *n* quaerenda.	1
+ quaeruntur *n*.	1
His habitis, circa...	
+ hanc partem...	
+ quaeruntur communia et propria.	1
+ quaeruntur *n*.	1
+ possunt quaeri quaedam communia.	1
+ praesentem lectionem...	
+ possunt quaeri *n*.	2
His suppositis, circa hanc lectionem quaeruntur *n*.	1
Possunt quaeri *n* iuxta intentionem *n* partium praesentis litterae.	1
Total	**10**

Table 19. Quaestiones. *The* Isagoge *commentary*

None of these diverse formulations find an exact parallel in any of the other commentaries.

In the commentary on the *Perihermeneias*, we find the following range of formulae:

Introductory formula	Occurrences
Circa illam lectionem *n* quaeruntur.	1
Quaeritur utrum...	3
Quaestio est...	
+ de...	1
+ utrum...	22
Total	**27**

Table 20. Quaestiones. *The* Perihermeneias *commentary*

As we can see, the prevalent formula here is *quaestio est utrum...* This way of beginning this section never occurs in any of the other commentaries.

Finally, we have the commentary on the *Book of Six Principles.* Here the section is introduced in one of the ways shown in table 21.

Introductory formula	Occurrences
Dubitatur...	3
Dubitatur hic primo...	1
Dubitatur primo...	1
Primo dubitatur...	2
Sed...	
+ dubitari potest...	1
+ dubitatur...	11
+ dubitatur hic...	1
+ dubitatur primo...	4
+ quaeritur...	2
+ primo...	
+ dubitatur...	1
+ quaeritur...	2
His habitis, ...	
+ dubitatur...	3
+ quaeritur...	5
His utique habitis quaeritur...	1
Total	**38**

Table 21. Quaestiones. *The* Six Principles *commentary*

As we can see, this commentator has a habit of opening the section with the conjunction *sed*. This is not done in any of the other commentaries. The use of *his habitis* in this context was also found in the *Isagoge* commentary, but there it is always followed by a determination beginning with *circa...*, which is never the case here.

The differences in formulation between the commentaries in the question section to some extent reflect differences in the way the commentators structure this section. As has been pointed out by David Piché, the question section in the commentary on the *Isagoge* reaches a degree of complexity which in many ways is closer to what one finds in question commentaries from the latter half of the thirteenth century than to what is found in *lectio* commentaries from the first half of the century.[6] Interestingly enough, this is a feature that is unique to this commentary among those contained in the Padua manuscript. Figure 9 shows an example from Lectio IV of the commentary.

---

[6] Piché, *Problème des universaux*, 134–35.

His suppositis, circa litteram quaeruntur quinque.
  Q1. Prima quidem quaestio est...
  Q2. Secunda quaestio est...
  Q3. Tertia quaestio est...
  Q4. Quarta quaestio est...
  Q5. Quinta et ultima quaestio est...

Q1. Circa primam sic proceditur.
  A. Et videtur quod...
    1. Videtur enim quod...
    2. Item...
    3. Ad idem est tertia ratio...
  B. Huius gratia quaeruntur quattuor quaestiones.
    1. Prima quaestio est...
    2. Secunda quaestio est...
    3. Tertia quaestio est...
    4. Quarta quaestio est...
  A. Ad quaestionem principalem dicendum est quod...
    1. Ad illud quod instas...
    2. Ad illud quod dicit...
    3. Ad aliud dicendum quod...
  B.
    1. Ad quaestionem dicendum quod...
    2. Ad secundam quaestionem dicendum quod...
    3. Ad tertiam quaestionem iam responsum est...
    4. Ad quartam quaestionem dicendum est quod...

Q2. Circa secundum quaeritur....

(...)

Figure 9. Quaestiones. *Example from the* Isagoge *commentary (ff. 13vb–14rb)*

As we can see, the commentator begins here, as he usually does, by listing the main questions to be addressed in the section. Then, the first question is raised and a number of objections to this question stated. In this case, four corollary questions are then asked. Next, the principal question is determined, the objections refuted and the corollary questions answered in turn. Subsequently, the commentator moves on to the second main question on his initial list. Quite apart from the length and complexity which questions sometimes reach in this commentary, the procedure of giving an initial list of questions to be raised is a unique feature of this commentary among the ones considered here.

In the commentary on the *Categories*, the question section consists usually of a series of alternating questions and answers, which may or may not be numbered. In about a third of the cases, these questions are initially divided into two main groups on the basis of various criteria, such as, for example, whether they concern the first or second half of the text, or whether they concern general philosophical points or purely exegetical matters. In these cases, the structure of the section becomes slightly more elaborate than usual in that the section is divided into two main parts. Figure 10 contains an example from the first *lectio*.

Ad dictorum evidentiam duo quaeruntur.
    I. Primum de quibusdam communibus.
    II. Secundum de dictis in littera.
I.
    Q1. Primum est an...
        a. Quod non videtur...
        b. Item...
        c. Item...
        a. Ad primum dicendum quod...
        b. Ad aliud...
        c. Ad ultimum dicendum quod...
(...)
    Q6. Sexto quaeritur quare...
        Dicendum quod...
        Aliter dicitur communiter quod...

II. Consequenter quaeritur de secundo.
    Q1. Et primo quare...
        Et dicendum quod...
(...)
    Q4. Consequenter quaeritur...
    Q5. Ultimo videtur...
        Ad ultimum dicendum quod...
        Ad aliud dicendum quod...

Figure 10. Quaestiones. *Example from the* Categories *commentary (ff. 24rb–25ra)*

Turning now to the commentary on the *Perihermeneias*. The question sections in this commentary are quite simple in terms of structure. The reason for this is that usually only one question is raised in each *lectio*. Figure 11 gives an example from Lectio x on the first book.

Q1. Quaestio est utrum... Et videtur quod non...
      1. Item...
      2. Item...
      3. Item...
      4. Item...
      5. Item...
   Ad quaestionem dicendum est quod...
    Ad argumenta.
      1. Respondeo ad primum quod...
      2. Ad secundum dicendum quod...
      3. Ad tertium dicendum quod...
      4. Ad quartum dicendum quod...
      5. Ad quintum dicendum quod...

Figure 11. Quaestiones. *Example from the* Perihermeneias *commentary (ff. 79rb–va)*

The one question raised is usually quite lengthy. It is raised without further ado and followed by a series of arguments to the negative (and sometimes also some further arguments to the affirmative). The question is then determined and the objections refuted one by one. On a few occasions, one or two short questions *circa litteram* are added after the main question has been determined and the objections refuted. Still, the number of questions in this commentary is remarkably small compared to the other commentaries.

Finally, there is the commentary on the *Book of Six Principles*. In this commentary, the question section is simply a (sometimes quite long) list of alternating questions and answers. The questions are not usually numbered, and there is never an initial list of the questions to be addressed as there is in the commentary on the *Isagoge*, nor is there any attempt to structure the section in the way it is sometimes done in the commentary on the *Categories*. Figure 12 shows the structure of the questions in Lectio VIII.

Q1. Sed dubitatur hic,
    quoniam...
    Item...
   Propter hoc quidam dicunt quod ..., sed dicimus quod...
    Responderi potest ergo ad praeobiecta in hunc modum, dicendo quod...
      Et si obiciatur quoniam...,
      dicendum quoniam...
      Potest dici aliter quod...
    Ad illud quod obicitur..., solutio patet per primam responsionem, quoniam...

Q2. Item. Videtur quod...
   Ad hoc dicendum est quod...

Q3. Item. Dicit auctor quod...
    Ad hoc dicendum quod...
    Potest tamen dici aliter quoniam...

Q4. Item. Quaeritur...
      Et videtur quod...
    Ad hoc dicendum quod...

Q5. Item. Videtur quod...
    Ad hoc potest dici quod...
    Potest tamen dici quod...

Q6. Item. Quaeritur...
    Ad quod posset dici quod...
    Potest autem dici aliter...

Q7. Sed dubitatur...
      Item.
    Et hoc quidem verum est,...

Figure 12. Quaestiones. *Example from the* Six Principles *commentary (ff. 108v–9v)*

One very prevalent feature of this commentary is that the author has a strong habit of offering two or three alternative solutions to a question (as can be seen in questions 1, 3, 5, and 6 in this particular example). This, of course, happens in the other commentaries as well, but never as frequently as is the case here.

As should now be abundantly clear, across the four commentaries contained in the Padua manuscript there are very clear differences in the application of the *lectio* format. These differences occur not only with respect to the nature, number, and order of the components of the *lectiones*, but also with respect to the concomitant terminology and formulae, and with regard to the structure and complexity of the section devoted to questions. There is, in other words, a definite diversity of style between all of these commentaries, and Gauthier's preliminary suggestion that because of their apparent unity of style they should be taken to constitute a single course on the *ars vetus* may safely be rejected.

Part Two
Edition

CHAPTER THREE
EDITOR'S PREFACE

1. RATIO EDENDI

The edition is based on a transcription made from black and white prints from a microfilm copy of MS Padua, Biblioteca Universitaria 1589 [*P*]. In cases of doubt, the manuscript was consulted in situ. Although the manuscript is in fairly good condition and the hand quite legible, the actual text is replete with errors of textual transmission. The sections containing the divisions of Aristotle's text especially have suffered many omissions by homoioteleuton due to the repetitive language in which they are formulated. Fortunately, in these cases, it has often been possible to reconstruct with some certainty the text that has been lost on the basis of the exposition (*sententia*) and literal exposition (*expositio litteralis*) of the same piece of text.

A fragment containing excerpts of the first four *lectiones* is found in MS Florence, Biblioteca Laurentiana Gadd. Plut. 89 Sup. 76 [*F*]. A full collation of this material was made from a microfilm copy of the manuscript, and all variants have been recorded in the critical apparatus. There would appear to be errors that are common to the two witnesses as well as errors that are peculiar to each of them. On occasion, the reading offered by *F* has been preferred to that of *P*.

The orthography has been standardized and mostly reflects that of Lewis and Short's *A Latin Dictionary*. This has been done on the assumption that it heightens legibility for readers who are not philologists and implies no judgement on the editor's part about the orthographical habits of the author.

I have imposed my own punctuation and paragraphing. The paragraphing is as a rule more fine grained than that of the manuscript, in which red *pieds-de-mouche* are used to this end. The sectioning into *lectiones* mirrors that of the manuscript, in which each new *lectio* is signalled by the opening words of the initial lemma of the part of Aristotle's text dealt with, written in letters larger than those of the body of the text, and with some occasional flourishing to the initial letter or the *pied-de-mouche* preceding it. The subsectioning into *divisio*, *sententia*, and *quaestiones* found in the edition is not distinguished from ordinary paragraphing in the manuscript.

Devices not found in the manuscript but introduced by the editor to help the reader see the structure of the text have been set in either **boldface** or <pointed brackets>. These include headings and numbering at different levels. The headings and subheadings supplied are based on the author's use. Since he frequently employs the term *lectio* to refer to the actual lecture, this term is used as a heading for these maximal units. As he mostly employs the terms *divisio* and *sententia* to refer to these parts of the lecture, they are used as subheadings. The gloss usually begins with the formula *expositio litteralis*, and this has been used as a subheading for this section. The term *quaestiones* was chosen for the fourth section due to the preponderance of the verb *quaeritur* is this section. Line numbers that restart with each page have been added to make for easy and precise referencing.

Italics are used to indicate Aristotelian lemmata. The manuscript uses <u>underlining</u> to mark out lemmata occurring in the running text. Its use of this device, however, is so faulty that it cannot be used as a guide as to what should be considered a lemma and what a gloss, often underlining what is clearly a gloss instead of what is the lemma. The technique of abbreviating words occurring in lemmata down to their initial letter is not employed in the manuscript. As far as can be gauged from the lemmata, the Latin translation used belongs to the French-Italian (*CsCh*) tradition of the *Editio composita* edited by L. Minio-Paluello in *Aristoteles Latinus* 1.2, with some readings from the *Translatio Boethii* incorporated. I have supplied all lemmata with a standard reference to Aristotle's text, that is, with a chapter number followed by column and line number of the Bekker edition of Aristotle.

2. SIGLA ET COMPENDIA

P	Padua, Biblioteca Universitaria 1589, ff. 24ra–67vb
F	Florence, Biblioteca Laurentiana Gadd. Plut. 89 Sup. 76, ff. 2ra–3rb
a	Aristoteles, *Categoriae* (translatio Boethii), ed. L. Minio-Paluello.
c	Aristoteles, *Categoriae* (editio composita), ed. L. Minio-Paluello.
a$_X$	$_x$ = codex cuius lectio memoratur in apparatu editionis **a**.
c$_Y$	$_Y$ = codex cuius lectio memoratur in apparatu editionis **c**.

[album]	*album* delendum censeo
\<album\>	*album* addendum censeo
†album†	*album* corruptum censeo
< * * * >	lacunam statuendam censeo
(...)	vox quam vel litterae quas legere nequivi

a.c.	ante correcturam
add.	addidit, addiderunt
al. man.	alia manus
comp.	compendium
coni.	coniecit
canc.	cancellavit
corr.	correxit
exp.	expunxit
in marg.	in margine
in ras.	in rasura
inser.	inseruit
inv.	invertit, inverterunt
iter.	iteravit, iteraverunt
om.	omisit, omiserunt
p.c.	post correcturam
s.l.	supra lineam
transp.	transposuit, transposuerunt
ut v.	ut videtur
!	sic
inf	infra
sup	supra

CHAPTER FOUR
JOHN PAGUS: *RATIONES SUPER PRAEDICAMENTA ARISTOTELIS*

Lectio I

\<Prooemium\>

"Ars imitatur naturam in quantum potest", scribitur in secundo *Physicorum*. Secundum igitur triplicem unitatem in rebus repertam triplex est unitas in sermone. Est enim unitas in rebus per indivisionem, ut in angelis. Alia est unitas ex unione materiae cum forma, ut est in rebus compositis, ut in elementatis. Tertia est quae attenditur penes ordinem et causalitatem, et sic partes mundi habent unitatem; ordinantur enim, et una causat aliam.

Huic triplici unioni correspondet triplex unitas in sermone. Unitati primae, quae est in rebus simplicibus, correspondet terminus; terminus enim habet unitatem per indivisionem, cum logicus ultra terminum non dividat. Item est secunda unitas in sermone, quae respondet secundae unitati in rebus, et haec unitas est in enuntiatione; enuntiatio enim componitur ex nomine et verbo sicut ex materia et forma; et haec unitas correspondet unitati quae est in compositis ex materia et forma, sicut in elementatis. Et est tertia unitas in sermone quae attenditur penes ordinem et causalitatem, et haec unitas est in syllogismo; est enim causalitas et ordo praemissarum ad conclusionem; et haec unitas respondet unitati universi.

Ex praedictis ergo patet divisio rationalis philosophiae quae logica appellatur. Nam quantum ad primam unitatem accipitur *Liber praedicamentorum*, ubi determinatur de incomplexo, quod habet unitatem per indivisibilitatem. Quantum ad secundam accipitur *Liber perihermeneias*, in quo determinatur de enuntiatione, quae habet unitatem per compositionem formae cum materia. Secundum tertiam unitatem accipiuntur alii libri in quibus de syllogismo determinatur, in quo est unitas per causalitatem et ordinem. Aliis autem omissis de *Libro praedicamentorum* intendimus, et quia scire est causam rei cognoscere, ad cognitionem causarum accedamus.

Causa materialis est dicibile incomplexum, et dicitur dicibile incomplexum ordinabile in genere vel ordinatum. Causa finalis duplex est, intra et extra. Intra ut

---

1 Arist. *Phys.* II 2.194a21–22, *ut apud* Anon. *Auct. Arist.* 2.60 (ed. Hamesse, 145)   **25–26**   *cf.* Nicolaus Parisiensis *Rat. sup. Praed.* I (Munich, Bayer. Staatsbibl. 14460, f. 42ra; 43vb)

---

2 est¹] *om.* F   **2** sermone] forma P   **3** enim] *om.* F   **3** in rebus] *om.* P   **3** alia est] est enim F   **3–4** unione...forma] unitate formae cum materia F   **4** ut¹] et haec unio F   **4** elementatis] elementis F P a.c.   **7–8** unitati...terminus¹] sermo enim incomplexus qui est terminus correspondet unitati primae quae est in rebus simplicibus F   **9** indivisionem] indivisibilitatem F   **10** est] *om.* F   **11** et¹] a P a.c.   **12** correspondet] respondet secundae F   **13** et] *om.* F   **13–14** ordinem] ordinis F   **14** ordo] ordinatio F   **15** praemissarum] praemissorum F   **15** ad] in F ut v.   **16** divisio] dictio F   **17** quantum ad] *add.* P *in marg.* : secundum F   **20** per compositionem] ex compositione F   **21** accipiuntur] accipitur P   **21** determinatur] agitur F   **21** quo] syllogismo *add.* F   **22** autem] *om.* F   **23** scire] *om.* F   **26** duplex est] *inv.* F

perlecto libro quae sunt utilia memoriae commendemus, extra ut ad totam logi-
cam, quia per hunc librum cognoscitur quae a quibus removentur et quae de quibus praedicantur. Efficiens fuit Aristoteles tradens hanc doctrinam. Titulus: *Incipiunt categoriae Aristotelis*, id est praedicamenta. Forma in duobus consistit, in
forma tractatus et forma tractandi. Forma tractandi est modus agendi, et est defi-   5
nitivus, divisivus et exemplorum positivus. Forma tractatus consistit in divisione
capitulorum et ordine. Ad cuius evidentiam ad libri divisionem accedamus.

\<Divisio\>

Iste liber dividitur in partes tres. In quarum prima determinat de principiis ipsius
dicibilis, id est de antepraedicamentis, in secunda de his per quae dicibile recipit divisionem, id est de praedicamentis, in tertia de consequentibus ipsius dici-   10
bilis, id est de postpraedicamentis. Secunda incipit: *Eorum quae secundum nullam
complexionem* (4.1b25), tertia ibi: *Quotiens autem* (10.11b16).

Prima in duas. Primo determinat principia ipsius dicibilis in se, secundo determinat principia ipsius secundum actualem ordinationem unius dicibilis ad alterum,
ut ibi: *Quando alterum* (3.1b10).   15

Prima habet tres. Primo determinat quae et quot sunt partes dicibilis, secundo
determinat naturam totius in partibus illis prout illud totum est de consideratione
f. 24rb   ipsius, tertio de|terminat naturam partium inter se prout sunt de consideratione
ipsius. Secunda ibi: *Eorum quae dicuntur* (2.1a16), tertia ibi: *Eorum quae sunt*
(2.1a20).   20

Prima in tres secundum tres partes dicibilis quas determinat. Dicibile enim aut
est in genere aut extra genus. Si extra genus, sic sunt dicibilia unum et ens, et sic est
aequivocum. Si in genere—et sic est dupliciter—aut sunt dicibilia de alio existente
in eodem genere, et sic univocum, aut de alio existente in alio genere, et sic denominativum. Primo ergo determinat de aequivocis, secundo de univocis, ibi: *Univoca*   25
(1.1a7), tertio de denominativis, ibi: *Denominativa* (1.1a13).

---

1 extra] enim *add. F ut v.*   1 ad] *om. F*   1 totam] tota *P*   2 per] *om. F*   2 cognoscitur]
cognoscuntur *F ut v.*   3 fuit] est *F*   4 id est] in *P*   4 forma] et forma *F ut v.*   5 forma³] et
forma *F ut v.*   6 positivus] expositivus *F*   8 partes tres] *inv. F*   9 id est] vel *F*   9 de his]
divisivis *F ut v.*   10 in tertia] tertio *F*   10–11 dicibilis] in suis partibus *add. F*   11 secunda]
om. F   12 tertia] secunda *F*   12 autem] solet opponi *add. F*   13–14 determinat principia
ipsius secundum] *om. P*   14 unius dicibilis ad alterum] ipsius dicibilis ad alterum *P* : ad alterum
dicibilis *F ut v.*   15 alterum] de altero *add. F*   16 habet tres] dividitur in tres *F*   16 dicibilis]
dicibiles *P* : declinabiles *F*   19 secunda] incipit *add. F*   19 ibi²] *om. F*   21 secundum] *om.*
P   21 dicibilis] dicibiles *P* : declinabiles *F*   21 dicibile] dicibilis *F*   22 dicibilia] declinabilia *F*
22 est²] *om. F*   23 si in genere et sic est] sed in genere *F*   25 ergo] *om. F*   25 aequivocis]
aequivoco *F*   25 univocis] univoco *F*   25–26 ibi univoca...denominativa] tertio de denominativo
secunda incipit univoca sunt tertia denominativa *F*   26 de denominativis] de nominativis *P*

Prima est praesentis lectionis et dividitur in partes duas. Primo definit aequivocum, secundo definitionem explanat per exempla, ibi: *ut animal homo* (1.1a2).

Secunda in duas. Primo ponit exempla, secundo ostendit exempla posita esse
competentia adaptando ea definitioni positae, ibi: *Quorum enim* (1.1a3).

<Sententia>

5   Circa primam sic procedit: Illa *dicuntur aequivoca*, id est res aequivocatae, *quorum*,
id est quarum rerum, *nomen*, supple secundum materiam, *commune est solum*, *se-*
cundum nomen vero ratio, id est definitio, *substantiae*, id est rei quae sub est, est
diversa.

Consequenter manifestat per exempla: *ut animal homo*, id est quod est homo,
10   *et quod pingitur*.

Consequenter ostendit exempla esse competentia: Bene dixi "animal homo et
quod pingitur", *enim*, pro quia, *solum nomen*, scilicet "animal", *est commune*, *vero*,
pro sed, *ratio*, id est definitio, *substantiae*, id est rei quae sub est, est *diversa se-*
cundum nomen. Bene dico "est diversa", quia *si quis assignet quod est utrumque*
15   *eorum*, id est animal quod est homo et quod pingitur, *quo*, id est in quantum, *sunt*
animalia, utrique *assignabit propriam rationem*, id est definitionem, *utriusque*.

Haec est sententia primae partis.

<Quaestiones>

Ad dictorum evidentiam duo quaeruntur. Primum de quibusdam communibus,
secundum de dictis in littera.

<1>

20   Primum est an de primis generibus possit esse scientia.

Quod non videtur. Omnis virtus naturaliter ordinatur ad obiectum; quod patet
inducendo. Et illa obiecti apprehensio est naturalis. Ergo virtus intellectiva naturaliter ordinatur ad apprehensionem primi obiecti. Sed decem prima genera sunt

---

1 est praesentis] *inv. F*   1 partes] *om. F*   2 definitionem explanat] *inv. F*   3 secunda] haec
secunda *F*   6 commune est] *inv. F*   6–7 secundum nomen vero] vero id est sed *F*   7 rei] res
P   7 sub est] est sub *P*   8 diversa] secundum idem nomen *add. F*   9 est homo] *inv. F*   10 et]
animal *add. F*   11 consequenter ostendit] *iter. F a.c. ut v.*   11 esse] *om. P*   12 pro] id est
F   12 quia] *iter. P*   12 scilicet] id est *F*   13 pro] id est *F*   13 id est rei quae sub est] *om.*
P   14 diversa] enim id est quia quod *add. F ut v.*   14 quis] id est aliquis *add. F*   14 assignet
quod est] assignat quid sit *F*   15 eorum] horum *F*   15 animal] animalis *F*   16 utrique] *om. F*
17 primae] *om. F*   11.18–12.5 ad dictorum...scientia] *om. F*

obiecta virtutis intellectivae, cum sint universalia, et universale est dum intelligitur, ut dicit Boethius. Ergo naturaliter ordinatur ad eorum apprehensionem. Non est ergo ars necessaria per quam dirigatur intellectus in eorum apprehensionem. Sed si sic, eorum erit superflua. Sed non est ponere artem superfluam. Ergo de ipsis non est scientia.

Item. "Scire est causam rei cognoscere", scribitur in primo *Posteriorum*. Solum ergo illorum est scientia quorum acceptio per causam est possibilis. Sed primorum decem generum non est possibilis acceptio per causam, cum sunt prima. Ergo de ipsis non est scientia.

Item. "In omni eo supra quod fundatur scientia est reperire statum", ut probatur in primo *Posteriorum*. In decem generibus non est status. Ergo de ipsis non est scientia. Minor patet, quia status est ad unum et non ad plura, et prima decem genera non sunt unum sed multa.

Ad primum dicendum quod non est ars necessaria per quam dirigatur intellectus in apprehensionem decem primorum generum, ut obicitur. Sed quia illam apprehensionem sequitur triplex operatio et in hoc intellectus errare poterat, ideo datae sunt tres partes formales logicae per quas reformatur intellectus in illam triplicem operationem. Quod ad istam apprehensionem sequitur triplex operatio | patet, quia ratio ordinat apprehensa, ordinata componit vel dividit et ex compositis vel divisis colligit aliud compositum vel divisum. Dicendum ergo quod haec doctrina non est dirigens intellectum in apprehensionem primorum decem generum, sed est dirigens ipsum quantum ad primam operationem, quae est ordinare; docet enim ordinare res unius generis in suo genere.

Ad aliud. Prima genera decem habent principia ex quibus componuntur, scilicet materiam et formam (et probat Aristoteles in *Metaphysica* quod habent principia supra se), et ideo possibilis est eorum acceptio per causas. Ad illud quod obicitur quod sunt prima est dicendum quod primum dicitur aut supra quod nihil, et sic non sunt prima, aut post quod aliud sequitur, et sic sunt prima. Vel aliter. Prima sunt respectu rerum compositarum et non respectu suorum principiorum.

f. 24va

1–2 Boeth. *Consol.* V 6.36, *ut apud* Anon. *Auct. Arist.* 25.89 (ed. Hamesse, 294) 6 Arist. *APo* I 2.71b10–12, *ut apud* Anon. *Auct. Arist.* 35.8 (ed. Hamesse, 311) 10–11 Arist. *APo* I 3.72b19–24 25–26 *cf.* Arist. *Metaph.* XII 4.1070b10–22; Averroes *in Metaph.* XII 22 (ed. Venet., 307vb)

3 sed] *lectio incerta* 7 causam] causas *P* 7 primorum] praedicamentum *F* 8 est possibilis] est *P* : possibilis *F* 9 ipsis] his *F* 10 ut probatur] *om. P* 11 ipsis] his *F* 11 est²] potest esse *F* 12 plura] multa *P* 14–23 ad...genere] *om. F* 17 tres] duae *P* 18 quod] quo *P* 18 triplex operatio] *iter. P* 24 aliud] primum dicendum est *F* : *om. P* 24 prima] primam *P* 24 genera] *om. P* 24 componuntur] exponuntur *P* 25 materiam] materia *P* 25 formam] forma *P* 25 et²] quod *F* 25 quod] quia *F ut v.* 26 et ideo] *om. F* 27 dicitur aut supra] est duplex ante *F* 28 aut] vel *F* 28 et] *om. F* 28 prima] supra *F* 29 prima sunt] *inv. F* 29 et] *om. F*

Ad ultimum dicendum quod haec scientia non est de decem praedicamentis, sed de dicibili incomplexo.

<2>

Secundo quaeritur an sit scientia una.

Quod non videtur. "Una scientia est cuius est unum genus subiectum", scribitur in primo *Posteriorum*. Sed decem genera non sunt unum sed multa. Ergo non est scientia una.

Item. Plus differunt duo genera ex opposito divisa quam duae species sub eodem genere existentes. Sed diversitas duarum specierum sub eodem genere existentium facit diversitatem in scientia. Ergo de istis non potest esse scientia una. Minor patet, quia geometria est de quantitate continua, arithmetica de discreta.

Ad primum. Haec scientia est una, quia non est de decem generibus ut de subiecto, sed de dicibili, quod est subiectum unum; est autem de his tanquam de partibus subiecti, cum dicibile dividatur per ista.

Ad secundum dicendum quod non est simile, quia mathematicus considerat continuum et discretum prout causantur ex diversis principiis (punctus enim est principium quantitatis continuae, unitas autem discretae), et quia habent principia diversa, diversas faciunt scientias. Sed rationalis philosophus considerat decem praedicamenta in quantum reducuntur ad unum principium, scilicet ad dicibile, et quia habent principium unum, potest esse scientia una.

<3>

Tertio videtur quod non spectet ad rationalem philosophum determinare de his.

Sermocinalis enim scientia est illa cuius subiectum est sermo vel pars sermonis. Decem autem prima genera non sunt sermo nec pars sermonis sed res. Ergo de his non potest esse scientia sermocinalis.

Item. Subiectum est in scientia cuius passiones in illa scientia inquiruntur. Sed in hac scientia non inquiruntur passiones sermonis sed rei. Ergo etc. Minor patet, quia suscipere contraria <et> magis et minus rei conveniunt, non sermoni.

Ad primum dicendum quod haec scientia non est de decem praedicamentis prout sunt res, sed prout sunt dicibilia. Sed quia dicibile in quantum tale cadit sub sermone, ideo rationalis philosophus de his pertractare potest.

4–5   Arist. *APo* I 28.87a38

---

3 scientia una] *inv. F*   4 scientia est] *inv. F*   5 unum] una *P*   7–10 item…discreta] *om. F*   8 diversitas] diversas *P*   10 quia] quod *P*   11 ad primum haec] responsio *F*   12 dicibili] incomplexo *add. F*   12 est²] *in marg. F*   13.14–16.10 ad secundum…imaginatum] *om. F*   24 subiectum] *iter. P*   26 quia] quod *P*

Ad secundum dicendum quod Aristoteles intendit hic de his in quantum per sermonem significantur, et sic sunt dicibilia. Unde decem genera possunt | dupliciter considerari: aut prout sunt res tantum aut prout sunt res sumptae sub vocibus vel significatae per voces. Propter hoc quaedam passiones probantur de his prout sunt res tantum, ut esse susceptibile contrariorum, quaedam prout sunt res sumptae   5 sub vocibus.

<4–5>

Quarto quaeritur quo modo differat haec doctrina a doctrina *Sex principiorum.*
  Quinto quaeritur <quare> hic tantum determinat de quattuor, ibi de sex.
  Ad primum. Hic determinat de ipsis secundum esse et essentiam quam habent in linea praedicamentali, unde determinat hic de his in quantum dicibilia, ibi autem   10 in quantum principia; et dicuntur principia in quantum veniunt ad constitutionem inferiorum, id est in quantum definitiva.
  Per dicta patet ad aliud, quoniam hic determinat de decem generibus <secundum> esse et essentiam quam habent in linea praedicamentali, et quia illa sex dependent ab istis quantum ad esse et oriuntur a specie eorum, cognitis principiis   15 cognoscuntur et alia per consequens.

<6>

Sexto quaeritur quare de illis sex in quantum principia est liber separatus potius quam de aliis, cum similiter illa sint principia.
  Dicendum quod illa significant formam extrinsecus advenientem, ista autem intrinsecus, et quia principium potius dicit rem extra, illa sunt in ratione principii   20 potius quam haec.
  Aliter dicitur communiter quod illa principia quattuor non sunt fundata supra res quantum ad quandam sui partem; excedunt enim res naturales, nam recipiuntur in rebus naturalibus <et in rebus non naturalibus>. Sed ista sex definitiva fundata sunt supra res vel supra principia naturalia, et ideo sunt principia secundum rem et   25 rationem <et> communicant materiam, quod non faciunt illa.

<7>

Consequenter quaeritur de secundo. Et primo quare non determinat hic de forma ut in *Libro sex principiorum* cum ista sint formae sicut et illa.

---

28 Anon. *LSP* I 1–15 (ed. Minio-Paluello, 35–38)

---

7 a] ad *P*

Et dicendum quod licet substantia, quantitas et alia dicantur formae loquendo communiter, non tamen ita proprie sicut illa de quibus agit in *Sex principiis*. Dicitur enim forma accepta proprie quasi foris manens, et ideo cum qualitas et quantitas intrinsecus adveniant, illa autem de quibus agit in *Sex principiis* extrinsecus, ideo illa dicuntur potius formae quam ista, et ideo de forma illic determinat et non hic.

<8>

Secundo quaeritur quare dicit "aequivoca" in plurali numero.

Solutio. Duplex dicitur aequivocum, scilicet aequivocans et aequivocatum. Hic definit aequivocatum in relatione ad aequivocans, et quia aequivocata sunt plura, dicitur "aequivoca" in plurali. Aequivocum dicitur ipsum nomen, aequivocata sunt res significatae.

<9>

Tertio quaeritur de eo quod dicit quod aequivoca habent nomen commune.

Contra. Differt nomen a voce, quia nomen est compositum ex voce et intellectu iuxta illud Aristotelis: "Nomen est vox significativa". Illa ergo quae communicant in voce sola non conveniunt in nomine. Sed sic se habent aequivoca. Ergo non conveniunt in | nomine.   f. 25ra

Et dicendum quod nomen dupliciter accipitur. Secundum speciem et secundum materiam. Nomen secundum materiam est vox, secundum speciem est vox coniuncta intellectui, et cum dicitur "nomen est commune", intelligendum est de nomine materia. Unde non est inconveniens unum nomen secundum materiam esse diversorum secundum speciem.

<10−11>

Consequenter quaeritur quare "animal" non aequivocatur ad animal verum et ad animal imaginatum sicut ad animal verum et ad animal pictum.

Ultimo videtur "animal" non esse aequivocum ad animal verum et ad animal pictum propter hoc quod natura animalis non convenit animali picto.

Ad ultimum dicendum quod nomen animalis est impositum picturae animalis secundum quod plures possunt comprehendere ipsum, et quia plures apprehen-

---

13   Arist. *Int.* 2.16a19−20

---

8 aequivocata] aequivoca *P*   **9** aequivocata sunt] aequivocans *P*   **10** significatae] signatae *P*
18 coniuncta] in *add. P*

dunt animal per figuram sensibilem picturae, erit "animal" aequivocum ad animal pictum et ad animal verum secundum quod plures eo utuntur et non secundum quod sapientes.

Ad aliud dicendum quod non aequivocatur "animal" ad animal verum et imaginatum sicut ad verum et pictum, et causa est quod animal pictum est species et res 5 sicut animal verum, sed quod est in anima species est tantum.

Item, animal pictum est similitudo animalis ex parte sensibilis figurae in ipso <per> quam plures comprehendunt animal, et utuntur nomine animalis quantum ad specialem materiam secundum quam non est nomen positum quo plures utantur. Et ideo non est aequivocum ad animal verum et ad animal imaginatum. 10

---

1 picturae] *lectio incerta*

Uɴɪᴠᴏᴄᴀ ᴅɪᴄᴜɴᴛᴜʀ ᴇᴛᴄ. (1.1a7)

<Dɪᴠɪsɪᴏ>

Determinato de aequivocis, determinat de univocis.

Et dividitur ista pars in duas. In prima definit univoca, in secunda subiungit exempla, ibi: *ut <animal> homo et bos* (1.1a8).

Secunda in duas. Primo ponit exempla, secundo ostendit exempla posita esse
5   competentia, ibi: *Si quis assignet* (1.1a11).

Haec est divisio lectionis.

<Sᴇɴᴛᴇɴᴛɪᴀ>

Circa primam partem sic procedit: Illa *dicuntur univoca*, scilicet nomina, *quorum* nominum secundum speciem *nomen est commune* secundum materiam, *ratio* vero *substantiae*, id est rei quae sub est, *eadem* est secundum nomen.

10   Consequenter manifestat per exempla: *ut animal homo* et *bos*, quia homo et bos univocantur in hoc nomine "animal". Et hoc est quod sequitur: *enim*, id est quia, *utraque*, id est homo et bos, *nuncupantur animalia communi nomine*, et non aequivoce scilicet, *et ratio substantiae eadem est*.

Consequenter ostendit exempla posita esse competentia: Ita bene dixi quod ra-
15   tio et nomen animalis sunt communia, quia *si quis assignet rationem*, id est defini-tionem, *utriusque*, dicens *quid sit utrumque quo*, id est in quantum, *sunt animalia*, *eandem assignabit rationem* animalis.

Haec est sententia partis.

<Qᴜᴀᴇsᴛɪᴏɴᴇs>

Ad dictorum evidentiam duo quaeruntur, primum de dictis in littera, secundum de
20   quibusdam communibus.

---

1 determinat] prosequitur *F*   **2** ista pars] *om. F*   **3** ibi ut] *inv. F*   **4** secunda] haec secunda *F*   **4** exempla] *om. P*   **4–5** esse competentia] *inv. F*   **5** ibi] ut ibi *F*   **5** quis] enim *add. F*   **7** dicuntur] esse *add. P*   **8** ratio vero] et ratio *F*   **9** est³] *om. F*   **10** exempla] hoc dicens *add. F*   **10** ut…bos] homo animal et bos animal *F*   **11–12** univocantur…bos] *om. P*   **13** est] *om. F*   **14** ita] contra *F*   **15** communia] enim *add. F*   **15** quis] id est aliquis *F*   **16** dicens] dicentem *F*   **16** id] *om. F*   **17** rationem] scilicet definitionem *add. F*   **19–20** ad…communibus] quaestio quaeritur de dictis in littera *F*

<1>

De primo. Dicit quod homini et bovi est unum nomen commune, scilicet "animal".

    Contra. "Omne nomen est a forma", ut scribitur in primo *Metaphysicae*. Er-
go diversum erit nomen a diversitate formae. Ergo genus secundum quod sumitur
sub diversis formis vel sub diversis differentiis nomen | diversum habebit. Sed non
potest esse genus sub diversis speciebus nisi prius sit sub diversis et oppositis dif-   5
ferentiis per quas contrahitur in species, et quod est sub differentiis oppositis non
habet nomen commune sed diversum. Ergo secundum quod est sub diversis speciebus non habebit nomen commune. Ergo hoc nomen "animal" non est nomen
commune bovi et homini.

    Et dicendum quod nomen generis potest esse commune speciebus.   10

    Ad obiectum dicendum quod duplex est forma, scilicet specialis et generalis;
specialis respectu cuius species est id quod est, et haec est forma quae non est eadem
in diversis speciebus sed alia et alia, et ideo nomen impositum ab ista forma non
potest esse in speciebus diversis, sed forma generis respectu cuius species dicitur
potest esse in diversis speciebus; ideo nihil impedit nomen generis esse commune   15
multis speciebus.

<2>

Secundo quaeritur, dato quod nomen generis possit esse commune in pluribus
speciebus, utrum definitio data secundum illud nomen possit esse communis.

    Quod non videtur. Scribitur in *Physicis* quod materia non potest esse simul sub
formis oppositis. Cum ergo genus se habeat per modum materiae et differentia   20
per modum formae, non potest genus esse sub differentiis oppositis. Sed ad hoc
quod sit in diversis speciebus oportet quod prius sit sub differentiis oppositis. Sed
non potest esse sub differentiis oppositis. Ergo neque in speciebus diversis. Si non
potest esse sub diversis speciebus, ergo nec eius ratio.

    Item. Scribitur ibidem quod sub alia et alia forma est <alia et alia> ratio materiae.   25
Ergo sub differentiis oppositis alia et alia erit ratio generis. Sed non potest esse sub
diversis speciebus quin fuerit sub differentiis oppositis. Ergo secundum quod est
sub diversis speciebus alia et alia est definitio. Non ergo communis.

---

1 Arist. *Cat.* 1.1a7–9   **2** *cf.* Arist. *Metaph.* VII 8.1033b16–19   **19–20** *cf.* Arist. *Phys.* I
7.190a13–21   **25** Arist. *Phys.* II 2.194b8–9

---

1 de primo] *om. F*   **4** vel] *ut F*   **4** nomen diversum habebit] diversis habebit nomen *F*   **6** et] *om.*
F   **6** differentiis] dupliciter *P, ut v.*   **8** habebit] habet *F*   **8** nomen³] *om. F*   **9** bovi et homini]
inv. F   **10** et] solutio et *F*   **10** esse commune speciebus] speciebus esse commune *F*   **18.11–**
20.5 ad obiectum… sumuntur] *om. F*   **11** generalis] accidentalis *P*   **12** specialis] substantialis *P*
17 commune] ratione *P*

f. 25rb

Ad primum. Ratio potest esse communis.

Ad obiectum. Non est simile de materia in natura et de genere quantum ad hoc, et causa est quia materia in natura est una, ut dicit Avicebron in *Libro fontis vitae*, sed quod est unum numero non est sub diversis formis et oppositis, quare materia non potest esse sub illis. Sed genus non est unum numero, quia unum numero est quod est in se indivisum et ab aliis divisum, genus vero non est ab aliis divisum—est enim unum in multis, ut scribitur in *Posterioribus*—, et quia non est unum numero, nihil impedit quin sit sub differentiis oppositis et sic ulterius in diversis speciebus, et ita ratio eius potest esse eis communis.

Ad aliud dicendum: Haec propositio, "Sub alia et alia forma est alia et alia ratio materiae", intelligitur de differentia constitutiva. Argumentum concludit de divisivis, quare non valet, quia diversitas in his differentiis non diversificat rationem sui superioris.

<3>

Consequenter quaeritur de secundo. Dicitur quod hic determinat de antepraedicamentis.

Contra. Ipsa praedicamenta sunt decem principia prima, ut dicit Porphyrius. Ergo nihil est ante quam ipsa.

Solutio. Praedicamenta dicuntur prima respectu suorum inferiorum et non respectu suorum principiorum, unde nihil ante praedicamenta in linea praedicamentali, sed illa | sunt priora sicut principium prius respectu suo principiato.   f. 25va

Vel aliter. Duplex est prius, ut dicitur in secundo *Physicorum*, naturaliter et quo ad nos; unde ista non sunt priora natura sed in via cognitionis.

<4–5>

Consequenter quaeritur de ordine ad partem praecedentem. Nam unum ante multa. Ergo univocum ante aequivocum.

Ultimo quaeritur quare non determinat de aliis differentiis sicut de istis.

Ad hoc ultimum dicendum quod hic determinat de praedicamentis prout sunt ordinabilia, et quia univocum, aequivocum et denominativum sunt differentiae ordinis et non aliae species nominis, solum de istis determinat.

---

3 *cf.* Avicebron *Fons vitae* IV 9–10 (ed. Baeumker, 230–32)   **7** *cf.* Arist. *APo* II 19.100a6–8; Anon. *Auct. Arist.* 35.124 (ed. Hamesse, 321)   **16** Porph. *Isag.* 6.7–8   **21–22** *cf.* Arist. *Phys.* I 1.184a16–24

---

4 quare] quia *P*   **6** in] a *P*   **6–7** est enim] ens est *P*   **12** rationem] ratione *P*

Ad aliud. Praedicamenta comparantur ad aliquid superius, et sic est aequivocum, quia nihil est supra ipsa, ut dicit Porphyrius, comparantur etiam ad sua inferiora, et sic est univocum, et ad collateralia, et est denominativum. Et prima comparatio ad superiora, secunda ad inferiora, tertia ad collateralia. Unde non ordinantur
penes unitatem et multitudinem sed penes comparationes quibus sumuntur.   5

---

2 Porph. *Isag.* 6.5–11

LECTIO III

DENOMINATIVA DICUNTUR ETC. (1.1a13)

\<DIVISIO\>

Hic prosequitur auctor de denominativis.

Et dividitur in partes duas. Primo definit denominativa, secundo definitionem explanat per exempla. Secunda ibi: *ut a grammatica* (1.1a14).

Consequenter sequitur illa pars, *Eorum quae dicuntur* (2.1a16), in qua determinat naturam totius in suis partibus (et quod hoc sit verum patet, quia determinat de dicibili prout habet istas partes sub se, dicibile cum complexione et sine). Et dividitur in duas. Primo ponit quandam divisionem, secundo manifestat eam per exempla, ibi: *ut homo currit* (2.1a17).

Haec est divisio lectionis.

\<SENTENTIA\>

Circa primam partem sic procedit: *Denominativa dicuntur* quae *ab aliquo* principali *solo casu*, id est sola cadentia formae ad subiectum, *differentia habent appellationem*, id est significationem, *secundum* illud *nomen*.

Et ponit exempla: *ut a grammatica grammaticus*, et sic de aliis.

Consequenter ponit quandam talem divisionem: Dicibilium quoddam est complexum et quoddam incomplexum.

Et ponit exempla: Complexum est *ut homo currit, homo vincit* (id est haec oratio simul coniuncta dicit complexum), incomplexum ut partes orationis per se sumptae, ut "homo" per se, "currit" per se.

Haec est sententia partis.

\<QUAESTIONES\>

Ad dictorum evidentiam duo quaeruntur. Primum est de prima parte, secundum de secunda.

---

1 prosequitur] deterquitur *! F*   1 de denominativis] de nominativis *P*   2 in partes] haec pars in *F*   3 secunda] ut *F*   5 suis partibus] *inv. F*   5 et] a *P a.c.*   5 quia] quod *P*   8 ibi] ut ibi *F*   10 aliquo] id est *add. F*   11 differentia] *ante* solo casu *F*   12 illud] *om. F*   14 talem divisionem] *inv. F*   14 quoddam] quiddam *F*   15 et] *om. F*   15 quoddam] quiddam *F*   16 complexum est] *om. P*   16 homo vincit] *om. F*   16 id est] *om. P*   18 currit per se] *om. F*   19 haec...partis] *om. P*   21.20–22.14 ad dictorum...secundo] *om. F*

<1>

De primo quaeritur in quo genere possunt reperiri denominativa.

Et videtur quod in qualibet forma separata et subiecto coniuncta est denominativum. Sed in quolibet genere est hoc invenire. Ergo in quolibet genere est denominativum. Patet minor in genere accidentis. Similiter patet in genere substantiae,
quia humanitas dicitur forma separata a subiecto, homo vero coniuncta.   5

Sed contra. Forma substantialis dat esse subiecto, ergo manente subiecto non
potest ab eo separari. Sed quod non est intelligere non contingit. Ergo non contingit
intelligere formam substantialem a subiecto separatam. Et forma separata faciebat
denominativum. Ergo denominativum non est in substantia.

Et dicendum quod in genere substantiae non est denominativum.   10

Ad obiectum dicendum quod forma a subiecto separata et subiecto coniuncta
non sufficit ad denominativum sed forma a subiecto separata et subiecto coniuncta
manente subiecto, sed hoc non potest esse in forma substantiali et suo subiecto.

<2>

Secundo quaeritur quare hic determinat de denominativis.

Et videtur quod non debeat hic determinare de his, quia denominativum est   15
dispositio secundum quam unum descendit ab alio et non secundum quam unum
est | dicibile de alio. Sed in hac doctrina solum agit de his quae sunt dicibilia. Ergo
non debet hic agere de denominativis.

Solutio. Denominativum dupliciter potest considerari, scilicet in comparatione
ad suam formam, et hoc modo est dispositio secundum quam unum descendit ab   20
altero, vel in comparatione ad subiectum quod continet, et hoc modo dico quod est
dispositio secundum quam unum de altero praedicatur, quia denominativum est
dicibile de subiecto quod continet; et hoc modo determinat de eo in hac doctrina.

f. 25vb

<3>

Tertio quaeritur de contrarietate quae videtur esse inter grammaticum et logicum.
Dicit enim grammaticus abstractum descendere a concreto, logicus e converso.   25

---

14 de denominativis] de nominativis *P*   **15** et] *om. F*   **15** non debeat hic] in hac doctrina non
debet *F*   **15** denominativum] denominatio *F ut v.*   **17** alio] altero *F*   **17** solum agit] *inv. F*
18 de denominativis] de nominativis *P*   **21** dico quod] *om. F*   **23** determinat] determinatur *F*
22.24–24.12 tertio…sunt] *om. F*

Et dicendum quod grammaticus considerat denominativum prout est dispositio nominum, logicus vero considerat ea in via essendi. Et quia hoc modo prius est abstractum, ideo dicit logicus concretum descendere ab abstracto.

Vel aliter. Grammaticus est artifex sensibilis et illa quae prius se offerunt sensui dicit esse priora, et quia concreta magis se offerunt sensui, ideo dicit ipsa esse priora, et <quia> posterius descendit a priori, ideo dicit abstracta descendere a concretis. Sed logicus est artifex intellectualis, et <quia> magis vel prius se offert intellectui abstractum quam concretum, ideo dicit concretum descendere ab abstracto.

<4>

Quarto quaeritur quare denominativa conveniunt in principio et differunt in fine, ut dicit Boethius.

Dicendum quod in dictione duo sunt, significatum et modus significandi, et significatum praecedit. Quia ergo denominativa et abstracta idem significant, conveniunt in principio, et quia diversimode, ad hoc denotandum differunt in fine, quia finalis terminatio multum valet ad distinguendum modos significandi.

<5>

Quinto quaeritur de eo quod dicit quod differunt solo casu. Per hoc enim videtur quod omnes obliqui sint denominativi, quia cadunt a recto.

Dicendum quod duplex est cadentia. Quaedam est ex parte rei, quaedam ex parte vocis secundum declinationem; et sic aequivocatur cadentia.

<6>

Ultimo quaeritur, cum denominativa dicantur concreta vel coniugata, adverbia autem ab his descendentia non, sed dicantur casus, quare hoc sit.

Et dicendum quod ista nomina, "albus", "alba", "album" et consimilia, dicuntur denominativa respectu formae principalis (est enim denominativum, id est de nomine itivum, ut a nomine principali), concreta autem quasi subiectum continentia dicuntur, coniugata quasi in significatione cognata, quia idem significant licet diversimode, vel sub eodem iugo posita, <ut> sub nomine principali. Sed adverbia ab

---

9–10   cf. Boeth. in Cat. 168a   15   Arist. Cat. 1.1a13–15

---

1 dispositio] aliis speciebus add. P   3 abstractum] abstract P   4 aliter grammaticus] inv. P   5 ideo dicit] inv. P   8 abstractum] abstract P   12 et abstracta] iter. P   23 continentia] an concernentia scr.?   24 cognata] an coniuncta scr.?

his descendentia dicuntur casus quia cadunt a significatione, quia adverbium non
significat ut principale.

<7>

De secundo quaeritur, cum haec divisio ponatur in *Libro Perihermeneias* et in isto,
et idem eodem modo sumptum poni in diversis scientiis non debeat, quo modo
differenter.   5

Et dicendum quod ibi dividitur intellectus, hic vero dicibile. Differunt etiam quo
ad finem, quia hic ponitur ut sumatur haec pars, dici sine complexione, ibi vero ut
sumatur altera, scilicet dici cum complexione.

<8>

Secundo quaeritur quare potius dicit "eorum quae dicuntur" quam "eorum quae
sunt". Nam videtur peccare cum haec divisio | sit entis.   10

Et dicendum quod licet hic dividatur ens, non tamen dividitur in quantum ens
sed in quantum dicibile, et ideo dixit "dicuntur" et non "sunt".

f. 26ra

<Litteralis expositio>

Litteralis expositio haec est: Ita dictum est de univocis et aequivocis, *vero*, id est
sed, illa *dicuntur denominativa quaecumque differentia ab aliquo* principali *solo casu*, id est sola cadentia formae ad subiectum, *habent appellationem*, id est   15
significationem, *secundum nomen*, principale supple.

Consequenter ponit exempla: *ut a grammatica grammaticus.*

Consequenter ponit quandam divisionem, dicens: *Eorum quae dicuntur*, id est
per sermonem significantur, *alia*, id est quaedam, *dicuntur secundum complexionem, vero*, <id est> sed, *alia* dicuntur *sine complexione.*   20

Et ea quae dicuntur secundum complexionem sunt, oratio supple coniuncta, *ut
homo currit, homo vincit, vero*, id est sed, *ea quae* dicuntur *sine complexione* sunt
ut homo, per se supple, *bos, currit, vincit*, intelligge divisim.

---

3 *cf.* Arist. *Int.* 1.16a13–18; Arist. *Cat.* 2.1a16–19   **9–10** Arist. *Cat.* 2.1a16

---

6 dividitur] definitur *P*   **13** ita] id est *F*   **13** vero id est] *om. P*   **14** aliquo] *P^{sup}c* : alio *P*
14 principali] a principali *F*   **17** consequenter] communiter *F ut v.*   **17** grammaticus] et forti-
tudine fortis *add. F*   **18** quae] *om. F*   **19** alia id est] *om. P*   **19–20** secundum...complexione]
cum complexione quaedam secundum incomplexionem *P*   **21** sunt] sunt ut currit homo *add. F*
21 ut] *om. F*   **22** homo²...est] *om. P*   **22** dicuntur–sunt] *transp. FP* **23** ut] *om. F* **23** supple]
et *add. F*   **23** divisim] *lectio incerta F* : diversimode *P*

Lectio IV

Eorum quae sunt alia sunt in subiecto etc. (2.1a20)

<Divisio>

Pars in qua ostendit principia ipsius dicibilis in se divisa fuit in tres. In prima determinat quae et quot sunt partes dicibilis, in secunda determinat naturam totius in partibus. His duabus habitis, sequitur tertia in qua determinat partium naturam inter se. Quia per divisionem quam ponit innuit triplicis ordinis habitudinem de qua est determinaturus (innuit enim ordinem substantiarum ad substantias et accidentium ad accidentia, et sic determinat naturam univoci; innuit etiam ordinem substantiarum ad accidentia, et sic determinat naturam denominativi), sed unaquaeque istarum ordinationum, scilicet substantiarum ad substantias et accidentium ad accidentia, habet capitulum per se, alia vero, scilicet substantiarum ad accidentia, non (quia cum sit medium et cognitis extremis cognoscantur media, ideo determinat de extremis et non de medio), ex hoc patet quod hic determinat naturam partium inter se, scilicet denominativi et univoci, quae sunt partes dicibilis.

Haec ergo pars dividitur in quattuor iuxta quattuor membra divisionis quam ponit. Secunda ibi: *alia autem in subiecto* (2.1a22), tertia ibi: *alia vero de subiecto* (2.1b1), quarta ibi: *alia vero neque de subiecto* (2.1b2).

Secunda in duas. Primo ponit membra divisionis, secundo explanat quoddam dictum dubium, ut ibi: *in subiecto autem esse* (2.1a23).

Haec secunda in duas. Primo explanat dubium, secundo membra dividentia manifestat per exempla, ibi: *ut quaedam grammatica* (2.1a25).

<Sententia>

Circa primam sic procedit: Eorum quae sunt alia dicuntur de subiecto et non sunt in subiecto. Et hoc manifestat per exempla: ut secundae substantiae; animal enim dicitur de homine, sed non est in homine.

Alia autem sunt in subiecto, sed non dicuntur de subiecto.

---

1 ostendit] oportet *F*   **1** principia…se] *conieci ex divisione in prima lectione data* : quae et quot sunt partes dicibiles (declinabiles *F*) *FP*   **2** partes] pars *F*   **2** dicibilis] dicibiles *P* : declinabilis *F*   **3** naturam] numerum *F*   **4** ordinis] cordis *F*   **5** determinaturus] determinandus *P*   **5–7** ad substantias…substantiarum] *om. P*   **6** etiam] enim *F*   **9** capitulum per] copulam pro *P*   **9** scilicet] *om. F*   **10** sit] sint *P*   **10** cognoscantur] cognoscuntur *F* : extrema et cum hoc etiam *add. P*   **11** de] *add. in marg. F*   **12** univoci] domus *F ut v.*   **12** partes] *om. P*   **12** dicibilis] dicibiles *P* : declinabilis *F*   **13** ergo] *om. F*   **14** secunda] incipit *add. F*   **14** ibi²] *om. F*   **15** ibi] *om. F*   **16** primo] in prima *F*   **16** secundo] in secunda *F*   **17** autem] *om. F*   **18** dividentia] divisionis *F*   **19** ibi] ut ibi *F*   **20** primam] primum *P*   **21** hoc] haec *F*   **21** secundae substantiae] *inv. P*   **23** alia…subiecto²] *om. P*   **23** dicuntur] dicitur *F*

Et quia aliquis posset dubitare quid est esse in subiecto, definit sic: Esse in subiecto dico quod est in aliquo non sicut quaedam pars eius sed impossibile est esse
sine eo in quo est.

Et hoc manifestat per exempla, dicens: ut accidentia particularia, sicut quaedam
grammatica, est in subiecto, ut in anima, sed non dicitur de subiecto.   5

Alia vero sunt quae sunt in subiecto et dicuntur de subiecto, ut accidentia universalia. Et ponit exempla: ut scientia est in anima et dicitur de grammatica ut de
subiecto.

Alia sunt quae neque dicuntur de subiecto neque sunt in subiecto, ut primae
substantiae. Et ponit exempla: ut aliquis homo et aliquis bos. Deinde dicit quod   10
nullum individuum dicitur de subiecto, sed quaedam sunt quae nihil prohibet esse
in subiecto; hoc dicit propter accidentia quae sunt in subiecto.

Haec est sententia partis.

<Litteralis expositio>

f. 26rb | Expositio haec est: *Eorum quae sunt alia*, id est quaedam, *dicuntur*, id est prae-
dicantur, *de quodam subiecto, vero*, id est sed, *in nullo subiecto sunt*, ut substantiae   15
universales. Consequenter ponit exempla, dicens: *ut homo dicitur*, id est praedicatur, *de aliquo homine subiecto, vero*, id est sed, *in nullo subiecto* ponitur sicut
accidens.

Consequenter ponit secundum membrum: Ita dixi "quaedam dicuntur de sub-
iecto etc.", *autem*, id est sed, *alia sunt in subiecto quidem*, ut accidentia particularia   20
supple, *vero*, id est sed, *de nullo subiecto dicuntur*.

Consequenter explanat quoddam dictum dubium, dicens: *dico*, id est expono,
illud *esse in subiecto quod cum sit in* alio *non* est in illo *sicut quaedam pars*, integralis
supple, sed *impossibile est esse sine eo in quo est*.

Consequenter explanat membrum divisionis per exempla, dicens: *ut quaedam*   25
grammatica est in subiecto, scilicet *in anima*, sed *de nullo subiecto dicitur*, ut subiecto inferiori supple. Consequenter ponit aliud exemplum: Ita dixi quod grammatica est in subiecto, *ut*, pro sicut, *quoddam album est in corpore*. Et hoc pro-

2 dico] est *P*   2 eius] *om. F*   3 quo est] quoque *P*   4 accidentia...sicut] *om. P*   5 subiecto ut
in] *om. F*   5 de] aliquo *add. F*   6–8 alia...subiecto] *om. P*   9 dicuntur de] sunt in *F*   9 sunt in]
dicuntur de *F*   9–10 primae substantiae] prima substantia *F*   10 exempla] exemplum *P*   10 bos]
equus *F*   11 prohibet] prohibent *F*   13 haec...partis] *om. P*   14 id est²] *om. F*   15 vero id
est] *om. P*   15 sunt] supple *add. F*   15 substantiae] *iter. F a.c. ut v.*   16 dicitur] dicuntur *F*
17 aliquo] quodam *P*   17 vero id est] *om. P*   17 ponitur] *om. F*   18 accidens] supple *add.*
F   19 membrum] divisionis *add. F*   19 dicuntur] dicitur *F*   20 autem id est] *om. P*   20 in
subiecto quidem] quidem in subiecto *F*   21 vero id est] autem id est *F* : *om. P*   21 nullo subiecto]
inv. P   22 explanat] *hic terminat textus in F*   27 ita] di *add. P*   28 ut] *P* : et *ac*   28 sicut] *iter.*
P

bat: quia *omnis color est in* subiecto *corpore,* sed *de nullo subiecto dicitur,* supple in abstractione.

Consequenter ponit tertium membrum: Ita dixi "quaedam sunt in subiecto etc.", sed alia *dicuntur de subiecto et sunt in subiecto,* ut universalia accidentia supple. Et ponit exemplum: *ut scientia est in subiecto,* scilicet *in anima,* et non solum est in subiecto, sed *dicitur de subiecto, ut de grammatica.*

Consequenter ponit aliud membrum: Ita dixi quod quaedam dicuntur de subiecto etc., sed *alia neque dicuntur de subiecto neque sunt in subiecto.* Et ponit exempla: *ut aliquis homo.* Consequenter probat hoc: Ita dixi quod aliquis homo non est in subiecto, quia *nihil horum,* id est particularium substantiarum, *neque est in subiecto neque dicitur de subiecto,* sed *nihil prohibet ea,* id est particularia accidentia, *esse in subiecto.* Et ponit exemplum: *quaedam enim grammatica est in subiecto.*

<QUAESTIONES>

Ad dictorum evidentiam <duo> quaeruntur. Primum est de modo procedendi, secundum de dictis in littera.

<1>

De primo sic: Idem eodem modo sumptum non habet determinari in diversis scientiis. Cum ergo haec divisio ponatur in *Libro sex principiorum* et hic, quaeritur quo modo differenter.

<2>

Secundo quaeritur: Cum hic ponantur quattuor membra, ibi tantum tria et dimittitur hoc membrum, <nec dici de subiecto nec> esse in subiecto, videtur vel quod hic sit superfluus vel ille deminutus.

<3>

Item. Membrum quod hic ponitur primum ponitur ibi ultimum. Videtur ergo quod hic est perversus in ordine aut ille. Propter hoc quaeritur de ordine istorum.

---

16 Anon. *LSP* I 11 (ed. Minio-Paluello, 37)

---

18 ibi] cui *P ut v.*   21 ultimum] secundum *P*

<4>

Item. Hic sunt duae dictiones, scilicet dici de et non dici de, esse in <et non esse in>. Quaeritur quare coniungat eas in simul.

<AD 1>

Ad primum dicendum quod in doctrina *Sex principiorum* dividitur forma communis ad substantialem et accidentalem, in hac autem dividitur ens prout habet continere omnem formam et primum subiectum, id est primam substantiam, et sic patet 5 quo modo differenter ponitur divisio hic et ibi.

Vel aliter. Hic dividitur res, quod patet per hoc quod dicit "Eorum quae sunt", ibi autem dividitur forma, ut patet per textum: *Forma alia quidem* etc. Et sic patet <quo modo> differenter.

<AD 2>

Ad secundum dicendum quod ibi agit de forma, et quia omnis forma vel est in sub- 10 iecto aut dicitur de subiecto, ideo ultimum membrum omittitur, scilicet nec dici de subiecto nec esse in subiecto, quia formae non competit. Alia autem tria ponuntur ibi quia formae competunt. Primum, scilicet dici de subiecto et esse in, competit formis accidentalibus universalibus, secundum, scilicet esse in et non dici de, competit formis <accidentalibus> particularibus, tertium, scilicet dici de et non esse in, 15 f. 26va formis | substantialibus universalibus. < * * * > Et ideo ponuntur hic tria membra formis competentia et ultimum competens primo subiecto. Et sic patet quod nec iste superfluus nec ille deminutus.

<AD 3>

Ad aliud dicendum quod <quia> de forma diversimode sumpta est intentio hic et ibi, ideo ista membra diversimode ordinantur. Ibi enim principaliter est intentio 20 de forma accidentali universali, quia de actione et passione etc., et ideo membrum ei competens primo ordinatur. Et quia forma accidentalis universalis essentialiter praedicatur de forma accidentali particulari et de substantia per accidens, ideo membrum competens formae substantiali tertio loco ordinatur. Hic autem est in-

---

8 Anon. *LSP* I 11 (ed. Minio-Paluello, 37).

---

3 dicendum] ita dixi *P*   3 dividitur] dicitur *P*   4 ad substantialem] *iter. P*   13 ibi] id est *P*
14 universalibus] substantialibus *P*

tentio de formis secundum ordinem praedicabilium. Sed praedicabilium triplex
est habitudo sive comparatio. Prima est substantiarum inter se, et ideo membrum
competens secundis substantiis primo ordinatur. Secunda est accidentium ad substantias, haec enim ordinantur ad primas substantias in quibus sunt, et ideo membrum competens accidentibus particularibus secundo loco ordinatur. Tertia est habitudo accidentium inter se, et ideo membrum competens accidentibus communibus tertio ordinatur. Quartum membrum ultimo ponitur quia dicitur omnino per
abnegationem aliorum.

<AD 4>

Ad ultimum dicendum quod coniungit illas duas dictiones ut det intelligere habitudinem triplicis ordinis, quia per hoc primum membrum, dici de et non esse in,
denotat ordinationem secundarum substantiarum ad primas (secundae enim substantiae dicuntur de primis et non sunt in primis), per secundum membrum denotat
ordinationem accidentium < * * * > inter se.

<5>

Item quaeritur de secundo: Dicit in littera quod animal dicitur de homine sed non
est in homine.

Hoc videtur esse falsum, quia dicit Aristoteles in quarto *Physicorum* quod superius est in suo inferiori. Ergo cum animal sit superius ad hominem, erit in
homine.

Propter hoc quaeritur quid sit dictum "esse in" et quot modis dicitur.

<6>

Item. Dicit quod esse in nihil differt ab eo quod impossibile est esse sine subiecto
in quo est.

Videtur esse falsum. Quia si aliquod corpus odoriferum diu teneatur in manu,
ipso ablato remanet odor in manu.

14–15 cf. Arist. *Cat.* 2.1a19–21 16–17 cf. Arist. *Phys.* IV 3.210a14–24; Anon. *Auct. Arist.*
2.123 (ed. Hamesse, 150); Boeth. *in Cat.* 172b–c 20–21 Arist. *Cat.* 2.1a23–25

2 se] haec enim ordinatur ad primas substantias in quibus sunt *add. P* 7 ultimo] universale *P*
11 denotat] denotas *P* 11 secundae enim] non secundae *P* 21 quo est] quoque *P*

\<7\>

Item. Videtur impossibile hoc quod dicit quod scientia est in anima.

Dicit enim Aristoteles in *Libro Physicorum* quod substantia \<composita ex\> materia et forma causa est omnium accidentium. Ergo accidens non potest esse nisi in composito ex materia et forma. Sed anima non est huiusmodi quia simplex. Quare nullum accidens potest esse in ea. Ergo nec scientia.   5

\<AD 5\>

Ad primum dicendum quod "esse in" dicitur multis modis, quos modos ponit Aristoteles in quarto *Physicorum*. Primus ut pars integralis in suo toto, secundus ut totum integrale in suis partibus, tertius ut superius in suo inferiori, quartus \<ut\> inferius in suo superiori, quintus ut forma in materia. Et hic est duplex secundum logicum, quia est forma substantialis et accidentalis. Primo modo dicitur anima   10
esse in corpore, secundo accidens in subiecto.

Ex hoc patet solutio ad obiectum, quia animal est in homine sicut superius in suo inferiori, et sic obicitur, sed non est in eo sicut accidens, et hoc modo sumitur
f. 26vb   hic "esse in", | et "dici de" sumitur sicut superius de inferiori.

\<AD 6\>

Ad aliud dicendum quod corpus odoriferum si diu teneatur in manu resolvitur a   15
calore, et per partes porosas exit odor cum partibus substantialibus resolutis a calore admixto, unde dicendum quod ipso ablato non remanet odor in manu sed in partibus suis a calore resolutis.

Aliter dicitur quod illud quod in manu relinquitur non est odor sed species odoris, sicut imago quae in speculo apparet non est imago sed species imaginis.   20

\<AD 7\>

Ad ultimum dicendum quod duplex est accidens. Quaedam enim sunt accidentia quae sunt sensibiles qualitates, ut albedo et similia, quaedam autem sunt spirituales, ut scientia et similia. Per hoc dicendum quod forma cum materia est causa accidentium quae sunt sensibiles qualitates, et ideo talia accidentia non habent esse nisi in

---

2–3   Arist. *Phys.* I 9.192a13–14, *ut apud* Anon. *Auct. Arist.* 2.30 (ed. Hamesse, 142)   **6–7**   Arist. *Phys.* IV 3.210a14–24; Anon. *Auct. Arist.* 2.123 (ed. Hamesse, 150); Boeth. *in Cat.* 172b–73c

---

16 calore] colore *P*   **16–17** calore] colore *P*

composito ex materia et forma, sed alia accidentia quae sunt spirituales qualitates possunt esse in eo quod non est compositum ex materia et forma, et ideo scientia in anima potest esse.

Lectio V

Quando autem alterum de altero etc. (3.1b10)

<Divisio>

Pars in qua determinat principia ipsius dicibilis vel de antepraedicamentis divisa in prima fuit < * * * > determinat principia ipsius dicibilis secundum quod unum dicibile naturalem habet ordinationem ad alterum, in secunda parte exsequitur, determinans ea per quae ipsum dicibile recipit divisionem, ibi: *Eorum quae secundum* (4.1b25).

5

Prima est praesentis lectionis et dividitur in duas. In prima ponit quandam maximam vel regulam secundum quod unum dicibile habet ordinationem ad alterum in eodem genere, secundo in diverso genere, ibi: *Diversorum generum* (3.1b17).

Prima in duas. Primo ponit regulam, secundo manifestat eam per exempla, ibi: *ut homo* (3.1b11).

10

Pars in qua ponit secundam regulam dividitur in duas. Primo ponit regulam, secundo exemplificat, ibi: *ut animalis et scientiae* (3.1b18).

Haec secunda in duas. Primo exemplificat per exempla, secundo per quandam additionem dubium removet, ibi: *Subalternorum vero* (3.1b21).

15

Haec est divisio lectionis, et sunt particulae quinque.

<Sententia>

Circa primam sic procedit: Quando alterum praedicatur de altero ut de subiecto, quidquid praedicatur de praedicato, praedicatur de subiecto.

Et hoc per exemplum manifestat, dicens: Homo praedicatur de quodam homine, ut de Socrate, et animal praedicatur de homine ut de subiecto, ergo praedicabitur de subiecto, quod est quidam homo.

20

Consequenter ponit aliam regulam, dicens quod diversa genera, si unum non ponitur sub altero nec ambo sub tertio, diversas habent species et differentias.

Et ponit exemplum: ut animal et scientia, quia animal habet has differentias, ut volatile, gressibile (et sumitur differentia communiter), sed scientia non habet has differentias, quia scientia non differt a scientia per aliquam istarum.

25

Ultimo, quia dixerat "et non subalternatim positorum", posset aliquis dubitare quare hoc membrum apposuit, et ideo dicit quod nihil prohibet quod genera subalternatim posita easdem habeant species et differentias. Et subiungit causam, dicens quod superiora praedicantur de inferioribus. Sed quicquid praedicatur de prae-

---

14 additionem] hoc *add. P*   **14** removet] removendo *P*   **21** regulam] divisionem *P*

dicato praedicatur de subiecto. Ergo differentiae quae de superiori praedicantur, de in|feriori etiam praedicabuntur, quare nihil impedit genera subalterna easdem habere differentias.

Haec est sententia lectionis.

\<Expositio litteralis>

Expositio litteralis haec est: *Quando alterum praedicatur de altero ut de subiecto*, id 5
est sub se iacto in linea praedicamentali, *quaecumque praedicantur de praedicato omnia dicuntur de subiecto.*

Et ponit exemplum, dicens: *ut homo praedicatur de homine quodam*, supple particulari, sed *animal* praedicatur *de homine*, quod est praedicatum supple, *ergo animal* praedicatur *de quodam homine*; et confirmat conclusionem quod *quidam* 10
homo et est homo et est animal.

Consequenter ponit aliam regulam: Ita dixi "Quando alterum etc.", sed *species et differentiae sunt diversae diversorum generum et non positorum subalternatim*, id est quod unum non ponatur sub altero nec ambo sub tertio.

Et ponit exempla: *ut animalis et scientiae.* Bene dico quod non, quia *scientia* 15
neque, pro non, *differt* a *scientia in eo quod* sit *bipes.*

Ultimo explanat regulam per additionem: Supra ita dixi quod genera non subalterna non habent easdem differentias, *vero*, pro sed, *nihil prohibet easdem differentias esse subalternorum generum.* Et subiungit causam: Quia *superiora praedicantur de* inferioribus (haec est maior sui argumenti). Et quod praedicatur de 20
praedicato (haec est minor supplenda) praedicatur de subiecto. *Quare*, id est ergo, *quaecumque fuerint differentiae praedicati, eaedem erunt etiam subiecti.*

\<Quaestiones>

Hic duo quaeruntur, primum de prima regula, secundum de secunda.

\<1>

De primo quaeritur quare non dicit "aliud de alio" sed dicit "alterum de altero".

Et dicendum quod praedicatum et subiectum non debent esse penitus diversa, 25
et quia "aliud" dicit diversitatem in substantia et accidente et sic denotat maximam diversitatem, ideo dicit "alterum", quod denotat diversitatem accidentium solum.

---

24 Arist. *Cat.* 3.1b10

---

22 fuerint] *ac* : sub *P*   **24** sed] sicut *P*

<2>

Secundo videtur superflue apponere hanc particulam "de subiecto", quia omne praedicatum semper dicitur de subiecto. Ergo superfluit dicere "de subiecto".

Et dicendum quod multipliciter dicitur subiectum. Uno modo sub alio iactum in linea praedicamentali. Aliter dicitur subiectum in quo sit † secundo † sive sit in
5   eadem linea sive non. Ut ergo denotet quia de subiecto primo modo loquitur, dicit "ut de subiecto".

<3>

Tertio quaeritur, cum superius dicta sit duplex divisio, scilicet dici de et non dici de et esse in et non esse in, cum det unam regulam penes dici de, quare non dat aliam penes esse in.
10   Et dicendum quod bene sequitur habitudo virtute eius quod est dici de. Bene enim sequitur, "Si medium dicitur de postremo et primum de medio, et primum de postremo". Sed non sequitur habitudo virtute eius quod est esse in. Quare? Quia non sequitur, "Citharizatio est in subiecto, scilicet Socrate, et bonitas in cithariza-tione, ergo bonitas est in Socrate", sed est fallacia accidentis. Quia ergo sequitur
15   habitudo penes dici de, ideo ponitur quaedam regula dicens istam habitudinem.

<4>

Quarto quaeritur, cum haec regula possit variari quadrupliciter: "Quidquid prae-dicatur de praedicato, et de subiecto", alio modo sic: "De quocumque praedicatur praedicatum, et subiectum", tertio modo sic: "De quocumque praedicatur subiec-tum, et praedicatum", alio modo sic: "Quidquid praedicatur | de subiecto, et de   f. 27rb
20   praedicato", quare non ponit nisi primam.

Et dicendum quod duae illarum sunt falsae et ideo non ponuntur, istae, scilicet, "Quicquid praedicatur de subiecto, et de praedicato", quia rationale praedicatur de homine et non de animali. Similiter haec est falsa: "De quocumque praedicatur praedicatum, et subiectum"; animal enim praedicatur de asino, homo tamen non
25   praedicatur de ipso. Aliae duae sunt verae, istae, scilicet, "Quicquid praedicatur de praedicato, et de subiecto" et "De quocumque praedicatur subiectum, et praedica-tum", sed non ponitur nisi prima, nam altera aequipollet illi et sic datur per illam intelligi.

---

5 denotet] denotat *P*   **10** est dici de] dicit de *P*   **13** citharizatio] cicarizano *P*   **13–**
14 citharizatione] cicarizatione *P*   **16** quadrupliciter] quare *P*   **18** praedicatum] praedicatur *P*
20 praedicato] quia rationale praedicatur *add. P*

<5>

Ultimo videtur regula habere instantiam. Nam genus praedicatur de animali et non praedicatur de homine.

Et dicendum quod duplex est praedicatio, substantialis et accidentalis. De prima loquitur auctor, de secunda tu obicis. Vel aliter. Aliquid praedicatur de altero dupliciter: aut quia utrumque cadit in eadem linea aut ita quod unum cadat in linea, reliquum transcendat. Secundo modo obicitur, quia genus transcendit omne praedicamentum. Primo modo loquitur auctor, et ideo dicit "ut de subiecto", id est sub alio iacto in linea praedicamentali.

<6>

De secundo quaeritur sic: Dicit quod "Diversorum etc."

Contra. Animal et planta sunt diversa genera et non subalternatim posita, et habent eandem differentiam, scilicet animatum.

Et dicendum quod dupliciter genera dicuntur subalterna: aut quia unum sub alio aut quia ambo sub tertio. Licet ergo animal non sit sub planta nec e converso, ambo tamen sub substantia sunt, et sic subalterna. Et sic solvo per interemptionem.

<7>

Secundo quaeritur sic: Cum det unam regulam per quam contingit a genere ad species et differentias descendere, quare non dat aliam per quam contingat descendere ad individua.

Et dicendum quod in hac doctrina agitur de dicibilibus, dicibilia autem sunt proprie genera, species et differentiae, et ideo de his debet dari regula et non de individuis, quia non sunt dicibilia proprie.

<8>

Tertio quaeritur, cum det unam regulam penes multitudinem generum, specierum, differentiarum, quare non dat aliam penes unitatem ipsorum.

Et dicendum quod non possit dari regula penes unitatem, et causa est quia licet esset unitas a parte generis, non potest tamen esse a parte specierum et differentiarum, quia unum genus, dicit Porphyrius, exigit plures differentias et species.

---

9 Arist. *Cat.* 3.1b17   **25–26** Porph. *Isag.* 7.1–3

<9>

Quarto quaeritur quare non ponit unitatem a parte generis et multitudinem a parte aliorum.

Et dicendum quod per primam regulam ordinatur unum dicibile ad aliud existens in eodem genere. Patet ergo quod hic intendit de diversis generibus, et propter hoc non ponit esse unitatem a parte generis. Quod hic intendit de diversis generibus patet, quia ponit principia dicibilis prout ordinatur ad principia alterius dicibilis.

<10>

Ultimo videtur regula habere instantiam

Nam prudentia est sub virtute, scientia <et> qualitate, et illa sunt diversa genera non subalternatim posita.

Similiter, scientia est sub qualitate et relatione.

Similiter, corpus sub substantia et quantitate.

Ad primum dicendum: Prudentia consideratur tripliciter, aut quantum ad esse formale, et tunc est electio boni et fuga mali et continetur sub virtute; si sumatur quantum ad esse materiale, quod est discretio boni a malo, | continetur sub scientia; in quantum autem comparatur ad subiectum et qualificat et denominat illud, qualitas est.   f. 27va

Ad aliud dicendum quod scientia comparatur ad scientem in quo est tanquam in subiecto quod denominat, et sic est qualitas; comparatur etiam ad scibile de quo est, et sic relatio.

Ad ultimum. Corpus diversimode sumitur. Uno modo corpus trina dimensio, et sic est quantitas. Aliter dicitur corpus res quae subest hac triplici dimensione, et sic est substantia. Licet ergo ista sunt sub diversis generibus, non tamen prout sumuntur eodem modo.

---

1 unitatem] unitas *P*   6 quia] quod *P*   7 regula habere instantiam] trahere aliam *P, ut v.*
15 qualificat] *lectio incerta*   20 diversimode] *lectio incerta*

Lectio VI

Eorum quae secundum nullam complexionem dicuntur

etc. (4.1b25)

\<Divisio\>

Habita parte in qua determinat principia ipsius diciblis, exsequitur partem secundam, determinans per quae ipsum dicibile recipit divisionem, scilicet substantiam,
quantitatem etc.

Haec pars in duas dividitur. Primo determinat de praedicamentis in generali,
5 secundo in speciali, ibi: *Substantia est quae proprie* (5.2a12).

Prima est praesentis lectionis et dividitur in partes duas. Primo ponit divisionem \<ipsius dicibilis, secundo probat quandam proprietatem vel passionem, ibi:
Singula igitur eorum (4.2a5).

Prima in duas. Primo ponit divisionem\>, secundo explanat eam per exempla,
10 ibi: *Est autem substantia* (4.1b27).

Pars in qua probat proprietatem vel passionem dividitur in duas. Primo ponit
ipsam per modum conclusionis, secundo probat eam, ut ibi: *Videtur enim omnis
affirmatio* (4.2a7).

Haec est divisio lectionis, et sunt quattuor particulae.

\<Sententia\>

15 Circa primam partem sic procedit: Dicibilium incomplexorum aliud significat substantiam, aliud quantitatem, et sic de aliis quae in littera ponuntur.

Consequenter manifestat hanc divisionem per exempla, dicens quod
\< * * * \>
ea quae dicta sunt dicibilia incomplexa non dicuntur secundum affirmationem;
20 et sic intellige de suo opposito, scilicet de negatione.

Ultimo probat hoc tali ratione, dicens: Omnis affirmatio est vera vel falsa. Nullum incomplexorum significat verum vel falsum. Ergo nullum incomplexorum
significat affirmationem vel negationem.

Haec est sententia partis.

Expositio litteralis

25 Ita dictum est de principiis dicibilis, sed *eorum*, id est de numero eorum, *quae se-*

cundum nullam complexionem dicuntur singulum sub genere existentium — et sic
non est in Deo — *aut significat substantiam* etc.

Consequenter explanat per exempla: Ita dixi "singulum incomplexorum etc.",
autem, id est sed, *substantia est, ut dicatur figuraliter*, id est exemplariter, *ut homo,
equus, quantitas ut bicubitum* etc.   5

Consequenter ponit quandam proprietatem vel passionem: Ita dixi "singulum
incomplexorum etc.", *igitur*, pro sed, *singula eorum quae dicta sunt*, id est dicibilium
incomplexorum, *ipsa secundum se*, accepta supple, *in nulla affirmatione dicuntur*,
sed *affirmatio fit in complexione*, id est compositione, *horum*, id est praedictorum,
ad se invicem.   10

Ultimo probat hoc: Ita dixi quod illa non dicuntur secundum affirmationem,
enim, id est quia, *omnis affirmatio videtur esse*, id est est, *vera vel falsa* (haec est
maior). *Vero*, id est sed, ea *quae secundum nullam complexionem dicuntur neque
sunt vera neque falsa*. Et ponit exempla: *ut homo* per se, *album* etc. Ergo, supple, non sunt affirmatio vel negatio. † Simili ergo tenetur illative prima incipias   15
conclusionem animal videtur quia ibi ponitur maior et minor. †

<Quaestiones>

Duo quaeruntur.

<1>

Primum de prima sic: Quaeritur cuiusmodi sit haec divisio, cum divisio varietur
f. 27vb   multis modis, ut | dicit Boethius.

Dicendum quod hic dividitur dicibile incomplexum ordinabile in genere, quod   20
est subiectum in hac scientia, in partes suas, scilicet in dicibile significans substantiam et quantitatem etc., et sic patet quod haec divisio est totius universalis in partes
suas.

<2>

Secundo quaeritur quare sic dividit: Incomplexorum aliud significat substantiam,
aliud quantitatem etc., et non sic: Aliud significat substantiam, aliud accidens, et   25
postea divideret accidens in quantitatem, qualitatem etc.

18–19 Boeth. *Divis.* 883d–84a (ed. Magee, 26–28)

---

6 quandam] quan *P*   **7** igitur] *P*^{sup}*ac* : ergo *P*   **7** singula] *P*^{sup}*ac* : signa *P*   **9** praedictorum]
praedictarum *P*   **13** sed] iter. *P*   **15** prima] *lectio incerta*   **24** aliud significat] alia significant *P*

Et videtur quod melius dixisset, cum omnis divisio sit bimembris, ut dicit
Boethius.

Et dicendum quod dividit incomplexum aequaliter per ista ad denotandum
quod illa sunt genera aequaliter et non secundum prius et posterius; unde magis
expressit sententiam quam si aliter dixisset.

Ad obiectum dicendum quod omnis divisio est bimembris vel reducibilis ad
bimembrem, et ita potest haec reduci sic: Incomplexorum aliud significat substantiam, aliud accidens; prima tamen divisio ponitur quia est magis sententiae
expressiva.

<3>

Item. Videtur regula habere instantiam.

Nam Deus est dicibile nec est in genere substantiae, quia tunc esset aliquid ante
ipsum, quod est impossibile, nec in aliquo aliorum. Idem est etiam de signis, quia
"omnis" et "nullus" et similia sunt incomplexa et non significant aliquod istorum.

Idem est de differentia et de puncto et de unitate.

Ad primum dicendum quod hic dividit dicibile incomplexum quod est in genere,
sed Deus et signa non sunt in genere sed transcendentia omne genus, quare non
comprehenduntur sub hac divisione.

Ad aliud dicendum quod differentia, punctus et unitas non sunt in praedicamento, sed sunt in genere. Nam praedicamentum est ordinatio praedicabilium secundum praedicationem et subiectionem, et hoc modo solum species et individua
sunt in praedicamento, sed esse in genere est quattuor modis. Uno modo quod participat rationem illius generis, et sic species et individua sunt in genere, et est participare participati definitionem suscipere, ut dicit Aristoteles in quarto *Topicorum*.
Secundo modo est aliquid in genere ut perfectivum eorum quae sunt in genere illo,
et sic differentia est in genere. Tertio modo est aliquid in genere ut via ad res illius
generis, et sic motus est in genere; quantum enim ad hanc speciem quae est generatio, est via ad res substantiae, quantum ad alterationem, in qualitate, et quantum
ad augmentationem, in quantitate. Ultimo est aliquid in genere sicut principium
eorum quae sunt in genere illo, et sic forma et materia sunt in genere substantiae.
Punctus et unitas et similia non sunt in praedicamento, sed sunt in genere.

1–2 Boeth. *Divis.* 883d–84a (ed. Magee, 26–28)   **22–23** Arist. *Top.* IV 1.121a10–14

---

17 hac] dictione *add. sed canc.* P   **21** sunt] sub P   **22** sunt] sub P

<4>

Consequenter quaeritur de secunda. Dicit quod incomplexa non sunt vera neque falsa.

Contra. Omne perfectum in sua specie est verum, dicit Anselmus. Quodlibet incomplexum est perfectum in sua specie. Ergo etc. Minor patet, quia scribitur in *Physicis* quod perfectum est quod attingit finem ad quem est. Cum ergo incomplexa 5 perfecte repraesentent illud ad quod sunt, erunt perfecta.

Et dicendum quod duplex est veritas, scilicet incomplexa, et nihil aliud est quam rei entitas secundum quod dicit Aristoteles quod ens et verum convertuntur, et sic veritas est in incomplexis, ut obicitur. Alia est veritas complexa, et de ista loquitur hic cum dicit quod in|complexa non significant verum. 10

Item. "Homo" est incomplexum, et similiter "currit", et si dicatur "Homo currit", significat verum vel falsum. Ergo incomplexa significant verum vel falsum.

Et dicendum quod incomplexa dupliciter sumuntur, aut per se, et sic non dicunt verum nec falsum, aut coniuncta cum altero, et sic dicunt verum vel falsum; primo modo loquitur, secundo obicis. 15

Item. Si dico "curro", verum vel falsum significo, et "curro" est incomplexum.

Et dicendum quod incomplexum est duplex, scilicet quantum ad substantiam et virtutem, et talia non significant veritatem vel falsitatem, et sic loquitur auctor. Aliud est incomplexum secundum substantiam tantum, est tamen complexum secundum virtutem, ut "curro", et hoc dicit Priscianus quod inest igitur nominativus 20 in ipsis verbis sine quo substantia significari non potest. Ergo patet quod verba primae vel secundae personae sunt complexa quantum ad rem et virtutem; et talia bene significant verum vel falsum, ut obicitur.

f. 28ra

1–2 Arist. *Cat.* 4.2a5–11 **3** *cf.* Anselmus *De veritate* 7 **4–5** Cf. Arist. *Phys.* VII 3.246a13–14; Anon. *Auct. Arist.* 2.187 (ed. Hamesse, 155) **8** Arist. *Metaph.* II 1.993b30–31 **20–21** Prisc. *Inst. gramm.* XVII 1.14 (ed. Hertz, vol. 2, 116–17)

---

3 perfectum] incomplexum *P* **4** quia] quod *P* **9** in incomplexis] in complexis *P a.c.* **11** si] sic *P* **13** non] est *add. sed exp. P* **16** et] cum *add. P*

LECTIO VII

\<DIVISIO\>

Determinato de his per quae ipsum dicibile recipit divisionem in generali, prosequitur de his in speciali.

Et haec pars dividitur in quinque. Primo determinat de substantia, secundo de
quantitate, ibi: *Quantitatis* (6.4b20), tertio de relatione, ibi: *Ad aliquid* (7.6a36),
5 quarto de qualitate, ibi: *Qualitatem* (8.8b25), quinto de aliis generibus in simul, ibi:
Recipit autem (9.11b1).

Prima in duas. Primo determinat de his quae ordinantur in praedicamento
substantiae secundum se, in secunda de quibusdam proprietatibus consequentibus
ipsam, ibi: *Commune est autem* (5.3a7).

10 Prima in duas. Primo determinat de his quae primo ordinantur in praedicamento substantiae definitive, sicut est de prima substantia et secundis, in secunda
ostendit tres proprietates in definitione primae substantiae positas ipsi convenire,
ut ibi: *Manifestum est autem* (5.2a19).

Prima est praesentis lectionis et dividitur in duas, quia omne quod principa-
15 liter ordinatur in praedicamento substantiae aut est prima substantia aut secunda. Primo definit primam substantiam, secundo secundam, ibi: *Secundae autem
substantiae* (5.2a14).

Haec est divisio lectionis, et sunt duae partes.

\<SENTENTIA\>

Circa primam sic procedit: Prima substantia est quae proprie et principaliter et
20 maxime dicitur substantia et non dicitur de subiecto neque est in subiecto. Et ponit
exempla: ut aliquis homo et aliquis equus.

Consequenter definit secundam substantiam, dicens: Secundae substantiae dicuntur species in quibus sunt primae substantiae et genera ipsarum specierum. Et
ponit exemplum: Ut aliquis homo, quod est prima substantia, est in hac specie
25 homo, quae est secunda substantia, et animal est genus illius speciei. Ex his concluditur quod homo et animal sunt secundae substantiae. Et potest extrahi argumentum a littera: Species in quibus primae substantiae sunt et genera specierum sunt
secundae substantiae, ergo homo et animal sunt secundae substantiae.

Haec est sententia partis.

---

20 dicitur] dividitur *bis* P   **24** quod] quidem P

Expositio litteralis

Ita dictum est "Singulum incomplexorum <aliud> significat substantiam etc.", vero, pro sed, *substantia*, supple prima, *est quae proprie, principaliter et maxime dicitur* substantia et *quae neque dicitur de subiecto*, quia non habet inferius, *neque est in subiecto*, quia non est accidens. Et ponit exemplum: *ut aliquis homo et aliquis equus*, resume non dicuntur de subiecto neque sunt in subiecto.   5

f. 28rb | Consequenter definit secundam substantiam. Continua: Ita dixi quid est prima substantia, sed *species dicuntur secundae substantiae, in quibus speciebus istae*, scilicet substantiae, *quae dicuntur principaliter substantiae insunt* sicut inferius in suo superiori, *et genera harum specierum*, supple dicuntur secundae substantiae. Haec est maior. Consequenter ponit exempla: *ut aliquis homo*, quod est prima   10 substantia, *est in homine*. Sed *animal est genus speciei*, scilicet hominis. Haec est minor. *Igitur secundae substantiae dicuntur homo et animal.*

<Quaestiones>

<1>

Primo quaeritur quare non dividit substantiam per primam et secundam antequam notificet quid unaquaeque istarum sit.

Et dicendum quod scribitur in quarto *Topicorum* quod divisio simul respicit   15 partes entis. Item, scribitur in *Praedicamentis* quod dividentia aliquid simul sunt in diviso et aequaliter participant divisum. Sed prima substantia et secunda non aequaliter participant substantiam sed secundum prius et posterius (hoc patet per textum, nam primae substantiae dicuntur principaliter substantiae). Substantia ergo non potest in his dividi.   20

<2–3>

Secundo quaeritur quare dicit "prima substantia" in singulari et "secundae" in plurali.

Tertio quaeritur quare prima definitur per verbum essendi et secunda per verbum dicendi.

Ad primum dicendum quod prima substantia est individuum et unum numero; ut ergo denotaret primae substantiae unitatem, definivit in singulari, quod dicit   25

15–16 *cf.* Arist. *Top.* VI 4.142b9–10   **16–17** *cf.* Arist. *Cat.* 12.14b31–15a7   **21–22** Arist. *Cat.* 5.2a12; 2a14

---

10 est²] sub *add.* P   **16** simul] quae *add.* P

unitatem. Sed quia secunda substantia multiplicatur per speciem et genus, ad denotandum hanc multiplicitatem definivit eam in plurali, quod dicit multiplicitatem
iuxta illud Prisciani "Plurale est geminatum singulare" .

Ad aliud. Omne individuum substantiae est substantia quantum ad modum
5 essendi et de nullo dicitur, sicut prima substantia; ut ergo denotet quod non est
reperire individuum substantiae quod non sit prima substantia, definivit primam
substantiam per hoc verbum "esse". Sed quaedam sunt universalia quae sunt substantiae quantum ad modum essendi et tamen non sunt secundae substantiae; ut
ergo denotet quod non omne universale est <secunda> substantia, definivit secun-
10 dam substantiam per "dici". Hic nota quod duo requiruntur ad hoc quod aliquid
sit secunda substantia, scilicet quod sit substantia quantum ad modum essendi et
dicendi.

<4>

Quarto quaeritur, cum quaelibet particula posita in definitione debeat separare
definitum ab alio, a quo separent primam substantiam istae particulae "proprie",
15 "principaliter" et "maxime".

Solutio. Per hanc differentiam "proprie" separatur a substantia considerata a
grammatico, qui extendit nomen substantiae ad omne illud quod potest reddere
suppositum verbo, quia substantia sic sumpta non sumitur proprie sed large. Per
li "principaliter" a secundis substantiis separatur, quia licet secundae substantiae
20 sint proprie substantiae, non tamen principaliter, quia non substant principaliter
sicut primae. Per li "maxime" separatur ab individuis accidentibus, quia licet haec
individua proprie substent et principaliter, non tamen maxime ut prima substantia,
quae omnibus substat, sed individua accidentia non substant omnibus quia non
primis substantiis sed e converso.

<5>

25 Quinto arguitur: "Universale est prius singulari per naturam", scribitur in primo
Posteriorum. Sed secundae substantiae sunt universalia, primae autem substantiae
singularia. Ergo secundae substantiae ante primas.

Et dicendum quod hic determinat de substantiis | sub illis intentionibus quae   f. 28va
sunt primum et secundum, <et> ideo prima substantia ante secundam. Argu-

---

3 cf. Prisc. *Inst. gramm.* V 9.47 (ed. Hertz, vol. 1, 172) **25–26** cf. Arist. *APo* I 2.71b33–72a6;
Anon. *Auct. Arist.* 35.15–18 (ed. Hamesse, 312)

---

3 prisciani] priscianus *P* **4** substantia] substantiae *P* **5** dicitur] dicuntur *P*

mentum autem procedebat ac si ordinarentur penes has intentiones: universale, singulare.

<6>

Sexto quaeritur: Species dicuntur secundae substantiae respectu individuorum, quae sunt primae. Cum ergo genera ponantur in tertio gradu respectu individuo-rum, debent dici tertiae substantiae. Aut quare non?   5

Et dicendum quod individua tripliciter possunt considerari: uno modo sub for-mis propriis, ut Socrates, Plato, alio modo sub formis suae speciei, ut hic homo, iste homo, tertio modo sub formis generis. Dicendum ergo quod sicut species habent individua immediate sibi correspondentia respectu quorum sunt secun-dae substantiae, similiter et genus. Dicendum ergo quod genus non dicitur esse   10
secunda substantia respectu speciei, quia sic sequeretur quod deberet dici tertia, ut obicitur, sed dicitur secunda substantia respectu individuorum immediate sibi correspondentium.

<7>

Ultimo quaeritur: Dicit quod primae substantiae sunt in secundis.

Contra. Primae sunt in secundis et secundae in primis. Ergo a primo primae   15
in primis, et ita idem in se ipso, quod est inconveniens. Minor patet, quia omne superius est in suo inferiori, ut scribitur in quarto *Topicorum*.

Et dicendum quod non secundum idem modum essendi in primae sunt in se-cundis et secundae in primis, quia secundae sunt in primis ut superius in suo infe-riori, sed primae sunt in secundis ut inferius in suo superiori, et propter hoc non   20
valet argumentum, quia aequivocatur "esse in".

---

14 Arist. *Cat.* 5.2a14–17   **16–17**   *cf.* Arist. *Top.* IV 1.120b12–21b23

---

11 deberet] deberent *P*   **18** secundum] est *P*

Lectio VIII

Manifestum est autem etc. (5.2a19)

\<Divisio\>

Habita parte illa in qua notificat ea quae ordinantur in praedicamento substantiae definiendo, sequitur in qua probat tres condiciones positas in definitione primae substantiae ei convenire.

Et dividitur in tres. In prima probat hanc differentiam quae est "principaliter", in secunda "maxime", ibi: *Secundarum vero substantiarum* (5.2b7), in tertia probat aliam quae est "proprie", ibi: *Merito autem* (5.2b30).

Prima est praesentis lectionis et dividitur in partes duas. In prima ad probandum quod intendit ponit quoddam medium et ipsum manifestat, in secunda ex medio manifestato concludit principale, ibi: *Non ergo existentibus* (5.2b6).

Prima in duas. Primo medium manifestat, secundo manifestatum concludit, ibi: *Quare omnia alia* (5.2b3).

Prima in duas. Primo manifestat medium per praedicta, secundo per subiunctionem exemplorum, ibi: *Hoc autem manifestum* (5.2a36).

Prima in duas. Primo ponit quaedam ex quibus infert medium, secundo concludit, ibi: *Alia praedicta ergo omnia* (5.2a32).

Prima in duas. Primo proponit, secundo per exempla manifestat, ibi: *ut hominis de subiecto* (5.2a21).

Haec est divisio lectionis, et sunt sex particulae.

\<Sententia\>

Circa primam sic procedit: Manifestum est ex his quae praedicta sunt, id est ex regula prius posita, scilicet "Quando alterum de altero praedicatur etc.", quod quaedam praedicantur de subiecto nomine et ratione. Quia si aliquid dicitur de subiecto, dicitur secundum nomen. Sed ratio praedicatur de nomine, quod est praedicatum. Ergo dicetur de subiecto.

Consequenter manifestat per exempla, dicens quod homo praedicatur de aliquo homine et secundum nomen et secundum rationem. Sed eorum quae sunt in subiecto quaedam nec secundum nomen nec secundum rationem praedicantur, et haec sunt accidentia abstracta, sed quaedam praedicantur secundum nomen | f. 28vb

---

19–20   Arist. *Cat.* 3.1b10–16

---

4 tres] duas *P*   **4** principaliter] maxime *P*   **5** maxime] proprie *P*   **6** proprie] principaliter *P*
8 quoddam] quodam *P*   **11** alia] anima *P*   **13** ibi] in *add. P*   **20** scilicet] quod *add. P*   **20** etc]
om. P

et non secundum rationem, ut accidentia concreta. Et ponit exemplum: ut album dicitur de subiecto, non autem definitio sua.

Ex his concludit medium manifestatum, dicens: Manifestum est quod omnia alia a primis substantiis aut dicuntur de primis aut sunt in primis.

Consequenter manifestat medium per subiunctionem exemplorum, dicens quod manifestum est per singula quod omnia alia sunt in primis aut dicuntur de primis, ut animal dicitur de homine, ergo de aliquo homine, quod est prima substantia, quod si non dicitur de aliquo homine, nec de homine. Similiter ponit exemplum in his quae sunt in, dicens quod color est in corpore, ergo in aliquo corpore, quod est prima substantia.

Ex his concludit medium, dicens quod ex dictis patet quod omnia <alia> a primis aut dicuntur de primis aut sunt in primis.

Ultimo ex medio manifestato concludit principale intentum sic: Omnia alia a primis aut sunt in aut dicuntur de. Ergo primae substantiae sunt substentamentum omnium aliorum et subiectum. Sed destructo subiecto destruuntur et quae sunt in eo. Ergo non existentibus primis impossibile est aliquod aliorum remanere. Si ergo primis destructis alia destruuntur, primae sunt principaliter substantiae.

Haec est sententia partis.

Litteralis expositio

Ita dictum est de prima substantia, *autem*, pro sed, *manifestum est ex his quae dicta sunt*, id est ex regula superius posita, scilicet "Quando alterum de altero praedicatur", *quoniam eorum*, id est earum substantiarum, *quae dicuntur de subiecto necesse est nomen et rationem de subiecto praedicari*. Quia si aliquid dicitur de subiecto, dicitur secundum nomen. Sed ratio praedicatur de nomine, quod est praedicatum. Ergo dicitur de subiecto per regulam.

Consequenter ponit exempla: *ut ratio hominis et nomen praedicatur de aliquo homine subiecto*, id est prima substantia. Continua: Bene dixi quod sic, *enim*, pro quia, *quidam homo et est homo et animal rationale mortale. Quare*, id est ergo, *nomen et ratio praedicabitur de subiecto*. Continua: Ita dixi de illis quae dicuntur de, *vero*, pro sed, *eorum quae sunt in subiecto*, <id est> accidentium, *neque nomen neque ratio praedicabitur* ut *in pluribus*, quia nunquam in abstractione. Ita dixi quod non, *autem*, id est sed, *nihil prohibet nomen praedicari in aliquibus*, id est in concreto, *vero*, id est sed, *impossibile est rationem de subiecto praedicari*. Et ponit exemplum: *ut album, cum sit in corpore subiecto, praedicatur de subiecto (enim*, <id

---

22 quia] quod *P*   **26** prima substantia] praedicabili *P*   **27** quia] *iter. P*

est> quia, *dicitur corpus album*), *vero*, id est sed, impossibile est rationem *albi de corpore* praedicari.

Concludit medium: Secundae substantiae dicuntur de primis, accidentia sunt in. Omnia alia a primis sunt talia et talia. Ergo *omnia alia*, a primis supple, *dicuntur*
5 *de aut sunt in.*

Sed *manifestum est hoc*, id est quod alia dicuntur de aut sunt in, *ex his quae* proponuntur; *ut animal*, quod est secunda substantia, *praedicatur de homine, ergo de aliquo homine*. Et probat consequentiam: *nam si de nullo aliquorum hominum* praedicatur, *nec de homine*. Et ita patet quod secundae substantiae dicuntur de.
10 *Rursus color*, quod est accidens, *est in corpore, ergo in aliquo corpore*. Et probat consequentiam: *nam si in nullo singulorum*, id est singularium, *nec omnino in corpore*. Et ita patet quod accidentia sunt in.

Consequenter concludit | medium ex his. Et sequitur sicut prius: *Quare*, <id   f. 29ra
est> ergo, *omnia alia* a primis *aut dicuntur de principalibus substantiis aut sunt in*
15 *eis.*

Ultimo concludit principale propositum ex medio probato. Et sequitur sic: Omnia alia aut sunt in primis aut dicuntur de. Ergo primae substantiae sunt substentamentum omnium aliorum et subiectum. Sed destructo subiecto destruuntur quae sunt in eo. *Ergo primis substantiis non existentibus impossibile est* aliquod *aliorum*
20 *esse, enim*, id est quia, *omnia alia dicuntur de eis subiectis aut sunt in eis*. Et ita primae substantiae sunt principaliter substantiae.

<QUAESTIONES>

<1>

Primo dubitatur quia in definiendo prius ponit hanc particulam, "proprie", deinde "principaliter", ultimo "maxime", in prosequendo autem ordinat modo contrario, quia primo probat convenire "principaliter" primis substantiis, secundo "proprie",
25 tertio "maxime".

Et dicendum quod ista possunt dupliciter ordinari: aut comparando ipsa ad invicem aut per relationem ad ea a quibus differt prima substantia per ipsa. Primo modo ordinat definiendo, quia si est substantia principaliter et maxime, est substantia proprie, et si est maxime, est principaliter, sed non e converso, et prius est
30 a quo non convertitur consequentia, ut scribitur in *Postpraedicamentis*. Secundo

---

22–23 Arist. *Cat.* 5.2a12–14   29–30 Arist. *Cat.* 12.14a30–35

---

13 concludit] principale propositum ex medio probato et sequitur sic *add. P*   **19** est aliquod] *inv.*
P   **22** definiendo] sententia *P*   **23** prosequendo] consequendo *P*   **27** differt] definitur *P*

modo ordinat in prosequendo, nam per "principaliter" differt a secundis substantiis, per "maxime" ab accidentibus, per "proprie" a substantia grammaticali, quam
logicus non considerat nisi per accidens; haec autem duo principaliter considerat,
et secunda substantia prius est quam accidens.

<2>

Secundo quaeritur de hoc quod dicit quod quaedam accidentia praedicantur se-   5
cundum nomen et non secundum definitionem.

Contra. Dicit Boethius: "De quocumque praedicatur definitio, et definitum, et
e converso". Ergo falsum dicit auctor.

Item. Dicitur in secundo *Topicorum* quod si dicatur accidens inesse alicui, vi-
dendum utrum ratio accidentis insit, quia si non, nec ipsum accidens. Ergo cui   10
convenit nomen, et ratio. Et ita a primo de quo praedicatur accidens secundum
nomen, de eodem praedicabitur secundum rationem.

Item. Scribitur in *Posterioribus* quod de quocumque praedicatur nomen, et
ratio.

Et dicendum quod duplex est definitio accidentis, una in quantum accidens, alia   15
in quantum tale accidens, ut definitio albi in quantum accidens est quod adest et
abest praeter subiecti corruptionem, sed in quantum tale accidens est corpus coloratum disgregativum visus; de prima definitione loquitur hic, de secunda obicitur.

Vel aliter. Accidens potest dupliciter definiri, ut album, scilicet per comparationem ad formam abstractam a qua descendit, et sic album est corpus coloratum   20
etc., et secundum hanc de subiecto praedicatur, ut hic obicitur; aliter definitur per
comparationem ad subiectum in quo est, et hoc est quod adest et abest praeter subiecti corruptionem, et secundum hanc non praedicatur de subiecto, et sic loquitur
auctor.

<3>

Tertio quaeritur qualiter intendit hanc definitionem.   25

Et dicendum quod praedicari est supponi, dicit Boethius, et quia accidens secundum illam definitionem quam recipit a subiecto non supponitur, ideo secundum
hanc non praedicatur.

5–6 Arist. *Cat.* 5.2a26–34   7–8 *cf.* Boeth. *Diff. Top.* II 5.5 (=1187a), III 3.2–3 (=1196c–d) (ed.
Nikitas, 23; 50); *in Top. Cic.* 1060a; Petrus Hispanus *Tractatus* V 6–7 (ed. de Rijk, 60–61)   **9–10**
cf. Arist. *Top.* II 2.109b30–10a9   **13–14** *locum non inveni*   26 Boeth. *in Isag.*[2] III 7 (ed. Brandt,
204)

---

2 grammaticali] generali *P*   **11** a] de *P*   **25** tertio] secundo *P ut v.*   **25** qualiter intendit] *lectio
incerta*   **26** boethius] dionysius *P*   **27** illam] primam *P*

\<4\>

Quarto quaeritur: Dicit quod destructis primis destruuntur alia quae sunt in ipsis.

Contra. Corruptio corruptibilis non est causa corruptionis incorruptibilis, ut per se patet. Cum ergo | primae substantiae sint corruptibiles et universalia incor-   f. 29rb
ruptibilia, corruptio in primis non erit causa corruptionis in universalibus. Ergo
5   ipsis destructis alia possunt remanere.

Item. Ad destructionem eius quod est hic et nunc non sequitur destructio eius quod est ubique et semper. Cum ergo singularia sint hic et nunc, universalia ubique et semper, ut scribitur in *Posterioribus*, ad destructionem singularium non sequitur destructio universalium.

10   Sed contra. Scribitur secundo *De anima*: "Data est virtus generativa in animalibus ut per eam continuetur divinum esse et appetibile, quod est esse speciei, ut quod in se salvari non poterat salvaretur \<in\> individuis". Ergo primae substantiae sunt causae continuationis ipsorum universalium. Sed omne illud quod per sui existentiam est causa continuationis alicuius in esse, per sui defectum est causa de
15   fectus \<eius. Ergo defectus\> singularium est \<causa\> defectus universalium, et ita primis substantiis non existentibus impossibile est aliquod aliorum esse.

Et dicendum quod universale duplex habet esse, naturae scilicet et rationis. \<Es­se\> naturae dicitur esse actuale quod habet in singularibus, et sic destructis primis destruuntur universalia. Esse rationis dicitur esse defectivum vel aptitudinale, et
20   sic destructis primis non destruuntur universalia sed sunt incorruptibilia iuxta illud Porphyrii, "ad destructionem inferiorum non sequitur destructio superiorum". Et per hoc patet solutio ad obiecta.

Sed contra hoc obicitur. Sicut se habet ars ad naturam, sic esse rationis ad esse naturae. Sed ars posterior est natura. Ergo esse rationis posterius est quam esse
25   secundum naturam, et ita esse naturae prius. Sed destructo priori destruitur posterius. Ergo destructo esse naturae destruitur esse rationis. Si igitur aliquid non sit secundum actum, quod est esse naturae, nec erit secundum aptitudinem, quod est esse rationis. Et sic solutio nulla.

Et dicendum: "Destructo priori destruitur posterius", hoc est necessarium si
30   prius et posterius sint in eodem genere, sed si non, falsum est. Sed esse secundum actum et esse secundum aptitudinem non sunt in eodem genere sed in diverso, quia esse secundum actum est in natura, reliquum in ratione. Unde patet quod non valet argumentum distinguendo prius et posterius ut dictum est.

---

1 Arist. *Cat.* 5.2b6–7 **7–8** *cf.* Arist. *APo* I 31.87b28–33; Anon. *Auct. Arist.* 35.92 (ed. Hamesse, 319) **10–12** *cf.* Arist. *An.* II 4.415a26–b7; Anon. *Auct. Arist.* 6.57–58 (ed. Hamesse, 179) **20–21** *cf.* Porph. *Isag.* 14.22–15.2

---

19 aptitudinale] actitudinale *P ut v.*   **24** posterior] posteriorum *P*   **24** est quam esse] esse est quam *P*

Lectio IX

Secundarum vero substantiarum etc. (5.2b7)

<Divisio>

Probato quod haec differentia "principaliter" conveniat primis substantiis, hic ostendit hanc differentiam "maxime" convenire eisdem. Sed quidam dicunt quod in prima parte determinavit de quibusdam proprietatibus primae substantiae, hic exsequitur de proprietatibus secundae substantiae.

Haec pars dividitur in duas et est praesentis lectionis. Primo probat quod primae substantiae sunt maxime substantiae per rationem sumptam per comparationem causae ad effectum, secundo per comparationem effectus ad causam, ibi: *Amplius principales* (5.2b15).

Prima in duas. Primo ponit minorem sui argumenti, secundo probat eam, ibi: *Propinquior enim* (5.2b9).

Haec secunda | in duas. Primo ponit minorem probationis, secundo probat ipsam, ibi: *Si quis enim* (5.2b9).   f. 29va

Pars in qua ponit secundam rationem in duas. Primo ponit rationem, secundo removet duas dubitationes, ibi: *Ipsarum vero specierum* (5.2b22).

Prima in duas. Primo ponit conclusionem probandam, secundo maiorem, ibi: *Sicut autem principales substantiae*, vel quidam habent: *Quemadmodum principales substantiae* (5.2b18).

Pars in qua removet dubium in duas penes duo quae removet. Secunda ibi: *Similiter autem* (5.2b26).

Haec est divisio lectionis, et sunt septem particulae.

<Sententia>

Circa primam sic procedit intendens tale argumentum: In quolibet genere est magis et minus per accessum ad maximum in illo genere. Sed species est magis substantia quam genus quia magis accedit ad primam substantiam. Ergo prima substantia est maxime in genere substantiae, et sic est maxime substantia. Huius rationis ponit minorem.

Consequenter probat eam. Et est ratio talis: Omne quod est propinquius primae substantiae est magis substantia. Species est propinquior primae substantiae. Ergo etc. Minorem ponit.

---

11 ponit] probat *P* **23** est] magis *add. P* **25** minorem] in duas secondarum substantiarum etc. *add. P*

Consequenter probat eam ratione tali: Illud quod convenientius dicit quid est
prima substantia est propinquius primae substantiae. Sed species sunt huiusmodi
(ut probat per exempla). Ergo etc.

Consequenter probat idem per comparationem effectus ad causam. Et est ratio
talis: Sicut se habent primae substantiae ad alia, ita se habent species ad genera. Sed   5
species dicitur magis substantia respectu generis quia pluribus substat. Ergo primae
substantiae respectu aliorum, cum omnibus substent, dicentur maxime substantiae.

Consequenter removet dubium. Quia dictum est quod species magis est substantia quam genus, posset aliquis dubitare utrum una species magis esset substantia quam alia. Ideo dicit quod non et ponit exempla.   10

Ultimo removet consimile dubium de primis substantiis.

Haec est sententia partis.

Expositio litteralis

Ita dixi quod prima substantia est principaliter substantia, *vero*, pro sed, *secunda-*
rum substantiarum species est magis substantia quam genus.

Et hoc probat: Bene dico quod est, *enim*, pro quia, *species propinquior est*   15
primae substantiae. Et format argumentum ut dictum est.

Consequenter probat hoc: Bene dixi "propinquior", quia *si quis assignet primam*
substantiam dicendo *quid est, assignabit evidentius*, id est manifestius, *et conve-*
nientius proferens speciem quam genus. Et ponit exempla: *ut*, pro sicut, assignans
quendam hominem quid est, *assignabit manifestius hominem quam animal.* Et red-   20
dit causam: *enim*, pro quia, *illud*, id est species, *est magis proprium*, id est propin-
quum, *alicuius hominis*, scilicet particularis, sed *hoc*, id est genus, est minus pro-
pinquum quia commune. Consequenter ponit aliud exemplum, dicens: *Si reddide-*
ris, id est si assignaveris, *aliquam arborem* assignando quid est, *manifestius assi-*
gnabis proferendo *arborem quam plantam*, quod est genus supremum. Et format   25
argumentum ut dictum est.

Consequenter ponit rationem per comparationem effectus ad causam, dicens:
Amplius principales substantiae, id est primae, *dicuntur maxime substantiae* eo, id
est ideo, *quod sunt subiectae omnibus aliis et*, pro quia, *omnia alia*, supple a primis,
aut praedicantur de eis, id est primis, *aut sunt in eis.*   30

f. 29vb   Consequenter probat istam conclusionem: Ita dixi quod primae substantiae |
sunt maxime, *autem*, pro quia, *sicut principales substantiae <ad alia omnia> se*

---

7 substent] subsint *P*   15 enim] *P*^{sup}*c* : vero *P*   15 quia] *iter. P*   15 propinquior] propinquorum
P   17 propinquior] propinquorum *P*   20 quendam] quaedam *P*   20 manifestius] *ac* : magis *P*
21 enim] *ac*_{Cs} : etiam *P*   24 manifestius] *c* : magis *P*   24–25 assignabis] assignabit *P*

habent, supple in substando, *sic se habent species ad genus*. Et hoc probat: *enim*, <pro> quia, *species* subiacent *generi*, supple sicut primae substantiae aliis. Et bene dixi "species subiacent generi", *nam genera praedicantur de speciebus, autem*, pro sed, *species non* convertitur, id est non conversim praedicatur, *de genere*. Littera

5 truncata: *Ex his* quae dicta sunt manifestum est quod *species magis est substantia genere*, id est quam genus.

Consequenter removet dubium: Ita dixi quod species magis est substantia quam genus, *vero*, id est sed, *ipsarum specierum quae non sunt genera*, <id est> *specialissimarum, alterum nihil*, pro non, *est magis substantia altero*. Et bene dico quod

10 non, *enim*, pro quia, nullus assignabit *familiarius hominem de aliquo homine quam equum de aliquo equo*.

Ultimo removet consimile dubium de primis substantiis: Ita dixi quod una species non est magis substantia, et non solum est hoc verum de speciebus, *autem*, pro sed, *principalium substantiarum*, id est primarum, <*alterum*> *nihil*, pro non, *est*

15 *magis substantia altero*. Et ponit exempla: *enim*, pro quia, *aliquis homo nihil*, pro non, *est magis substantia quam aliquis bos*.

<QUAESTIONES>

<1>

Primo quaeritur: Dicit quod species est magis substantia quam genus. Quaeritur ergo utrum una substantia sit magis substantia quam alia.

Dicit auctor quod sic.

20 Sed contra. Magis et minus sunt in quolibet genere per accessum maiorem et minorem ad unum terminum et recessum maiorem et minorem a termino contrario, ut innuit Aristoteles in secundo < * * * >, ut hoc dicitur magis album per accessum ad maxime album et per recessum a contrario, quod est maxime nigrum. Ergo magis et minus non possunt esse nisi in eis in quibus est reperire contrarios

25 terminos. Sed in substantiis non est reperire contrarios terminos, quia substantiae nihil est contrarium. Ergo etc.

Item. Dicit auctor in sequentibus quod substantia non suscipit magis et minus.

Ad oppositum. Omne quod comparatur recipit magis et minus. Sed omne univocum comparabile, scribitur in primo *Topicorum*. Ergo omne univocum recipit

30 magis et minus. Sed substantia est univoca. Ergo etc.

---

17 Arist. *Cat.* 5.2b7–22 **22–23** *cf.* Arist. *Top.* III 5.119a27–32; Anon. *Auct. Arist.* 36.55 (ed. Hamesse, 325) **27** Arist. *Cat.* 5.3b33–4a8 **28–29** Arist. *Top.* I 15.107b17

---

4 conversim] conversum *P*

Et dicendum quod de substantia contingit loqui dupliciter: aut quantum ad esse, et sic non suscipit magis et minus, ut habetur in sequentibus, aut in comparatione ad actum suum qui est substare, et sic bene suscipit magis et minus, ut substantia quae pluribus substat est magis substantia et quae paucioribus minus.

Per hoc patet solutio ad obiecta. Nam argumenta quae probant quod non recipit   5
magis et minus procedunt quantum ad esse.

Ad argumentum in contrarium dicendum quod sophisticum.

Ad aliud dicendum quod duplex est comparatio. Quaedam secundum aeque, et ista est univoca, sicut homo et equus aequaliter comparantur ad animal (nam aequaliter sunt homo et equus species), et de ista loquitur in primo *Topicorum*. Alia   10
est secundum magis et minus, et ista est solum in accidentibus, ut dicit Boethius. Cum ergo dicitur "Omne quod comparatur etc.", hoc est verum de comparatione secundo modo, sed cum assumis "Omne univocum comparabile", iam aequivocas in comparatione, quare non tenet.

<2>

Consequenter quaeritur: Dicit quod species magis substantia quam genus.   15

Sed contra. Omne quod est causa alteri ut sit, magis est ens in genere illo. Sed genus in genere substantiae est | causa speciei, ut dicit Porphyrius et Boethius. Ergo magis est ens in genere substantiae genus quam species.

f. 39ra

Item. Forma est magis substantia quam materia, scribitur in octavo *Physicorum*. Ergo quod magis est forma magis est substantia per illam considerationem   20
secundi *Topicorum*: "Si simpliciter ad simpliciter etc." Sed genus est magis forma quam species. Ergo magis substantia. Minor patet: Forma est divinum et appetibile et multiplicata est per materiam. Ergo forma quae est magis multiplicata est magis forma. Sed forma generis est huiusmodi. Ergo est magis forma et ita magis substantia.   25

Et dicendum quod species est magis substantia, ut dicit auctor.

Ad primum dicendum quod ens dividitur multipliciter. Uno modo per materiam et formam, alio modo per causam et causatum, alio per simplex et compositum. Cum ergo obicitur, "Genus est causa speciei, ergo verius est ens, et ita verius est substantia", dicendum quod verum est per relationem ad hanc divisionem entis,   30

---

11 Boeth. *Top. Diff.* I 5.30 (=1178c) (ed. Nikitas, 12)   **15** Arist. *Cat.* 5.2b7–22   **16–17** *cf.* Boeth. *in Isag.*[2] I 9 (ed. Brandt, 158)   **19–20** *potius* Arist. *Phys.* II 1.193b6–8; Anon. *Auct. Arist.* 2.55 (ed. Hamesse 145)   **20–21** Arist. *Top.* II 11.115b4–9   **22–23** *cf.* Arist. *An.* II 4.415a26–b7; Anon. *Auct. Arist.* 6.57–58 (ed. Hamesse, 179)

---

2 aut] alio modo *P*   **15** quaeritur dicit] *inv. P*   **17** substantiae] substantia *P*   **22** divinum] divisum *P*

aliud causa, aliud causatum, sed falsum est quantum ad istam, aliud simplex, aliud compositum, quia sic verius est ens species quam genus.

Ad secundum, quod magis est forma generalis quam specialis magis est ens, dicendum quod verum est quantum ad hanc divisionem entis, aliud forma, aliud materia, sed falsum quantum ad istam, aliud simplex, aliud compositum, et etiam quantum ad actum qui est substare, et sic loquitur hic.

<3>

Consequenter quaeritur de ordine ad partem sequentem, quia prius comparat speciem ad genus quam species ad alias species.

Videtur ordinem pervertere. Nam una species non dicitur magis species quam altera. Magis ergo convenit species cum specie quam cum genere. Et ita pars sequens ante istam.

Et dicendum quod contingit de genere et specie loqui dupliciter: aut quantum ad id quod sunt aut quantum ad actum substandi. Secundo modo plus convenit species cum specie quam cum genere, ut obicitur, sed quantum ad id quod sunt plus convenit genus cum specie quam species cum specie, quia genus totaliter salvatur in specie et non una species in alia; et ideo prius comparat speciem ad genus quam speciem ad speciem.

<4>

Consequenter quaeritur quare comparat speciem ad speciem et primam substantiam ad primam potius quam genus ad genus.

Et dicendum quod genus est quoddam totum, species autem et primae substantiae sunt partes, ut dicit Porphyrius. Quia totum in quantum tale est completum quid, pars in quantum tale est quid incompletum, ideo partes plus dependent quam totum.

Sed obicitur. Sicut genus non dependet ab alio genere, sic nec species ab alia specie nec prima substantia a prima substantia. Ergo qua ratione non comparat genus ad genus non debet comparare speciem ad speciem.

Et dicendum quod non est simile, quia genus non dependet ab aliquo genere nec ambo a tertio; sed licet una species ab alia non dependeat, ambae tamen dependent a tertio, ut a genere.

20–21 Porph. *Isag.* 7.27–8.3

---

4 ad] regulam *add. P*   **7** prius] primo *P*   **15** quia] et *P*

Vel aliter. Magis videtur quod una species est magis substantia quam alia et
similiter de primis substantiis quod dicerentur | magis substantiae inter se quam
de generibus, et quia probat de istis, etiam per consequens probat de generibus per
locum a maiori.

<5>

Consequenter videtur quod una species sit magis substantia quam alia, licet oppo-   5
situm dicat auctor.

Quia genus per differentias dividitur oppositas quarum una respectu alterius se
habet per modum habitus, reliqua per modum privationis, ut animal dividitur per
rationale et irrationale, et rationale habet se per modum habitus, irrationale per
modum privationis. Sed habitus verius est ens quam privatio. Ergo species consti-   10
tuta ex differentia quae habet se per modum habitus magis est ens quam species
constituta ex differentia quae per modum privationis se habet. Et ita una species
magis est ens quam alia, et ita magis substantia.

Et dicendum quod contingit loqui de speciebus dupliciter: aut per relationem
ad sua principia formalia, et ita illa quae est per modum habitus verius est ens, ut   15
obicitur; sed species comparando ad suum genus et ad sua individua una non est
magis species quam alia in substantia, quia aequaliter species sunt sub suo genere
iuxta illud *Praedicamentorum*, "Dividentia aliquod tertium aequaliter sunt in illo et
aequaliter habent individua sibi correspondentia", et sic loquitur hic.

5–6 Arist. *Cat.* 5.2b22–26   **18–19** *cf.* Arist. *Cat.* 13.14b31–15a4

---

16 sed] scilicet *P*   **18** sunt] sub *P*   **19** habent] sibi *add. P*

Lectio X

\<Divisio\>

In hac parte, ut dictum est, ostendit hanc differentiam, "proprie", convenire primis substantiis.

Et dividitur in duas partes penes duas rationes quas ponit. Secunda ibi: *Amplius principales substantiae* (5.2b38).

Prima in duas. Primo proponit quod intendit et probat illud, secundo concludit propositum probatum, ut ibi: *Ergo merito* (5.2b37).

Prima in duas. Primo proponit, secundo propositum probat, ibi: *Sola enim haec* (5.2b31).

Haec secunda in duas. Primo probat minorem argumenti, secundo manifestat eam per exempla, ibi: *Aliquem enim hominem* (5.2b32).

Pars in qua ponit rationem secundam in duas. Primo ponit conclusionem probandam, secundo probativam maiorem ipsius ponit, ibi: *sicut autem primae substantiae* (5.3a1).

Haec est divisio lectionis, et sunt particulae sex.

\<Sententia\>

Circa primam sic procedit et intendit tale argumentum: Species et genus sunt secundae substantiae et solum, quia indicant hae solae quid est prima substantia. Cum ergo species et genera respectu aliorum dicantur proprie substantiae, prima substantia respectu aliorum est proprie substantia. Primo proponit huius rationis quod intendit, dicens quod sola species et genera dicuntur secundae substantiae.

Consequenter probat hoc sic: Quaecumque indicant primam substantiam, solum sunt secundae substantiae. Genus et species sunt huiusmodi solum (hanc ponit). Ergo etc.

Consequenter probat minorem per exempla sicut patet.

Deinde concludit ex dictis quod sola species et genera dicuntur secundae substantiae respectu aliorum. Et ex hoc ulterius infert quod primae substantiae sunt proprie substantiae.

Consequenter ponit aliud argumentum. Et est tale: Sicut se habent primae substantiae ad alia, ita se habent species et genera ad omnia alia. Sed genus et species dicuntur proprie substantiae respectu aliorum. Ergo prima substantia respectu

---

25 infert] instat *P*

f. 39va   aliorum dicetur proprie | substantia. Primo ponit conclusionem, secundo maiorem
et eam per exempla manifestat.

Haec est sententia partis.

EXPOSITIO LITTERALIS

Ita dictum est quod primae substantiae sunt maxime, *autem*, <pro> sed, *post prin-*
cipales, id est primas, *sola aliorum*, id est de numero aliarum, *<species et genera>*   5
dicuntur secundae substantiae.

Consequenter probat hoc: Bene dixi "dicuntur secundae substantiae", *haec*
enim sola, id est species et genera, *eorum quae praedicantur indicant*, supple substantialiter (nam accidentia indicant accidentaliter), *principalem*, id est primam,
substantiam. Argumentum formatur ut dictum est.   10

Consequenter probat hoc per exempla: Ita dixi "sola haec indicant etc.", *enim*, id
est quia, *si quis assignaverit aliquem hominem quid sit, familiarius*, id est evidentius, *assignabit speciem quam genus, et*, id est quia, *faciet manifestius* quid sit aliquis
homo *assignando hominem*, quod est species supple, *quam animal.* Et quia compa-
rativum relinquit suum positivum, per hoc quod dicit quod species facit manifestius   15
innuit quod genus faciat manifestum. *Vero*, pro sed, *quicquid quilibet assignaverit*
<aliorum>, a substantia supple, *assignabit extranee*, id est improprie, *velut*, id est
sicut, *reddens*, id est respondens, *album* etc.

Consequenter concludit: *Ergo solae hae*, id est species et genera, *dicuntur merito*
secundae substantiae, et proprie supple. Ex hoc concludit ulterius † aliam   20

primictem † conclusionem probandam, dicens: *Amplius principales*, id est primae, *substantiae dicuntur proprie eo*, id est ideo, *quod*, id est quia, *omnibus aliis*
subiacent.

Consequenter probat hoc, dicens: *Autem*, pro sed, *sicut primae substantiae se*
habent ad omnia alia, ita species et genera principalium, id est primarum, *se habent* 25
ad omnia alia, quae *praedicantur de his*, id est specie et genere. Et ponit exemplum:
enim, <id est> quia, *aliquem <hominem>* dicens *grammaticum esse, et hominem et*
animal dicis esse *grammaticum*; sic et in aliis.

7–8 haec enim sola] $P^{sup}c$: hae enim solae P 8 praedicantur] praedicatur P 11 sola haec] solae
hae P

<Quaestiones>

<1>

Primo quaeritur de eo quod dicit quod sola genera et species substantiae indicant primam substantiam.

Contra. Accidentia indicant primam substantiam. Ergo non solum genera et species. Maior patet. Scribitur enim in primo *De anima*: "Accidentia maximam partem conferunt ad cognoscendum subiectum".

Et dicendum quod duplex est esse, scilicet esse naturae, et tale constat ex principiis naturalibus, aliud est cognitionis, secundum quod dicit Porphyrius quod individua constant ex septem proprietatibus. Et secundum quod duplex habet esse, dupliciter potest indicari. Nam primum esse est substantiale, secundum accidentale. Dicendum ergo quod solum species et genera indicant primam substantiam substantialiter, et sic loquitur auctor. Accidentia, ut obicitur, indicant primam substantiam accidentaliter, quare non valet obiectio.

<2>

Secundo quaeritur de eo quod dicit quod species magis indicant primam substantiam quam genus.

Contra. Potior est cognitio quae est per causam quam quae per effectum; nam, ut scribitur primo *Posteriorum*, "Scire est causam etc." Sed genus est causa speciei, ut dicit Porphyrius. Ergo etc.

Ad idem. | In quaestione quid est non est ire in infinitum, quia dicit Plato quod   f. 39vb
non contingit infinita pertransire. Ergo est ibi status. Verior est cognitio per illud in quo est status quam per illud in quo non est status. In specie autem non. Ergo etc.

Et dicendum quod cognoscens per speciem verius cognoscit quam cognoscens per genus, et causa est quia in specie intelligitur genus et non e converso, unde cognoscens per speciem cognoscit per genus, sed non convertitur; propter hoc verior est cognitio per speciem quam per genus.

1–2   Arist. *Cat.* 5.2b30–32   **4–5**   Arist. *An.* I 1.402b21–22; Anon. *Auct. Arist.* 6.7 (ed. Hamesse, 174)   **7–8**   *sententia apud* Porph. *non invenitur, sed cf. Isag.* 7.21–24; Boeth. *in Isag.*² III 11 (ed. Brandt, 234–36); *et praesertim* Anon. *Auct. Arist.* 30.12–13 (ed. Hamesse, 300).   **13–14**   Arist. *Cat.* 5.2b32–35   **15–16**   Arist. *APo* I 2.71b10–12, *ut apud* Anon. *Auct. Arist.* 35.8 (ed. Hamesse, 311)   **16–17**   *cf.* Boeth. *in Isag.*² I 9 (ed. Brandt, 158)   **18–19**   *cf.* Porph. *Isag.* 6.13–16; Anon. *Auct. Arist.* 30.11 (ed. Hamesse, 300)

9 dupliciter] duplex *P*   **18** est ire] convenire *P*   **19** cognitio] ergo *P*

Ad obiecta dicendum quod verior esset cognitio per genus quam per speciem nisi genus in specie intelligeretur.

<3>

Tertio quaeritur: Dicit quod omnia alia praedicantur de specie et genere.

Contra. Scribitur in primo *Veteris ethicae* quod omnis actio circa singularia, et passio similiter. Ergo actio et passio non sunt circa universalia. Sed si praedicentur   5
de universalibus, sunt in ipsis. Ergo non praedicantur de ipsis.

Et dicendum quod actio et cetera accidentia possunt inesse alicui dupliciter, scilicet prius aut posterius. Dicendum ergo quod actio et cetera accidentia possunt inesse alicui dupliciter, ut dictum est, et sunt in primis substantiis primo modo, et sic loquitur Aristoteles, sed ex consequenti et per posterius insunt substantiis se-   10
cundis, et ideo per posterius praedicantur de ipsis, et sic loquitur hic. Et hoc est quod dicit Porphyrius quod accidentia per prius sunt in individuis, per posterius in speciebus.

---

3 Arist. *Cat.* 5.3a1–6   4 Arist. *EN* II 7.1107a31–32; Anon. *Auct. Arist.* 12.43 (ed. Hamesse, 235); *cf.* Arist. *Metaph.* I 1.981a16–17; Anon. *Auct. Arist.* 1.5 (ed. Hamesse, 115)   11–13 Porph. *Isag.* 13.18–21

---

1 esset] est *P*

LECTIO XI

COMMUNE EST AUTEM ETC. (5.3a7)

‹DIVISIO›

Habita prima parte in qua determinat de his quae ordinantur in praedicamento substantiae penes substantialia, incipit pars in qua determinat de proprietatibus accidentalibus consequentibus ad haec.

Haec pars dividitur in duas quia substantia dupliciter potest considerari, scilicet in quantum res sub sermone, et sic dicibile, aut in quantum res tantum sive in quantum res naturalis, quod idem est. Unde primo determinat proprietates substantiae prout est res sub sermone, secundo prout est res solum, ibi: *Inest autem substantiis nihil illis* (5.3b25).

Prima in duas. Primo ponit proprietates communes secundis substantiis et quibusdam aliis, sicut differentiis, secundo ponit proprietates proprias, ibi: *Inest autem substantiis et differentiis* (5.3a33).

Prima praesentis est lectionis et dividitur in duas. Primo ponit quandam proprietatem communem, secundo removet quoddam dubium, ut ibi: *Non ‹vero› vos conturbent* (5.3a28).

Prima in duas. Primo ponit proprietatem et probat eam primis et ‹secundis› substantiis convenire, secundo extendit eam ad differentias. Secunda ibi: *Non est autem hoc substantiae proprium* (5.3a21).

Prima in duas. Primo ponit proprietatem, secundo probat eam substantiis convenire, ibi: *Principalis namque substantia* (5.3a7).

Haec secunda in duas. Primo probat eam convenire primis substantiis, secundo secundis. Secunda ibi: *Secundarum vero substantiarum* (5.3a10).

Haec secunda in duas. Primo probat istam proprietatem convenire secundis substantiis per inductionem, secundo per syllogismum. Secunda ibi: *Amplius autem* (5.3a15).

| Pars in qua ostendit istam proprietatem convenire differentiis dividitur in duas.   f. 40ra
Primo probat hoc per inductionem, secundo per syllogismum, ibi: *Ratio quoque differentiae* (5.3a26).

Haec est divisio lectionis, et sunt particulae septem.

---

1 ordinantur] determinantur *P, sed cf. divisionem in* Lectio VII *datam*   **13** vos] *P hic et infra* : nos *ac*   **16** eam] ex *add. P*   **19** principalis] ma *add. P a.c.*   **20** eam] *iter. P a.c.*

\<Sententia\>

Circa primam sic procedit, proponens quod commune est omni substantiae in subiecto non esse.

Consequenter probat hoc de primis substantiis. Et est ratio talis: Nihil quod non est in subiecto nec de subiecto dicitur, est in subiecto. Sed prima substantia est huiusmodi (hanc ponit). Ergo etc.   5

Consequenter probat hoc idem de secundis substantiis per inductionem, dicens quod \<neque\> homo, qui est species, nec \<animal, quod est\> genus, sunt in subiecto. Et omnis secunda substantia est genus vel species. Ergo nulla \<secunda\> substantia est in subiecto.

Consequenter probat hoc per syllogismum talem: Nihil quod est in subiec-   10 to praedicatur nomine et ratione. Secundae substantiae praedicantur nomine et ratione. Ergo non sunt in subiecto.

Consequenter probat hoc differentiis convenire. Et primo per inductionem, dicens quod bipes et gressibile dicuntur de subiecto et non sunt in subiecto. Similiter aliae differentiae. Et ita differentia non est in subiecto.   15

Consequenter probat hoc per syllogismum talem: Differentiae praedicantur nomine et ratione. Sed nihil quod est in subiecto praedicatur nomine et ratione. Ergo etc.

Ultimo removet dubium. Quia dixit quod substantia non est in subiecto et videtur quod partes substantiae essent in subiecto quia sunt in toto, ideo hoc removens   20 dicit quod non conturbent vos partes substantiae quia ita sunt in toto ac si essent in subiecto, quia illa quae sunt in aliquo sicut partes in toto non sunt in subiecto, per hoc volens quod aequivocetur modus essendi in prout dicitur pars esse in toto et accidens in subiecto.

Haec est sententia partis.   25

Expositio litteralis

Ita dictum est quod est substantia, *autem*, id est sed, *non esse in subiecto*, id est haec proprietas, *est commune omni substantiae*.

Et hoc probat primo de primis. Bene dico "commune est etc.", *namque principalis*, id est prima, *substantia neque dicitur de subiecto neque est in subiecto*, sicut accidens supple. Argumentum formatur ut dictum est.   30

Consequenter probat hoc convenire secundis substantiis. Ita dixi quod prima substantia non est in subiecto, sed *constat*, id est manifestum est, *secundarum sub-*

---

13 hoc] *iter. P a.c.*   **19** quia] *iter. P a.c.*   **27** commune] P*sup/inf*c : communis P *stantiarum quidem*, id est quoniam, *non sunt in subiecto*; *enim*, id est quia, *homo*, quod est species supple, *dicitur de aliquo homine subiecto*, *autem*, id est sed, *in nullo subiecto est*. Et bene dico quod non est etc., *enim*, pro quia, *homo non est in aliquo homine* sicut accidens in subiecto.

Consequenter probat hoc per syllogismum, dicens: *Amplius nomen eorum quae sunt in subiecto nihil prohibet aliquotiens*, in concretione, supple, et non in abstractione, *praedicari de subiecto*, *vero*, pro sed, *rationem*, id est definitionem, *impossibile est* praedicari. *Vero*, pro sed, *ratio*, id est definitio, *secundarum substantiarum et nomen praedicatur de subiecto*; et ratio, *nam*, id est quia, *hominis rationem*, id est definitionem, *de aliquo homine praedicabis*. Ex his concludit: *Ergo secunda non est ex his quae sunt in subiecto*. Forma argumentum ut dictum est.

Consequenter probat hoc convenire differentiis. Ita dixi quod substantia non est in subiecto, *autem*, pro sed, *hoc*, id est non esse in | subiecto, *non est proprium* f. 40rb
substantiae. Et probat hoc per inductionem, dicens: *namque*, id est quia, *differentia est eorum quae non sunt in subiecto*, ut *bipes et gressibile dicitur de* aliquo *homine*, *autem*, pro sed, *in nullo subiecto est*. Et bene dico "in nullo", *enim*, pro quia, *bipes*, quod est differentia supple, *non est in* aliquo *homine neque gressibile*. Similiter intellige de aliis.

Consequenter probat hoc per syllogismum, dicens: *Ratio*, id est definitio, *differentiae dicitur de eo de quo ipsa differentia praedicatur*, *velut si gressibile* praedicatur *de homine, et ratio gressibilis de homine praedicabitur*. Et ponit exemplum. Argue ut dictum est.

Ultimo removet dubium: Ita dixi quod nulla substantia est in subiecto, *vero*, id est sed, *partes substantiarum non conturbent vos*, *quae*, partes scilicet, *ita sunt in toto quasi in subiecto sint*, quare non *cogamur eas*, id est partes substantiae, *non esse substantias <confiteri>*, quia partes, resume, *non dicuntur esse in subiecto quae sunt in aliquo tanquam* in toto. Quasi dicat: Non est idem modus essendi in.

<\QUAESTIONES>

<1>

Primo quaeritur de ordine ad partem praecedentem.

Dicit Dionysius: "Nulla substantia sensibilis vel intelligibilis comprehendi potest per intellectum nisi cognitio per accidentia praevia sit". Sed cognitio per istas proprietates est per accidentia. Ergo debet esse praevia.

29–30 *cf.* Dion. *Cael. Hier.* I 3 (ed. Migne, PG 3, 122c–d)

---

3 homo] *ac* : animal *P*

Ad idem. Dicit Nicomachus quod omnis rei certitudo consistit in accidentibus. Et ita idem quod prius.

Et dicendum quod multiplex est via cognoscendi in scientiis: una doctrinae et una disciplinae; † et est post via doctrinae est actio in docente, ut dicit †

Item. Dicit alibi: Doctrina est actio doctoris in discipulum, disciplina est pas- 5 sio in discipulo recipiente. Scientia est cognitio rei per causam infallibilem, ars est exitus a scientia in operationem. Et hoc dicit † Morebus. †

Dicendum ergo quod <in> via disciplinae, quae est quantum ad discipulum, co- gnitio rei per accidentia debet esse praevia quia per ea quae magis sensui se of- ferunt, et secundum hunc respectum argumenta procedunt; sed in via doctrinae 10 est e converso, nam docens intendit habere rei cognitionem per ea quae dicunt rei quidditatem quia per substantialia, et secundum hunc respectum loquitur hic, quia prior est cognitio per substantialia.

<2>

Secundo quaeritur de eo quod innuit quod substantia sit ens per se.

Sed contra. Dicit Plato quod nihil est infra Primum cuius ortum causa legitima 15 non praecesserit. Quia nihil est causa sui ipsius, ergo nihil est citra Primum quod non habet esse per causam. Sed nihil quod habet esse per causam est ens per se, sed ab alio ut a sua causa. Ergo nihil erit citra Primum ens per se.

Item. Dicit Iohannes Chrysostomus: "Omne quod est a semetipso eo ipso est ab aeterno". Sed nihil est ab aeterno citra Primum. Ergo nihil est a se ipso citra 20 Primum. Ergo omne quod est est <ab> alio. Et ita idem quod prius.

Ratione huius quaeritur, cum ens per se conveniat substantiae et Primae Causae, quo modo differenter.

f. 40va   Ad hoc ultimum | dicendum quod ens per se dicitur uno modo quod non est ab alio nec in alio, et sic Prima Causa est ens per se, secundo modo dicitur quod non 25 est in alio sed est ab alio, ut substantia.

Rationes autem procedunt prout per se est quod non est ab aliquo nec in alio, et sic non loquitur hic, unde aequivocatur ens per se.

---

1 cf. Boeth. *Inst. arith.* I 1.1–2 (ed. Guillaumin, 6)   5 cf. Arist. *Phys.* III 3.202b1–22; Averroes *in Phys.* III 20–22 (ed. Venet., 94ra–95ra); Haly *Commentum super Librum tegni Galieni* I 1 (ed. Venet., 1ra)   15–16 Plato *Tim.* 28a, Transl. Calcidii (ed. Waszink et Jensen, 20); Anon. *Auct. Arist.* 27.2 (ed. Hamesse, 296)   19–20 cf. Richardus de S. Victore *De trinitate* I 6 (ed. Migne, PL 196, 894a)

---

1 nicomachus] nasicheus *P*   5 doctoris] doctioris *P*   23 differenter] different *P*

\<3\>

Consequenter quaeritur: Innuit quod differentia non est substantia.

Sed contra. Dicit Commentator supra primum *Physicorum* quod omnis perfectio nobilior est suo perfectibili. Et dicit Commentator supra primum *De anima* quod nullum accidens nobilius est substantia. Ergo nullum accidens potest esse perfectio substantiae. Sed differentia est perfectio, dicit Porphyrius et etiam Boethius. Ergo differentia non est accidens. Ergo substantia.

Item. Omne quod est aut est substantia aut accidens. Differentia non est accidens. Ergo est substantia. Minor patet, quia "Nullum accidens dat esse substantiae", scribitur in primo *Physicorum*. Differentia dat esse substantiae, ut dicit Porphyrius. Ergo differentia non est accidens.

Et dicendum quod substantia dicitur tribus modis: materia, forma et compositum, ut dicit Aristoteles in *Libro de anima*. Cum autem Aristoteles dicit quod differentia non est substantia, verum est si accipiatur substantia pro composito; est autem substantia quae est forma, ut obicitur; et ita substantia aequivocatur.

Vel aliter. Substantia duplicem habet modum, scilicet essendi (est enim ens per se) et modum dicendi (quia praedicatur in quid). Dicendum ergo quod differentia substantiae cum sit ens per se, est substantia quantum ad modum essendi, sed non est substantia quantum ad modum dicendi, quia praedicatur in quale, ut dicit Porphyrius. Primo modo obicitur, secundo modo loquitur auctor.

\<4\>

Sed modo obicitur. Scribitur in septimo *Topicorum* quod si definitio praedicatur in quid, et partes eius, scilicet genus et differentiae. Ergo differentia habet modum dicendi ipsius substantiae, quod est contra solutionem.

Et dicendum quod praedicari in quid est dupliciter: proprie et communiter. Primo modo non praedicatur differentia in quid, et sic loquitur in solutione, secundo modo obicitur. Et dico in quid proprie quod praedicatur essentialiter et habet individua sibi immediate correspondentia, et quia differentia non habet individuum sibi immediate respondens, ideo non praedicatur in quid. Praedicari in quid com-

---

1 Arist. *Cat.* 5.3a21–28 **2–3** *cf.* Averroes *in Phys.* II 4 (ed. Venet., 50ra) **3–4** Averroes *in An.* II 2.16–20 (ed. Crawford, 130); Anon. *Auct. Arist.* 6.113 (ed. Hamesse, 183) **5** *cf.* Porph. *Isag.* 10.15–17; Boeth. *in Isag.*² IV 8 (ed. Brandt, 260) **8–9** *cf.* Arist. *Phys.* I 6.189a32–35 **9** *cf.* Porph. *Isag.* 12.2–4 **11–12** Arist. *An.* II 1.412a6–9; II 2.414a14–16; Anon. *Auct. Arist.* 6.37 (ed. Hamesse, 177) **18–19** Porph. *Isag.* 3.5–12; 3.17–19; 11.7–12; 15.2–4; 18.16–17 **20–21** Arist. *Top.* VII 3.153a15–22

---

5 etiam] autem *P* **8** quia] quod *P*

muniter est praedicari in quale substantiale, unde differentia praedicatur in quid quia in quale substantiale.

<5>

Quinto quaeritur: Innuit quod partes substantiae sunt substantiae.

Quod non videtur. Ens in potentia est ens quod non habet esse distinctum ab alio. Sed partes substantiae non habent esse distinctum. Ergo sunt in potentia. Sed   5
nihil quod est tantum in potentia est substantia actu. Ergo partes substantiae non sunt substantiae actu.

Item. Omnis substantia aut est prima aut est secunda. Partes substantiae non sunt prima neque secunda. Ergo etc.

Ad oppositum. Omne quod dat esse substantiae est substantia. Partes substan-   10
tiae dant ei esse. Ergo etc. Minor patet: Dicit Commentator supra primum *De anima* quod nullum accidens est nobilius substantia. Sed illud quod dat esse est nobilius. Ergo illud quod dat esse non est accidens. Minor patet: Dicit Commentator supra primum *Physicorum* quasi in principio quod partium compositio est forma totius. Cum ergo forma dat esse, partes per naturam substantiae compositionis   15
dant esse toti.

Quod concedo cum auctore.

Ad primum obiectum dicendum: Cum dicitur quod impossibile est quod ens tantum in potentia sit substantia actu, et ita cum partes substantiae sint potentia tantum, non erunt res actu, dicendum quod ens actu dicitur dupliciter. Uno modo   20
quod habet esse distinctum ab alio, et sic partes substantiae non sunt substantiae vel substantiae actu, ut obicitur. Aliter dicitur ens actu quod habet esse com|pletum in suo toto. Si enim ens actu dicatur quod habet esse completum in se et non in alio, sic partes substantiae non sunt actu, et sic non sunt substantiae, ut obicitur. Sed si ens actu dicatur quod habet esse completum in alio, sic partes substantiae sunt   25
substantiae actu.

<6>

Sexto quaeritur an pars sit eadem cum toto.

Quod non videtur. Quia si una esset eadem cum suo toto, eadem ratione et alia.

---

3 Arist. *Cat.* 5.3a29–32   **11–12** Averroes *in An.* II 2.16–20 (ed. Crawford, 130); Anon. *Auct. Arist.* 6.113 (ed. Hamesse, 183)   **13–15** *cf.* Averroes *in Phys.* I 17 (ed. Venet., 13v–14r); Anon. *Auct. Arist.* 2.43 (ed. Hamesse, 144)

---

1 quale substantiale] quali substantiali *P*   **3** substantiae²] substantia *P*   **18** dicitur] dicit *P*
20 dupliciter] tripliciter *P*   **22** substantiae] substantia *P*

f. 40vb

Sed quae uni et eidem sunt eadem, ipsa inter se sunt eadem, scribitur in *Elenchis*.
Ergo una pars erit eadem alteri. Quod falsum est.

Et dicendum, ut dicit Commentator supra primum *Physicorum*, quod pars secundum se non est eadem toti sed coniuncta cum aliis, unde omnes partes simul
5   sumptae sunt materia totius, compositio earum est forma.

<7>

Sed modo quaeritur an sit aliud a toto.

Quod non videtur. † Quia omnis acceptio eius quod est aliud ab hoc et non est
hoc. † Ergo quod est aliud est. Sed pars non est, dicit Philosophus. Ergo non est
aliud a toto.

10   Item. Pars est aliquid totius et deficit a toto. Sed in quantum est aliquid totius
non est a toto aliud sed convenit cum eo, nec in quantum deficit quia defectus dicit
non esse, sed quod est aliud est; ergo ratione illius defectus non est aliud a toto.
Ergo nullo modo est aliud.

Quod concedo. Unde improprie dicitur quod pars est aliud a toto, sed deberet
15   dici quod non est eadem toti. Unde est aliud dicere "est aliud ab hoc" et "non est
hoc", nam de non ente posset dici "non est hoc", non tamen est aliud ab hoc, quia
non est.

<8>

Consequenter quaeritur specialiter an pars subiectiva sit eadem cum suo toto.

Quod non videtur. Quaecumque sic se habent quod unum ab altero deminuit et
20   alterum excellit, non sunt eadem. Pars subiectiva et suum totum sunt huiusmodi.
Ergo etc. Ex hoc possum inferre hanc esse falsam, "Homo est animal", nam omnis
affirmativa vera propter identitatem praedicati ad subiectum.

Et dicendum quod duplex est identitas, completa et incompleta, et utraque sufficit ad hoc quod propositio affirmativa sit vera. Dicendum ergo quod pars subiectiva
25   et suum totum sunt eadem identitate incompleta, non tamen identitate completa.

---

1 Arist. *SE* 6.168b31–32   **3–5** *cf.* Averroes *in Phys.* I 17 (ed. Venet., 13v–14r); Anon. *Auct.*
Arist. 2.43 (ed. Hamesse, 144)   **8** *cf.* Arist. *Phys.* VII 5.250a24–25

---

1 eidem] eadem *P*   **4** coniuncta] cum iuncta *P*   **8** sed] si *P*   **15** unde] non *add. P*   **22** vera]
vere *P*   **24** vera] vere *P*

\<9\>

Ultimo quaeritur an una pars sit eadem cum alia parte.

Et dicendum quod idem habent esse commune, scilicet esse quod habent in toto, tamen diversa habent esse propria. Propter hoc possunt solvi omnes rationes quae possunt ad utramque partem induci, esse ut dictum est distinguendo.

\<10\>

Gratia dictorum quaeritur quare dicit Philosophus partem tantum esse in potentia.   5

Et dicendum quod omne quod est \<est unum\>, iuxta illud Porphyrii: "esse unicuique est unum". Sed dicit Boethius: "Unum est quod est in se indivisum \<et ab aliis divisum\>". Quia ergo pars non est ab aliis divisa, non dicitur esse unum proprie.

---

5   *cf.* Arist. *Phys.* VII 5.250a24–25   **6–7**   Porph. *Isag.* 9.21–22; Anon. *Auct. Arist.* 30.17 (ed. Hamesse, 301)   **7–8**   *hoc adagium a magistriis frequenter citatur, fons autem verus incertus est*

LECTIO XII

INEST AUTEM SUBSTANTIIS ETC. (5.3a33)

<DIVISIO>

Determinavit superius proprietatem quae convenit substantiae communiter sumptae, consequenter determinat proprietatem quae convenit substantiae secundum
alteram partem sui.

Et primo ponit proprietates substantiae prout est aliquid secundum rationem,
secundo prout est aliquid secundum naturam, ut ibi: *Inest autem substantiis nihil
illis* (5.3b25).

Prima est praesentis lectionis et dividitur in partes duas. Primo ponit proprieta-
tem quae convenit | secundis substantiis et differentiis ita quod non primis, secundo   f. 41ra
ponit proprietatem quae convenit primis ita quod non secundis, ibi: *Videtur autem
omnis substantia* (5.3b10).

Prima in duas. Primo proponit quod intendit, secundo probat, ibi: *A principali
namque substantia* (5.3a36).

Haec secunda in duas. Primo probat hoc <non convenire primis, secundo
probat hoc> convenire secundis substantiis et differentiis, ibi: *Secundarum vero
substantiarum* (5.3a37).

Pars in qua ponit proprietatem quae convenit primis ita quod non secundis dividitur in duas. Primo proponit quod intendit, secundo probat, ibi: *Et in primis
quidem* (5.3b10).

Haec secunda in duas. Primo probat hoc convenire primis substantiis, secundo
non convenire secundis, ibi: *In secundis vero* (5.3b12).

Haec secunda in duas. Primo facit quod dictum est, secundo removet quoddam
dubium incidens ex quodam dicto, ibi: *Non enim quale quid* (5.3b18).

Haec secunda in duas. Primo facit quod dictum est, secundo removet aliud
dubium incidens ex quodam dicto, ibi: *Plus autem in genere* (5.3b21).

Haec est divisio lectionis, et sunt octo particulae.

<SENTENTIA>

In prima parte sic procedit, proponendo quod intendit, <dicens quod> univoce
praedicari convenit differentiis et secundis substantiis ita quod non primis.

Consequenter probat. Et est ratio talis: Nihil quod non praedicatur, univoce
praedicatur. Prima substantia de nullo praedicatur (hanc ponit). Ergo etc.

---

22 incidens] manens *P*

Consequenter probat hoc convenire secundis substantiis et differentiis. Et est ratio talis: Secundae substantiae et differentiae praedicantur nomine et ratione. Sed praedicari univoce est praedicari secundum nomen et secundum rationem. Ergo secundae substantiae et differentiae praedicantur univoce.

Consequenter ponit proprietatem quae convenit primis substantiis ita quod non secundis. Et primo proponit quod intendit, dicens: Omnis substantia videtur hoc aliquid significare.   5

Et probat hoc de primis. Ratio talis est: Omne quod significat singulare et unum numero significat hoc aliquid. Primae substantiae sunt huiusmodi. Ergo etc.

Consequenter removet hoc a secundis, dicens quod licet secundae substantiae videantur hoc aliquid significare, tamen non significant hoc aliquid sed quale quid. Et est ratio talis: Nullum non significans unum numero et singulare significat hoc aliquid sed quale quid. Nulla substantia secunda significat unum numero et singulare. Ergo nulla substantia secunda significat hoc aliquid sed quale quid.   10

<Et quia dixit quod secunda substantia significat quale quid>, crederet aliquis quod significaret quale quid sicut album. Ideo hoc removet, dicens quod non, quia album solum qualitatem significat, sed secunda substantia determinat qualitatem circa substantiam primam.   15

Et quia dixit quod secunda substantia determinat qualitatem circa primam, crederet aliquis quod hoc esset aequaliter. Hoc removet, dicens quod plus est determinatio in genere quam in specie. Et probat hoc tali ratione: Quod magis complectitur magis est determinativum. Genus plus complectitur quam species. Ergo etc.   20

Haec est sententia partis.

Expositio litteralis

Ita posui proprietatem communem, *autem*, id est sed, secundis *substantiis*, supple ita quod non primis, *et differentiis inest omnia univoce praedicari*, id est haec proprietas, *ex his*, id est de primis substantiis, *enim*, pro quia, *omnia quae praedicata <sunt> ex his*, id est ex primis substantiis, *aut praedicantur de individuis* tantum, ut species, *aut de speciebus* et individuis, ut genus et differentia.   25

Consequenter probat hoc non convenire primis: Ita dixi quod non convenit primis, *nam*, id est quia, *nulla est praedicatio a principali substantia*. Et hoc probat: *enim*, <id est> quia, *de nullo subiecto*, id est | sub aliquo iacto in linea praedicamentali, *dicitur*. Argue ut dictum est.   30

Consequenter probat hoc convenire secundis substantiis et differentiis: Ita dixi non convenire hoc primis, *vero*, id est sed, *secundarum substantiarum species*

---

16 removet] removens *P*   **34** vero] *P^{sup} **ac*** : autem *P*

praedicatur, supple univoce, *de* individuis, et *genus de specie et individuo; similiter differentiae praedicantur de speciebus.* Et *primae substantiae* recipiunt *rationem generis* sicut nomen. Et probat quod similiter recipiant rationem generis sicut nomen: Bene dixi "similiter", *enim*, id est quia, *quaecumque de praedicato dicuntur, eadem*
5 *dicuntur de subiecto.* Sed ratio praedicatur de praedicato. Ergo et de subiecto. Et ita recipiunt rationem similiter sicut nomen. Idem probat de differentiis, dicens: *Species et individua suscipiunt rationem differentiarum. Autem*, pro sed, *univoca sunt quorum nomen est commune et ratio eadem. Quare*, id est ergo, *omnia quae sunt ex substantiis*, supple secundis, *et differentiis dicuntur univoce.*

10 Consequenter ponit proprietatem quae convenit primis: Ita dixi "praedicari univoce inest etc.", *autem*, id est sed, *omnis substantia videtur significare hoc aliquid. Et in primis substantiis est indubitabile et verum quoniam hoc aliquid* significant.

Et hoc probat: Bene dixi "non est dubium", *enim*, id est quia, *quod significatur*, supple per primam substantiam, *est individuum et unum numero.* Argue ut dictum
15 est.

Consequenter probat hoc non convenire secundis: Ita dixi quod convenit primis, *vero*, id est sed, *in secundis substantiis videtur similiter* sicut in primis *hoc aliquid significare sub figura appellationis*, id est sub similitudine vocis significantis ad se ipsam appellantem (videtur enim significare hoc aliquid; dictio enim commu-
20 nis commune appellat, non tamen hoc aliquid). Vel aliter: *sub appellationis figura*, id est sub similitudine quam habet in appellando cum prima substantia, quia sicut prima appellat hoc aliquid, ita et secunda. Et ponit exempla: ut *quando quis dixerit hominem vel animal.* Et licet sic videatur, *tamen non est verum, sed magis significat quale* quid, id est commune. Et hoc probat: *enim*, id est quia, illud *quod est sub-*
25 *iectum*, id est per secundam substantiam significatum, *neque*, pro non, *est unum quemadmodum prima substantia, sed homo dicitur de pluribus et animal.*

Et quia dixit quod secundae substantiae quale significant, crederet aliquis quod significaret quale sicut "album". Ideo hoc removet, dicens: Ita dixi quod significant quale, *vero*, id est sed, *non* significant *quale simpliciter quemadmodum album*;
30 *enim*, id est quia, *album nihil aliud significat*, id est determinat, *quam qualitatem*, *autem*, id est sed, *species et genus determinant qualitatem circa substantiam* (*enim*, id est quia, *quandam substantiam qualem significant*, id est determinant).

Ultimo, quia dixit quod genus et species qualitatem determinant, ne crederet aliquis quod aequaliter, ideo hoc removet, dicens: *Autem*, id est sed, *determinatio fit*
35 *plus in genere quam in specie*, *enim*, id est quia, *dicens "animal"* plura *complectitur quam* "homo".

---

19 enim] *an* autem *scribendum?* **21** cum] est *P* **25** significatum] significatuum *P* **29** vero] *!* *P* : enim *P^{sup}* : autem *ac*

\<Quaestiones\>

\<1\>

Primo quaeritur de ordine.

Definiendo substantiam prius prosequitur de prima quam de secunda. Ergo ponendo proprietates prius deberet ponere proprietates primae substantiae quam secundae. E converso facit.

Et dicendum quod in prima substantia duo sunt, scilicet primum et particulare,   5
et in secunda similiter alia duo, | secundum et universale. Unde si ordinantur quantum ad has condiciones, primum et secundum, prima substantia praecedit. Si vero ordinantur quantum ad has condiciones, particulare et universale, cum universale simpliciter sit prius particulari, ut scribitur in primo *Posteriorum*, sic secunda substantia ante primam, et sic ordinat hic.   10

\<2\>

Ad evidentiam dictorum in littera duo quaeruntur, primum de prima proprietate, secundum de secunda.

De primo sic: Videtur quod praedicari univoce non solum convenit secundis substantiis et differentiis.

Quia in quolibet genere est reperire praedicari nomine et ratione. Sed praedi-   15
cari nomine et ratione est praedicari univoce. Ergo in quolibet genere est reperire univoce praedicari. Non ergo solum substantiis et differentiis convenit.

Et dicendum quod praedicari univoce simpliciter non solum convenit substantiis et differentiis sed cum hac determinatione "de primis". Unde res aliorum generum licet praedicentur univoce, non tamen univoce de primis substantiis.   20

\<3\>

Iuxta hoc quaeritur utrum omnis differentia praedicetur univoce.

Quod non videtur. Omne quod praedicatur univoce praedicatur secundum nomen et rationem. Sed omnis ratio datur per genus et differentias, dicit Boethius. Ergo et ratio differentiae. Sed tunc quaeritur de differentia definitiva utrum praedicetur nomine et ratione. Si non, habeo propositum. Si sic, ergo habet rationem   25
per genus et differentiam datam, et sic est ire in infinitum, quod falsum est. Ergo

---

8–9   *cf.* Arist. *APo* I 2.71b33–72a6; Anon. *Auct. Arist.* 35.15–18 (ed. Hamesse, 312)   **23**   Boeth.
in Int.[1] I 2 (ed. Meiser, 46)

---

2 prius] primo *P*

oportet dare aliquam differentiam quae non habeat rationem, et ita non praedicatur secundum rationem, cum ipsam non habeat. Ergo est aliqua differentia quae non univoce praedicatur.

Et dicendum quod ratio multipliciter datur. Uno modo per genus et differentias, et haec dicitur formalis. Alio modo datur per causam materialem et formalem, sicut haec: "Homo est compositum ex anima et corpore". Prima est logica, secunda naturalis. Alia est in qua definitur potentia per suum actum, secundum quod habetur in *Libro de anima* quod potentiae definiuntur per actus. Licet ergo differentia non habeat definitionem quae est per genus <et> differentias, habet tamen definitionem quae est per suum actum, ut "rationale" "quod est aptum natum ratiocinari" et sic de aliis.

Per hoc patet ad obiectum, scilicet quod omnis definitio datur per genus et differentias, quia haec propositio simpliciter falsa est, ut dictum est, sed solum est vera de formali, et illam definitionem differentia non habet; et ideo argumentum non procedit.

<4>

Consequenter quaeritur utrum aliquis homo sit prima substantia; saepe enim vult auctor quod sic.

Contra. De quocumque praedicatur species, ut homo, et de eisdem praedicatur aliquis homo. Ergo aequalis est ambitus cum sua specie, et ita est universale. Ergo non est prima substantia.

Et dicendum quod in hoc quod est aliquis homo duo sunt, scilicet aliquis, quod est intentio substantiae primae, et homo, per quod designatur intentio substantiae secundae. Unde si aliquis homo consideretur a parte eius quod est homo, non differt a specie et de tot praedicatur sicut sua species, ut obicitur. Si consideretur a parte eius quod est aliquis, quod habet convenire in parte, sic est prima substantia et sic de nullo praedicatur.

<5>

De secunda proprietate sic quaeritur. Quid sit dictum quod homo et quodlibet universale significat quale quid | et quo modo hoc habeat intelligi?   f. 41vb

---

7–8   Arist. *An.* II 4.415a16–20; Anon. *Auct. Arist.* 6.56 (ed. Hamesse, 179)

---

2 non²] est *add.* P   **18** species] et genus *add.* P   **24** et] a P   **27** quodlibet] quolibet P *ut. v.*
28 quale] quali P

<6>

Iuxta hoc quaeritur: Dicit quod "album" solam qualitatem significat.

Contra. "Album" significat qualitatem adiunctam substantiae et utraque claudit in se, quod patet per Priscianum dicentem "album, id est alba res".

<7>

Ratione huius quaeritur qualiter habeat intelligi hoc quod dicit <quod> secunda substantia determinat qualitatem circa substantiam, album vero non.   5

<8>

Ultimo quaeritur: Dicit quod plus est determinatio in genere quam in specie.

Superius dixit contrarium, quod si aliquis assignet primam substantiam dicendo quid sit, manifestius assignabit per speciem quam per genus; et ita species est magis determinativa.

<Ad 5>

Ad primum. Dicit auctor in *Metaphysica*: "Omne habens formam pluribus com-   10
munem dicitur quale"; et sic omne universale est quale. Sed istorum quae quale significant quaedam habent individua immediate sibi correspondentia de quibus illa qualitas essentialiter praedicatur; et haec praedicantur in quid. Huiusmodi solum sunt secundae substantiae. Genus ergo et species significant quale quia commune quid significant et praedicantur essentialiter de individuis immediate sibi   15
correspondentibus.

<Ad 6>

Per hoc patet ad alia, quia album non dicitur significare solam qualitatem quia non significet substantiam cum qualitate, sed dicitur significare solam qualitatem, id est quale, quia commune significat sed non significat quid, quia non habet individua immediate sibi correspondentia de quibus illa communitas vel qualitas praedicetur   20
essentialiter. Unde li "solum" non excludit li "substantiam" sed "significare quid", ut visum est.

---

1 Arist. *Cat.* 5.3b19–21 **3** *cf.* Prisc. *Inst. gramm.* II 3.18 (ed. Hertz, vol. 1, 55) **6** Arist. *Cat.* 5.3b21–23 **7–8** Arist. *Cat.* 5.2b8–14; 2b32–35 **10–11** Arist. *Metaph.* III 6.1003a8–9

---

3 priscianum] priscianus *P* **8** species] speciem *P* **9** determinativa] determinativum *P* **19** sed] haec *P ut v.* **21** li²] si *P*

Aliter dicitur quod album accipitur pro albedine quae secundum veritatem solam dicit qualitatem. Et si obicitur quod est nomen, dicendum quod nomen est secundum grammaticum, qui modos significandi considerat, et quia modus substantiae est significare per modum subiecti, dicit omne nomen significare substantiam nomen substantiae excedendo. Sed logicus veritatem rei speculatur, quare dicit album, id est albedinem, solam qualitatem significare.

Aliter dicitur quod dictio exclusiva addita termino generali non excludit aliud, unde non sequitur "tantum qualitas est, ergo substantia non est", quia qualitas non habet esse nisi in substantia. Quare non sequitur "significat solam qualitatem, ergo non substantiam".

<Ad 7>

Ad aliud dicendum—scilicet qualiter intelligitur quod secunda substantia determinat qualitatem circa substantiam, album vero non—quod qualitas designata per substantiam praedicatur essentialiter de prima substantia et ideo dicitur determinare qualitatem circa primam substantiam, album vero non, ut dictum est.

<Ad 8>

Ad ultimum. Omne superius est terminus inferioris. Sed duplex est natura termini, scilicet continere et notum facere. Quantum ad primam naturam plus est determinatio in genere quam in specie, et sic loquitur hic, quia genus plura continet, sed quantum ad hanc naturam quae est notum facere plus est determinatio in specie quam in genere, quia genus in specie intelligitur et non e converso. Ergo cognoscens per speciem cognoscit per genus et non e converso, et ita maior est determinatio in specie quantum ad cog|nitionem quam in genere, et sic loquitur superius.   f. 42ra

---

5 quare] quia *P*

Lectio XIII

Inest autem substantiis etc. (5.3b25)

\<Divisio\>

Determinatis proprietatibus substantiae prout est res rationis, determinat eius proprietates prout est aliquid secundum naturam.

Haec pars dividitur in duas. Primo ponit proprietates communes substantiae et aliis, secundo proprietatem propriam, ibi: *Maxime autem* (5.4a10).

Prima est praesentis lectionis et dividitur in duas secundum duas proprietates. Secunda ibi: *Videtur autem substantia* (5.3b33).

Prima in duas. Primo ponit proprietatem, secundo probat, ibi: *Primae autem substantiae* (5.3b25).

Haec secunda in duas. Primo probat hoc convenire substantiis, secundo extendit hoc ad quantitatem, ut ibi: *Non est autem hoc substantiae* (5.3b27).

Haec secunda in duas. Primo ponit extensionem, secundo removet dubium, ibi: \<*nisi quis forte* (5.3b31).

Pars in qua ponit secundam proprietatem in duas. Primo ponit proprietatem, secundo removet dubium, ibi:\> *Dico autem hoc* (5.3b34).

Haec secunda in duas. Primo removet dubitationem, secundo explanat per exempla quaedam dicta, ibi: *sicut album* etc. (5.4a1).

Haec est divisio lectionis, et sunt septem particulae.

\<Sententia\>

Circa primam sic procedit, dicens nihil esse contrarium substantiis.

Secundo probat hoc tali ratione: Primae substantiae nihil est contrarium, secundae substantiae nihil est contrarium. Omnis substantia vel prima vel secunda. Ergo substantiae nihil est contrarium.

Consequenter extendit quantitati, dicens: Hoc convenit quantitati. Et probat tali ratione: Quantitati continuae, ut bicubito, nihil est contrarium nec discretae, ut decem. Omnis quantitas talis vel talis. Ergo etc.

Consequenter removet dubium, dicens quod alicui videtur multa esse contraria paucis vel magnum parvo, quod non est verum.

Consequenter ponit secundam proprietatem, dicens quod substantia non videtur suscipere magis et minus.

---

6 autem] prima *add.* P   6 substantia] esse causa alterius ut habere contrarium est causa quare aliquid recipit magis et minus et causa ante causatum dicit priscianus quare patet ordo *add.* P
7 autem] omne *add.* P

Consequenter removet dubium. Quia dixit superius quod species magis est substantia quam genus, et ita videtur substantia suscipere magis, quod negat, ideo dicit quod substantia secundum id quod est non recipit magis et minus, et sic loquitur hic, sed secundum hunc actum qui est substare loquitur superius.

Ultimo manifestat per exempla quae dicuntur magis et minus et quae non, dicens quod album dicitur magis et minus et bonum et similia, sed substantia non. Et ponit exempla.

Haec est sententia partis.

Expositio litteralis

Ita posui proprietates < * * * > *inest substantiis.*

Et hoc probat. Bene dico <quod> convenit illis, *autem,* <id est> quia, *primae substantiae quid est contrarium*? Quasi dicens: Nihil. Et bene nihil, *enim,* id est quia, *alicui homini,* quod est prima substantia supple, *nihil est contrarium, at vero nec homini,* quod est species, et *animali,* quod est genus, *nihil est contrarium.*

Consequenter extendit quantitati. Ita dixi quod hoc inest substantiis, *autem,* pro sed, *hoc,* id est non habere contrarium, *non est proprium substantiae,* supple convertibile, *sed multorum aliorum, ut quantitatis.* Et hoc probat: *enim,* id est quia, *bicubito,* quod est quantitas continua supple, *nihil est contrarium, at vero nec decem,* quod est discreta.

Consequenter removet dubium. Ita dixi quod quantitas non habet contrarium, *nisi quis,* id est aliquis, *dicat multa contraria <esse> paucis. Vero,* id est sed, *determinatorum,* id est praedictorum, *nullum | nulli est contrarium (nulli,* id est alicui; superfluit negatione).

Consequenter ponit secundam proprietatem, dicens: Non solum dicta proprietas convenit substantiae, *autem,* id est sed, alia, nam *substantia videtur non suscipere <magis et minus>* (et dicit "videtur" sub dubitatione).

Quia uno modo suscipit magis, alio non, et nondum est solutum qualiter contingit, removet dubium. Ita dixi "Videtur autem substantia etc.", nam *dico hoc,* id est non suscipere magis et minus, *non quia substantia non est magis et minus a substantia,* id est substando suscipit, (*autem,* id est sed, *dictum est hoc quia est* id quod est); *sed* dico hoc *quoniam unaquaeque substantia hoc ipsum quod est non dicitur magis et minus,* unde *haec substantia homo non est magis et minus nec ipse a se* sub diversis temporibus *nec* ipse *ab altero* in eodem tempore. Bene dico quod non, *enim,* id est quia, alterum *non est magis* et minus, supple substantia, ab *altero.*

---

3 secundum id quod est] id quod est substantia *P* **12** quod est] *iter. P, ut v.*

f. 42rb

Ultimo manifestat per exempla quae dicuntur magis et minus et quae non, dicens: *album est magis album altero* etc., *et ipsum*, id est illud album, *dicitur magis et minus a se*, supple in diversis temporibus. Et ponit exempla: Ut *homo* non *dicitur magis* et minus *nunc quam prius nec quicquam aliorum quae sunt substantiae*; 5 *quapropter* etc.

<h2 style="text-align:center"><Quaestiones></h2>

Ad dictorum evidentiam duo quaeruntur. Primum est de prima proprietate, secundum de secunda.

<h3 style="text-align:center"><1></h3>

Quantum ad primam. Dicit quod substantiae nihil est contrarium.

Contra. Scribitur in *Libro de morte et vita*: "Impossibile est habenti materiam 10 non habere contrarium". Sed substantia, composita adminus, habet materiam. Ergo habet contrarium.

< * * * >

Item. Scribitur in primo *Physicorum* quod in quolibet genere est una prima contrarietas. Ergo in genere substantiae.

15 Item. Scribitur in *Libro de generatione* quod ignis aquae contrariatur; et tamen utrumque est substantia.

Item. Omne quod corrumpitur corrumpitur per contrarium. Substantia corrumpitur. Ergo etc.

Iuxta hoc quaeritur quare substantiae nihil est contrarium.

20 Et dicendum quod substantiae sunt subiectum et sustentamentum totius contrarietatis et omnium aliorum, unde alia sunt in ipsis et ipsa non in aliis. Sed contraria nata sunt fieri in substantia. Ergo si substantiae essent contrariae, essent natae fieri in alia substantia, quod est falsum.

Alia ratio est quod contraria nata sunt fieri circa idem. Ergo si substantiae essent 25 contrariae, essent in alia tertia et illa tertia cum suo contrario in alia tertia, et ita in infinitum.

Ad obiecta dicendum quod duplex est contrarietas, completa et incompleta. Completa est illorum quae posita sub eodem genere maxime a se distant et mutuo se

---

8 Arist. *Cat.* 5.3b25–32 **9–10** Arist. *Long.* 3.465b11–12; Anon. *Auct. Arist.* 7.109 (ed. Hamesse, 204) **13–14** Arist. *Phys.* I 6.189a14 **15** Arist. *Gen.* II 4.331a14–18; Anon. *Auct. Arist.* 4.38 (ed. Hamesse, 170)

---

8 quantum…dicit] *add. al. ma. in marg.* **10** composita] compacta *P* **23** falsum] subiectum *P* **25** tertia¹] materia *P*

expellunt quia sunt opposita secundum essentiam et operationes; et ista tanguntur in definitione: per "maxime a se distant" tangitur quod sint contraria per essentiam, per li "mutuo se expellunt" tangitur quod sint contraria secundum operationes. Et est alia contrarietas secundum essentiam sed non secundum operationem, et haec est in substantiis, quia maxime a se distant sed non mutuo se expellunt. Quod sic   5
confirmo, nam complete contraria habent fieri circa idem et utrumque per excellentiam corrumpit alterum, et hoc non est in substantiis. Quod patet, quia omne

f. 42va | excellens est magis. Substantia autem non recipit magis, ut dicit auctor. Quare completa contrarietas non est in substantia.

Per hoc patet ad obiecta in parte, quia cum dicitur, "Impossibile est habenti   10
materiam etc.", verum est de contrarietate completa.

Per hoc etiam patet ad secundum.

Ad tertium dicendum quod tria sunt naturae principia: materia, forma et privatio. Quia in qualibet mutatione est subiectum mutationem recipiens, et dicitur materia, et illud a quo fit mutatio, id est forma quae privatur, et illud quod introducitur, et hoc est forma, et quia hoc est in quolibet genere, dicitur esse in quolibet   15
una contrarietas, quae nihil aliud est quam forma et privatio; sed haec contrarietas est incompleta, ut dictum est.

Ad aliud dicendum quod ignis et aqua in quantum substantiae non contrariantur, sed per naturam suarum qualitatum, quae sunt accidentia, quia ignis calidus   20
et siccus, aqua frigida et umida; et ideo non sequitur quod substantiae aliquid sit contrarium, licet earum qualitates et operationes sint contrariae.

Ad ultimum. Scribitur in *Libro Physicorum* quod omnia quae corrumpuntur aut sunt contraria aut ex contrariis. Dicendum ergo quod corrumpi a contrario est multipliciter: uno modo quia habet contrarium, ut album nigrum; alio quia componitur ex contrariis, et sic accidentia destructa substantia corrumpuntur; tertio per   25
defectum suae naturae sive in se sive sui, et sic intelligere corrumpitur; quarto quod est in corruptibili per defectum suae naturae, et sic corrumpitur bonitas intellectus; ultimo corrumpitur ab excellenti, secundum quod scribitur in *Libro de anima*: "Excellentia sensibilium corrumpit sensum", et sic corrumpitur a tempore quicquid est   30
in tempore. Et ita patet quod non valet argumentum. Substantia enim corrumpitur, non quia habeat contrarium, sed quia composita est ex contrariis. Unde procedit a superiori ad inferius affirmando.

---

8 Arist. *Cat.* 5.3a33–4a9   **13–14** *cf.* Arist. *Phys.* I 7.191a8–17   **23–24** Arist. *Phys.* I 5.188b22–26   **29–30** Arist. *An.* II 12.424a28–30; III 13.435b7–9; Anon. *Auct. Arist.* 6.104; 6.179 (ed. Hamesse, 182; 189)

---

6 utrumque] utramque *P a.c.*   **16** dicitur esse] *iter. P*   **21** aliquid] aliquis *P*   **23** ultimum] tertium *P*

\<2\>

Consequenter quaeritur, cum non habere contrarium conveniat quantitati et relationi, utrum per eandem causam, et si per differentem, quo modo sit differens.

Et dicendum quod per differentem, quia convenit substantiae secundum quod est ens per se, contraria autem non entia per se sed in alio; unde patet quod natura
5   substantiae repugnat naturae contrariorum, et \<propter\> hoc substantia non habet contrarium, sed est subiectum contrarietatis. Quantitas etiam non habet contrarium, quia inter accidentia quantitas immediatius se tenet cum substantia, et ideo a substantia contrahit quod sit subiectum contrarietatis sicut substantia. Ad aliquid dictis similiter non contingit habere contrarium, quia contraria nata sunt fieri circa
10 idem, sed non simul, sed relativa non habent esse in eodem subiecto et sunt simul, et ita natura contrariorum eis repugnat.

\<3\>

De secundo quaeritur: Dicit quod substantia non recipit magis et minus.

Contra. Dixit superius quod species magis est substantia quam genus.

Item. Dicit Priscianus quod si aliquis augetur, substantia sui suscipit magis.
15 Item. Scribitur in *Topicis* quod ignis flamma magis est ignis quam ignis carbo, et lux quam flamma. Et utrumque substantia. Ergo substantia recipit magis.

Et dicendum quod contingit loqui de substantia dupliciter, scilicet quantum ad suas operationes et quantum ad id quod est. Primo modo recipit magis, sed non recipit qualitatem sed quantitatem, et dico qualitatem, id est non praedicatur essen-
20 tialiter (per hoc patet ad obiecta), sed magis et minus quantitatem, id est secundum extensionem.

Per hoc patet ad primum et ad tertium. Nam species quantum ad hanc operationem quae est substare est magis substantia, ut obicitur. Similiter flamma | quantum   f. 42vb
ad istum actum qui est lucere est magis ignis quam carbo, et lux quam flamma.
25 Ad secundum. Priscianus appellat substantiam passionem. Unde licet substantia possideatur, in quantum possidetur naturam accidentis habet, quia haec passio habetur et natura substantiae est habere, et quia passio habet naturam accidentis, potest suscipere magis.

---

12 Arist. *Cat.* 5.3a33–4a9   13 Arist. *Cat.* 5.2b7–22   14 *fortasse* Prisc. *Inst. gramm.* XVII
12.78 (ed. Hertz, vol. 2, 153)   15–16 *cf.* Arist. *Top.* V 5.134b28–35a5

---

2 differentem] differentiae *P*   3 differentem] differentiae *P*   5 repugnat] repugna *P*   5 naturae]
natura *P*   10 simul[1]] sunt *P*   10 sunt simul] ideo non simul *P*   14 augetur] auget *P*   18–19 sed]
secundum *P bis*   22 tertium] secundum *P*

Lectio XIV

Maxime vero etc. (5.4a10)

<Divisio>

Determinatis proprietatibus quae conveniunt substantiae et aliis, determinat proprietatem substantiae maxime propriam.

Haec pars in duas. Primo ponit proprietatem et probat, secundo ad maiorem manifestationem ponit instantias, ibi: *In aliis autem nullum tale* (5.4a21).

Haec secunda in duas. Primo ponit instantias, secundo solvit, ibi: *Sed et si quis* (5.4a27).

Prima praesentis est lectionis et dividitur in duas. Primo ponit proprietatem, secundo ipsam manifestat, ibi: *In aliis quidem non habebit* (5.4a11).

Haec secunda in duas. Primo probat hanc proprietatem aliis a substatia non convenire, secundo ostendit eam substantiae convenire, ibi: *Substantia vero* (5.4a17).

Haec est divisio lectionis.

<Sententia>

Circa primam partem sic procedit, dicens quod maxime proprium substantiae est quod cum sit una numero et eadem, susceptiva sit contrariorum.

Consequenter probat aliis a substantia non convenire, dicens quod in aliis non sit aliquod manens unum et idem quod recipiat contraria, ut color non est unus et idem numero albus et niger, et actio prout est prava et studiosa (et est studiosus quem labor non invenit otiosum).

Consequenter probat hoc substantiae convenire, dicens quod substantia cum sit unum et idem numero recipit contraria, ut aliquis homo aliquando albus, aliquando niger etc.

Ultimo ponit instantias, dicens quod eadem oratio videtur susceptiva veri et falsi, ut haec oratio, "Socrates sedet", est vera eo sedente, sed ipsa eadem est falsa eo surgente. Sed verum et falsum sunt contraria. Ergo oratio recipit contraria. Et tamen oratio non est substantia. Eadem instantia est et de opinione.

Haec est sententia partis.

---

5 instantias] *lectio incerta*   **10** substantia] $P^{inf}c$: substantiae *P*   **23** vera] vere *P*

Expositio litteralis

Dictum est de proprietatibus quae conveniunt substantiae et aliis, *vero*, id est sed, *proprium maxime*, id est convertibile, *substantiae videtur esse* hoc quod sequitur: *quod cum sit* una *et* eadem *numero, est* susceptiva *contrariorum*.

Consequenter probat hoc non convenire aliis a substantia: Ita dixi <quod> hoc convenit substantiae, *autem*, id est sed, *in aliis quaecumque non sunt substantiae*   5 *non habebit quis quod proferat*, vere supple, *quod cum sit unum et idem numero sit susceptibile contrariorum*, sicut *color* cum sit *unum et idem numero, non erit* albus *et* niger, *neque eadem actio* est *prava et studiosa*. Non solum ita est in istis, *autem*, id est sed, etiam *in aliis similiter quaecumque non sunt substantiae*.

Consequenter ostendit hanc proprietatem substantiae convenire: Ita dixi quod   10 non substantiae non recipiunt contraria, *vero*, pro sed, *substantia cum sit unum et idem numero est* susceptibile *contrariorum*. Et ponit exempla. Littera patet.

Ultimo ponit instantias: Ita dixi quod recipere contraria solum convenit substantiis, sed *in aliis*, a substantia supple, non *videtur aliquid tale*, scilicet quod recipiat contraria, *nisi* aliquis *instet dicens orationem et visum*, id est opinionem, quae   15 non sunt substantiae supple, *esse huiusmodi*, <id est> susceptiva contrariorum. Et bene dixi "nisi quis instet", *enim*, id est quia, *eadem oratio et idem visus videtur esse* verus *et* falsus, sicut haec *oratio*, "*aliquem sedere*", id est "aliquis sedet", *si sit vera* eo sedente, cum eadem sit oratio, *erit falsa | eo surgente*. Et non solum sic est de oratione, *autem*, id est sed, *similiter de opinione*. Exemplum ponit. Littera patet.   20

<Quaestiones>

<1>

Ad dictorum evidentiam primo quaeritur de expositione huius proprietatis.

Quia dicit quod hoc est maxime proprium substantiae, ergo debet convenire omni et soli secundum Porphyrium. Sed videtur quod non convenit omni. Probatio: Quia intelligentiae non sunt susceptibiles contrariorum. Et sunt substantiae. Ergo etc.   25

Item. In igne est claritas, et non est susceptibilis oppositi, quod est obscuritas. Et tamen ignis est substantia. Ergo etc.

Item. Natura formae est suscipi et non suscipere; habet enim suscipi in materia

f. 43ra

---

22   Arist. *Cat.* 5.4a10–11   **22–23**   Porph. *Isag.* 12.17–22

---

5 autem] *! P* : quidem *P^{sup}* **ac**   **12** contrariorum] contra contrariorum *P*   **13** quod] non *add. P a.c.*   **14** in aliis] quaecumque *add. P*   **14** a] *add. s.l. P*   **18** vera] **ac** : vere *P*   **20** autem] **ac** : *comp.* u^m *habet P*

et non suscipere. Ergo forma non suscipit contraria. Et tamen forma est substantia. Ergo non omnis substantia recipit contraria.

Item. Dicit in littera quod haec proprietas convenit substantiae quae est una et eadem numero solum. Sed dixit superius quod substantia secunda non est unum et idem numero. Ergo haec proprietas non ei convenit, et ita omni substantiae non convenit.

Item. Si haec proprietas omni substantiae convenit, sequitur quod anima non possit peccare. Minor patet. Anima enim non movetur, dicit auctor *Sex principiorum*. Ergo non transmutatur.

Et dicendum cum auctore quod haec proprietas omni substantiae convenit, cum sit maxime propria.

Ad primum obiectum dicendum quod dupliciter est considerare intelligentias, scilicet per relationem ad voluntatem creatoris, et sic bene intelligentiae sunt incorruptibiles et ita determinatae ad bonum quod nullo modo ad malum, et sic non sunt susceptibiles contrariorum; sed per relationem ad sui naturam, sic. Et hoc patet. Dicit enim Philosophus quod nihil est perfectum et non egens alterius perfectione nisi quod vere est perfectissimum. Patet ergo quod in quantum relinquuntur naturae propriae susceptibiles sunt contrariorum, et quod non sunt corruptibiles, hoc est per voluntatem sui creatoris. Et haec solutio patet per dictum Platonis in persona creatoris loquentis. Dicit enim: "Dii deorum quorum ego opifex sum et pater, natura vestra dissolubiles estis, voluntate autem mea indissolubiles. Vegetatior enim est nexus meus ad aeternitatis vestrae custodiam quam ea ex quibus vestra aeternitas est compacta". Item. Scribitur in *Causis* quod omnes intelligentiae fixionem habent per bonitatem puram quae Deus est.

Ad secundum dicendum quod hoc intelligitur, "nisi alterum insit determinate a natura", quod est de igne, quia claritas inest igni determinate a natura et nigredo corvo et similia.

Ad tertium dicendum quod non est inconveniens si respectu diversorum forma sit suscipiens et suscepta; suscipitur enim in materia et ipsa existens suscipit contraria.

Ad quartum dicendum quod secunda substantia per se non est unum numero sed per primam substantiam; dependet enim a prima substantia quantum ad actum

3–4 Arist. *Cat.* 5.4a10–21 **4–5** *cf.* Arist. *Cat.* 5.3b16–18 **8–9** *cf.* Anon. *LSP* II 16–18 (ed. Minio-Paluello, 38–39) **15–17** *cf.* Arist. *Metaph.* V 16.1021b12–22a3 **19–23** Plato *Tim.* 41a, Transl. Calcidii (ed. Waszink et Jensen, 35); Anon. *Auct. Arist.* 27.12 (ed. Hamesse, 297) **23–24** Anon. *Liber de causis* VIII 79 (ed. Pattin, 66); Anon. *Auct. Arist.* 11.8 (ed. Hamesse, 231)

8 peccare] omne nomen quod recipit contraria *add. sed canc.* P **26** claritas] caliditas P **26** igni] igitur P

existendi <secundum quod> dicit auctor *Sex principiorum* quod omnis communitas a singularitate procedit. Quia ergo esse suum habet a prima substantia, ideo per primam substantiam est unum numero, et ita prout est in prima substantia susceptiva est contrariorum, et non per se. Distingue ergo quod contingit de secunda substantia loqui dupliciter: aut per se aut prout est in prima. Primo modo non est   5
unum numero nec recipit contraria, ut obicitur, sed secundo modo, sicut visum est.

Ad ultimum, cum dicit quod anima non movetur, dicendum quod aliquid movetur dupliciter: aut quia motus est in ipso tanquam in subiecto aut in causa effi-
f. 43rb   ciente, et sic anima movetur | et potest transmutari et recipere contraria. Primo
modo loquitur auctor.   10

Vel aliter. Dupliciter movetur aliquid: aut primo aut ex consequenti (vel per se vel per accidens). Primo modo anima non movetur, sed secundo. Quod patet. Nam anima est in corpore sicut nauta in navi. Unde sicut nauta movet navem et navi mota movetur nauta, ita anima movet corpus, quo moto movetur et ipsa, prout in *Topicis* scribitur quod moventibus nobis moventur ea quae sunt in nobis.   15

<2>

Consequenter arguitur quod non conveniat soli, quia linea est susceptiva recti et curvi. Et ista sunt contraria. Ergo linea suscipit contraria, et tamen non est substantia.

Et dicendum quod si linea susceptibilis est contrariorum, non tamen secundum sui mutationem sed subiecti. Eo enim quod subiectum est sic dispositum, scilicet   20
curvum vel rectum, ideo linea dicitur curva vel recta. Recipere ergo contraria cum hac condicione, "secundum sui mutationem", solum convenit substantiae.

<3>

Consequenter quaeritur: Videtur quod si hoc sit maxime proprium, sequitur inconveniens, scilicet Primam Causam esse in praedicamento.

Quia maxime proprium convertitur cum eo cuius est proprium. Ergo quicquid   25
est susceptibile contrariorum, est substantia. Deus est huiusmodi. Ergo Deus est substantia, et ita in praedicamento. Minor patet. Nam Deus est omnipotens. Ergo potest recipere contraria.

_____

1–2 Anon. *LSP* I 9 (ed. Minio-Paluello, 37), *ut apud* Anon. *Auct. Arist.* 33.5 (ed. Hamesse, 306)
14–15 *cf.* Arist. *Top.* II 7.113a29–30; Anon. *Auct. Arist.* 36.31 (ed. Hamesse, 324)

_____

25 quicquid] quid *P*   26 huiusmodi] ergo etc. *add. P*

<4>

Gratia huius quaeritur utrum Deus sit in praedicamento.

Quod non videtur, quia aliquid esset ante ipsum, scilicet generalissimum in illo genere, et hoc est impossibile.

Sed contra. Singulum incomplexorum aut significat substantiam aut quantitatem etc. Sed Deus non significat aliquid aliorum. Ergo substantiam. Ergo est in praedicamento substantiae.

<AD 3>

Ad primum dicendum quod Deus non potest recipere contraria. Et cum dicitur "est omnipotens etc.", non sequitur, quia talis potentia potius est impotentia quam potentia; sicut non sequitur, "Deus potest omnia, ergo peccare" (immo est fallacia secundum quid et simpliciter), quia talis potentia peccandi est potius impotentia quam potentia, quia peccatum provenit ex defectu corruptae naturae.

<AD 4>

Ad aliud dicendum quod Deus non est in praedicamentum.

Ad obiectum dicendum quod haec divisio singulum incomplexorum datur de causatis, non de causa; unde cum Deus sit causa omnium, sub dicta divisione non comprehenditur.

<5>

Solet quaeri quare dixit "videtur".

Et dicitur quod causa est quia positurus est instantias.

<6>

Ultimo quaeritur quare dicit substantiam susceptibilem aliquando, aliquando capacem, et quo modo haec differenter.

Et dicendum quod "susceptibilis" dicit possibilitatem quae est a parte formae, "capax" quae complectitur utrumque; possibilitas enim suscipiendi contraria est in substantia a parte materiae et a forma paratur ut ducatur illa potentia ad actum; ex hoc sequitur quod compositum actu suscipiat contraria.

---

16 Arist. *Cat.* 5.4a10

---

11 corruptae] corruptionis *P*   **22** et a forma paratur] a forma et paratur *P*   **23** sequitur quod compositum] consequitur quod positum *P*

LECTIO XV

SED ET SI QUIS HOC SUSCIPIAT (5.4a27)

<Divisio>

Positis instantiis, solvit eas.

Haec pars in duas. Primo solvit distinguendo, secundo interimendo. Vel aliter: Primo solvit, secundo solutionem resumit ut ipsam addendo confirmet. Quocumque modo dicatur, secunda incipit ibi: *Si quis enim hoc recipiat* (5.4b4).

5   Prima in duas. Primo ponit solutionem, secundo ipsam manifestat, ibi: *nam ea quae in substantiis* (5.4a28).

Haec secunda in duas. Primo ponit maiorem suae rationis, secundo minorem, ibi: | *Oratio autem et opinio* (5.4a35).   f. 43va

Pars in qua solvit interimendo in duas. Primo proponit solutionem, secundo
10 probat, ibi: *Oratio namque* (5.4b6).

Haec secunda in duas. Primo probat solutionem, secundo concludit principale intentum, ibi: *Quare proprium erit substantiae* (5.4b16).

Haec est divisio lectionis.

<Sententia>

Circa primam partem sic procedit, dicens quod si aliquis dicat quod oratio et opinio
15 recipiunt contraria, tamen differunt. Non enim recipiunt quia ipsa varientur sed subiecta.

Consequenter probat hoc. Ratio talis est: Quaecumque sunt susceptibilia contrariorum eo modo quo substantia, recipiunt mutationem. Oratio et opinio non recipiunt mutationem. Ergo non recipiunt contraria eo modo quo substantia.
20 Maiorem et minorem probat.

Consequenter concludit principale propositum, dicens quod postquam hoc soli substantiae convenit et omni, proprium erit substantiae secundum sui mutationem recipere contraria.

Consequenter solvit interimendo, dicens: Si aliquis dicat orationem et opinio-
25 nem recipere contraria, non est verum.

Consequenter probat hoc. Ratio talis est: Oratio et opinio non recipiunt contraria secundum sui mutationem sed secundum mutationem rei. Sed illa quae re-

---

3 solutionem] resolutionem *P*   **4** enim] *!* *P* : vero P^{inf} : autem etiam **c** : autem ac_{Cs} **8** oratio] P^{inf}**c** : omnia *P, ut v.*

cipiunt contraria ipsa recipiunt secundum sui mutationem, ut patet in substantia. Ergo oratio et opinio non recipiunt contraria.

Ultimo concludit principale propositum, dicens, ex quo soli substantiae convenit et omni, quod proprium erit substantiae quod manens eadem numero secundum sui mutationem recipit contraria. 5

Haec est sententia partis.

Expositio litteralis

Ita dixi "oratio et opinio videntur recipere contraria", *autem*, pro sed, *si quis suscipiat hoc*, scilicet quod recipiunt contraria, *tamen* differunt in *modo* recipiendi.

Bene dixi "differunt in modo recipiendi", *nam*, id est quia, *ea quae sunt in substantiis*, id est de numero substantiarum (vel aliter: sicut inferius in suo superiori), *sunt ipsa susceptibilia contrariorum mutata*, id est secundum mutationem sui. Bene dixi "secundum sui mutationem", *enim*, id est quia, *frigidum de calido factum* etc. Et non solum sic est in istis, *similiter autem et in aliis*, supple substantiis, *unumquodque susceptibile contrariorum est suscipiens mutationem*. 10

Ita est in substantia, *autem*, id est sed, *oratio et opinio perseverant immobilia omnino*, id est universaliter, per se supple. Et bene dixi "per se", *vero*, id est quia, *cum res movetur, contrarium circa eam fit*, id est orationem. Ita dixi "res movetur, non oratio", *nam oratio permanet eadem eo quod aliquis sedeat* vel non sedeat, sed *<cum> res mota sit, fit*, oratio supple, et *aliquando vera* et *aliquando falsa*. Non solum sic est in oratione, *autem*, <id est> sed, *similiter in opinione*. Consequenter concludit: Ex quo haec proprietas convenit omni substantiae et soli, *quapropter*, id est ergo, *proprium est substantiae quod secundum* sui *mutationem* capax *sit contrariorum*. 15

Consequenter solvit interimendo: Ita dixi "oratio et opinio non recipiunt contraria", *vero*, id est sed, *si quis recipiat hoc, dicens orationem et opinionem susceptibilia esse contrariorum*, supple secundum sui mutationem, *non est hoc verum*. 25

Consequenter probat hoc: Bene dixi "non est hoc verum", *namque*, id est quia, *oratio et opinio non dicuntur susceptibilia contrariorum in eo quod aliquid* | *recipiant*, supple secundum sui mutationem, *sed eo quod passio*, id est mutatio, *facta sit circa alterum*. Bene dico "alterum", *nam in eo quod res est* etc., *non in eo quod ipsa sit susceptibilis contrariorum*. Bene dixi "oratio et opinio non recipiunt contraria secundum sui mutationem", nam *oratio neque opinio a nullo simpliciter movetur* et per se, sed per rem. Ex quo concludit: Non recipiunt contraria per se sed per aliud, 30

f. 43vb

7 autem] *! P* **14** unumquodque] *c* : unum quod est *P* **19** sit] fit *P* **19** vera] vere *P* **19** falsa] false *P*

quare, id est ergo, *non erunt susceptibilia contrariorum*, supple oratio et opinio, *cum nulla passio sit facta in eis*. Ita dixi "oratio et opinio non recipiunt contraria per se sed per rem", *verum*, id est sed, *substantia dicitur susceptibilis contrariorum in eo quod ipsa recipit contraria*. Bene dixi "recipit contraria", quia *suscipit languorem*

5   etc.

Ultimo concludit principale propositum: Ex quo soli substantiae convenit haec proprietas et omni, *quare*, id est ergo, *proprium est substantiae* etc. Littera patet.

<\QUAESTIONES>

<1>

Primo quaeritur quare potius ponit instantiam in oratione et opinione quam in aliis.

Et dicendum quod magis videtur de istis quod recipiant contraria quam de aliis.
10   Quod patet, quia opinio idem est quod visus interior vel intellectus, et intellectus sunt signa rerum, scribitur in primo *Perihermeneias*, et oratio similiter est signum intellectus, habetur ibidem, et per consequens rei. Sed signum proportionatur significato, dicit Boethius. Quia ergo significata, id est res, recipiunt contraria, videtur quod signa similiter, scilicet opinio et oratio, et ideo potius instat in istis quam
15   in aliis.

<2>

Secundo quaeritur: Dicit quod oratio eadem numero est susceptiva veri et falsi.

Contra. Proferatur haec oratio, "Socrates currit", ipso currente, vera est. Proferatur ipso non currente, falsa est. Probatio quod non eadem: Scribitur in capitulo de quantitate: "Quod semel dictum est non potest amplius sumi". Ergo non est
20   eadem oratio nunc prolata et prius. Idem patet per Horatium: "evolat, emissum semel, irrevocabile verbum".

Et dicendum quod contingit loqui de oratione dupliciter: in quantum est res a tempore mensurata, et sic non est eadem, ut obicitur; secundo <modo> loquimur de ea in quantum signum, et sic est eadem, quia signum semper idem significat, et
25   sic loquitur hic.

10–11 *cf.* Arist. *Int.* 1.16a6–8   **11–12** Arist. *Int.* 1.16a3–4   **12–13** *locum non inveni*   **16** Arist. *Cat.* 5.4a23–26   **18–19** Arist. *Cat.* 6.5a32–36, *ut apud* Anon. *Auct. Arist.* 31.19 (ed. Hamesse, 303)   **20–21** Hor. *Ep.* I 18.71

---

1 ergo] quia *P*   **10** visus] et *add. P*   **16** secundo] *Franceschini* : sed *P*   **17** vera] vere *P*

\<3\>

Tertio quaeritur: Dicit quod illa quae sunt in substantiis recipiunt contrarietatem, quod est contra ipsum.

Et dicendum quod aliquid est in substantia dupliciter: aut sicut in subiecto, et sic accidentia sunt in substantiis, aut sicut inferius in superiori, et sic inferiores substantiae sunt in substantia. Cum ergo obicitur "Quaecumque sunt in substantiis   5 recipiunt contraria", verum est secundo modo, sed cum assumis "Accidentia sunt in substantia", verum est sicut in subiecto; et sic aequivocatur "esse in".

\<4\>

Quarto quaeritur utrum eadem sit veritas rei et orationis.

Quod sic videtur. Nam eadem est sanitas quae est in animali et in urina secundum substantiam, sed differunt secundum rationem solum, quia in animali est   10 ut in subiecto, in urina ut in signo. Pari ergo ratione eadem erit veritas secundum substantiam in re et oratione, in re ut in subiecto, in oratione ut in signo.

Sed contra. Scribitur in *Libro de articulis fidei* quod idem non est causa sui ipsius. Sed veritas rei est causa veritatis orationis. Ergo non est eadem veritas.

f. 44ra   Item. Dicit Iohannes Chrysostomus: "Omne quod est | a semetipso est ab ae-   15 terno". Sed nihil est ab aeterno nisi Primum. Ergo nihil est a seipso nisi Primum. Sed veritas orationis est a veritate rei. Ergo non est eadem veritas.

Item. Scribitur in *Timaeo*: "Nihil est \<cuius\> ortum causa legitima non praecesserit". Et ita idem quod prius.

Ad haec omnia dicendum quod eadem est veritas rei et orationis secundum   20 substantiam, differens tamen secundum rationem; nam est in re ut in subiecto, in oratione ut in signo.

Ad obiectum dicendum quod veritas rei non est causa veritatis orationis, sed est causa \<quare\> praeest in oratione, ut ego non sum causa quare sum, sed sum causa quare sum hic.   25

\<5\>

Consequenter quaeritur: Dicit "ab eo quod res est vel non est etc".

---

1 Arist. *Cat.* 5.4a29–30   **13–14** Nicolaus Ambianensis *Ars fidei catholicae* I, prop. 8 (ed. Dreyer, 81)   **15–16** *cf.* Richardus de S. Victore *De trinitate* I 6 (ed. Migne, PL 196, 894a)   **18–19** Plato *Tim.* 28a, Transl. Calcidii (ed. Waszink et Jensen, 20); Anon. *Auct. Arist.* 27.2 (ed. Hamesse, 296) **26** Arist. *Cat.* 5.4a8–10

---

4 inferius in superiori] superius in inferiori *P*   **22** oratione] ratione *P ut v.*

<Contra.> Haec oratio, "Chimaera est Chimaera", vera est. Sed non est aliqua res existens per istam orationem significata. Ergo non semper dicitur oratio vera ab eo quod res est.

Praeterea. Dictiones syncategorematicae causant veritatem in oratione, et tamen non significant res.

Ad primum. "Res" uno modo dicitur a "ratus", "rata", "-tum", et sic solum dicitur res quod habet entitatem, id est existentiam actualem, et sic sumendo rem haec non est vera, "Chimaera est Chimaera"; non sic sumitur hic. Aliter sumitur "res" a "reor", "reris", quod est "opinor", "-ris", et sic, cum opinio non solum sit de ente actu sed potentia, res appellatur ens in anima vel secundum animam; et sic accipitur hic. A re tali haec oratio est vera, "Chimaera est Chimaera".

Ad secundum dicendum quod res sumitur dupliciter. Proprie, et sic signa non dicuntur res, vel communiter, extendendo nomen rei ad rem et modum rei, et sic large sumitur hic res. Et quia signa in oratione dicuntur rei modi, potest ab eis causari veritas vel falsitas in oratione.

<6>

Sexto quaeritur quid sit veritas.

Si dicatur cum Anselmo: "Veritas est rei perfectio in sua specie", contra. Si veritas est perfectio rei in sua specie, ergo perfectio rei est vera. Sed omnis oratio est perfecta in sua specie. Ergo omnis oratio est vera. Maior patet: Perfectum est id quod attingit id propter quod est. Sed omnis oratio est talis. Ergo omnis oratio perfecta. Sed veritas est rei perfectio. Ergo omnis oratio est vera. Quod cum sit falsum, perfectio rei non est veritas quae est in oratione.

Item. Si dicatur cum Boethio: "Veritas est adaequatio vocis cum intellectu", et haec est veritas quae est in oratione, contra. Removeamus nomina aequivoca, et tunc erit verum quod tot sint signa quot significata. Si ergo adaequatio vocis cum intellectu veritas est quae est in oratione, erit reperire veritatem in quacumque oratione. Sed in omni oratione in qua non ponitur aequivocum est reperire adaequationem vocis cum intellectu. Ergo omnis oratio in qua ponitur nomen aequivocum est falsa. Quod falsum est.

Item. Si dicatur quod unio praedicati ad subiectum quantum ad affirmationem et divisio praedicati a subiecto quantum ad negationem est veritas quae est in oratione, contra. Scribitur in *Posterioribus*: "Si aliquid est in aliquibus pluribus, inest

---

17 *cf.* Anselmus *De veritate* 7   **23** *locum non inveni* **95.32–96.1** *cf.* Arist. *APo* I 23.84b3–12

---

7 entitatem] unitatem *P*   **13** modum] modium *P*   **18** vera] verum *P*   **28–29** in...falsa] in qua non ponitur aequivocum est vera *malim*   **28** nomen] unde *P ut v.*

eis per eandem causam non per diversam". Cum ergo unio et divisio sint causae diversae, haec non erunt causa quare veritas est in oratione. Ergo indivisio praedicati
a subiecto vel divisio | non est veritas quae est in oratione. Ergo quaeritur quid sit.

Et dicendum quod non est perfectio rei in sua specie, ut probat prima ratio,
quia illa definitio data est de veritate incomplexa quae est rei entitas. Sed veritas   5
orationis est adaequatio vocis cum intellectu, ut dicit Boethius, vel divisio praedicati
a subiecto quantum ad negationem vel indivisio quantum ad affirmationem.

Ad argumentum quod probat quod adaequatio vocis cum intellectu non est veritas quae est in oratione dicendum quod aequivocatur adaequatio vocis cum intellectu. Uno enim modo dicitur adaequatio vocis cum intellectu quia tot sunt signa   10
quot significata, et sic omnis oratio vera in qua non ponitur aequivocum, ut obicitur; et sic non sumitur hic. Alio modo dicitur adaequatio vocis cum intellectu
quando in re praedicatum est unitum subiecto et sic per orationem enuntiatur, et
tunc est adaequatio vocis cum re sive cum intellectu, sed quando est in re divisum
<et> per orationem significatur compositum, tunc est inadaequatio.   15

Ad argumentum quod probat quod indivisio praedicati vel divisio non est veritas quae est in oratione dicendum quod illa propositio, "in aliquibus pluribus etc.",
intelligenda est de illis pluribus quae sunt in eodem genere, et ideo, quia affirmatio
et negatio non sunt in eodem genere, non tenet in istis.

5–6   *locum non inveni*

---

7 negationem] veritatem *P*   11 ponitur] praedicatur *P*   15 inadaequatio] ante adaequatio *P*
17 in] ab *P*

Lectio XVI

Quantitatis autem etc. (6.4b20)

\<Divisio\>

Determinato de substantia, quae est fundamentum aliorum et ex qua alia causantur, prosequitur de aliis praedicamentis, et primo de quantitate.

Et dividitur haec pars in partes duas. Primo determinat de quantitate penes substantialia eius, secundo penes eius accidentia, ut ibi: *Amplius quantitati nihil est contrarium* (6.5b12).

Prima in duas. Primo determinat de quantitatibus quae sunt proprie quantitates, secundo de quantitatibus per accidens, ibi: *Proprie autem quantitates* (6.5a39).

Prima in duas. Primo ponit duas divisiones, secundo explanat membra dividentia. Secunda ibi:

\< * * * \>

Et aliud quidem (6.4b21).

Haec est divisio lectionis, et sunt particulae tres.

\<Sententia\>

Circa primam sic procedit: Quantitas quaedam est continua, quaedam discreta.

Consequenter ponit aliam divisionem, dicens: Quaedam est quantitas quae constat ex partibus habentibus positionem ad se, alia quae constat ex partibus quae non habent positionem.

Ultimo explanat membra primae divisionis, dicens: Discreta quantitas est numerus et oratio, continua est superficies etc.

Haec est sententia partis.

Expositio litteralis

Ita dictum est de substantia, *autem*, pro sed, *quantitatis aliud continuum, aliud discretum*. Quasi dicens: Quaedam est quantitas continua, quaedam discreta.

Et aliud, hoc est quaedam quantitas, *constat ex partibus habentibus positionem ad se*, id est inter se, *invicem*, in suo toto supple, sed *aliud*, id est alia quantitas, constat *ex non habentibus positionem*.

Ultimo explanat membra primae divisionis: Ita dixi "aliud continuum etc.", *autem*, id est sed, *discreta quantitas est numerus et oratio*, \<*vero*, id est sed, *continua*

---

11 et aliud quidem] et ad quod *P*

f. 44va   *est linea, superficies, corpus>*, et non | tantum istae supple, sed *praeter haec tempus et locus.*

<Quaestiones>

Ad dictorum evidentiam duo quaeruntur, primo de modo procedendi, secundum de quibusdam dictis in littera.

<1>

De primo sic. Videtur quod qualitas ante quantitatem.   5

Nam qualitas est proprietas consequens formam, quantitas proprietas consequens materiam, ut habetur secundo *Physicorum.* Sed forma <est> dignior materia, cum sit nobilior. Ergo proprietas consequens naturam formae erit prior, et sic qualitas ante quantitatem.

Et dicendum quod quam cito res est, tam cito est vel una vel plures et sic quanta,   10
non autem tam cito est qualis. Quia ergo immediatius et prius inhaeret substantiae, ideo immediatius post substantiam ordinatur. Et sic solvit Boethius in Commento. Quod autem inhaereat immediatius patet. Nam qualitas non inhaeret substantiae nisi mediante superficie, et ita superficies immediatius inhaeret.

Alia causa est quia magis convenit cum substantia quam qualitas. Quod patet,   15
quia sicut substantiae nihil est contrarium, ita nec quantitati, sed qualitas habet contrarium.

Ad obiectum dicendum quod duplex est prius: in via cognitionis et naturae. Unde licet forma in via cognitionis praecedat, secundum viam naturae non praecedit; nam prius est materia quam a forma informetur. Et sic quantitas consequens   20
naturam materiae prior.

<2>

Secundo quaeritur quare non definit quantitatem.

Si dicatur, et bene, quod definitio per priora est, sed quantitas, cum sit generalissimum, non habet prius, tunc quaeritur quare non definitur per relationem ad suum concretum sicut qualitas; quia diceretur: "Quantitas est secundum quam quanti   25
dicimur", sicut dicitur: "Qualitas est secundum quam quales dicimur".

6–7 *fortasse* Arist. *Phys.* I 9.192a13–14; Anon. *Auct. Arist.* 2.30 (ed. Hamesse, 142)   **11–12** Boeth. *in Cat.* 201d–2b   **26**   Arist. *Cat.* 8.8b25–26

---

10 vel²] *add. P s.l.*   **13** inhaereat] inhaerent *P a.c.*   **20** a] alia *P*   **23** sit] *add. in marg. P* **24** definitur] definit *P*   **25** quia] quod *P*

Et dicendum quod non est simile. Nam omnes qualitates comparantur uniformiter ad concretum, sed non quantitates (non enim a quantitatibus omnibus dicimur quanti, sed solum a continua; a discreta vero dicimur quoti), quare non potest sic quantitas definiri.

<3>

Tertio quaeritur quare determinando de substantia incipit ab inferiori, hic determinando de quantitati incipit a superiori, quare est sibi contrarius in modo procedendi hic et ibi.

Et dicendum quod non, quia proprietas substantiae est substare, et ideo incipit ab inferiori substantia, quae magis substat, unde magis hanc proprietatem participat. Sed quantitas est accidens, cuius proprietas est inhaerere iuxta illud Boethii: "Accidentis esse etc.", et ideo prius determinat de quantitate superiori quia plus hanc proprietatem participat.

<4>

Quarto quaeritur quare non dividit quantitatem per primam et secundam sicut substantiam.

Et dicendum quod primum in genere est individuum. Sed individuum primo et per se convenit substantiae, aliis vero per accidens; quod patet, quia alia non individuantur nisi prius individuata substantiae ratione. Et quia primum dependet a secundo, ideo primum et secundum insunt substantiae primo er per se, in aliis autem sunt per accidens; et hinc est quod substantia dividitur per primam et secundam et non aliquod aliorum.

Haec quaeruntur de primo.

<5>

De secundo quaeritur: Dividendo quantitatem praeponit continuum, prosequendo postponit, quare videtur ordinem pervertere.

Et dicendum quod continuum et discretum possunt dupliciter considerari: uno modo per relationem ad suum definiens, alio modo in quantum habent rationem

---

10–11 cf. Boeth. *in Cat.* 170d–71a (*hoc adagium,* "Accidentis esse est inesse", *quandoque Boethio, quandoque Aristoteli a magistriis attribuitur; cf.* Thomas Aquinas *Expositio Libri posteriorum* I 2.40 (ed. Leonina, 11) *cum nota editoris in apparatu fontium*) **22** Arist. *Cat.* 6.4b20 **22–23** Arist. *Cat.* 6.4b25–5a14

---

22 praeponit] proponit *P*

mensurae. Primo modo continuum praecedit. Quod patet, quia continuum est cuius partes copulantur ad aliquem terminum communem, discretum quod non habet terminum communem ad quem eius particulae copulentur, et ita definitio

f. 44vb continui se habet per | modum habitus, discreti per modum privationis, et habitus ante privationem. Sed in quantum <habent> rationem mensurae, sic discretum 5 praecedit, quia in pluribus reperitur. Nam mensura quantitatis discretae reperitur in superioribus et inferioribus (potest enim dici unus angelus), sed mensura continui solum in inferioribus reperitur. Primo modo ordinat dividendo, secundo prosequendo.

<6>

Secundo quaeritur: Dicit "quantitatis" et non "quantitatum". 10

Nam videtur contra Priscianum, dicentem in primo *Constructionum*: "Si dividentibus verba singulariter reddantur, oportet genitivum pluralem divisum praecedere". Cum ergo sit sic, in proposito debet poni genus in genitivo plurali. Vel quare non?

Et dicendum quod essentia generis est una in se, unde animalia non est genus, 15 sed animal. Ut ergo denotaret essentiae generis unitatem, dixit "quantitatis" potius in numero singulari.

Vel aliter. "Animal" est proprium nomen generis et "homo" speciei, scribitur in primo *Constructionum*. Sed proprium nomen loquendo proprie non habet plurale. Quare dividit genus in singulari et non in plurali. 20

Ad obiectum dicendum quod Priscianus loquitur in rebus animatis, quare non valet hoc argumentum.

Et cum haec responsio fatua videatur, dicendum aliter quod duplex est constructio: quaedam ratione significati, alia gratia expressionis sententiae. Primo modo loquitur Priscianus, secundo hic auctor quia voluit ostendere unitatem essentiae 25 generis et hoc magis expressit per singulare, ut visum est.

<7>

Tertio quaeritur quare dicit "aliud" et non "alia", cum dividentia identitatem habent in genere diviso; male ergo dicit.

---

10 Arist. *Cat.* 6.4b20   **11–13** Prisc. *Inst. gramm.* XVII 4.28 (ed. Hertz, vol. 2, 125)   **18–19** cf. Prisc. *Inst. gramm.* XVII 5.35 (ed. Hertz, vol. 2, 130)   27 Arist. *Cat.* 6.4b20–22

---

1 mensurae] mensuratae *P*   **11** priscianum] priscianus *P*   **12–13** praecedere] *lectio incerta* **13** genus] genitivus *P*   **15** essentia] essentiam *P*

Et dicendum, ut prius, quod dicit "aliud" gratia expressionis sententiae, quia dicit Porphyrius quod differentiae specificae faciunt aliud. Ut ergo denotaret quod continuum et discretum sunt nunc specificatae et haec divisio datur per tales differentias, ideo dixit "aliud continuum" et non "alia".

<8>

5   Quarto quaeritur quare ponit notam diversitatis inter species quantitatis continuae.

Et dicendum quod tempus et locus rem mensurant extrinsece, aliae vero intrinsece; ad quam diversitatem explicandam notam diversitatis interposuit.

Vel aliter. Tempus et locus mensurant rem sub esse accidentali, alia vero sub esse substantiali; et ut haec explicaretur diversitas, diversitatis interposuit notam.

10   Veritates istarum solutionum patent sumendo sufficientiam continuae quantitatis.

---

1 *cf.* Q6 *immediate supra*   **1–2** Porph. *Isag.* 8.19–21   **5** *cf.* Arist. *Cat.* 6.4b23–25   **10** *cf.* Lectio XIX, Q8

---

3 nunc] *lectio incerta*   **8** accidentali] *lectio incerta, cf. autem* Lectio XIX, Q8   **9** substantiali] *comp.* "spâli" *habet P, cf. autem* Lectio XIX, Q8

Lectio XVII

Partium etenim numeri (6.4b26)

<Divisio>

Notificatis membris primae divisionis per exempla, notificat ipsa per descriptionem.

Haec pars in duas. Primo notificat speciem quantitatis discretae, secundo continuae, ibi: *Linea vero continua est* (6.5a1).

5 Prima est praesentis lectionis et dividitur in duas. Primo enim notificat numerum, secundo orationem, ibi: *Similiter autem oratio* (6.4b31).

Prima in duas. Primo ponit minorem certam rationis, secundo ex ipsa concludit propositum, ibi: *Quapropter numerus* (6.4b30).

Pars in qua notificat orationem in duas. Primo proponit quod intendit, secundo
10 exsequitur propositum, ibi: *Quia etenim quantitas* (6.4b34).

Illa secunda in duas. Primo probat quod oratio est quantitas, secundo quod sit quantitas discreta, ibi: *Ad nullum enim* (6.4b36).

<Sententia>

Sic procedit circa primam: Omnis quantitas cuius partes ad nullum terminum communem copulantur est discreta. Numerus est huiusmodi. <Ergo etc.> | Minorem f. 45ra
15 cum eius explanatione ponit et conclusionem.

Consequenter prosequitur de oratione. Primo proponit intentum, scilicet quod oratio est quantitas discreta.

Consequenter probat quod sit quantitas: Omne illud cuius partes mensurantur est quantitas. Oratio est huiusmodi. Ergo etc.

20 Ultimo probat quod sit quantitas discreta tali ratione: Cuius partes non copulantur ad terminum communem est discreta. Oratio est huiusmodi. Ergo etc.

Haec est sententia partis.

Expositio litteralis

Ita dixi quod numerus est quantitas discreta, *enim*, id est quia, *nullus est terminus communis ad quem partes* numeri copulentur. Et ponit exempla: *ut quinque et*
25 *quinque, si*, id est quamvis, sint partes decem, *ad nullum* tamen *terminum commu-*

---

4 continua] $P^{inf}ac_{Cs}$: continuorum P : continuum c   **6** secundo] secund P   **13** terminum] quod add. P a.c.

nem copulantur quinque et quinque, sed sunt semper discreta, id est sunt semper dispertita vel separata vel distincta. Et non solum sic est in istis, *sed tria et septem ad nullum terminum communem copulantur, sed semper discreta et separata sunt.*

Concludit: Ex quo partes non copulantur ad aliquem terminum communem, *quapropter*, id est ergo, *numerus est* discretus.   5

Consequenter prosequitur de oratione. Primo proponit quod intendit, dicens: Non solum numerus est discreta quantitas, *autem*, pro sed, etiam *oratio similiter est discretorum.*

Et probat quod sit quantitas: Bene dixi quod est quantitas, *etenim*, id est quia, *manifestum est* quod *oratio est quantitas, enim*, id est quia, *syllaba longa et bre-*   10 *vis mensuratur.* Et exponit de qua oratione intendit: Ita dixi "oratio est quantitas", *autem*, id est sed, *dico*, id est expono, *orationem voce prolatam.*

Ultimo probat quod oratio sit quantitas discreta: Bene dico quod oratio est quantitas discreta, *enim*, id est quia, *partes eius ad nullum terminum communem copulantur*, nullus *enim est terminus ad quem syllabae*, quae sunt partes orationis   15 supple, copulentur, *sed unaquaeque*, scilicet syllaba, *est divisa secundum se ipsam.*

<Quaestiones>

Ad evidentiam dictorum duo quaeruntur, primum de prima, secundum de secunda.

<1>

De prima sic. Quaeritur utrum numerus sit quantitas.

Videtur quod sic per auctorem. Omne illud secundum quod aliquid dicitur ae-quale vel inaequale alicui est quantitas (quia hoc est maxime proprium quantitati,   20 ergo convenit omni et soli). Sed secundum numerum dicuntur aliqua aequalia vel inaequalia. Ergo numerus est quantitas.

Sed contra. Duplex est numerus, scilicet res numerata et quo numeramus. Sed nec sic nec sic est quantitas. Ergo nullo modo est quantitas. Minor patet, quia numerus qui est res numerata est ipsa substantia (si enim accidens numeratur, hoc   25 non est nisi quia substantia numeratur). Sed genera sunt impermixta, scribitur in primo *Posteriorum*. Ergo, cum res numerata sit substantia, non erit quantitas.

Item. Nec numerus quo numeramus est quantitas, quia omnis quantitas aliquid est secundum rem iuxta illud Boethii: "Decem sunt genera prima rerum significan-

---

19 *cf.* Arist. *Cat.* 6.6a26–35   **26–27**   Arist. *APo* I 15.79b6–12, *ut apud* Anon. *Auct. Arist.* 35.68 (ed. Hamesse, 317)   **104.29–105.1**   *cf.* Boeth. *in Cat.* 161a

---

9 etenim] P^{sup}c : certe P *ut* v.

tia". Sed numerus quo numeramus solum est secundum animam et non est aliquid secundum rem (quod patet, quia est nutus corporeus vel motus ipsius animae). Ergo nullo modo est quantitas.

Et dicendum quod numerus est quantitas utroque modo.

5 Ad primum obiectum dicendum quod res numerata duplicem habet numerum, scilicet essentialem, et iste est numerositas suorum substantialium, et sic est substantia res numerata. Habet etiam numerum accidentalem, et ita quod est in se indivisum et ab aliis divisum facit | cum aliis numerum, et sic est quantitas. Primo   f. 45rb
modo procedit ratio.

10 Ad secundum. Cum dicimus numerum cum quo numeramus, duo tanguntur, scilicet operatio numerantis, et tangitur quaedam natura qua mediante nutus corporeus transit supra res numeratas, et haec natura dicitur binarius, ternarius, et huiusmodi; et haec natura bene est quantitas. Per hoc patet ad obiectionem, quia numerus quo numeramus non solum est nutus corporeus ut obicitur, sed est
15 quaedam natura quae est aliquid secundum rem, et haec natura est quantitas.

Patet ergo quod secundum quosdam res numerata est quantitas. Aliter dicitur quod triplex est numerus, scilicet numeratus, et talis numerus dicitur res numeratae, quae substantiae sunt, ut obicitur. Secundo modo dicitur numerus numerans, et hoc est ipsa anima, et sic adhuc substantia. Tertio modo numerus quo numera-
20 mus, et iste nihil aliud est quam nutus corporeus transiens super res numeratas, et sic quantitas est. Ad obiectum dicatur ut dictum est.

<2>

Secundo quaeritur utrum numerus possit constitui ex suis partibus.

Quod non videtur. Unum quod est totum constat ex suis partibus coniunctis secundum quod dicit Commentator supra primum *Physicorum* quod partes con-
25 iunctae sunt materia totius. Sed earum coniunctio est forma. Ergo impossibile est constitui aliquod discretum ex suis partibus.

Item. Contraria est via generationis viae resolutionis. <Sed> via resolutionis respicit partes separatas ad ipsasque terminatur (hoc patet). Ergo via generationis respicit partes unitas et ad ipsas terminatur. Ergo in generatione totius ex partibus
30 oportet partes esse unitas, et ita idem quod prius.

Et dicendum quod numerus potest constitui ex suis partibus, ut dicit auctor.

24–25   *cf.* Averroes *in Phys.* I 17 (ed. Venet., 13v–14r); Anon. *Auct. Arist.* 2.43 (ed. Hamesse, 144)

---

8 indivisum] divisa *P*   **8** divisum] diversa *P*   **13** obiectionem] opinionem *P*   **26** discretum]
totum *P*   **27** via resolutionis] *add. al. man. in marg.*

Et ut pateat obiectorum solutio, notandum quod unum dicitur sex modis. Primo modo unum compositione, ut forma et materia sunt unum. <Secundo modo
unum> continuatione, ut partes alicuius continui. Tertio modo unum contigua-
tione, ut duo corpora secundum plura contigua. Quarto modo unum colligatione,
ut terra aquae coniuncta. Quinto <modo> unum in situ, ut plantae pars abscisa et   5
alteri plantae unita. Sexto modo unum aggregatione, ut acervus lapidum.

Cum ergo obicitur quod generatio totius sit ex partium unione, hoc est verum si
illud totum sit unum continuatione; sed quia numerus est unum aggregatione, non
valent rationes. Unde partes numeri non dicuntur separatae ita quod ex eis non
possit fieri unum aggregatione, sed quia ex eis non potest fieri unum continuatione.   10

<3>

Tertio quaeritur utrum unitates sint partes numeri.

Quod sic videtur. Omne quod est principium alicuius materiale et formale est
pars ipsius. Unitas est huiusmodi. Ergo etc. Minor patet, quia ex unitatibus fit
numerus, et sic est materiale, et apposita unitate resultat species numeri, et ita est
formale.   15

Quod est verum.

Sed modo quaeritur utrum linea possit similiter constare ex punctis. Et videtur quod sic, cum punctus sit principium quantitatis continuae sicut numerus
discretae; ergo sicut numerus fit ex unitatibus, sic linea ex punctis.

Contra. Scribitur in primo *Posteriorum* quod ex impartibilibus non fit partibile.   20
Sed punctus est impartibilis, linea vero partibilis. Ergo etc. Minor patet. Punctus
enim est cuius pars non est, dicit Boethius in *Arithmetica*, | et ita est indivisibilis.
Item. Linea est continuum, et omne continuum divisibile in infinitum, scribitur in
tertio *Physicorum*.

Et dicendum quod linea non est ex punctis. Et causa est <quia est> continuum   25
et ideo habet esse per unitatem partium et contactum. Sed puncti ad punctum
non fit unio neque contactus. Quare ex punctis non fit linea. Quod autem puncti
ad punctum non sit contactus probat Aristoteles sic: Omnis contactus aut est in
medio aut in extremis. Si in medio, ergo est in puncto aliquid medium et extrema,
et ita indivisibile habet partes, quod falsum est, et si in extremis, similiter.   30

Alia causa est <quia> quaelibet pars lineae est linea, et cum linea sit continuum
et sic divisibile, punctus autem indivisibilis, et sic non est pars lineae.

f. 45va

---

20 *locum non inveni*   **21–22** Boeth. *Ars geometriae* (ed. Friedlein, 374)   **23–24** Arist. *Phys.*
III 7.207b16–17; Anon. *Auct. Arist.* 2.108 (ed. Hamesse, 148)   **27–30** Arist. *Phys.* VI 1.231a21
sqq.

---

13 ipsius] unita *add. P*   **13** quia] quod *P*   **27** unio] via *P*   **29** puncto aliquid] positione ad *P*
32 autem] aut *P*

Ad obiectum dicendum quod non est simile, quia numerus cum sit unum aggregatione, potest esse ex unitatibus, quae sunt materia et forma, ut visum est. Sed linea est continuum et ita habet esse in partium unione, puncti autem ad punctum non est unio, et ideo linea non fit ex punctis.

<4>

5 Quarto quaeritur quare partes numeri non possunt ad terminum communem copulari.

Et dicendum quod ad hoc quod aliqua uniantur termino communi oportet quod habent unitatem per continuationem ad terminum communem ad quem copulantur.

10 Haec de primo quaeruntur.

<5>

De secundo sic. Quaeritur utrum oratio sit in praedicamento.

Quod non videtur. Nullum transcendens vel communiter se habens ad omnia praedicamenta est determinatum ad aliquod illorum. Oratio est huiusmodi, quia per ipsam repraesentatur res cuiuslibet praedicamenti. Ergo non est determinate
15 in aliquo genere.

Et dicendum quod oratio triplex est, dicit Boethius in Commento: in scripto, in mente, in prolatione. Tertio modo loquitur hic, ut dicit in littera, et haec est in generibus determinatis diversis secundum quod diversimode accipitur.

Ad obiectum dicendum quod non valet, quia sicut anima existens vere substan-
20 tia in corpore dicitur quodam modo <omnia> quia species omnium quodam modo ingerit se, et tamen non sequitur quod anima transcendat omne genus, similiter oratio existens in genere qualitatis vel quantitatis potest repraesentare rem cuiuslibet praedicamenti, et tamen non sequitur quod quodlibet transcendat.

Vel aliter. Contingit loqui de oratione dupliciter: aut de ipsa id quod est aut in
25 quantum ei accidit rem significare. Primo modo est in genere, secundo transcendit, ut obicitur. Et est simile de anima, quae secundum se substantia est, comprehendit tamen omnia in quantum omnium habet virtutes cognitivas.

16–17 *potius* Boeth. *in Int.*² I 1 (ed. Meiser, 29)   **17**   Arist. *Cat.* 6.4a35–36

---

14 repraesentatur res] reputantur *P* : manifestatur res *add. al. man. in marg.* (*cf. autem responsionem ad obiectum*)   **20** in corpore] incorpora *P ut v.*

<6>

Secundo quaeritur in quo praedicamento sit.

Quod in substantia videtur. Oratio est vox, vox autem aer, aer autem substantia; ergo vox est substantia. Sed oratio de qua hic loquitur est vox, ut dicit in littera. Ergo est substantia.

Quod qualitas videtur. Omne immutativum sensus particularis est passio vel   5
passibilis qualitas. Sed vox est immutativa sensus particularis (est enim suum sensibile aurium). Ergo qualitas. Sed genera sunt impermixta, scribitur in primo *Posteriorum.* Ergo non est quantitas.

Et dicendum quod oratio tripliciter potest considerari: uno modo prout est obiectum sensus particularis, et sic est qualitas, ut probat secunda ratio; vel prout   10
habet partes quae non possunt copulari ad aliquem terminum communem, et sic est quantitas; vel ad | materiam in qua generatur, ut ad aerem, et sic est substantia. Et sic patet ad obiecta.

f. 45vb

<7>

Consequenter quaeritur de secundo argumento. Dicit: "Partes orationis mensurantur, ergo est quantitas". Eadem ratione substantia erit quantitas, cum mensuretur.   15

Et dicendum quod duplex est mensura: quaedam est per aequidistantiam, id est per aequalem distantiam, mensurae ad mensuratum, ut bracchii ad pannum; alia est per partes aliquotas, id est quae aliquotiens sumptae reddunt suum totum, ut unitas quae est pars numeri et sumpta multotiens reddit suum totum, et haec mensura appropriatur quantitati discretae, et sic non est instantia de substantia.   20
Sic littera legatur: *Syllaba longa et brevis mensuratur* (6.4a33), supple per partes aliquotas, id est per litteras, quae sumptae aliquotiens reddunt syllabam, et syllaba longa et brevis sunt partes aliquotae orationis.

<8>

Sed quaeritur quare potius probat de oratione quod sit quantitas quam de aliqua alia specie.   25

Et dicendum quod de illa erat magis dubium. Quod patet, quia uno modo omne genus transcendit, alio est in praedicamento qualitatis, alio substantiae, alio quantitatis. Non similiter autem erat in aliis.

---

3   *cf.* Arist. *Cat.* 6.4a35–36   **7–8**   Arist. *APo* I 15.79b6–12, *ut apud* Anon. *Auct. Arist.* 35.68 (ed. Hamesse, 317)   **14–15**   *cf.* Arist. *Cat.* 6.4a31–5a1

---

27 omne] *add. s.l.* P

Lectio XVIII

Linea <vero> continua est (6.5a1)

<Divisio>

Determinato de quantitate discreta, determinat de quantitate continua.

Haec pars in duas. Primo determinat de quantitatibus intrinsice mensurantibus, secundo extrinsice, ibi: *Est autem tempus* (6.5a6).

Prima in tres. Primo prosequitur de linea, secundo de superficie, tertio de
5 corpore. Secunda ibi: *et superficiei* (6.5a3), tertia ibi: *Similiter et in corpore* (6.5a4).

Pars in qua determinat de mensurantibus extra dividitur in duas. Primo determinat de tempore, secundo de loco, ibi: *Rursus locus* (6.5a8).

Haec secunda in duas. Primo proponit quod intendit, secundo prosequitur probando, ibi: *Locum enim quendam* (6.5a8).

10 Haec secunda in duas. Primo ponit probationem, secundo concludit intentum, ibi: *Quapropter locus* (6.5a13).

Haec est divisio lectionis, et sunt partes septem.

<Sententia>

Circa primam sic procedit: Omnis quantitas cuius partes copulantur ad aliquem terminum communem est continua. Linea est huiusmodi. Ergo etc.

15 Ratio eadem est de superficie, corpore, tempore.

Consequenter probat de loco. Primo proponit quod locus est continuus, secundo probat. Ratio talis est: Singulae partes loci quae obtinent singulas particulas corporis copulantur ad illum terminum ad quem corporis particulae. Sed corporis particulae copulantur ad terminum communem. Ergo et particulae loci.

20 Ex hoc concludit quod locus est continua quantitas, cum eius partes copulentur ad terminum communem.

Haec est partis sententia.

Expositio litteralis

Ita dixi de quantitatibus discretis, *autem*, pro sed, *linea est continua*, *enim*, id est quia, *potes sumere communem terminum*, *id est punctum*, *ad quem*, scilicet
25 punctum, *particulae eius*, id est lineae, *copulantur*.

---

9 enim] $P^{inf}c$: vero P   **22** partis] partes P

Consequenter probat hoc de superficie: Resume "potes sumere communem terminum", *superficiei*, scilicet *lineam*. Et hoc probat: *enim*, id est quia, *particulae plani*, id est superficiei, *copulantur ad quendam terminum communem*. Hic nota quod
triplex est superficies: plana, concava et convexa.

Consequenter probat hoc de corpore, dicens: Non solum quantitates dictae sunt   5
continuae, *autem*, id est sed, *similiter poteris*, o lector, *su|mere communem termi-
num*, id est superficiem, *in corpore ad quam*, id est *superficiem*, copules *particulas
corporis*.

Et non solum ita est in istis, *autem*, pro sed, *tempus et locus*, supple divisim, *est
talium*, id est de numero continuorum.   10

    < * * * >

Et hoc probat: *enim*, id est quia, *particulae corporis obtinent quendam locum,
quae particulae*, scilicet corporis, *copulantur ad* aliquem *terminum communem*,
scilicet superficiem. Consequenter infert ex hoc: Ex quo particulae loci copulantur
ad eundem terminum ad quem particulae corporis, et particulae corporis copu-   15
lantur ad superficiem, *ergo et loci particulae*, quae, scilicit loci particulae, *obtinent
singulas particulas corporis, copulantur ad* superficiem.

Ultimo infert intentum: Ex quo ita est, *quapropter*, id est ergo, *locus est continuus*; *enim*, id est quia, *particulae eius*, id est loci, *copulantur ad unum communem
terminum*.   20

\<Quaestiones\>

\<1\>

Ad dictorum evidentiam primo quaeritur utrum punctus sit in genere quantitatis.

Quod sic videtur. Supposito quod non sit in genere substantiae, tunc arguo:
Quod est in genere posteriori non est principium eorum quae sunt in genere priori
(hoc patet, quia principium praecedit principiatum). Sed quantitas praecedit alia
praedicamenta iuxta illud Boethii in Commento quod quantitas immediatius in-   25
haeret substantiae quia quam cito res est, tam cito est quanta. Cum ergo punctus
sit principium specierum quantitatis, scilicet lineae, non erit in alio praedicamento
accidentium. Ergo in quantitate.

Sed contra. Maxime proprie proprium quantitatis est secundum eam aequale vel inaequale dici, ut dicit in sequentibus. Ergo convenit omni. Sed secundum   30
punctum nihil dicitur aequale vel inaequale. Ergo non est quantitas.

25–26 *cf.* Boeth. *in Cat.* 201d–2c   **29–30** Arist. *Cat.* 6.6a26–35

27 alio] aliquo *P ut v.*

f. 46ra

Item. De omni eo quod est in genere quantitatis praedicatur quantitas. De puncto non praedicatur quantitas. Ergo etc. Minor patet: Punctus nec est quantitas continua nec discreta, de quibus solum praedicatur quantitas quia omnis quantitas continua vel discreta.

Et dicendum quod aliquid est in genere dupliciter: uno modo sicut participans rationem illius generis, et sic species et individua sunt in genere; secundo modo ut principium illorum quae sunt in genere illo, et sic forma et materia sunt in genere substantiae et punctus in genere quantitatis.

Per hoc patet ad obiecta quia omnes rationes probant punctum non esse in genere sicut participans rationem illius generis, sed est punctus in genere quantitatis tanquam principium eorum quae sunt in genere quantitatis.

<2>

Consequenter quaeritur: Dicit quod partes corporis et loci copulantur ad eundem terminum communem.

Contra. Diversarum quantitatum diversi sunt termini. Corpus et locus diversae sunt quantitates. Ergo diversos habent terminos. Non ergo copulantur ad eundem terminum.

Item. Si copulantur ad superficiem, aut ergo ad superficiem corporis aut loci aut utriusque. Non ad alteram tantum, quia non est maior ratio de una quam de alia. Si ad utramque, cum illae duae sint diversae, non copulantur ad eundem terminum sed ad diversos.

Contra. Ut habemus ab Euclide, si aliqua | linea protrahatur et ei alia linea coniungatur in continuum et directum, totum fit una linea. Ergo pari ratione si una superficies coniungatur alteri, totum fiet una. Sed partes corporis copulantur ad superficiem propriam et partes loci similiter ad propriam, et istae sunt una, ut probatum est. Ergo partes loci et corporis copulantur ad eandem superficiem, et ita ad eundem terminum communem.

Quod concedo. Et dicendum quod est locus duplex, scilicet res locans, et sic locus dicitur corpus locans; secundo modo est locus quo locans locat, et sic definitur in *Physicis*: "Locus est ultima superficies corporis ambientis". Primo <modo obicitur>, secundo modo loquitur hic. Dicendum ergo quod si locus et locatum considerentur quantum ad istam dimensionem quae est longitudo, cum haec sit in utroque, copulantur ad punctum, si vero secundum latitudinem, partes eorum copulantur ad lineam.

f. 46rb

12–13 Arist. *Cat.* 6.5a9–13   **21–22** *cf.* Euclides *Elementa* I, post. 1   **28–29** Arist. *Phys.* IV 4.212a20–21; *cf.* Anon. *Auct. Arist.* 2.120 (ed. Hamesse, 149)

Ad obiectum dicendum quod superficies loci et locati dupliciter possunt considerari: uno modo in relatione ad illa quorum sunt superficies propriae, et sic quia corpora sunt diversa, diversae erunt superficies; aliter considerantur in quantum sunt unitiva istorum duorum, et quia ea quae uniuntur uniuntur per indivisibilia, indivisibilia unita fiunt unum. Patet ad obiecta, quia uno modo sunt unum, alio   5
modo non, ut visum est.

<3>

Consequenter quaeritur: Dicit quod praeteritum et futurum copulantur ad praesens.

Contra. Terminus plus participat naturam individualitatis quam pluralitatis. Ergo haec duo non possunt ad unum idem copulari.   10

Item. Unius quantitatis unus est terminus. Tempus est una quantitas. Ergo etc. Sed praeteritum et futurum non sunt unum sed duo. Ergo ipsa ad tempus praesens non copulantur.

Quod concedo. Unde dicendum quod ibi est hypallage, ut visum est in sententia.

<4>

Sed tunc quaeritur: Videtur quod impossibile sit praeteritum et futurum copulari   15
ad praesens.

Nihil quod est terminus est idem cum illo cuius partes ad ipsum copulantur. Sed partes temporis copulantur ad praesens. Ergo praesens non est tempus. Quod falsum est. Gratia huius quaeritur qualiter praeteritum et futurum copulantur ad praesens.   20

Et dicendum quod quando incipit esse praesens, tunc praeteritum terminatur, sed quando praesens terminatur, tunc incipit esse futurum; et ita quantum ad sui finem est terminus initialis futuri, quantum ad sui principium terminus finalis praeteriti.

Vel aliter. Medium participat naturam extremorum. Sed dicit Priscianus quod   25
tempus est praesens cuius pars praeterit, pars est in instanti parsque futura est. Ergo quantum ad sui principium est idem cum praeterito, quantum ad posterius

---

7–8   Arist. *Cat.* 6.5a6–8 (*dicit tamen Aristoteles quod praesens tempus copulatur et ad praeteritum et ad futurum*)   **14**   *nihil dictum est de hoc in sententia nec in litterali expositione; notandum autem est quod litteralis expositio lacunam habere videtur*   **25–26**   cf. Prisc. *Inst. gramm.* VIII 10.51 (ed. Hertz, vol. 1, 414)

---

5 quia] quod *P*   5 unum^2] unde *P*   9 terminus] *ex* terminis *corr. al. man.*   9 individualitatis] *lectio incerta*   21–22 praeteritum–futurum] *transp. P, sed corr. al. man.*

idem cum futuro, et sic praesens tempus est medium utriusque, cum ipsa uniendo naturam sapiat utriusque.

Ad obiectum dicendum quod duplex est medium, scilicet continuans et continuatum, aliud est continuans et non continuatum, ut punctus. Cum ergo obicitur quod terminus non est idem | cum eo cuius est terminus, dicendum quod verum est de termino continuante <et non continuato et non de termino continuante> et continuato, unde cum ad talem terminum copulentur partes temporis, non tenet ratio de tempore.

<5>

Ex iam dictis incidit quaestio: Cum aliae quantitates continuae copulentur ad medium continuans et non continuatum, quae est causa quare tempus non copulatur ad tale medium sed ad medium continuans et continuatum.

Et dicendum quod causa est quia tempus non habet permanentiam in partibus sicut aliae quantitates, sed habet tempus partes successivas. Successivum autem respicit prius et posterius. Talis autem terminus est continuans et continuatus. Quia ergo praesens tempus rationem prioris respicit, praeteritum rationem posterioris, ideo ad ipsum partes possunt copulari. Non est autem sic in aliis quantitatibus.

Aliter dicitur quod praesens tempus appellatur hic instans, et quia tempus respicit prius et posterius cum sit successivum, et instans dicitur indivisibile, ideo instans non est tempus. Concedunt ergo argumentum quod praesens prout hic sumitur non est tempus.

f. 46va

---

1 uniendo] *lectio incerta*   **4** obicitur] obicit *P*   **9** dictis] *add. P in marg.*   **18** dicitur] dividitur *P*

Lectio XIX

Amplius quidem (6.5a15)

<Divisio>

Notificatis membris primae divisionis, notificat membra secundae.

Haec pars in duas. Primo resumit divisionem quam probare intendit, secundo probat, ibi: *<ut> lineae quidem* (6.5a17).

Et haec secunda in duas. Primo probat primum membrum divisionis, secundo secundum, ibi: *<De> numero autem* (6.5a24).

Prima in quattuor iuxta quantitates de quibus determinat. Secunda ibi: *<Similiter autem> et particulae plani* (6.5a20), tertia ibi: *Sed et soliditatis* (6.5a23), quarta ibi: *Similiter et loci* (6.5a23).

Pars in qua explanat secundum membrum in tres penes tres species quantitatis. Secunda ibi: *sed nec ipsa quae sunt temporis* (6.5a27), tertia ibi: *sed et oratio similiter* (6.5a33).

Haec est divisio lectionis, et sunt particulae octo.

<Sententia>

Circa primam sic procedit: Quaedam quantitates constant ex partibus habentibus positionem, quaedam ex partibus non habentibus positionem.

Consequenter probat hoc de linea, dicens: Omnes quantitates quarum partes habent continuationem et sunt alicubi habent positionem in partibus. Linea est huiusmodi. Ergo etc.

Eadem est ratio de superficie et corpore.

Consequenter explanat secundum membrum, et primo in numero. Ratio talis: Nulla quantitas cuius partes non habent situm alicubi nec continuantur ad invicem habet positionem in partibus suis sed magis ordinem. Numerus est huiusmodi. Ergo etc.

Consequenter idem probat de tempore. Ratio talis: Nulla quantitas cuius partes non permanent habet positionem in partibus. Tempus est huiusmodi. Ergo etc. Et quia dixit quod partes temporis habent ordinem, incidenter dicit quod similiter partes numeri.

Consequenter probat idem de oratione. Ratio talis est: Nulla quantitas cuius partes non permanent habet positionem in suis partibus. Oratio est huiusmodi.

---

10 oratio] $P^{inf}c$: ea *P* **12** octo] VII *P* **25** temporis] *add. P (fortasse al. man.) in marg.* **27** nulla quantitas] *inv. P*

Ergo etc. Minorem probat. Ratio talis: Omnis quantitas cuius partes dictae non possunt amplius sumi non habet particulas permanentes. Oratio est huiusmodi. Ergo etc.

Ultimo concludit propositum probatum, ex quo linea et similia habent positionem in partibus, numerus autem et consimilia non habent, quod quaedam quantitates habent positionem et quaedam non habent.

Haec est sententia lectionis.

Expositio litteralis

Non solum dicuntur de quantitate quae dicta sunt, *autem*, pro sed, aliae quanti-
f. 46vb tates *constant ex particulis quae sunt in eis*, particulis, | dico, *habentibus positio-
nem*, id est continuationem et permanentiam, *ad se invicem*; *autem*, id est sed, aliae, quantitates supple, constant *ex non habentibus positionem*.

Probat primum membrum: Ita dixi "quaedam habent positionem", *ut*, pro sic-
ut, *particulae lineae habent positionem ad invicem, namque*, pro quia, *singulum eorum*, id est earum partium, *est situm alicubi*, id est in superficie, *et habes unde sumas et assignes unumquodque*, id est unamquamque partem, *ubi* sita *est*, scilicet *in plano*, id est in superficie, *et*, habes unde sumas, resume, *ad quam particulam*, scilicet ad punctum, *particulae* eius copulantur. Et nota quod particula dicitur hic terminus continuans non continuatus, et non dicitur proprie, quia punctus non est pars lineae.

Consequenter probat hoc de superficie: Non solum ita est de linea, *autem*, id est sed, *particulae plani habent quandam positionem similiter*, supple sicut partes lineae. Bene dico quod sic, *autem*, id est quia, *similiter* ostendetur *ubi iacet*, id est habet situm, *unumquodque*, id est unaquaeque pars, *et quae*, scilicet particulae, *copulantur*, id est continuantur, *ad invicem*.

Non solum ita est de istis, *sed quoque*, id est similiter, *soliditatis*, id est corporis, particulae, supple, copulantur ad invicem et habent situm. *Similiter et loci*, supple particulae.

Consequenter probat secundum membrum divisionis: Ita dixi quod dictae quantitates habent partes copulatas ad eundem terminum, *autem*, id est sed, *quis-
quis*, id est aliquis, *non poterit* conspicere de *numero tanquam*, id est quo modo, *particulae* eius, scilicet numeri, habent *ad invicem positionem aliquam ut sit situm alicubi aut*, pro vel, *aliquae particulae*, numeri supple, conectuntur, id est continuantur, *ad invicem*.

< * * * > nec habent situm, *enim*, id est quia, *particulae temporis nihil*, pro non,

---

2 sumi] sui *P*   **26** supple[1]] similiter *P*   **26** et[2]] *P^{sup}c* : ut *P*   **29–30** quisquis] *c* : siquis *P*

permanent, autem, pro sed, *quod non est permanens quo modo aliquam positionem habebit*? Quasi dicat: Nullo modo. *Sed magis dices* particulas *habere quendam ordinem* ideo *quod aliud*, id est alia pars, *temporis prius, aliud vero posterius*, et, supple, prius et posterius dicunt ordinem. (Et nota quod li "magis" tenetur elective,
5 non comparative.) Non solum ita est de tempore, *sed* etiam *de numero eo quod* unum *numeretur prius quam duo et duo quam tres. Et ita habebunt* partes numeri *quendam ordinem, vero*, pro sed, *non multum*, id est omnino, *percipies positionem*.

Nec ita est de istis solum, *sed similiter oratio*. Et hoc probat: *enim*, id est quia, *particulae eius*, <id est> orationis, *nihil*, pro non, *permanent*.
10 Ultimo concludit propositum probatum: Postquam linea et similia habent positionem, sed numerus et similia non, et istae sunt quantitates, *itaque* aliae, id est quaedam quantitates, *constant* etc. Littera plana est.

<QUAESTIONES>

Ad evidentiam dictorum duo quaeruntur, primum de quantitatibus habentibus positionem, <secundum de non habentibus positionem>.

<1>

15 Circa primum sic. Dicit quod partes lineae sunt sitae alicubi; ergo in aliquo loco.

Sed contra. Scribitur in quarto *Physicorum* quod soli corpori debetur locus. Ergo quod non est corpus non est in loco. Linea non est corpus. Ergo etc.

Gratia huius quaeritur quo modo partes lineae sunt sitae alicubi, id est in superficie, cum esse in dicatur multipliciter.
20 Ad quaestionem dicendum quod esse in dupliciter sumitur ad praesens, sicut locatum in loco et sicut pars in toto. Secundo modo sunt partes lineae in superficie, quia linea ratione dimensionis est pars | superficiei; linea enim est longitudo sine latitudine, superficies vero longitudo <et> latitudo sine profunditate.   f. 47ra

Per hoc patet ad obiectum, quia cum dicitur: "Partes lineae sunt sitae alicubi",
25 verum est ut partes in toto, et cum concluditur: "Ergo sunt in loco", aequivocatur esse in.

Vel aliter. Locus debetur alicui duobus modis, scilicet per se et per accidens. Primo modo solum corpus est in loco, secundo omnia accidentia sunt in loco, ut albedini non debetur locus per se in corpore existenti sed per corpus.

---

15 Arist. *Cat.* 6.5a17–20   **16** *cf.* Arist. *Phys.* IV 1.209a26–27; Anon. *Auct. Arist.* 2.119 (ed. Hamesse, 149)

---

3 alia…prius] prius alia pars temporis *P*   **4** elective] *lectio incerta*   **24** dicitur] dicit *P*   **24** alicubi] alicui *P*   **25** concluditur] concludit *P*

<2>

Consequenter quaeritur in quo sit locus tanquam in subiecto; et loquamur de loco quo locans locat.

Et videtur quod sit in corpore locato, quia accidens est in eo ut in subiecto quod denominatur quale ab ipso, sicut patet in singulis. Sed corpus locatum denominatur a loco. Ergo in eo ut in subiecto.   5

Sed contra. Locus est superficies corporis locantis. Sed superficies rei locantis est eius prima passio. Sed prima passio est in eo cuius est, ut patet de risibili. Ergo superficies est in re locante ut in subiecto. Non ergo in locata.

Et dicendum quod locus dupliciter potest considerari, scilicet in quantum superficies vel in quantum mensura. Si in quantum est superficies, quia est superfi-   10
cies solum rei locantis, sic est in re locante. Si in quantum mensura, quia est solum mensura locatae rei, sic est in re locata ut in subiecto. Et sic utrasque rationes concedo.

<3>

Consequenter quaeritur de secundo, et primo quid exigitur ad hoc quod quantitas positionem habeat; et quaeritur iuxta hoc quo modo per defectum illorum quae   15
exiguntur haec tria, scilicet numerus, tempus et oratio, dicantur positionem non habere.

Ad primum. Ad habere positionem duo requiruntur. Primum quod habeat permanentiam in partibus suis, secundum quod habeat terminum communem ad quem eius particulae copulentur, ut innuit auctor in littera.   20

A primo deficit tempus (nam habet partes successivas, non permanentes), a secundo deficit numerus, ab utroque deficit oratio.

<4>

Consequenter quaeritur quare dicit "in numero non multum perspicies". Quare dicit "multum"?

Ad hoc patet per dicta, quia numerus habet unam illarum dictarum condicio-   25
num quae exiguntur ad habendam positionem (habet enim permanentiam in partibus, quia in duo permanent unitates), et deficit ab altera et non ab utraque illarum condicionum.

---

23 Arist. *Cat.* 6.5a30–32

---

4 ab] ad *P a.c.*   **4** sicut patet] licet pateat *P*   **8** locata] locato *P*

\<5\>

Consequenter quaeritur quare inter omnes quantitates continuas solum tempus deficit a condicione quae exigitur ad habendam positionem in partibus.

Hoc autem patet, quia non habet partes permanentes, sed aliae quantitates continuae non deficiunt ab aliqua illarum condicionum, quia habent permanentiam in partibus.

Vel aliter. Inter omnes quantitates continuas solum tempus participat numerum. Numerus autem est discretus. Discretum autem non habet positionem. Hinc est quod neque tempus.

\<6\>

Sed modo quaeritur utrum tempus sit quantitas continua et discreta.

Quod sic videtur, quia prima passio non derelinquit suum subiectum. Sed longum et breve sunt primae passiones continui, multum et paucum quantitatis discretae. Sed omnia ista in tempore reperiuntur. Ergo in tempore est natura continui et discreti.

Item. "Tempus est mensura motus secundum prius et posterius", scribitur in quarto *Physicorum*. Prius et posterius dicunt dualitatem, et dualitas | discretionem.   f. 47rb
Et haec est in tempore. Ergo tempus est discretum.

Quod concedo.

\<7\>

Sed modo quaeritur, cum tempus sit continuum et discretum, a quo naturam habeat continui et a quo discreti; quare etiam, cum habeat naturam continui et discreti, dicitur potius quantitas continua quam discreta.

Ad primum. Tempus comparatur ad motum cuius est mensura. Sed motus est continuum a parte magnitudinis spatii supra quod exercetur. Quia ergo propria mensura adaequatur mensurato, erit adaequatio in tempore per comparationem quam habet ad motum comparatum ad magnitudinem supra quam exercetur, et sic non inest ei discretio. Item comparatur ad mobile cum iam pertransit actu, et quia simul et semel non potest esse in diversis locis, sed secundum prius et posterius, et in his est natura dualitatis et in dualitate discretio, ideo tempus comparatum sic ad mobile participat naturam discreti.

14–15   *cf.* Arist. *Phys.* IV 11.219b1–2; Anon. *Auct. Arist.* 2.137 (ed. Hamesse, 151)

---

11 quantitatis] quantitas *P a.c.*

Ad aliud dicendum quod tempus per prius et immediatius comparatur ad motum quam ad mobile secundum quod dicit Aristoteles in *Physicis*, quia quicquid est mobile, est per motum. Sed secundum quod comparatur ad motum naturam participat continui, ut visum est. Hinc est quod potius dicitur quantitas continua quam discreta.   5

<8>

Ultimo quaeritur quo modo accipitur numerus specierum quantitatis.

Et dicendum quod omnis quantitas aut est quantitas continua aut discreta, dicit auctor. Si discreta, aut est habens aliquo modo permanentiam in partibus aut non. Primo modo numerus, secundo oratio. Si continua, aut mensurat substantiam sub esse essentiali aut sub esse accidentali. Si sub esse essentiali, quia est mensu-   10
rare substantiam secundum quod corpus habet tres dimensiones, dicit Priscianus in *Orthographia*, scilicet longitudinem, latitudinem et profunditatem, aut mensuratur secundum longum tantum, et sic linea, aut secundum latum et longum, et sic superficies, aut secundum longum, latum et profundum, et sic corpus; linea enim est longitudo sine latitudine et profunditate, superficies longitudo et latitu-   15
do sine profunditate, corpus autem habet istas tres dimensiones. Si est mensurans substantiam sub esse accidentali, aut prout est in motu aut in quiete. Primo modo tempus, secundo locus. Per hoc patet qualiter ponitur nota separationis inter species quantitatis continuae.

---

2 *cf.* Arist. *Phys.* III 2.202a7–8   **10–12**   *cf.* Prisc. *Inst. gramm.* I 2.4 (ed. Hertz, vol. 1, 6)

---

3 mobile] per mobile *P*   **16** si] en *! P*

Lectio XX

Proprie autem quantitates (6.5a39)

‹Divisio›

Determinato de quantitatibus per se, quae sunt proprie quantitates, determinat de quantitatibus per accidens.

Haec pars in duas. Primo enim quasi supposita quadam divisione proponit quod intendit, secundo probat, ibi: *Ad haec autem* (6.5b1).

Haec secunda in duas. Primo probat, secundo probatum concludit, ibi: *Quare solae proprie* (6.5b7).

Prima in duas. Primo probat quae sunt quantitates per accidens, secundo qualiter sunt quantitates secundum accidens, ibi: *Neque enim singulum* (6.5b3).

Prima in duas. Primo ponit minorem suae rationis, secundo probat per exempla, ibi: *ut multum dicitur album* (6.5b2).

Haec est divisio lectionis.

‹Sententia›

Circa primam partem sic procedit: Quantitates praenominatae solum sunt quantitates proprie, sed aliae sunt quantitates per accidens.

Et hoc probat tali ratione: Omne illud quod est quantitas per relationem ad praedictas | est quantitas per accidens. Omnis autem quantitas a praedictis est huiusmodi. Ergo etc. Minorem ponit.   f. 47va

Consequenter probat eam per exempla: ut album dicitur multum per superficiem multam etc.

Consequenter ostendit qualiter quantitates sunt per accidens, dicens: Si aliquis assignet quanta sit actio, assignabit quanta sit per tempus; similiter assignabit quantum est album per superficiem.

Ultimo concludit: Ex quo aliae sunt quantitates per istas, ergo supradictae sunt proprie quantitates, aliae vero quantitates per accidens.

Haec est sententia partis.

Expositio litteralis

Ita dictum ‹est› de quantitatibus per se, *autem*, id est sed, quantitates *hae solae quas diximus sunt proprie quantitates*, supple continuae, scilicet linea, superficies, corpus, tempus et locus. Ita est de illis, *vero*, pro sed, *omnia alia*, id est omnes aliae quantitates, supple sunt quantitates, *secundum accidens*.

Nam, id est quia, *ad haec aspicientes*, ad supradicta scilicet, *dicimus alias quantitates*, per accidens scilicet.

Et ponit exempla: *ut album dicitur multum* quia *superficies multa, et actio longa eo*, id est ideo, quia *tempus longum et motus multus*. Hic nota: Multum, prima passio continui, convenit tempori.

Bene dixi quod actio est longa per tempus et motus multus, *enim*, id est quia, *singulum horum*, id est actio et motus, *neque*, pro non, *dicitur quantitas per se*, sed per tempus mensurans, *ut si quis assignet quanta sit actio, definiet*, id est assignabit, *tempore*, id est per tempus, *annuam vel* alio modo, *et assignans quantum sit album definiet* per superficiem. Bene dico quod sic, *enim*, id est quia, *quanta fuerit superficies*, supple in qua est albedo, *tantum* erit *album*.

Ultimo concludit propositum probatum: Ex quo praedictae solum sunt proprie quantitates et aliae per istas, *quare*, id est ergo, *solae ipsae quantitates quae dictae sunt dicuntur*, supple quantitates, *proprie et* per *se*. Ita est de istis, *vero*, id est sed, *nihil aliorum*, id est aliarum quantitatum, *per se* dicitur quantitas *sed per accidens*.

<Quaestiones>

<1>

Ad dictorum evidentiam primo quaeritur quare non dividit quantitatem quod alia per se, alia per accidens, sed supposita divisione exsequitur de dividentibus.

Et dicendum quod dividentia debent aequaliter participare divisum. Quia ergo per se et per accidens in eodem genere non aequaliter participant ipsum genus, hinc est quod non dividitur quantitas per haec.

<2>

Secundo quaeritur quare dicantur quantitates per accidens et quo modo.

Et videtur quod nullo modo, quia sicut se habet quale ad qualitatem, ita quantum ad quantitatem. Sed quale non dicitur ad qualitatem per accidens. Ergo nec quantum.

f. 47vb Et dicendum quod quantitas dicitur per accidens quia per se non mensurat sed per aliud, ut patet simile in ulna. Nam si pannus mensu|retur ab ulna, ulna est mensura per se, sed si cum panno mensurato alius mensuretur, ille non est mensura

---

5

10

15

20

25

per se sed per ulnam. Similiter tempus primo et per se mensurat annum, <annus>
autem actionem secundo mensurat et per aliud quia per tempus.

Ad obiectum dicendum quod non est simile, quia quale in quantum quale non
dicitur per accidens qualitas sicut quantum dicitur per accidens quantitas quia
secundo mensurat, id est per alia.

Vel aliter. Non est simile, quia omnis qualitas per se et non per aliud facit quale,
sed non omnis quantitas per se mensurat, sed quaedam per alia, ut visum est.

<3>

Consequenter quaeritur: Dicit quod tempus est quantitas per se et motus per
accidens.

In *Libro metaphysicae* dicitur oppositum.

Et dicendum quod tempus dupliciter consideratur. Uno modo per relationem
ad primum mobile, scilicet ad caelum stellatum, prout movetur, et sic est in ipso,
id est caelo, sicut accidens in subiecto, ab ipso aeternitatem recipiens, et sic motus
primo mensurat primum mobile, et quia tempus est propria mensura motus, per
motum mensurat primum mobile, et sic motus est quantitas per se, tempus vero
per accidens, et sic loquitur in quinto. Quod autem tempus habeat aeternitatem a
primo mobili prout movetur patet, quia scribitur in primo *Meteorum* quod motus
superior est causa motus inferiorum; unde quam cito corrumpetur motus iste, corrumpetur tempus et quodlibet inferius. Aliter consideratur tempus per relationem
ad motum inferiorum, et sic, quia tempus est mensura ipsorum et per ipsum motus,
sic tempus quantitas est per se, motus vero per accidens, et sic loquitur hic.

<4>

Consequenter quaeritur: Hic dicit quod superficies est quanta.

Contra. Scribitur in secundo *Topicorum* quod nullum genus denominative
praedicatur de sua specie. Male ergo dicitur "superficies est quanta", cum quantitas
sit genus superficiei.

Item. Idem non praedicatur de aliquo secundum concretionem et abstractio-
nem, ut album et albedo. Cum ergo quantitas praedicetur de superficie, quantum
non praedicabitur de ipsa.

8–9 Arist. *Cat.* 6.5b3 **10** Arist. *Metaph.* V 13.1020a31–32 **17–18** Arist. *Met.* I 2.339a30–32
22 Arist. *Cat.* 6.5b6 **23–24** Arist. *Top.* II 2.109b5–7, *fere ut apud* Anon. *Auct. Arist.* 36.21 (ed.
Hamesse, 323).

---

2 autem actionem] *inv.* P **7** visum est] mensurae P **17** meteorum] metaphysicae P *ut v.*
20 motus] motum P

Et dicendum quod quadruplex est praedicatio. Uno modo secundum quod superius praedicatur de inferiori, ut animal de homine. Secundo quando praedicatur prima passio de proprio subiecto, ut risibile de homine. Tertio causa de effectu vel e converso, ut solis est lucere super terram de die. Alio ut mensuratum de mensura, ut quantum de superficie.

Per hoc patet ad aliud. Verum est quod idem non praedicatur in concretione et abstractione secundum eundem modum praedicandi, sed secundum diversos, ut visum est.

<5>

Ultimo quaeritur: Dicit quod tanta est albedo, quanta est superficies.

Instantia de pica. Nam superficies totam ipsam complectitur, ergo et albedo. Quod falsum est.

Et dicendum quod littera sic exponitur: tanta est albedo, quanta est superficies in qua est ipsa albedo.

---

9 Arist. *Cat.* 6.5b6–7

---

3 effectu] effective *P ut v.* **4** mensuratum] de mensuratum *add. P a.c.*

Lectio XXI

Amplius quantitati nihil est contrarium (6.5b12)

\<Divisio\>

Notificata quantitate | per eius essentialia, ipsam notificat per eius accidentalia.

Haec pars in duas. Primo ponit consequentia communia quantitati et aliis, secundo consequens maxime proprium vel proprietatem quantitatis, ibi: *Proprium autem maxime* (6.6a26).

5 Prima in duas. Primo ponit hanc proprietatem quantitatis: non habere contrarium, secundo non suscipere magis et minus, ibi: *Sed non videtur quantitas* (6.6a20). Et quia prima proprietas est causa secundae, patet ordo.

Prima in duas. Primo ponit illam proprietatem, secundo ad maiorem manifestationem quasdam instantias adducit, ibi: *nisi multa paucis* (6.5b15).

10 Haec secunda in duas penes duas \<instantias\>. Secunda ibi: *Maxime videtur esse circa locum* (6.6a12). Prima plus habet quam secunda, et signum est quia ad primam respondet, ad secundam autem non, quare patet ordo.

Prima in duas. Primo instat, secundo solvit, \<ibi: *Horum autem nihil* (6.5b16).

Haec secunda in duas. Primo solvit,\> ostendens quod illa in quibus data est
15 instantia non sunt quantitates, secundo quod non recipiant contraria, ibi: *Amplius sive aliquis ponat* (6.5b30).

Prima in duas. Primo probat quod non sunt quantitates absolute, secundo in comparatione ad quantitates determinatas, ibi: *Amplius bicubitum* (6.5b26).

Prima in duas. Primo ponit minorem suae rationis, secundo probat, ibi: *Per se*
20 *enim nihil* (6.5b17).

Haec secunda in duas. Primo probat de magno et parvo, quae videntur esse quantitates continuae, secundo de multo et pauco, ibi: *Rursus in vico* (6.5b23).

Pars in qua probat ista non esse contraria in duas. Primo probat hoc per rationem ostensivam, secundo per rationes ducentes ad impossibile, ibi: *Amplius*
25 \<*si*\> *magnum* (6.5b33). Prima cum praecedentibus est praesentis lectionis, et sunt particulae septem.

\<Sententia\>

Circa primam sic procedit: Quantitati nihil est contrarium. Et probat hoc per inductionem: ut bicubito etc.

---

3 proprietatem] proprietates *P*   9 nisi] $P^{inf}c$: ut *P*   18 comparatione] comparationes *P*
19 minorem] in *P*

Consequenter ponit instantias, dicens quod aliquis dicet esse contraria multa paucis et magnum parvo, et dicet ista esse quantitates, et ita quantitati esse
contrarium.

Consequenter solvit, dicens quod non sunt quantitates. Et probat sic: Nihil
quod est ad aliquid est quantitas. Magnum et parvum sunt huiusmodi. Ergo etc.   5
Minorem ponit.

Consequenter probat eam tali ratione: Quaecumque secundum id quod sunt ad
aliud referuntur sunt ad aliquid. Haec sunt huiusmodi, ut probat in monte et milio.
Ergo etc.

Consequenter probat hoc de multo et pauco, dicens: Multi homines dicuntur   10
esse in vico sed in civitate pauci licet plures sint in civitate; etiam in domo multos
dicimus esse et in foro paucos licet sint plures in foro. Sed hoc non esset verum
nisi multum et paucum essent ad aliquid. Ergo sunt ad aliquid et non quantitates.
Minorem ponit.

Consequenter probat per relationem ad determinatas. Ratio talis: Bicubitum   15
et tricubitum significant quantitatem, et etiam aliae quantitates. Parvum et magnum non significant quantitatem sed magis ad aliquid. Ergo sunt ad aliquid et non
quantitates.

Ultimo probat quod ista non sunt quantitates ratione tali: Nulli quod per se
non sumitur sed solum in relatione ad alterum est aliquid contrarium. Illa sunt   20
huiusmodi. Ergo nihil est eis contrarium, et ita unum non contrariatur alteri.

Haec est sententia partis.

Expositio litteralis

f. 48rb   Non solum dicuntur de quantitate | quae dicta sunt, autem, id est sed, *amplius*
quantitati nihil est contrarium. Bene dico quod non est, *manifestum est enim in*
definitis, id est in prima specie et in secunda (vel: *in definitis*, id est in determinatis),   25
quoniam nihil est contrarium, quantitati supple. Et hoc manifestat: *ut bicubito* etc.
nihil est contrarium.

< * * * > nisi quis dicat multa paucis esse contraria.

Consequenter solvit ad ista: Ita forte dicetur, *autem*, pro sed, *nihil horum*, in
quibus instat supple, *est quantitas, sed magis*, elective, *sunt ad aliquid*.   30

Enim, id est quia, *nihil dicitur magnum* et *parvum per se*, id est nisi in relatione
ad alterum vel absolute, *sed* magis dicuntur in relatione *ad aliud*; namque, id est
quia, *mons parvus dicitur* et *milium magnum eo quod hoc*, scilicet milium, *sit maius*

---

1 aliquis dicet] aliquid *P*   7 quaecumque] sunt *add. P*   7 secundum id] *inv. P*   10 hoc de] *inv.*
P   24 in] *iter. P*   25 id est¹] ibi *P*   30 instat] est contra *add. P*   30 elective] *lectio incerta*

omnibus *sui generis*, sed *illud*, id est mons, *minus sui generis*. Ex hoc concludit: *ergo relatio*, id est respectus, *eorum est ad* aliquid. Et causam subiungit conclusionis: *nam*, id est quia, *si magnum* et *parvum diceretur per se ipsum*, id est non in relatione ad alterum, *nunquam mons* etc.

Et non solum sic est de istis: *Rursus nos dicimus plures homines esse in vico* sed *in civitate paucos cum sint eorum multiplices*, id est multo plures, et ita, supple, ad aliquid. Aliud exemplum ponit. Planum est.

Consequenter ponit aliam rationem: Non solum per dicta probatur quod non sunt quantitates, autem, id est sed, *amplius bicubitum* etc. significant *quantitatem* etc., sed *magnum* et *parvum non significant quantitatem*. Et causam subiungit: *quoniam magnum et parvum* spectant *ad* aliquid; *quare manifestum est* etc.

Ultimo probat quod non sunt contraria: Ita probavi quod non sunt quantitates, *amplius sive aliquis ponat* etc., *nihil erit illis contrarium*. Et hoc probat: autem, id est quia, *quod non potest sumi* etc., *quo modo huic erit aliquid contrarium*? Quasi dicens: Nullo modo.

<Quaestiones>

Ad dictorum evidentiam duo quaeruntur, primum de modo procedendi, secundum de dictis in littera.

<1>

De primo sic. Superius posuit quaedam consequentia quae conveniunt primis substantiis et non secundis, quaedam quae conveniunt secundis et non primis. Quare ergo non ponit proprietates quae conveniant quantitati continuae et non discretae, discretae et non continuae? Videtur deminutus.

Et dicendum quod substantia dicitur per prius et posterius de prima et secunda, et ita non aequaliter substantiam participant. Propter hanc diversitatem possunt quaedam ita convenire primis ut non secundis et e converso, et quia quantitas aequaliter dicitur de continua et discreta, ideo non habet tantam diversitatem, quia non assignavit proprietates de continua quin assignarentur de discreta et e converso; patet ergo quod non est simile.

18–19 Arist. *Cat.* 5.3a33–b24

---

15 nullo] *ex* ullo *corr.* P   **24** ut] et P

<2>

Consequenter quaeritur: Sicut non esse in subiecto convenit substantiae, sic esse
<in subiecto> convenit quantitati. Ergo sicut illud ponitur proprietas substantiae,
sic et hoc debet poni proprietas quantitatis.

    Et dicendum quod non est simile, quia quod est commune non debet alicui
proprium assignari, sed soli substantiae convenit non esse in subiecto.   5

<3>

Consequenter quaeritur: Dicit: "Quantitati nihil est contrarium".

    Contra. Scribitur in *Physicis*: "Omnis motus a contrario in contrarium". Cum
f. 48va   ergo in quantitate sit motus, ut | ab augmento in deminutionem vel e converso,
quantitati erit aliquid contrarium.

    Et dicendum quod duplex est motus, scilicet in termino et ad terminum. Motus   10
in termino est quando fit motus ab una qualitate in aliam, ut in alteratione, et in tali
motu est propositio, et quia talis motus solum est in qualitate, ideo contrarietas solum erit in qualitate. Motus ad terminum est quando fit mutatio quantitatis incom-
pletae in eandem completam vel qualitatis similiter, et talis motus est in quantitate,
et in tali motu licet sit contrarietas, non tamen gratia quantitatum. Patet ergo quod   15
aequivocatur motus.

<4>

Consequenter quaeritur: Videtur quod magnum sit quantitas, quod negat auctor.

    Omnes mathematicae sunt de quantitate. Sed geometria est de magnitudine.
Ergo magnitudo est quantitas. Ergo et magnum per naturam magnitudinis.

    Et dicendum: Cum dicitur "Omnes mathematicae sunt de quantitate", verum   20
de subiecto est, sed cum assumis "Geometria est de magnitudine", hoc verum est
tanquam de propria passione subiecti; et ita aequivocatur esse de. Et quod sit verum patet, quia geometria est de quantitate continua, et magnum et parvum sunt
propriae passiones continui.

---

2 Arist. *Cat.* 5.3a7–32   6 Arist. *Cat.* 6.5b12   7 Arist. *Phys.* V 2.226b2–3, *ut apud* Anon.
Auct. Arist. 2.157 (ed. Hamesse, 153)   17 Arist. *Cat.* 6.5b16–30

<5>

Ultimo quaeritur: Dicit quod relativis non est contrarietas.

In capitulo de relativis dicit oppositum.

Et dicendum quod quaedam in genere sunt relationis ita quod non in alio genere, et talibus nihil est contrarium. Alia sunt quae possunt esse in alio genere, et hoc
5   dupliciter. Aut enim illud genus naturam contrarietatis participat aut non. Si non, adhuc relativis nihil est contrarium. Si sic, aliquid est eis contrarium, et hoc est per naturam illius generis, ut patet in exemplis ab Aristotele positis, scilicet in virtute et vitio, quae sunt in genere qualitatis. Primo et secundo modo loquitur hic, ultimo in sequentibus.

<6>

10   Sed modo quaeritur quare contrarietas non potest esse in genere relationis.

Et dicendum quod contraria nunquam possunt esse simul, sed relativa sunt simul natura.

Item. Contraria mutuo se expellunt. Sed relativa se ponunt. Quare natura contrarietatis relativis repugnat.

---

1 Arist. *Cat.* 6.5b30–33   2 Arist. *Cat.* 7.6b15–16   7–8 Arist. *Cat.* 7.6b15–16

---

1 dicit] dicitur *P*

Lectio XXII

Amplius si magnum et parvum (6.5b33)

\<Divisio>

Probavit ostensive quod magnum et parvum non sunt contraria, hic probat ducendo ad impossibile.

Haec pars in duas. Primo ponit impossibilia ad quae ducit, secundo deducit ad illa, ibi: *Contingit enim idem esse parvum* (6.5b36).

Haec secunda in duas. Primo ducit ad hoc impossibile quod contraria essent simul in eodem, secundo ad hoc quod idem sibi contrarium, ibi: *Et eadem sibi* (6.6a5).

Prima in duas. Primo ducit ad dictum impossibile, secundo probat hoc esse impossibile, ibi: *Sed nihil est quod videatur* (6.6a1).

Consequenter sequitur pars in qua ponit secundam instantiam. Et dividitur in duas. Primo ponit ipsam instantiam, secundo ipsam confirmat per rationes, ibi: *Sursum enim* (6.6a12).

Haec secunda in duas penes duas rationes. Secunda ibi: *Videtur autem et aliorum* (6.6a16).

Haec est divisio lectionis, et sunt particulae septem.

\<Sententia>

Circa primam sic procedit: Si magnum et parvum sunt contraria, accidit idem simul recipere contraria et idem sibi esse contrarium, et utrumque istorum est impossibile.

Consequenter ducit ad primum impossibile. Ratio talis est: Si magnum et parvum sunt contraria, cuicumque insunt ista insunt contraria. Sed eidem insunt ista. Ergo eidem insunt contraria. Minorem ponit et probat.

| Consequenter probat hoc esse impossibile per locum a maiori. Ratio talis: Substantia, de qua videtur magis, non suscipit simul contraria. Ergo multo fortius nec alia.   f. 48vb

Consequenter ducit ad secundum impossibile. Ratio haec: Si aliquid est parvum et magnum, in quantum parvum est contrarium est sibi magno. Sed idem est magnum et parvum. Ergo etc.

Consequenter ponit secundam instantiam, dicens quod contrarietas videtur multum esse circa locum.

Et hoc probat. Ratio haec: Quaecumque maxime a se distant, sunt contraria. Sursum et deorsum, quae sunt differentiae loci, sunt huiusmodi. Ergo etc.

Ultimo probat per aliam rationem: Quaecumque sunt in eodem genere et maxime a se distant, sunt contraria. Sursum et deorsum sunt huiusmodi. Ergo etc.

EXPOSITIO LITTERALIS

Ita dixi magnum et parvum non esse contraria, *amplius, si magnum et parvum sunt contraria*, hoc dato, *contingit idem simul contraria recipere et* idem *esse* contrarium *sibi*, et utrumque, supple, est impossibile.

Bene dixi quod contraria erunt simul in eodem, *enim*, id est quia, *contingit idem* etc. Et hoc probat: *enim*, id est quia, *aliquid est parvum ad hoc*, id est comparatum ad unum, *vero*, id est sed, *idem ipsum est magnum* etc., *quare simul contraria* recipiet, idem supple.

Consequenter probat hoc esse impossibile: Ita sequitur contraria esse in eodem, *sed nihil est quod videatur* etc.; *ut substantia videtur esse susceptibilis contrariorum, sed non suscipit* etc., *nam nullus est simul sanus et aeger* etc. Et concludit: Ex quo substantia non suscipit, ergo *nihil aliud* a substantia.

Consequenter ducit ad aliud impossibile: Ita sequitur illud impossibile, *contingit* idem *sibi esse* contrarium, quia *si magnum et parvum* sunt contraria, *autem*, id est sed, *idem est magnum et parvum, erit ipsum*, id est idem, *sibi contrarium. Sed impossibile est* idem *esse contrarium sibi.* Ergo *magnum non est contrarium parvo*. Ex hoc concludit ulterius: Ex quo magnum non est contrarium parvo, *quare*, id est ergo, *si quis* dixerit magnum et parvum *non esse relativa, quantitas tamen* etc.

Consequenter ponit aliam instantiam: Ita est de magno et parvo, sed *contrarietas quantitatis videtur esse* etc.

Et hoc probat: *enim*, id est quia, *ponunt*, philosophi supple, *sursum* esse *contrarium ad id quod est deorsum dicentes locum quod est in medio*, id est centrum, *deorsum.* Et quare ponunt ista contraria, quaeret aliquis. *Eo quod multa sit distantia medii ad terminos mundi*, id est ad sua extrema vel ad firmamentum.

Ultimo ponit aliam rationem: Non solum per praedicta probantur contraria, *autem*, id est sed, *videtur proferre*, id est accipere ad hoc probandum, *definitionem aliorum contrariorum ab his*, id est sursum et deorsum; *enim*, id est quia, *determinant*, philosophi supple, *contraria* etc.

---

1 haec quaecumque] *inv. P*   **12** recipiet] recipiat *P a.c.*   **25** ponunt] *ac* : probant *P, sed cf. immediate infra*   **25** supple] *post* dicentes *transp. P*   **28** medii] mundi *canc. P et* medii *add. in marg.*

\<Quaestiones\>

\<1\>

Ad dictorum evidentiam primo quaeritur: Dicit quod magnum et parvum non sunt contraria.

Contra. "Omnis motus a contrario in contrarium", scribitur in *Physicis*. Sed augmentum est motus. Ergo est a contrario in contrarium. Sed est a parvo in magnum.
5 Ergo parvum et magnum sunt contraria.

Item. Scribitur in *Physicis* quod quidam philosophi ponebant principia esse contraria, et ipsa enumerat: ut magnum, parvum. Ergo magnum et parvum sunt contraria.

Et dicendum quod magnum et parvum pos|sunt tripliciter considerari. Uno   f. 49ra
10 modo ratione quantitatis supra quam radicantur (est enim magnum continuum permanens et parvum similiter); sic sunt quantitates, et quia quantitati nihil est contrarium, ideo non contrariantur. Aliter considerantur ratione excessus et deminutionis quae adducunt supra quantitatem quam supponunt, et sic sunt ad aliquid (quia excessus et deminutio dicuntur ad aliquid vel in respectu), et sic non sunt
15 contraria, et est magnum continuum permanens cum excessu, parvum cum deminutione. Tertio modo per relationem ad terminum ad quem sunt isti motus, et quia augmentum est ad perfectionem, deminutio ad imperfectionem, et perfectum et imperfectum sunt contraria, sic magnum et parvum sunt contraria, ut argumenta probant.

\<2\>

20 Consequenter quaeritur de suo secundo argumento: "Hoc est magnum respectu huius et est parvum respectu illius, ergo est magnum et parvum".

Videtur quod non valet, quia scribitur in *Elenchis* (in primo) quod non sequitur, "Hoc est duplum huius et non est duplum illius, ergo est duplum et non duplum". Ergo a simili non valet hic, sed est ignorantia elenchi \<ut\> ibi.

25 Ad hoc dicendum est quod rerum quaedam sunt quorum esse potest esse absolutum, et si aliquando sumantur in comparatione, non propter hoc earum esse destruitur; et in talibus non tenet argumentum. Alia sunt quorum esse semper est in comparatione, et illa si comparatione careant, esse eorum destruitur, et ista sunt

---

1–2 Arist. *Cat.* 6.5b33–36 **3** Arist. *Phys.* V 2.226b2–3, *ut apud* Anon. *Auct. Arist.* 2.157 (ed. Hamesse, 153) **6–7** *cf.* Arist. *Phys.* I 4.187a12–20 **20–21** Arist. *Cat.* 6.5b36–38 **22–23** *cf.* Arist. *SE* 5.167a21–25

---

15 magnum] et *add.* P   **25** rerum] rectum P *a.c.*   **28** si] in *add.* P

relativa; et in istis tenet argumentum, ut "Iste est pater huius et est filius illius, ergo est pater et filius".

<3>

Consequenter quaeritur de secunda <instantia>, et primo quare ponit ipsam et non solvit, quia qua ratione solvit primam, secundam debet solvere. Vel quare non?

Et dicendum quod ibi est fallacia aequivocationis, quia duplex est distantia, sci-   5
licet localis et substantialis. Contraria maxime a se distant distantia essentiali, sursum et deorsum distantia locali. Sed scribitur in *Elenchis* quod loci aequivocationis
sunt publicissimi. Quia ergo ridicula est ibi aequivocatio et manifesta, ideo non
solvit.

Vel aliter. Quod sursum et deorsum uno modo sunt contraria appellando con-   10
traria quae maxime a se distant, quaecumque sit illa distantia, sed non sunt contraria proprie; et dico contraria proprie quae maxime a se distant et mutuo se
expellunt. Quia ergo argumentum uno modo concludit, ideo non solvit.

<4>

Consequenter quaeritur: Videtur quod male posuit exemplum de sursum et deorsum, quia sursum et deorsum sunt differentiae positionis. Non igitur loci, cum "Di-   15
versorum generum etc." Maior patet, quia situs est ordinatio vel positio partium, ut
dicit auctor *Sex principiorum*, sed haec ordinatio est secundum sursum et deorsum,
ut homo habet caput sursum et pedes deorsum.

Et dicendum quod sursum et deorsum dupliciter considerantur. Uno modo
prout dicunt ordinem partium eiusdem totius in suo toto, et sic sunt differentiae   20
positionis, ut obicitur. Aliter considerantur prout dicunt ordinationem vel respectum partium diversorum totorum, et sic sunt differentiae loci, et sic loquitur hic,
quod per exempla patet; dicit enim quod terra est deorsum et caelum sursum, et
illa sunt diversa tota.

<5>

Consequenter quaeritur utrum sursum et deorsum sint contraria.   25

f. 49rb Quod sic videtur, quia sunt sub eodem genere et ma|xime a se distant; ergo sunt
contraria.

7–8 *cf.* Arist. *SE* 1.165a1–5   **15–16** Arist. *Cat.* 3.1b17–18   **16–17** *cf.* Anon. *LSP* VI 60 (ed. Minio-Paluello, 48)

---

1 ut iste est pater] *iter. P*   **7** quod] quia *P*   **8** ridicula] ridi^lia *P ut v.*   **16** quia] quod *P*   **17** est] *iter. P a.c.*

Si dicatur quod distant locali distantia et non essentiali, ut dictum est prius, quod hoc nihil sit videtur. Contrariorum motuum contrarii sunt termini. Sed motus sursum et deorsum sunt contrarii. Ergo et eorum termini. Sed sursum est terminus motus superioris et deorsum inferioris. Ergo sursum et deorsum sunt contraria. Maior patet de se. Probatio minoris: Scribitur in quarto *Meteorum* quod contrariarum causarum contrarii sunt effectus. Sed motus superior causatur a levitate, motus inferior a gravitate. Sed leve et grave sunt contraria. Ergo et eorum effectus, scilicet motus superior et inferior.

Et dicendum quod duplex est natura loci. Una quae est continere, et per hanc naturam locus est quantitas et non habet contrarium. Alia est attrahere, prout scribitur in tertio *Physicorum*: "Mirabilis est loci potentia per quam attrahit locatum", quia sursum attrahit levia et deorsum gravia, et dicitur in eodem quod unumquodque non prohibitum fertur ad locum proprium, et sic locus est substantia qualificata, quia sursum et deorsum qualitates participant contrarias, et sic per naturam qualitatis sunt contraria, et sic argumentum procedit.

Aliquando dicitur quod locus non contrariatur loco in quantum locus sed in quantum unum sursum, alterum deorsum, sicut ignis contrariatur aquae, dicit Philosophus, non quia ignis sed quia calidus.

<6>

Consequenter quaeritur: Dicit quod medium mundi maxime distat ab extremis terminis.

Videtur male dicere, quia magis distat terminus a termino quam medium ab extremis. Ergo deberet dicere quod maxima est distantia termini ad terminum et non medii ad terminos.

Et dicendum quod duplex est distantia. Una est situalis, alia est localis. Dicendum ergo quod magis distat medium ab extremis quam termini inter se distantia situali (quod patet, quia partes terminorum de quibus hic loquitur continuantur ad invicem, sicut partes firmamenti), et sic loquitur hic, sed si loquimur de distantia locali, plus distant termini quam medium ab ipsis.

1 Q3 *supra* **5–6** *cf.* Arist. *Met.* IV 7.384b2–3; Anon. *Auct. Arist.* 5.20 (ed. Hamesse, 173) **10–11** *re vera* Arist. *Phys.* IV 1.208b34–35 **12–13** *re vera* Arist. *Phys.* IV 1.208b11–12 **17–18** *cf.* Arist. *Gen.* II 4.331a14–18; Anon. *Auct. Arist.* 4.38 (ed. Hamesse, 170); *cf. etiam* Averroes *in Phys.* V 10 (ed. Venet., 216r) **19–20** Arist. *Cat.* 6.6a12–16

5 meteorum] methav^orum *P ut v.* **9** est²] *add. s.l. P* **19** mundi] medii *P* **21** medium] terminus *P*

Lectio XXIII

Sed non videtur quantitas suscipere (6.6a20)

\<Divisio\>

Posita una proprietate quae convenit quantitati et aliis, in parte ista ponit aliam, et sequitur illa pars in qua ponit proprie proprium. Et sic sunt duae partes lectionis. Secunda ibi: *Proprium autem maxime* etc. (6.6a26).

Prima in duas. Primo ponit proprietatem et ipsam probat, secundo infert propositum probatum, ibi: *Quare quantitas* etc. (6.6a25).

Prima in duas. Primo ponit proprietatem, secundo probat, ibi: *ut bicubitum* (6.6a20).

Pars in qua ponit proprie proprium in duas. Primo ponit proprietatem et probat, secundo infert propositum probatum, ibi: *Quare proprium quantitatis* (6.6a33).

Prima in duas. Primo ponit, secundo probat, ibi: *Singulum earum* (6.6a27).

Haec secunda in duas. Primo probat quod convenit omni quantitati, secundo quod non aliis, ibi: *In ceteris vero* (6.6a30).

Haec est divisio lectionis, et sunt particulae septem.

\<Sententia\>

Circa primam sic procedit: Quantitas non suscipit magis et minus.

Consequenter probat sic: Omnis quantitas aut est continua aut est discreta. Sed neutra istarum recipit magis | et minus. Ergo etc. Minorem ponit et manifestat et etiam conclusionem.   f. 49va

Consequenter ponit proprie proprium, dicens quod maxime proprium quantitatis est dici secundum eam aequale vel inaequale.

Et hoc probat. Et primo quod convenit omni: Omnis quantitas est vel continua vel discreta. Secundum quamlibet aliquid dicitur aequale vel inaequale. Ergo omni quantitati convenit dici secundum eam aequale vel inaequale. Minorem ponit et manifestat.

Consequenter probat quod convenit soli: Omnis proprietas quae convenit omni quantitati et non aliis convenit soli. Haec proprietas est huiusmodi. Ergo etc. Minorem ponit et manifestat.

Ultimo concludit propositum probatum: Ex quo haec proprietas convenit omni et soli, ergo proprium est quantitati secundum eam aequale vel inaequale dici.

Haec est sententia partis.

---

10 earum] $P^{inf}c$: eorum P   24–25 omni] suum P *ut v.*

Expositio litteralis

Non solum dicta proprietas quantitati convenit, *sed quantitas non videtur suscipere* etc.

Et hoc probat inducendo: *ut bicubitum,* quod est continuum permanens; *enim,* id est quia, *aliud* non dicitur *magis bicubitum alio.* Non solum ita est in isto, *nec in numero,* qui est quantitas discreta, est magis et minus, *ut ternarius* non est magis numerus ternario neque *quinarius* etc. Non solum ita est in istis, vero, pro sed, *tria* neque, pro non, *dicentur magis* et minus quam quinque, *nec tria potius* etc. *Nec tempus,* quod est continuum successivum, *dicitur magis et minus. Nec omnino,* id est universaliter, *in his quae dicta sunt* etc.

Concludit: Ex quo quantitas nec continua nec discreta recipit magis et minus, *quare,* id est ergo, *quantitas non suscipit* etc.

Consequenter ponit proprie proprium: Ita posui proprietates non convertibiles, sed *proprium maxime,* id est convertibile, *quantitatis est quod dicitur,* aliquid, supple, secundum eam, *aequale* vel *inaequale.*

Consequenter probat quod hoc convenit omni quod est quantitas. Continua: *Singulum earum quantitatum quae dictae sunt et aequale dicitur et inaequale.* Et ponit exempla: *ut corpus aequale et inaequale* dicitur, *et numerus,* qui est quantitas discreta, *aequalis et inaequalis dicitur, et tempus* etc. Non solum sic est in istis, *autem,* id est sed, *in singulis aliis,* supple speciebus quantitatis, aliquid *dicitur aequale* vel *inaequale.*

Sed in aliis *quae non sunt quantitates non videtur multum,* quia non per se sed per aliud vel per accidens, *dici aequale* vel *inaequale.* Bene dico quod non, *enim,* <id est> quia, *affectio,* quae est qualitas, *et dispositio non* dicuntur *multum,* id est per se, *aequalis et inaequalis sed magis similis.* Similiter dicit de albo.

Ultimo infert: Ex quo haec proprietas convenit omni et soli, *quare,* id est ergo, *proprium est quantitatis* etc.

<Quaestiones>

Ad dictorum evidentiam duo quaeruntur, primum de prima proprietate, secundum de secunda.

---

7 quinque] *lectio incerta*   **14** aequale] quale *P*   **16** aequale] quale *P*   **22** dici] *ac* : dicitur *P*
24 albo] albedo *P*

<1>

De primo sic. Dicit Boethius quod affirmatio prius est negatione. Cum ergo secunda proprietas dicatur per affirmationem, prima per negationem, secunda ante
primam.

    Et dicendum: Cum dicit Boethius quod affirmatio ante negationem, dicendum
5 quod intelligit "si sunt eiusdem", et quia in proposito non sunt eiusdem, non | habet   f. 49vb
haec ratio locum.

<2>

Sed quaeritur quare sic ordinentur.

    Et dicendum quod secunda proprietas est propria quantitati, sed aliae sunt
communes, quia conveniunt qualitati et aliis; et quanto communius, tanto prius.

<3>

10 Consequenter quaeritur: Dicit quod quantitas non recipit magis et minus.

    Contra. Quaecumque recipiunt augmentum et deminutionem recipiunt magis
et minus. Quantitas est huiusmodi. Ergo etc.

    Et dicendum quod magis et minus dicitur modo uno secundum extensionem
dimensionis, alio secundum qualitatem, id est secundum praedicationem essentia-
15 lem. Primo modo quantitas recipit magis et minus, ut obicitur, secundo non. Licet
enim una quantitas protrahitur magis et minus quam alia, non tamen una est magis
quantitas alia.

<4>

De secundo quaeritur: Dicit quod maxime proprium est quantitatis secundum eam
aequale etc. Quare non dicit "esse" sicut "dici"?

20   Et dicendum quod hic loquitur de quantitate prout est dicibile, ut patuit superius, et non secundum esse. Quod volens exprimere, dixit "dici" et non "esse".

---

1   Boeth. *in Cat.* 181b; *cf. etiam in Int.*² I 1 (ed. Meiser, 16); II 5 (ed. Meiser, 98–99)   **10**   Arist.
Cat. 6.6a20–25   **18–19**   Arist. *Cat.* 6.6a26–27   **20–21**   *cf.* Lectio I, Q3

---

1 prius] primo *P*

<5>

Consequenter quaeritur an haec proprietas competat quantitati.

    Et quod non videtur. Aequale et inaequale respiciunt terminos. Sed infinito non est terminus. Ergo nec aequale nec inaequale. Minor: Scribitur in quarto *Physicorum*, "Infinitum est cuius quantitatem sumentibus semper est aliquid sumere extra", et nullum tale terminum habet. Arguo ulterius: Omnis quantitas est infinita. Ergo   5 in quantitate non est terminus. Ergo nec aequale nec inaequale. Quod quantitas sit infinita patet: Scribitur in eodem quarto quod infinitum congruit quantitati.

    Et dicendum quod contingit de quantitate loqui dupliciter, scilicet quantum ad naturam partium intrinsecarum, et sic non habet principium nec ultimum vel terminos, quia quaelibet eius pars est divisibilis in infinitum; et sic secundum eam non   10 dicitur aequale vel inaequale, ut obicitur. Sed si loquamur de ipsa per naturam partium extrinsecarum, habet principium et ultimum et sic terminos, sicut per litteram patet; et sic secundum eam dicitur aliquid aequale vel inaequale.

    Per hoc patet ad obiectum, quia cum dicitur "quantitas est infinita", hoc est verum per naturam partium intrinsecarum, et sic concedo quod non habet terminos,   15 sed haec infinitas non est nisi potentia. Sed per aliam naturam habet terminos, ut visum est.

<6>

Consequenter videtur quod haec proprietas non solum competat quantitati.

    Quia secundum aequalitatem vel inaequalitatem dicitur aliquid aequale vel inaequale. Sed aequalitas et inaequalitas sunt in genere relationis vel qualitatis.   20 Ergo haec proprietas convenit relativis. Non ergo solum quantitati.

    Et dicendum quod haec praepositio, "secundum", potest dicere habitudinem causae efficientis, et sic sumitur cum dicitur: "Proprium est quantitatis etc." Quantitas enim est causa efficiens aequalitatis et inaequalitatis. Vel potest dicere circumstantiam causae formalis, et sic sumitur cum dicitur: "Secundum aequalitatem   25 vel inaequalitatem dicitur aliquid aequale vel inaequale". Aequalitas enim est forma aequalis. Et sic est ibi aequivocatio in hoc quod dico, "secundum", ut visum est. |

f. 50ra

3–4   *re vera* Arist. *Phys.* III 6.207a7–8   7   *re vera* Arist. *Phys.* I 2.185b2

---

4 semper] sed *P* 9 naturam] numerum *P* 11 naturam] numerum *P* 14 dicitur] dicit *P* 20 vel qualitatis] *an delendum?* 27 est²] capitulum *add. P*

Lectio XXIV

Ad aliquid vero talia dicuntur (7.6a36)

\<Divisio\>

Determinato de substantia et quantitate, prosequitur de tertio praedicamento, quod est relatio.

Haec pars in duas. Primo determinat de relatione secundum aliorum opinionem, secundo secundum propriam (vel aliter: Primo de relativis secundum dici, secundo de relativis secundum esse), ibi: *Habet autem dubitationem* (7.8a14).

Prima in duas. Primo determinat de relativis penes substantialia, secundo penes accidentalia, ibi: *Inest autem contrarietas* (7.6b15).

Prima in duas. Primo proponit definitionem, secundo per exempla explanat, ibi: *ut maius* (7.6a38).

Haec secunda in duas. Primo ponit exempla coniunctim et competentia dictis, secundo divisim, ibi: *At vero sunt* (7.6b1).

Haec secunda in duas. Primo facit quod dictum est, secundo removet dubium, ibi: *Sunt autem accubitus* (7.6b11).

Prima in duas. Primo exemplificat de ad aliquid dictis in genitivo, secundo in aliis casibus, ibi: *vel quomodolibet aliter* (7.6b7).

Haec est divisio lectionis, et sunt quinque particulae.

\<Sententia\>

Circa primam sic procedit: Illa dicuntur ad aliquid quaecumque secundum esse habent respectum ad aliquid.

Et ponit exempla coniunctim: ut maius etc.

Consequenter explanat divisim et primo de ad aliquid dictis in genitivo. Dicit ergo quod habitus et disciplina et huiusmodi dicuntur in genitivo et non in alio casu.

Consequenter ponit exempla de dictis ad aliquid in aliis casibus: ut mons dicitur magnus ad alium montem et simile dicitur ad aliquid in dativo.

Consequenter removet dubium. Quia dixerat quod positio est ad aliquid, crederet aliquis quod denominativa positionis. Dicit quod non, quia statio, sessio et huiusmodi sunt positiones, sed iacere, stare et sedere et similia dicuntur denominative a positionibus, sed non sunt positiones.

Haec est sententia partis.

---

11 at] P^{inf}**ac** : aliquid P

Expositio litteralis

Dictum est de substantia, quantitate etc., *vero*, pro sed, *talia dicuntur ad aliquid quaecumque hoc ipsum* etc., id est secundum suum esse, *dicuntur aliorum*, id est in genitivo, *vel quomodolibet aliter*, id est in alio casu, dicuntur *ad aliud*.

Et ponit exempla: *ut maius hoc ipsum quod est*, id est secundum suum esse, *dicitur alterius*; *enim*, id est quia, *maius aliquo*, scilicet minore, *et duplum dicitur*   5
alicuius, scilicet dimidii. Non solum sic est in istis, *autem*, id est sed, *similiter* etc.

Consequenter ponit exempla divisim: Vel dicuntur praedicta ad aliquid, *at vero illa quae sequuntur sunt, ut habitus* etc. *Enim*, id est quia, *omnia haec quae dicta sunt hoc ipsum quod sunt*, id est secundum suum esse, *aliorum dicuntur* in genitivo *et non* dicuntur *ad aliud aliter* quam genitive. Ex hoc concludit quod habitus et   10
similia, postquam habent respectum in genitivo, sunt ad aliquid: *Ergo hoc ipsum quod sunt*, scilicet secundum suum esse, in genitivo *dicuntur* ad aliquid.

Consequenter exemplificat in aliis casibus: Ita dixi "dicta ad aliquid genitive sunt ad aliquid", *vel* illa sunt ad aliquid quae dicuntur *ad aliud quomodolibet aliter*, id est in quolibet alio casu, *ut mons* etc.   15

Ultimo removet dubium: Ita dixi "positio est ad aliquid etc.", *autem*, id est sed, *accubitus* etc. *sunt positiones*, sed *positio* dicitur *ad aliquid*, *autem*, id est sed, *iacere*
f. 50vb   etc. *non sunt positiones* sed *dicuntur denominative a positionibus | quae*, scilicet positiones, *dictae sunt*.

\<Quaestiones\>

\<1\>

Primo quaeritur: Videtur quod relatio non possit esse unum genus divisum contra   20
alia.

Nihil quod se habet ad plura dividitur ex opposito illis. Relatio est huiusmodi. Ergo etc. Minor patet, quia relatio causatur ex substantia, ut a patre et filio, et ex quantitate, ut aequalitas, inaequalitas, et a qualitate, ut similitudo, dissimilitudo.

Et dicendum quod aliqua sunt in genere tripliciter ad praesens. Uno modo sicut   25
participantia rationem generis, sicut species et individua. Alio modo sicut intentiones consequentes ea quae sunt in ipso genere et non sicut res, et sic istae intentiones, species et genus, sunt in quolibet genere. Tertio modo sicut effectus in sua causa, et sic relatio est in generibus aliis.

Ad obiectum dicendum quod entia in genere sicut genus participantia non di-   30
viduntur ex opposito contra alia, et quia sic non est in relatione, potest dividi ex opposito contra alia.

<2>

Consequenter quaeritur: Videtur quod prius deberet determinare de qualitate.

Quia qualitas habet salvari in uno absoluto, relatio autem in uno comparato vel in duobus ita quod in uno sit sicut in subiecto, in alio sicut in termino. Sed unum ante multa et absolutum ante comparatum. Ergo qualitas prior.

5   Item. Causa praecedit causatum et principium principiatum. Sed a qualitate causatur relatio, sicut similitudo, <et albedo>, quae est qualitas, est principium relationis. Ergo qualitas prior.

Et dicendum quod relatio primo ordinatur. Et causa est, ut dicit Boethius, quia in capitulo de quantitate dixerat quod multum et paucum sunt ad aliquid. Ne er-
10   go animus auditoris remaneat in suspenso, ignorans quid esset dictum ad aliquid, immediate post capitulum de quantitate determinat de relatione.

Alia causa est quia relatio magis convenit cum substantia et quantitate quam qualitas. Quod patet, quia sicut substantia et quantitas non habent contrarium nec magis aut minus suscipiunt, sic nec relatio; in qualitate est contrarium.

15   Alia causa est quia relatio reperitur in rebus corporeis et incorporeis (quod patet, quia in angelis est dualitas, et ubi dualitas, ibi duplum, et sic relatio), sed qualitas solum est in rebus corporeis. Et ideo ratione maioris communitatis praeponitur.

Per hoc patet ad obiecta, quia non ordinatur per relationem ad has condiciones, scilicet causa, causatum, absolutum et comparatum, sed prout magis et minus et
20   contrarium non suscipit, cum substantia convenit, et secundum quod in pluribus invenitur.

<3>

Consequenter quaeritur, cum nominet alia praedicamenta nomine simplici, ut "substantia", "quantitas" etc., quare nominet hoc praedicamentum nomine composito "ad aliquid dictum".

<4>

25   Iuxta hoc quaeritur, cum definiat alia in abstractione, quare hoc definivit in concretione; nam "ad aliquid dictum" concretionem dicit.

8–9 *cf.* Boeth. *in Cat.* 217a

---

5 principiatum] principatum *P a.c.*

\<Ad 3\>

Ad primum. Alia genera habent | esse in uno absoluto. Hinc est quod potuerunt nomine simplici nominari. Sed relatio non est in uno absoluto sed comparato, quare non debuit nomine simplici nominari.

\<Ad 4\>

Ad aliud. Sicut est in rebus quod in quibusdam actum praecedit potentia, ut in generabilibus et corruptibilibus, in aliis actus et potentia simul sunt, ut in intelligentiis 5
prout scribitur in *Libro fontis vitae*: "Omnis substantia spiritualis simul est in sua potentia et actu existens", similiter est in generibus, quia quaedam consequuntur materiam tantum, ut quantitas, quaedam formam tantum, ut qualitas, quaedam compositum, ut relatio. Quia ergo concretio solum est in compositis et relatio respicit compositum, in quo est concretio, ideo relatio in concretione definitur, alia 10
vero in abstractione.

\<5\>

Consequenter quaeritur quare definit relativa in plurali.

\<6\>

Iuxta hoc quaeritur quare definiuntur per verbum "dici".

\<Ad 5\>

Ad primum. Substantiae relativorum sunt diversae sed uniuntur in hoc quod est referri. Sed ubi diversitas, ibi pluralitas. Ut ergo denotet diversitatem substantia- 15
rum in relativis, dixit "quaecumque" in plurali, sed ut denotet unitatem ipsorum in hoc quod est referri, dixit "hoc ipsum" in singulari.

\<Ad 6\>

Ad aliud quod definivit per verbum "dici" ut innuat hanc definitionem non esse datam secundum opinionem suam sed aliorum. Vel aliter, ut innuat hanc definitionem esse datam de relativis secundum dici. 20

6–7 *locum non inveni* **12** Arist. *Cat.* 7.6a36–38 **13** Arist. *Cat.* 7.6a36–38

<7>

Consequenter quaeritur de expositione huius quod est "aliorum".

Nam exponit Boethius: "id est genitive".

Littera contra dicit quod "maius dicitur alterius", et tamen non dicitur ad aliud genitive, immo ablative.

5 Et dicendum quod genitivus et ablativus dicunt habitudinem causae efficientis, sed genitivus substantiae, ablativus accidentis vel passionis, dicit Petrus Elye. Quia ergo imponuntur ab eadem generali habitudine, speciali diversa, a Latinis distinguuntur. Boethius ergo, qui habet librum translatum, ad Graecorum imitationem genitivum pro ablativo posuit, dicens quod "maius alterius dicitur".

<8>

10 Consequenter quaeritur quare aliqua non dicuntur ad aliquid in nominativo vel in vocativo.

Et dicendum quod ad aliquid respectum importat quo nominativus et vocativus carent quia sunt absoluti † et non sicut alia quae dicantur prius ad aliquid quam ista, ideo etc. †

<9>

15 Consequenter quaeritur: Dicit quod habitus est ad aliquid.

Contra. "Diversorum generum etc". Cum ergo habitus sit species qualitatis, non erit in genere relationis.

Iuxta hoc quaeritur quo modo differenter sit species qualitatis et in genere relationis, praedicamentum et postpraedicamentum.

20 Et dicendum quod habitus quadrupliciter potest considerari. Uno modo prout est de difficili mobilis qualitas qualificativa et denominativa subiecti, et sic est in prima specie qualitatis. Aliter accipitur comparatio eorum quae sunt circa corpus ad ipsum corpus contentum, et sic est praedicamentum, quod patet per eius definitionem. Aliter sumitur prout dicit comparationem dispositionis ad dispositum, 25 id est ad habentem, et sic est relatio. Quarto modo dicitur dispositio cuiuslibet rei quae habetur, et sic est postpraedicamentum.

---

1 Arist. *Cat.* 7.6a37 sqq. 2 *cf.* Boeth. *in Cat.* 217d 3 Arist. *Cat.* 7.6a38 5–6 *cf.* Petrus Helias *Summa sup. Prisc.* (ed. Reilly, 391) 15 Arist. *Cat.* 7.6b1–6 16 Arist. *Cat.* 3.1b17 23–24 *cf.* Anon. *LSP* VII 69 (ed. Minio-Paluello, 51)

---

12 quo] quia *P*

<10>

Ultimo quaeritur: Dicit quod stare et huiusmodi dicuntur denominative a positio-
nibus sed non sunt in genere relationis sicut | positio.

  Contra. Dicit Nicolaus Logicus in *Quaestionibus* suis: "Si primum conferat virtutes secundo, operatur utique secundum sicut et primum". Sed principale est primum in quolibet genere et denominativum secundum. Ergo si principale conferat 5
virtutem denominativo, quod poterit principale per illam virtutem poterit denominativum. Sed principale per suam significationem habet esse in genere tali. Ergo
denominativum erit in eodem.

  Et dicendum quod denominativum cum suo principali est in eodem genere. Sed
sedere et iacere et huiusmodi praeter id quod significant rem sui principalis habent 10
quod significant illam in actu et fieri, et quia omne tale est in genere actionis, ideo
sunt in genere actionis et non relationis.

f. 50vb

1–2 Arist. *Cat.* 7.6b11–14 **3–4** *locum non inveni*

Lectio XXV

Inest autem contrarietas (7.6b15)

\<Divisio\>

Notificatis dictis ad aliquid per substantialia, ipsa notificat per accidentalia, ponens eorum proprietates.

Et primo ponit proprietates \<communes\>, secundo \<proprietates proprias\>, ibi: *Omnia autem relativa* (7.6b27).

Prima est praesentis lectionis et dividitur in partes duas penes duas proprietates. Secunda ibi: *Videntur autem et magis et minus* (7.6b20).

Prima in duas. Primo ponit proprietatem et eam per exempla manifestat, secundo ostendit hanc proprietatem omnibus relativis non convenire, ibi: *Non autem omnibus relativis* (7.6b17).

Pars in qua secundam proprietatem ostendit in duas. Primo ponit ipsam et per exempla explanat, secundo ostendit quod non convenit omnibus relativis, ibi: *Non autem omnia relativa* (7.6b23).

Haec est divisio lectionis, et sunt particulae quattuor.

\<Sententia\>

Circa primam sic procedit: Contrarietas in relativis reperitur, ut virtus contraria est vitio et utrumque est ad aliquid; similiter est de scientia et ignorantia.

Consequenter dicit quod hoc omnibus relativis non convenit, quia duplo nihil est contrarium neque triplo.

Consequenter ponit aliam proprietatem, dicens quod relatio suscipit magis et minus, sicut simile et inaequale.

Ultimo dicit quod hoc non convenit omnibus relativis, quia duplum neque subduplum non suscipit magis et minus, et tamen sunt ad aliquid.

Haec est sententia partis.

Expositio litteralis

Continua: Ita dictum est quod dicuntur ad aliquid etc., *autem*, pro sed, *contrarietas est in relatione, ut virtus* etc.

Ita dixi "contrarietas est in relatione", *autem*, pro sed, *contrarietas non est in omnibus relativis, enim*, id est quia, *duplici* etc.

---

6 videntur] *P*^{inf}*ac* : videtur *P*   **21** tamen] causa *P ut v.*   **26** duplici] *ac* : duplum *P*

Consequenter ponit aliam proprietatem: Non solum dicta proprietas convenit relativis, *autem*, id est sed, *relativa videntur suscipere magis et minus.*

Ita dixi quod hoc convenit relativis, *autem*, id est sed, *non omnia relativa suscipiunt.* Bene dixi quod non, *enim*, id est quia, *duplex*, quod est ad aliquid, *non dicitur magis et minus.*   5

<QUAESTIONES>

<1>

Primo quaeritur: Dicit "Contrarietas est in relatione".

In capitulo de quantitate dicit contrarium.

Item. Omnia contraria habent esse in eodem subiecto, simul autem non possunt esse in illo, ut patet per eorum definitionem. Sed nulla relativa habent esse in eodem, et simul sunt, ut dicit auctor in littera. Ergo nulla relativa possunt esse   10
contraria.

Item. Posito uno relativorum, ponitur reliquum. Sed posito uno contrariorum, non ponitur reliquum sed potius removetur. Ergo etc.

Ad hoc dicendum quod in relativis quae tantum sunt relativa non est contra-
f. 51ra   rietas, sed in illis quae sunt in relatione et in alio genere, | cui generi admixta est   15
contrarietas, est contrarietas, ut virtus et vitium sunt in relatione quantum ad modum dicendi sed in qualitate quantum ad modum essendi, unde in quantum sunt in genere qualitatis habent contraria et non in quantum relativa. Quod patet, quia si virtus in quantum relatio tantum habet contrarium, cum dicatur ad virtuosum, erit contrarium virtuoso, sed non est, immo vitio. Per hoc patet ad obiecta.   20

Vel aliter. Relativa secundum esse non habent contraria, et sic loquebatur superius, sed relativa secundum dici possunt habere contraria, et sic loquitur hic; sed non est in quantum relativa sed in quantum in genere qualitatis, ut visum est.

<2>

Item. Dicit quod scientia et ignorantia sunt contraria.

Alibi dicit quod sunt privativa. Ergo est sibi contrarius.   25

Iuxta hoc quaeritur quo modo differenter sunt contraria et privativa, quare etiam quaedam sunt tantum privativa, quaedam tantum contraria, quaedam contraria et privativa, et in quibus potest hoc esse.

---

6 Arist. *Cat.* 7.6b15–16   **7** Arist. *Cat.* 6.5b30–33   **9–10** Arist. *Cat.* 7.7b15–22   **24** *cf.* Arist. *Cat.* 7.6b16   **25** *cf.* Arist. *Top.* VI 9.147b26–31

---

15 generi] generis *P*   **27** privativa] quare *add. P*

Ad haec omnia dicendum quod quaedam sunt oppositionis extrema quorum utrumque est natura aliqua; et talia tantum sunt contraria, ut albedo et nigredo. Alia sunt quorum est unum natura aliqua, aliud purus defectus, ut visio et caecitas; talia sunt tantum privativa. Alia sunt quorum unum est natura aliqua, aliud autem
5 partim natura partim defectus, ut virtus et vitium; et talia possunt esse contraria et privativa. Quod patet, quia virtus est natura quaedam, vitium autem partim est natura, partim est defectus, quia vitium in quantum dicit virtutis defectum est purus defectus, in quantum autem habet in proprio subiecto radicari est natura quaedam. Et hoc est quod scribitur in *Libro de anima*, quia in nobis potentia duplex est, sen-
10 sus et ratio, et scribitur quod quando praedominatur ratio <et> succumbit ancilla sensualitas, tunc bene operatur homo, si e converso, male; et sic patet quod vitium habet principia in subiecto radicata. Similiter est de scientia et ignorantia.

9–10 *cf.* Arist. *An.* III 3.427a17–b13   **10–11**   *cf.* Arist. *EN* I 6.1098a3–17; *cf. etiam* Alanus de Insulis, *Liber Poenitentialis* (ed. Migne, PL 210, 284a); Anon. *Liber de stabilitate animae* (ed. Migne, PL 213, 919c)

---

10 quando] aut *P ut v.*

Lectio XXVI

Omnia autem relativa ad convertentiam dicuntur (7.6b27)

<Divisio>

Determinatis communibus, determinat propria.

Haec in duas. Primo determinat propria eorum quae dicuntur ad aliquid, secundo eorum quae sunt ad aliquid, ibi: *Videtur autem ad aliquid simul esse natura* (7.7b15).

Prima in duas. Primo determinat de his quibus convenit haec proprietas, secundo de quibus extranee convenit, ibi: *Omnia ergo quae ad aliquid dicuntur* (7.7a22).

Prima est praesentis lectionis et dividitur in duas quia primo ostendit hanc proprietatem dictis ad aliquid convenire et qualiter, et quia propter nomine carentia videbatur non omnibus convenire, in secunda parte ostendit hoc eis convenire, ibi: *Aliquotiens autem forte* (7.7a5).

Prima in duas. Primo ostendit hoc relativis convenire, secundo <qualiter eis convenit, ibi: *At vero aliquotiens* (7.6b36).

Prima in duas. Primo ponit proprietatem et eam per exempla manifestat, secundo> removet dubium, ibi: *sed casu aliquotiens differunt* (7.6b32).

Secunda pars principalis in duas. Primo ostendit hanc proprietatem dictis ad aliquid convenire, secundo ponit generale documentum ad fingendum nomina, ibi: *Sic autem fortasse* (7.7a18).

Haec est divisio lectionis, et sunt particulae quinque.

<Sententia>

Circa primam sic procedit: Dicit quod omnia relativa dicuntur ad convertentiam et ponit exempla: ut servus domini servus etc.

Consequenter removet dubium. Posset alicui videri quod dicuntur ad convertentiam secundum eundem | casum. Hoc removet, dicens quod non, quia disciplina dicitur disciplinati in genitivo et disciplinatum ad disciplinam in ablativo.

Consequenter dicit qualiter eis convenit, quia si convenienter assignetur. Nam si assignans peccet, tunc non convertuntur, ut si ala assignetur avis, ala autem non dicitur avis secundum convertentiam, male assignatum est. Quod probat: Quia ala non dicitur avis in eo quod avis sed in eo quod alata; sunt enim quae non sunt aves alas habentia, ut pisces, serpentes et huiusmodi.

f. 51rb

---

3 esse] *ac* : est *P*   9 nomine carentia] nomen carentiam *P*   22 quod] quia *P*

Consequenter probat hoc convenire quibus nomina non sunt imposita, dicens quod si nomen non est impositum ad quod assignetur relativum, oportet fingere ipsum ad hoc quod convertatur; sicut remus si assignetur navis, non convertuntur, nam sic assignatio non est conveniens (nam sunt naves quarum non sunt remi), sed si assignetur convenienter, convertuntur, ut remus si assignetur remitae. Similiter   5 in aliis.

Ultimo dat documentum fingendi nomina, dicens quod ex nomine primo imposito et illo ad quod convertitur debet nomen fingi, ut ab ala alatum etc.

Haec est sententia partis.

Expositio litteralis

Non solum dictae proprietates conveniunt relativis, *autem*, id est sed, *omnia rela-*   10 *tiva ad convertentiam dicuntur*. Et ponit exempla: *ut servus* etc.

Consequenter removet dubium: Ita dixi "dicuntur ad convertentiam", *sed dif-ferunt*, convertentia supple, *casu secundum locutionem*, id est secundum sermonem. Et nota quod casus triplex: uno modo inflectio vocis a voce, alio cadentia formae ad subiectum, ut denominativa, alio definitur a Boethio: "Casus est inopi-   15 natae rei eventus per intellectum agentis". De primo loquitur hic. Et ponit exempla: *ut disciplina* etc.

Consequenter dicit qualiter eis convenit: Ita dixi hoc relativis convenire, *vero*, id est sed, *non videtur converti*, id est dici ad convertentiam, *nisi* illud *ad quod dicitur convenienter assignetur*. Bene dico quod non, *enim*, id est quia, *si his qui assignat*   20 *peccet, non* convertuntur, *ut si ala assignetur avis*, dicendo *ut sit avis alae*. Bene dico "non convertuntur", quia *prius neque*, pro non, *est assignatum convenienter ala avis*. Bene dixi quod est male assignatum, *enim*, id est quia, *neque*, pro non, *ala dicitur avis in eo quod avis, sed in eo quod alata est*. Dico quod non in eo quod avis, *etenim*, id est quia, *alae sunt aliorum quae non sunt aves*. Ex hoc concludit: 25 Ex quo inconveniens assignatio impedit quod ala non convertit cum ave, *quare* per oppositum *si convenienter assignetur* etc.

Consequenter dicit hoc convenire quibus nomen non est impositum: Ita dixi relativa converti si convenienter assignentur, *autem*, id est sed, *aliquotiens* etc., *ut remus si assignetur* navi, *non erit conveniens assignatio*. Beno dico quod non, *enim*,   30 id est quia, *remus neque*, pro non, *dicitur eius*, id est navis, *in eo quod navis; sunt enim naves* etc.; *quare*, cum non assignetur convenienter, *non convertitur. Sed as-*

15–16   Boeth. *Consol.* V 1.18 (ed. Bieler, 89); Anon. *Auct. Arist.* 25.79 (ed. Hamesse, 293)

---

9 partis] par *P*   **14** nota] secundum locutionem *add. P*   **20** qui] *add. P s.l.*   **32** sed] *ac* : si *P*

signatio erit convenientior < * * * > | Et bene dico "quomodolibet aliter", *enim*, id est   f. 51va
quia, *nomen non est positum.* Vero, pro sed, *convertitur si assignetur convenienter*
etc. Non solum sic est de istis, *autem*, id est sed, *similiter et in aliis, <ut> caput* etc.

Ultimo docet nomina fingere: Ita dixi quod oportet fingere nomina, *autem*, id
est sed, in illis in *quibus nomen non est positum sumitur*, supple nomen, *facilius*
fortasse, sicut dictum est, *si* sumuntur *ab his quae sunt prima*, id est a primitivis, *et*
non a quibuscumque, sed *ab his ad quae convertuntur*. Vel aliter: *ab his quae sunt*
prima, id est a primitivis, *et ab his ad quae convertuntur*, id est a re, *ut in his quae*
praedicta sunt, ut *ab ala alatum* etc.

<Quaestiones>

<1>

Primo quaeritur quare haec proprietas differat a sequenti, quia scribitur in *Post-*
praedicamentis: "Simul natura sunt quaecumque convertuntur subsistendi consequentiam, ut relativa". Ergo simul esse natura et dici ad convertentiam idem
sunt.

Et dicendum quod triplex est convertentia. Quaedam est a parte suppositorum,
sicut equus et hinnibile sunt convertibilia quia pro eisdem supponunt, et huiusmodi convertibilitas idem est quod aequipollentia, et haec potest esse in terminis et
propositionibus. Aliter dicitur convertentia secundum subsistendi consequentiam,
id est quod unum substet alteri in consequendo. Tertio modo dicitur dependentia a
parte significati, ipsam per obliquitatem exprimendo, et de ista loquitur hic, quia significatum "patris" dependet a significato "filii" et e converso. Per hoc patet solutio
ad obiectum, nam aequivocatur convertentia.

Per hoc etiam patet ad aliud quod solet obici: Videtur quod hoc non sit proprium relativis, quia homo et risibile sunt convertibilia et tamen non sunt ad aliquid.
Solutum est, nam aequivocatur convertentia.

<2–3>

Consequenter quaeritur quare assignando proprietatem dicit "relativa dicuntur" et
definiendo dixit "ad aliquid dicta".

Iuxta hoc quaeritur in quo differunt ad aliquid et relativa.

10–12 Arist. *Cat.* 13.14b27–30   **25** Arist. *Cat.* 7.6b29   **26** Arist. *Cat.* 7.6a36

---

2 nomen non est positum] *ac* : unum est compositum *P*   **5** positum] *ac* : compositum *P*
5 sumitur supple] *inv. P*   **6** primitivis] primitivi scilicet *P*   **10** proprietas] non *add. P*

Ad primum. Duplex est via in relativis. Una a primo in ultimum cum reflec-
tione, ut pater filii; et "relativum" dicit hanc viam. Propter hoc assignando hanc
proprietatem potius ponit "relativa" quam "ad aliquid dicta". Sed quia "ad aliquid"
dicit aliam viam, et haec via magis participat unitatem, cum definitio dicat esse et
unitatem rei, ideo potius ponit in definitione "ad aliquid" quam "relativa".   5

Per hoc patet ad aliud.

<4>

Consequenter quaeritur, cum quaedam relativa dicantur secundum casum similem
et quaedam secundum dissimilem, qualiter differant.

Et dicendum quod quaedam sunt relativa quorum utrumque dicitur ad aliud
secundum propriam formam, ut pater filii et filius patris, et talia dicuntur per casum   10
similem. Alia sunt quorum unum dicitur ad aliud secundum propriam formam,
alterum non sed secundum formam prioris, ut disciplina dicitur ad aliud secundum
propriam formam, disciplinatum non sed secundum formam disciplinae, et talia
dicuntur secundum casum dissimilem.

<5>

Consequenter quaeritur: Dicit "Animalia quaedam sunt capita non habentia".   15
Quaeritur quae sunt illa et quare caput non habent.

f. 51vb   Et | dicendum quod natura nihil facit frustra nec deficit in necessariis, dicit Ari-
stoteles in *Libro de anima*. Quia ergo quaedam sunt animalia quae non habent
alimentum sibi coniunctum, et talia habent caput positum in loco eminentiori in
quo sunt quinque sensus situati propter hoc ut per sensus sibi alimenta acquirant,   20
sed alia sunt quae habent alimentum sibi coniunctum, quare capite non indigent
nec sensibus situatis in ipso quibus mediantibus sibi alimentum acquirant.

Sed quod hoc nihil sit et quod animal non sit sine capite videtur, quia scribitur
in *Libro de anima* quod non est animal sine gustu, et gustus est quidam tactus in
lingua radicatus et per consequens in capite. Omnia ergo habent caput, ut videtur.   25

Ad hoc dicendum est quod non oportet quod omnia habeant omnes sensus nec
caput, sed sufficit quod habeant aliquid loco oris per quod alimenta recipiant, et hoc
modo est in conchylibus et huiusmodi; sunt enim animalia largos poros habentia,

---

15 Arist. *Cat.* 7.7a17 **17–18** Arist. *An.* III 9.432b21–23; Anon. *Auct. Arist.* 6.168 (ed. Hamesse,
188) **23–24** *cf.* Arist. *An.* III 12.434b21–24; Anon. *Auct. Arist.* 6.176 (ed. Hamesse, 189) **27–28**
cf. Boeth. *in Cat.* 224b

---

11 aliud] aliquid *P* **17** deficit] defuit *P* **18** quae] *ex* quaedam *corr. P* **23** sine] *add. P in marg.*
25 per] quia *P*

et per eos attrahunt nutrimentum. Et est simile de puero in matrice, qui nutritur
de sanguine menstruali, qui non semper attrahit ipsum per os, sed per umbiculum,
quod est ei loco oris.

<6>

Consequenter quaeritur an impositio nominum pertineat ad logicum.

Quod non videtur. "Grammatica est de sermone ordinato ad significandum",
dicit Isaac. Ergo grammatici est considerare significationem ipsius nominis. Sed
significatio nominis idem est quod impositio. Ergo grammatici est considerare
nominis impositionem. Non ergo dialectici, ut videtur.

Et dicendum quod non est inconveniens idem a diversis scientiis considerari
differenter. Dicendum ergo quod impositio nominum per prius grammatico spectat
et per posterius logico et per accidens. Quod patet, quia logicus non tractat de
nominum impositione nisi ut ostendat qualiter relativum nomen dicitur ad aliud
cui nomen non est impositum. Et sic patet solutio ad obiectum.

Aliter dicitur quod spectat ad grammaticum nominum impositio in quantum
supra ipsam naturam congruitas radicatur, sed ad logicum in quantum est principium veritatis.

<7>

Consequenter quaeritur, cum logicus supponat principia grammatici, quare non
supponit nominum impositiones sed docet quo modo nomina imponenda se habeant ad nomina iam inventa.

Et dicendum quod dictum est, quod ipsa supponit primo et principaliter, unde
si de ipsis determinet, hoc est per accidens, ut patuit.

<8>

Ultimo quaeritur: Dicit in fine lectionis "ab his quae prima sunt et ab his quae
convertuntur". Ratio quaeritur quare addit "et ab his quae convertuntur".

Et dicendum quod denominativa dicuntur quae descendunt a suis principalibus
sed tamen eis non convertuntur; unde ad differentiam illorum addit "et ab his quae
convertuntur". Vel dicas ut dictum est.

5–6 *hoc adagium a magistriis frequenter Isaac attribuitur, fons autem verus incertus est* **22–23**
Arist. *Cat.* 7.7a20–22 **26** *cf. expositionem litteralem supra*

---

4 consequenter quaeritur] *inv.* P **20** unde] nomen P *ut v.* **23** ratio] *lectio incerta*

Lectio XXVII

Omnia ergo quae ad aliquid dicuntur (7.7a22)

<Divisio>

Determinata hac proprietate, dici ad convertentiam, respectu eorum ad quae dicitur proprie, prosequitur de ipsa respectu eorum ad quae dicitur extranee.

| Haec pars in duas. Primo proponit quod intendit, secundo propositum mani-   f. 52ra
festat, ut ibi: *Dico autem* (7.7a25).

Haec secunda in duas penes duo proposita quae explanat. Secunda ibi: *Amplius si convenienter* (7.7a31).

Haec secunda in duas. Primo proponit primo propositum, secundo propositum per exempla explanat, ibi: *ut servus si ad dominum* (7.7a35).

Haec secunda in duas. Primo proponit exempla, secundo concludit quod per totam lectionem probare intendit, ibi: *Quare oportet assignare* (7.7b10).

Haec est divisio lectionis, et sunt particulae quinque.

<Sententia>

Circa primam sic procedit: Ad aliquid dicta, si assignentur recte, ad convertentiam dicuntur, sed si non, non.

Consequenter probat ultimum, dicens quod dicta ad aliquid non convertuntur si assignentur ad aliquod extraneum. Et ponit exemplum: ut si servus non assignetur ad dominum sed ad hominem, non convertitur, quia male fuit assignatum.

Consequenter proponit primo propositum, dicens quod si dictum ad aliquid convenienter assignetur ad id ad quod dicitur, semper cum ipso convertetur.

Consequenter ponit exempla: ut si servus dicitur ad dominum, circumscripto a domino esse hominem et similia, relicto solo domino, servus semper dicetur ad ipsum, et si servus convenienter non assignetur, ut si assignetur ad hominem, circumscripto domino, non convertetur cum homine, quia male fuit assignatum. Similiter est de ala et ave.

Ultimo concludit quod si dictum ad aliquid convenienter assignetur ad illud <ad> quod dicitur, semper dicetur conversim, et si est <nomen> impositum, facile est assignare, et si non, imponatur, ut dictum est.

---

7 primo propositum] quod *P*   20 a] *add. P s.l.*   22 quia] quod *P*

Expositio litteralis

Ita dictum est quod conveniens assignatio facit quod dicta ad aliquid convertuntur, *ergo omnia quae dicuntur ad aliquid* etc. Bene dico "si assignentur convenienter", *nam*, id est quia, *si assignentur*, dicta ad aliquid supple, *ad quodlibet aliud et non ad illud* ad quod dicuntur, *non convertuntur*.

Bene dico "non convertuntur", *autem*, id est sed, *dico* hoc ideo *quoniam*, pro quod, <*nec*, pro> non, *horum* etc., *si* assignentur *ad aliquid eorum quae sunt accidentia*, et appellatur aliquid extraneum, id est illud quod non dependet ab alio secundum suum esse, ut homo a domino, *et non ad ea* etc. 5

Ita dixi "si non assignetur convenienter, non convertitur", *autem*, id est sed, *si assignetur*, aliquod relativum supple, *convenienter* etc. 10

Et ponit exemplum: *ut servus si dicatur ad dominum*. Littera plana.

Ultimo concludit: Postquam dicta ad aliquid convertuntur si convenienter assignentur, *quare*, id est ergo, *oportet assignare*, dictum ad aliquid supple, *ad id quod convenienter* assignatur; *et si nomen* est impositum etc. Littera plana.

<Quaestiones>

<1>

Primo quaeritur quare non determinet de aliis praedicamentis secundum opinionem aliorum et propriam, sicut de dictis ad aliquid. 15

Et dicendum quod maior incidebat error inter philosophos circa dicta ad aliquid quam circa alia, et quia non vitatur malum nisi cognitum, dicit Boethius, de relativis ponit aliorum opinionem erroneam ut eam rectificet. Quod autem maior | error circa hoc incidit patet. Nam relatio causatur a rebus aliorum praedicamentorum, ut simile a qualitate et aequale a quantitate. Ergo cum in aliis dicta ad aliquid radicentur, opinati sunt quidam omnia alia esse in relatione. 20

f. 52rb

<2>

Consequenter quaeritur quare non determinet de relativis per se et per accidens, sicut de quantitate; nam videtur per simile quod deberet.

Et dicendum per interemptionem. Nam relativa secundum dici sunt relativa per accidens, sed relativa secundum esse sunt relativa per se. In hoc ergo quod determinat de istis sufficienter de relativis tractatur. 25

---

18 *cf.* Boeth. *Top. Diff.* II 2.15 (=1184b) (ed. Nikitas, 23)

---

4 dicuntur] nec pro *add.* P   **12–13** assignentur] assignetur P   **25** per] quod P

<3>

Sed ex hac solutione dubium oritur.

    Nam in capitulo quantitatis primo prosequitur de quantitate per se, ultimo
per accidens. Ergo si relativa secundum dici sunt relativa per accidens et relativa
secundum esse sunt per se, deberent relativa secundum esse praeordinari.

5   Et dicendum quod per se et per accidens possunt dupliciter ordinari, scilicet secundum naturae ordinem, et sic per se praecedit per accidens, <vel per> relationem
ad has condiciones, vitium et virtus, et quia per accidens est vitium et obliquitas
contra per se, sic prius per accidens iuxta illud Boethii: "Antequam inserantur virtutes, sunt vitia exstirpanda". Hunc ordinem hic auctor intendit, primum vero in
10 quantitate.

<4>

Consequenter quaeritur: Videtur quod non sint relativa secundum dici quin sint
relativa secundum esse.

    Quia decem genera sunt <principia> in essendo (quod patet, quia Aristoteles
in *Metaphysica* de ente et de principiis entis determinat; cum ergo determinet de
15 decem generibus, decem sunt principia entis). Sed ad aliquid est unum ex illis. Ergo
est principium in essendo. Arguo ulterius: In nullo quod est principium in essendo
est natura determinata secundum dici solum.

    Item. Omne quod est in aliis generibus est in eis secundum modum essendi et
non secundum modum dicendi solum. Ergo pari ratione relativa non possunt esse
20 secundum dici quin sint secundum esse.

<5>

Ratione huius quaeritur, cum ea quae sunt in aliis generibus sunt in eis secundum
esse et non secundum dici solum, quare in relatione secundum dici sunt quaedam
et quaedam secundum dici et esse.

<AD 4>

Ad primum. Omnia alia genera a relatione sunt naturae aliquae, sed relatio est qui-
25 dam respectus causatus a natura aliqua. Sed si natura a qua causatur illa relatio sit

---

8–9 *locum apud Boethium non inveni, cf. autem* Isidorus *Sententiae* II 36.6: "Prius vitia exstirpanda
sunt in homine, deinde inserendae virtutes."

---

9 sunt] *iter. P a.c.*   9 auctor intendit] *lectio incerta*   16 nullo] illo *P ut v.*

talis cui non sit admixtus aliquis respectus in re, tunc sunt relativa secundum dici.
Sed si illi naturae sit admixtus respectus in re, tunc sunt relativa secundum dici et
secundum esse, ut duplum et dimidium. Unde relativa non dicuntur secundum dici
quia nullo <modo> sint secundum esse, sed quia causantur a natura aliqua cui non
est admixtus aliquis respectus in re, sicut partes substantiae.   5

Ad obiecta dicendum quod non possunt esse relativa secundum dici quin sint
relativa secundum esse, et concedo argumenta, sed quare dicantur secundum dici
et secundum esse dicta est causa.

<AD 5>

Ad ultimum dicendum quod, sicut dictum est, omnia alia genera naturas habent
aliquas, et propter hoc ea quae sunt in ipsis insunt secundum esse et secundum dici,   10
sed relatio dicit respectum causatum | a naturis aliorum, ratione cuius respectus
habet quod sint in eo quaedam relativa secundum esse et quaedam secundum dici,
ut visum est.

f. 52va

<6>

Consequenter quaeritur: Dicit quod homo est accidens.

Contra. Non adest et abest etc. Ergo non est accidens.   15

Item. Homo est in praedicamento substantiae. Ergo erit substantia. Ergo non
accidens.

Et dicendum quod accidens ad praesens dicitur tripliciter. Uno modo omne
illud quod non est substantia, et sic novem genera dicuntur accidentia. Alio modo
dicitur quod adest et abest etc., et sic est unum de quinque universalibus. Ultimo   20
dicitur extraneum, id est illud quod secundum suum esse ab alio non dependet, ut
homo est accidens domino cum secundum esse suum a domino non dependeat.
Per hoc patet ad obiectum, quia aequivocatur accidens.

Vel aliter. Duplex est accidens, simpliciter vel in respectu, ut homo accidit So-
crati respectu tertii et quodlibet superius inferiori, ut patet hic: "Homo est species;   25
Socrates est homo; ergo Socrates est species". Est enim homo accidens rei subiectae. Et hoc est quod habetur in *Elenchis*, quod triangulus accidit aequilatero, quod
est species eius, respectu huius passionis quae habere est tres.

---

14 Arist. *Cat.* 7.7a25–31   **27** *potius* Arist. *Top.* II 3.110b22–26; *cf. autem* Arist. *SE* 6.168a40–b6

---

3 secundum dici] *inv. P*   **27** aequilatero] aequilatio *P ut v.*

Lectio XXVIII

Videtur autem ad aliquid simul esse natura (7.7b15)

<Divisio>

Posita proprietate relativorum secundum dici, ponit proprietatem relativorum secundum esse.

Haec pars in duas. Primo ponit proprietatem, secundo ponit quasdam instantias contra ipsam, ut ibi: *Non autem in omnibus relativis* (7.7b22).

Prima in duas. Primo ponit proprietatem et explanat per exempla, secundo probat ipsam relativis convenire, ibi: *Simul autem haec auferunt* (7.7b20).

Pars in qua ponit instantias in duas penes duas instantias. Secunda ibi: *Similiter autem his* (7.7b35).

Prima in duas. Primo ponit instantiam in generali, secundo applicat ad specialia, ibi: *Scibile enim scientia* etc. (7.7b23).

Haec secunda in duas penes duas rationes quas ponit. Secunda incipit ibi: *Amplius scibile ablatum* (7.7b26).

Haec secunda in duas. Primo ponit substantiam rationis, secundo probat medium, ut ibi: *ut circuli* (7.7b31).

Haec secunda in duas. Primo probat medium per exemplum geometricum, secundo per naturale, ut ibi: *Amplius animali sublato* (7.7b32).

Pars in qua ponit secundam instantiam in duas. Primo ponit eam, secundo probat, ut ibi: *Nam sensibile interemptum* (7.7b37).

Haec secunda in duas penes duas rationes. Secunda ibi: *Amplius sensus quidem simul cum* (7.8a7).

Prima in duas. Primo ponit substantiam suae rationis, secundo probat medium, ut ibi: *Sensus enim circa corpus* (7.7b38).

Haec secunda in duas. Primo probat unam partem medii, secundo aliam, ut ibi: *Sensus autem sensibile* (7.8a3).

Haec est divisio lectionis, et sunt particulae duodecim.

<Sententia>

Circa primam sic procedit: Dicta ad aliquid videntur simul esse natura (et dicit "videntur" quia positurus est instantias). Et ponit exemplum: ut duplum et dimidium etc.

---

6 haec] *ac* : hoc *P*   **19–20** quidem simul cum] *ac* : et in seneuco *! P*   **21** ponit] in *add. P*

Consequenter probat hoc sic: Quaecumque sese auferunt sunt simul natura. Duplum et dimidium et consimilia sunt huiusmodi. Ergo etc.

Consequenter ponit primam instantiam, dicens quod haec proprietas non videtur omnibus relativis convenire, ut scibilia, scientiae.

Et hoc probat sic: Illa quorum unum est prius altero non sunt simul natura.   5
Scientia et scibile sunt huiusmodi. Ergo etc.

< * * * >

f. 52vb   Consequenter probat medium: | Ut quadratura circuli est scibile, et eius non est scientia (et hoc est verum tempore Aristotelis).

Consequenter idem probat per exempla naturalia sic: Quando aliqua duo sic se   10
habent ad tertium quod destructo illo tertio unum illorum destruitur et non alterum, illud quod non destruitur est prius. Sed destructo animali destruitur scientia et non scibile. Ergo scibile est prius.

Consequenter ponit instantiam secundam: Similiter est de sensu et sensibili, nam sensibile prius est quam sensus.   15

Quod probat: Illud quo interempto interimitur alterum et non e converso est prius altero. Sensus et sensibile sunt huiusmodi. Ergo etc.

Consequenter probat quod sensibile interemptum interimit sensum sic: Sensus est circa corpus. Sed sensibile interemptum interimit corpus et corpus interemptum sensum. Ergo a primo sensibile interemptum interimit sensum.   20

Consequenter probat quod non est e converso: Animali perempto perimitur sensus et non sensibile ut corpus. Ergo perempto sensu non perimitur sensibile.

Ultimo probat propositum quod sensibile sit prius sic: Si aliqua duo simul habent esse, si aliquod praecedit unum, et alterum. Sed animal et sensus sunt simul, et sensibile prius quam animal. Ergo prius quam sensus.   25

Haec est sententia partis.

Expositio litteralis

Non solum dicta proprietas convenit relativis, *autem*, id est sed, *ad aliquid*, id est ea quae sunt ad aliquid, *videntur simul esse natura*, id est natu vel origine, dicit Augustinus. *Et verum est in aliis pluribus*, sicut in vere relativis supple. Bene dico quod sic, *enim*, id est quia, *duplum est simul* etc.   30

< * * * > Non solum sic est in istis, *autem*, id est sed, *similiter* est *in aliis*, scilicet relativis, *quaecumque sunt talia*, id est vere relativa.

28–29   *cf.* Ps.-Aug. *Categoriae decem* 98 (ed. Minio-Paluello, 155)

---

3 primam] *ex* secundam *corr. P ut v.*   **3** instantiam] *add. P in marg.*   **9** verum] quod *add. sed canc. P et unam vocem quam legere nequeo add. al. man. in marg.*   **28** natu] nata *P*   **29** verum est] **ac** : videtur esse *P*

Consequenter ponit instantiam: *Ita videntur relativa simul esse natura, autem*, id est sed, *simul natura*, id est illa proprietas, *non videtur omnibus relativis* convenire.

Bene dico non, *enim*, id est quia, *scibile prius videtur esse scientia*; *namque*, id est quia, *accipimus scientias in pluribus* existentibus, sed *in paucis vel nullis* etc. Et dicit "in paucis" propter quasdam res quae solum consistunt in imaginatione, ut Chimaera; nam in talibus non est prius scibile quam scientia.

Consequenter ponit aliam rationem: *Amplius scibile sublatum* etc. Bene dico quod sic, *nam*, id est quia, *si scibile non sit* etc.

Et ponit exemplum: *ut quadratura circuli est* scibilis, *scientia quidem nondum est eius, vero*, id est sed, *illud*, id est quadratura, *est scibile*.

Consequenter ponit aliud medium: Bene dixi quod scibile prius est, *enim*, id est quia, *animali sublato* etc.

Non solum sic est in istis, *autem*, id est sed, *similiter his*, id est scientiae et scibili, *se habent ea quae sunt de sensu*, id est sensus et sensibile.

< * * * >

Bene dico sic, *enim*, <id est> quia, *sensus* est *circa corpus* quantum ad exteriorem *et in corpore* quantum ad interiorem, *autem*, pro sed, *perempto sensibili corpus est peremptum*. Bene dico sic, *enim*, id est quia, *sensibile corpus est* etc.

Consequenter probat quod non est e converso: Beno dico "sensibile interimit sensum", *autem*, id est sed, *sensus non perimit sensibile*. Bene dico non, *enim*, id est quia, | *sensibile erit* etc.   f. 53ra

Ultimo ponit aliam rationem quod sensibile prius: *Amplius sensus fit simul cum sensato*. Bene dico quod sic, *enim*, id est quia, *ignis et aqua* etc.

<Quaestiones>

Ad removendam obiectionem frivolam nota quod sensus dicitur dupliciter. Uno modo potentia sensitiva per quam animal apprehendit speciem in materia, et sic simul cum animali est, et sic loquitur auctor. Aliter dicitur sensus ipsa operatio virtutis, et sic animal prius.

<1>

Primo quaeritur qualiter sumitur hic natura.

Dicit quod relativa sunt simul natura.

Contra. Scribitur in *Libro Physicorum*: "Omnium generabilium et corruptibi-

---

30 Arist. *Cat.* 7.7b15   **163.31–164.1**   *cf.* Arist. *Phys.* II 1.193a29–31

---

31 contra] quia *P*

lium materia idem est quod natura". Ergo omnia generabilia et corruptibilia habent simultatem in natura. Non ergo convenit solum relativis simul esse natura si natura dicatur materia. Cum ergo haec proprietas solum competat relativis, natura materia non dicetur.

Item. Dicit Isidorus quod natura prima causa appellatur, non quia aliunde sit   5
nata, sed quia alia ab ea nascuntur. Et patet quod hic non intendit de tali natura. Quaeritur ergo de qua natura loquitur.

Et dicendum ut dicit Augustinus in *Praedicamentis*: Relativa simul sunt natura, unde natura idem est quod natus vel ortus vel quaedam origo quae est principium unius relativi et alterius. Quod patet per quandam quaestionem quam movet ibi-   10
dem. Quaerit enim an dominus fuerit dominus ab aeterno, et dicit quod non, sed cum incepit esse servus, tunc incepit esse dominus. Patet ergo quod illud quod est principium nascendi unius relativorum est principium nascendi utriusque.

Patet ergo ad obiecta. Nam hic non intelligitur de natura superiori ac de natura quae est forma nec quae est materia nec de natura quae est virtus insita rebus per   15
quam res natae sunt continuare se eadem in specie cum hae se eadem in numero salvare non poterant (et haec natura dicitur virtus seminativa), sed intelligitur de natura quae <est> ortus vel origo, ut dictum est.

<2>

Consequenter quaeritur: Videtur quod haec proprietas omnibus relativis non conveniat, quia unum definitur per alterum, dicit Porphyrius. Sed definientia sunt   20
priora, scribitur in sexto *Topicorum*. Ergo prius unum altero.

Item. Ordinantur causae sicut effectus. Sed generans est causa paternitatis, generatum causa filiationis. Ergo sicut generans ante generatum, sic paternitas ante filiationem. Et ista sunt relativa. Ergo non omnia relativa simul sunt natura.

Item. Prius et posterius, causa et causatum, dicuntur ad aliquid, et non sunt   25
simul natura, ut patet. Et ita idem quod prius.

Ad primum. Duplex est definitio. Quaedam indicans esse causae formalis, et in tali definientia priora, ut obicitur. Alia est terminans respectum, et talem habent relativa, et de tali non tenet argumentum.

Ad aliud. Generans non est causa sufficiens paternitatis, sed substantia patris et   30
filii exigitur ad esse paternitatis, et utriusque substantia exigitur ad esse filiationis.

5–6 Isidorus *Etym.* XI 1.1 (ed. Lindsay, vol. 2)   **8–10**   *cf.* Ps.-Aug. *Categoriae decem* 98 (ed. Minio-Paluello, 155)   **10–12**   *cf.* Ps.-Aug. *Categoriae decem* 98 (ed. Minio-Paluello, 155)   **20** *cf.* Porph. *Isag.* 4.4–9; Boeth. *in Isag.*² III 2 (ed. Brandt, 201–3)   **20–21**   *cf.* Arist. *Top.* VI 4.141b25–29; Anon. *Auct. Arist.* 36.93 (ed. Hamesse, 328)

---

13 utriusque] similitudinis *add. P*   **16** se¹] sed *P*   **28** priora] prius *P*

Patet ergo quod argumentum falsum supponit quod generans est causa sufficiens paternitatis, quod falsum est.

Ad ultimum. Prius et posterius etc. possunt dupliciter considerari. Uno modo secundum id quod sunt, et sic unum prius altero, ut obicitur, et sic non dicuntur ad aliquid. Aliter sumuntur sub his inten|tionibus, prioritatis, causalitatis etc., et sic unum non est prius altero, et sic sunt ad aliquid et sunt simul. f. 53rb

Per hoc solvitur quaestio quaedam quae fit hic, quare ponit instantias et non solvit, quia si scibile et scientia considerentur secundum id quod sunt, scibile est prius, et sic rationes quas ponit procedunt, et quia hac via verum concludunt, eas insolutas relinquit; sed si considerentur scibile et scientia sub his intentionibus, scibile non est prius scientia, sed simul sunt.

<3>

Sed modo quaeritur quare ponit instantias sophisticas.

Et dicendum: Ad denotandum quod haec proprietas non convenit relativis secundum id quod sunt, et sic instat, sed convenit relativis secundum suum esse.

<4>

Consequenter quaeritur quare dicit quod destructo scibili destruitur scientia.

Contra. Destructo posteriori non destruitur prius. Sed scibilia inferiora sunt posteriora quam scientia quae est prius in Primo. Ergo destructis inferioribus remanebit scientia quae est in Primo. Et ita destructo scibili remanebit scientia.

<Ad> oppositum. Omne quod per sui praesentiam est causa alicuius, per sui non existentiam est causa non existentiae eiusdem. Sed scibile per sui praesentiam est causa scientiae. Ergo per sui non existentiam est causa non existentiae eiusdem. Destructo ergo scibili scientia destruetur.

Ad primum. Duplex est scientia. Quaedam est causa rerum, et haec est scientia Primi. Alia est scientia quae est causata a rebus. Sed tu obicis de scientia res causante.

Alia ponitur instantia: Nos habemus scientiam de eclipsi lunae, eclipsi non existente scibili; non propter hoc scientia destruetur.

Et dicendum quod duplex est scientia. Quaedam per quam scitur res, alia per quam scitur res esse. Aliud est enim scire rem et scire rem esse, ut artifex antequam aedificet habet scientiam de domo, non tamen scit domum esse, cum adhuc non sit.

---

15   Arist. *Cat.* 7.7b26–32

---

18 primo] prima *P*   **26** nos] non *P*   **30** tamen scit] causa sit *P*

Cum ergo dicat auctor: "Destructo scibili destruitur scientia", loquitur de scientia per quam scitur res esse, sed tu obicis de alia.

Vel aliter. Aliquid potest esse dupliciter. Vel in essendo vel in fiendo. Licet enim eclipsis non sit in essendo, est tamen in fiendo, quia quam cito recedit a puncto in quo est quando eclipsatur, tam cito circulum peragendo appropinquat per motus 5 varios ad eundem punctum.

<5>

Consequenter quaeritur: Dicit quod destructa scientia non destruitur scibile.

Contra. Destructa forma perfectiva alicuius destruitur ipsum. Scientia est forma perfectiva scibilis. Ergo scientia destructa destruitur scibile.

Et dicendum quod scibile potest nominare rem tantum, et sic non est ad aliquid 10 nec destructa scientia destruitur scibile, et sic loquitur auctor, quia substantia scibilis non destruitur scientia destructa. Si vero nominet substantiam sub actu sciendi, destructa scientia destruitur scibile, sed non scibile secundum substantiam sed sub hac forma quae est scientia, et sic obicitur.

<6>

f. 53va   Ultimo quaeritur: Dicit quod destructo | animali <destruitur scientia. 15

Contra. Destructo animali> remanet anima. Quae est perfectibilis virtutibus et scientiis, dicit Philosophus. Ergo adhuc scientia poterit esse in ipsa.

Item. Ad Primum paratum est quantum est de se influere scientiam aequaliter et suam ineffabilem bonitatem; et hoc est quod habetur in *Libro de causis*: "Prima causa non cessat influere in causata". Ergo scientia potest esse in anima, et animali 20 destructo potest scientia in anima remanere.

Et dicendum quod duplex est scientia. Quaedam est a Primo habita per inspirationem et illuminationem et influentiam bonitatis, alia est quae causatur ex memoria, scribitur in *Posterioribus*. Et quia sensus et memoria non sunt in anima a corpore separata, ideo anima a corpore separata non potest perfici nisi prout corpori est unita. De prima scientia obicitur, circa secundam auctoris intentio nunc 25 versatur.

1 Arist. *Cat.* 7.7b26–32   7 Arist. *Cat.* 7.7b26–35   15 Arist. *Cat.* 7.7b33–34   **16–17** *locum non inveni*   **19–20** *cf.* Anon. *Liber de causis* V 58 (ed. Pattin, 59)   **23–24** *cf.* Arist. *APo* II 19.100a3–b6; Anon. *Auct. Arist.* 35.125 (ed. Hamesse, 321)

7 non] *add. P s.l.*   **10** nominare] ordinare nominare vel *P*

Lectio XXIX

Habet autem quaestionem utrum nulla substantia (7.8a14)

<Divisio>

Determinato de relativis secundum aliorum opinionem, de ipsis secundum propriam prosequitur.

Haec pars in duas. Primo praemittit quandam quaestionem ex cuius explanatione ducit ad impossibile si dicta definitio bene est assignata, secundo ipsam corrigit
5 suam definitionem ponendo, ibi: *Si autem non sufficienter* (7.8a31).

Prima in duas. Primo ponit quaestionem, <secundo concludit inconveniens, ibi: *Si igitur sufficienter* (7.8a28).

Prima in duas. Primo ponit quaestionem> ad utramque partem contradictionis continentem, secundo ipsam explanat de parte utraque explanando, ut ibi: *Nam in*
10 *primis* (7.8a16).

Haec secunda in duas. Primo prosequitur de illis quae <non> videntur esse ad aliquid, secundo de illis quae videntur esse ad aliquid, ut ibi: *In aliquibus vero* (7.8a25).

Prima in duas. Primo explanat quaestionem in primis substantiis quae non
15 videntur esse ad aliquid, secundo in secundis, ut ibi: *Similiter autem in secundis* (7.8a21).

Pars in qua ponit definitionem secundum opinionem propriam in duas. Primo ponit ipsam, secundo infert correlarium vel, secundum alios, ponit quandam proprietatem relativorum, ut ibi: *Ex his ergo manifestum est* (7.8a35).

20 Prima praesentis est lectionis et dividitur in duas. Primo definit, secundo ponit differentiam ad definitionem superius assignatam, ibi: *Prior autem definitio* (7.8a33).

Haec est divisio lectionis, et sunt particulae septem.

<Sententia>

Circa primam sic procedit: Quaeritur utrum nulla substantia dicatur ad aliquid,
25 sicut videtur, an sint quae dicantur ad aliquid.

Consequenter explanat quaestionem, et primo in primis, dicens quod primae substantiae non dicuntur ad aliquid. Et probat sic: Si dicerentur ad aliquid, hoc esset secundum partem vel secundum totum. Sed nec sic nec sic dicuntur ad aliquid. Ergo etc. Minorem ponit et explanat per exempla.

18–19   *cf.* Boeth. *in Cat.* 237a–b

---

11 esse] omne *P*   **12** quae] non *add. P a.c.*   **12** aliquibus] *P^{inf}ac* : quibus *P*   **29** explanat] *ex* exempla *corr. P*

Consequenter manifestat idem in secundis substantiis, dicens quod quaedam substantiae, sicut illae quae designant totum, non dicuntur ad aliquid. Et ponit exempla: ut homo, bos etc.

Consequenter quaestionem explanat in illis quae videntur ad aliquid dici, dicens quod dubium est in secundis substantiis; nam substantiae quae partes designant videtur quod dicantur ad aliquid. Et ponit exemplum: ut caput etc.

f. 53vb   Consequenter concludit inconveniens, dicens | quod si dicta definitio est conveniens, difficile erit solvere quod nulla substantia dicatur ad aliquid.

Consequenter ponit definitionem secundum opinionem propriam, dicens quod si dicta definitio non est conveniens sed assignetur ista, "Ad aliquid dicta sunt quae secundum suum esse dependent ab esse alterius", responderi poterit ad obiecta.

Ultimo comparat definitiones, dicens quod prima definitio convenit omnibus relativis, non tamen dicit esse eorum sicut secunda.

Haec est sententia partis.

Expositio litteralis

Ita dictum est de relativis, *autem*, id est sed, *utrum nulla substantia dicatur ad aliquid, quemadmodum*, pro sicut, *<videtur>*, *habet quaestionem*, *an contingit hoc*, id est dici ad aliquid, *secundum quasdam* etc.

Continua. Bene dixi "Videtur nulla substantia dici ad aliquid", *nam*, id est quia, *in primis substantiis* videtur quod non sint ad aliquid. Bene dico quod non, *nam*, id est quia, *neque totae* etc. Vere "nec totae nec partes", *nam*, id est quia, *aliquis homo*, id est prima substantia † per haec quam ponitur haec oratio †, *non dicitur* etc., id est non refertur ad aliud aliquid secundum se, ut Socrates non dicitur alicuius Socrates. Non solum sic est de istis, *autem*, id est sed, *partes*, id est primae substantiae partes designantes, *similiter*, non dicuntur ad aliquid supple. Bene dico quod non, *enim*, id est quia, *quaedam manus* etc.

Non solum ita est in primis, *autem*, id est sed, ita est *in secundis substantiis* quod non dicuntur ad aliquid, *atque*, pro et, *hoc in pluribus*, esse videtur supple, *ut homo* etc. Et hoc concludit: Ex quo secundae substantiae, ut homo, quae totum designant non dicuntur ad aliquid, *ergo in huiusmodi*, id est in his secundis substantiis quae totum designant, *manifestum est* etc.

Ita est in istis, *vero*, pro sed, *in aliquibus secundis substantiis* quae partem designant *habet* dubium, nam videntur dici ad aliquid supple, *ut caput* etc., *quare haec ad aliquid videntur*, quod est inconveniens.

---

15 substantia] *add. P in marg.*   **32** videntur] videtur *P*

Continua. Ita sequitur inconveniens ex dicta definitione, *igitur si definitio eo-rum quae sunt ad aliquid est assignata sufficienter*, id est convenienter, *nimis difficile* erit *solvere* etc.

Bene "nimis difficile erit solvere", *autem*, id est sed, *si non sufficienter* est dicta definitio assignata, quod videtur, *sed* haec *sunt ad aliquid quibus hoc ipsum esse*, id est suum esse, *<est> se habere ad aliquid quodam modo*, id est per se, etc., forte ad obiecta sic *aliquid dicetur*. Quasi dicens: Responderi poterit ad obiecta.

Ita sunt positae duae definitiones, *autem*, id est sed, *prior definitio sequitur omnia relativa*, id est convenit omnibus relativis, *non tamen* etc.

<QUAESTIONES>

<1>

Primo quaeritur de ordine partis huius ad partem praecedentem.

Ars imitatur naturam. Sed in natura esse rei praecedit accidens. Ergo et in eius arte. Sed definitio dicit esse rei, dicit Aristoteles, proprietas vero ipsius acciden-tis rei. Ergo definitio praecedit proprietatem. Pars ergo praecedens, in qua ponit proprietatem, deberet istam subsequi in qua ponit definitionem.

Item. Superius determinando de his quae dicuntur ad aliquid prius posuit definitionem quam proprietatem. Quare hic facit e converso?

Et dicendum quod <quia> haec definitio causatur a praecedenti proprietate, ideo ponitur posterius sicut causatum post causam quod ab ipsa causatur. Patet quod nullus | possit perfecte scire quid sint relativa nisi sciat quo modo esse ha-beant relativa, et hoc docetur in praecedenti lectione (dicit vero quod relativa sunt simul natura). f. 54ra

Ad obiectum dicendum quod duplex est definitio. Quaedam est principalis, non orta ab aliqua proprietate, et talis praeordinatur, ut obicitur, et talis est definitio eorum quae dicuntur ad aliquid superius assignata, quare praeordinatur. Alia est definitio orta ab aliqua proprietate, et haec debet posterius ordinari, sicut est hic.

<2>

Consequenter quaeritur quare in principio lectionis praeponitur negatio affirma-tioni, cum dicat Boethius quod affirmatio praecedit.

---

12 *cf.* Arist. *Top.* VI 3.140a33–b7   **26–27** Arist. *Cat.* 8a14–16   **27** Boeth. *in Cat.* 181b; *cf. etiam in Int.*² I 1 (ed. Meiser, 16); II 5 (ed. Meiser, 98–99)

---

2 assignata] si *add. P*   **6** se habere] *c* : sed habet *P*   **15** prius] primo *P*   **15–16** posuit definitionem] ponit definitionem vel posuit definitionem *P*

Et dicendum quod sub istis intentionibus, affirmatio et negatio, affirmatio, cum dicat habitum, praecedit, ut obicitur. Sed hic ordinantur penes has condiciones, universale et particulare, et quia negatio universalior, praeponitur. Vel alia est causa quia magis ei consentit auctor.

<3>

Consequenter quaeritur: Dicit quod quaedam substantiae secundae videntur dici   5
ad aliquid et non primae.

Contra. Sicut secundae dependent a primis, ita primae a secundis. Ergo qua ratione una dicitur ad aliquid, et alia. Vel quare non?

Et dicendum quod non est simile, quia scribitur in capitulo de substantia quod prima substantia non est in nec dicitur de, sed omnia alia dicuntur de ipsis aut sunt   10
in. Quare ergo, cum primae substantiae sint fundamentum aliorum, debet esse fixum et stabile, non dependens, scribitur in *Orthographia*. Propter hoc primae substantiae non dicuntur nec videntur esse ad aliquid, sed quia alia dicuntur de aut sunt in, magis participant naturam dependentiae.

Vel aliter. Dicit Priscianus quod propria nomina substantias et qualitates pri-   15
vatas significant, id est alicui appropriatas. Sed quod est uni appropriatum ab aliis non dependet. Sed nomen commune significat substantiam et qualitatem genera-lem. Quod autem est generale a pluribus participatur et sic a pluribus dependet. Quare dici ad aliquid secundis substantiis magis convenit quam primis.

Alia est causa quia singulare dependet ab universali quantum ad exitum in es-   20
se; unde scribitur in *Libro de vegetabilibus* quod universale dat esse singularibus et denominationem. Universale autem dependet a singularibus quantum ad esse con-tinuationis; universale enim in se non habet continuari sed in suis singularibus. Et sic singulare et universale adaequantur in hac dependentia. Sed praeter hoc uni-versale dupliciter dependet a singularibus. Primo quantum ad cognitionem, quia in   25
certitudine in universali non est status, dicitur in secundo *Topicorum*, sed est deve-nire in singulare ut reddatur certitudo. Secunda dependentia est quantum ad actum existendi, quia cum universale sit forma et esse formae est in alio, ideo universale habet esse in suo singulari. Ergo quia universale in duplici dependentia dependet a suo singulari, ideo secundae substantiae per hanc duplicem dependentiam potius   30
ponitur esse ad aliquid quam primae.

5–6 Arist. *Cat.* 7.8a25–29; 8a16–21   9–11 Arist. *Cat.* 5.2a12–14; 32–36   11–12 *cf.* Prisc. *Inst. gramm.* I 3.7 (ed. Hertz, vol. 1, 8)   15–16 Prisc. *Inst. gramm.* II 5.25 (ed. Hertz, vol. 1, 58) 21–22 *locum non inveni*   25–27 *locum non inveni*

---

3 est] de *P*   19 quare dici] praedici *P*   20 quia] quare *P*   22–23 esse continuationis] *an* continuationem in esse vel sim. scribendum?*

<4>

Consequenter quaeritur quare secundae substantiae quae sunt partes dicuntur ad
aliquid | et non quae sunt totae.   f. 54rb

   Videtur enim quod sicut hae sunt ad aliquid, ita illae, quia sicut pars dicitur ad
totum, ita totum ad partem. Ergo si secundae substantiae quae sunt partes dicuntur
5 ad aliquid, pari ratione et totae.

   Item. Posterius dependet a priori et non e converso. Cum ergo totum sit posterius partibus, totum dependet a partibus. Ergo propter huiusmodi dependentiam
magis debet totum esse ad aliquid quam partem.

   Et dicendum quod totum et perfectum idem, scribitur in *Physicis*. Sed perfec-
10 tum est quod nullo indiget. Quare totum in quantum tale nullo indiget, et ideo
non habet ad aliud dependentiam. Sed pars non habet esse completum nisi in toto. Propter hoc secundae substantiae quae sunt partes ponuntur ad aliquid et non
secundae quae sunt totum.

   Ad primum obiectum dicendum quod pars et totum possunt dupliciter consi-
15 derari, scilicet secundum id quod sunt vel secundum has intentiones, partialitas et
totalitas. Si secundo modo, unum dicitur ad aliud et e converso. Si primo, cum
totum habeat esse perfectum et completum, nullo indiget nec dependet a parte,
sed quia pars non habet esse completum nisi in toto, et incompletum secundum id
quod est dependet a completo, ideo pars secundum id quod est dicitur ad totum, et
20 propter hoc dicitur ad aliquid.

   Ad aliud dicendum quod in via essendi prius est pars quam totum, et sic procedit, sed in via completionis et nobilitatis prius est totum partibus.

<5>

Consequenter quaeritur quare potius ponit instantias in praedicamento substantiae
quam in aliis.
25 Et dicendum, ut dicit Philosophus, quod ducit ad impossibile, et manifestius
impossibile est quod substantia dicatur ad aliquid quam quantitas vel aliquid aliud
aliorum. Et hoc patet quia substantia maxime per se stans, relatio maxime dependens, sed alia, cum sint accidentia et accidentis esse est inesse, habent quodam
modo naturam dependentiae.

---

9 *cf.* Arist. *Phys.* III 6.207a13–14   **25** Arist. *Cat.* 7.8a28–31

---

16 si¹] sed *P*   **21** sic] non *P*   **26** aliquid aliud] aliud aliud *P*

<6>

Consequenter quaeritur: Dicit quod homo non dicitur alicuius homo.
 Hoc est contra usum loquendi solitum.
 Et dicendum quod homo sumitur improprie pro servo vel subdito.

<7>

Consequenter quaeritur: Dicit quod difficile est solvere aut impossibile etc.
 Contra. Dicit Boethius disiunctivas artis esse veras pro utraque parte. Sed hoc   5
non est huiusmodi, quia si est difficile et impossibile, et impossibile, quod falsum
est. Propter hoc quaeritur qualiter intelligitur.
 Et dicendum quod substantia dupliciter sumitur. Per se aut in respectu, sicut
quaedam prima, quaedam secunda. Si secundo modo, impossibile est solvere quod
nulla substantia dicatur ad aliquid secundum primam definitionem. Si per se con-   10
sideretur et probetur sic quod dicatur ad aliquid substantia: "In quantum accipitur
in respectu dicitur ad aliquid, ergo substantia dicitur ad aliquid", sic est fallacia accidentis, et sic erit difficile solvere, cum sit haec fallacia difficilis ad solvendum prout
scribitur in *Elenchis* quod per hanc scientes ab insciis arguuntur.

<8>

Ultimo quaeritur: Videtur quod definitio quam ponit sit male assignata sicut prima.   15
 Quia prima est inconveni|ens eo quod aliis a relativis convenit. Simile est de
ista. Probatio: Substantiae quae sunt partes non habent esse completum nisi in
toto. Ergo id quod sunt est ad aliud. Ergo definitio data convenit istis, et non sunt
relativa secundum esse.
 Et dicendum, cum dicit "esse relativorum etc.", hoc quod est "ad aliud" nominat   20
illud ad aliud quod est in genere relationis, sed licet id quod est pars substantiae sit
ad aliud, id tamen ad aliud non est relatio sed substantia, et ita aequivocatur ibi "ad
aliud".

f. 54va *(left margin, line 16)*

---

1   Arist. *Cat.* 7.8a22   **4**   Arist. *Cat.* 7.8a30   **5**   *locum non inveni*   **13–14**   Arist. *SE* 6.168b4–10

---

1 non] est *add. P*   **1** dicitur] *add. in marg. P*   **5** contra dicit] cum dicat *P*   **20** cum] ut *P*

Lectio XXX

\<Divisio\>

Posita definitione relativorum quae solum vere convenit relativis, sequitur pars in qua concludit correlarium incidens ex iam dictis.

Quae in tres dividitur. Primo ponit correlarium, secundo rediens supra dubitationem prius positam solvit ad ipsam, tertio de insufficientia se excusat. Secunda incipit: *Caput vero et manus* (7.8b15), tertia: *Fortasse autem difficile* (7.8b21).

Prima in duas. Primo ponit correlarium et ipsum probat, secundo ipsum probatum concludit, ut ibi: *Quapropter palam est* (7.8b13).

Prima in duas. Primo proponit, secundo propositum probat, ut ibi: *Palam itaque* (7.8a38).

Haec secunda in duas. Primo propositum probat per quandam rationem, secundo per exempla, ut ibi: *Sed in singulis* (7.8b4).

Prima in duas. Primo probat propositum per quandam rationem, secundo probat consequentiam a destructione consequentis, ibi: *Si enim non* (7.8b2).

Haec est divisio lectionis, et sunt particulae septem.

\<Sententia\>

Circa primam sic procedit, dicens quod si aliquis cognovit per definitionem aliquid eorum quae sunt ad aliquid, per definitionem scit illud ad quod dicitur.

Et probat sic: Nihil cuius esse est ad aliud se habere potest nosci definitione quin noscatur id ad quod dicitur. Sed unumquodque quod est ad aliquid est huiusmodi. Ergo etc.

Consequenter probat consequentiam a destructione consequentis, \<dicens\> quod si non novit illud ad quod dicitur, nec id quod dicitur ad ipsum; ergo si non novit hoc, nec illud.

Consequenter probat idem per exempla, dicens quod si aliquis novit per definitionem quid est duplum, et novit respectu cuius sit duplum. Et hoc probat a destructione consequentis sic: Si non novit respectu cuius sit duplum, nec novit quod duplum sit ad aliquid.

Consequenter concludit quod postquam ita est in his et in aliis etiam relativis, manifestum est quod si quis novit unum definite, et reliquum.

---

13 destructione] ant *add. P a.c.*   **17** esse] *iter. P*

Consequenter supra dubitationem redeundo prius positam solvit ad eam, dicens quod caput et manus potest sciri definite ignorato illo ad quod dicuntur, et propter hoc, quia definite potest sciri unum sine reliquo, non erunt haec ad aliquid. Ratio potest esse: Quaecumque sic se habent quod unum potest sciri definite sine altero non sunt ad aliquid. Caput, manus et similia sunt huiusmodi. Ergo etc. Ex hoc 5 concludit per locum a maiori ex consequenti: Ex quo ista de quibus magis videtur non sunt ad aliquid, ergo nulla substantia est ad aliquid.

Ultimo de insufficientia se excusat, dicens quod determinare sufficienter de his est difficile, et ideo labori studentium relinquatur; nam "dubitare de singulis etc."

f. 54vb   Haec est sententia partis. | 10

Expositio litteralis

Ita dictum est quae sunt ad aliquid, vero, id est sed, *manifestum est ex his*, id est quae sequuntur, quoniam *si quis*, id est aliquis, scit *definite*, id est per definitionem, *aliquid* horum etc., sciet *definite*, id est per definitionem, *illud ad quod dicitur*, id est ad quod per se refertur.

Itaque, id est ergo, *palam est*, quod dixi supple, *ex hoc* quod sequitur, quia *si* 15 *aliquis novit* quoddam quod *est ad aliquid*, *autem*, id est sed, *esse* eius erit *ad aliquid quodam modo se habere*, id est per se, *et novit illud ad quod se habet*, id est illud ad quod idem refertur, *aliquo modo*, id est per se.

Et probat hoc a destructione consequentis: Et vere sic est, *enim*, id est quia, *si non novit* illud *ad quod* dicitur *quodam modo*, id est ad quod idem per se refertur, 20 *neque*, pro non, novit qualiter *se habet ad* illud.

Consequenter idem probat per exempla: Non solum sic ostenditur quod dictum est, *sed palam est* etiam per exempla, *ut si quis* etc. Et probat consequentiam a destructione consequentis: Vere sic est, *enim*, id est quia, *si nihil*, pro non, *novit definite* ad quid *duplum sit*, id est illud respectu cuius dicitur duplum, *neque*, pro 25 non, *novit si est duplum* ad aliquid. Non solum sic est in istis, *autem*, id est sed, *similiter* etc.

Ex hoc concludit propositum: Ex quo ita est in istis et in aliis vere relativis, *quapropter*, id est ergo, *palam est* etc.

Ita est de vere relativis, *vero*, id est sed, *caput et manus* etc. *potest sciri definite*, 30 *autem*, id est sed, *non est necessarium scire ad quod* dicitur; *enim*, id est quia, *cuius hoc caput* etc. Ex hoc concludit: Ex quo bene potest sciri definite sine alio, *quare*,

---

9   Arist. *Cat.* 7.8b23–24

---

1 prius positam] propositum *P*   8 insufficientia] *syllabam* in *add. P s.l.*   23 consequentiam] consequentia *P*   24 si nihil pro non] nihil pro non si non *P*   31 cuius] *ac* : cum *P*

id est ergo, *non erunt haec ad aliquid*, vere supple, et *si* haec *non sunt relativorum,
verum erit dicere*, per locum a maiori, quod *nulla substantia* sit ad aliquid.

Ita dictum est de relativis, *autem*, id est sed, determinare *confidenter*, id est sufficienter, etc. *de huiusmodi rebus* etc. Vere sic est, *autem*, id est sed, *dubitare de
singulis non* est *inutile*, id est habere aequales ad utramque partem rationes, quia
qui sic dubitat est proprie videre verum, ut scribitur in *Elenchis*.

<Quaestiones>

<1>

Primo quaeritur: Dicit quod si quis definite novit unum correlativorum, et reliquum.

Contra. Scribitur in secundo *Topicorum* quod unum contingit solum intelligere,
plura autem scire. Ergo impossibile est simul intelligere duo relativa vel cognoscere.

Item. Impossibile est anima simul et in eodem tempore plura apprehendere vel
cognoscere. Et sic idem quod prius.

Et dicendum quod anima dupliciter apprehendit, scilicet primo et per se, et sic
non potest plura apprehendere, ut obicitur, secundo unum per se et aliud per accidens, et sic plura potest apprehendere. Quod patet, quia sicut relativa uno nomine significantur, ita per unum nomen apprehenduntur, quia sicut hoc nomen,
"pater", principaliter patrem significat, per consequens autem filium, eodem modo
apprehenduntur unum per se et aliud per accidens.

Vel aliter. Duo rerum genera distinguuntur absolute et respective. Unum solum
contingit intelligere, supple absolute, sed simul possunt plura intelligi respective.

<2>

Consequenter quaeritur quae est causa quod si unus definite novit unum relativo-
rum, et re|liquum.   f. 55ra

Et dicendum quod scribitur in sexto *Metaphysicae*: "Ab eodem res habet esse
et cognosci". Cum ergo unum relativorum non habet <esse> nisi in respectu ad
alterum, ut dicit auctor, ergo nec cognosci. Quia ergo definitio dicit esse, si quis
novit per definitionem unum, et reliquum.

6 *potius* Arist. *Top.* I 2.101a34–36   **7–8** Arist. *Cat.* 7.8a35–b12   **9–10** Arist. *Top.* II
10.114b34–35; Anon. *Auct. Arist.* 36.34 (ed. Hamesse, 324)   **23–24** *cf.* Arist. *Metaph.* II
1.993b30–31   **25** *cf.* Arist. *Cat.* 7.8a31–35

2 verum erit] *ac* : videtur enim *P*   **13** dupliciter] aliquid *P*   **24–25** ad alterum] aliquid *P*

<3>

Consequenter quaeritur utrum unum possit per alterum definiri.

Quod non videtur. Scribitur in sexto *Topicorum* quod contrarium non potest per suum contrarium definiri quia simul sunt natura. Sed ubi eadem causa, idem effectus. Cum ergo relativa sint simul natura, non potest unum per alterum definiri.

Item. Dicit Boethius: "Unumquodque definientium est in plus, totum autem in aeque" (et etiam Philosophus in secundo *Posteriorum*). Cum ergo unum relativorum non sit in plus quia dicuntur ad convertentiam, unum per alterum non poterit definiri.   5

Iuxta hoc quaeritur quare unum per alterum definitur.

Ad hoc ultimum dicendum quod definitio dicit esse, scribitur in sexto *Topicorum*. Cum ergo unum relativum non habeat esse nisi in respectu ad alterum, ergo nec unum nisi per alterum definitur.   10

Ad primum obiectum dicendum: Relativa dupliciter possunt sumi. Uno modo secundum suum esse, et sic sunt simul natura, ut obicitur, et unum per alterum nullatenus definitur. Aliter sumuntur per relationem ad proprietates quas acquirunt, et hoc modo, quia relativum definiens est finitum et finiens alterius dependentiam, et relativum quod definitur est infinitum, et finitum ante infinitum, ideo unum relativum definiens est alterum, et sic potest unum per alterum definiri.   15

Ad aliud. Quaedam est definitio data per formas praedicabiles, et datur per genus et differentias. Alia est data per formalem causam materiali coniunctam, et haec competit naturali, ut "Homo est quid compositum ex corpore tanquam ex materia et anima tanquam ex forma". Alia est per partes integrales, ut "Domus est quid compositum ex tecto, pariete etc." Alia est per actum vel per finem, prout scribitur in *Libro de anima*: "Potentiae definiuntur per actus", et sic definiuntur omnia nomina potentiarum ad actum significandum ordinata, ut "mortale" "aptum natum mori". Alia est terminans respectum, ut in relativis. Per hoc patet ad obiectum, quia cum obicitur, "Unumquodque definientium etc.", verum est de definitione data per formas praedicabiles, ut per genus et differentias, et non de aliis, et talis non competit relativis.   20

25

2-3 *cf.* Arist. *Top.* VI 4.142a23–25   **5-6** *locum non inveni*   **6** Arist. *APo* II 13.96a32–35, *potius ut apud* Robertus Grosseteste *in APo* II 4.112–14 (ed. Rossi, 369)   **10-11** Arist. *Top.* VI 3.140a33–b1   **23-24** *cf.* Arist. *An.* II 4.415a16–20; Anon. *Auct. Arist.* 6.56 (ed. Hamesse, 179)

---

16 relativum] relatio *P*   **25** significandum] significantia *P*

<4>

Consequenter quaeritur, habito quod possit per alterum definiri, utrum sit e converso.

Quod non videtur. Scribitur in *Libro de articulis fidei*: "Nihil est causa sui ipsius", "Nihil est prius et posterius se ipso", "Nihil est notius se ipso". A qualibet
5 istarum sumi potest argumentum. A prima sic: Si pater definitur per filium, cum definiens sit causa definiti, filius erit causa patris, et si filius per patrem, pater erit causa filii. Ergo a primo, cum quicquid est causa causae est causa causati, pater erit causa patris, et sic idem sui ipsius causa, quod est impossibile. Similiter ab aliis propositionibus sumi potest argumentum.

10 Item. "Inconveniens est circulo demonstrare", scribitur in *Libro posteriorum*. Ergo similiter et definire. Sed si definitur unum per alterum et e converso, | erit   f. 55rb definitio circularis.

Et dicendum quod paternitas duos habet respectus. Unum ad substantiam in quo est, et sic magis notum, alium ad terminum, scilicet ad filium, et sic minus
15 notum. Similiter est de aliis formis correlativis. Dicendum ergo quod definitum semper sumitur prout forma ad terminum comparatur, et sic minus notum, sed definiens sumitur prout forma ad subiectum comparatur, et sic magis notum; et ita minus notum semper per magis notum definitur.

Per hoc patet ad obiecta, quia non sequitur idem esse causam sui nec quod sit
20 definitio circularis. Quia licet pater secundum sui substantiam idem sit cum definitur et est definiens, tamen differt quantum ad proprietates, quia prout definitur est minus notum et infinitum, finibile tamen, secundum autem quod est definiens est magis notum et finitum alterius dependentiam finiendo. Unde patet quod non valet argumentum, quia medium variatur in comparatione ad extrema. Nam cum
25 dicitur "pater definitur per filium", li "pater" sumitur in quantum minus notum et infinitum, tamen finibile per adiunctum, sed cum dicitur "pater definit filium", li "pater" sumitur prout est finitum et magis notum, alterum, filium scilicet, finiens, et non sumitur sicut prius; et sic medium variatur.

Per hoc patet ad alia, quia non est inconveniens idem esse prius et posterius,
30 notum et ignotius, diversimode acceptum.

3–4 Nicolaus Ambianensis *Ars fidei catholicae* I, prop. 8 (ed. Dreyer, 81) **4** Nicolaus Ambianensis *Ars fidei catholicae* I (ed. Dreyer, 79) **4** *locum non inveni* **10** *cf.* Arist. *APo* I 3.72b25–73a6; Anon. *Auct. Arist.* 35.33 (ed. Hamesse, 313); Robertus Grosseteste *in APo* I 3 (ed. Rossi, 105)

---

7 quicquid] aliquod *P* **26** tamen] et non *P*

<5>

Ultimo quaeritur: Dicit quod dubitare de singulis etc.

Contra. Scribitur in secundo *Topicorum*: "Si oppositum in opposito, et propositum in proposito". Cum ergo singula scire sit utile, dubitare de singulis est
inutile.

Et dicendum quod duplex est ignorantia, scribitur in primo *Posteriorum*. Quae-   5
dam est simplex, ut illa quae causatur extra per defectum rationis, et haec est in
rusticis qui solum asserunt bipedalem non assignantes aliquam rationem. Alia est
composita, ut illa quae causatur ex conflictu rationum concurrentium, et hanc appellat Aristoteles deceptionem factam per syllogismum. A simili in proposito duplex est dubitatio. Quaedam est simplex et est per defectum rationis, et talis oppo-   10
nitur huic quod est scire et est mala, ut obicitur, et de tali hic non intendit. Alia est
composita et per conflictum rationum ad utramque partem concurrentium, et talis
est via in scientiam et non opponitur scire, et de tali hic intendit; et hoc est quod in
Elenchis scribitur, quod qui dubitat est proprie videre verum.

---

1 Arist. *Cat.* 7.8b23–24   **2–3** *potius* Arist. *Top.* IV 3.124a9; Anon. *Auct. Arist.* 36.60 (ed.
Hamesse, 326)   **5**   Arist. *APo* I 16.79b23–24, *ut apud* Anon. *Auct. Arist.* 35.69 (ed. Hamesse, 317)
8–9   Arist. *APo* I 16.79b23–25   **13–14**   *potius* Arist. *Top.* I 2.101a34–36

---

2 et] a *P*   **3** sit] sic *P*   **6** rationis] ratione *P*

Lectio XXXI

Qualitatem autem dico etc. (8.8b25)

\<Divisio\>

Prosecuto de aliis quibusdam praedicamentis, prosequitur de qualitate.

Et haec pars in duas. Primo determinat de qualitate penes substantialia, secundo \<penes accidentalia, ibi: *Inest autem contrarietas* etc. (8.10b12).

Prima in duas. Primo determinat de qualitate, secundo\> de his quae ab ipsa denominantur, ut ibi: *Qualia vero* (8.10a27).

Prima in duas. Primo determinat de qualitate definitive, secundo divisive, ut ibi: *Est autem qualitas* (8.8b26).

Haec secunda in duas. Primo ponit quod intendit, secundo propositum manifestat, ut ibi: *Una quidem species* (8.8b27).

Haec secunda in quattuor penes quattuor species qualitatis. | Secunda ibi: *Aliud vero genus qualitatis* (8.9a14), tertia ibi: *Tertia vero species* (8.9a28), quarta ibi: *Quartum vero genus* (8.10a11).

Prima cum duabus praecedentibus praesentis est lectionis. Et dividitur in duas. Primo proponit quod intendit, secundo prosequitur, ut ibi: *Differt autem habitus a dispositione* (8.8b28).

Haec secunda in duas. Primo comparat habitum ad dispositionem sub differentia, secundo sub convenientia, ibi: *Sunt autem habitus* (8.9a10).

Prima in duas. Primo proponit differentiam et ipsam manifestat, secundo concludit propositum, ibi: \<*Quare differt habitus* (8.9a8).

Prima in duas. Primo proponit differentiam, secundo ipsam manifestat, ibi:\> *Tales vero sunt scientiae* (8.8b30).

Haec secunda in duas. Primo \<ponit exempla de habitu, secundo dicit quid est dispositio, ibi: *Affectiones vero* etc. (8.8b35).

Haec secunda in duas. Primo\> manifestat per exempla quid est dispositio, secundo reddit causam quare dicantur dispositiones, ibi: *Afficitur enim* (8.8b36).

Haec secunda in duas. Primo \<facit quod dictum est, secundo removet dubium, ibi: *Nisi forte* etc. (8.9a1).

Haec secunda in duas. Primo\> removet dubium, secundo reddit causam cuiusdam dicti, ut ibi: *Manifestum est autem* (8.9a4).

Haec est divisio lectionis.

---

9 quidem] est *add. P*   **21** scientiae] sci + *fere duas litteras in ras. P*

f. 55va

\<Sententia\>

Circa primam partem sic procedit: Illae res dicuntur qualitates a quibus denominamur quales.

Consequenter prosequitur, proponens quod qualitas dicitur multipliciter.

Et ponit unam speciem, dicens quod una species est habitus et dispositio.

Consequenter dicit quod differt quia habitus est permanentior et diuturnior   5
quam sit dispositio.

Consequenter ponit exempla de habitu, dicens: Scientiae et virtutes sunt habitus. Et reddit causam: Quia scientia habet permanentiam in subiecto et de difficili ab ipso separatur. Ratio sic potest extrahi: Omnis qualitas habens permanentiam in subiecto et \<quae\> difficile ab ipso separatur est habitus. Scientia et   10
virtus sunt huiusmodi. Ergo etc. Et quia dixit "separabile de difficili", posset credi
quod a subiecto non posset separari. Ideo dicit quod si fiat grandis permutatio circa
subiectum, ut ab aegritudine, potest scientia removeri.

Consequenter dicit quod est dispositio, dicens quod qualitas quae facile separatur a subiecto dispositio nominatur, ut calor accidentalis et frigiditas et huiusmodi.   15

Consequenter reddit causam quare huiusmodi dicantur dispositiones, dicens
quod subiectum existens sub aliquo istorum cito ad aliud permutatur, ut ex calido
fit frigidus etc.

Consequenter removet dubium. Quia dixit simpliciter quod quaedam aegritudo est dispositio, et non dixit quod aliqua sit habitus, ideo ostendit quod aliqua   20
quandoque fit habitus quamquam primo fuerit dispositio; et hoc est per moram
temporis.

Consequenter reddit causam quare haec dicuntur habitus, dicens: Quia haec
sunt diuturna et difficile mobilia, habitus nominantur. Quod probat per oppositum:
Quia illa quae parvo tempore durant non sunt habitus cum sint facile mobilia, ergo   25
per oppositum reliqua quae sunt de difficili mobilia sunt habitus.

Consequenter concludit propositum: Ex quo habitus est de difficili mobilis et
dispositio facile, ergo differt habitus a dispositione.

Ultimo comparat sub convenientia, dicens quod habitus sunt dispositiones et
non e converso. Et hoc exemplificat.   30

f. 55vb   Haec est sententia partis. |

Expositio litteralis

Dico illam rem esse *qualitatem secundum quam dicimur*, id est denominamur,
quales.

---

1 qualitates] qual + *fere tres litteras in ras.* P

Ita dixi quod est qualitas, sed *qualitas est eorum quae multipliciter dicuntur*, id est habent diversa nomina sub eadem specie, ut *habitus* et *dispositio dicitur una species qualitatis*.

Autem, id est sed, *habitus differt a dispositione*, quia, habitus supple, *est permanentior* quantum ad difficultatem separationis *et diuturnior* quantum ad moram temporis.

Vere habitus diuturnior, *vero*, id est sed, *scientiae* et *virtutes sunt tales*, id est habitus, nam, id est quia, *scientia videtur esse permanentium et eorum quae moventur difficile* (et dicit "videtur" quia non quaelibet scientia est habitus sed exercitio confirmata), *ut si quis sumat scientiam vel*, pro etiam, *mediocriter*, illa, supple, scientia est ei habitus et non ab ipso separabilis, *nisi* fiat circa ipsum *grandis permutatio* etc. Non solum sic est in istis, *autem*, id est sed, *similiter virtus* etc., <quae> est habitus supple, *posse moveri* etc., de facili supple.

Ita dixi quid est habitus, *vero*, id est sed, illae qualitates *dicuntur affectiones*, id est dispositiones, *quae sunt faciles*, id est quae facile separantur, *et cito permutabiles, ut calor* etc. Et loquitur hic de calore accidentali ab extrinseco causato, ut ab aeris intemperie vel aliquo huiusmodi, et non de naturali.

Vere sunt dispositiones, *enim*, <id est> quia, *homo afficitur circa eas quodam modo*, id est aliquo tempore et non diu. Et non solum ita est de istis, sed *similiter in aliis*, ut aegritudo et similia sunt dispositiones et cito transmutantur.

Nisi forte in his, supple dispositionibus, in quibus *contingit transferri*, id est converti, *per longitudinem temporis in naturam cuiusque*, <id est> in habitum ut iam naturalia videantur, *ut affectus existat insanabilis* et *difficile mobilis, quem quilibet vocet*, supple propter temporis longitudinem, *habitudinem*, id est habitum, nam est ista conversa in habitum.

Autem, id est quia, *manifestum est quoniam haec volunt nominari habitudines*, id est habitus, *quae sunt* etc. Bene dico quod sic, *nam*, id est quia, *in disciplinis non multum retinentes*, id est illi qui parum retinent, *non dicuntur habere habitus*, quia facile mobiles eorum scientiae sunt, supple, *quamvis* etc.

Ex quo habitus est difficile mobilis et dispositio facile, *quare*, id est ergo, *habitus* etc. *quod*, id est quia, *hoc*, id est dispositio, *facile* etc.

Ultimo ponit convenientiam: Ita dictum est quod differunt, *autem*, id est sed, *habitus sunt dispositiones*, id est habitus praecedit dispositionem, *enim*, id est quia, *qui retinent habitum* etc.

---

8 scientia videtur] *ac* : scientiae videntur *P* (videtur *autem habet mox infra*)   **9** quia] quod *P*
9 exercitio] *ex* excitatio *corr. P*   **22** naturam] natura enim *P a.c.*   **26** autem] *P^{sup} ac* : quod *P ut v.*   **31** est²] quia *add. P a.c.*

<Quaestiones>

<1>

Primo quaeritur de ordine ad partem subsequentem. Quando et ubi causantur
a quantitate. Sed quantitas praecedit qualitatem. Ergo et haec deberent ipsam
praecedere.

Et dicendum quod ordinantur ista genera secundum quod universalius vel minus universaliter substantiam consequuntur. Sed ubi solum consequitur substan-   5
tiam cor|poream (nam soli corpori debetur locus, dicit auctor *Sex principiorum*),
sed quando ipsum tempus vel ipsas res a tempore mensuratas. Sed qualitas sequitur omnem substantiam corpoream et quandam incorpoream, animam scilicet, et
ita cum universalius substantiam consequatur, quando et ubi praeponitur.

<2>

Consequenter quaeritur quare dixit "qualitatem dico" et non "dicitur".   10

Et dicendum quod dixit "dico" ut denotet quod prosequitur de ipsa secundum
opinionem propriam. Nam si dixisset "dicitur", videretur quod prosequeretur de
ipsa secundum opinionem aliorum, sicut fecerat de ad aliquid. Unde ne animus
auditoris maneat in suspenso, credens Aristotelem aliam definitionem ponere, dixit
"dico".   15

<3>

Tertio quaeritur quare ipsam definit per relationem ad nos, dicens "dicimur".

Et videtur quod male, quia dicit Boethius quod definitio omni debet convenire
et soli. Sed non secundum quamlibet qualitatem dicimur quales, sicut secundum
qualitatem lapidis. Est ergo inconveniens, ut videtur.

Et dicendum, sicut dicut Augustinus, quod homo quodam modo est omnia,   20
nam cum omnibus participat: cum inanimatis in essendo, cum plantis in vege-
tando, cum brutis in movendo, cum angelis in intelligendo; et sic homo quodam
modo omnes participat qualitates, ad quod designandum dixit "dicimur".

---

6 *cf.* Anon. *LSP* V 54 (ed. Minio-Paluello, 47); Anon. *Auct. Arist.* 33.20 (ed. Hamesse, 307)   **10**
Arist. *Cat.* 8.8b25   **16**   Arist. *Cat.* 8.8b25–26   **17–18**   *cf.* Boeth. *in Cat.* 165a–d   **20–22**   *cf.*
Ps.-Aug. *De spiritu et anima* 6 (PL 40, 783)

---

10 et non] *iter. P*   **12** dixisset] videtur quod non *add. P*   **18** quamlibet] sui *add. P*   **21** plantis]
brutis *P*   **22** brutis] plantis *P*   **22** movendo] vivendo *P*

Item. Dicit Philosophus quod sumus quodam modo finis omnium; unde omnia propter hominem. Sicut ergo ad hominem quodam modo ordinantur, sic omnes aliae qualitates ad qualitatem rationalis substantiae ordinantur; ideo dicit "dicimur".

Ad obiectum dicendum quod secundum quamlibet qualitatis speciem dicimur quales, sed non secundum numerum, ut obicitur.

<4>

Consequenter quaeritur: Et videtur definitio inconveniens.

Scribitur in sexto *Topicorum* quod definitiones fiunt causa innotescendi vel faciendi notum. Sed omnis cognitio per priora. Ergo et definitio. Sed qualitas in se accepta definitur hic per qualitatem substantiae unitam. Ergo haec definitio data est per posterius, et ita inconveniens.

Et dicendum quod haec non est definitio sed potius descriptio.

Ad obiectum dicendum: Scribitur in primo *Physicorum* quod prius dicitur quo ad nos et quo ad naturam. Unde definitio proprie loquendo datur per priora simpliciter, ut obicitur, sed descriptio per priora quo ad nos. Et sic est hic, quia secundum naturam prius qualitas per se accepta quam substantiae unita, sed secundum nostram cognitionem est penitus e converso.

<5>

Consequenter quaeritur: Dicit "Qualitas dicitur multipliciter".

Contra. Omne genus praedicatur univoce et non multipliciter, dicit Porphyrius. Cum ergo qualitas sit genus, non dicetur multipliciter.

Et dicendum quod duplex est multipliciter. Quoddam ratione significatorum, et tale est aequivocum et non potest definiri. Aliter dicitur multiplex ratione suarum specierum vel partium, et tale non impedit definitionem. Unde qualitas dicitur multipliciter non multiplicitate significationis, sed quia multas habet species.

Sed haec solutio conveniens non videtur, | quia eadem ratione quantitas, cum   f. 56rb
multas species habeat, multipliciter diceretur. Dicendum ergo aliter quod qualitas dicitur multipliciter non multiplicitate significationis, sed quia quaelibet eius species duplici nomine nominatur.

---

1 Arist. *Phys.* II 2.194a34–35; Anon. *Auct. Arist.* 2.63 (ed. Hamesse, 145) **7–8** Arist. *Top.* VI 1.139b14–15 **12–13** *cf.* Arist. *Phys.* I 1.184a16–24 **17** Arist. *Cat.* 8.8b26–27 **18** *cf.* Porph. *Isag.* 6.8–12

---

5 quales] *ex* qualitas *corr.* P   **21** ratione] ratio P

<6>

Consequenter quaeritur: Dicit quod habitus et dispositio sunt una species qualitatis, sed habitus est difficile mobilis, dispositio facile.

Sed facile mobile et difficile sunt opposita. Ergo habitus et dispositio unam speciem non constituunt.

Et dicendum quod habitus et dispositio super eandem essentiam radicantur et respectu eiusdem subiecti. Quod patet, nam si facis elemosinam semel vel bis, ex his operationibus causatur in te virtus secundum dispositionem, et per frequentiam earundem operationum quod fuit dispositio in habitum convertetur. Unde si operationes multiplicatae sunt bonae, et habitus derelictus bonus, et si malae, malus. Et hoc est quod scribitur in primo *Ethicae veteris* quod quales sunt operationes, tales sunt habitus ex operationibus derelicti in anima. Patet ergo quod habitus et dispositio super eandem essentiam radicantur et respectu eiusdem subiecti; et propter hoc possunt esse una species qualitatis.

Ad obiectum dicendum quod facile mobile et difficile solum differunt penes modos accidentales, et talis diversitas non impedit identitatem in specie.

<7>

Ultimo quaeritur: Dicit quod omnis habitus dispositio.

Contra. Habitus est difficile mobilis et dispositio facile. Si ergo habitus est dispositio, difficile mobile erit facile mobile.

Propter hoc quaeritur quo modo habitus potest esse dispositio et non e converso.

Et dicendum quod qualitas habet esse in subiecto. Aut ergo complete aut incomplete (et dico "complete" quia non habet fluxibilitatem ad terminum, id est non potest recipere magis et minus, ut patet in albissimo, et dico "incomplete" ita quod fluxibilitatem habeat ad terminum, ut patet in albo). Primo modo habitus nominat qualitatem, scilicet in subiecto existentem et non habentem ad terminum fluxibilitatem, sed dispositio dicit qualitatem in subiecto existentem et habentem fluxibilitatem ad terminum. Ex hoc patet quod quicquid habet dispositio, habet habitus, et non e converso, quia utrumque dicit qualitatem in subiecto existentem, sed habitus superaddit terminum terminantem fluxibilitatem illius qualitatis, et propter hoc est quod omnis habitus est dispositio, sed non convertitur (sicut hic: "Quicquid habet homo, habet animal"), ut dictum est litteram exponendo.

1–2 Arist. *Cat.* 8.8b26–28   9–11 *cf.* Arist. *EN* II 1.1103b21–22; Anon. *Auct. Arist.* 12.26 (ed. Hamesse, 234)   16 Arist. *Cat.* 8.9a11–13

---

7 frequentiam] quod *add. P a.c.*   31 animal] sed non convertitur ut dicatur *add. P*

<8>

Sed quaeritur qualiter habitus est species qualitatis et praedicamentum et postpraedicamentum et ad aliquid.

Hoc autem in tractatu relativorum pro meo modulo exquisitum.

---

3 *cf.* Lectio XXIV, Q9

Lectio XXXII

Aliud vero genus qualitatis (8.9a14)

\<Divisio\>

Notificata prima specie, prosequitur de secunda.

Haec pars in duas. Primo proponit, | dicens quae sunt in secunda specie,   f. 56va
secundo prosequitur propositum, ibi: *Non enim quoniam sunt dispositi* (8.9a16).

Haec secunda in duas. Primo manifestat propositum per exempla animatis
5   competentia, secundo per exempla quae competunt inanimatis, ut ibi: *Similiter
autem his* (8.9a25).

Et haec est divisio lectionis, et sunt tres particulae.

\<Sententia\>

Circa primam sic procedit, dicens quod secunda species qualitatis est potentia vel
impotentia naturalis.

10   Consequenter prosequitur, dicens quod illi qui denominantur a potentiis naturalibus non dicuntur tales quia sunt dispositi sed quia habent naturalem potentiam
vel impotentiam hoc facere vel pati; similiter est de sanatione et aegrotatione.

Ultimo ponit alia genera exemplorum, dicens quod aliquid molle dicitur quia
habet naturalem potentiam ut non possit resistere secationi; et est durum, ut scribi-
15   tur in quarto *Meteorum*, quod de difficili cedit impressioni, molle vero quod cedit de
facili non circumfluendo (et dicit "non circumfluendo" propter aquam et huiusmodi
alia umida).

Haec est sententia partis.

Expositio litteralis

Dictum est de prima specie, *vero*, pro sed, secundum *genus qualitatis est* etc., *sim-
20   pliciter*, id est universaliter, *quaecumque dicuntur*, id est denominantur, *secundum
potentiam* etc. Quasi dicens: Omnis naturalis potentia vel impotentia est res huius
generis.

Ut cursor etc. sunt huiusmodi, *autem*, id est sed, cursor et pugilator *non* dicuntur *huiusmodi quoniam sunt dispositi* etc. *sed quod*, id est quia, unumquodque ha-
25   bet *naturalem potentiam* etc. Non solum sic est de istis, *autem*, id est sed, *sanativi*

14–16   Arist. *Met.* IV 4.382a11–13

---

8 est] *add. P s.l.*   13 quia] quod *P*

etc. *ut nihil patiantur* etc., id est de facili non laedantur, *a quibuslibet accidentibus*, extrinsecus supple, ut ab aere corrupto et huiusmodi, sed *aegrotativi dicuntur* qui habent naturalem *impotentiam nihil patiendi*, quin laedantur supple.

Non solum sic est de istis, *autem*, id est sed, *similiter his*, id est sicut est in his, *durum, molle* etc. Vere sic est, *enim*, id est quia, *durum dicitur quod habet* etc., 5 sed *molle* dicitur *quod*, id est quia, habet *impotentiam eiusdem*, quia non potest resistere sectioni.

<QUAESTIONES>

<1>

Primo quaeritur quare nominat nomine duplici species qualitatis cum sic non nominaverit species aliorum.

Et dicendum quod contrarietas est proprie in qualitate, unde si in aliis inveni- 10 tur, hoc est per naturam qualitatis, ut ignis contrariatur aquae quia calidus et aqua frigida. Illud autem quod habet contrarium prius habet esse incompletum quam completum, ut cum ignis agit in aquam non potest subito imprimere formam suam propter resistentiam contrarii. Unde Galenus: "Omne repentinum naturae inimi-cum"; non enim repentinas patitur mutationes. Ut ergo illud duplex esse denotetur, 15 duplici nomine nominatur. Quod patet per exempla: Prima species est habitus et dispositio, et habitus dicit esse completum et dispositio dicit esse incompletum.

<2>

Consequenter quaeritur quare primam et tertiam nominet nomine speciei, secun-dam vero et quartam nomine generis.

Et dicendum quod magis conveniunt quae in specie et in genere conveniunt 20 quam quae in genere tantum. Quia ergo magis conveniunt quae in prima et tertia sunt specie quam quae in aliis, ideo primam et tertiam nomine speciei, secundam vero et quartam nomine generis nuncupavit. Quod ita sit patet: Dispositio via est in habitum quia ex operationis frequentia in habitum convertetur, similiter est de passione et passibili qualitate, sed naturalis potentia vel impotentia non sic se habet 25 nec forma vel figura, quia unum | non est via ad alterum nec potest unum ab altero generari.

f. 56vb

14–15   *cf. potius* Hippocrates, *Aphorismi* II 51 (ed. Venet., 12)

---

12 prius] primo *P*   **13** aquam] aqua *P*   **14** galenus] g. *P*   **18** tertiam] secundam *P*   **18–19** secundam] tertiam *P*   **21** tertia] secunda *P*   **22** tertiam] secundam *P*   **22** secundam] tertiam *P*   **26** via] in via *P ut v.*

\<3\>

Consequenter quaeritur quare quaedam species coniunguntur per coniunctionem copulativam, quaedam vero per disiunctivam.

Et dicendum quod copulativa coniunctio, dicit Priscianus, inter ea ponitur quae possunt esse simul, sed disiunctiva inter ea quae nullo modo possunt esse simul.

5   Idem dicit Boethius per hoc: "Sapit coniunctio disiunctiva etc." Patet ergo quod magis conveniunt quae copulantur per coniunctionem coniunctivam quam quae per disiunctivam. Quia ergo prima et tertia species plus conveniunt, ut visum est, ut signum significato correspondeat, coniunctione copulativa connectuntur vel copulantur, alia vero disiunctiva.

\<4\>

10 Consequenter quaeritur: Videtur quod naturalis potentia vel impotentia non faciant unam speciem.

Nam opposita non possunt constituere unam speciem. Haec sunt huiusmodi. Ergo etc. Minor patet. Scribitur in quarto *Meteorum*: "Contrariarum causarum contrarii sunt effectus". Sed naturalis potentia causatur a bona complexione, scilicet

15 ab umorum adaequatione, naturalis impotentia a mala, scilicet ab umorum inadaequatione, ut scribitur in secundo *Topicorum*. Sed adaequatio vel inadaequatio sunt contraria.

Et dicendum quod in quantum sunt opposita non constituunt unam speciem, ut obicitur, sed in quantum unum est incompletum respectu alterius et alterum com-

20 pletum, et in quolibet genere incompletum reducitur ad completum, sic poterant constituere unam speciem prout unum ad alterum reducetur.

\<5\>

Consequenter quaeritur: Dicit quod naturalis potentia est qualitas.

Contra. Dicit Commentator supra primum *Physicorum* quod omnis perfectio nobilior est perfectibili. Sed nullum accidens nobilius substantia, dicit Commenta-

---

3–4   *cf.* Prisc. *Inst. gramm.* XVI 1.1–2; 7–8 (ed. Hertz, vol. 2, 93–94; 97–98)   5   Boeth. *Hyp. syll.* III 11.7 (= 876c) (ed. Obertello, 388)   13–14   Arist. *Met.* IV 7.384b2–3; *Gen.* II 10.336a30–31; Anon. *Auct. Arist.* 5.20 (ed. Hamesse, 173)   14–16   *locum non inveni*   22   *cf.* Arist. *Cat.* 8.9a14–27   23–24   *cf.* Averroes *in Phys.* II 4 (ed. Venet., 50ra)   189.24–190.1   Averroes *in An.* II 2.16–20 (ed. Crawford, 130); Anon. *Auct. Arist.* 6.113 (ed. Hamesse, 183)

---

6 coniunctivam] *add.*   *P in marg.*   15–16 inadaequatione] *syllabam* ad *add.*   *P s.l.* 19 incompletum] incomplexum *P*   20 poterant] poterat *P*

tor supra *Librum de anima*. Ergo nullum accidens est perfectio substantiae. Cum
ergo differentiae substantiae, sicut rationale, a naturali potentia oriantur, naturalis
potentia non erit accidens. Ergo substantia. Male igitur species ponitur qualitatis.

Et dicendum quod duplex est naturalis potentia. Quaedam est in esse constituens et producens, et a tali potentia substantiae differentiae oriuntur, et talis   5
substantia est. Alia est quae consequitur rem in esse constitutam, sicut pugnan-
di potentia naturalis vel aliquid huiusmodi, et quia omne illud quod advenit alicui
post eius esse completum est accidens, ut dicit Philosophus, naturalis potentia ad
accidens reducetur, et sic est species qualitatis.

<6>

Ultimo quaeritur de hoc quod per actum potentiam monstrat cum dicit: "Naturalis   10
potentia vel impotentia est etc." (Cursores enim et huiusmodi dicunt actum).

Nam omnis manifestatio per priora. Sed actus posterior. Igitur inconveniens.
Minor patet: Omne quod elicitur ab alio est posterius ipso. Actus elicitur a potentia,
dicit Philosophus. Ergo actus posterior.

Item. Via naturaliter prior est quam finis ad quem est. Sed dicit Commentator   15
super undecimum *Metaphysicae*: "Actus est finis ad quem est", id est potentia. Ergo
prior erit potentia sicut via.

Et dicendum quod prius dicitur dupliciter, scribitur in *Physicis*. Secundum naturam et quo ad nos. Licet ergo secundum naturam, sicut probant argumenta, potentia ante actum, tamen secundum viam cognoscendi actus prioritatis possidet   20
principatum; et sic potentia per actum potest manifestari.

7–8 *locum non inveni*   **10–11** *cf.* Arist. *Cat.* 8.9a14–27   **13–14** *locum non inveni*   **15–16**
cf. Averroes *in Metaph.* IX 15 (ed. Venet., 241rb)   **18–19** *cf.* Arist. *Phys.* I 1.184a16–24

---

5 et talis] et aliis *P ut v.*   **8** post eius esse] *lectio incerta*

Lectio XXXIII

Tertia vero species qualitatis etc. (8.9a28)

\<Divisio\>

Hic prosequitur de tertia specie qualitatis.

Haec pars in duas. Primo ponit ipsam, secundo per exempla explanat, ibi: *Sunt autem huiusmodi* (8.9a30).

Haec secunda in duas. Primo explanat | per exempla, secundo probat exempla   f. 57ra
esse competentia, ibi: *Et quoniam hae* etc. (8.9a31).

Haec secunda in duas. Primo probat quod sunt qualitates, secundo quod tales
sunt passibiles, ibi: *Passibiles vero* (8.9a36).

Haec secunda in duas. Primo facit quod dictum est, secundo innuit differentiam
inter passibiles qualitates, ut ibi: *Albedo enim et nigredo* (8.9b10).

Prima in duas. Primo exstirpando vitia removet falsitatem, secundo virtutes
inserendo explicat veritatem, ibi: *Sed quoniam eorum* (8.9b5).

Pars in qua innuit differentiam in duas. Primo differentiam ponit, secundo
quoddam suppositum manifestat, ibi: *Quoniam ergo* (8.9b12).

Haec est divisio lectionis, et sunt particulae sex.

\<Sententia\>

Circa primam partem sic procedit: Tertia species qualitatis est passio et passibilis
qualitas.

Et ponit exempla: ut dulcedo, amaritudo etc.

Consequenter probat quod sunt qualitates sic: Omnia illa secundum quae se
suscipientia dicuntur qualia sunt qualitates. Haec sunt huiusmodi. Ergo etc. Minorem ponit et exemplificat.

Consequenter probat quod sunt passibiles. Et primo removet falsitatem, dicens quod non dicuntur passibiles qualitates quia eorum subiecta per ipsas aliquid
patiantur, ut ostendit per exempla.

Consequenter inserit virtutes ponendo veritatem, dicens quod dicuntur passibiles quia inferunt sensui passionem; quod in littera manifestat.

Ultimo ponit differentiam, dicens quod albedo et alii colores non dicuntur
qualitates quia sensui inferant passionem sicut supradicta, sed quia a quibusdam
passionibus inferantur.

Haec est sententia partis.

---

5 esse] *add. P s.l.*   **13** quoddam] *ex quiddam corr. P*   **16** qualitas] *ex qualitatis corr. P*

Expositio litteralis

Non solum sunt qualitates species supradictae, *vero*, id est sed, *tertia species* etc.

Vere sic est in istis, *autem*, id est sed, *dulcedo et amaritudo* etc. *sunt huiusmodi*; ergo etc.

Bene dico quod sic, *quoniam hae qualitates manifestum est*; *enim*, id est quia, *quaecumque*, id est subiecta, *ista*, id est supradicta, *<susceperint> dicuntur qualia*   5 etc., et non sunt qualitates.

Vero, pro sed, *dicuntur passibiles qualitates non* propterea quod illa quae ipsa suscipiunt, id est subiecta eorum, *aliquid patiantur*; nam, id est quia, *mel neque*, pro non, *dicitur dulce* eo quod *aliquid sit passum*, a dulcedine supple. Quasi dicens: Non infert dulcedo melli passionem.   10

Sed singulum eorum quae dicta sunt dicuntur passibiles qualitates quoniam, id est quia, *sunt perfectiva secundum* qualitates, id est diversitates, sensuum. Continua. Vere sic est, nam, id est quia, *dulcedo efficit passionem* gustui.

Ultimo ponit differentiam: Ita dictum est de illis, vero, id est sed, *albedo, nigredo et alii colores non dicuntur passibiles qualitates similiter his quae dicta <sunt>*, id   15 est sicut praedicta inferunt passiones, *sed* propter *hoc*, resume dicuntur passibiles qualitates, *quod*, id est quia, *ab aliquibus passionibus innascuntur*, id est inferuntur.

<Quaestiones>

<1>

Primo quaeritur an differat passio prout hic sumitur et prout est genus distinctum contra alia.

Quod non videtur, quia passio prout genus infertur a principio extra, scilicet ab   20 actione agentis, dicit auctor *Sex principiorum*. Similiter prout hic sumitur causatur a principio extra, scilicet ab obiecto.

Et dicendum quod differunt. Nam passio sumitur dupliciter. Uno modo idem est quod ens derelictum immediate ex actione agentis dum ipse agens est in motu, et sic est unum praedicamentum, ut patet per eius definitionem. Aliter sumitur prout   25 est in quiete in subiecto existens. Quod potest exemplariter exemplari: Si aliquis f. 57rb   ad ignem se calefaceret, calor receptus immediate ab igne | est passio quae est praedicamentum, sed si ab igne recedat, calor in quiete existens est species qualitatis.

20–21   *cf.* Anon. *LSP* III 29 (ed. Minio-Paluello, 41); Anon. *Auct. Arist.* 33.11 (ed. Hamesse, 307)

---

4 id est quia] quoniam *P*   **11** quoniam] *lectio incerta*   **12** sensuum] nam gustus quandam infert passionem sensui quandam aliis sensibus *add. P*   **17** qualitates] qua *P*   **20** videtur] quod *add. P*   **25** unum] *lectio incerta*   **28** existens est] *inv. P*

Alia est differentia, nam passio sumitur hic prout est via in passibilem qualitatem; nam per continuationem obiecti passio fit passibilis qualitas.

Ad obiectum dicendum quod, sicut obicitur, conveniunt in hoc quod utrumque infertur a principio extra, unde idem nomen ratione huius convenientiae sortiuntur, sed ratione dictarum differentiarum unum ab altero sumitur separatum.

<2>

Consequenter quaeritur quare dicat "passibiles" in plurali.

Et dicendum quod duplex est causa in hoc specie propter quam dicantur aliqua passibiles qualitates, ut patet in littera. Ad denotandum ergo in istis causam duplicem, ut signum signato correspondeat, hanc speciem denominat in plurali.

<3>

Consequenter quaeritur, cum calor et frigus sint in prima specie qualitatis, et idem sub diversis speciebus esse non potest, quare dicit quod sub hac specie continentur.

Et dicendum quod non est inconveniens idem diversimode acceptum esse sub diversis speciebus. Dicendum ergo quod frigidum et calidum relata ad subiecta prout sunt ab eis facile vel difficile mobilia sunt in prima specie qualitatis, sed prout tactui inferunt passionem sub hac specie continentur.

<4>

Consequenter quaeritur utrum sensus sit virtus activa vel passiva, quia vult in littera quod passiva.

Et hoc videtur. Quia omnis virtus quae est ut in ea aliquid fiat est virtus passiva. Virtus sensitiva est huiusmodi, quia recipitur obiecti species in ea. Ergo est virtus passiva.

Item. "Triplex est mobile", scribitur in *Physicis*. Movens non motum, sicut Prima Causa; movet enim omnia et ab aliquo non movetur, nam stabilis manens dat cuncta moveri, dicit Boethius. Aliud est motum movens, ut natura a primo motu mota movet inferiora; et hoc est quod scribitur secundo *Physicorum*: "Natura est principium motus in eo in quo est per se et non secundum accidens". Aliud est

---

6 Arist. *Cat.* 8.9a29; a36; b4; b7; b11 **16–17** *cf.* Arist. *Cat.* 8.9b5–10 **21** *cf.* Arist. *Phys.* VIII 5.256b14–24 **22–23** Boeth. *Consol.* III m. IX.3 (ed. Bieler, 51); Anon. *Auct. Arist.* 25.47 (ed. Hamesse, 290) **24–25** Arist. *Phys.* II 1.192b20–23; Anon. *Auct. Arist.* 2.50 (ed. Hamesse, 144)

---

11 speciebus esse] *inv. P* **13** subiecta] sua causa *P ut v.*

motum et non movens, ut inferiora. Per hoc patet quod in quocumque genere est
motum et movens <et movens> non motum erit tertium, scilicet motum et non
movens. Sed in genere sensus sunt tria: sensus, obiectum et medium per quod de-
fertur species obiecti in sensum. Cum ergo obiectum sit movens non motum (quia
movens medium et non motum ab alio) et medium sit movens (movet enim sen-   5
sum) et sit motum ab obiecto, relinquitur quod erit ibi motum et non movens, et
hoc non potest ibi reperiri nisi sensus. Ergo sensus erit motum et non movens. Sed
omne tale est huiusmodi. Ergo etc.

   Quod autem sit activa et passiva videtur. Sensus in duobus consistit, scilicet in
receptione et iudicio; recipit enim species et iudicat de receptis. Sed omne quod   10
recipit in quantum huiusmodi est virtus passiva et omne quod iudicat in quantum
huiusmodi est virtus activa. Cum ergo sensus haec duo habeat facere, erit virtus
activa et passiva.

   Quod concedo, quia virtus sensitiva in quantum recipit species virtus passiva
est solum, ut obicitur, sed in quantum de receptis iudicat est virtus activa. Con-   15
siderando ergo virtutem sensitivam in quantum ad utrumque, sub utroque poterit
comprehendi.

<5>

Consequenter quaeritur: Sicut habitus est difficile mobilis, sic et passibilis qualitas, et sicut dispositio est facile mobilis, sic et passio. Quare ergo non dicit quod
passibiles qualitates sint passiones, sicut habitus dispositiones?   20

f. 57va | Et dicendum quod ad omnem passibilem qualitatem non sequitur passio, si-
cut ad dulcedinem, nec ad multa alia, sicut ad omnem habitum sequitur dispositio. Quia ergo non est verum universaliter quod ad passibilem qualitatem sequatur
passio, sicut ad habitum dispositio, ideo hoc non dixit.

<6>

Consequenter quaeritur, cum nigredo et alii colores visui passionem inferant sicut   25
dulcedo gustui, quare dicit quod non dicuntur similiter qualitates passibiles; nam
videtur dicere falsum.

   Et dicendum quod quantum ad hoc non intendit ponere differentiam sed quo ad
hoc quod albedo et alii colores ab aliquibus passionibus innascuntur. Sed dulcedo
et huiusmodi alia non inferuntur a passionibus, et quo ad hoc intendit differentiam   30
assignare.

---

6 sit] sic *P*

Lectio XXXIV

Quoniam ergo fiunt per aliquam etc. (8.9b12)

\<Divisio\>

Assignata differentia inter qualitates passibiles, quoddam suppositum manifestat, scilicet quod colores causantur a passionibus.

Haec pars in duas. Primo facit quod dictum est, secundo ponit differentiam inter passiones et passibiles qualitates, ut ibi: *Quaecumque igitur talium* (8.9b20).

Prima in duas. Primo proponit quod manifestare intendit, secundo manifestat, ibi: *erubescens* (8.9b13).

Haec secunda in duas. Primo manifestat propositum, secundo infert correlarium, ibi: *Quare si quis* (8.9b14).

Pars in qua ponit differentiam in duas. Primo dat differentiam passionum ad passibiles qualitates quae sunt a parte corporis, secundo earum quae sunt a parte animae, ut ibi: *Similiter autem his* (8.9b34).

Prima in duas. Primo dicit quae sunt passibiles \<qualitates\>, secundo quae sunt passiones, ut ibi: *Quaecumque vero ex his* (8.9b27).

Pars in qua dat differentiam passionum animae ad passibiles qualitates in duas. Primo dicit quae sunt passibiles qualitates, secundo quae sunt passiones, ibi: *Quaecumque vero ex his* (8.10a6).

Haec est divisio lectionis, et sunt particulae septem.

\<Sententia\>

Circa primam sic procedit: Diversi colores causantur a passionibus in corpore existentibus.

Consequenter probat hoc: Propter verecundiam fit aliquis rubeus, propter timorem pallidus. Sed timor et verecundia sunt passiones, pallor et rubor colores. Ergo a passionibus causantur colores.

Consequenter infert correlarium sic: Postquam ex verecundia et timore causantur colores et illae sunt passiones, ergo multo fortius, si patiantur aliquid naturaliter, habent colorem illi similem quam haberent si accidentaliter paterentur; ut si aliquis naturaliter patiatur aliquid propter quod sanguis ad interiora currat, naturaliter erit pallidus, si autem naturaliter aliquid patiatur propter quod sanguis ad exteriora discurrat, naturaliter erit rubeus.

---

17 septem] VI *P*

Consequenter dicit quod est passibilis qualitas: Omnes qualitates quae innascuntur a passionibus naturalibus vel accidentalibus difficile mobilibus et diu
permanentibus sunt passibiles. Et de hoc ponit exempla.

Consequenter dicit quae sunt passiones, quia illae quae nascuntur a parum
durantibus et facile mobilibus. Et hoc per exempla demonstrat.   5

Idem dicit de passibilibus qualitatibus animae et passionibus.

Haec est sententia partis.

Expositio litteralis

Ita dixi quod albedo et similia a quibusdam passionibus inferantur, *ergo*, pro sed,
<quoniam> multae colorum mutationes, id est diversi colores, *fiunt per aliquam*
passionem, id est ab aliqua passione, in corpore supple, | *manifestum est*.   10

   Enim, id est quia, *aliquis erubescens factus est rubeus*, propter verecundiam
supple, *et timens* factus est *pallidus* propter etc.

   Continua. Huiusmodi passiones accidentales sunt causae quorundam acciden-
talium colorum, *quare*, id est ergo, *si quis est passus naturaliter*, id est propter aliquam naturalem passionem, *aliquid talium passionum*, *oportet eum habere*, na-   15
turalem supple, *colorem similem*. Bene dico quod sic, *enim*, id est quia, *affectio*,
id est quae est statio, *circa corpus ad verecundiam*, id est per quam est passio accidentalis, *eadem*, id est similis, *affectio*, id est dispositio, *fiet secundum naturalem*
passionem, id est causatam a naturali passione, *ita ut naturalis color sit similis*, accidentali supple. (Et dicit naturalem quae causatur a passione naturali, accidentalem 20
quae causatur a passione accidentali).

   Ita dictum est qualiter colores causantur a passionibus, *igitur*, pro sed, *quaecum-*
que talium casuum, id est modorum, sumpserunt *principium ab aliquibus passioni-*
bus etc., *dicuntur passibiles qualitates*. Et quia illa a quibus causantur possunt esse
naturalia vel accidentalia, subiungit: *sive secundum naturalem substantiam*, id est 25
ab aliqua naturali passione, *facta*, ut *pallor aut nigredo, dicuntur qualitates*. Et hoc
probat: *enim*, id est quia, *quales* etc., *sive propter aegritudinem longam* sive *propter*
aestum aut aliquid talium, id est propter aliquam proprietatem accidentalem, *con-*
tingit vel nigredo etc. *et permanet in vita*, id est diu, ista *dicuntur qualitates*; autem,
id est quia, *dicimur quales secundum eas*, supple sicut secundum naturales.   30

   Ita dictum est de passionibus, *vero*, id est sed, *quaecumque* sunt *ex his* etc. *di-*
cuntur passiones; *non <enim dicimur secundum eas> quales*; *enim*, id est quia, ille
<qui> propter verecundiam etc., *sed magis* dicitur *quod aliquid sit passus*. Ex hoc

---

16 supple] *post* talium *transp.* P   **17** quam] quae P   **26** qualitates] supple *add.* P   **28** aut] *c* :
autem P   **30** dicimur] *ac* : dicuntur P

concludit: Ex quo huiusmodi <a> passionibus facile mobilibus oriuntur, *quare*, id est ergo, *huiusmodi dicuntur passiones*, *vero*, id est sed, *minime*, id est non, dicuntur *qualitates*, cum secundum ea non dicamur quales.

Ita dictum est de passibilibus qualitatibus corporis, *vero*, id est sed, *passibiles*
5   *qualitates* etc. *dicuntur similiter his* quae sunt a parte corporis; *enim*, <id est> quia, *quaecumque fiunt ab aliquibus passionibus mox in nascendo*, id est quando aliquis nascitur, *dicuntur qualitates*, *ut dementia* etc. Et hoc probat: *Quales enim* etc. Non solum sic est de creatis a naturalibus passionibus, sed *similiter quaecumque aliena-tiones*, id est qualitates passibiles, *sunt factae ab aliquibus casibus non* naturali-
10 bus, id est non a causis naturalibus sed accidentalibus, et *difficile* praetereuntibus, *sunt qualitates passibiles*. Quasi dicens: Non solum causatae a naturalibus causis sunt passibiles, sed causatae ab accidentalibus, dummodo istae permaneant diu in subiecto.

Ita dictum est quae sunt passibiles, *vero*, id est sed, *quaecumque* sunt etc., *dicun-*
15 *tur passiones* etc., *ut si quis contristatus iracundior fit*; *non enim iracundus dicitur* etc.

<QUAESTIONES>

<1>

Primo quaeritur: Dicit quod accidentalia facile dissolvuntur et cito transeunt; gratia cuius quaeritur an possint corrumpi.

Quod non videtur. Accidens, cum est forma, est simplex et invariabile, dicit
20 auctor *Sex principiorum*. Sed nullum tale corruptibile. Ergo etc. Minor patet, quia corruptio est dissolutio, dissolutio autem non est nisi compositi.

<Ad> idem. Accidens est invariabile, ut dictum est. Cum ergo omne quod corrumpitur varietur, accidens non corrumpetur.

| Sed contra. Omne quod progreditur de non esse in esse est per naturam re-   f. 58ra
25 gressibile in non esse. Accidens est huiusmodi. Ergo etc. Ergo per naturam omne accidens corrumpetur.

Quod concedimus. Unde corruptio multis modis dicitur, ut dictum est in praedicamento substantiae, ibi: *Inest autem substantiis nihil illis esse contrarium* (5.3b25); ubi patet quot modis accidens corrumpatur.

30 Ad obiectum primum dicendum quod simplex dicitur dupliciter. Vel quia non est ex aliquibus compositum, et sic accidens simplex cum non habeat materiam ex

---

17 Arist. *Cat.* 8.9b27   **19–20** *cf.* Anon. *LSP* I 1 (ed. Minio-Paluello, 35); Anon. *Auct. Arist.* 33.1 (ed. Hamesse, 306)   **197.31–198.1** *locum non inveni*

---

11 qualitates] sunt *add. P a.c.*   **15** quis] *add. P s.l.*   **23** corrumpitur] ai *add. P a.c.*   **25** non] *add. P in marg.*

qua, ut dicit Boethius. Alio modo dicitur simplex quod non est alii coniunctum, et
sic accidens non est simplex. Similiter compositum duplex. Vel quia < * * * > aliis
coniunctum ut compositum. Isto ultimo modo accidens est compositum.

Ad aliud. Invariabile duplex. Vel quia non est subiectum variationis, et sic accidens invariabile, vel quia non est terminus variationis; et sic accidens, non sicut   5
subiectum, sed sicut terminus variatur.

<2>

Consequenter quaeritur quare propter verecundiam fit homo rubeus et quare propter timorem pallidus.

Ad primum. Verecundia provenit ex apprehensione alicuius turpis vel apparentis <talis>. Natura autem non deficit in necessariis — intendit enim suum subiectum   10
cooperire, licet impium detegat — et reducit sanguinem, qui est amicalis naturae,
dicit Galenus, et educit ipsum ad partes exteriores et maxime ad faciem, ubi potest
post verecundia apparere.

Ad aliud. Timor provenit ex apprehensione alicuius terribilis vel apparentis talis.
Natura autem intendit sibi salvationem subiecti, unde faciendo quod potest reducit   15
sanguinem, qui est sibi amicalis, ad partes interiores et maxime ad illam partem ubi
viget principalius salus hominis, scilicet ad cor. Quia ergo membra exteriora sunt
sanguine exinanita, qui per sui praesentiam erat causa ruboris, per sui absentiam
contrarium operatur.

<3>

Consequenter quaeritur: Dicit quod secundum passionem non dicimur quales.   20

Contra. Qualitas est secundum quam quales dicimur. Sed definitio convenit omni, dicit Boethius. Cum ergo passio sit qualitas, secundum ipsam dicemur
quales.

Si dicatur quod passio non est qualitas, ut dicit auctor, contra. Genus de qualibet
sua specie praedicatur. Ergo qualitas de passione, cum sit eius species, praedicatur.   25

Ad primum. Dupliciter possumus dici quales, scilicet secundum actum et habitum vel secundum actum tantum; et dico secundum habitum secundum famam
communem, et sic a passione non dicimur quales, et dico secundum actum tantum
in praesenti dum dominatur illa passio, et sic obicitur.

---

12 *cf.* Isaac Israeli *Liber febrium* II 8 (ed. Lyon, 214vb)   **20** Arist. *Cat.* 8.9b29–34; 10a6–10
21–22 *cf.* Boeth. *in Cat.* 165a–d   **24** Arist. *Cat.* 8.9b29–34; 10a6–10

---

9 ex apprehensione] *add. P in marg.*

Vel aliter. A passione non dicimur quales simpliciter, et sic loquitur, sed secundum quid tantum, et sic obicitur.

Per hoc patet ad aliud, quia passiones non sunt qualitates a quibus dicamur quales simpliciter, et sic loquitur auctor, sed sunt qualitates a quibus dicimur quales
5 secundum quid, ut visum est.

<4>

Consequenter quaeritur: Dicit quod passiones quaedam sunt animae.

Contra. Dicit auctor *Sex principiorum* quod anima nullo motu movetur. Sed si non movetur, non patitur, et si non patitur, non sunt in ipsa passiones. Male ergo dicit auctor asserendo.

10 Et dicendum quod motus potest esse in aliquo dupliciter. Aut sicut in causa efficiente aut sicut in subiecto. Licet ergo motus non sit in anima, ut obicitur, sicut in subiecto, est tamen in anima ut in causa ef|ficiente, et eo modo quo motus est in   f. 58rb
ipsa erit passio in eadem.

Vel aliter. Non movetur per se sed per accidens, scilicet corpore moto; unde eo
15 modo quo movetur patitur.

<5>

Ultimo quaeritur, cum sint quaedam naturales potentiae a parte animae, quaedam a parte corporis, quare sicut passiones et passibiles qualitates dividuntur quod quaedam sunt a parte corporis, quaedam a parte animae, quare naturalis potentia vel impotentia non similiter dividantur.

20 Et dicendum quod non est simile, quia naturalis potentia, sive sit a parte corporis sive animae, uniformiter dicitur (et naturalis potentia a parte utriusque est quando habet potentiam aliquid facile faciendi), sed passiones et passibiles qualitates non formantur modo simili a parte utriusque, sed a parte corporis sumuntur quia in sensum inferunt passiones, a parte vero animae quia in animam inferunt
25 passiones.

---

6 Arist. *Cat.* 8.10a6–10   **7** *cf.* Anon. *LSP* II 16–18 (ed. Minio-Paluello, 38–39)

---

2 quid] in aliquo *add.* P   **24** animam] anima P

Lectio XXXV

Quartum vero genus (8.10a11)

<Divisio>

Hic prosequitur de quarta specie qualitatis.

Haec pars in duas. Primo ponit constitutiva quartam speciem, secundo epilogat, ut ibi: *Qualitates itaque* (8.10a27).

Prima in duas. Primo facit quod dictum est, secundo de insufficientia se excusat, ibi: *Et fortasse alii* (8.10a25).

Prima in duas. Primo notificat ipsam speciem, secundo probat exempla posita esse qualitates, ibi: *Secundum vero unumquodque* (8.10a13).

Haec secunda in duas. Primo probat quod sunt qualitates, secundo removet dubium, ibi: *Rarum vero et spissum* (8.10a16).

Et sequitur illa pars in qua de quali prosequitur. Et dividitur in duas, quia primo definit quale, secundo definitionem explanat, ibi: *ut a candore candidus* (8.10a30).

Haec secunda in duas. Primo explanat definitionem, <secundo eam manifestatam concludit, ibi: *Quae ergo dicuntur* (8.10b10).

Prima in duas. Primo explanat definitionem> in his quae denominative dicuntur quia nomen est impositum qualitati, secundo in his quae non dicuntur denominative, <ibi: *In aliquibus vero* (8.10a31).

Haec secunda in duas. Primo explanat in his quae non dicuntur denominative quia nomen non est impositum qualitati, secundo in his quae non dicuntur denominative> licet nomen sit impositum qualitati, ibi: *Aliquando autem et posito nomine* (8.10b6).

Haec est divisio lectionis, et sunt particulae decem.

<Sententia>

Circa primam sic procedit. Quartum genus qualitatis est forma et figura circa ipsam constans, et rectitudo et curvitas sub hoc genere continentur.

Consequenter probat quod sunt qualitates: Omne illud secundum quod aliquid dicitur quale est qualitas. Haec sunt huiusmodi. Ergo etc. Minorem ponit et manifestat.

Consequenter removet dubium quod rarum et spissum etc. non sunt qualitates licet videantur. Quod sic probat: Nihil cuius partes habent positionem in toto est qualitas sed potius positio. Rarum etc. sunt huiusmodi. Ergo etc. Minorem ponit et per eorum definitiones manifestat.

Consequenter de insufficientia se excusat, dicens quod aliae apparebunt esse species qualitatis quam quae dictae sunt, sed hae sunt maxime usitatae.

Consequenter epilogat, dicens quod species qualitatis sunt superius nominatae.

Consequenter definit quale sic: Qualia sunt quae dicuntur denominative a qualitatibus supradictis vel quomodolibet aliter quam denominative, ut a candore   5 candidus etc.

Consequenter dicit quod quaedam non dicuntur denominative a qualitatibus, ut cursor et pugilator non dicuntur denominative a potentiis naturalibus, cum eis non sint imposita nomina. Ex hoc crederet aliquis quod non similiter dicerentur denominative ab arte pugilatoria vel cursoria, quod removet, dicens quod | ab il-   10 lis dicuntur denominative, nam et illis disciplinis nomina sunt imposita. Et nota quod termini sunt in prima specie qualitatis, nam scientiae a quibus dicuntur sunt habitus; prout dicuntur a naturali potentia, sub secunda specie continentur.

Consequenter dicit quod alia sunt qualia quae non dicuntur denominative a qualitatibus licet nomina sint eis imposita, ut studiosus non dicitur denominative a   15 virtute.

Ultimo concludit definitionem manifestatam quod qualia dicuntur denomina- tive a dictis qualitatibus vel quomodolibet aliter quam denominative.

Expositio litteralis

Ita dictum est de aliis speciebus, *vero*, id est sed, *quartum genus qualitatis est forma et figura constans circa aliquid*, id est circa formam; *autem*, id est sed, *amplius ad*   20 *haec*, id est praeter haec, *rectitudo* etc. sunt in hoc genere qualitatis.

Vere sunt qualitates, nam, id est quia, *quid*, id est aliquid, *dicitur quale secun- dum unumquodque eorum*. Bene dico quod sic, vero, id est quia, *triangulum* etc. *di- citur quale quid*, <id> est species qualitatis (Vel expone: *quid*, id est aliquid, *dicitur quale* secundum *triangulum* etc.)   25

Ita est de istis, *vero*, id est sed, *rarum* etc. *putabuntur*, supple a quibusdam, *significare* qualitates, *sed putantur*, a nullo supple, rarum et *huiusmodi esse aliena a divisione quae est circa qualitatem*, id est a speciebus dividentibus qualitatem. Vere videntur esse aliena, *enim*, id est quia, *videntur* significare *quandam positionem partium quodammodo*, id est in toto. Bene dico quod sic, enim, id est quia, *spissum*,   30 id est corpus compactum vel non porosum, dicitur *eo quod partes* etc., sed *rarum* dicitur *eo quod* distant, partes resume, *a se invicem*. Et hoc est corpus porosum etc., *quod*, id est quia, *partes iaceant* etc., id est aequaliter sint porrectae, *et asperum quod haec pars*, id est quaedam, *superat*, id est supereminet, *illa vero* etc.

---

27 significare] *ac* : significationibus *P ut v.*   **32** a] *ac* : ad *P*

Continua: Ita dictae sunt species qualitatis, *et fortasse alii modi*, id est aliae species, apparebunt quibusdam *qualitatis* quam quae dictae sunt, *sed hi sunt* etc.

Ex hoc concludit: *Qualitates itaque* etc.

Ita dictum est de qualitate, *vero*, id est sed, *qualia* sunt *quae dicuntur denomi-*
native ab his, id est secundum praedictas qualitates, *vel quomodolibet*, supple quam denominative, *ut candidus a candore* dicitur denominative *et a grammatica* etc.

Ita dictum est de istis, *vero*, id est sed, *in aliquibus*, scilicet qualitatibus, *non contingit ea quae dicuntur ab eis*, scilicet qualitatibus, *dici denominative eo*, id est propter hoc, *quod*, id est quia, *nomina non sunt qualitatibus* imposita, *ut cursor etc.*
qui dicuntur secundum naturalem valetudinem, id est potentiam, *a nulla qualitate dicitur denominative. Et non est mirum, enim*, id est quia, *nomina non sunt* impo-
sita *valetudinibus*, id est potentiis naturalibus, *secundum quas*, scilicet valetudines, *isti*, id est cursor etc., *dicuntur quales.* Vere nomina non sunt eis imposita, *sicut in disciplinis*, id est in scientiis acquisitis, supple sunt nomina imposita, *secundum quas dicuntur pugilatores* etc. *secundum affectionem*, id est secundum potentiam acquisitam. Bene dico quod nomina sunt eis imposita, *enim*, id est quia, *dicitur*, id est nominatur, *disciplina pugilatoria, vero*, id est sed, *hi qui afficiuntur* eis, id est disciplinis, *dicuntur denominative ab his.*

Ita est in his, *autem*, id est sed, *<aliquando> non dicitur denominative*, a qua-
litate | supple, *nomine* imposito, illi qualitati supple, *quod dicitur quale secundum*   f. 58vb
eam, ut studiosus a virtute, supple non dicitur denominative licet dicatur quale ab ipsa; *enim*, id est quia, *habendo virtutem dicitur studiosus, sed non denominative* dicitur hoc nomen "studiosus" *a virtute*, id est ab hoc nomine. Ita est in istis, *au-*
tem, id est sed, *hoc tale*, id est quod sumantur ab aliqua qualitate et non dicantur ab illa denominative si nomen sit eis impositum, *non inest pluribus.*

Ultimo concludit: Ex quo candidus dicitur denominative a candore et cursor et similia dicitur aliter quam denominative, *ergo quae dicuntur qualia* etc.

<Quaestiones>

<1>

Primo quaeritur in quo differt forma a figura et qualiter intelligatur quod figura sit constans circa aliquid.

Ad primum. Forma est proprie dispositio exterior in rebus animatis, figura vero in rebus inanimatis.

Vel aliter. Forma dicitur dispositio interior quae lineis clauditur, sicut illa con-

---

2 qualitatis] *ac* : qualitatibus *P*   **2** hi sunt] *ac* : his *P*   **4–5** denominative] dicuntur *add. P a.c.*
30 forma] *add. P in marg.*

cavitas vel convexitas quae est in medio, figura vero dicitur applicatio linearum ad illud quod continetur; unde figura terminat ipsam formam.

Per hoc patet ad aliud. Cum figura semper constet circa formam, constans est circa aliquid, id est circa formam quam terminat.

<2>

Consequenter quaeritur quare haec species nomine generis nuncupetur.   5

Et dicendum quod magis conveniunt quae sunt in prima et tertia specie qualitatis quam quae sub quarta specie continentur. Quod patet. Dispositio enim est via in habitum et per moram temporis in habitum convertetur; similiter passio in passibilem qualitatem. Sed figura in formam vel e converso nullatenus convertetur. Quia ergo conveniunt magis quae sunt sub eadem specie quam quae sub eodem   10 genere tantum, ut signum signato correspondeat, quarta nomen generis, sed prima et tertia speciei nomina sortiuntur.

<3>

Consequenter quaeritur, postquam secunda species nomen sortitur generis sicut ista, quare nomina huius copulantur coniunctione copulativa, illa vero per disiunctivam.   15

Et dicendum quod coniunctio copulativa, ut dicit Priscianus, res copulat quae simul esse possunt; unde magis conveniunt quam ea quae per coniunctionem disiunctivam copulantur. Et quia magis conveniunt quae sunt in quarta quam quae in secunda, ideo per copulativam coniunctionem copulantur. Quod magis conveniant patet, quia naturalis potentia et impotentia sic se habent quod una non terminat   20 reliquam, secus autem est in proposito.

<4>

Consequenter quaeritur quare dicit "amplius ad haec rectitudo et curvitas" interponendo notam diversitatis.

Et dicendum quod ad designandum quod sicut in formis est concavitas vel convexitas, similiter in lineis debet esse.   25

---

5 Arist. *Cat.* 8.10a11   **14–15** Arist. *Cat.* 8.9a14; 10a11   **16–17** *cf.* Prisc. *Inst. gramm.* XVI 1.1–2 (ed. Hertz, vol. 2, 93–94)   **22–23** Arist. *Cat.* 8.10a12

---

1 applicatio] *lectio incerta*   **3** figura] cum *add. P a.c.*   **3** est] *add. P s.l.*   **7** quae] sunt *add. P a.c.*   **17** possunt] *add. P in marg.*   **17** unde] unum *P*

\<5\>

Consequenter quaeritur: Dicit quod rarum et spissum non sunt qualitates.

Auctor *Sex principiorum* in tractatu de positione dicit oppositum.

Et dicendum quod rarum et spissum prout dicunt ordinem partium in toto sic sunt positiones. Si vero considerentur ratione rei prout sensum immutant, cum
5   omne immutans sensum in quantum tale sit in tertia specie qualitatis, sic sunt qualitates, et sic loquitur auctor *Sex principiorum*. Primo modo loquitur iste.

\<6\>

Consequenter quaeritur: Dicit quod alii apparebunt esse modi qualitatis. Quaeritur qui sint isti modi et quare dixit "fortasse".

Et dicendum quod \<quia\> quantitatis continuae passiones, ut rectitudo et curvi-
10   tas, continentur in hac quarta specie qualitatis, quidam existimaverunt quod simili-
ter passiones discretae quantitatis, ut paritas et imparitas, novam speciem qualitatis generarent, | et quia horum opinio falsa est, ideo dixit "fortasse"; unde si istae sunt   f. 59ra
qualitates, in prima specie continentur.

\<7\>

Consequenter quaeritur quare determinat de qualitate et quali cum in capitulo
15   quantitatis de quanto non fecerit mentionem.

Et dicendum quod quaedam proprietates conveniunt quali ita quod non quali-
tati et e converso — et hoc est quod infra dicet, quod iustitia et sanitas et similia non suscipiunt magis et minus, sed ea quae dicuntur qualia ab istis, ut grammaticior — quare distinctim de qualitate et quali determinat; sed eaedem proprietates
20   conveniunt quantitati et quanto. Consimilis est quaestio de relatione et relativo.

\<8\>

Consequenter quaeritur quare manifestat quale per qualitatem et superius qualitatem per quale notificat; nam videtur notificatio circularis.

Iuxta hoc quaeritur, cum omnis notificatio per priora, qualiter notificetur qualitas per quale et e converso.
25   Ad hoc dicendum quod prius dicitur dupliciter, scribitur in primo *Physicorum*.

---

1 Arist. *Cat.* 8.10a16–25   **2** *cf.* Anon. *LSP* VI 61–62 (ed. Minio-Paluello, 48–49)   **7** Arist. *Cat.* 8.10a25–26   **21** Arist. *Cat.* 8.10a29–31   **21–22** Arist. *Cat.* 8.8b25–26   **205.25–206.1** *cf.* Arist. *Phys.* I 1.184a16–24

Quo ad nos et quo ad naturam. Unde manifestatur qualitas per qualia, quae nobis sunt notiora, et quale per qualitatem, quae prioritatis naturae possidet principatum, et sic semper notificatio per priora.

Patet etiam quod non est circularis, quia non est processus ab eodem uniformiter in eodem.   5

\<9>

Consequenter quaeritur quare potentiis naturalibus non sunt nomina imposita, cum ars imitetur naturam, scribitur in secundo *Physicorum*. Cum ergo potentiae naturales sint in natura, deberent eis esse nomina imposita. Vel quare non?

Et dicendum quod quia grammaticus est artifex sensibilis et ei spectat nominis impositio, non imponit nomina nisi rebus sensibilibus et notis maxime. Sed dicit   10
Boethius: "Felix qui potuit rerum cognoscere causas". Quia ergo rerum potentiae naturales sunt nobis occultae, sicut in psilothro, cum quo si capillorum radices coniungantur, eradicantur penitus, dicit Ali, et similiter de aliis potentiis naturalibus, ideo grammaticus eis nomina non ponit.

\<10>

Ultimo quaeritur quare studiosus non dicitur denominative a virtute.   15

Et dicendum, ut dicit Boethius, quod denominativum et principale conveniunt in principio quantum ad vocem et differunt in fine. Et quia virtus et studiosus non sunt huiusmodi, patet quod † vox iterum et significatio † Nam quaedam qualia comparantur et causantur a qualitate a qua dicuntur in duplici causalitate, efficienti scilicet et formali, et quia omnis denominatio a forma, dicit Philosophus in *Metaphysi-*   20
ca, ideo qualia relata ad qualitates in causalitate formali ab eis dicuntur denominative. Sed studiosus refertur ad virtutem in causalitate effectiva tantum; nam virtus per sui frequentiam reddit hominem studiosum sed non est eius causa formalis, sed virtus est forma virtuosi et studium studiosi. Quare studiosus denominative non dicitur a virtute. (Unde virtus significat virtutem sine multiplicitate, virtuosus autem   25
cum multiplicitate; unde dicit Priscianus: "'-osus' plena notat").

---

7   Arist. *Phys.* II 2.194a21–22, *ut apud* Anon. *Auct. Arist.* 2.60 (ed. Hamesse, 145)   **10–11**   *cf. potius* Verg. *Geor.* II 490   **12–13**   Haly *Commentum super Librum tegni Galieni* II 12 (ed. Venet., 17rb)   **15**   *cf.* Arist. *Cat.* 8.10b6–9   **16–17**   *cf.* Boeth. *in Cat.* 168a   **20–21**   *cf.* Arist. *Metaph.* VII 8.1033b16–19   **26**   *cf.* Prisc. *Inst. gramm.* IV 7.37 (ed. Hertz, vol. 1, 138)

Lectio XXXVI

Inest autem contrarietas secundum <quod> quale etc.
(8.10b12)

<Divisio>

Notificatis qualitate et etiam quali penes substantialia, notificat penes accidentalia.

Haec in duas. Primo ponit proprietates non convertibiles, secundo convertibiles, ibi: *Simile vero* (8.11a16).

Prima in duas <secundum duas proprietates quas ponit. Secunda ibi: *Suscipit autem* (8.10b25).

Prima in duas. Primo ponit proprietatem, secundo additionem, ibi: *Amplius si* (8.10b17).

Prima in duas. Primo ponit proprietatem, secundo ostendit quod non convenit omnibus, ibi: *Non autem in omnibus* (8.10b16).

Pars in qua ponit secundam proprietatem in duas.> Primo ponit proprietatem, secundo ostendit quod non convenit omnibus, ibi: *Non tamen omnia* (8.10b30).

Haec secunda | in duas. <Primo ostendit quod non convenit abstractis, secundo quod qualia recipiunt magis et minus, ibi: *Sed tamen ea* (8.11a2). f. 59rb

Haec secunda in duas.> Primo ostendit quod qualia recipiunt magis et minus, secundo excipit quaedam qualia quibus haec proprietas non competit, ibi: *Triangulus vero* (8.11a5). Ubi praesens lectio terminatur, et sunt particulae sex.

<Sententia>

Circa primam sic procedit. Contrarietas inest qualitatibus abstractis et etiam concretis; de utroque ponit exemplum.

Consequenter dicit quod hoc non convenit cuilibet qualitati, sicut rubeo et aliis coloribus mediis nihil est contrarium.

Consequenter ponit additionem, dicens quod si unum contrariorum erit in genere qualitatis, reliquum erit in eodem; et ponit exempla.

Consequenter ponit secundam proprietatem, dicens quod qualitas, scilicet concreta, recipit magis et minus; et ponit exempla.

< * * * >

Consequenter dicit quod recipientia istas qualitates recipiunt ipsas secundum magis et minus; et ponit exempla.

Et in hoc terminatur sententia lectionis.

---

17 qualitatibus] qualibus *P* **28** et] ut *P*

Expositio litteralis

Ita dictum est de speciebus qualitatis, *autem*, id est sed, *contrarietas inest secundum quod quale*, id est qualitati in abstractione, *ut iustitia* etc. Non solum haec proprietas convenit abstractis, *autem*, id est sed, *similiter* alia *quae dicuntur qualia secundum eas*, id est qualia vel concreta, sunt contraria, *ut iustum* etc.

Ita haec proprietas convenit istis, *autem*, id est sed, *hoc*, scilicet accipere contrarium, *non est in omnibus*, supple qualitatibus. Bene dico quod non, *enim*, id est quia, *rubeo* etc. *aut huiusmodi coloribus*, mediis supple, etc.   5

Consequenter ponit additionem: Non solum convenit hoc qualitati, *amplius si* unumquodque *ex contrariis fuerit quale*, id est in genere qualitatis, *palam est* etc. Vere palam est, *nam*, id est quia, *si iustitia est contraria iniustitiae* etc. Non solum   10
sic est in abstractis, *autem*, id est sed, *similiter* est *in aliis quae sunt secundum quale*, id est similiter est in quolibet.

Continua: Non solum convenit haec proprietas qualitati, *autem*, id est sed, *qualitas*, supple concreta, *suscipit magis et minus*; *album enim* etc. Continua: Non solum alterum est magis album altero, *sed* etiam *ipsa*, id est eadem, recipiunt   15
crementum diversis temporibus.

Ita qualitas recipit magis et minus, *tamen non omnia*, id est non omnis qualitas, *sed plura*, id est solum concreta, recipiunt magis et minus. Quod non abstracta probat: *namque*, id est quia, *quilibet potest ambigere* (quasi dicens: non est verum) *si iustitia* una *dicatur magis et minus a iustitia*, alia supple. Non solum sic est in   20
istis, *autem*, <id est sed>, *similiter in aliis affectionibus*, id est in aliis qualitatibus abstractis. Bene dico "similiter in aliis", *enim*, id est quia, *quidam dubitant de talibus*, id est de abstractis; *namque*, id est quia, *non multum aiunt* etc., *et alios affectus*, id est alias disciplinas.

Ita est de abstractis, *tamen ea qualia quae dicuntur secundum eos affectus*, id est   25
secundum illas disciplinas, *recipiunt magis et minus indubitanter*. Bene dico quod sic, *enim*, id est quia, *grammatior* etc.

<Quaestiones>

<1>

Primo quaeritur: Dicit quod contrarietas est in qualitate.

Et dicit Aristoteles quod si affirmationem secundum quid opponitur negatio

---

28   Arist. *Cat.* 8.10b12–16   **208.29–209.1**   *locum non inveni*

---

21 autem] *lectio incerta*   **27** grammatior] *! Pc$_{EbMüVa}$* : grammaticior *malim*

secundum quid, et negatio simpliciter affirmationi simpliciter. Ergo et similiter si qualitas simpliciter, sicut albedo, opponitur qualitati simpliciter, sicut nigredini, et qualitas per accidens opponetur qualitati per accidens. Quaeritur ergo quid opponitur albedini Socratis. Aut enim sibi opponitur nigredo in ipso existens aut in alio.

5 | <Quod> non nigredo in ipso existens planum est; nam sic essent opposita in eodem. Nec nigredo in alio, ut videtur, quia scribitur in *Postpraedicamentis*: "ab uno contrariorum contingit ire in alterum, et est ibi regressus". Sed ab albedine Socratis non est ire in nigredinem Platonis nec e converso. Iuxta enim Boethium accidentia indignantis sunt naturae; permutari quidem possunt, sed minime separari. Sic

10 albendini Socratis nihil est contrarium.

Et dicendum quod albedini in Socrate non contrariatur nigredo in Platone, ut obicitur, sed nigredo in ipso. Et non est inconveniens contraria esse in eodem ita quod unum sit actu, reliquum vero potentia; et hoc scribitur in secundo *Topicorum*.

Quod hoc nihil sit dicitur communiter. Dicitur enim quod nihil ens actu est

15 idem cum aliquo solum in potentia existente, quia sic sequeretur idem esse actu et potentia tantum, quod est impossibile. Ergo per simile in contrariis nihil ens in actu est contrarium existenti in potentia tantum. Nulla igitur est solutio, ut videtur.

Et dicendum quod non est simile. Nam aliqua esse eadem est potentia et constructio quaedam, sed aliqua esse contraria est corruptio quaedam; nam corrup-

20 tio per contrarium. Sed scribitur in *Topicis* quod in quolibet facilius est destruere quam construere. Pauciores ergo condiciones sufficiunt ad destruendum quam ad construendum, et per consequens pauciores ad contrarietatem quam ad identitatem. Et ideo non sequitur quod si aliquid actu existens non possit esse idem cum existente in potentia tantum, quod non possit contrariari.

<2>

25 Consequenter quaeritur quare in naturalibus medium non contrariatur extremis sicut in moralibus.

Et videtur quod contrarietur. Nam dicit Philosophus quod medium ad alterum extremum comparatum accipitur pro altero. Ergo rubeum ad album comparatum est sicut nigrum. Sed nigrum contrariatur albo. Ergo rubeum albo contrariatur.

30 Et dicendum quod in naturalibus medium conficitur ex extremis, et quia exigitur

---

6–7 *cf.* Arist. *Cat.* 10.13a18–31   **8–9** *cf.* Boeth. *in Cat.* 172d–73c   **13** *cf.* Arist. *Top.* II 3.111a14–32   **20–21** Arist. *Top.* VII 5.154b13–14; Anon. *Auct. Arist.* 36.111 (ed. Hamesse, 330)   **27–28** *cf.* Arist. *Phys.* V 1.224b30–35; Anon. *Auct. Arist.* 2.148 (ed. Hamesse, 153)

---

2 sicut¹] sit *P*   **7** contrariorum] praedictorum *P*   **9** permutari...separari] perminus quidem possunt sed minime separari permutari *P*

quod naturam suscipiat extremorum, ideo non contrariatur illis. Sed in moralibus medium non conficitur ex extremis. Quod patet, quia largus non dicitur qui dat danda et retinenda retinet, secundum quod communiter attestatur, sed quia respicit condiciones quae debent respici in quolibet dono: quid cui des, videas, cur, quo modo, quando. Sapiens ergo ordinare debet et non ordinari, ut scribitur in *Metaphysica*. Ergo a prodigo vel avaro non ordinatur sed a propria ratione, ut scribitur in *Ethicis*: "Virtus est medium secundum rationem". 5

Ad obiectum dicendum quod verum est quod medium comparatum ad extrema est sicut alterum et sic opponitur sicut alterum, et quia tunc non est medium simpliciter, talis oppositio est secundum quid, unde est ibi fallacia secundum quid et simpliciter; et sic patet solutio ad obiectum. 10

<3>

Modo quaeritur quare in naturalibus medium conficitur ex extremis, in moralibus vero non.

Et dicendum quod in naturalibus extrema contrariorum mutuo se expellunt. Quia ergo unum expellit alterum et e converso, et in tali expellatione potest aliquid 15
f. 59vb de uno | et alio remanere et uniri in unum, et tunc fit medium, ut patet sensibiliter in collisione corporum solidorum, sed in moralibus non agunt et patiuntur ad invicem, quare in illis non potest medium confici ex extremis.

<4>

Consequenter quaeritur: Dicit quod qualitas suscipit magis et minus.

Non videtur esse verum de abstractis. Albedo et nigredo sunt species. Sed dicit 20
Porphyrius quod species constituitur ex differentia faciente aliud, quae non recipit magis et minus. Si ergo constituentia suum esse non recipiunt magis et minus, scilicet genus et differentia, nec ipsa species suscipiet.

Quod concedo, quod in abstracto species non suscipiunt magis et minus.

Sed contra. Hoc nomen, "albedo", aut imponitur formae in termino aut citra. 25
Si in termino, cum album dicatur denominative ab ea, dicet albedinem in termino. Sed dicit auctor *Sex principiorum* quod ultra terminum non potest progredi. Ergo album dicet albedinem quae non poterit intendi usque ad terminum et sic nec recipere magis.

5–6 Arist. *Metaph.* I 2.982a17–19; Anon. *Auct. Arist.* 1.13 (ed. Hamesse, 116) **6–7** *cf.* Arist. *EN* II 6.1107a6–7 **19** Arist. *Cat.* 8.10b25 **20–22** Porph. *Isag.* 8.19–9.23 **27** *cf.* Anon. *LSP* VIII 93 (ed. Minio-Paluello, 57)

---

4 des] det *P* **5–6** metaphysica] thiᵒ *P* **7** virtus] vir cuius *P*

Item. In albo duo sunt, forma et suppositum. Sed constat quod non recipit magis et minus ratione suppositi, cum sit substantia; substantia enim non recipit etc. Ergo gratia formae. Sed propter quod unumquodque tale, et illud magis. Ergo forma abstracta potest intendi.

5 Item. Contrarietas est causa intentionis et remissionis. Sed posita causa ponitur effectus. Cum ergo forma abstracta habeat contrarium, intenditur.

Et dicendum quod albedo et qualibet forma consimilis potest dupliciter considerari, scilicet prout est inclinata ad subiectum vel prout non est inclinata sed per se stans. Secundo modo habet modum substantiae et est species, <et sic> nec potest
10 intendi nec remitti. Primo modo habet modum accidentis iuxta illud Boethii: "Accidentis esse est inesse", et sic potest intendi et remitti, et sic intentio et remissio, dicit auctor *Sex principiorum*, est secundum accessum et recessum ad puritatem speciei. Item, scribitur in *Topicis*: "Albius est quod est nigro impermixtius".

Ad primum obiectum dicendum quod nec sic nec sic imponitur, cum habeat
15 modum substantiae, ut visum est, et imponi in termino vel citra terminum sint condiciones modum habentium accidentis et non substantiae.

Ad aliud. Album gratia formae suscipit magis et minus, sed non gratia cuiuscumque formae sed formae ut est inclinata ad subiectum, et sic non significatur per hoc nomen, "albedo".

20 Ad ultimum. Contrarietas secundum sui essentiam non est causa quare aliquid intenditur et remittitur, sed solum secundum suas operationes, ut patet in igne et aqua; nam quanto ignis effectus suos in aquam imprimit, tanto plus aquae frigiditas remittitur. Et ita secundum suas operationes mutuo se expellunt et sunt causae intentionis et remissionis. Sed non possunt se expellere nisi permisceantur. Non
25 autem permiscentur nisi in subiecto. Ergo a primo si recipiunt magis et minus, sunt in subiecto, et ideo solum in concretione recipiunt magis et minus.

---

3   Arist. *APo* I 2.72a29–30   **10–11**   *cf.* Boeth. *in Cat.* 170d–71a (*hoc adagium*, "Accidentis esse est inesse", *quandoque Boethio, quandoque Aristoteli a magistriis attribuitur*; *cf.* Thomas Aquinas *Expositio Libri posteriorum* I 2.40 (ed. Leonina, 11) *cum nota editoris in apparatu fontium*)   **11–13** *cf.* Anon. *LSP* VIII 90 (ed. Minio-Paluello, 56)   **13**   Arist. *Top.* III 5.119a27–32; Anon. *Auct. Arist.* 36.55 (ed. Hamesse, 325)

---

13 albius] *cum fonte* : album *P*   **13** impermixtius] *cum fonte* : impermixtum *P*   **18** sic] similiter *P*   **23** operationes] et ita *add. P*

TRIANGULUS VERO ETC. (8.11a5)

<DIVISIO>

Ostenso quod qualia recipiunt magis, probat quod hoc non convenit cuilibet quali.

Haec pars | in duas. Primo proponit quod intendit et probat, secundo infer   f. 6ora
correlarium, ibi: *Horum itaque* (8.11a15).

Prima in duas. Primo proponit, secundo probat, ibi: *Quaecumque enim defini-*
5 *tionem* (8.11a7).

Et sequitur pars in qua ponit proprium convertibile. Et in duas dividitur. Primo
enim ostendit quod hoc non convenit aliis, secundo concludit hoc esse proprium
qualitatis, ibi: *Quare id proprium erit* (8.11a18).

Et sequitur pars in qua movet quaestionem. Et in duas dividitur. Primo quaerit,
10 secundo solvit, ibi: *Paene enim in talibus* (8.11a22).

Secunda in duas. Primo ponit solutionem satisfacientem quaestioni, secundo
opinioni. Vel aliter: Primo solvit secundum opinionem Platonis, secundo secundum propriam, ibi: *Amplius si contingat* (8.11a37).

Prima in duas. Primo solvit, secundo solutionem manifestat, ibi: *Nam cum*
15 *disciplina* (8.11a25).

Haec secunda in duas penes duo proposita in solvendo quae exemplificat. <Se-
cunda> ibi: *Eorum vero* (8.11a26).

Haec secunda in duas. Primo probat <per> inductionem species non esse ad
aliquid, secundo secundum rationem, ibi: *Dicimur enim quales* (8.11a33).

20 Prima in duas. Primo facit quod dictum est, secundo removet dubium, ibi: *Sed*
forte secundum genus (8.11a28).

Haec est divisio lectionis, et sunt particulae duodecim.

<SENTENTIA>

Circa primam sic procedit: Triangulus, quadrangulus et aliae species figurarum
non recipiunt magis et minus.

25 Consequenter probat hoc sic: Nullum quod recipit magis et minus participatur aequaliter secundum definitionem. Triangulus etc. sunt huiusmodi. Ergo etc.
Triangulus enim participatur aequaliter, ergo non recipit magis et minus. Consequenter probat idem de non participantibus definitionem. Magis enim et minus
sunt in eadem specie. Sed quadratum vel altera parte longior non sunt in specie

---

4–5 definitionem] *ac* : definitione *P*   16 quae] quem *P*   19 dicimur] *P^{inf}ac* : dicuntur *P*
21 forte] et *add. P*

circuli. Ergo non sunt circulus secundum magis et minus. Similter est de aliis quod si aliqua duo non participant definitionem tertii nec sunt in eadem specie cum illo, non participant illud secundum magis et minus.

Consequenter concludit: Ex quo dictae proprietates omni non congruunt neque soli, non sunt propriae qualitati.

Consequenter ponit proprie proprium, dicens quod dici simile vel dissimile proprium est qualitatis, et causa est quia secundum aliud non dicimur similes vel dissimiles.

Consequenter concludit quod ex quo aliis non competit, erit proprium qualitatis.

Consequenter movet quaestionem, dicens quod nullus conturbetur quamvis quasdam qualitates cum relatione interposuerimus, ut habitus et dispositiones, licet "Diversorum generum etc".

Consequenter solvit quod genera habituum dicuntur ad aliquid et non species.

Consequenter explanat hoc, dicens quod disciplina, cum sit genus, dicitur ad aliquid.

Consequenter dicit quod species eorum non dicuntur ad aliquid, ut grammatica etc.

Et quia crederet aliquis quod nec secundum se nec secundum genus dicantur ad aliquid, hoc removet, <dicens> quod sub generis nomine ad aliquid dicuntur.

Consequenter probat per rationem speciem non esse ad aliquid: Illa secundum quae dicimur quales sunt qualitates et non ad aliquid. Speciales scientiae sunt huiusmodi. Ergo etc. Minorem ponit et conclusionem, ibi: *Quare haec erunt* (8.11a35).

Ultimo ponit aliam solutionem, dicens quod non est inconveniens idem esse in diversis generibus diversimode acceptum.

Haec est sententia partis.

Expositio litteralis

Dictum est quod qualia recipiunt magis, *vero*, id est sed, *triangulus* etc. *non videtur suscipere magis et minus*; et | non solum sic est de istis, sed *nec aliquid* etc.

Enim, id est quia, *quaecumque* etc., *similiter*, id est aequaliter, vel: *similiter*, id est secundum eandem rationem et non secundum magis et minus. Ita est de istis recipientibus definitionem, *vero*, id est sed, *eorum quae non recipiunt*, definitionem

f. 60rb

13   Arist. *Cat.* 3.1b17–24

2 non] *add. P in marg.*   15 quod] quia P   22 qualitates] species sunt qualitates *add. P a.c.* 30 vel] *lectio incerta*

supple, *alterum* non *dicitur magis* participare *altero* illud. Bene dico quod non, *enim*, id est quia, *quadratum* non *est magis circulus quam forma*, supple quantitativa, *altera parte longior*; *enim*, id est quia, *nullam suscipit*, triangulus vel quadrangulus supple, *rationem circuli*. Non solum sic est de istis, *autem*, id est sed, *simpliciter*, id est generaliter, *si utraque non recipiunt*, id est si sunt duo quorum neutrum recipit, *huius propositi*, id est circuli, *rationem*, *non dicetur* etc., quia proprie non fit comparatio nisi inter participantia communi proprietate. Ex hoc concludit: Ex quo huiusmodi qualia non recipiunt magis, *non ergo* etc.

Ex quo dictae proprietates non competunt omni nec soli, *itaque*, id est ergo, *horum quae dicta sunt* etc.

Vere non sunt propria qualitatis, *vero*, id est sed, *dicuntur*, aliqua supple, *similia* etc., *autem*, id est sed, *alterum* etc. *nisi secundum id quale est*, id est secundum qualitatem.

Concludit: Ex quo haec proprietas qualitati convenit et non aliis, *quare*, id est ergo, *id erit proprium* etc.

Ita dictum est de qualitate, *autem*, id est sed, *non decet contubari ne quis dicat* etc., *propositionem*, id est tractatum propositum, *interposuisse multa de relativis*; *enim*, id est quia, *habitus et dispositiones dicebamus* etc., et ista sunt qualitates.

Ita possit aliquis obicere, vero, id est sed, *genera dicuntur ad aliquid in talibus paene* (et dicit "paene" propter quaedam quae non sunt ad aliquid, ut frigus, calor et similia), sed *nihil horum quae singularia sunt*, id est nulla species istorum generum, dicitur ad aliquid.

Vere genus est ad aliquid, *enim*, id est quia, *cum disciplina* etc.

Bene dixi "species non dicuntur ad aliquid", *vero*, pro quia, *eorum quae singularia sunt nihil ipsum* etc.

Ita dixi species per se non dici ad aliquid, *sed dicuntur ad aliquid*, species supple, *secundum genus*, id est per nomen sui generis, *forte* (et dicit "forte" quia non sunt vere relativa). Et ponit exempla: *ut grammatica* etc. Et concludit: *Quapropter*, id est ergo, ea *quae sunt* singularia *non sunt ad aliquid*, sed qualitates supple, *per se*, sed per accidens, quia secundum nomen generis.

Vere sunt qualitates, *enim*, id est quia, *secundum* singularia *dicimur quales* etc.; *enim*, id est quia, *dicimur scientes* etc.; *secundum quas*, id est secundum illas, *dicimur quales*.

Non solum isto modo solvitur, *amplius si contingat hoc ipsum*, id est idem, *esse quale et relativum*, *nihil*, pro non, *est inconveniens* annumerari, diversimode supple.

---

4 supple rationem circuli] rationem circuli supple *P*   8 non²] ut *P*   19 possit] ponit *P*   21 nulla] nullas *P*   29 singularia] *lectio incerta*   29 se] non *add. P*   31 singularia] *lectio incerta*   32 dicimur] *ac* : dicuntur *P*   35 relativum] *add. al. man.* : rel + *aliquid quod legere nequeo in ras. P*

<Quaestiones>

<1>

Primo quaeritur quare qualitates quae continentur sub quarta specie qualitatis non habent contrarium nec possunt intendi nec remitti.

Et dicendum quod huiusmodi qualitates sunt fundatae in quantitate et causantur a quantitate. Quod patet, nam linea gratia subiecti sic dispositi habet talem formam. Sed dicit auctor *Sex principiorum* in capitulo de quantitate quod si causa non suscipit magis et minus, nec effectus. | Quia ergo quantitas non recipit magis et minus nec habet contrarium, ideo nec huiusmodi qualitates. Hoc per Philareti sententiam in *Libro de pulsibus* confirmatur dicentis: "Quanto plus dominatur virtus causarum, tanto validior fit effectus".

f. 60va

<2>

Consequenter quaeritur: Dicit quod proprium est qualitati secundum eam simile vel dissimile dici.

Cum ergo secundum similitudinem etc., similitudo et dissimilitudo erunt qualitates, quod non est verum, sed potius relationes.

Et dicendum quod in quantum li "secundum" dicit habitudinem causae efficientis sic est proprium qualitatis secundum eam simile vel dissimile dici; nam qualitas est istorum efficiens causa (quod patet per Boethium; est enim similitudo rerum differentium eadem qualitas). Sed cum obicitur "secundum similitudinem etc.", hoc est verum prout li "secundum" dicit habitudinem causae formalis et non efficientis; nam similitudo est forma similis, sicut albedo albi. Et sic aequivocatur haec praepositio, "secundum".

<3>

Consequenter quaeritur: Dicit quod species habituum non possunt esse ad aliquid, sed eorum genera ad aliquid esse possunt.

Contra. Scribitur in quarto *Topicorum* quod in quocumque est species, et genus. Rursum in secundo: "Non est ponere genus sine specie". Ergo in quocumque praedicamento erit genus, in eodem erit species, ut videtur.

5–6 *cf.* Anon. *LSP* V 56 (ed. Minio-Paluello, 47) **7–9** Philaretus *Liber pulsuum* (ed. Venet., 4ra) **10–11** Arist. *Cat.* 8.11a15–19 **16–17** Boeth. *Top. Diff*. III 3.14 (= 1197c) (ed. Nikitas, 52–53) **21–22** Arist. *Cat.* 8.11a20–37 **23–24** Arist. *Top.* IV 1.121a5–9 **24** *locum non inveni*

---

4 subiecti] situs naturalis *P* **12** similitudinem] dissimilem *P* **23** species] specie *P*

Item. Scribitur in *Antepraedicamentis*: "Quicquid praedicatur de praedicato, et de subiecto". Cum ergo de grammatica disciplina dicatur, et relatio disciplinae conveniat, ergo et grammaticae conveniet, ut videtur.

Et dicendum quod loquendo secundum veritatem et esse in quocumque praedicamento est genus, et species, ut obicitur. Genera tamen habituum possunt esse in genere relationis secundum dici, licet non sint species in eodem.

Vel aliter. Dicendum quod sunt in eodem praedicamento secundum opinionem Aristotelis, licet Platonicorum sententia non consentiat.

<4>

Consequenter quaeritur: Dicit quod idem potest esse in generibus diversis.

Quod non videtur. Nam "Diversorum generum etc."

Et dicendum quod intelligit secundum diversos respectus, sicut patet de disciplina, quia accepta absolute prout subiectum denominat et qualificat est in praedicamento qualitatis, in quantum vero est actio doctoris in discipulum, ut Ali attestatur, quia tunc non habet suum esse in doctore absolute acceptum sed etiam prout a discipulo recipitur, sic est in praedicamento relationis.

1–2 Arist. *Cat.* 3.1b10–16 **9** Arist. *Cat.* 8.11a37–39 **10** *cf.* Arist. *Cat.* 3.1b17–24 **13–14** Haly *Commentum super Librum tegni Galieni* I 1 (ed. Venet., 1ra)

---

2 de grammatica] *inv. P a.c.* **12** absolute] absoluta *P a.c.* **13–14** ali attestatur] alii attestantur *P*

Lectio XXXVIII

Suscipit autem facere et pati etc. (9.11b1)

‹Divisio›

Notificatis quattuor membris, de aliis sex breviter se expedit.

Haec pars in duas. Primo determinat de actione et passione in simul, secundo de residuis, ibi: *Dictum est autem* (9.11b8).

Prima in duas. Primo ponit proprietates communes actioni et passioni, secundo 5 ipsas per exempla manifestat, ibi: *Calefacere enim* (9.11b2).

Haec secunda in duas. Primo manifestat primam proprietatem, secundo secundam, ut ibi: *Sed magis et minus* (9.11b5).

Pars in qua de aliis prosequitur in duas. Primo de ipsis prosequitur, secundo recapitulat de praedictis, ibi: *De propositis itaque* (10.11b15).

10 Prima in duas. Primo determinat de situ, secundo de aliis, ibi: *De reliquis autem* (9.11b10).

Haec est divisio lectionis, et sunt sex particulae.

‹Sententia›

Circa primam sic procedit: Actio et passio contrarietatem recipiunt et magis et minus.

15 Consequenter manifestat primam proprietatem: ut calefactio, quod est actio, habet contrarium, | et calefieri, quod est passio.   f. 60vb

Deinde manifestat de secunda proprietate, dicens quod calefacere, quod est actio, recipit magis et minus, et similiter calefieri, quod est passio.

Deinde determinat de aliis, dicens quod de situ dictum est in capitulo de ad 20 aliquid, ubi dicitur quod a positione dicitur denominative.

Sed de ubi et quando et habere, quia manifesta sunt per praedicta, non dicetur aliud quam quae dicta sunt in principio libri; nam ibi dictum est quod habere est ut esse calciatum et similia.

Ultimo recapitulat, dicens quod de praedictis sufficiant quae dicta sunt.

---

20 Arist. *Cat.* 7.6b11–14   **22–23** Arist. *Cat.* 4.1b27–2a5

---

7 sed magis et minus] suscipit autem P   **17** manifestat] emanifestat P   **19** de²] *ex* si *corr.* P
19 ad] *add.* P *s.l.*

Expositio litteralis

Ita dictum est de aliis praedicamentis, sed *facere recipit,* id est habet, non quia subiectum sed alterum extremorum, *contrarietatem* etc.

Vere recipiunt contraria, *enim,* id est quia, *calefacere,* quod est actio, *contrarium est* etc., *et calefieri,* quod est passio, contrarium est *ad frigidum fieri* etc.

Non solum contrarietatem recipiunt, *sed magis et minus.* Et hoc probat: *Enim,* 5
<id est> quia, *calefacere,* quod est actio, *et calefieri,* quod est passio, id est facere et pati, etc. Consequenter recapitulat, dicens: *De his,* supple duobus, *tanta dicantur.* Quasi dicens: De his non plura dicemus.

Ita dictum est de istis, *autem,* id est sed, *de situ dictum est in his quae sunt ad aliquid,* id est in capitulo relationis, ita dictum est de istis supple, *quia dicuntur* 10
denominative etc.

Et ita dictum est de situ, *autem,* id est sed, *de reliquis* etc., *quam quae dicta sunt* etc., *in principio,* huius libri supple; et haec sunt dicta, *quod habere significat* etc., *sed* etiam *alia* sunt manifesta *quae de his* etc.

<Quaestiones>

<1>

Primo quaeritur: Dicit quod pati et facere recipiunt magis et minus. 15
Ergo et comparationem. Quod falsum est.

Et dicendum quod actio et passio secundum id quod sunt non recipiunt magis et minus nec contrarietatem, nam hae proprietates soli competunt qualitati, tamen aliquando sumitur agere ut terminatum est ad qualitatem, cui qualitati debetur contrarium, et sic gratia illius qualitatis dicitur suscipere magis et minus, ut dealbare 20
et cetera similia. Verbum igitur de natura sui significati non recipit magis et minus, sed ratione qualitatis ad quam terminatur, et sic loquitur hic.

<2>

Et quaeritur quare non determinat hic diffuse de istis sicut de aliis.
Solutio. Dicunt quidam quod de istis ideo breviter hic se expedit quia proposuit de his tractatum facere specialem, ut *Librum sex principiorum.* Sed "loquendum 25

---

15 Arist. *Cat.* 9.11b1–2   24–25 *cf.* Anon. D'Orvillensis, *in Cat.* (ed. Ebbesen, 374)   **220.25–**
221.1 *cf.* Arist. *Top.* II 2.110a15–19; Anon. *Auct. Arist.* 36.26 (ed. Hamesse, 323)

---

4 frigidum] *ex* frigum *corr. P*   9 sed] *iter. P*   10 quia] quae *P*   14 quae] *c* : quod *P ut v.*
17 secundum] *add. P s.l. ut v.*   18 qualitati] *ex* qualitate *corr. P*   24 hic] sic *P*

ut plures", scribitur secundo *Topicorum*. Cum igitur ab omnibus librum istum ab
Aristotele non esse compositum dicatur, aliter dicamus quod Aristoteles determinat
in libro isto de decem praedicamentis secundum <esse et> essentiam quam habent
in linea praedicamentali, et illa sex ab illis quattuor dependent secundum esse, cum
oriantur a speciebus eorundem; ideo cognitis quattuor primis ex consequenti et
alia cognoscuntur. Et quod ista sex oriantur a speciebus aliorum quattuor patet,
quia quando et ubi oriuntur a speciebus quantitatis, ut a tempore quando et a loco
ubi, passio et actio a speciebus qualitatis, ut a naturali potentia actio, ab impotentia
passio, habitus et situs a relatione, nam habitus est adiacentia eorum quae sunt ad
aliquid, ut eorum quae sunt circa corpus ad corpus, sed situs est ordinatio partium
ad aliquid, ut ad totum. Et hoc est quod dicit in fine lectionis, quod de his nihil aliud
dicetur quam quae dicta sunt in principio de primis quattuor, quia primis cognitis
secundum esse ex consequenti habetur cognitio aliorum.

<3>

Consequenter quaeritur quare ponit proprietates actionis | et passionis et non   f. 61ra
aliorum.
    Et dicendum quod facere et pati retinent proprietatem eorum a quibus causan-
tur, ut habetur in principio lectionis, sed alia non retinent proprietates eorum a quibus causantur; quod patet, quia situs et habere dicuntur a relatione, sed relativorum
proprietas est esse simul natura, eis autem non convenit.

<4>

Consequenter quaeritur quare ponit istas proprietates simul.
    Et dicendum quod ista ab eodem genere qualitatis generantur, ut a naturali po-
tentia vel impotentia. Quia ergo ab eodem has habent proprietates, simul ipsas
ponit.

<5>

Consequenter quaeritur quare simul determinat de actione et passione.
    Et dicendum ut dicitur in tertio *Physicorum*: Omne agens physice dum movet

---

11–12 Arist. *Cat.* 9.11b10–14   **14–15** Arist. *Cat.* 9.11b1–7   **17** *cf.* Arist. *Cat.* 9.11b1–7 *et*
Q1 *supra*   **221.25–222.1** *cf.* Arist. *Phys.* III 1.201a20–25; 2.202a4–9. *cf. etiam* Anon. *Auct. Arist.*
2.100 (ed. Hamesse, 148)

---

2 esse] est *P*   **8** actio] situs habitus *add. P*   **9** relatione] *ex* relationes *corr. P*

movitur et dum agit patitur, et e converso. Ad quam convenientiam exprimendam de his simul pertractavit.

<6>

Consequenter quaeritur, cum alia praedicamenta notificaverit per species, quare ista per species explanare recusavit; nam videtur quod male faceret, cum ista species habeant ut praedicta.   5

    Et dicendum quod actio et passio ab eodem principio oriuntur, ut visum est, scilicet ab eadem specie. Cum earum principium non distinguatur per species, ut effectus causae proportionetur, non est necesse ut ista per species multiplicet.

<7>

Sed modo quaeritur, cum effectus causae proportionetur, cum ergo causa sit in uno praedicamento, ergo effectus, scilicet actio et passio, non erunt diversa praedica-   10 menta.

    Et dicendum quod res non distinguuntur penes causas efficientes sed penes causas formales, iuxta illud Aristotelis: "Formae operatio est triplex: dare esse, distinguere unum ab altero, ordinare in opus". Licet ergo actio et passio ab eodem efficienti causentur, quia tamen diversas habent formas, diversa poterunt constituere   15 praedicamenta.

<8>

Consequenter quaeritur quare nominet ista genera nomine concretionis.

    Et dicendum quod istae proprietates, ut dictum est, eis non competunt nisi ratione qualitatis ad quam terminantur. Quia ergo non competunt eis nisi in concretione ad qualitatem et non per se, huiusmodi genera concretionis nomine   20 nuncupavit.

13–14 *locum non inveni*   **17**   Arist. *Cat.* 9.11b1; b7   **18–19**   Q1 *supra*

---

7 scilicet] sed P   **9** causa] + *fenestra fere unius vocis capax* P   **17** nominet] *ex* nomine *corr.* P

Lectio XXXIX

Quotiens autem solet opponi etc. (10.11b17)

\<Divisio\>

Hic prosequitur de postpraedicamentis.

Haec pars in quinque secundum quinque postpraedicamenta. Secunda ibi: *Prius autem* (12.14a26), tertia ibi: *Simul autem* (13.14b24), quarta ibi: *Motus* (14.15a13), quinta ibi: *Habere autem* (15.15b18).

⁵ Prima in duas. Primo ponit prooemium, secundo prosequitur, ibi: *Opponitur autem* (10.11b20).

Haec secunda in duas. Primo prosequitur in generali, secundo in speciali, ibi: *Quaecumque igitur* (10.11b25).

Haec secunda in duas. Primo prosequitur de oppositis secundum se, secundo ad ¹⁰ invicem comparando, ibi: *Quoniam autem privatio et habitus non sic opponuntur* (10.12b15).

Prima in quattuor secundum quattuor genera oppositionis. Secunda ibi: *Illa vero quae ut contraria* (10.11b33), tertia ibi: *Privatio vero et habitus* (10.12a26), quarta ibi: *Non est autem neque quod sub affirmatione* (10.12b5).

¹⁵ Prima in duas. Primo definit relativa, secundo definitionem explanat, ut ibi: *ut duplum hoc ipsum quod est* (10.11b26).

Haec secunda in duas. Primo exemplificat, secundo concludit definitionem, ibi: *Quaecumque ergo opposita* (10.11b32).

Pars in qua determinat de contrariis in duas. Primo ostendit quod quaedam ²⁰ proprietas assignata de relativis contrariis non competit, secundo quasi supposita divisione de membris dividentibus prosequitur, ut ibi: *Quaecumque vero talia* (10.11b37).

Haec secunda in duas. Primo ponit membra ipsa enumerando, secundo per exempla exemplificat, ibi: *ut languor et sanitas* (10.12a4).

²⁵ Prima in duas penes duo membra. | Secunda ibi: *Quorum vero* (10.12a3).　　f. 61rb

Pars in qua manifestat per exempla in duas. Primo exemplificat primum membrum, secundo secundum, ibi: *Quorum vero \<non\> est necessarium* (10.12a9).

Haec est divisio lectionis, sub qua novem particulae continentur.

---

14 non est autem neque quod sub affirmatione] P^{inf}**c** : non est autem secundum affirmationem *P*
28 novem] 4 *P ut v.*

\<Sententia\>

Primae partis sententia haec est: Dicendum est quot modis aliquid alii opponatur. Et modos enumerat, dicens quod sunt quattuor, et ipsos manifestat et pertransit.

Consequenter prosequitur in generali exempla ponendo, dicens quod relativa sunt ut duplum, dimidium etc.

Consequenter prosequitur in speciali, et primo de relativis, dicens quod illa opponuntur relative quae secundum sui esse referuntur ad sua relativa in genitivo vel in quolibet alio casu.   5

Et ponit exempla: ut duplum etc. (littera plana est), et pertransit.

Consequenter concludit quod illa sunt relative opposita quae referuntur ad aliquid in genitivo vel in quolibet alio casu.   10

Consequenter dicit quod unum contrariorum secundum se non dicitur ad aliquid contrarium, sed si dicatur, hoc est secundum hoc nomen commune, "contrarium", ut malum non dicitur malum boni licet dicatur bono contrarium.

Consequenter, divisione supposita, dicit quod talia contraria in quibus necesse est alterum subiecto inesse ipso manente sunt immediata, sed talia quorum non est   15
necessarium alterum inesse sunt mediata.

Consequenter ponit exemplum de immediatis: ut languor et sanitas.

Et haec est sententia partis.

Expositio litteralis

Quotiens solet opponi etc. *Dicendum est quotiens*, id est quot modis etc.

Vere hoc est dicendum, *autem*, id est quia, *unumquodque istorum opponitur, ut*   20
sit figuratim dicere, id est exemplariter, *ut relativa*, opponuntur supple, *ut duplum*
et dimidium etc.

Ita dictum est quod < * * * > *ut relativa opponuntur, ea ipsa* quod *sunt*, id est secundum suum esse, *dicuntur*, id est referuntur, *oppositorum*, id est ad sua relativa in genitivo casu, *aut quomodolibet aliter*, id est in alio casu, *ut duplum* etc. Et non   25
solum duplum, *sed et disciplina* etc.

Ex quo duplum et similia dicuntur ad aliquid quia esse eorum est ad aliquid se habere, *ergo quaecumque sunt opposita* etc.

Ita dictum est de relativis, *vero*, id est sed, *illa quae* opponuntur *ut contraria*
ipsa quae sunt, id est secundum suum esse, *nullo modo dicuntur ad se invicem*, id   30
est non referuntur ad aliquid secundum se, sed *dicuntur contraria sibi invicem*, id
est dicuntur ad aliquid secundum hoc nomen, "contrarium". Vere sic est, *enim*, id
est quia, *bonum* non *dicitur mali bonum, sed contrarium; nec album* etc.

---

6 quae] sunt *add. P*   23 ut] *exp. P ut v., sed videtur potius quod lacuna statuenda est*

Ita est in contrariis, *vero*, id est sed, eorum *contrariorum quaecumque sunt talia ut alterum sit* necesse *inesse in quibus nata sunt fieri et de quibus praedicantur*, id est in substantiis, talium *nihil est medium*.

Vere haec sunt immediata, *vero*, id est sed, *quorum*, scilicet contrariorum, *non est necessarium* etc., *aliquid est medium*.

Et ponit exempla: *ut languor et sanitas*, quae sunt contraria immediata supple, habent *fieri* etc. Non solum sic est de istis, *sed par et impar* etc.

<Quaestiones>

<1>

Primo quaeritur: Cum in *Libro perihermeneias* de oppositione determinaverit, videtur haec pars superfluere. Aut qualiter dicit differenter hic et ibi?

Et dicendum quod oppositio est passio rerum. Cum ergo quaedam sint complexae et quaedam incomplexae, et in hoc libro determinet de dicibili incomplexo, hic determinat de oppositione quae est a parte rei incomplexae, sed in *Libro perihermeneias* determinat de complexo, scilicet de enuntiatione, quare determinat de oppositione quae est a parte rei complexae; quare neuter superfluit.

<2>

Iuxta hoc quaeritur quare | ibi ponit tantum tres modos, hic autem quattuor; nam ibi deminutus vel hic superfluus videtur.   f. 61va

Ad primum. Subiectum oppositionis de qua agitur in *Libro perihermeneias* est enuntiatio. Sed subiectum non variatur nisi tripliciter. Aut enim enuntiatur in utraque aliquid uniformiter aut deformiter. Si uniformiter, aut enuntiatur in utraque aliquid universaliter aut particulariter. Si universaliter, sic contrariae. Si particulariter, sic subcontrariae. Si autem deformiter, sic sunt contradictoriae. Quia ergo enuntiatio pluribus modis variari non potest, in *Libro perihermeneias* non sunt nisi tres species oppositionis.

Ad aliud. Oppositio quaelibet est inter duo ad minus. Aut ergo utrumque significat ens simpliciter aut unum ens simpliciter, reliquum non. Si primo modo, aut sunt simul natura, et sic sunt relativa, aut non, et sic contraria. Si <secundo modo, aut> unum significat ens simpliciter et reliquum secundum quid, et sic privativa, aut unum significat ens simpliciter, reliquum nihil ponit, et sic contradictoria.

---

8   *cf.* Arist. *Int.* 7.17a38–18a12

---

5 est²] *ac* : inesse *P*   **6** supple] non *add. P*   **9** qualiter dicit] *inv. P*   **16** superfluus] *ex* superflue *corr. P*   **19** enuntiatur] essentiatur *P*

<3>

Si quaeritur quare sic ordinentur, patet.

Nam ordinantur secundum quod magis conveniunt. Sed relativa magis conveniunt quam contraria. Quod patet, quia utrumque relativorum significat ens simpliciter et sunt simul natura, sed licet contraria significent ens simpliciter, non tamen sunt simul natura, quare contraria minus conveniunt.   5

Item, contraria plus conveniunt quam privativa, quia contraria mutuo se expellunt et sunt in subiecto ordine regressibili, sed privativa sunt in subiecto ordine irregressibili, ut habetur in littera.

Item, privativa plus conveniunt quam contradictoria, quia privatio ponit aliquid, scilicet subiectum, iuxta illud Boethii: "Qui habet privationem, habet habitum   10 quodam modo, id est secundum quid", sed non sic est in contradictoriis.

<4>

Consequenter quaeritur, cum ad aliquid sit praedicamentum, quo modo sit post-praedicamentum.

Et dicendum quod relativa prout sunt in diversis substantiis, cum oppositionem non habeant, constituunt praedicamentum, sed prout sunt in eadem substantia,   15 opponuntur, et sic postpraedicamentum.

<5>

Item, obicitur quod cumplura sint genera oppositionis.

Nam homo et asinus sunt opposita, et non sunt relative opposita, nam esse unius non dependet ab esse alterius, nec sunt contraria, cum se mutuo non expellant nec habeant fieri circa idem, nec sunt contradictoria nec privativa, ut patet. Ergo plura   20 sunt genera oppositionis quam quattuor.

Et dicendum quod licet homo et asinus non sint contraria, opponuntur tamen ut contraria. Unde aliud est dicere quod sunt contraria et aliud quod opponuntur ut contraria. Et sic opponuntur; habent enim contrarias differentias ipsa constituentes, scilicet rationale et irrationale — non tamen quod huiusmodi differentiae   25 sint contrariae secundum operationes, quia non mutuo se expellunt, sed secundum essentiam tantum.

7–8   Arist. *Cat.* 12a26–29; *cf.* Lectio XL   **10–11**   *cf.* Boeth. *Divis.* 883a (ed. Magee, 24)

---

6 item] *ex* inter *corr. P*   **9** item] *ex* inter *corr. P*   **11** secundum quid] subiectum *P*   **18** asinus] equus *P*   **20** habeant] habent *P*   **26** operationes] oppositiones *P*

Aliter potest dici quod contrarietas hic large sumitur, ut non solum proprie contraria sed etiam disparata comprehendat. Quia ergo species sunt disparatae, sub contrarietate oppositio earum continetur.

<6>

Item, quaeritur quare dividit contraria per mediatum et immediatum et non alia genera oppositionis.

Nam videtur quod debeat alia sic dividere. Est enim aliquid ad quod non dicitur pater neque | filius. Ergo inter relativa cadit medium. f. 61vb

Item, aliquid est quod neque est caecum neque est videns, ut catulus ante tempus determinatum. Ergo inter privativa est medium.

Et dicendum quod multiplex est medium. Quoddam enim est medium secundum speciem, sicut medium confectum ex extremis novam speciem constituens, et de tali loquitur hic, et solum competit contrariis. Aliud est medium non secundum speciem, et tale est in relativis et privativis, ut obicitur, quia medium inter patrem et filium est medium secundum subiectum, non confectum ex extremis; similiter in privativis est medium secundum tempus. Quia ergo medium de quo hic loquitur solum competit contrariis, ideo divisio per mediatum et immediatum solis competit contrariis.

<7>

Sed modo quaeritur quare medium secundum speciem solum competit contrariis.

Et dicendum quod quando ex extremis fit medium aliquod, oportet quod utrumque extremorum aliquid ponat, et sic est ibi motus ab uno in alterum et conflictus, ut patet quando aqua fit tepida. Sed quia utrumque extremorum privationis non ponit aliquid, quia privatio non ponit nisi secundum quid, ideo ex talibus extremis non potest fieri tale medium. Eadem ratio est in contradictoriis. Item, scribitur in *Physicis* quod in ad aliquid non est motus; ergo nec tale medium.

<8>

Consequenter quaeritur: Videtur oppositio inter physicum et logicum, quia physicus inter sanum et aegrum ponit medium, logicus autem non.

4–5 *cf.* Arist. *Cat.* 10.11b37–12a4   **24**   Arist. *Phys.* V 2.225b10–13; 226a24–27

---

3 contrarietate] s *add. P*   **22** quia] nisi *P*   **24** ad] *add. P in marg.*

< * * * > Ergo si considerentur secundum se, cum sanitas sit temperamentum, dicit Iohannitius, et aegritudo intemperamentum (et idem scribitur in *Topicis*: "Sanitas est umorum adaequatio, et inadaequatio aegritudo"), cum inter haec non sit medium, erunt contraria immediata; et sic loquitur logicus. Si considerentur per comparationem ad effectus, scilicet ad operationes, cum sanitas sit ex qua omnes operationes salvae fiunt, dicit Avicenna, sed aegritudo facit operationum sensibilem laesionem, dicit Iohannitius, et inter haec cadit medium quia aliquando est laesio sensibilis et tamen omnes operationes salvae, ideo comparando ad operationes cadit medium.

<9>

Consequenter quaeritur: Cum non faciat mentionem de numero imperfecto, sed de abundanti et perfecto, videtur procedere deminute.

Iuxta hoc quaeritur quid appellatur numerus perfectus, abundans et imperfectus.

Et dicendum quod in numero duo sunt genera partium, aliquotae et non aliquotae, quae sumptae aliquotiens reddunt suum totum.

Unde numerus perfectus appellatur cuius partes aliquotae simul sumptae reddunt suum totum, neque plus neque minus, ut patet in sex; nam unitas est pars aliquota, nam sexiens sumpta reddit suum totum, similiter tria geminatum reddit sex, sed quattuor et quinque non sunt aliquotae partes, ut patet; solum ergo unum, duo, tria sunt partes aliquotae, et haec omnia simul sumpta reddunt sex, neque plus neque minus.

Item, numerus dicitur imperfectus quando omnes partes simul sumptae aliquotae non reddunt suum totum sed minus, ut patet in decem, quia partes aliquotae solum sunt unum, duo, quinque, et omnia ista simul sumpta non | reddunt nisi octo.

Item, numerus dicitur abundans quando omnes partes aliquotae simul sumptae reddunt suum totum et plus, ut patet in duodeviginti, cuius partes aliquotae sunt unum, duo, tria, sex, novem, et haec omnia simul sumptae faciunt unum et viginti.

Per hoc patet ad obiectum, quia per numerum abundantem dat intelligere imperfectum.

Aliter solvitur communiter quod hic appellatur numerus perfectus numerus par, numerus vero abundans numerus impar, et quia omnis numerus vel talis vel talis, sub his poterit comprehendi.

f. 62ra

1–2   Iohannitius *Isagoge ad Techne Galieni* 58 (ed. Maurach, 164)   **2–3** *cf.* Arist. *Top.* VI 2.139b21–22; VI 6.145b8–9   **5–6** Avicenna *Liber Canonis* I 1.1 (ed. Venet., 1)   **6–7** Iohannitius *Isagoge ad Techne Galieni* 58 (ed. Maurach, 164)   **10–11** *cf.* Arist. *Cat.* 10.12a6–9   **30–31** *cf.* Anon. D'Orvillensis, *in Cat.* (ed. Ebbesen, 388)

---

6 facit] fac *P ut v.* 6 operationum] *lectio incerta* **11** et] *ex a corr.* P **29** imperfectum] deminutum P

Lectio XL

<Divisio>

Notificatis contrariis immediatis per exempla, notificat mediata.

Haec pars in duas. Primo notificat ipsa exemplariter in extremis, secundo in mediis, dicens quae sunt mediata, ibi: *Sed horum medium* (10.12a17).

Haec secunda in duas. Primo facit quod dictum est, secundo infert correlarium, ibi: *In aliquibus itaque* (10.12a20).

Et sequitur pars in qua determinat de privativis. Et in duas dividitur. Primo notificat ipsa, secundo ponit dubitationem, ibi: *Privari vero et habere habitum* (10.12a35).

Prima in duas. Primo notificat ipsa per definitionem, secundo per quandam proprietatem, ibi: *Privari autem unumquodque* (10.12a29).

Pars in qua ponit dubitationem in duas. Primo ponit ipsam, secundo probat, ibi: *Nam si esset eadem* (10.12a40).

Haec secunda in duas. Primo ponit rationem, secundo inter illa convenientiam assignat, ibi: *Opposita etiam* (10.12b1).

Haec est divisio lectionis, et sunt particulae octo.

<Sententia>

Circa primam sic procedit: Illa contraria in quibus non est necesse alterum inesse susceptibili sunt mediata, ut album et nigrum habent <esse> circa corpus, et non est necesse alterum inesse determinate; similiter est de pravo et studioso.

Consequenter dicit quae sunt illa media, dicens quod albi et nigri fuscum et pallidum et alii colores medii, sed pravi et studiosi est medium per abnegationem utriusque, ut quod neque pravum neque studiosum.

Ex hoc concludit quod in aliis mediis nomina sunt posita, ut fusco et pallido, sed in aliquibus nomina non sunt posita sed sumuntur per negationem utrorumque extremorum, ut boni et mali quod neque bonum neque malum.

Consequenter definit privativa, dicens quod privatio et habitus habent fieri circa idem ordine irregressibili, ut visio et caecitas etc.

Consequenter ponit proprietatem, dicens quod unumquodque dicimus privari quando illud quod natum est habere non habet, ut edentulum dicimus non quia non habeat dentes sed quia non habet quando natus est habere; similiter est de caeco.

---

10 autem unumquodque] vero utrumque *P*　**16** necesse] est *add. P a.c.*　**28** habere] et *add. P*
29 quando] quod (*ex* quia *correctum*) *P*

Consequenter ponit dubitationem, dicens quod privari non est idem quod privatio nec habere habitum idem quod habitus.

Consequenter probat: Quaecumque sunt eadem, praedicantur de eodem. Sed ista non praedicantur de eodem. Ergo non sunt eadem. Minorem ponit et probat.

Ultimo ponit convenientiam, dicens quod privari et habere habitum opponun- 5
tur sicut privatio et habitus, et hoc manifestat.

Et terminatur sententia lectionis.

Expositio litteralis

Dictum est quae sunt contraria immediata, *vero*, id est sed, *eorum* contrariorum *quorum* etc. Non solum sic est de istis, *sed pravum et studiosum praedicantur quidem* etc.   10

f. 62rb | Sed *horum*, <id est> praedictorum, *est medium* etc., *albi quidem et nigri fuscum et pallidum*, sunt, supple, medium, *et quicumque sunt alii colores* etc.

Ex hoc concludit: Ex quo album et nigrum habent media quibus nomina sunt posita et pravum et studiosum habent media quibus nomina non sunt posita, *itaque*, pro ergo, *in aliquibus* contrariis *nomina sunt posita, ut* in *his quae sunt media* 15
albi et nigri etc. Sed *in aliquibus non est assignare nomina in medio, sed determinantur*, id est denominantur, *per negationem utrorumque*, scilicet extremorum, *ut quod neque bonum neque malum*, est medium, supple, inter bonum et malum, etc.

Ita dictum est de contrariis, *vero*, id est sed, *privatio* etc. quod est *circa aliquid idem*, ordine supple, *ut visio et caecitas circa oculum*. Bene dixi "ordine", *autem*, id 20
est quia, *est*, id est contingit, *dicere universaliter in quo habitus nascitur fieri, circa hoc*, id est circa idem, *dicitur utrumque eorum* fieri *ordine*, excepto quod habitus primo, deinde privatio, vel ordine irregressibili, supple.

Ita dictum est quid est privatio, *autem*, id est sed, *dicimus unumquodque susceptibilium privari quando* non *habet id quod natum est habere*. Vere sic est, *enim*, id 25
est quia, *edentulum dicimus*, aliquem supple, *non* quia *non habet dentes, nec caecum* etc., *sed* quia *non habet quando contingit habere. Quaedam enim generationes* etc., id est res generatae.

Ita dictum est quid est privatio et habitus, *vero*, id est sed, *privari non est privatio et habere habitum* non est *habitus*. Bene dico quod non, *enim*, id est quia, *visus est* 30
habitus, vero, id est sed, *caecitas* est *privatio* etc.

Et bene dico quod non sunt eadem, *nam*, id est quia, *si* essent eadem, *praedicarentur de eodem*; *vero*, id est sed, *minime*, pro non, praedicantur de eodem. Et hoc probat: *Sed homo dicitur caecus, caecitas vero* etc.

---

10 quidem] *ac* : quod *P*   **20** circa] *ac* : etc *P*   **26** dicimus aliquem supple] supple dicens aliquem *P*

Continua: Ita dixi quod differunt, sed *haec, id est privari et habere habitum,*
videntur esse opposita, id est sunt, *tanquam privatio et habitus*; *enim,* id est quia,
idem est modus oppositionis, supple in istis et in illis. Et hoc probat: *Nam,* id est
quia, *caecitas est opposita* etc.

<Quaestiones>

<1>

5   Primo quaeritur de ordine ad partem praecedentem, quia immediatum dicitur per
privationem mediati. Sicut ergo habitus ante privationem, sic contraria mediata
ante immediata.

Et dicendum quod non secundum istum respectum ordinantur, sed <quia> contraria immediata ad sui esse non exigunt nisi duo, mediata vero ad minus tria, et
10 dualitas ante ternarium, ideo sic ordinantur; unde ordinantur secundum quod plura
vel pauciora exigunt ad sui esse.

<2>

Consequenter quaeritur: <Dicit> quod inter bonum et malum est medium.

Contra. Malum et non ens, bonum et ens, convertuntur. Sed inter ens et non
ens nihil est medium. Ergo <nec> inter bonum et malum, cum convertantur cum
15 non ente et ente.

Et dicendum quod duplex est bonum, naturale scilicet et morale. Bonum naturale est rei entitas, unde "omnia bonum appetunt", id est esse, et inter tale bonum
et malum nihil est medium, ut obicitur. Aliud est bonum morale, scilicet bonum
acquisitum, de quo scribitur in *Ethicis* quod non qui facit bona bonus est, sed qui
20 bonum facit et hoc ipso gaudet | bonus est; de eodem scribitur ibidem quod tria   f. 62va
requiruntur ad hoc ut simus boni: scire, velle, impermutabiliter operari. Homo ergo qui semper bona facit et hoc ipso gaudet, habet bonum acquisitum vel morale,
quod idem est, sed ille qui semper promptus est ad malum et ipsum operatur, malum habet acquisitum, et inter haec cadit medium, nam puer incunabulus neque
25 bonum neque malum operatur; et de tali obicitur.

---

12 *cf.* Arist. *Cat.* 10.12a20–25   **17** *cf.* Arist. *Top.* III 1.116a20; Anon. *Auct. Arist.* 36.38 (ed.
Hamesse, 324)   **19–20** *cf.* Arist. *EN* I 9.1099a17–18; II 2.1104b4–10   **20–21** *cf.* Arist. *EN* II
3.1105a28–33

---

10 secundum] *ex* 6 *vel sim. corr.* P *ut v.*   **13** contra malum et non ens] contrarium et ens *P*
14 convertantur] convertatur *P*

<3>

Gratia huius quaeritur quare homines ut in pluribus sunt mali, boni autem ut in paucioribus, ut scribitur in secundo *Topicorum*.

Oppositum videtur. Triplex est virtus in homine: vegetativa, sensitiva et intellectiva vel rationalis, quod idem est. Sed non quaelibet istarum est perfectio hominis, sed intellectiva tantum. Ergo homo dicitur a virtute intellectiva. Sed intellectus   5
est semper rectus in sui operatione, scribitur in tertio *De anima*. Ergo homo dictus a tali virtute semper est rectus in sui operatione. Omnes ergo homines semper rectum operantur, et sic nullus pravus.

Solutio. Dicendum quod duplex est virtus animae, scilicet sensus et ratio. Et quando dominatur sensualitas <et> succumbit ratio, homo male operatur, ut scribi-   10
tur in *Ethicis*, sed e converso, bene, quod dicit Augustinus: "Hospicium male disponitur quando ancilla dominatur". Sed probatio quod frequentius dominetur sensualitas rationem quam e converso, et sic plures mali quam boni: Operatio proveniens a sensualitate praedominante naturalis est, sed proveniens a ratione praedominante voluntaria est; ratio enim voluntarie operatur, cum sit libera, dicit Priscianus. Sed   15
natura violentior est in suis operationibus et frequentius operatur quam ratio. Ergo frequentius fit operatio praedominante sensualitate quam praedominante ratione, et ideo in pluribus mali.

Ad obiectum dicendum quod intellectus semper est rectus in sui operatione quantum est de se, et sic ratio praedominetur, non tamen si succumbat, ut dictum   20
est. Quando ergo concluditur, "Ergo homo a tali virtute dictus semper est rectus", verum est eo modo quo intellectus dicebatur rectus. Sed hoc erat solum in quantum praedominatur ratio. Quia ergo succumbit frequentius, ideo plures mali.

<4>

Consequenter quaeritur quare quaedam contraria habent medium nominatum et quaedam non, et breviter ad hoc discernatur.   25

Et dicendum quod grammaticus, cui spectat nominum impositio, est artifex sensibilis, et ideo imponit solum illis nomina quae sunt maxime in sensu. Quia ergo sunt contraria ex parte animae quorum media artifici sensibili sunt ignota in quan-

---

1–2   Arist. *Top.* II 6.112b11–12; Anon. *Auct. Arist.* 36.30 (ed. Hamesse, 324)   5–6   *cf.* Arist. *An.* III 10.433a26; Anon. *Auct. Arist.* 6.169 (ed. Hamesse,188)   9–11   *cf.* Arist. *EN* I 6.1098a3–17; *cf. etiam* Alanus de Insulis, *Liber Poenitentialis* (ed. Migne, PL 210, 284a); Anon. *Liber de stabilitate animae* (ed. Migne, PL 213, 919c)   11–12   *cf.* Aug. *in Iohannis evangelium tractatus* 14 (ed. Migne, PL 35, 1395)   15   *cf.* Prisc. *Inst. gramm.* VIIII 1.8 (ed. Hertz, vol. 1, 455–56)

---

10 sensualitas] *ex* sensus alitas *corr. P ut v.*   10 ratio] o *add. P*   13 quam] in *add. P a.c.*   22 erat] in *add. P*   27 sensu] anima *P*   28 sunt[1]] *ex* sub *corr. P*   28 artifici] *comp.* ar[a] *P*

tum talis est, eis nomina non imponit, ut patet in bono et malo et consimilibus. Ergo per contrarium, cum contraria quae sunt a parte corporis habeant medium quantum ad sensum maxime notum, eis nomina imponit.

Vel aliter. Quaedam sunt contraria in quibus medium conficitur ex extremis; quia ergo talia media dicunt positionem, ideo eis nomina imponuntur. Alia sunt contraria in quibus medium non conficitur ab extremis, sed per eorum remotionem in medium devenitur; quia ergo non sunt media nisi per remotionem extremorum, ut signum signato correspondeat, per eorum privationem talia nuncupantur.

<5>

Consequenter quaeritur quae magis conveniant, an privativa an contraria; nam dictum est quod contraria.

Contra. Opposita privative non se expellunt mutuo, quia privatio expellit | habitum et non e converso. Sed illa quorum unum expellit alterum et non e converso magis conveniunt quam alia illa quorum unum expellit alterum et e converso. Igitur privativa magis conveniunt quam contraria.

Item. Privative opposita semper fiunt circa idem, ut patet in singulis, contraria vero non semper fiunt circa idem sed aliquando in una parte, aliquando in alia. Cum ergo magis conveniant quae semper fiunt circa idem quam alia illa quae aliquando circa idem, aliquando non, plus conveniunt privativa quam contraria.

Et dicendum quod magis convenire uno modo dicitur secundum naturam, et sic privativa plus conveniunt cum habeant fieri circa idem, id est circa eandem naturam; et sic argumenta procedunt. Contraria vero plus conveniunt secundum formam, et dico "secundum formam" quia utrumque potest ponere ens completum, sed privatio non ens nisi quodam modo, ut Boethius attestatur.

<6>

Ultimo privatio habitum videtur praecedere, licet auctor dicat oppositum.

Quia privatio dicit non esse, habitus vero dicit esse. Sed in quolibet generabili et corruptibili non esse praecedit esse. Igitur privatio ante habitum.

Et dicendum quod duplex est non esse. Quoddam quod praecedit esse et quoddam quod subsequitur esse. Cum ergo dicitur quod non esse praecedit esse, hoc

f. 62vb

9–10 *cf.* Lectio XXXIX, Q3   **23** *cf.* Boeth. *Divis.* 883a (ed. Magee, 24)   **24** *cf.* Arist. *Cat.* 10.12a29–35

---

4 sunt] media *add. P a.c.*   **13** alia] *exp. P secundario, nota autem quod eadem lectio et immediate infra invenitur, ubi non deleta est*   **17** conveniant] conveniat *P*   **24** praecedere] *ex* procedere *corr. P*

verum est de non esse primo <modo>, sed cum dicitur ulterius quod privatio dicit non esse, verum est de non esse secundo modo; et ita est aequivocum non esse. Et hoc habetur in littera, quod non potest esse privatio nisi prius fuerit habitus vel potuerit esse.

Aliter dicitur quod argumentum peccat secundum consequens a superiori ad inferius, unde non sequitur, "Non esse est prius esse, ergo hoc non esse". 5

1 dicitur] dicit *P*

Lectio XLI

\<Divisio>

In hac parte prosequitur de oppositis secundum affirmationem et negationem.

\<Haec pars in duas. Primo ponit differentiam oppositorum secundum affirmationem et negationem> ad ea quae sunt sub ipsis, secundo ponit convenientiam, ibi:
Concedantur (10.12b10).

5   Et sequitur pars in qua comparat opposita ad invicem, et incipit ibi: *Quoniam
autem privatio et habitus* (10.12b15). Et dividitur in tres. Primo comparat relativa
ad privativa, secundo contraria ad privativa, tertio contradictoria ad alia. Secunda
ibi: *Quoniam autem neque \<ut> contraria* (10.12b26), tertia ibi: *Quaecumque vero
tanquam affirmatio* (10.13a37).

10   Prima in duas. Primo probat quod privativa non sunt relativa, secundo confirmat per proprietatem relativorum, ibi: *Amplius omnia reciproca* (10.12b22).

Pars in qua comparat contraria ad privativa in duas. Primo ponit proprietates
contrariorum in relatione ad subiectum, secundo idem facit in relatione ad tempus
\<regrediendi> et non regrediendi, ibi: *Amplius in contrariis* (10.13a18).

15   Prima in duas. Primo ponit proprietates contrariorum, secundo ipsas removet
a privativis, ibi: *In privatione vero et habitu* (10.13a3); ubi lectio terminatur.

Prima in duas. Primo ponit proprietatem contrariorum immediatorum, \<se-
cundo mediatorum>, ibi: *Quorum vero aliquid est medium* (10.12b32).

Haec secunda in duas. Primo ponit proprietatem, secundo, quia non convenit
20   omnibus, excipit ipsam verificando, ibi: *Praeter ea quibus unum* etc. (10.12b37).

Haec est divisio lectionis, et sunt particulae septem.

\<Sententia>

Circa primam sic procedit: Illud quod est sub affirmatione et negatione non est
idem ut affirmatio et negatio. Et hoc probat: Affirmatio est oratio affirmativa et
negatio negativa. Sed illud quod est sub affirmatione et negatione non est oratio.
25   Ergo etc.

Consequenter ponit convenientiam, dicens quod idem modus oppositionis est
in his et in affirmatione et negatione.

Consequenter comparat privativa ad relativa, probans quod ipsa non sunt relativa sic: Quaecumque sunt ad aliquid unum dicitur ad aliud in genitivo vel quo-

---

11 proprietatem] definitionem *P*   **13** contrariorum] relativorum *add. P*   **15** contrariorum]
relativorum *P*   **23** et²] ex *P*

modolibet aliter. Sed habitus non dicitur sic vel sic ad privationem nec e converso.
Ergo privativa non sunt relativa.

Consequenter probat | idem per proprietatem relativorum sic: Quaecumque
sunt ad aliquid dicuntur ad convertentiam. Sed privativa non dicuntur ad convertentiam, ut probat. Ergo etc.   5

Consequenter comparat contraria ad privativa, et primo immediata, dicens
quod contraria non opponuntur secundum privationem et habitum. Quod probat de immediatis: Contrariorum immediatorum necessarium est alterum inesse
susceptibili ipso manente. Sed hoc modo non est in privatione et habitu, ut patet
in catulo ante tempus determinatum. Ergo etc.   10

Consequenter idem probat de mediatis sic: Contrariorum mediatorum nunquam necessarium est alterum inesse susceptibili ipso manente. Sed in privativis
aliquando est necesse quia post tempus determinatum. <Ergo> etc.

Et quia dixit quod in contrariis mediatis nunquam est necesse alterum inesse
susceptibili ipso manente, et hoc falsum est in quibusdam, ideo excipit, dicens quod   15
in talibus in quibus contingit unum contrariorum a natura determinate, necesse est
ipsum subiecto semper inesse. Et ponit exempla.

Haec est sententia partis.

Expositio litteralis

Ita dictum est de aliis generibus oppositionis, *autem*, id est sed, *quod iacet sub affirmatione et negatione* etc. Bene dico quod non, *enim*, id est quia, *affirmatio est*   20
oratio affirmativa etc.

Ita dixi quod differt, sed *haec*, id est quae sunt sub affirmatione et negatione,
concedantur esse opposita etc.

Ita dictum est de oppositis secundum se, *autem*, id est sed, *manifestum est*, per
ea quae sequuntur supple, *quoniam*, pro quod, *habitus et privatio non sic opponun-*   25
tur ut ad aliquid. Bene dico quod non, *enim*, id est quia, *visus non est visus caecitatis*
genitive *nec alio ullo modo*, id est in aliquo casu.

Et non solum hoc est verum, autem, id est sed, *omnia* reciproca *dicuntur*, id est
ad convertentiam, etc.

Non solum differunt privativa a relativis, *autem*, id est sed, *manifestum est ex*   30
his, quae sequuntur supple, *quoniam*, pro quod, *ea quae dicuntur* etc. *neque*, pro
non, *opponuntur ut contraria*; *enim*, id est quia, *contrariorum quorum nihil est me-*
dium necessarium *alterum inesse semper in quibus nata sunt fieri*, id est in substan-

---

31 pro quod] propter *P*   33 fieri] circa *add. P*   **236.33–237.1** substantiis] relativis *P*

tiis, et *de quibus* praedicantur; et per hoc tangit constantiam subiecti. Vere sic est, *enim*, id est quia, *horum* contrariorum *nihil est medium* etc.

Ita dictum est de immediatis, *vero*, pro sed, *quorum*, scilicet contrariorum, *est aliquid medium nunquam alterum* etc., *horum nihil prohibet aliquid esse medium*.
5 Bene dico quod non, *autem*, id est quia, *horum erat aliquid medium*, supple cum superius tractabatur de his, *quorum non est necessarium* etc.

Vere oportet alterum inesse, *praeter* ea, id est illis exceptis, *unum* etc., *autem*, id est quia, *contingit alterum inesse determinate in his* in *quibus inest unum naturaliter et non alterutrum*, id est hoc vel illud indifferenter. Bene dico "non alterutrum", *non*
10 *enim possibile est* etc.

<Quaestiones>

<1>

Primo quaeritur quare non determinat in *Sex principiis* de istis postpraedicamentis.

Et dicendum quod postprincipium et postpraedicamentum differunt secundum rationem, licet sint idem secundum rem, quia postpraedicamentum dicitur in quantum res respicit rationis (quod patet, quia postpraedicamentum respicit praedica-
15 mentum; cum praedicamentum sit unio praedicabilium, ideo est res rationis), sed postprincipium dicitur in quantum res respicit naturae. Quia ergo hic determinat de praedicamentis in quantum dicibilia, et dicibile rem dicit rationis, ideo hic determinat de postpraedicamentis et non ibi.

<2>

Sed modo quaeritur: Ibi determinat de magis et minus, hic autem non.
20 Et dicendum quod magis et minus causantur a naturae principiis, id est a mixtione umidorum vel consimilium. Quia ergo principaliter res naturae respiciunt et non res rationis, ibi de his determinat et non hic.

<3>

Consequenter quaeritur quare non com|parat relative opposita ad contraria; nam   f. 63rb
videtur quod deberet cum alia comparet ad invicem.

5–6   *cf.* Lectio XL   **19**   Anon. *LSP* VIII 80–93 (ed. Minio-Paluello, 53–57)

---

4 nunquam] *c* : quorum   *P*   **9** alterutrum¹] *ac* : alterum   P   *(sed cf. immediate   infra)*
9 id…indifferenter] et hoc velut differenter P   **19** quaeritur ibi] hic *exp.*   *et* quaeritur ibi
add. in marg. P

Et dicendum quod quaestio falsum supponit; nam comparavit superius ubi de contrariis pertractavit, ibi scilicet: *Illa vero quae ut contraria opponuntur* (10.11b33).

<4>

Consequenter <quaeritur>: Dicit quod unum contrariorum expellit alterum nisi insint determinate a natura.

Secundum hoc videtur quod contraria nunquam se possunt expellere, quia "nihil est", dicit Plato, "cuius ortum causa legitima non praecesserit". Ergo si albedo et nigredo insunt a natura in subiecto in quo sunt, erunt ergo inseparabilia. Sed hoc est falsum. Ergo et illud quod dicit auctor.

Et dicendum quod esse a natura est dupliciter. Uno modo quia semper habet causam in ipso subiecto ipso manente, ut caliditas in igne, unde quia causa non potest separari, nec effectus; et sic loquitur hic. Alio modo dicitur esse a natura quia habet causam in subiecto naturalem, separabilem tamen ab ipso ipso manente, et quia illa causa potest separari, et eius effectus; et de talibus obicitur.

<5>

Consequenter quaeritur: Vult quod contraria possunt eidem inesse.

Sed contra. Quod potest inesse possibile est inesse. Sed habetur in *Prioribus*: "Possibile est quo posito <inesse> nullum sequitur impossibile". Sed est impossibile contraria eidem inesse. Minor patet, quia sic accideret contraria inesse simul actu eidem, quod est impossibile.

Solutio. Verum dicit auctor quod contraria nata sunt fieri circa idem, et hoc scribitur in secundo *Topicorum*.

Ad obiectum. Dicendum quod, "Possibile est quo posito inesse nullum sequitur impossibile", hoc verum est si ponatur inesse eodem modo quo sit possibile, sed cum dicit auctor quod contraria possunt eidem inesse, intelligit successive et non simul, et si hoc modo ponatur inesse, inconveniens non sequetur.

4–5   *cf.* Arist. *Cat.* 10.12b26–13a3   6–7   Plato *Tim.* 28a, Transl. Calcidii (ed. Waszink et Jensen, 20); Anon. *Auct. Arist.* 27.2 (ed. Hamesse, 296)   15   *cf.* Arist. *Cat.* 10.12b26–13a3   16–17   *cf.* Arist. *APr* I 13.32a19–20; Anon. *Auct. Arist.* 34.12 (ed. Hamesse, 309)   20–21   Arist. *Top.* II 7.113a34–35; *cf.* Anon. *Auct. Arist.* 36.32 (ed. Hamesse, 324)

---

4 quod] quare *P ut v.*   5 insint] in sta *! P ut v.*   11 causam] et anima *P*

<6>

Consequenter quaeritur: Dicit quod ignis non est susceptibilis contrariorum.

Sed contra. Dictum est in capitulo de substantia quod proprium est substantiae esse susceptibile contrariorum. Cum ergo ignis sit substantia, contraria suscipiet.

Item. Scribitur in secundo *Topicorum* quod si unum contrariorum non potest inesse, reliquum non inest. Ergo per consequentiam e converso si unum inest, reliquum poterit inesse, et ita ignis, cum sit calidus, poterit fieri frigidus.

Et dicendum quod quia causa caloris in igne nunquam potest ab eo removeri, nec per consequens effectus.

Ad obiectum. Dicendum quod <quando> dicit quod substantia recipit contraria, intelligit secundum materiam, et sic ignis poterit contraria recipere; nam materia quae subiacet igneitati poterit subiacere aquositati, et ita materia quae subiacet caliditati poterit subiacere frigiditati (et hoc est quod scribitur in primo *Meteorum* quod elementa corrumpuntur et generantur ad invicem, et unum est in potentia et alterum). Sed quando dicit hic quod ignis non recipit contraria, intelligit secundum formam, quia materia ignis sub igneitate non remaneret si contraria reciperet.

Ad secundum. Verbum Aristotelis tenet quando alterum non inest determinate a natura.

Aliter dicitur ad primum quod substantia recipit contraria si illa sint in substantia ut accidens in subiecto, unde quia caliditas non est in igne sicut accidens in subiecto sed sicut forma et principium ipsum definiens, ideo ignis non recipit contraria.

<7>

Consequenter quaeritur, cum aqua possit calefieri, quare ignis non queat frigefieri.

Et dicendum: Scribitur in quarto *Meteorum*, "Cum quattuor sint qualitates, duae passivae, aridum et umidum, et duae activae, calidum et frigidum, calidum est maxime activum". Huic consonat Philaretus, quod calidum | est facile mobile et sic facile activum. Cum ergo ignis est maxime activus, per oppositum erit minime passivus, et quia maxime activus, potest effectum suum in aquam imprimere, et quia minime passivus, minime effectus recipit aliorum.

Alia causa est. Scribitur in *Libro de morte et vita* quod maior flamma destruit

f. 63va

---

1 *cf.* Arist. *Cat.* 10.12b37–13a3 **2–3** Arist. *Cat.* 5.4a10–11 **4–5** *cf.* Arist. *Top.* II 7.113b9–11 **12–14** *cf.* Arist. *Met.* I 3.339a37–b1 **23–25** *cf.* Arist. *Met.* IV 1.378b10–13; Anon. *Auct. Arist.* 5.17 (ed. Hamesse, 173) **25–26** Philaretus *Liber pulsuum* (ed. Venet., 3vb) **239.29–240.1** Arist. *Long.* 3.465b23–25; Anon. *Auct. Arist.* 7.110 (ed. Hamesse, 204)

---

22 quare] quia *P*

minorem in ipsam agendo et non e converso. Ergo magis activum agit in minus imprimendo effectum suum et non e converso. Et ita reddit quod prius.

  Alia causa est a parte materiae. Nam aqua est maxime corporea (quod patet, nam inferius situatur), et quia maxime corporea, maxime poterit recipere contraria. Sed ignis inter corpora magis appropinquat incorporeitati, et illud quod est   5 incorporeum non potest alterari et ita non potest recipere contraria. Propter hoc ergo ignis non potest recipere contraria, cum incorporeitati maxime appropinquet.

Lectio XLII

In privatione vero et habitu etc. (10.13a3)

\<Divisio\>

Positis proprietatibus contrariorum, separat

< * * * >

eadem ab immediatis, secundo a mediatis, \<ibi:\> *Sed neque quorum est medium* (10.13a7).

Haec secunda in duas. Primo ponit maiorem et explanat, secundo minorem, ibi: *In contrariis autem* (10.13a12).

Sequitur pars in qua ponit proprietates contrariorum in comparatione ad tempus regrediendi vel non. Et in duas dividitur. Primo ponit maiorem cuiusdam rationis, secundo minorem, ibi: *In privatione et habitu* (10.13a30).

Prima in duas. Primo ponit maiorem, secundo per exempla manifestat, ibi: *Namque quod sanum est* (10.13a21).

Haec secunda in duas. Primo ponit exempla, secundo post exempla posita quoddam dubium manifestat, ibi: *Pravus enim* (10.13a23).

Haec est divisio lectionis, et sunt particulae septem.

\<Sententia\>

Circa primam sic procedit: Proprietates dictae de contrariis non competunt privativis. Quod probat sic: Quaecumque sunt contraria immediata necesse est alterum inesse susceptibili < * * * > post tempus determinatum, et non alterum determinate sed hoc vel illud indifferenter.

Sed in contrariis mediatis non est necesse alterum inesse susceptibili nisi quando alterum inest a natura, et tunc alterum inest determinate. Igitur privativa non opponuntur ut contraria mediata.

Consequenter ponit aliam rationem talem: In contrariis fit motus ab uno in aliud et e converso, nisi alterum insit per naturam. Sed in privatione et habitu non fit motus in alterum. Ergo privativa non opponuntur ut contraria. Primo ponit maiorem < * * * >

Consequenter explanat qualiter ex pravo fit studiosus, dicens quod per continuationem bonorum operationum a vitio declinabit et augmentabitur in virtute nisi tempus fuerit interruptum.

Ultimo ponit minorem et explanat.

Haec est sententia partis.

---

3 secundo] secundum *P*

Expositio litteralis

Ita dictum est de contrariis, autem, id est sed, *nihil eorum quae dicta sunt,* de contrariis supple, *est verum in privatione et habitu.* Bene dico quod non, *enim,* id est
quia, *neque,* pro non, *est necessarium, enim,* id est quia, *nondum habet naturam.*
Ex hoc concludit: Ex quo in contrariis immediatis necesse est alterum inesse et non
in privatione et habitu, *ideoque,* pro ergo, *haec,* id est privatio et habitus, *non erunt*   5
talium contrariorum etc., id est non erunt contraria immediata.

    Non solum hoc dico de immediatis, *sed neque* privativa sunt contraria *quorum*
f. 63vb   contrariorum *est medium.* | Et hoc probat: *Enim,* id est quia, *necessarium est al-*
terum eorum in privatione et habitu *inesse susceptibili,* intellige post tempus determinatum; hoc est quod sequitur: *Quando enim iam natum fuerit ad habendum*   10
visionem, id est priusquam pervenerit ad effectum perfectum vel debitum tempus,
aut dicetur caecum etc. *Et* eorum, id est privative oppositorum, *non contingit* inesse susceptibili *alterum,* id est privationem vel habitum, *sed alterutrum,* id est hoc
vel illud indifferenter. Nota quod per hoc quod dicit "eorum etc." differunt privatio
et habitus a mediatis quorum unum est naturaliter et determinate.   15

    Continua. Ita est in privativis, *autem,* id est sed, *in contrariis* etc., *sed* in *ali-*
quibus, id est quando inest alterum a natura, *et his determinate unum,* quod non
contingit in privatione et habitu. Ex hoc concludit: Ex quo non opponuntur ut
contraria mediata nec immediata, et non sunt plura genera contrarietatis, *palam*
quod *secundum neutrum* etc., id est neque sicut mediata neque sicut immediata.   20

    Amplius in contrariis quidem etc.

    Et hoc exemplificat: *Namque,* pro quia, *quod sanum est* etc., *et ex pravo possibile*
est fieri studiosum.

    Vere pravus potest fieri studiosus, *enim,* id est quia, *pravus deductus* etc., *vel,*
id est saltem, *proficiet modicum,* id est aliquantulum, *ut sit melior,* quam pravus   25
supple, et *si* sumpserit *semper,* id est continue, *vel,* <id est> saltem, *modicum cre-*
mentum, palam est quia aut perfecte mutabitur, id est a vitio declinabit, *aut sumet*
multum, id est magnum, *crementum,* in virtute supple; *si enim bene* etc., restitue-
tur <in> pravum supple, *dum hoc,* id est crementum, *fit semper,* id est continue, *in*
contrarium habitum, id est virtutem, *nisi forte* tempus *sit suspensum,* id est nisi fiat   30
interruptio in tempore.

    Ita dictum est de contrariis, *vero,* id est sed, *in privatione et habitu* etc.

---

7 privativa] relativa *P*   **10** natum] *c* : natus *P*   **14** quod²] *add. P in marg.*   **15** a] ab *P*   **21** etc]
esse *P*

<Quaestiones>

<1>

Primo quaeritur: Dicit quod necessarium est semper privationem vel habitum susceptibili inesse.

Contrarium dicit in hac lectione, dicens quod in hoc differunt a contrariis immediatis quia in his contrariis necesse est semper alterum susceptibili inesse, non 5 autem in privatione et habitu.

Et dicendum quod loquitur post tempus determinatum, quia est necesse alterum inesse; prius vero loquitur ante tempus determinatum.

<2>

Consequenter <quaeritur>: Dicit quod pravus potest fieri studiosus.

Contra. Scribitur in *Ethicis* quod non in principio habitum denominamus, sed 10 in fine ipsi habitus denominantur. Ergo postea cum denominetur, non potest fieri regressus. Ergo pravus non fiet studiosus nec e converso.

Et dicendum quod habitus in quantum tales semper denominantur quantum est de se, sed habitus per operationes contrarias continuatas debilitari potest et paulatim a subiecto separari, et hoc est quod dicitur in littera quod exigitur ne fiat 15 interruptio temporis. Idem scribitur in *Ethicis*, quod tria requiruntur ut simus boni: scire, velle et impermutabiliter operari; et ibidem dicit: "Quales sunt operationes, tales sunt habitus ex illis in anima derelicti". Patet ergo quod per temporis interruptionem contrariarum operationum potest habitus debilitari, et per consequens potest contrarius habitus introduci.

<3>

20 Consequenter quaeritur: Dicit quod a privatione in habitum non contingit regredi.

Contra. Ignorans potest fieri sciens et talis commutatur

< * * * >

<Item.> In *Libro de anima* scribitur quod caecus est aptus natus videre et non videns. Ergo caecus habet potentiam videndi et non videt. Sed dicitur alibi quod

---

1–2 Arist. *Cat.* 10.13a8–10   3–5 Arist. *Cat.* 10.13a3–7   8 Arist. *Cat.* 10.13a22–31   9–10 *cf.* Arist. *EN* I 6.1098a18–20   14–15 Arist. *Cat.* 10.13a30–31   15–16 *cf.* Arist. *EN* II 3.1105a28–33   16–17 *cf.* Arist. *EN* II 1.1103b21–22; Anon. *Auct. Arist.* 12.26 (ed. Hamesse, 234)   20 Arist. *Cat.* 10.13a31–36   23–24 *cf.* Arist. *An.* I 4.408b20–22   243.24–244.1 *cf.* Arist. *Phys.* II 6.197b22–27

---

3 a contrariis] a con *add. P a.c.*   16 ibidem] sub *P*   19 contrarius] esse *P*

f. 64ra frustra est potentia quae non | reducitur ad actum. Cum ergo natura nihil faciat
frustra, oportet quod potentia videndi quae est in caeco reducatur ad actum, et ita
a privatione in habitum fiet regressus, ut videtur.

Et dicendum quod habitus est duplex: naturalis et accidentalis. Similiter est
duplex privatio. Dicendum ergo quod a privatione naturali in habitum non fit   5
regressus.

Per hoc patet ad primum. Instat vero de privatione et habitu accidentali.

Ad secundum. Dicendum quod duplex est calvities, scilicet naturalis et accidentalis. Calvities naturalis est per defectum caliditatis et umiditatis, et talis est in
senibus, in quibus frigiditas et siccitas dominantur, et a tali privatione nunquam in   10
habitum fit regressus.

Ad aliud. Duplex est potentia. Quaedam enim est potentia actum praecedens,
ordinata tamen ad actum, et de tali verum est, ut obicitur, "frustra enim est potentia
etc."; nam illa potentia quam aliquis habet antequam sit privatus potest ad actum
reduci, et potest fieri videns, ut patet in catulo ante tempus determinatum. Alia est   15
potentia post actum ut post privationem, et illa non potest ad actum per naturam
reduci, et de tali loquitur hic.

<4>

Consequenter quaeritur: Dicit quod caecus non potest videre.

Contra. Haec est vera: "Quidam videns potest esse caecus". Ergo et sua conversa: "Quidam caecus potest esse videns".   20

< * * * > sicut oculo quem non habes tu potes videre. Ergo tu existens caecus
potest videre.

Item. Scribitur in *Libro de animalibus*: "Si quis crepuerit columbo parvo oculos,
adhuc poterit videre". Ergo neutrum oculum habens poterit videre.

Ad primum dicendum quod aliter convertitur "Aliquis videns potest esse cae-   25
cus", sic: "Aliquis qui potest esse caecus est videns" vel sic: "Caecus in futuro potest
nunc esse videns". Similiter convertitur "Quidam puer erit senex": "Quidam futu-
rus senex est modo puer". Quod sic debeant converti patet. Nam conversio debet
esse respectu eiusdem temporis. Sed haec oratio, "Homo puer erit senex", idem significat cum hac, "Homo qui modo est puer in futuro erit senex". Ergo sic debet   30
converti: "Homo senex in futuro est modo puer".

Ad secundum. Maior falsa est et probatio peccat secundum figuram dictionis;
et hunc paralogismum ponit Aristoteles in secundo *Elenchorum* inter paralogismos

---

18 Arist. *Cat.* 10.13a33–34   **23–24** *cf.* Arist. *HA* VI 5.563a12–16; *GA* IV 6.774b27–34   **244.33–
245.1** Arist. *SE* 22.178b8–10

---

8 quod duplex] dicendum *P*   **28** conversio] *ex* convertio *corr. P*   **32** secundum[1]] ultimum *P*

figurae dictionis. Cum enim dicitur: "Uno solo oculo tu potes videre et non habes unum solum oculum, verum est, < * * * > ergo quem non habes tu potes videre"; nam mutas ad aliquid in substantiam. Ideo non valet "Tu vides uno solo oculo et non habes unum solum oculum, ergo tu vides oculo quem non habes", sed "ut non habes".

Ad ultimum. Non est simile de parvo catulo et homine, quia omnis virtus quae est in animali a calore provenit naturali. Cum ergo columbus sit animal maxime calidum, et calor ipsius plus abundet in catulo, propter hoc si aliquis crepuerit ei oculos, ex abundantia caloris possunt ei oculi reformari, et potest iterum videre. Sed non est sic de homine, cum in homine non abundet calor naturalis. Et dicit "parvo columbo" et non "seni", quia calor naturalis plus abundat in parvo quam in magno.

2 habes] habet *P*   8 plus] *lectio incerta*   8 catulo] ca^te *P*   9 ei] *lectio incerta*

Lectio XLIII

Quaecumque vero ut affirmatio et negatio (10.13a37)

<Divisio>

Hic comparat contradictoria ad alia.

Haec pars in duas. Primo facit quod dictum est, secundo repetit de contrariis (vel determinat de contrariis moralibus secundum alios), ibi: *Contrarium | autem bono* (11.13b36); ubi praesens lectio terminatur.   f. 64rb

5   Prima in duas. Primo proponit quod intendit, secundo propositum demonstrat, ibi: *In solis vero istis* (10.13b1).

Haec secunda in duas. Primo probat propositum, secundo probatum concludit, ibi: *Quare in his solis* (10.13b33).

Prima in duas. Primo attribuit quandam proprietatem contradictoriis, secundo 10 illam removet ab aliis, ibi: *Neque enim in contrariis* (10.13b3).

Haec secunda in duas. Primo removet illam proprietatem a contrariis incomplexis et ab aliis oppositis, secundo a complexis, ibi: *Sed maxime videbitur* (10.13b12).

Prima in duas. Primo ponit minorem suae rationis, secundo manifestat per 15 exempla, ibi: *ut sanitas et languor* (10.13b6).

Haec secunda in duas. Primo ponit exempla, secundo probat ipsa esse competentia, ibi: *Omnino autem eorum* (10.13b10).

Pars in qua removet illam proprietatem a contrariis complexis in duas. Primo facit hoc, secundo quasi recapitulando dicit quod haec proprietas tantum convenit 20 contradictoriis, ibi: *In affirmatione vero et negatione* (10.13b26).

Prima in duas. Primo removet hoc a contrariis complexis, secundo quasi incidenter ponit differentiam inter contraria et privativa, ibi: *In privatione <vero> et habitu* (10.13b20).

Haec est divisio lectionis, et sunt particulae novem.

<Sententia>

25   Circa primam sic procedit, dicens: Opposita secundum affirmationem et negationem non opponuntur sicut alia opposita.

---

3 Nicolaus Parisiensis *Rat. sup. Praed.* X (Munich, Bayer. Staatsbibl. 14460, f. 58va); *cf. etiam* Robertus Kilwardby *Not. sup. Praed.* XVII (Madrid, Bibl. Univ. 73, f. 35vb)

---

8 solis] $P^{inf}ac$: solum P **12** videbitur] $P^{inf}c$: videtur P **19** dicit] dicens P **20** in affirmatione vero] $P^{inf}ac$: ut in affirmatione P **24** novem] VII P

Consequenter hoc sic probat: Quaecumque opponuntur sicut affirmatio et negatio necesse est semper alterum eorum esse verum et alterum falsum. Sed in aliis
oppositis hoc non est necessarium. Maior ponitur ibi: *In solis enim istis* (10.13b1).

Consequenter manifestat minorem sic: Languor et sanitas sunt contraria et
neutrum verum vel falsum est.   5

< * * * > Omnia praedicta sunt incomplexa. Ergo non sunt vera vel falsa.

Consequenter dicit quod licet maxime conveniat contrariis complexis quod
unum extremorum sit verum, ut per exempla manifestat, hoc tamen est solum
subiecto permanente.

Consequenter ponit differentiam inter complexa contraria et privativa, dicens   10
quod in privatione et habitu non semper oportet subiecto manente alterum esse
verum, alterum esse falsum, sicut erat in contrariis. Et hoc per exempla manifestat.

Consequenter quasi epiloquendo dicit quod in oppositis secundum affirmationem <et negationem> semper est alterum verum, alterum falsum, sive subiectum
sit sive non. Et hoc per exempla manifestat.   15

Ultimo concludit propositum iam probatum.

Haec est sententia lectionis.

Expositio litteralis

Ita dictum est de aliis oppositis, vero, id est sed, *quaecumque ut affirmatio* etc.,
nullo praedictorum modorum sunt opposita.

Bene dico quod non, *enim*, id est quia, *in solis istis*, id est contradictoriis, *necesse*   20
est etc.

Vere "in solis", *enim*, id est quia, *neque*, pro non, *in contrariis est necessarium*
etc.

Et ponit exempla: *ut sanitas* etc.

Vere ista non dicunt verum vel falsum, *autem*, <id est> quia, *omnino*, id est ge-   25
neraliter, *eorum quae secundum nullam complexionem dicuntur*, id est incomplexa,
neque verum etc. Sed *omnia quae dicta sunt porro*, id est certe, non *dicuntur* secundum complexionem, id est sunt incomplexa. Ergo nullum dictorum significat
verum vel falsum.

Ita est in istis, *sed hoc tale*, id est quod unum extremorum sit verum vel falsum,   30
videbitur maxime contingere in his quae dicuntur contraria secundum complexio-
nem, id est in contrariis complexis. Hoc videbitur, *namque*, id est quia, *Socratem*
f. 64va   *esse sanum ac languere sunt contraria*, et quia sunt immediata, videtur alterum |

---

semper esse verum. Ita videtur, *sed neque in his*, id est contrariis complexis, videbitur *alterum semper verum*. Bene dico quod non, *enim*, id est quia, *<cum> Socrates
sit*, quoddam, id est alterum, *est verum, aliud autem falsum*. Continua: Ita dictum
est "dum Socrates est", *vero*, pro sed, *cum non sit*, supple Socrates, *ambo sunt fal-*
5 *sa*; *enim*, id est quia, *cum ipse Socrates non sit omnino*, id est nullo modo, *neque*
languere neque sanum esse, Socratem supple, *est verum*.

Ita est in contrariis si subiectum sit quod altera est vera, altera falsa, *vero*, id est
sed, *in privatione et habitu, cum* subiectum *non sit, neutrum*, id est nec privatio
nec habitus, *est verum, et si sit*, subiectum supple, *non erit alterum verum*, alterum
10 falsum, sed post tempus determinatum. Exempla ponit, littera plana est.

Continua. Ita non est necessarium in contrariis nec in privativis, *vero*, id est sed,
in affirmatione et negatione, sive sit sive non sit, subiectum supple, *aliud quidem* etc.
Et ponit exempla, littera plana est.

Ultimo concludit. Continua: Ex quo alterum verum alterum falsum esse semper
15 contingit in contradictoriis et non in aliis, *quare*, id est ergo, *in his solis* etc.

<QUAESTIONES>

<1>

Primo quaeritur: Dicit quod in omnibus contradictoriis semper est alterum verum
etc.

Contrarium scribitur in *Perihermeneias* quod in singularibus et futuris non est
determinata veritas et falsitas, et cum sunt contradictoria, ut cum dico: "Socrates
20 currit", "Socrates non currit".

Et dicendum quod cum dicit hic "in omnibus contradictoriis etc.", loquitur coniunctim ut sit disiunctio inter terminos, nam quaelibet est vera vel falsa coniunctim,
sed in *Perihermeneias* loquitur divisim et determinate, et ita non est contradictio.

<2>

Consequenter quaeritur: Videtur quod in contradictoriis non sit necessarium sem-
25 per alterum esse verum, alterum falsum.

Nam istae contradicunt: "Socrates est", "Socrates non est". Aut ergo antequam
Socrates esset haec fuit semper vera, "Socrates est", aut haec, "Socrates non est".

16–17 Arist. *Cat.* 10.13b1–3 **18–19** Arist. *Int.* 9.18a33–34; *cf.* Anon. *Auct. Arist.* 32.13 (ed.
Hamesse, 305)

---

1 semper] in *add. P* **1** videtur] videre *P* **3** quoddam] quodam *P* **4** vero] *c* : enim *P* **4** sit]
sic *add. P* **7** quod] quia *P* **14** alterum] est *add. P*

Sed non haec, "Socrates non est" (ex hoc arguo: "Semper" circuit omne tempus). Ergo si haec semper fuit vera, "Socrates est", Socrates semper fuit; nam verum et ens convertuntur. Ergo fuit ab aeterno, quod falsum est vel erroneum, cum unum solum fuerit ab aeterno.

Et dicendum quod haec oratio, "Socrates non est", antequam Socrates esset,   5
semper fuit vera in re. Sed ista veritas nihil est aliud quam rei non entitas; † potest enim Socratem non esse unum † causatur propter rei non existentiam. Sic ergo non sequitur: "Habuit non entitatem ab aeterno, ergo fuit ab aeterno", quia praemissa ponit ens non esse et conclusio ab aeterno fuisse. Sic non sequitur: "Fuit vera ab aeterno", loquendo de tali veritate, "ergo fuit ab aeterno".   10

<3>

Consequenter quaeritur quare prius de relativis quam de contrariis determinavit; prius enim oportet comparare relativa ad contradictoria quam contraria, e converso autem facit.

Et dicendum quod superius ordinavit ea in quantum eorum extrema magis conveniunt, et quia extrema relativorum plus conveniunt, ut superius patuit, ideo prae-   15
ordinantur. Aliter hic ordinantur, scilicet in quantum opposita maiorem habent convenientiam, et quia magis conveniunt contraria cum contradictoriis quam relativa, ideo primo comparat ipsa. Quod magis conveniunt patet, quia sicut <in> contradictoriis necesse est semper unum esse verum alterum falsum, sic in contrariis immediatis subiecto existente, sed in relative oppositis non est necesse semper   20
alterum inesse, ut in littera attestatur.

<4>

Consequenter quaeritur quare non comparat contraria mediata ad contradictoria sicut immediata; nam videtur per simile quod deberet.

Et dicendum quod licet non comparet ipsa explicite, satis habetur eorum comparatio ex consequenti eo quod comparat contraria immediata ad contradictoria;   25
nam magis videtur in contrariis immediatis alterum semper subiecto inesse quam
f. 64vb   de mediatis, et quia hoc non est necesse in istis, multo | minus in illis.

12–13 Arist. *Cat.* 10.13b4–10   **15** *cf.* Lectio XXXIX, Q3   **20–21** Arist. *Cat.* 10.13b5–9

---

3 unum] non *P*   **11** prius] ut *add. P*   **11** determinavit] oportet *add. P a.c.*   **12** enim] *add. P s.l.*   **17** convenientiam] convenientias *P*   **19–20** contrariis] contradictoriis *P*   **21** inesse] sed solum post tempus determinatum *add. P*   **23** per] quod *P*   **27** illis] istis *P*

<5>

Consequenter quaeritur: Dicit quod in solis contradictoriis semper est necesse esse
alterum <verum> alterum falsum.

Superius dixit quod in contrariis immediatis oportet alterum esse verum alterum falsum. Ergo non solum competit contradictoriis.

5   Et dicendum quod cum dixit superius quod in contrariis immediatis etc., intel-
legit tantum existente susceptibili, hic autem loquitur sive sit susceptibile sive non;
unde alterum esse verum alterum esse falsum subiecto existente vel non existente
solum contingit in contradictoriis.

<6>

Consequenter quaeritur quare non comparat relativa complexa ad contradictoria
10   sicut contraria complexa.

Et dicendum quod relativa complexa non sunt opposita, ut patet in binario,
quod est duplum respectu unitatis et subduplum respectu quaternarii. Cum ergo hic comparet opposita ad invicem in quantum opposita, relativa complexa ad
contradictoria non debuit comparare.

1–2 Arist. *Cat.* 10.13b33–35   3–4 Arist. *Cat.* 10.12b26–32

LECTIO XLIV

CONTRARIUM AUTEM ETC. (11.13b36)

<DIVISIO>

Postquam comparavit opposita ad invicem, repetit de contrariis. Alii dicunt quod hic determinat de contrariis moralibus.

Haec pars in duas. Primo removet quasdam dubitationes circa contraria, secundo comparat contraria ad sua genera, ibi: *Palam vero* (11.14a15).

5 Prima in duas. Primo comparat contraria inter se, secundo ipsa comparat ad substantiam, ibi: *Amplius <contrariorum* etc. (11.14a7).

Haec secunda in duas. Primo comparat contraria incomplexa, secundo complexa, ibi: *Amplius> si <Socratem> sanum esse* (11.14a11).

Pars in qua comparat contraria ad sua genera in duas. Primo comparat ad genus
10 subiectum, secundo ad genus praedicabile, ibi: *Necesse est autem* (11.14a18).

Haec est divisio lectionis, et sunt particulae quinque.

<SENTENTIA>

Circa primam sic procedit: Dixit superius quod bonum est contrarium malo. Ex hoc crederet aliquis quod malum esset contrarium bono et non alii. Hoc removet, dicens quod bonum de necessitate opponitur malo, sed malum non semper est
15 contrarium bono sed aliquando alii malo. Et hoc per exempla manifestat.

Consequenter removet dubitationem comparando contraria ad substantiam. Dictum fuit superius quod in contrariis non est necesse alterum inesse susceptibili. Ex hoc crederet aliquis quod si unum inest subiecto, non est necesse alterum non inesse. Hoc removet, dicens quod in contrariis incomplexis necesse est si unum
20 inest, alterum non inesse. Et hoc per exempla manifestat.

Consequenter dicit idem de complexis et hoc per exempla manifestat.

Consequenter comparat contraria ad genus subiectum, dicens quod

< * * * >

contraria vel sunt in eodem genere vel in contrariis vel sunt aliorum genera. Et
25 hoc manifestat per exempla.

Haec est sententia partis.

1–2 Nicolaus Parisiensis *Rat. sup. Praed.* X (Munich, Bayer. Staatsbibl. 14460, f. 58va); *cf. etiam* Robertus Kilwardby *Not. sup. Praed.* XVII (Madrid, Bibl. Univ. 73, f. 35vb)   **12**   *cf.* Arist. *Cat.* 10.11b20–24   **17–18**   *cf.* Arist. *Cat.* 10.12a3–4; 12a9–20; 12b32–13a2

---

24 sunt²] secundum *P*

Expositio litteralis

Ita dictum est de generibus oppositionis, *autem*, id est sed, bonum *est contrarium* malo de *necessitate*. Dicit "de necessitate" non quia bonum non potest malo non esse contrarium, sed quia nihil nisi malum est bono contrarium. Vere sic est, *autem*, id est quia, *hoc palam est per inductionem singulorum, ut languor*, quod est malum, supple est contrarium, *sanitati*, quae est bonum, *et* iustitia etc. Non solum sic est   5 de istis, *autem*, id est sed, *similiter in aliis*. Ita dixi quod malum est tantum bono contrarium, *sed* malum *est contrarium* bono et *aliquando* malo (hic non probat, sed relinquit improbatum quia ita est manifestum). Videtur malum malo esse contrarium, *enim*, id est quia, *egestati cum sit malum superabundantia est contraria, cum ipsa sit malum. Sed quilibet inspiciet in paucis hoc tale*, quod malum contrarium   10 malo, *in pluribus vero est* etc.

    Amplius contrariorum etc.

    Amplius si Socratem languere etc.

    Ita dictum est de contrariis, *vero*, id est sed, *palam est quod* contrarietas habet *fieri* natura, id est per naturam, *circa idem specie aut genere*, ut *languor* etc. Vere   15 sic est, *autem*, id est sed, *nigredo et albedo* sunt *in corpore simpliciter*; et dicit "in corpore" quia albedo non solum contingit cor|pori quod est animal, sed aliis sicut lapidi.

    Bene dixi "habent fieri circa idem etc.", *autem*, id est quia, *necessarium est contrarium* etc., *virtus enim genus huius*, id est iustitiae, sed *nequitia huius*, id est   20 vitii.

f. 65ra

<Quaestiones>

<1>

Primo quaeritur quare potius repetit de contrariis quam de aliis.

    Et dicendum quod intendit quasdam removere dubitationes circa ipsa contraria; ut ergo ipsas removeat, occasionaliter de ipsis repetit.

<2>

Consequenter quaeritur: Dicit quod malum opponitur bono et malo.   25

---

25 *cf.* Arist. *Cat.* 11.14a2–5

---

2 quia] quod *P* **8** relinquit improbatum] reliquum probat *P* **10** sed] *c* : et *P* **11** vero] *c* : non *P* **16** autem] *c* : enim *P* **17** corpori] corpore *P a.c.* **22** quaeritur quare] *inv. P*

Contra. Scribitur in *Libro perihermeneias*: "Tantum unum uni opponitur". Nihil ergo dicit "duo opponuntur uni".

Et dicendum quod duo opponuntur uni secundum diversos respectus. Unde bonum et malum opponuntur ratione generum † quia medium inest extremis tanquam virtus extrema tanquam vitium † sed virtus et vitium sunt diversa genera, et ideo dixit quod malum et bonum opponuntur ratione generum. Sed malum opponitur malo ratione differentiarum, unde quia ista duo, avaritia et superfluitas, opponuntur, ideo superabundantia et egestas. Non est ergo inconveniens diversis respectibus unum opponi duobus.

<3>

Consequenter videtur quod bonum sit contrarium bono.

Nam lex praecipit: Si alicuius filius sit suspensor, et pater eius delictum commiserit, suspendatur per filium. Natura vero negat. Cum ergo lex et natura sint bona, bonum bono erit contrarium.

Et dicendum quod est duplex bonum: simpliciter et secundum quid. Primo modo loquitur hic, secundo tu obicis. Nam lex non est bonum nisi secundum quid, simpliciter vero bonitas naturalis, ut scribitur in secundo *Topicorum*; unde scribitur in *Ethicis*: "propter ea quae sunt a natura neque laudandum neque vituperandum".

<4>

Consequenter quaeritur quare bonum bono non contrariatur.

Et dicendum quod bonum dicitur uno modo, scribitur in *Ethicis*, malum vero multifarie; nam quando volumus sumus mali, scribitur ibidem. Quia ergo bonum dicitur uno modo, alii bono non opponitur, sed quia malum multifarie, malum malo opponitur.

Vel aliter. Bonum est quoddam constructibile, malum vero destructibile. Si ergo bonum erit bono contrarium, cum contrarium destruat contrarium, unum bonum aliud bonum destruet; quod est contra eius naturam.

---

1 *cf.* Arist. *Int.* 7.18a8–9; Anon. *Auct. Arist.* 32.14 (ed. Hamesse, 305)   **15–16**   *cf.* Arist. *Top.* II 11.115b11–35   **16–17**   *cf.* Arist. *EN* II 4.1106a6–10   **19–20**   *cf.* Arist. *EN* II 5.1106b34–35   **20** *cf.* Arist. *EN* III 7.1113b16–17

---

2 opponuntur] opponitur *P*   **19** vero] alio *P ut v.*

<5>

Consequenter quaeritur: Dicit quod contraria sunt in contrariis generibus.

In capitulo qualitatis dixit quod sunt in eodem genere. Ergo sibi contrariatur hic et ibi.

Et dicendum quod duplex est genus, scilicet proximum et remotum. Dicendum <ergo> quod contraria sunt in contrariis generibus proximis; nam genus proximum   5
iustitiae est virtus et proximum iniustitiae est vitium, et sic loquitur hic, sed sunt in eodem genere remoto, ut in qualitate, et sic loquitur superius.

<6>

Consequenter quaeritur: Dicit quod bonum et malum non sunt in genere.

Contrarium scribitur in primo *Topicorum*, ubi vult quod sint in genere.

Item. Dicit quod sunt genera.   10

Contra. Scribitur in secundo *Topicorum* quod nullum genus praedicatur deno-minative. Sed bonum et malum dicuntur denominative. Ergo non sunt genera.

Item. Si sunt genera, aut quantum ad naturalem aut logicum aut moralem. Non quantum ad naturalem, quia bonum et ens convertuntur et malum et non ens; cum ergo ens et non ens non sint genera secundum naturalem sed transcendunt omne   15
genus, sic nec bonum nec malum. Item, secundum logicum et moralem sub habitu
f. 65rb   continentur; ergo per consequens sub | qualitate. Et sic nullo modo erunt genera, ut videtur.

Ad primum. Duplex est genus. Genus praedicabile et genus subiectum. Cum ergo dicit hic <quod> non sunt sub genere, verum est sub genere subiecto, sed cum   20
dicitur in *Topicis* quod sunt in eodem genere, intelligit de genere praedicabili, et sic non est contradictio hic et ibi. Sed dicuntur esse genera; nam in moralibus om-nes contrarietates ad bonum et malum reducuntur. Non ergo sunt in genere alia-rum contrarietatum moralium sed eorundem genera, cum ad eorum contrarietates omnes aliae contrarietates reducantur.   25

Per hoc patet ad secundum. Nam contingit loqui de accidentibus dupliciter. Uno modo per comparationem ad sua inferiora, de quibus essentialiter praedi-cantur, et sic non praedicantur denominative, ut obicitur. Aliter comparantur ad subiecta in quibus habent esse, et tunc praedicantur denominative. Primo modo loquitur in *Topicis*, secundo hic.   30

---

1 Arist. *Cat.* 11.14a19–21   2 *cf.* Arist. *Cat.* 8.10b17–24   8 Arist. *Cat.* 11.14a24–25   9
fortasse Arist. *Top.* I 14.105b13–15 10 Arist. *Cat.* 11.14a24–25 11–12 Arist. *Top.* II 2.109b5–7

---

6 est²] ut *P*

Vel aliter. Cum dicitur "genus non praedicatur etc.", verum est de genere praedicabili et non de genere subiecto, cuiusmodi sunt bonum et malum.

Ad ultimum. Concedo quod non quo ad naturalem, sed quo ad logicum vel moralem.

Ad obiectum dicendum quod auctor non dicit simpliciter quod non sint in genere — sunt enim in qualitate, ut obicitur — sed negat quod non sunt in genere contrarietatum moralium, sed, ut visum est, sunt genera earundem. Littera ergo sic exponitur: *Bonum et malum non sunt in genere*, supple moralium contrarietatum, *sed sunt genera* aliorum, id est aliarum contrarietatum moralium, cum ad illa, <ut> visum est, aliae contrarietates reducantur. Vel aliter secundum primam solutionem: *Bonum et malum non sunt in genere* praedicabili secundum moralem, sed sunt genus subiectum.

<7>

Ultimo quaeritur quare non est summum malum sicut summum bonum.

Et dicendum quod quaecumque sunt cum creatione participant entitatem, et sic per consequens omnia entia in quantum entia participant bonitatem; nihil est ergo ita malum quin naturam sapiat bonitatis. Quia ergo illud esset summe malum quod nullo modo participaret naturam bonitatis, impossibile est summe malum inter entia reperire. Sed quia aliquid est ita bonum quod nunquam participat malum, ut Prima Causa, erit reperire summe bonum; ab eo enim relegata est omnis invidia et nequaquam bonitati purissimae licet quicquam facere nisi pulchrum, ut Platonis sententia attestatur.

7–8 Arist. *Cat.* 11.14a24–25 **19–21** Plato *Tim.* 30a–b, Transl. Calcidii (ed. Waszink et Jensen, 23)

LECTIO XLV

PRIUS AUTEM QUADRUPLICITER DICITUR ETC. (12.14a26)

<DIVISIO>

Habito de oppositis, hic prosequitur de priori.

Haec pars in duas. Primo ponit modos a philosophis usitatos, secundo modum inusitatum superaddit, ibi: *Videtur autem praeter hos* (12.14b10).

Prima in duas. Primo dicit qui et quot sint modi prioris, secundo exsequitur,
5 ibi: *Primo quidem* (12.14a27).

Et ista secunda in quattuor secundum quod sunt quattuor modi prioris. Secunda ibi: *Secundo autem* (12.14a30), tertia ibi: *Tertio vero* (12.14a35), quarta ibi: *Amplius supra* (12.14b4).

Pars in qua superaddit modum inusitatum in duas. Primo dicit quod est alius
10 modus, secundo ipsum per exempla explanat, ibi: *Quod autem sint quaedam* (12.14b13).

Haec secunda in duas. Primo facit quod dictum est, secundo infert correlarium, ibi: *Ideoque* (12.14b22).

Haec est divisio lectionis, et sunt octo particulae.

<SENTENTIA>

15 Circa primam sic procedit: Unum potest esse prius altero quattuor modis.

Consequenter prosequitur de primo modo, dicens: Primo modo est aliquid prius | altero secundum tempus.

Secundo modo dicitur prius a quo non convertitur consequentia. Et hoc per exempla manifestat.

20 Tertio modo dicitur prius secundum ordinem, sicut in mathematicis praemissae praecedunt conclusionem secundum ordinem et in grammatica litterae praecedunt syllabas.

Quarto modo dicitur prius quod est honorabilius, secundum quod quidam consueverunt magis dilectos morum negotiis dicere priores. Concludit quod isti sunt
25 modi prioris a philosophis usitati.

Consequenter modum inusitatum superaddit, dicens quod alius est modus prioritatis praeter dictos, scilicet quando aliqua convertuntur secundum consequentiam et alterum est causa alteri ut sit; nam id quod est causa est prius.

Consequenter explanat per exempla illum modum, dicens quod huiusmodi sunt
30 res et oratio per quam illa res significatur. Nam si oratio vera est < * * * > in re, et

f. 65va

---

14 octo] X *P* **18** prius] alterum *add. P* **27** aliqua] aliquando *P*

e converso, sed veritas rei est causa veritatis orationis et non e converso, et ideo veritas rei est causa veritatis in oratione.

Ultimo concludit quod alterum altero prius est quinque modis.

Haec est sententia partis.

Expositio litteralis

Ita dictum est de oppositis, *autem*, id est sed, *alterum* etc., *quadrupliciter*, id est   5
quattuor modis.

Primo et proprie secundum tempus, secundum quod, scilicet tempus, *dicitur aliquid senius* etc.

Ita dictum est de primo, *autem*, id est sed, *secundo* modo dicitur prius *quod non convertitur secundum* essendi *consequentiam*, id est secundum consequentiam vel   10
conversionem existentiae quae facta est secundum esse, *ut* unum *est prius duobus.*
Bene dico quod sic, *enim*, id est quia, *duobus existentibus consequens est*, id est consequitur, *unum esse*, vero, id est sed, *uno existente non est necessarium duo esse*;
idcirco consequentia non convertitur; *autem*, id est sed, *illud videtur esse prius a quo consequentia non convertitur in eo quod est esse*, id est facta in eo quod est esse,   15
id est facta secundum esse (dicitur autem facta secundum esse consequentia in qua est simpliciter, ut "Si homo est, animal est").

Ita dictum est de secundo modo, autem, id est sed, *tertio* modo *dicitur prius*, alterum altero supple, *secundum ordinem quendam*, id est secundum ordinem causatum a ratione, *quemadmodum in disciplinis*, id est mathematicis, *inest prius et*   20
posterius ordine. Bene dico quod sic, *enim*, id est quia, *elementa*, id est praemissae, *sunt priora his* propositionibus *quae describuntur secundum ordinem*, id est quae probantur per † figurarum continuam descriptionem †. Non solum sic est in geometria, *sed in grammatica elementa*, id est litterae, *sunt priora syllabis*, supple ordine; *similiter in oratione*, prosaica supple, *prooemium est prius narratione per*   25
ordinem etc.

Amplius praeter ea quae dicta sunt, id est praeter dictos modos prioris, *videtur esse prius quod melius est* etc. *Consueverunt* enim *plurimi* etc., *et hic modus*, quidquid est supple, *est paene alienissimus*. Ex hoc concludit: Ex quo isti modi consueti, *itaque modi qui dicti sunt*, a philosophis supple, vel usitati, *isti sunt*.   30

Non solum his modis dicitur prius, *autem*, id est sed, *praeter eos qui dicti sunt videtur* etc. Et dicit "videtur etc.", quia

< * * * >

---

28 plurimi] *c* : plu + *fenestra fere I–II vocum capax P*

ANONYMUS PATAVINUS

Commentarii in Praedicamenta Aristotelis fragmentum

(MS PADUA, BIBLIOTECA UNIVERSITARIA 1589, ff. 65va–67vb)

<*Videtur autem praeter eos* (12.14b10)> Iste est quintus modus quem superaddit Aristoteles, qui est quando convertitur aliquid secundum consequentiam existendi et unum est causa alterius, sed alterum alio modo causa est ad alterum, et quod est causa secundum intellectum prius, licet non in sensu. Sic enim convenit | de re et
        f. 65vb
5 oratione indicante de re; nam si res est, vera est oratio, et si oratio, et res, sed veritas orationis non est causa rei, sed e converso; nam si res est et illud significat oratio, et ipsa consequenter vera. Sed quia non solum res causa videtur, verum etiam et proferens orationem, ideo dicit Philosophus *res etiam quodammodo causa* (12.14b20). Idem est etiam de latione solis et die, quia latio cum sit causa, prius est. Eadem est
10 ratio de omni causa mediata coniuncta effectui, et tunc ambo convertuntur.

<QUAESTIONES>

Primo quaeritur propter quid Aristoteles determinet de priori.

    Secundo de ordine prioris ad simul.

    Tertio de ordine modorum prioris.

    Quarto opponitur: Si prius et posterius sunt ad aliquid, peccare videtur Aristo-
15 teles ex omissione modorum posterioris.

<SOLUTIO>

Ad primum eorum quae dicta sunt dicimus quod Philosophus in *Praedicamentis* praeordinavit genera speciebus et dixerat quo modo prius; idcirco ad plenam cognitionem praedicamentorum modos supponit prioris ut per assignationem ipsorum notetur modus secundum quem genera priora sunt speciebus. Dicitur quod
20 dictum fuerat quod habitus prior erat privatione, et ignorabatur secundum quem modum, ideo etiam distinguit Philosophus modos prioris; nam tempore antecedit habitus privationem a natura, secundum vero secundum modum genera sunt priora speciebus.

    Ad secundum dicimus quod ratione <generum> de priori, de simul vero ratione
25 tione specierum; ideo rationaliter ordinatur prius priusquam simul sicut genera speciebus.

---

10 coniuncta] *lectio incerta*

Ad tertio quaesitum dicimus quod omne quod prius est aut est secundum rem aut est secundum intellectum. Si secundum rem, aut secundum tempus dicitur primus modus, si autem non secundum tempus simpliciter, aut secundum ordinem disciplinarum aut non. Si secundum ordinem disciplinarum, est tertius modus, si vero non secundum ordinem sed per accidens, est quartus modus, quia dicitur melius vel honorabilius sive aliquid huiusmodi, et iste talis modus appellatur. Si autem fuerit prius secundum intellectum, aut secundum consequentiam, et tunc quintus modus, aut secundum inconvertibilitatem, et iste est secundus. Ordo autem istarum ad invicem est quod quattuor propter consuetudinem et antiquitatem eorum anteferuntur quinto, et primus aliis propter veritatem et proprietatem sui, sed secundus aliis quia ipse est determinator aliorum, tertius vero quarto propter abusionem ipsius quarti.

Ad quartum obiectum dicunt quidam quod bene determinat Aristoteles de posteriori, quia de simul. Nos autem dicimus quod non determinat de posteriori loquendo de simul; non enim quaecumque simul sunt posteriora sunt, ut relativa et multa alia. Verum tamen dicimus quod Aristoteles per prius intelligit posterius, quia sunt quasi eiusdem cognitionis, et ars debet circa difficile et bonum esse; ideo obticuit modos posterioris.

17 *cf.* Arist. *EN* II 2.1105a9; II 5.1106b31–32; Anon. *Auct. Arist.* 12.33 (ed. Hamesse, 235)

5 est quartus modus] incensum *P ut v.* **8–9** autem] aut *P* **10** quinto] quo *P* **10** primus] primum *P ut v.* **10** aliis] alii + *signum quod interpretari nequeo P*

Lectio

Simul autem dicuntur simpliciter etc. (13.14b24)

Postquam Philosophus determinavit modos prioris, ad plenam cognitionem prae-dicamentorum nunc determinat modos eorum quae dicuntur simul. Qui sunt tres.

Primus est secundum tempus, quo modo illa dicuntur esse simul quorum gene-5 ratio fit in eodem tempore omnino; et illorum neutrum prius et posterius dicitur. Et hoc est quod ait Philosophus: *Simul itaque haec dicuntur* etc. (13.14b26). Illatio est a sufficiente divisione quae fieri intelligitur, quae est: Quaecumque sunt, aut prius <aut posterius> aut simul dicuntur. Sed quorum generatio fit in eodem tempore, nec prius nec posterius. Sequitur a divisione quod simul dicantur.

10 *Naturaliter autem simul sunt* etc. (13.14b27). Secundus modus | eorum quae   f. 66ra sunt simul est secundum quem dicuntur simul quaecumque convertuntur secun-dum consequentiam essendi et alterum alteri non est causa ut sit, sicut se habent relativa ut duplum et dimidium; illa enim convertuntur secundum consequentiam essendi et alterum alteri non est causa ut sit.

15 *Dicuntur naturaliter simul quaecumque dividuntur* etc. (13.14b31). Nunc se-quitur tertius modus secundum quem simul esse dicuntur quaecumque dividun-tur opposito modo ab eodem genere, ut sunt differentiae dividentes idem genus, ut gressibile, aquatile, volatile; similiter et species a genere dividuntur mediantibus differentiis, et illae etiam simul dicuntur.

20 *Genera enim priora sunt* (13.15a4). Probatio est quod species et differentiae dividuntur a genere, quod est quod genera priora sunt, et posterius non dividitur in priora sed e converso.

Simul ergo per naturam dicuntur quaecumque convertuntur (13.15a7). Infert Philosophus ab inductione exempla praedicta dici simul connumerando praedictos 25 tres modos, praeferendo secundum aliis et tertium primo, considerans intellectus dignitatem et convertibilitatem et inconvertibilitatem.

<Quaestiones>

Primo quaeritur propter quid determinat Philosophus de simul.

Secundo quaeritur de ordine simul ad motum.

Tertio quaeritur de numero et ordine modorum eorum quae simul sunt.

---

17 opposito] opposita P *ut v.*   **18** aquatile] similiter *add.* P   **18** dividuntur] dividitur P **18** mediantibus] mediantur P

Quarto, cum aliis multis modis dicuntur quaedam simul esse, ut in loco generali, velut in domo et in regno et similibus, et in potestate et in fine, et sicut contraria nata sunt fieri simul in eodem subiecto, ergo insufficiens erit Aristoteles in determinatione eorum quae sunt simul.

Quinto quaeritur: Dicit Aristoteles quod in relativis alterum alteri non est causa ut sit. Sed certum est quod pater est causa filii et dimidium dupli et disciplina disciplinati et causa effectus, et cum haec omnia sint ad aliquid, ergo etc.

\<Solutio\>

Ad primum dicimus quod quia species subiectae erant generibus et in eis simul ordinatae, et ignorabatur quo modo erat in eis simultas, ideo ad cognitionem praedictorum Aristoteles de speciebus simul pertractat; quia etiam ea quae erant ad aliquid dicta erant simul natura.

Ad secundum dicimus, sicut diximus, quod propter plenam cognitionem specierum et relativorum distinguuntur modi eorum quae simul dicuntur. Motus vero determinatur propter actionem et passionem et propter quaedam tacta de actione et passione in specie tertia qualitatis. Ex his ergo patet causa ordinationis. Nam simul cognitum universalius currit in cognitionem praedictorum, motus vero non adeo universaliter.

Ad tertium et quartum dicimus quod quaecumque simultatem habent aut secundum rem se habent, et illa sunt quorum generatio est in eodem tempore, aut secundum intellectum, et tunc aut secundum consequentiam erunt aut species et differentiae et quaecumque e diverso dividuntur, et quia prius quod est secundum tempus per prius et verius est ceteris, propter hoc eisdem antefertur, et quia secundus dicitur secundum convertibilitatem, tertius vero minime, sub tali ordine disponuntur.

Ad quartum obiectum dicimus quod proprie dicuntur simul esse quae immutabilia sunt, sed quae sunt in loco generali mutare possunt locum illum et potestatem et finem, et licet duo contraria nata sint fieri circa idem subiectum, non tamen simul | nata sunt fieri circa idem subiectum (dici potest quod iste modus continebatur sub ultimo modorum).

Ad quintum dicimus supradicta quodammodo causas esse et effectus, sed modo alio minime, scilicet materialiter causae sunt et effectus, formaliter vero minime, et sic intellexit Philosophus.

f. 66rb

5

10

15

20

25

30

5–6   *cf.* Arist. *Cat.* 13.14b27–31

---

2 potestate] *lectio incerta* (po^{te} P)   **20** aut^2] ut P   **21** dividuntur] dividunt P   **22** antefertur] auferunt P   **25** proprie] non *add.* P   **26** potestatem] *lectio incerta* (po^{tem} P)

Lectio

Motus species sunt sex etc. (14.15a13)

\<Divisio\>

Visis tribus partibus tertiae partis principalis, in quarum prima naturae oppositionum lucescunt, in secunda patuit natura prioris per assignationem modorum, in tertia vero similiter patuit natura simul, nunc quarta pars sequitur. In qua determinat naturam motus, primo ostendendo quae et quot sunt species motus in genere et speciebus suis. Sunt autem species motus hae: generatio, corruptio, augmentum, deminutio, alteratio, secundum locum mutatio.

Alii itaque motus palam etc. (14.15a15). Supposito numero specierum et eorum nuncupationibus, nunc in secundo loco intendit Aristoteles ostendere supradictas species diversificari. Quarum diversitatem ostendit inferendo ab effectu divisionis quae intelligitur per suppositionem specierum, et ab his quae sequuntur illatio videtur.

Non enim generatio est corruptio etc. (14.15a16). Ostensio est diversitatis specierum supradictarum, scilicet quod generatio non est corruptio neque augmentum neque deminutio nec aliqua dictarum specierum est secundum locum mutatio.

Similiter autem etc. (14.15a18). Quasi dicens: Nec generatio nec corruptio nec augmentum nec deminutio similiter comparando alias species ad invicem.

In alteratione vero habet quandam quaestionem etc. (14.15a18). Quia in aliis speciebus ab alteratione manifesta erat natura diversitatis, ideo supposuit sed non probavit. Sed in alteratione movet quaestionem ut eam solvat, quia ipsa videtur habere dubitationem utrum alteratio sequatur alias species motus vel e converso; et hoc est quod dicit littera ista: *Ne forte necesse sit id quod alteratur per aliquam* etc. (14.15a19).

Hoc autem non est verum (14.15a20). Philosophus respondet effectui dubitationis, ex quo apparebat consequi identitas alterationis cum aliis speciebus, quod verum non est.

Paene secundum omnes passiones aut plures etc. (14.15a21). Si ergo est diversitas alterationis ad alias species motus, hoc modo secundum plures passiones accidit nobis alterari, quae sunt ira et dementia et consimiles animae et corporis passiones, nulla alia superveniente mutatione; non enim necesse est quod alterationem harum passionum sequatur generatio aut aliqua aliarum specierum.

Sed quia dixit Philosophus "aut plures" quia aliquotiens ex passionibus animae

---

3 simul] prioris *P*   **14** secundum] *add. P in marg.*   **20** species motus] specifico motu *P ut v.*   **26** paene] penes *P a.c.*   **26** omnes] animi *add. P*

et corporis saepe movetur animal ad delectabile et fugit a tristabili et corruptibili, sed hoc non est necessarium, ideoque dicit Philosophus aliam speciem esse a
praedictis: *Nam neque augeri necesse est* etc. (14.15a22).

Nam si eadem esset etc. (14.15a25). Per exemplum diversitatem ostendit in-
f. 66va ter alterationem et augmentum, quod est quia si eaedem | essent species, oporteret   5
id quod augetur alterari semper, sed non est hoc. Immo sunt quaedam crescen-
tia quae non alterantur, ut quadrangulus circumposito gnomone; est enim gno-
mon augmentum quadranguli a tribus partibus, et semper est quadrangulus licet
augmentum sumpserit. Cum ergo augmento videtur nulla alteratione facta.

Similiter autem et in aliis (14.15a31). Non est magis ratio de diversitate altera-   10
tionis et augmenti quam alterationis et aliarum; ideo dixit sic esse in aliis.

Quare alii sunt etc. (14.15a31). Illatio est ab inductione eorum quae dicta sunt
quod aliae sunt species motus.

Est autem simpliciter quod motui quies contrarium etc. (14.15b1). Modo Philosophus tertio loco inquirit contrarium motus et specierum eius. Et hic ordo valde   15
artificialis est, quia primo est determinare de re per se, deinde per accidens. In-
quirere enim numerum specierum motus et diversitatem ipsarum est velut inquisi-
tio secundum se, perscrutari contrarium motus et specierum eius est determinatio
motus per accidens. Motui autem in genere quies contraria est propter effectus
contrarios; de quibus magis patebit in solutionibus quaestionum.   20

His vero quae per singula sunt etc. (14.15b1). Nunc ostenduntur contraria specierum motus. Generationi corruptio contraria est per effectus contrarios; nam generatio esse producit, corruptio vero non esse. Similiter augmento deminutio contraria est; nam augmentum perfectionem efficit, deminutio vero imperfectionem.
Sed mutationi locali opposita videtur quies secundum locum vel in contrarium lo-   25
cum mutatio, ut mutationi quae sursum est mutatio quae inferius est contraria est;
similiter in dextris, sinistris, ante, retro.

Reliquo vero assignatorum motuum etc. (14.15b7). Difficultatem ostendit in
assignatione oppositi alterationis, quia nullum videtur habere contrarium.

Nisi quis in hoc secundum qualitates etc. (14.15b9). Dubitative assignat quieta-   30
tem secundum qualitatem esse contrariam alterationi aut mutationi in contrariam
qualitatem; verbi gratia, dealbari contrarium est denigrari, et sanari aegrum fieri, et
sic de aliis.

Sicut in mutatione secundum locum quietem (14.15b10). Similitudinem inducit
Philosophus in contrario mutationis localis et in contrario alterationis.   35

---

5 alterationem] alteritatem *P* **14** est] *add. P s.l.* **23** deminutio] deminutioni *P* **34** in mutatione
secundum] *c* : mutationis *P*

\<Quaestiones\>

Primo quaeritur propter quid determinat Philosophus de motu.

Secundo de ordine motus ad habere.

Tertio quaeritur de modo determinationis motus, scilicet quare hic non definitur motus sed solum per species et contrarium eius notificatur.

Quarto quaeritur quid sit motus et quies et quot habet species.

Quinto quaeritur in quo praedicamento sit motus et quies, oppositio, prius, simul, punctus, instans et unitas.

Sexto quaeritur de numero et ordine specierum motus.

Septimo opponitur: Aristoteles probat in *Physicis* quod generatio et corruptio non sunt motus. Cuius probatio est haec: Omnis motus est de aliquo ente ad aliquod ens; nam omne motum oportet habere naturale principium ens et finem praeter motus circulares. Sed generatio procedit a non ente et tendit ad ens, e converso corruptio incipit ab ente et terminatur in non ens. Ergo generatio et corruptio non sunt motus. Praeterea, nihil aliud est generatio quam formae substantialis datio, et corruptio ablatio formae, et hoc totum fit subito sine motu et tempore, quare non sunt motus.

\<Octavo\> opponitur: Dicit Aristoteles quod alius motus est alteratio praeter alios motus. Sed quod idem sit motus | probatur: In illa materia generatur forma ubi prius disponitur; similiter in augmentatione et deminutione et corruptione et in mutatione locali. Et talis dispositio alteratio est.

Nono opponitur: Videtur quod quaedam alteratio non sit motus, ut mutatio contrariorum immediatorum, verbi gratia, sanitatis et aegritudinis; simile videtur de ignorantia et scientia. Aut enim oportet nos fateri contraria immediata habere medium — quod non est dicendum — per quod sit vel supradicta contraria mutari secundum tempus et motum.

\<Decimo\> opponitur: Si augmentum est motus de minori quantitate ad maiorem et perfectam, et hoc fit mediante incremento † quod tantum disponitur quod assimilatur omnibus membris omnia membra nigreditur † et sic oportet totum corpus augeri secundum omnes suas partes. Sed hoc non accidit in triangulo; non enim crementum recipit secundum se totum, quia non secundum duas partes. Ergo illud augmentum non est motus naturalis et hic supponuntur cuiusque motus species, non solum naturales.

f. 66vb

9–10 Arist. *Phys.* V 2.225a26–27   17–18 Arist. *Cat.* 14.15a18–31

---

9 in] ethicis *add. P*   11 et] a *P ut v.* (*in* ad *corr. al. man.*)   32 non] sed *P*

Undecimo opponitur: Dicit hic Aristoteles, "quies contraria est motui". Sed in *Physicis* dicit quod quies est privatio motus. Sed diversa est oppositio habitus et privationis et contrariorum. Quare videtur sibi contradicere.

Duodecimo opponitur: Aristoteles videtur dubitare de contrarietate alterationis, quia sibi dubie assignat duo contraria. Sed nihil est quod duo contraria habeat. Idem est de mutatione locali. Quare sequitur: Aut alteratio aut mutatio localis nullum habet contrarium aut alterum tantum; et quaeratur illud et propter quam causam.

<Solutio>

Ad primum eorum quae dicta sunt dicendum quod agere et pati non sunt sine motu, et quia natura motus videbatur esse in tertia specie qualitatis, et etiam quia de contrarietate tactum fuerat in *Praedicamentis* et *Postpraedicamentis*, ad quam motus sequitur, ideo ad pleniorem memorationem eorum quae nunc dicta sunt in parte illa pertractat Philosophus de motu.

Ad secundum quaesitum dicimus quod universalior est utilitas cognitionis motus quam habendi; ideo rationabiliter motus habere praecedit. Non enim habere valet ad cognitionem praedicamentorum nisi gratia huius praedicamenti, habere, quod latius suo loco dicemus.

Ad tertium quaesitum dicimus quod de motu non est hic sermo principaliter, sed magis in naturalibus eius principalis versatur intentio. Ideo qualicumque modo nobis pateat sine definitione de motu per species et oppositum de ipso perquirit; nam definitionem motus non est leve assignare et cognoscere.

Ad quartum dicimus quod motus est exitus de potentia ad actum; quod in speciebus motus manifestum est multis. In philosophia generatio proprie sumpta terminus est generationis vel datio formae substantialis, sed prout hic sumitur generatio est praeparatio ad finem generationis, et corruptio proprie est terminus corruptionis sive ablatio formae substantialis, sed prout hic sumitur corruptio est praeparatio ad finem corruptionis. Augmentum vero est motus de minore quantitate ad maiorem, deminutio est motus de maiore quantitate ad minorem. Alteratio vero est motus in qualitate et maxime secundum tertiam speciem, et huius alterationis tot sunt species quot qualitates in tertia specie universales. Sed mutatio localis est mutatio de loco ad locum aut secundum totum aut secundum partes; secundum totum, ut in omni motu recto, proprie est duplex, unus est a deorsum in sursum, alius

---

1 Arist. *Cat.* 14.15b1 **1–2** Arist. *Phys.* V 6.229b25; Anon. *Auct. Arist.* 2.161 (ed. Hamesse, 153) **17** *cf. lectionem sequentem*

---

6 aut mutatio] *iter.* P **24** prout] quod P

est a sursum in deorsum, secundum vero partes, ut in omni motu circulari, sicut in
caelo et in aliis | quae moventur, velut in rota molendini; nam ista talia secundum   f. 67ra
totalitatem non mutantur de loco ad locum sed solum secundum partes, illud vero
totum semper remanet in eodem loco, sed secundum partes mutatur situs. Quies
5 vero est privatio exitus de potentia ad actum, et cum ipsa quies privatio est, ipsa non
est ens, et species non entis non sunt; idcirco species quietis proprie non dicuntur
existere. Dici tamen potest quod quot sunt species motus, tot sunt species quietis,
et per illos motus significantur species quietis.
    Ad quintum quaesitum dicimus quod motus non est in uno praedicamento per
10 se, sed in pluribus propter plures intentiones eius; aut enim comparatur ad finem
aut ad causas suas. Nam si ad causas suas, aut in comparatione ad agentem, et tunc
in actione firmabitur vel ordinabitur, aut in comparatione ad subiectum in quo est,
et tunc idem est quod passio. Si vero ad finem comparatur motus, aut ad quantitatem, et tunc dicitur augmentum et deminutio, aut ad qualitatem, et tunc dicitur
15 alteratio, aut ad ubi, et tunc dicitur mutatio localis; et sic in tribus praedicamentis
praedictis continetur motus propter finium diversitatem. In quibus omnibus apta-
bitur quies propter motus privationem. Avicenna tamen dicit quod motus ratione
finis est in quattuor praedicamentis, in quantitate, qualitate, ubi et situ. Aristoteles
non nominat situm, comprehendens sub ubi vel sub qualitate, Avicenna Aluceus
20 vero, considerans aliqualem diversitatem, situm ab aliis segregavit. Quidam tamen
dicunt sententiam Avicennae esse falsam. Quidam etiam dicunt quod quies cum sit
privatio, non est in praedicamento. De oppositione, autem, priori et simul dicimus
quod generaliter spectant ad praedicamentum relationis, sed specialia opposita non
omnia. De instante, puncto et unitate dicimus quod per privationem dicuntur, qua-
25 re non sunt in praedicamento; nam punctus est cuius pars non est respectu partium
lineae, et unitas similiter dicitur cuius pars non est respectu partium numeri, et instans etiam dicitur cuius pars non est respectu temporis. Dici tamen potest quod
haec tria spectare possunt ad praedicamentum quantitatis cum suos reddant effectus; nam punctus intellectus facit lineam esse continuam, sed unitas est quoddam
30 sine quo numerus esse non potest, similiter instans intellectum facit tempus esse
continuum, et haec more qualitatum videntur recipere divisionem suorum subiec-
torum. Verbi gratia, tempus divisum ostendit divisionem instantis; nam sicut tempus aliud praesens, aliud praeteritum, aliud futurum, sic et instans. Eodem modo
accidit de puncto et linea; nam cum in ea intelligatur punctus unus et ipsa divisa in

---

17–18   Avicenna *Liber primus naturalium* II 3 (ed. Janssens et al., 206)   **20–21**   *cf.* Averroes *in Phys.* IV 45 (ed. Venet., 144r)

---

3 mutantur] mensurantur *P*   **11** agentem] *litteram* a *add. P s.l.*   **11** et tunc] actum *P*   **18** situ] sita *P a.c.*   **19** aluceus] ! *P*   **24–25** quare] quae *P*   **29** quoddam] quodam *P*   **32** instantis] puncti *P*

duas partes, tunc illas partes duo puncta sequuntur. Similiter de numero et unitate;
nam multiplicato numero necesse est unitatem multiplicari.

Ad sextum dicimus quod motus large dictus, ut hic sumitur, sicut iam dicemus,
aut fit in substantia aut in quantitate <aut in qualitate> aut in ubi, et si in substantia, aut tendit ad esse, et ita est generatio, aut ad non esse, et est corruptio; si vero   5
fit in quantitate, aut tendit ad perfectionem, et illud est augmentum, aut ad imperfectionem, et illud dicitur deminutio; si vero in qualitate fit motus, tunc generali
nomine alteratio dicitur; si vero motus fit in ubi, dicitur secundum locum mutatio.
Ideoque sex sunt species mutationis. De ordine autem dicimus quod substantia di-
gnitate | praefertur accidentibus et quantitas aliis accidentibus et qualitas ubi; ideo   10
tali ordine species mutationis disponuntur.

Ad septimum obiectum dicimus: Concedimus rationes de generatione et corruptione esse veras; et sic sequitur quod generatio et corruptio non sunt motus, et
tamen Philosophus appellat eas esse motus. Quare dicendum est quod motus hic
non sumitur stricte sed large et improprie pro mutatione. Ipsa generatio non appel-   15
latur hic finis generationis nec corruptio finis illius motus sed ipsae praeparationes
ad praedictos terminos, et hoc modo generatio et corruptio sunt motus.

Ad octavum dicimus quod alteratio dupliciter sumitur, scilicet generaliter et
specialiter. Sed de speciali alteratione intelligit Philosophus quando vocat eam esse
speciem motus, et illa est alteratio sumpta tantum in qualitatibus quae sunt in tertia   20
specie qualitatis, sed generalis alteratio non est alia a speciebus motus, et ita est ista
mutatio de qua determinat Philosophus hic.

Ad nonum obiectum dicimus quod large potest dici quod mutatio contrariorum
immediatorum est alteratio, sed proprie et per se non est alteratio, immo reducitur ad generationem et corruptionem; bene enim potest dici quod dispositio ad   25
sanitatem et aegritudinem, et sic est de aliis, est alteratio, et illa fit per multa media.

Ad decimum obiectum dicimus additionem quadranguli non esse augmentum
propter rationem assignatam, sed est additio quaedam quae notior est pluribus
quam augmentum naturale, ideoque cognitionis causa pro supradicto augmento
naturali additionem reddit memoratam.   30

Ad undecimum obiectum dicimus quod large sumit hic Aristoteles contrarium
sive verum contrarium sive privatio, sed in *Physicis* loquitur proprie et per se, ideoque illic appellavit quietem privationem motus esse. Vel aliter dicimus quod Aristoteles hic large sumit motum in inferioribus, sed in <*Physicis* stricte in> caelis,
quorum motus vere est privatio quies, quare nulla sequitur contradictio impediente   35
ignorantia elenchi.

---

3 dictus] est *add. P*   **8** si] quia *P*   **8** motus] locus *P*   **8** secundum] quod *P*   **9–10** dignitate]
dig^e *P*   **13** sic] *iter. P*   **24–25** reducitur] reducuntur *P*

f. 67rb

Ad duodecimum obiectum dicimus quod proprie et per se alterationi contraria est quies secundum qualitatem; similiter mutationi locali quies secundum locum contraria est. Speciali vero alterationi, ut denigrationi vel dealbationi, duo apparebunt contraria convenire, scilicet quies secundum illam qualitatem et mutatio in contrariam qualitatem, non tamen verum est principaliter, sed est unum per se et immediate, alterum per accidens; nam quies secundum illam qualitatem contraria est per se, ut dealbationi quies secundum illam qualitatem contraria est, cum potest accidere mutatio in nigredinem, et sic de aliis qualitatibus. Eodem modo se habet de mutatione locali, verbi gratia ei mutationi quae est superius simpliciter contraria est quies secundum locum illum, et ei potest accidere mutatio in contrarium locum, scilicet mutatio in locum inferiorem; eadem est ratio in aliis loci differentiis, quae sunt ante, retro, dextrum, sinistrum. Et quia bene apte iudicare de supradictis non erat facile, ideo sub quodam modo dubitationis locutus est Philosophus, volens nos reddere sollicitos ad studium et laborem.

---

1 alterationi] alteratione *P a.c. ut v.*   2 mutationi] mutatione *P a.c. ut v.*   5 est²] et *P*   11 in locum] *iter. P*

LECTIO

HABERE AUTEM MULTIS MODIS DICITUR ETC. (15.15b17)

\<DIVISIO\>

Determinatis quattuor partibus tertiae partis generalis, nunc sequitur quinta et ultima, in qua ponuntur modi eius quod est habere. Nam primus est penes qualitatem,
secundus penes quantitatem, tertius penes corpora continentia | totum vel partem,   f. 67va
quartus penes partes integrales, quintus penes corpora contenta a continente, sex-
5   tus penes possessiones, septimus et ultimus est penes habitum uxoris a viro et e
converso.

Habere autem dicitur multis modis etc. (15.15b17). Et hoc ut significetur
secundum quem praedicamentum habendi.

Aut enim tanquam habitum et affectionem (15.15b17). Sic ergo est primi modi,
10   qui est supra qualitatem, et quia magis appetimus qualitates secundum primam
speciem habere, ideo primo nominat eam.

Aut aliam qualitatem etc. (15.15b18). Si ergo est quod non refert de qualitate,
secundus modus, qui per quantitatem sumitur.

Aut ea quae sunt circa corpus (15.15b22). Tertius modus habendi est qui est
15   circa corpora per continentiam.

Ut vestimentum etc. (15.15b22). Exempla sunt tertii modi.

Aut in membro etc. (15.15b22). Quidam dicunt quod iste alius modus est.
Quod non concedimus, quia non est separandus a tertio modo propter eandem
intentionem; nam sive res habita contineat totum sive partem, non tamen mutat
20   intentionem habendi.

Aut ut membrum etc. (15.15b23). \<Quartus modus, qui est penes partes
integrales.

Aut ut in vase etc. (15.15b25).\> Quintus modus sequitur, qui est penes corpora
contenta a vase vel a loco.

Aut ut possessionem etc. (15.15b27). Sextus modus, qui est penes possessiones
25   sive sint res mobiles sive immobiles.

Aut ut vir uxorem etc. (15.15b28). Septimus modus, qui est penes uxorem
habitam a viro vel e converso.

Videtur alienissimus etc. (15.15b28). Istum ultimum modum despicit Philoso-
30   phus propter maximam improprietatem eius quod est habere; non enim dicitur vir
proprie habere uxorem vel e converso nisi translative, quare habere sumitur pro
cohabitare.

---

7 autem] *P^{sup}c* : enim *P*   12 qualitate] aut quantitate *add. P*   19 sive¹] si non *P*   24 vase] veste
P   26 mobiles] mo^{les} *P*   26 immobiles] immo^{les} *P*   30 maximam] *lectio incerta*   30 quod]
quae *P*

Forte alii apparebunt etc. (15.15b31). Arrogantiam renuit, dicens modo dubitationis alios apparere modos eius quod est habere, velut ostendeat causam non
esse necessariam de numero modorum habendi; et hoc est quod dixit: *sed qui
consueverunt dici* etc. (15.15b32).

\<Quaestiones\>

Primo quaeritur propter quid determinet Philosophus de habere.   5
    Si dicatur ut significetur modus secundum quem habere est unum generalissi-
morum, secundo quaeritur secundum quem modum habere dicitur unum generalissimorum, et quaeritur quare non secundum alios.
    Tertio quaeritur de numero et ordine modorum assignatorum.

\<Solutio\>

Ad primum eorum quae dicta sunt dicimus quod quia diversimode diceretur habe-   10
re, ignorabatur secundum quem modum faceret praedicamentum, ideoque in co-
gnitione habendi et etiam aliorum ad praesens eius quod est habere distinguuntur
modi.
    Ad secundum quaesitum dicimus quod habere facit praedicamentum secun-
dum tertium modum, qui est penes corpora continentia totum vel partem, ut calcia-   15
tum esse vel armatum esse et his similia. Et quia habitus proprie non est nisi corpo-
rum et nunquam accidentium, immo talis habitus dicitur informatio, similiter nec
partes integrales proprie haberi dicuntur, immo dicuntur esse in suo toto tanquam
perfectiva in perfecto suo, nec etiam quae in vase sunt proprie haberi dicuntur, sed
tantum contineri, similiter nec possessiones proprie haberi dicuntur, sed velut pos-   20
f. 67vb   sideri, rursus | nec uxor nec vir habet vel haberi dicitur proprie, sed ille habitus est
cohabitatio, secundum nullum praedictorum habere dicitur praedicamentum.
    Ad tertium quaesitum dicimus quod omne quod quocumque modo habetur aut
est substantia aut \<qualitas aut\> quantitas, et sub his comprehenduntur alia quae
haberi dicuntur. Si vero substantia habeatur, aut continue aut non, et si continue,   25
tunc dicuntur haberi partes quae sunt continuae, si autem non continue, aut contingue aut separatim. Si contingue, aut secundum quod res habita continetur, et hoc
ut lagenam vinum habere et modicum granum, aut quod habetur separatum est ab
habente, et hoc duobus modis, aut quodammodo proprie aut multum improprie.
Si vero quodammodo proprie, hoc est habere possessionem, si autem improprie,   30
iste est modus ultimus, secundum quem vir dicitur uxorem habere et e converso.

---

18 haberi] habere *P*

Ideoque propter divisionem dictam septem modi ostenduntur eius quod est habere. De ordine autem dicimus quod iam patuit secundum quod ideo primus aliis
antefertur dignitate qualitatum quae sunt scientiae virtutes. In re vero sequitur secundus propter affinitatem habitus accidentalis. Qui sequitur tertius praesentis est
speculationis, sed quartus ratione continuationis sequentibus antefertur. Quintus
propter contiguationem reliquis est praeponendus, sed sextus septimo praeponitur
propter minorem improprietatem et maiorem modi septimi, secundum quem vir
dicitur habere uxorem vel e converso.

BIBLIOGRAPHY

Alan of Lille. *Liber poenitentialis*, ed. J.P. Migne. Patrologia Latina 210. Paris: Migne, 1855.

Albert the Great. *De Praedicamentis*, ed. Silvia Donati and Carlos Steel. Opera Omnia 1.1b. Münster: Aschendorff, forthcoming.

—. *Meteora*, ed. Paul Hossfeld. Opera Omnia 6.1. Münster: Aschendorff, 2003.

Alexander of Hales. *Summa theologica*, ed. Collegium S. Bonaventurae. 4 vols. Quaracchi: Collegium S. Bonaventurae, 1924–48.

Ammonius. *On Aristotle's Categories*, trans. S. Marc Cohen and Gareth B. Matthews. Ancient Commentators on Aristotle. London: Duckworth, 1991.

Andrews, Robert. *Peter of Auvergne's Commentary on Aristotle's* Categories: *Edition, Translation, and Analysis.* PhD diss., Cornell University, 1988.

—. "Question Commentaries on the *Categories* in the Thirteenth Century." *Medioevo* 26 (2001): 265–326.

—. "Thomas of Erfurt on the *Categories* in Philosophy." In *Was ist Philosophie im Mittelalter?*, ed. Jan A. Aertsen and Andreas Speer, 801–8. Miscellanea Mediaevalia 26. Berlin: Walter de Gruyter, 1998.

Andrews, Robert, and Timothy B. Noone. "Willelmus de Montoriel: *Summa libri Praedicamentorum.*" *Cahiers de l'Institut du Moyen-Âge Grec et Latin* 64 (1994): 63–100.

Anonymous. *Dialectica Monacensis*, ed. L.M. de Rijk. In de Rijk, *Logica Modernorum*, vol. 2.2, 453–638.

—. *Liber de causis*, ed. Adriaan Pattin. Leuven: Uitgave van Tijdschrift voor Filosofie, 1967.

—. *Liber de stabilitate animae*, ed. J.P. Migne. Patrologia Latina 213. Paris: Migne, 1855.

—. *Liber sex principiorum*, ed. L. Minio-Paulello. Aristoteles Latinus 1.7. Bruges: Desclée de Brouwer, 1966.

—. *Logica "Cum sit nostra"*, ed. L.M. de Rijk. In de Rijk, *Logica Modernorum*, vol. 2.2, 413–51.

—. *Logica "Ut dicit"*, ed. L.M. de Rijk. In de Rijk, *Logica Modernorum*, vol. 2.2, 375–411.

—. *Ripoll Compendium*, ed. Claude Lafleur and Joanne Carrier. In Claude Lafleur and Joanne Carrier, *Le "Guide de l'étudiant" d'un maître anonyme de la faculté des arts de Paris au XIIIᵉ siècle: Édition critique provisoire du ms. Barcelona, Arxiu de la Corona d'Aragó, Ripoll 109, ff. 134ra–158va*. Publications du Laboratoire de Philosophie Ancienne et Médiévale de la Faculté de Philosophie de l'Université Laval 1. Québec: Faculté de Philosophie, Université Laval, 1992.

—. *Tractatus Anagnini*, ed. L.M. de Rijk. In de Rijk, *Logica Modernorum*, vol. 2.2, 215–332.

Anonymous of D'Orville. *Commentary on Aristotle's* Categories, ed. Sten Ebbesen. In Ebbesen, "Anonymus D'Orvillensis," 251–423.

Anonymous Porretanean. *Commentary on Aristotle's* Categories, ed. Sten Ebbesen. In Ebbesen, "A Porretanean Commentary," 45–88.

Anselm. *De veritate*, ed. F.S. Schmitt. Opera Omnia 1.1. Stuttgart-Bad Cannstatt: Friedrich Frommann, 1968.

Aristotle. *Aristoteles Latinus*, ed. L. Minio-Paluello et al. Bruges: Desclée de Brouwer, 1951–.

—. *Categoriae et Liber de interpretatione*, ed. L. Minio-Paluello. Oxford: Clarendon Press, 1949.

—. *Categories and De Interpretatione*, trans. J.L Ackrill. Clarendon Aristotle Series. Oxford: Clarendon Press, 1963.

—. *Complete Works of Aristotle: The Revised Oxford Translation*, ed. Jonathan Barnes. 2 vols. Bollingen Series. Princeton: Princeton University Press, 1995.

—. *Kategorien*, trans. Klaus Oehler. Aristoteles: Werke in Deutscher Übersetzung 1.1. Berlin: Akademie Verlag, 2006.

Ashworth, E. Jennifer. "*Catégories*, 1 dans le '*Guide de l'étudiant.*'" In Lafleur and Carrier, *L'enseignement de la philosophie*, 281–95.

Asztalos, Monica. "Boethius on the *Categories*." In *Boèce ou la chaîne des savoirs*, ed. Alain Galonnier, 195–205. Leuven: Peeters, 2003.

Averroes. *Commentarium in libros Metaphysicorum Aristotelis*. Aristotelis Opera cum Averrois Commentariis 8. Venice, 1562. Reprint, Frankfurt am Main: Minerva, 1962.

—. *Commentarium in libros Physicorum Aristotelis*. Aristotelis Opera cum Averrois Commentariis 4. Venice, 1562. Reprint, Frankfurt am Main: Minerva, 1962.

—. *Commentarium magnum in Aristotelis De anima libros*, ed. F.S. Crawford. Corpus Commentariorum Averrois in Aristotelem. Versionum Latinarum 6.1. Cambridge, MA: The Mediaeval Academy of America, 1953.

—. *Commentum medium super libro Praedicamentorum Aristotelis*, ed. R. Hissette. Averrois Opera, Series B; Averroes Latinus 11. Leuven: Peeters, 2010.

Avicebron. *Fons vitae: Ex arabico in latinum translatum ab Iohanne Hispano et Dominico Gundissalino*, ed. C. Baeumker. Beiträge zur Geschichte der Philosophie des Mittelalters 1.2–4. Münster: Aschendorff, 1895.

Avicenna. *Liber Canonis*. Venice, 1507. Reprint, Hildesheim: Georg Olms, 1964.

—. *Liber primus naturalium. Tractatus secundus. De motu et de consimilibus*, ed. J. Janssens, S. Van Riet, and A. Allard. Avicenna Latinus 1.10. Leuven: Peeters, 2006.

Barnes, Jonathan. "Les catégories et les *Catégories*." In Bruun and Corti, *Les* Catégories *et leur histoire*, 11–80.

Biard, Joël, and Irène Rosier-Catach, eds. *La tradition médievale des catégories (XIIe–XVe siècles): Actes du XIIIe Symposium européen de logique et de sémantique médiévales.* Philosophes médiévaux 45. Leuven: Peeters, 2003.

Boethius. *Commentarii in librum Aristotelis Perihermeneias*, ed. C. Meiser. Leipzig: Teubner, 1877–80.

—. *De divisione liber*, ed. John Magee. Philosophia Antiqua 77. Leiden: Brill, 1998.

—. *De hypotheticis syllogismis*, ed. L. Obertello. Brescia: Paideia, 1969.

—. *De institutione arithmetica. De institutione musica. Geometria*, ed. G. Friedlein. Leipzig: Teubner, 1867.

—. *De topicis differentiis kai hoi buzantines metafraseis ton Manouel Holobolou kai Prochorou Kudone*, ed. D.Z. Nikitas. Athens: Academy of Athens, 1990.

—. *In Categorias Aristotelis*, ed. J.P. Migne. Patrologia Latina 64. Paris: Migne, 1860.

—. *In Isagogen Porphyrii Commenta*, ed. Samuel Brandt. Corpus Scriptorum Ecclesiasticorum Latinorum 48.1. Vienna: F. Tempsky, 1906.

—. *In Topica Ciceronis commentaria*, ed. J.C. Orelli. In Cicero, *Opera Omnia* 5.1. Turin: Orelli, Fuesslini & Co., 1833.

—. *Institution Arithmétique*, ed. J.-Y. Guillaumin. Paris: Les Belles Lettres, 1995.

—. *Opuscula theologica*, ed. C. Moreschini. 2nd ed. Munich: K.G. Saur, 2005.

—. *Philosophiae consolatio*, ed. Ludwig Bieler. Corpus Christianorum Series Latina 94. Turnhout: Brepols, 1984.

Braakhuis, H.A.G. *De 13de eeuwse tractaten over syncategorematische termen: Inleidende studie en uitgave van Nicolaas van Parijs'* Sincategoreumata. 2 vols. Meppel: Krips Repro, 1979.

—. "Obligations in Early Thirteenth Century Paris: The *Obligationes* of Nicholas of Paris(?) (MS Paris, B. N. lat., 11.412)." *Vivarium* 36 (1998): 152–233.

—. "The Chapter on the *Liber Peryarmenias* of the Ripoll '*Student's Guide*': A Comparison with Contemporary Commentaries." In Lafleur and Carrier, *L'enseignement de la philosophie*, 297–323.

Brower, Jeffrey E. "Medieval Theories of Relations." In *The Stanford Encyclopedia of Philosophy* (Winter 2010 Edition), ed. Edward N. Zalta. URL = <http://plato.stanford.edu/archives/win2010/entries/relations-medieval/>.

Bruun, Otto, and Lorenzo Corti, eds. *Les* Catégories *et leur histoire.* Paris: Vrin, 2005.

Callus, D.A. "The Date of Grosseteste's Translations and Commentaries on Pseudo-Dionysius and the Nicomachean Ethics." *Recherches de Théologie ancienne et médiévale* 14 (1947): 186–210.

Cao, G.M., C. Casagrande, M.A. Casagrande Mazzoli, D. Ciccarelli, S. Gavinelli, and S. Vecchio. *Catalogo di manoscritti filosofici nelle biblioteche italiane.* Vol. 7, *Novara, Palermo, Pavia.* Corpus Philosophorum Medii Aevi, Subsidia 8. Florence: Leo S. Olschki, 1993.

Chenu, Marie-Dominique. "Maîtres et Bacheliers de l'Université de Paris v. 1240: Description du Manuscrit Paris, Bibl. Nat. lat. 15652." In *Études d'Histoire Littéraire et Doctrinale du XIIIe siècle.* Publications de l'Institut d'Études Médiévales d'Ottawa 1 (1932): 11–39.

Conti, Alessandro D. "Thomas Sutton's Commentary on the *Categories* according to MS Oxford, Merton College 289." In Lewry, *The Rise of British Logic*, 173–213.

Courtenay, William J. "Radulphus Brito: Master of Arts and Theology." *Cahiers de l'Institut du Moyen-Âge Grec et Latin* 76 (2005): 131–58.

—. *Teaching Careers at the University of Paris in the Thirteenth and Fourteenth Centuries.* Texts and Studies in the History of Mediaeval Education 18. Notre Dame: University of Notre Dame, 1988.

Dalgaard, Karen Elisabeth. "Peter of Ireland's Commentary on Aristotle's *Perihermeneias.*" *Cahiers de l'Institut du Moyen-Âge Grec et Latin* 43 (1982): 3–44.

de Haas, Frans A.J. *John Philoponus' New Definition of Prime Matter.* Philosophia Antiqua 69. Leiden: Brill, 1997.

de Libera, Alain. *L'art des généralités.* Paris: Aubier, 1999.

—. "Le traité *De appellatione* de Lambert de Lagny (Lambert de Auxerre)." *Archives d'Histoire Doctrinale et Littéraire du Moyen Age* 48 (1982): 227–85.

—. "Les *Appellationes* de Jean Le Page." *Archives d'Histoire Doctrinale et Littéraire du Moyen Age* 51 (1984): 193–255.

de Rijk, L.M. "The Aristotelian Background of Medieval *transcendentia*: A Semantic Approach." In Pickavé, *Die Logik des Transzendentalen*, 3–22.

—. *Logica Modernorum: A Contribution to the History of Early Terminist Logic*. 2 vols. Assen: Van Gorcum, 1962–67.

Denifle, Heinrich, and Emile Châtelain. *Chartularium Universitatis Parisiensis*. 4 vols. Paris: Delalain, 1899.

Dexippus. *On Aristotle Categories*, trans. John Dillon. Ancient Commentators on Aristotle. London: Duckworth, 1990.

Dod, Bernard G. "Aristoteles Latinus." In Kretzmann, Kenny and Pinborg, *Cambridge History*, 45–79.

D'Ors, Angel. "Petrus Hispanus O.P., Auctor Summularum (II): Further documents and problems." *Vivarium* 39 (2001): 209–54.

Doucet, Victorin. "La date des condemnations parisiennes dites de 1241: Faut-il corriger le Cartulaire de l'Université?" In *Mélanges Auguste Pelzer*. Recueil de Travaux d'Histoire et de Philologie 3ᵐᵉ Série, 26ᵐᵉ Fascicule, 183–93. Leuven: Éditions de l'Institut Supérieur de Philosophie, 1947.

Dreyer, Mechthild. *Nikolaus von Amiens: Ars fidei catholicae; Ein Beispielwerk axiomatischer Methode*. Beiträge zur Geschichte der Philosophie und Theologie des Mittelalters, Neue Folge 37. Münster: Aschendorff, 1993.

Ebbesen, Sten. "A Porretanean Commentary on Aristotle's *Categories*." *Cahiers de l'Institut du Moyen-Âge Grec et Latin* 72 (2001): 35–88.

—. "Anonymus D'Orvillensis' Commentary on Aristotle's *Categories*." *Cahiers de l'Institut du Moyen-Âge Grec et Latin* 70 (1999): 229–423.

—. *Commentators and Commentaries on Aristotle's Sophistici Elenchi: A Study of Post-Aristotelian Ancient and Medieval Writings on Fallacies*. 3 vols. Leiden: Brill, 1981.

—. "*Communia Visitatio* and *Communia Feminae*." *Cahiers de l'Institut du Moyen-Âge Grec et Latin* 73 (2002): 167–258.

—. "Concrete Accidental Terms: Late Thirteenth-Century Debates about Problems Relating to such Terms as 'album.'" In *Meaning and Inference in Medieval Philosophy: Studies in Memory of Jan Pinborg*, ed. Norman Kretzmann, 107–74. Dordrecht: Kluwer, 1988.

—. "Les *Catégories* au moyen âge et au début de la modernité." In Bruun and Corti, *Les* Catégories *et leur histoire*, 245–74.

—. "The Paris Arts Faculty: Siger of Brabant, Boethius of Dacia, Radulphus Brito." In *Medieval Philosophy*, ed. John Marenbon, 269–290. Vol. 3 of *Routledge His-*

tory of Philosophy, ed. G.H.R. Parkinson and S.G. Shanker. London: Routledge, 1998.

—. "Two Nominalist Texts." *Cahiers de l'Institut du Moyen-Âge Grec et Latin* 61 (1991): 429–40.

—. "What Counted as Logic in the Thirteenth Century?" In *Methods and Methodologies*, ed. Margaret Cameron and John Marenbon, 93–107. Leiden: Brill, 2011.

Franceschini, Ezio. "Giovanno Pago: Le sue *Rationes super Praedicamenta Aristotelis* e la loro posizione nel movimento Aristotelico del secolo XIII." *Sophia* 2 (1934): 172–82; 329–50; 476–86.

Frede, Michael. "Categories in Aristotle." In Frede, *Essays in Ancient Philosophy*, 29–48. Originally appeared in *Studies in Aristotle*, ed. D.J. O'Meara, 1–24. Washington, DC: The Catholic University of America Press, 1981.

—. *Essays in Ancient Philosophy*. Oxford: Clarendon Press, 1987.

—. "The Title, Unity, and Authenticity of the Aristotelian *Categories*." In Frede, *Essays in Ancient Philosophy*, 11–28. Originally appeared as "Titel, Einheit und Echtheit der aristotelischen Kategorienschrift" in *Zweifelhaftes im Corpus Aristotelicum*, ed. Paul Moraux and Jürgen Wiesner, 1–29. Berlin: Walter de Gruyter, 1983.

Gabbay, Dov M., and John Woods, eds. *Handbook of the History of Logic*. Vol. 2, *Mediaeval and Renaissance Logic*. Amsterdam: Elsevier, 2008.

Gorman, Michael, and Jonathan J. Sanford, eds. *Categories: Historical and Systematic Essays.* Studies in Philosophy and the History of Philosophy 41. Washington, DC: The Catholic University of America Press, 2004.

Grabmann, Martin. "Die Logischen Schriften des Nikolaus von Paris und ihre Stellung in der Aristotelischen Bewegung des XIII. Jahrhunderts." In Martin Grabmann, *Mittelalterliches Geistesleben*, vol. 1, 222–48. Munich: Max Hueber, 1926.

Gracia, Jorge, and Lloyd Newton. "Medieval Theories of the Categories." In *The Stanford Encyclopedia of Philosophy (Summer 2006 Edition)*, ed. Edward N. Zalta URL = http://plato.stanford.edu/archives/sum2006/entries/medieval-categories/

Gründel, Johannes. "Die Sentenzenglosse des Johannes Pagus (circa 1243–1245) in Padua, Bibl. Ant. 139." *Münchener Theologische Zeitschrift* 9 (1958): 171–85.

Haly. *In librum Tegni Galeni*. In *Articella*. Venice, 1493.

Hamesse, Jacqueline. *Les Auctoritates Aristotelis: Un florilège médiéval; Étude historique et édition critique.* Philosophes médiévaux 17. Leuven: Publications Universitaires, 1974.

Hansen, Heine. "Anonymus Domus Petri 206's Commentary on Aristotle's *Categories.*" *Cahiers de l'Institut du Moyen-Âge Grec et Latin* 78 (2008): 111–203.

—. "Strange Finds, or Nicholas of Paris on Relations." In *Logic and Language in the Middle Ages*, ed. Jakob L. Fink, Heine Hansen, and Ana María Mora Márquez. Leiden: Brill, forthcoming.

Harari, Orna. "The Unity of Aristotle's Category of Relatives." *Classical Quarterly* 61 (2011): 521–37.

Henninger, Mark G. *Relations: Medieval Theories 1250–1325.* Oxford: Clarendon Press, 1989.

Henri d'Andeli. *The Battle of the Seven Arts: A French Poem by Henri d'Andeli, Trouvère of the Thirteenth Century*, ed. and trans. Louis John Paetow. Memoirs of the University of California, vol. 4.1, History, vol. 1.1. Berkeley: University of California Press, 1914.

Hippocrates. *Aphorismi cum commento Galieni.* In *Articella.* Venice, 1493.

Isaac Israeli. *Omnia Opera Isaac.* Lyon, 1515.

Isidore of Seville. *Etymologiae*, ed. W.M. Lindsay. 2 vols. Oxford: Clarendon Press, 1911.

Johannitius. *Isagoge ad Techne Galieni*, ed. Gregor Maurach. In *Sudhoffs Archiv* 62 (1978): 148–74.

John Duns Scotus. *Quaestiones in librum Porphyrii Isagoge et Quaestiones super Praedicamenta Aristotelis*, ed. R. Andrews, G. Etzkorn, G. Gál, R. Green, T. Noone, and R. Wood. *Opera Philosophica* 1. St. Bonaventure, NY: The Franciscan Institute, 1999.

Kant, Immanuel. *Critique of Pure Reason*, trans. and ed. P. Guyer and A.W. Wood. Cambridge: Cambridge University Press, 1998.

Kneepkens, C.H. "*Significatio generalis* and *significatio specialis*: Notes on Nicholas of Paris' Contribution to Early Thirteenth-Century Linguistic Thought." In *Medieval Analyses in Language and Cognition*, ed. Sten Ebbesen and Russell L. Friedman, 17–43. Copenhagen: The Royal Danish Academy of Sciences and Letters, 1999.

Kretzmann, Norman, Anthony Kenny, and Jan Pinborg, eds. *The Cambridge History of Later Medieval Philosophy.* Cambridge: Cambridge University Press, 1982.

Lafleur, Claude, and Joanne Carrier. "La *Philosophia* d' Hervé le Breton (alias Henri le Breton) et le recueil d'introductions à la philosophie du ms. Oxford, Corpus Christi College 283 (Première partie)." *Archives d'Histoire Doctrinale et Littéraire du Moyen Age* 61 (1994): 149–226.

—, eds. *L'enseignement de la philosophie au XIIIe siècle: Autour du "Guide de l'étudiant" du ms. Ripoll 109*. Studia Artistarum 5. Turnhout: Brepols, 1997.

—. "*L'Introduction à la philosophie* de maître Nicolas de Paris." In Lafleur and Carrier, *L'enseignement de la philosophie*, 447–65.

—. "Un instrument de révision destiné aux candidats à la licence de la Faculté des arts de Paris, le *De communibus artium liberalium* (vers 1250?)." *Documenti e studi sulla tradizione filosofica medievale* 5 (1994): 129–203.

—. "Une figure métissée du platonisme médiéval: Jean le Page et le Prologue de son Commentaire (vers 1231-1240) sur l'*Isagoge* de Porphyre." In *Une philosophie dans l'histoire: Hommages à Raymond Klibansky*, ed. Bjarne Melkevik and Jean-Marc Narbonne, 105–60. Québec: Les Presses de l'Université Laval, 2000.

Lagerlund, Henrik. "The Assimilation of Aristotelian and Arabic Logic up to the Later Thirteenth Century." In *Handbook of the History of Logic*, ed. Dov M. Gabbay and John Woods, vol. 2, *Mediaeval and Renaissance Logic*, 281–346.

Lambert of Lagny [Auxerre]. *Logica (Summa Lamberti)*, ed. Franco Alessio. Florence: La Nuova Italia Editrice, 1971.

Lewry, P. Osmund. "Robert Kilwardby on Meaning: A Parisian Course on the *Logica vetus*." In *Sprache und Erkenntnis im Mittelalter*, ed. Jan P. Beckmann et al. Miscellanea Mediaevalia 13, vol. 1, 376–84. Berlin: Walter de Gruyter, 1981.

—. *Robert Kilwardby's Writings on the* Logica Vetus: *Studied with Regard to their Teaching and Method*. PhD diss., University of Oxford, 1978.

—, ed. *The Rise of British Logic*. Papers in Mediaeval Studies 7. Toronto: Pontifical Institute of Mediaeval Studies, 1985.

Lohr, Charles. "Medieval Latin Aristotle Commentaries: Addenda et Corrigenda." *Bulletin de Philosophie Médiévale* 14 (1972): 116–26.

—. "Medieval Latin Aristotle Commentaries: Authors Narcissus–Richardus." *Traditio* 28 (1972): 281–396.

Marenbon, John. *Medieval Philosophy: An Historical and Philosophical Introduction*. London: Routledge, 2007.

McMahon, William E. "The Medieval Sufficientiae: Attempts at a Definitive Division of the Categories." *Procedings of the Society for Medieval Logic and Metaphysics* 2 (2002): 12–25.

—. "Radulphus Brito on the Sufficiency of the Categories." *Cahiers de l'Institut du Moyen-Âge Grec et Latin* 39 (1981): 81–96.

—. "Reflections on Some Thirteenth- and Fourteenth-Century Views of the Categories." In Gorman and Sanford, *Categories*, 45–57.

—. "Some Non-Standard Views of the Categories." In Biard and Rosier-Catach, *La tradition médiévale des catégories*, 53–67.

Minio-Paluello, L. *Aristoteles Latinus: Codices. Pars posterior*. Cambridge: Cambridge University Press, 1955.

Morrison, Donald. "Le statut catégoriel des differences dans l'*Organon*." *Revue philosophique de France et de l'Etrangér* 183 (1993): 147–78.

Nicholas of Paris. *Philosophia*, ed. Claude Lafleur and Joanne Carrier. In Lafleur and Carrier, "*L'Introduction à la philosophie*," 454–65.

—. *Rationes super Porphyrium*. In MS Munich, Bayerische Staatsbibliothek Clm. 14460, ff. 1ra–20vb.

—. *Rationes super Praedicamenta*. In MS Munich, Bayerische Staatsbibliothek Clm. 14460, ff. 42ra–62ra.

Nicolaus Damascenus. *De plantis: Five Translations*, ed. H.J. Drossaart Lulofs and E.L.J. Poortman. Aristoteles Semitico-Latinus. Amsterdam: North-Holland Publishing Company, 1989.

Otte, James K. *Alfred of Sarashel's Commentary on the Metheora of Aristotle: Critical Edition, Introduction, and Notes*. Studien und Texte zur Geistesgeschichte des Mittelalters 19. Leiden: Brill, 1988.

Pasnau, Robert, ed. *The Cambridge History of Medieval Philosophy*. 2 vols. Cambridge: Cambridge University Press, 2010.

Pelster, Franz. "Literargeschichtliches zur Pariser theologischen Schule aus den Jahren 1230 bis 1256." *Scholastik* 5 (1930): 46–78.

Peter of Auvergne. *Quaestiones super Praedicamentis*, ed. Robert Andrews. *Cahiers de l'Institut du Moyen-Âge Grec et Latin* 55 (1987): 3–84.

Peter Helias, *Summa super Priscianum*, ed. Leo Reilly. Studies and Texts 113. 2 vols. Toronto: Pontifical Institute of Mediaeval Studies, 1993.

Peter of Ireland, *Expositio et Questiones in Librum Aristotelis Peryermenias seu de Interpretatione*, ed. Michael Dunne. Philosophes Médiévaux 34. Leuven: Peeters, 1996.

Peter of Spain. *Tractatus*, ed. L.M. de Rijk. Assen: Van Gorcum, 1972.

Philaretus. *De pulsibus*. In *Articella*. Venice, 1493.

Piché, David. *Le problème des universaux à la Faculté des arts de Paris entre 1230 et 1260*. Paris: Vrin, 2005.

Pickavé, Martin, ed. *Die Logik des Transzendentalen: Festschrift für Jan A. Aertsen zum 65. Geburtstag*. Miscellanea Mediaevalia 30. Berlin: Walter de Gruyter, 2003.

Pini, Giorgio. *Categories and Logic in Duns Scotus: An Interpretation of Aristotle's* Categories *in the Late Thirteenth Century.* Studien und Texte zur Geistesgeschichte des Mittelalters 77. Leiden: Brill, 2002.

—. "The Transcendentals of Logic: Thirteenth-Century Discussions on the Subject Matter of Aristotle's *Categories.*" In Pickavé, *Die Logik des Transzendentalen,* 140–59.

Plato. *Timaeus,* trans. Calcidus; ed. J.H. Waszink and P.J. Jensen. Plato Latinus 4. London: The Warburg Institute; Leiden: Brill, 1962.

Porphyry. *Introduction,* trans. Jonathan Barnes. Oxford: Clarendon Press, 2003.

—. *Isagoge,* ed. L. Minio-Paluello. Aristoteles Latinus 1.6–7. Bruges: Desclée de Brouwer, 1966.

—. *On Aristotle Categories,* trans. Steven K. Strange. Ancient Commentators on Aristotle. London: Duckworth, 1992.

Priscian. *Institutiones grammaticae,* ed. Martin Hertz. 2 vols. Grammatici Latini 2–3. Leipzig: Teubner, 1855–59.

Ps.-Augustine. *Categoriae decem,* ed. L. Minio-Paluello. Aristoteles Latinus 1.5. Bruges: Desclée de Brouwer, 1961.

Radulphus Brito. *Quaestiones subtillissimae Magistri Rodulphi Britonis super arte veteri.* Venice, 1499.

Robert Kilwardby. *Notulae super Librum Porphyrii.* In MS Cambridge, Peterhouse 206, ff. 33ra–42ra; MS Madrid, Biblioteca Universitaria 73, ff. 1ra–10vb.

—. *Notulae super Librum Praedicamentorum.* In MS Cambridge, Peterhouse 206, ff. 42ra–65va; MS Madrid, Biblioteca Universitaria 73, ff. 10vb–43vb.

—. *Notulae super Librum Perihermeneias.* In MS Cambridge, Peterhouse 206, ff. 65vb–79rb (incomplete); MS Madrid, Biblioteca Universitaria 73, ff. 44ra–66va; MS Venice, Biblioteca Marciana L.VI.66 [2528], ff. 1r–18v.

Roger Bacon. *Summulae dialectices I-II: De termino, De enuntiatione,* ed. Alain de Libera. *Archives d'Histoire Doctrinale et Littéraire du Moyen Age* 53 (1986): 139–289.

Schmidt, Robert W. *The Domain of Logic According to Saint Thomas Aquinas.* The Hague: Martinus Nijhoff, 1966.

Schoonheim, Pieter L. *Aristotle's* Meteorology *in the Arabico-Latin Tradition: A Critical Edition of the Texts, with Introduction and Indices.* Aristoteles Semitico-Latinus 12. Leiden: Brill, 2000.

Sedley, David. "Aristotelian Relativities." In *Le style de la pensée,* ed. Monique Canto-Sperber and Pierre Pellegrin, 324–52. Paris: Les Belles Lettres, 2002.

Shields, Christopher. *Aristotle*. London: Routledge, 2007.

Simplicius. *On Aristotle's Categories 1–4*, trans. Michael Chase. Ancient Commentators on Aristotle. London: Duckworth, 2003.

—. *On Aristotle's Categories 5–6*, trans. Frans A.J. de Haas and Barrie Fleet. Ancient Commentators on Aristotle. London: Duckworth, 2001.

Steel, Carlos. "Albert's Use of Kilwardby's *Notulae* in his Paraphrase of the *Categories*." In *Via Alberti: Texte, Quellen, Interpretationen*, ed. Ludger Honnefelder, Hannes Möhle, and Susana Bullido del Barrio, 481–506. Münster: Aschendorff, 2009.

Studtmann, Paul. "Aristotle's Category of Quantity: A Unified Interpretation." *Apeiron* 37 (2004): 69–91.

Tabarroni, Andrea. "Lo Pseudo Egidio (Guglielmo Arnaldi) e un'inedita continuazione del commento di Tommaso al *Peryermenias*." *Medioevo* 14 (1988): 371–427.

Thom, Paul. *Logic and Ontology in the Syllogistic of Robert Kilwardby*. Studien und Texte zur Geistesgeschichte des Mittelalters 92. Leiden: Brill, 2007.

Thomas Aquinas. *De ente et essentia*, ed. R.M. Spiazzi. Opuscula Philosophica. Turin: Marietti, 1954.

—. *Expositio Libri peryermenias: Editio altera retractata*, ed. Leonina. Opera Omnia 1.1. Rome: Commissio Leonina, 1989.

—. *Expositio Libri posteriorum: Editio altera retractata*, ed. Leonina. Opera Omnia 1.2. Rome: Commissio Leonina, 1989.

—. *In duodecim libros Metaphysicorum Aristotelis expositio*, ed. M.-R. Cathala and R.M. Spiazzi. Turin: Marietti, 1964.

—. *In octo libros Physicorum Aristotelis expositio*, ed. P. M. Maggiolo. Turin: Marietti, 1965.

—. *Scriptum super libros Sententiarum*, ed. P. Mandonnet and M.F. Moos. 4 vols. Paris: Lethielleux, 1929–1956.

—. *Sentencia Libri de anima*, ed. Leonina. Opera Omnia 45.1. Rome: Commissio Leonina, 1984.

—. *Summa Theologiae*, ed. Leonina. Opera Omnia 4–12. Rome: Commissio Leonina, 1888–1906.

van Steenberghen, Fernand. *Aristotle in the West: The Origins of Latin Aristotelianism*. Leuven: E. Nauwelaerts, 1955.

Walter of Châtillon. *Alexandreis*, ed. Marvin L. Colker. Padua: Antenore, 1978.

Wedin, Michael. *Aristotle's Theory of Substance: The* Categories *and* Metaphysics Zeta. Oxford: Clarendon Press, 2000.

Weijers, Olga. *Le maniement du savoir: Pratiques intellectuelles à l'époque des premières universités (XIIIe-XIVe siècles).* Studia Artistarum, Subsidia. Turnhout: Brepols, 1996.

—. *Le travail intellectuel à la Faculté des arts de Paris: Textes et maîtres (ca. 1200–1500),* vols. 1–6, Studia Artistarum 1, 3, 6, 9, 11, 13. Turnhout: Brepols, 1994–2005.

Westerhoff, Jan. *Ontological Categories: Their Nature and Significance.* Oxford: Clarendon Press, 2005.

Wielgus, Stanisław. "Quaestiones Nicolai Peripatetici." *Mediaevalia Philosophica Polonorum* 17 (1973): 57–155.

William of Conches. *Glosae super Boetium,* ed. Lodi Nauta. Corpus Christianorum Continuatio Mediaevalis 158. Turnhout: Brepols, 1999.

Wippel, John F. "Thomas Aquinas's Derivation of the Aristotelian Categories (Predicaments)." *Journal of the History of Philosophy* 25 (1987): 13–34.

INDEX LOCORUM

This index lists all the authoritative passages explicitly referred to by Pagus in his commentary. The references are to the page and line where the author or work is mentioned. Parentheses around a name, e.g., (Plato), indicate that Pagus attributes the quotation to this author on the basis of the authoritative passage preceding the name. Square brackets around a name, e.g., [Galen], indicate that Pagus misattributes the quotation to this author. Cruces around a name, e.g., † Morebus †, indicate that I take the transmitted text to be corrupt.

ARISTOTELES, PSEUDO
De vegetabilibus

AUGUSTINUS
in Iohannis evangelium

AUGUSTINUS, PSEUDO
Categoriae decem

De spiritu et anima

AVERROES
in De anima

in Metaphysica

in Physica

AVICEBRON
Fons vitae

APPENDIX

INDEX QUAESTIONUM

This index lists all the questions found in Pagus' commentary. Page numbers indicate the page where the question is raised. When the same or partly the same question is found in one or more of the contemporary commentaries by the Anonymous of Peterhouse 206 (**A**), Nicholas of Paris (**N**), and Robert Kilwardby (**K**), a reference to these commentaries is given in a square bracket following the question. These references are given as follows: roman numerals refer to *lectiones* and are followed by arabic numerals referring to questions; **N** VI.2, for example, means that the same or partly the same question is found in Nicholas of Paris' commentary as the second question of the sixth *lectio*. Following in parentheses is the number of the page or folio where that question is raised (references to the Anonymous of Peterhouse are to the edition in Heine Hansen, "Anonymus Domus Petri 206's Commentary on Aristotle's *Categories*," *Cahiers de l'Institut du Moyen-Âge Grec et Latin* 78 (2008): 119–203; references to Nicholas of Paris are to MS Munich, Bayerische Staatsbibliothek Clm. 14460; and references to Robert Kilwardby are to, first, MS Cambridge, Peterhouse 206 and, second, MS Madrid, Biblioteca Universitaria 73). Note that in order to facilitate indexing the titles of the questions have often been abbreviated.

Lectio XXVIII (*Cat.* 7.7b15–8a13)

Lectio XXIX (*Cat.* 7.8a14–35)

Lectio XXX (*Cat.* 7.8a35–b24)

APPENDIX

DE WULF-MANSION CENTRE
ANCIENT AND MEDIEVAL PHILOSOPHY

Series 1

XV.   *Henry of Ghent. Proceedings of the International Colloquium on the occasion of the 700ᵗʰ Anniversary of his Death (1293)*. Ed. W. VANHAMEL, 1996, XII-458 pp.

XVI.   P. PORRO, *Forme e modelli di durata nel pensiero medievale. L'aevum, il tempo discreto, la categoria "quando,"* 1996, VII-532 pp.

XVII.   *Henricus Bate. Opera astronomica* (in preparation).

XVIII.   *Galenus. De virtute alimentorum* (in preparation).

XIX.   *Ptolemaeus. Iudicialia ad Syrum sive Quadripartitum* (in preparation).

XX.   *Iohannes Scottus Eriugena. The Bible and Hermeneutics. Proceedings of the Ninth International Colloquium of the Society for the Promotion of Eriugenian Studies*, Leuven-Louvain-la-Neuve, June 7-10, 1995, edited by G. VAN RIEL – C. STEEL –J. MCEVOY, 1996, XXII-408 pp.

XXI.   *Henricus Bate. Speculum divinorum et quorundam naturalium. Parts XIII-XVI. On Thinking and Happiness*. Ed. G. GULDENTOPS, 2002, LV-409 pp.

XXII.   *Henricus Bate. Speculum divinorum et quorundam naturalium. Parts XVII-XIX*. Ed. M. VAN DER LUCHT (in preparation).

XXIII.   *Henricus Bate. Speculum divinorum et quorundam naturalium. Parts XX-XX-III. On the Heavens, the Divine Movers and the First Intellect*. Ed. C. STEEL - G. GULDENTOPS, 1996, LVI-563 pp.

XXIV.   *The Perennial Tradition of Neoplatonism*. Ed. J.J. CLEARY, 1997, XXXIV–578 pp.

XXV.   *Tradition et traduction. Les textes philosophiques et scientifiques grecs au moyen-âge latin. Hommage à F. Bossier*, édité par R. BEYERS – J. BRAMS – D. SACRÉ – K. VERRYCKEN, 1999, VIII-377 pp.

XXVI.   *Proclus et la Théologie Platonicienne. Actes du Colloque International de Louvain (13-16 mai 1998)*, édité par A.-Ph. SEGONDS - C. STEEL, 2000, LXI-699 pp.

XXVII.   S. PERFETTI, *Aristotle's Zoology and its Renaissance Commentators (1521-1601)*, 2000, X –258 pp.

XXVIII.   *Avicenna and his Heritage. Acts of the International Colloquium. Leuven – Louvain-la-Neuve (Sept. 8-11, 1999)*. Ed. J. JANSSENS – D. DE SMET, 2002, XII-341 pp.

XXIX.   G. GALLE, *Peter of Auvergne. Questions on Aristotle's De Caelo. A Critical Edition with an Interpretative Essay*, 2003, 1000 pp.

XXX.   *History and Eschatology in John Scottus Eriugena and his Time. Proceedings of the Tenth International Conference of the Society for the Promotion of Eriugenian Studies, Maynooth – Dublin (August 16-20, 2000)*. Ed. J. McEvoy – M. Dunne, 2002, XVIII-645 pp.

XXXI.   *Henry of Ghent and the Transformation of Scholastic Thought*. Ed. G. GULDENTOPS – C. STEEL, 2003, XII-436 pp.

XXXII.   *Platonic Ideas and Concept Formation in Ancient and Medieval Thought*. Ed. G. VAN RIEL – C. MACÉ, 2004, XXV-259 pp.

XXXIII.   G. ROSKAM, *On the Path to Virtue. The Stoic Doctrine of Moral Progress and its Reception in Middle-Platonism*, 2005, VIII-508 pp.

XXXIV. *Platons Timaios als Grundtext der Kosmologie in Spätantike, Mittelalter und Renaissance. Plato's Timaeus and the Foundations of Cosmology in Late Antiquity, the Middle Ages and Renaissance.* Ed. T. LEINKAUF – C. STEEL, 2005, XXVI-492 pp.

XXXV. *The Eucharist in Theology and Philosophy. Issues of Doctrinal History in East and West from the Patristic Age to the Reformation.* Ed. I. PERCZEL – R. FORRAI – G. GERÉBY, 2005, XXVII-474 pp.

XXXVI. J.C. FLORES, *Henry of Ghent: Metaphysics and the Trinity. With a Critical Edition of question six of article fifty-five of the Summa Quaestionum Ordinariarium,* 2006, VIII-240 pp.

XXXVII. J.P. DOYLE, *Collected Studies on Francisco Suárez, S.J. (1548-1617).* Ed. V. Salas, 2010, XVIII-408 pp.

XXXVIII. *Miroir et savoir. La transmission d'un thème platonicien, des Alexandrins à la philosophie arabo-musulmane.* Ed. D. DE SMET, M. SEBTI, G. DE CALLATAŸ, 2008, X-310 pp.

XXXIX. *Platonic Stoicism – Stoic Platonism. The Dialogue between Platonism and Stoicism in Antiquity.* Ed. M. BONAZZI – C. HELMIG, 2007, XVI-312 pp.

XL. J. MÜLLER, *Willensswäche in Antike und Mittelalter. Eine Problemgeschichte von Sokrates bis Johannes Duns Scotus,* 2009, 816 pp.

XLI. *Ancient Perspectives on Aristotle's* De Anima. Ed. G. VAN RIEL – P. DESTRÉE, 2009, XIV-198 pp.

XLII. M. BIENIAK, *The Soul-Body Problem at Paris, ca. 1200-1250. Hugh of St-Cher and His Contemporaries,* 2010, XII-246 pp.

XLIII. *Les dialogues platoniciens chez Plutarque. Stratégies et méthodes exégétiques.* Ed. par X. BROUILLETTE-A. GIAVATTO 2010, VIII-164 pp.

XLIV. J.P. DOYLE, *On the Borders of Being and Knowing. Some Late Scholastic Thoughts on Supertranscendental Being.* Ed. V. Salas, 2012, XVIII-326 pp.

Series 2
HENRICI DE GANDAVO OPERA OMNIA
Editionibus curandis praeest G. A. Wilson

I. R. MACKEN, *Bibliotheca manuscripta Henrici de Gandavo. I. Catalogue A-P,* 1979, XVIII-677 pp.

II. R. MACKEN, *Bibliotheca manuscripta Henrici de Gandavo. II. Catalogue Q-Z. Répertoire,* 1979, XIX-XXII + 678-1306 pp + 34 extra-textual plates (pp. XXIII-LIV).

V. *Quodlibet I* (R. MACKEN), 1979, XCIV + 262 pp. + 12 extra-textual plates.

VI. *Quodlibet II* (R. WIELOCKX), 1983, XLVIII-166 pp.

VII. *Quodlibet III* (K. EMERY, Jr.) (in preparation).

Series 3
FRANCISCI DE MARCHIA
OPERA PHILOSOPHICA ET THEOLOGICA
Editionibus curandis praeest R. L. Friedman

II,1.   *Quaestiones in secundum librum Sententiarum (Reportatio)*, Quaestiones 1-12
         (T. SUAREZ-NANI, W. DUBA, E. BABEY, G.J. ETZKORN), 2008, LXXXIX-272 pp.

II,2.   *Quaestiones in secundum librum Sententiarum (Reportatio)*, Quaestiones 13-27
         (T. SUAREZ-NANI, W. DUBA, E. BABEY, G.J. ETZKORN), 2010, XCIX-314 pp.

II,3.   *Quaestiones in secundum librum Sententiarum (Reportatio)*, Quaestiones 28-49
         (in preparation).

CORPUS LATINUM
COMMENTARIORUM IN ARISTOTELEM GRAECORUM

I.   *Thémistius. Commentaire sur le Traité de l'âme d'Aristote. Traduction de Guil-
         laume de Moerbeke.* Ed. G. VERBEKE, 1957, XCVII-322 pp.

II.   *Ammonius. Commentaire sur le Peri Hermeneias d'Aristote. Traduction de Guil-
         laume de Moerbeke.* Ed. G. VERBEKE, 1961, CXX-515 pp.

III.   *Jean Philopon. Commentaire sur le De anima d'Aristote. Traduction de Guil-
         laume de Moerbeke.* Ed. G. VERBEKE, 1966, CXIX-172 pp.

IV.   *Alexandre d'Aphrodisias. Commentaire sur les Météores d'Aristote. Traduction
         de Guillaume de Moerbeke.* Ed. A. J. SMET, 1968, CXXXIV-526 pp.

V,1.   *Simplicius. Commentaire sur les Catégories d'Aristote. Traduction de Guillaume
         de Moerbeke.* Vol. 1, ed. A. PATTIN, 1971, LIV-282 pp.

V,2.   *Simplicius. Commentaire sur les Catégories d'Aristote. Traduction de Guillaume
         de Moerbeke.* Vol. 2, ed. A. PATTIN, 1975, pp. 283-765.

VI,1.   *The Greek Commentaries on the Nicomachean Ethics of Aristotle in the Latin
         Translation of Robert Grosseteste, Bishop of Lincoln († 1253).* Vol. 1, *Books
         I-IV.* ed. H.P.F. MERCKEN, 1973, 135*-371 pp.

VI,3.   *The Greek Commentaries on the Nicomachean Ethics of Aristotle in the Latin
         Translation of Robert Grosseteste, Bishop of Lincoln († 1253).* Vol. 3, *Books
         VII-X*, ed. H.P.F. MERCKEN, 1991, 72*-478 pp.

VII,1.   *Commentators and Commentaries on Aristotle's Sophistici elenchi. A Study of
         Post-Aristotelian Ancient and Medieval Writings on Fallacies.* Vol. 1: *The Greek
         Tradition*, by S. EBBESEN, 1981, IX-355 pp.

VII,2.   *Commentators and Commentaries on Aristotle's Sophistici elenchi. A Study
         of Post-Aristotelian Ancient and Medieval Writings on Fallacies.* Vol. 2: *Greek
         Texts and Fragments of the Latin Translation of "Alexander's" Commentary*, by
         S. EBBESEN, 1981, XXXVII-556 pp.